THE RUSSIAN FASCISTS

The Russian Fascists

TRAGEDY AND FARCE IN EXILE

1925-1945

John J. Stephan

1817

HARPER & ROW, PUBLISHERS

NEW YORK

HAGERSTOWN

SAN FRANCISCO

LONDON

Permission to reproduce photographs is gratefully acknowledged to the Hoover Institution on War, Revolution, and Peace for photos from *Nash Put* and *Natsiya* (identified in parentheses after the captions); to the Slavonic Division, New York Public Library, Astor, Lenox and Tilden Foundations for photos from *Fashist;* to Hara Shobō, Inc. for the portrait of General Araki Sadao; to Andre A. Vonsiatsky for photos of his father with Prince Theodore Romanov, of his father with Marion Ream Vonsiatsky, and of Nakamura Fusako; and to the Hartford *Courant* for photos of Vonsiatsky with Donat Kunle and Alexander Tzuglevich, and of Thomas J. Dodd.

FIRST EDITION

Designed by Sidney Feinberg

Library of Congress Cataloging in Publication Data

Stephan, John J
The Russian fascists.
Bibliography: p.
Includes index.
1. Russia—Politics and government—1917–1936.
2. Russia—Politics and government—1936–1953.
3. Russians in foreign countries.   4. Fascism—Russia.
I. Title.
DK269.S73   322.4′2′0947   77–11804
ISBN 0–06–014099–2

---

78 79 80 81 82 10 9 8 7 6 5 4 3 2 1

FOR DAD

Contents

Photographs

Marion Ream Vonsiatsky at sixty-two
Vonsiatsky with fellow fascists Donat Kunle and Rev. Alexander Tzu-
    glevich, July 1937
Masthead of Vonsiatsky's paper *Fashist*
Staff and students of New York's Russian Fascist Bible School

(Pictures following page 326)

Swastika-topped fascist headquarters building in northwest Manchuria
November 7, 1935, issue of Rodzaevsky's newspaper *Nash Put*
Cover of fascist theoretical journal, *Natsiya*
Natsiya cover based on 1915 French war-bond poster
Japanese General Araki Sadao
September 13, 1936, issue of *Nash Put* hailing fascist leaders
Rodzaevsky poses with followers in Harbin, 1940
The *Admiral Ushakov,* flagship of Vonsiatsky's "navy"
Russian Fascist Christmas party in Shanghai, 1939
June 10, 1942, Hartford *Times* headlining Vonsiatsky espionage
    indictment
Thomas J. Dodd, who prosecuted case against Vonsiatsky
Anastase and Marion Vonsiatsky, Tucson, 1962
Vonsiatsky burial crypt near Putnam, Connecticut

MAPS

Acknowledgments

No amount of appreciation can repay the time and effort contributed by many individuals to this study. I owe a special debt of gratitude to those whose own lives play a part in this book: Andre Anastase Vonsiatsky, Vladimir Konstantinovich Rodzaevsky, Nicholas and Lydia Petlin, Neonilla Yalisheva, Nikita Nikitivich Romanoff, Alexis Sherbatoff, Andrei Lobanov-Rostovsky, Boris de Rosmaritza, Lydia B. Schmüser, Albert E. Kahn, Professor Thomas J. Dodd, John W. Ream, Fred Portunato, and Wesley Griswold. Residents of Putnam and Thompson, Connecticut, provided vivid glimpses into what no written source could have imparted. Particularly helpful were Millicent Beausoleil, John Bigelow, C. F. Cunningham, James W. B. Kelley, Anne V. Kenny, Prudence Kwiecien, Irving Myron, Beatrice Peloquin, Helen and Natalie Roshak, Robert Rovatti, Richard E. Snow, and the late Thomas Watson.

Archivists and librarians have provided invaluable services in making material available. I am deeply grateful to Jerome Bakst of the Anti-Defamation League; Arline Paul and Hilja Kukk of the Hoover Institution on War, Revolution, and Peace; Paul T. Heffron of the Manuscript Division, Library of Congress; Milton O. Gustafson, R. Michael McReynolds, and Henry J. Wolfinger of the National Archives; James K. Owens of the Federal Archives and Records Center; Joseph H. Doherty and Matthew J. Smith of the Providence College Library; Nicholas A. Slobodchikoff of the Museum of Russian Culture, San Francisco; Dr. Weinandy of the Foreign Ministry Political Archive, Bonn; Kurihara Ken and Togawa Yukie of the Foreign Ministry Archives, Tokyo; R. Kato of the National Diet Library, Tokyo; the staffs of the Slavonic Collection, New York Public Library, and of the Public

Record Office, London; and Ellen Chapman, Eleanor Au, Masato Matsui, Pat Polansky, Misao Shibayama, and Takumi Tashima of the University of Hawaii Library.

For their cooperation in releasing classified documents, I am grateful to Clarence M. Kelley, Henry E. Petersen, Clair A. Cripe, and Richard Thornburgh of the U.S. Department of Justice; to Captain L. E. Connall of the Naval Investigative Service, Department of Defense; to Dr. Pasquale J. Ciccone of the Medical Center for Federal Prisons; and to Milton E. Noble, Registrar of Brown University.

A number of scholars have given helpful advice on historiographical and bibliographical matters. I should particularly like to acknowledge the generosity of Professor Dr. Erwin Oberländer of the University of Cologne for sharing his extensive knowledge of Russian fascism. Thanks are also due to Professors George Akita, Peter Berton, Gary Best, Alexander Dallin, Basil Dmytryshyn, Igor A. Latyshev, Michael A. Ledeen, George A. Lensen, Herbert Margulies, Albert O. Parry, Dmitrii V. Petrov, Don C. Rawson, Alexander V. Riasanovsky, Nicholas V. Riasanovsky, Hans Rogger, the late Joseph Schiebel, Harry Shukman, Michael Speidel, Richard Storry, Donald W. Treadgold, Robert Valliant, John A. White, and Robert C. Williams.

For clarifying specific points of information, I am obliged to Ali Block, Olga Bodisco, Virginia Brooks, Irene Bulazel, Elizabeth Conze, Ariadna Delianich, Kay Doherty, John C. Franklin, J. Gershevich, Alexander Goriansky, Nikolai Kalugin, Eugene J. Kerno, George Mihailoff, Leona de Nikanov, Olga Moncks Pertzoff, Andrei Sedych, Ivan Toropovsky, and A. S. Troubetzkoy.

Heartfelt thanks are due to William Reiss of Paul R. Reynolds, Inc., and to my editor, Nahum Waxman, for their valued criticism, suggestions, and encouragement.

My father, John Stephan, and my wife, Barbara, have been constantly supportive during the travels and travails of making this book, for the shortcomings of which the author assumes full responsibility.

Note

Japanese personal names are rendered in the Japanese fashion. The surname precedes the given name.

A coherent, comprehensive system of transliteration of Russian names in a book about Russian émigrés is an illusory ideal. Consistency has been sacrificed for the sake of accuracy, as many émigrés have anglicized (Nikolai to Nicholas) or gallicized (Muraviev to Mouravieff) their names. Moreover, for the sake of nonspecialists, names of well-known personages (e.g., Nicholas and Alexandra, Wrangel) are spelled according to popular usage. At the risk of ruffling purists, endings that various systems of transliteration render as "ii," "yi," or "iy" have been simplified to "y," and the apostrophe (') denoting the soft sign has been omitted.

Foreword

Russian *fascists?* To most people the words have a discordant, even
unnatural ring. The term might be an anti-Soviet epithet wielded
by cold warriors in the 1950s or a slogan of the Chinese in the 1960s
and 1970s, or it might simply be a bit of facetious nonsense. Few
would think of a full-fledged political movement replete with dogma,
marching songs, swastika arm bands, its own führer, and a global
constituency. The historical reality of such an improbable apparition
is the subject of this book.

Who were the Russian fascists? That most people have not heard
of them is no surprise. Card-carrying Russian fascists never numbered
more than ten thousand, although their leaders claimed twice that
many followers. Being émigrés or the offspring of émigrés, they lived
in Russian enclaves scattered around the world. Their ranks included
tsarist army officers, Cossacks, Orthodox priests, maverick academics,
disgruntled bourgeois, and displaced proletarians, seasoned with bogus aristocrats, a preadolescent Romanov, various convicted felons,
and a sprinkling of Soviet agents. During their twenty-odd years, this
strange band brewed a quixotic crusade to take over the Soviet Union
and build a fascist Russia that would surpass Mussolini's Italy and
Hitler's Germany. During the 1930s, they operated in Berlin and
Buenos Aires, Tientsin and Tokyo, Cairo and Chicago, Valparaiso
and Vienna, Paris and Putnam, Connecticut. They courted young
exiles, cultivating their agonized patriotism and their half-hostile fascination with the way Mussolini and Hitler crushed domestic Communists and seemingly breathed vitality into Italy and Germany. They
collaborated with anyone who would cater to their illusions: Chinese
warlords, Japanese generals, Nazi satraps, a Chicago tycoon's heiress,

the Connecticut State Police, and Josef Stalin. In 1941, the climactic year of their movement, Russian fascists feverishly prepared to "inherit" their motherland from the Third Reich's conquering legions. But their dreams evaporated at the threshold of apparent fulfillment, leaving only a residue of betrayal and death.

Karl Marx once remarked that history repeats itself, first as tragedy and thereafter as farce. Tragedy and farce repeat each other contrapuntally in the annals of the Russian fascists. Rootless and impotent in expatriate limbo, they anesthetized themselves to the futility of their cause by living in a world of illusions. One worshiped Stalin, convinced that the Great Leader nurtured untapped reservoirs of anti-Semitism. Another issued commands to a phantom network of agents throughout the USSR and staged military maneuvers with toys and pet animals on a Connecticut farm. The Russian fascists aped German and Italian regalia to the point of parody, adoringly decorating lampshades, trouser buttons, wastebaskets, and even Santa Claus with swastikas. Yet their absurd antics were symptoms of a tragic predicament. The sad fact is that the Russian fascists did not know how to serve their motherland by any other means than allying with their enemies. Patriotic traitors, they became almost everyone's targets and stooges.

Why has the word "fascist" been attached to this particular group of Russians? Mainly because they called themselves fascists. The term is notoriously difficult to define, but a brief discussion of its usages should clarify how the Russian fascists fit into broader historical patterns.

The word "fascist" surfaces ubiquitously in current parlance. It is perhaps most commonly heard to describe Mussolini's Italy, Nazi Germany, Spain under Franco, Japan between 1931 and 1945, and Chile after the fall of Allende. Political organizations of a violently nationalist and militarist persuasion, such as the Rumanian Iron Guard or the Hungarian Arrow Cross movement, have also been called fascist.

In addition to being a descriptive term for certain regimes and organizations, "fascist" has cropped up as an expletive hurled at anything and anyone from a political rival to disciplinarian parents. Thomas E. Dewey was labeled "fascist" by some domestic critics. A Manchester *Guardian* columnist recently condemned U.S. foreign policy for practicing "external fascism." A Pentagon analyst declared in 1975 that the Defense Department's alleged protection of corporate contractors "is fascism, pure and simple." During her sojourn with the Symbionese Liberation Army, Patricia Hearst denounced the "fascist pig" media.

As a term of invective, "fascist" has also been applied to the left. Anti-Communist publicists talked of "Red fascism" in the 1950s. In 1973, Italian Communist Party leader Enrico Berlinguer denounced his country's radical Marxists as "objective fascists." During the 1930s, the Communist Party of the Soviet Union (CPSU) referred to deviant comrades as "social fascists." That particular phrase has returned to haunt the Kremlin, for Peking now lambasts the Soviet leaders as "social fascists" and in 1976 characterized the CPSU as a "bourgeois fascist party." (Stalin, whom the Chinese exempt from criticism, was called a "crypto-fascist" by Mussolini in 1938. But the Duce did not mean it as an insult.)

Fascism's amorphous perimeters, protean guises, and pejorative associations make it an elusive phenomenon to grasp. Webster's Third International Dictionary defines fascism as "any tendency for setting up a centralized, autocratic national regime with severely nationalistic policies, exercising regimentation of industry, commerce, and finance, rigid censorship, and forcible suppression of opposition." This broad formulation still leaves room for debate. Lenin characterized fascism—together with imperialism—as the highest stage of capitalism, and Marxists have since postulated that fascism has a bourgeois class character. To many non-Marxists, however, confining fascism to a particular class or mode of production overlooks fascist movements with a peasant character (such as those in Rumania and Yugoslavia). Indeed, some observers, ranging from the Italian political economist Renzo Bertoni to Leon Trotsky, perceived Stalinist Russia in the 1930s as exhibiting the basic traits of a paradigmatic fascist regime: an authoritarian, antiliberal state under a charismatic leader, one-party rule, authoritarian control of the means of production by a managerial bureaucracy, domesticated labor unions, planned industrialization aimed at economic autarchy, ruthless suppression of internal opposition, and (in 1939–40) territorial expansion. Of course, such a proposition is anathema inside the USSR. Soviet commentators have reacted by adding corollaries to the Leninist definition of fascism. Professor Nikolai S. Derzhavin declared in 1941 that "Fascism is the worst foe of Slavism." Ilya Ehrenburg spoke more directly: "There are different varieties of Fascists. Some like beer, some like wine. . . . But you can always tell them if they bitterly hate the Soviet Union."

Even among non-Marxists, there is no consensus about the nature of fascism. Benedetto Croce regarded fascism as an intoxication with activism, a short-lived, cataclysmic outburst of childish adventurism, a temporary aberration in the stream of European thought. Others have emphasized fascism's continuity with past patterns. Some commentators treat fascism as a political or economic system. Others look for a psychological explanation. Historians and social scientists often adopt different approaches to the subject and disagree about the utility of an abstract "model" of fascism. There are even those who would question whether fascism can be defined in a general sense, so disparate were the anatomies and experiences of individual fascist movements.

This history will treat Russian fascism as a movement drawing on a wide variety of socioeconomic groups in the 1920s and 1930s, groups afflicted by political desperation, national humiliation, economic displacement, and cultural nostalgia. Russian fascists, exalted the authoritarian state, followed charismatic leaders, invoked national spirit and traditional cultural values, and glorified combat, but not all of them embraced anti-Semitism. Russian fascists defined their own variety of fascism as "a synthesis of the lessons to be drawn from the failure of the White* movement, the experience of Italian, German, and Japanese fascism, Russia's glorious past, and the present postrevolutionary reality." Russian fascists were unique in another respect: They operated outside their own nation, developing what perhaps was the only "cosmopolitan" fascist movement. Yet their global scope, forced upon them by their being exiles, proved to be a fatal disability. It put them at the mercy of foreign patrons and drove them into extravagant fantasies.

Despite an extensive literature about fascism, the full story of the Russian fascists has never been told. Libraries have been written on Hitler and Mussolini. Scholars have analyzed fascist impulses among Americans, Argentinians, Japanese, Irish, French, Swedes, Spanish,

---

* In this context, "White" refers to partisans of the old tsarist regime and to followers of one or another of the many anti-Bolshevik generals who raised armies during the Russian Civil War. However, during the 1920s, the expression "White Russian" came to be applied loosely to all Russian émigrés, regardless of their political affiliations, who left their homeland during the February and October revolutions and Civil War (1917–22).

Dutch, Danes, Chinese, Norwegians, Swiss, and many others. Amid all this activity, why has the Russian fascist experience been accorded so little attention?

First, information about Russian fascists is hard to get. Konstantin Vladimirovich Rodzaevsky and Anastase Andreivich Vonsiatsky, the movement's self-proclaimed leaders, are dead. Their surviving followers, no longer interested in publicity, have camouflaged their pasts. Party records have been lost, destroyed, or buried in inaccessible vaults of Soviet archives. The full scope of the subject can be glimpsed only by piecing together fragmentary accounts in multiple languages from repositories scattered throughout the world.

Second, Soviet historians are uncannily silent about Russian fascism, although they might be expected to make much of an anti-Communist conspiracy dripping with German, Japanese, and American associations. Could ethnic sensitivities inhibit the admission that *Russian* fascists existed? Or is the silence related to those uncomfortable parallels of structure and rhetoric between the Russian Fascist Party and the Communist Party of the Soviet Union, parallels that Peking, already denouncing Kremlin leaders as "social fascists," might leap to exploit? Whatever the constraint, Soviet writers refer to "Russian fascists" about as often as they talk about "German national socialists." On rare occasions when Russian fascist leaders such as Rodzaevsky and Vonsiatsky are mentioned in print, they are lumped together with Cossack atamans, tsarist generals, and other vintage counterrevolutionaries under the all-embracing rubric "White Guard."

Third, those who lived among Russian fascists remain discreetly silent. Most Russian émigrés had nothing to do with fascism in any form, and many actively opposed it. But for some, the subject of fascism rattles skeletons in the closet.

"That's a sensitive, delicate subject," observed Berkeley historian Professor Nicholas V. Riasanovsky upon hearing about this study in 1975. There is little doubt that during the 1920s and early 1930s, fascism appealed to a number of young Russian exiles eager to overthrow the Soviet regime and impatient and disillusioned with monarchism, liberalism, and milder varieties of socialism. Where the monarchist movement had shown itself to be anachronistic and stultifying, fascism seemed youthful and dynamic. Where liberalism had already betrayed its weakness in Russia between 1905 and 1917, fascism promised to mobilize national power and unity—if given a chance. Where socialism tended toward internationalism, fascism elevated the nation above class, and many émigrés felt an aching need for a national affiliation. Had not fascism saved Italy—and later Germany—from communism? Did not fascism offer the most efficacious, if not the only, means to destroy Bolshevism? Today, with Auschwitz still fresh in the collective memory, few would care to admit to having been moved by such thoughts forty or fifty years ago. Consequently, a number of firsthand sources on the Russian fascist movement have lapsed into defensive muteness.

I first learned about Russian fascists in 1971 while browsing through copies of a prewar Japanese illustrated magazine called *Pictorial Orient* in the University of Hawaii Library. My attention was caught by an article in a 1941 issue entitled "Russian Fascists in Harbin," written by Amar Lahiri, an Indian apologist for what was then called the New Order in East Asia. The photographs of Slavic storm troopers posing solemnly beneath portraits of Nicholas and Alexandra in the presence of a Japanese adviser, of the fascist "Duce" Konstantin Rodzaevsky gazing Christ-like from beneath a scraggly beard, and of a neon swastika blinking defiantly on the Soviet-Manchurian frontier struck me as at once incongruous, absurd, pathetic, and irresistible. I made a mental note of the article as a bizarre tidbit for lectures.

In the summer of 1972, while engaged in research at the Portugal Street Annex of London's Public Record Office, I came across several folios on White Russians in the Far East, deposited with recently declassified Foreign Office files on China for the years 1938–45. One folio contained a 1941 report by the late Oxford orientalist G. F. Hudson about Japan's patronage of a Russian fascist movement. Another yielded letters and telegrams sent by Rodzaevsky from Manchuria in June 1941, ordering his European representatives to set up fascist cells in Soviet territory occupied by the Wehrmacht. Intercepted by British Imperial Censorship, Rodzaevsky's instructions prompted a secret British investigation of émigré reactions to Hitler's anti-Soviet crusade. These folios indicated that the Russian fascists were more than exotic trivia. I resolved to explore the subject systematically.

Two weeks later, I was in the USSR. Conversations in Leningrad, Moscow, Irkutsk, and Khabarovsk revealed a vivid consciousness of

"White Guards" among older generations of Soviet citizens but almost no admitted awareness of a Russian fascist movement as such.

Reaching Tokyo, via Siberia, I inquired at the Foreign Ministry Archives and was shown four bundles of reports and correspondence labeled "White Russian Fascist Activities (1925–1944): Secret." The contents consisted not only of dispatches from Japanese diplomatic officials in Manchuria and China but copies of Home Ministry police reports detailing Rodzaevsky's official and unofficial Japanese contacts. References in the Foreign Ministry Archives to the Gestapo and FBI suggested that more material might exist in American and German repositories.

German archives did indeed contain useful material on the Russian fascists. Nazi Party, SS, and Ostministerium* records provided glimpses of Russian fascists inside the Reich. Foreign Ministry Archives at Bonn contained data on Russian émigrés gathered by the German embassy in Bern, Switzerland. The files of Stuttgart's Deutsches Ausland-Institut opened useful perspectives through its reports on ethnic Germans in Manchuria.

American repositories turned out to hold rich and diverse material on Russian fascists operating in the United States. The Justice, State, and War departments had each kept files on the subject, and these are now deposited in the National Archives in Washington. Vonsiatsky's Justice Department file also includes data from the Immigration and Naturalization Service as well as detailed FBI reports. Although four FBI reports dated between 1939 and 1941 were at first withheld, an appeal submitted to the Department of Justice on June 25, 1975, under the terms of the Freedom of Information Act, resulted in their release on June 15, 1976.** The Federal Archives and Records Center in Waltham, Massachusetts, contained transcripts of Vonsiatsky's grand jury hearing in 1942. Nearly complete sets of Russian fascist newspapers, journals, and pamphlets were located at the Hoover Institution on War, Revolution, and Peace (notably in the Boris I. Nicolaevsky Collection) and in the Slavonic Collection of the New York Public Library.

In addition to searching for written records, I attempted to trace surviving friends and followers of Rodzaevsky and Vonsiatsky. The

* Reich Ministry for Occupied Eastern Territories.
** Confidential reports were simultaneously released by the Criminal Division, Department of Justice, and the Naval Investigative Service, Department of Defense.

task was littered with obstacles. Time had claimed some lives and shrouded others. A notice placed in the New York Russian daily, *Novoye Russkoye Slovo,* provided a number of leads. Inquiries at state bureaus of vital statistics for death records yielded the names and addresses of relatives. Before long, I was writing to émigrés around the world, from France to Tasmania. In order to interview particularly valuable informants, I made several trips to New York and San Francisco. By 1974, I had visited Rodzaevsky's and Anastase Vonsiatsky's families, the former in San Francisco, the latter in St. Petersburg—Florida.

During this period, three trips were also made to Putnam, Connecticut, once touted as "The Center" of the All-Russian Fascist Party. Dozens of local residents generously consented to share their recollections about Vonsiatsky. Valuable data surfaced in unlikely places: in probate court files at nearby North Grosvenor Dale, in a crypt at the West Thompson Cemetery, and in an abandoned cottage once known as the Russian Bear. By an extraordinary coincidence, my father learned that four crates of documents dug up on Vonsiatsky's former estate during conversion of a hen coop into a girls' dormitory had been donated to Providence College (Providence, Rhode Island) and deposited in the college archives. Examined and collated by the author in 1975, the "guano archives" yielded not only private papers and photographs but additional Russian fascist publications available in none of the major repositories in the United States, Europe, and Japan.

Much material on the Russian fascist movement (particularly in the Far East) still remains to be seen. Records of the Russian Fascist Union in Harbin, Manchuria, were seized by the Red Army and Soviet security organs in 1945 and are presumably in the USSR today, but there is little likelihood of these sources being made available for research. This being the case, the present study can be regarded as only an attempt to explore a subject that others will someday hopefully develop with greater refinement and detail.

THE RUSSIAN FASCISTS

CHAPTER I

The Russian Diaspora

All émigrés, cut off from the living environment to which they
have belonged, shut their eyes to avoid seeing bitter truths, and
grow more and more acclimatised to a closed, fantastic circle
consisting of inert memories and hopes that can never be realized.
—ALEXANDER HERZEN (1848)

For more than a century, Russians have abandoned their homeland
to escape repression, violence, or destitution. The years 1918 to 1922
saw an exodus of epic proportions. Convulsed by revolution, civil
war, foreign intervention, and famine, Russia spewed out more than
two million refugees. They left in waves, spreading in all directions.
A northern wave headed toward Finland and the arctic ports of Mur-
mansk and Archangel. A southern wave passed through the Ukraine
and the Crimea, depositing thousands of refugees in Turkey and the
Balkans. A westward wave slipped through civil war battlefronts to
the Baltic republics and to Poland and Czechoslovakia. Some 560,000
Russians had flocked to Germany by 1920, and most of these later
gravitated to France, which in the 1930s emerged as a mecca for
displaced Russians. An eastward wave of about 250,000 people rolled
across Siberia to the Far East. Some 100,000 settled in Manchuria,
which already had a sizable Russian population before 1917, and
others continued on to China proper and to Korea and Japan. Elements of all three waves reached Canada (40,000), the United States
(20,000), South America (3,000), and Australia (1,700).

Contrary to popular fancy, the Russian emigration was more than
a parade of ballerinas, operatic basses, grand dukes, and would-be
Anastasias. Although well seasoned with artists and aristocrats, the
emigration had basically a working- and middle-class character. Thousands of Cossacks and soldiers from the defeated White armies im-

1

parted a military coloration. Politicians, journalists, lawyers, doctors, engineers, priests, professors, businessmen, and shopkeepers contributed a bourgeois flavor. Muzhiks fleeing famine added a peasant element, and a dash of *Lumpenproletariat* and criminal flotsam mingled with the general flow.

Whatever their class backgrounds, the Russians who fled their homeland between 1918 and 1922 experienced shocks that left them dazed, disoriented, and embittered. While the February and October revolutions had been relatively bloodless, the Civil War unleashed a storm of savagery. Reds and Whites alike committed atrocities that left ugly and unhealing scars of hatred. Baron Pyotr Nikolaevich Wrangel's Cossacks carved notches in their rifle butts for each Bolshevik they slew. Roman Fyodorovich von Ungern-Sternberg (nicknamed the "Bloody Baron" for his sanguine hair and sanguinary tastes) took a thousandfold revenge for his wife's rape and murder by stuffing suspected Bolsheviks alive into locomotive boilers on the Trans-Siberian Railroad. The brutal liquidation of Tsar Nicholas II and his family in the basement of a merchant's house in Ekaterinburg on July 16, 1918, provided the haunting specter of the fourteen-year-old hemophilic tsarevich writhing over the punctured bodies of his parents and sisters until a Cheka lout discharged a pistol into the boy's ear. Even the most hardened soul flinched when told how the executioners had then celebrated their regicidal efficiency around a campfire of truncated, benzine-soaked imperial corpses.

The fugitive from revolution and civil war felt that he may have escaped death but was not sure that he had found life. Exile lay somewhere between the two. Memories of a shattered universe haunted him, a once secure and seemingly immutable universe that had suddenly transmogrified into a nightmare of betrayed loyalties, lost loved ones, confiscated property, and ruined careers. In seeking asylum abroad, the Russian refugee gained physical safety but sacrificed spiritual roots. For some, such a wrenching transplantation amounted to death by installment.

Stumbling into their new, alien environments, the Russian émigrés met scant understanding. As long as their predicament retained an aura of novelty, it elicited curiosity and in some cases sympathy. The YMCA, the League of Nations, and various philanthropic groups offered assistance to thousands of refugees. But as time passed, their misfortunes came to be taken for granted, or even made the butt of jokes.

Surviving Romanovs found themselves treated as exotic creatures who had outlived their epoch. Western liberals openly blamed them for Russia's woes, and even potentially sympathetic statesmen kept their distance, careful to avoid any contact that might prove damaging to their own political careers. When Grand Duke Alexander (cousin and brother-in-law of Nicholas II) tried to see Woodrow Wilson, Robert Lansing (Wilson's secretary of state), and Colonel E. M. House during the Versailles Conference in 1919, he was repeatedly put off until an American friend, General Charles G. Dawes, bluntly advised him: "Don't even try to see the Mighty; they won't receive you, they've got no use for fallen men." Barred without explanation from entering England, Alexander sought an interview with Arthur Balfour during one of the British foreign secretary's visits to Paris. Although the Russian grand duke did finally extract an appointment with Balfour at the latter's inconspicuous hotel room, he never quite got to meet him. He did, however, catch sight of him ducking out the fire escape while a flushed assistant stammeringly informed the visitor that "Mr. Balfour deeply regrets that a conference of the utmost importance is depriving him of the pleasure of talking to Your Imperial Highness." Asked if he cared to leave a message, Alexander replied: "Yes, by all means. Tell him that a man of his age should use the elevator." A wry sense of humor helped many a dispossessed aristocrat stay sane.

Even more galling was the behavior of European royalty to whom the Romanovs were related by blood and marriage. England's George V and Rumania's Queen Marie treated their Russian cousins generously. Others, however, begrudged even token help. Denmark's King Christian X chafed at having to put up his aunt, the Empress Dowager Marie, who returned to her native land after fifty years in Russia as consort of Tsar Alexander III and mother of Nicholas II. Oblivious to the old lady's traumatic losses, he pestered her to consume less electricity and made no secret of his suspicions that she was pawning his parlor trinkets.

Royal coldness stung more than royal miserliness. A number of Windsors, Savoias, and Glücksbergs adopted a strained, distant attitude as if their Russian relatives, rather than being victims of Bolshevism, carried some contagious vulnerability to it. Indeed, surviving Romanovs did feel that they possessed a certain expertise on revolutions, an expertise that they were all too ready to share with royalty in Copenhagen, Windsor, and Madrid. However annoying to their hosts, Romanov exiles took a wry pleasure in nodding knowingly at the sight of a strike or procession of unemployed workers, as if to say: "Ah yes, I've seen this before. Your turn, affectionate cousins, is only a matter of time."

Émigrés of every class were exploited economically, and their helplessness made them easy targets. A once well-to-do gentleman who had lost everything in Russia returned with anticipated relief to the Paris landlord to whom he had entrusted a sizable quantity of possessions six years previously. The landlord greeted him with a six-year rent bill, payment of which was required to release the now depleted belongings in his care. Émigrés forced to sell their jewels learned that Bond Street and Rue de la Paix merchants bought precious stones at only a fraction of their value. Grand Duke Alexander parted with his numismatic collection in 1919 for 5 percent of its prewar catalogue price. Ten years later, he came across an advertisement in *The* [*London*] *Times* in which the same Swiss dealer represented one of the coins as having been purchased from "a member of the Russian Imperial Family" for a sum a hundred times as large as that paid to Alexander for the entire collection.

Exile also meant isolation. Thrown together in their misfortune, Russian émigrés clustered in insular communities throughout the world, communities as elegant as Paris' Passy or as seedy as Shanghai's Hongkew. They clung to each other for comfort, security, and attachment to dwindling vestiges of a lost homeland. Their isolation was often compounded by the cool attitude of society around them. Andrei Lobanov-Rostovsky had scores of French friends from his student days in a Nice *lycée*, but when he returned to France in 1920, "my former friends and even people whom I had known since childhood became strained in my presence. I felt myself a leper amongst them and began to avoid them." The late novelist Vladimir Nabokov vividly recalled his own isolation in *Speak, Memory:* ". . . in the course of almost one-fifth of a century [1920–40] spent in Western Europe I have not had, among the sprinkling of Germans and Frenchmen I knew (mostly landladies and literary people), more than two good friends all told." Nor did even the handful of Russian émigrés with full social calendars necessarily feel liked and respected as human beings. Grand Duke Alexander sardonically recalled how American hostesses invited him to dinner because they wanted to embellish their soirées with a "tragic" titled Russian.

Hard to bear were the pervasive misconceptions about Russia. Nabokov bridled at how his intellectual acquaintances at Cambridge uncritically acclaimed Lenin and breezily lumped émigrés "from peasant Socialist to White general" under the pejorative rubric "tsarist elements." Imperial Russia's contributions to the Allied cause in World War I went unrecognized or, worse, were held up to ridicule. Far from acknowledging how a sacrificial Russian offensive in August 1914 had diverted the Germans from Paris, Frenchmen self-righteously blamed émigrés (who were conveniently at hand) for the "treason" of Brest-Litovsk.* Asked in 1920 by an American lady about his activities during World War I, Lobanov-Rostovsky replied that he had served in the Imperial Russian Army. "Oh!" she marveled, "I did not know Russia had been in War," then added as an afterthought, "I guess you Russians didn't do very much, did you?"

For the exiled Russian war veteran, there was no more humiliating spectacle than the Allied victory parade held in Paris on November 11, 1919. For three years (1914–17), Russia had faithfully fought as an ally of Britain and France. Russia had sacrificed three million lives and millions of casualties, absorbing German blows that would otherwise have fallen on the western front. Watching from the sidelines along the Champs-Élysées, survivors of Tannenberg and the Masurian Lakes mutely savored the irony of a triumphal pageant that included not a single Russian soldier yet glittered with proud contingents from Montenegro and San Marino.

Economic destitution deprived most émigrés of the chance to indulge in nostalgic charades, but the more prescient rich families had stashed away a portion of their assets in British, French, or even German banks before the deluge. Some affluent exiles squandered their money at Biarritz and Cannes in pathetic attempts to recapture prerevolutionary life-styles. Prince Felix Yusupov, sole heir to Russia's largest industrial fortune—estimated at $350 million—managed to salvage a million dollars' worth of jewelry, two Rembrandts, and a collection of antique snuffboxes from the revolutionary conflagration. Living by installment as he sold off possessions, Yusupov and his wife, Princess Irina—only daughter of Grand Duke Alexander—threw extravagant parties at which the prince regaled guests with stories

* The Treaty of Brest-Litovsk (March 3, 1918), concluded between the Bolsheviks and the Central Powers, took Russia out of World War I and enabled the Germans to concentrate their forces on the western front.

of how he had helped murder Gregory Rasputin, the peasant-monk whose hypnotic influence over the tsarina imparted a lurid tinge to the Romanov twilight. Handsome types with dash and enterprise, such as Grand Duke Dmitry,* recouped financial losses (or made fortunes) by marrying wealthy American heiresses. But such windfalls were so rare that they became legendary.

"Nothing," wryly remarked Grand Duke Alexander, "is so useful to an exile as his hard-earned ability to recite the Cinderella story in reverse." Some abused that ability. Many more resorted to it as a desperate ploy to land a job.

Russian émigrés quickly discovered that no amount of good breeding or higher education guaranteed employment commensurate with expectations. To be sure, luminaries such as Bunin, Nabokov, Kandinsky, Chagall, Stravinsky, Rachmaninoff, Balanchine, Pavlova, Koussevitzky, and Sikorsky eventually demonstrated that exiles of extraordinary brilliance could pursue successful careers. A number of scholars found congenial havens at Stanford, Cornell, Chicago, Columbia, Harvard, the Sorbonne, and Prague. But taken in the context of the entire emigration, those cases were exceptional. For the vast majority, exile meant a loss of status and a stab of personal nonfulfillment.

Most Russian aristocrats adjusted to hard economic realities with remarkable grace, resourcefulness, and humor. Aside from a handful such as Empress Dowager Marie, who received direct support from her royal relatives in Denmark and England, even genuine Romanovs tried to fend for themselves. Refusing a lucrative offer to autograph dinner invitations for the financier Alfred Lowenstein, Grand Duke Alexander gamely took up the uncertain career of a peripatetic lecturer, starting with an address on "Old Russia" delivered at the New Baptist Church in Grand Rapids, Michigan. Grand Duchess Marie, sister of Grand Duke Dmitry, braved formidable competition and embroidered dresses in Paris. Notwithstanding a comfortable income from his American spouse, Audrey Emery ("Princess Ilinskaya"), Grand Duke Dmitry sold champagne for a Rheims firm in Palm Beach, Florida. While living off the sale of Rembrandts, snuffboxes, and a $375,000 settlement from Metro-Goldwyn-Mayer for a libelous movie about Rasputin insinuating that the guru had enjoyed Princess Irina's sexual favors, the Yusupovs ran a chain of couturiers in Paris, London,

---

* Grand Duke Dmitry (1891–1942), first cousin of Nicholas II, had been involved with Prince Yusupov in Rasputin's murder.

and Berlin. Prince Lobanov-Rostovsky juggled figures for an insurance company before joining the UCLA faculty. Rumor had it that a certain "Prince Golitsyn" waited on tables in New York well into the 1930s. The "prince," however, could well have been another member of the species exemplified by Harry F. Gerguson, better known as "Michael Romanoff" (shortened from "Prince Dmitry Michael Obolensky-Romanoff"), who used his grandiloquent alias to cash forged checks before opening a restaurant in Hollywood.

Some émigrés combined imagination and practical skills to find work. The more entrepreneurial types opened restaurants, cafes, grocery stores, dress shops, and newspapers in such oases as Paris, Berlin, Belgrade, Shanghai, and Harbin. Priests gathered new congregations in Russian communities. Lawyers and doctors resumed interrupted practices. Skilled engineers were more fortunate than most professionals and generally found employment in foreign firms. Some, but not all, writers, artists, and musicians found their creative talents in demand. One émigré went into professional wrestling, called himself "The Angel," and crushed 175 consecutive challengers from Strangler Lewis to the Great Gaman.

Thousands of Cossacks who had fought under Denikin, Kolchak, and Wrangel in a losing struggle against the Bolsheviks began exile with crippling disadvantages. Destitute and often poorly educated, they were ill-prepared to begin new lives abroad. Had not life in Russia conditioned them to hardship, they probably could not have endured the fates awaiting them in exile, which commonly started in one of the refugee camps set up by the British and French at Gallipoli, Lemnos, and Alexandria. Thereafter, the tsar's loyal fighters scattered throughout the world doing just about anything to keep body and soul together. They built roads and cleared forests in Yugoslavia, tilled fields in Bulgaria and Peru, hacked cabs in Paris, shoveled coal in Montevideo, played bit roles in Hollywood, served in the French Foreign Legion, and hired themselves out as bouncers and bodyguards in China. In one instance, a group of Don Cossacks stayed intact, maintaining strict discipline as if still in the tsar's service. They worked as porters at Paris' Gare du Nord, marching to and from the station like a severed but still vibrant limb of Old Russia.

Fate sometimes played jokes on émigrés, thrusting many of them into absurd—or pathetic—situations. The monk Iliodor, for example, who had stirred thousands with his fiery oratory before the Revolution, wound up a Baptist janitor in New York's Metropolitan Life Insurance Building. Had not Iliodor's archrival Rasputin been stuffed under the Neva River ice in 1916, the two ecclesiastics might have spent their dotage reminiscing on a Central Park bench. A colonel who in exile promoted himself to general ("because Americans expected nothing short of the highest ranks and titles") groomed horses in the American Express Company's New York freight stables; briefly operated a restaurant called the Double Headed Eagle; became a protégé of Gloria Swanson, who procured him minor roles in Metro-Goldwyn-Mayer films; and finally opened a cafe on Hollywood Boulevard, which was demolished in an explosion caused by defective gas valves. The "general's" colleague, former commander of the Imperial Guard Artillery's First Regiment, bobbed hair in a Sunset Boulevard beauty parlor.

Exile's most onerous burdens often fell on women. Violence-torn Russia cast off thousands of wives, widows, and waifs with no visible means of support. Women bore the triple responsibility of raising children, supporting an unemployed or underemployed husband, and holding together a displaced family. Many worked in factories, entered domestic service, or wore out their eyes as seamstresses. Some sold themselves. Russian prostitutes had populated Peking and Singapore brothels well before 1917, but their numbers swelled in the 1920s to the point that "Russian girl" came to mean "Caucasian harlot" in the tenderloin lingo of Harbin, Shanghai, and Kobe. It can only be conjectured how many Tanyas, Olgas, and Valentinas catered to customers seeking exotic gratification. In *Snow Country,* the late Nobel laureate Kawabata Yasunari portrayed a squalid, prematurely aged Russian woman peddling trinkets at a Japanese hot springs resort. Asked by a guest where she came from, she only repeated, "Where am I from? Where am I from?" Her question echoed throughout the Russian diaspora.

A humiliating awareness of utter dependence hurt as much as social ostracism and economic deprivation. Instead of feeling relief while he was being borne to safety by a British cruiser, Grand Duke Alexander was mortified that his former antagonists (he had been an admiral during the heyday of Anglo-Russian rivalry) were rescuing him from his own countrymen. Nabokov spoke for thousands of compatriots who fled from the Bolsheviks through the German-occupied Ukraine in 1918 protected by the Kaiser's army, which only months earlier had been their national enemy. "Patriotic Russians were torn between the animal relief of escaping native executioners and the necessity of owing their reprieve to a foreign invader—especially to the Germans."

Statelessness gutted the émigré's sense of security. When the Soviet government deprived Russians living abroad of citizenship in 1921, exiles found themselves wallowing in legal limbo. Governments looked askance at granting visas to refugees and closed their ears to appeals for naturalization, no matter how imploringly couched. "Nansen passports," sickly green identity cards issued to stateless Russians by the League of Nations, only codified the bearers' rootlessness and drew suspicion upon them as fugitives outside any national administration. Holding a Nansen passport, recalled Nabokov, was like being a criminal on parole or a child born out of wedlock.

In the Far East, statelessness carried an element of physical risk. China denied Russian émigrés extraterritorial privileges accorded to other Europeans, thereby exposing them to the whims of every warlord and petty official. It was not exceptional in Shanghai or Harbin for a Chinese or Japanese policeman to beat a White Russian in the streets like a coolie. With no one to protect them, they were anyone's fair game.

Such conditions took a psychological toll. Unable to relinquish the past or to deal with the present, some Russian émigrés fell prey to colossal fantasies. In extreme cases, the exile refused to recognize that a revolution had even occurred. Empress Dowager Marie shrugged off reports of the murders of her two sons (Tsar Nicholas and Grand Duke Michael) and her five grandchildren (Nicholas' son and heir, Alexis, and four daughters). Instead, she withdrew into a dream world at Hvidore, an estate in her native Denmark, which before 1917 had been the scene of big, happy, "family reunions" of Romanovs, Glücksbergs, Windsors, and Hohenzollerns. On December 5, 1924, seven years after the October Revolution and ten months after the death of Lenin, Marie complained to her nephew, Grand Duke Alexander: "Christmas is nearly here and there are many gifts to be distributed around the Hvidore, but the Department of Imperial Estates has not forwarded my check as yet. I cannot imagine what the nature of this strange delay could possibly be." Not daring to break the old lady's spell, Alexander promptly remitted all the money that he could afford.

Marie's state of mind was by no means unique. Thousands lived with their "bags packed" (a popular phrase), convinced that at any moment they could return home and resume normal lives. The Bolshevik triumph was only a temporary aberration. The Soviet regime would collapse momentarily. Kremlin leaders kept a special train in readiness to make good their escape upon the outbreak of the inevitable counterrevolution. French and German landlords and grocers were repeatedly assured that bills would be paid "as soon as we get back to Russia." Every stray rumor of economic breakdowns or popular uprisings within the Soviet Union was eagerly seized and consumed as grist for voracious imaginations.

As years passed, the mists of false hope evaporated, leaving a residue of acrid frustration. The highly touted offensives of Yudenich, Kolchak, Denikin, and Wrangel each faltered after coming tantalizingly close to success. The foreign expeditionary forces withdrew from Russia, triggering indecorous evacuations from Odessa, Sevastopol, and Vladivostok, the last citadels of White resistance. The popular uprisings never materialized. Baffled and hurt, émigrés vented their anger on each other in an orgy of recriminations.

In 1919, three men seated at separate tables in a Paris cafe suddenly recognized each other. One was Grand Duke Alexander. The second was Alexander Kerensky, the radical socialist politician who had headed the short-lived Provisional Government in 1917. The third, Boris Savinkov, was a notorious Social Revolutionary terrorist whose victims had included Alexander's cousin, Grand Duke Sergei. The three defeated men glared at each other in speechless hostility, unable to laugh at the irony of their common fate. All had seen their cherished hopes destroyed. None could safely return to Russia. None could pay the cafe bill without calculating his dwindling resources. Each regarded the other two as responsible for his own predicament. Collectively, they personified the Russian diaspora.

Uprooted and outraged, the Russian émigrés made eager joiners. A welter of organizations sought to channel the exiles' inchoate passions into visionary programs. Some groups descended from parties of the Duma, a prerevolutionary legislative assembly—the Social Democrats (including the Mensheviks), the Social Revolutionaries (SRs), and the Constitutional Democrats (Kadets). Others arose as ad hoc responses to revolution, such as the Committee of Russian Ambassadors and the Russian Armed Services Union. Some thrived on hatred of communism and boasted of conducting terrorism within the Soviet Union. Others professed that Bolshevism was evolving into democracy and urged reconciliation with Stalin. Some pledged to resurrect the Russian Empire. Others swore to dismember the USSR along nationality lines.

The émigrés suffered commonly from a congenital inability to work together. It has been said, perhaps unfairly, that within every Russian lurks an anarchist. The uncertainties and frustrations of exile unleashed a virulent sectarianism that infected even the most innocuous enterprises. Grand Duchess Marie discovered that many fellow exiles refused to be associated with her in charity work because they regarded the Romanovs as responsible for Russia's—and their own—misfortunes. Socialists bickered among themselves as Alexander Kerensky blamed practically everybody but himself for the failure of the February Revolution. Ukrainian nationalists split into pro-German hetmanites backing Paul Skoropadsky and pro-French republicans supporting Simon Petliura. Already fragmented by old regional ties, Cossacks found themselves wooed by competing atamans (leaders), ranging from the philo-Teutonic Pyotr Krasnov to the Japanese favorite, Grigory Semenov. Orthodox prelates haggled over expatriate jurisdictions and shrunken congregations. During the 1920s, maverick Bolsheviks such as Leon Trotsky joined the emigration, adding yet another dissonant note to the general din.

Although supposedly united around the goal of a Romanov restoration, the monarchists split into rival factions backing different candidates for the title of tsar of Russia (in exile). The order of succession to the Romanov throne was difficult to establish, because the Bolsheviks had systematically eliminated the obvious heirs: Nicholas' only son, Alexis; his only living brother, Michael; and his surviving uncle, Paul. Male Romanovs who escaped abroad were cousins or nephews of the last tsar. Neither custom nor law clearly prescribed who should inherit the throne under such extraordinary circumstances. This nebulous situation gave birth to a heated controversy over "legitimism" revolving around, but not limited to, two imperial pretenders.

Grand Duke Nikolai Nikolaevich (1856–1929) was the grandson of Tsar Nicholas I and an avuncular cousin of Nicholas II. He had an emperor's physique: a towering six-foot-six-inch frame, immaculately trimmed silver hair, a sternly lean but expressive face, and an erect, majestical bearing. Yet "Nikolasha," as relatives and intimate friends called him, felt ambivalent about his own imperial pretensions. Worse, surviving members of the Romanov family entertained doubts about him. He was blamed for having exerted a baneful influence on the last tsar. Some never forgave "Uncle Nikolasha" for advising Nicholas to issue the October Manifesto* in 1905 and to abdicate in 1917. Grand Duke Alexander wryly speculated that: "Had Nikolasha advised the Czar on March 2 [old style], 1917 to remain with the army and to accept the challenge of the revolution, Mr. Stalin would not have been entertaining G. B. Shaw in the Kremlin in 1931."

Such handicaps notwithstanding, Grand Duke Nikolai enjoyed considerable support among Russian monarchists throughout the world. His quiet dignity, unquestioned integrity, and simple patriotism appealed to exiles in the 1920s, much as similar qualities in Dwight D. Eisenhower appealed to Americans in the 1950s.

The other leading imperial candidate, Grand Duke Cyril Vladimirovich (1876–1938), was a grandson of Tsar Alexander II, a nephew of Alexander III, and a first cousin of Nicholas II. He had played the insouciant court dandy until the Russo-Japanese War, when a harrowing brush with death as an officer aboard the mined battleship *Petropavlovsk* transformed him into a pensive fatalist. Cyril avoided sharing his cousin's fate by fleeing to Finland in June 1917 with his expectant wife, Victoria, princess of Saxe-Coburg, and infant daughter, Kira. After a graciously nomadic existence in Finland, Switzerland, and southern France, Cyril settled at Villa Edinburgh, his wife's family estate near Coburg in northern Bavaria. Like Nikolasha, Cyril felt diffident about politics. Left to himself, he would have found contentment in golf, gardening, and sports cars. But Victoria ("Ducky"), an ambitious and strong-willed German, had grander plans for her husband than genteel retirement. Well before the Revolution, Victoria and her mother-in-law, Princess Marie of Mecklenburg-Schwerin, had barely concealed their restiveness at the Romanov throne's being occupied by a weakling with a hemophilic heir when eminently eligible "Vladimiroviches" (the male offspring of Grand Duke Vladimir and Princess Marie, of whom Cyril was the eldest) were waiting in the wings. In exile, Victoria became convinced that German support could not only further her spouse's imperial pretensions but might someday

* A decree issued under strong liberal pressure on October 30, 1905. It granted Russia a constitution, extended the franchise and civil liberties, and enlarged the legislative powers of the Duma.

restore the monarchy in Russia. Mobilizing her charm and her family's money, she cultivated the emigration's extreme right wing and through General Erich Ludendorff helped finance Adolf Hitler's fledgling National Socialist German Workers' Party (NSDAP). Hitler himself visited Coburg in 1922 to attend a "German Day" rally sponsored by Victoria's family. Ducky returned the future Führer's attention by gracing a number of SA (storm trooper) rallies.

Under Victoria's prodding, Cyril issued a manifesto "to the Russian people" on August 8, 1924, proclaiming himself the only legitimate pretender to the throne and leader of the monarchist movement. Three weeks later, he formally declared himself Cyril I, tsar of Russia. Cyril's most vociferous devotees clustered in Munich, where they established the Russian Legitimist-Monarchist Union to challenge the Supreme Monarchist Council, which backed Grand Duke Nikolai. The Bavarian government, however, took a dim view of Cyril's pretensions and obliged the "Coburg tsar" to sign a statement renouncing further political activities.

Denied freedom of action in Germany, Cyril and Victoria moved to France in 1927, settling in the village of St. Briac on the rocky coast of Brittany. From an unprepossessing country house, Cyril solemnly set about administering an invisible empire. He issued orders, signed promotions, bestowed imperial praise and pardon, and waited for the call of destiny. St. Briac became a phantom capital. Thousands of letters from throughout the world poured into the village post office, overwhelming the local *facteur,* whose job it was to haul sackfuls of mail to the resident tsar from his scattered "subjects." Cyril gravely studied each letter, determined to rule as a conscientious mail-order sovereign. His correspondents offered information, asked for advice, and sought favors. From America, a former captain of the Guards turned dishwasher in a Midwestern hashery complained that he had not been promoted although several of his friends who had left Russia as lieutenants were now colonels. A Cossack in Bolivia, an officer in Manchuria, a general in India each requested imperial guidance on the propriety of serving in foreign armies. The Russian colony in Harlem, subsisting in grinding poverty, asked for a word of monarchical encouragement. A former Moscow Supreme Court justice working in a Canadian pulp factory confidentially advised that a certain fellow émigré was a dangerous radical who must not be allowed back to Russia after the restoration.

At St. Briac, Cyril surrendered to the conviction that history would someday turn the ridiculous into the sublime. His fantasy world was described with gentle humor by the perennial skeptic, Grand Duke Alexander: "Pathos intermingled with comedy and blindness goaded on by hope from the backbone of this segregated world of make-believe. Nothing is real, everything is a prop."

No amount of whimsical choreography could dispel nagging doubts about Cyril, even among the most enthusiastic monarchists. His unvarnished Germanophilia angered and embarrassed Slavic pride. Victoria's awkward marital record (she had divorced the late Tsar Nicholas' brother-in-law), her refusal to convert from Lutheranism to the Russian Orthodox Church, and her flagrant Nazi sympathies were all damaging liabilities. Worst of all, Cyril's questionable behavior during the February Revolution plagued him in exile. Even before Nicholas had abdicated, the future St. Briac tsar had marched with unseemly haste at the head of the Marine Guards to Petrograd's Tauride Palace and had broken his oath of loyalty to his cousin and sovereign by swearing allegiance to the Provisional Government. If not treason to an empire, it was the betrayal of a family. Few Romanovs forgot or forgave.

The exiled military caste tended to favor Grand Duke Nikolai, who had been a popular if incompetent commander in chief of the Russian Army in 1914–15. General Baron Pyotr Nikolaevich Wrangel, magnetic leader of the Volunteer Army, which made the Whites' last stand in southern Russia, established a Russian Armed Services Union in Paris in 1923 to preserve a semblance of unity and continuity among defunct imperial units. Although designed to remain aloof from politics, the Union was monarchist and pro-Nikolasha to the core. Only naval veterans and some pro-German army officers pledged fealty to Grand Duke Cyril.

Racked by endemic divisiveness and paranoiac mistrust, the Russian diaspora never reached a consensus on how to cope with exile. In the words of Grand Duke Alexander: "Pink and reddish, green and whitish, they were all waiting for the Bolsheviks to fall so that they could go back to Russia and resume their feuds interrupted by the October Revolution."

Disillusioned, most émigrés eventually abandoned all hope of ever seeing Russia again. They turned their attention to seeking assimilation in adopted homelands. As a middle-aged refugee living in Los

Angeles remarked in 1927: "I don't hope to go back to Russia. I don't recognize Russia now. Russia and my past are somewhere in my dreams. My present life is just to live, no ambitions, no thoughts about the future. I am going to be a citizen next month and try to be an American."

Others, however, clung to the vision of a counterrevolution that would enable them to return home and resume their former lives and careers. From among these emerged the Russian fascists.

CHAPTER II

Genesis of the Émigré Right in Europe

We do not want to convert the Russians to National Socialism, but to make them into our tools.

—ADOLF HITLER

At the diaspora's right fringe clustered a motley assortment of ex-officers, politicians, former landowners, and *enragé* intellectuals who formed a bridge between the prerevolutionary radical right and the self-proclaimed fascists who are the subject of this book. Some of these were Russian chauvinists with monarchist inclinations. Others were dispossessed Baltic Germans (ethnic Germans from the Russian Baltic provinces of Courland and Livonia) who looked askance at Slavs. Still others were Ukrainian separatists possessed of arcane grievances and grandiose pretensions. Regardless of their varied backgrounds—and often their mutual hostility—nearly all shared an anti-Semitic streak. Some ascribed the recent catastrophes that had befallen Russia not only to Jews but also to Masons and Asiatics.

Some of the rightists also appear to have been members of a prerevolutionary organization called the Union of Russian People (URP). Founded in 1905 as a response to liberal and revolutionary challenges to tsarist autocracy, the URP and its secret military arm, the Black Hundreds, anticipated subsequent totalitarian movements in Italy and Germany. The Union echoed Nicholas I by calling for "orthodoxy, autocracy, nationality" but departed from conservative tradition by practicing a militant, demagogic political style. Deliberately tailoring its appeal to peasants and bourgeois (the URP distrusted aristocrats as liberals), the Union assiduously fanned popular prejudices. It blamed foreigners, intellectuals, and above all Jews for

16

Russia's afflictions. It agitated noisily for the execution of a Kiev Jew named Beilis, accused in 1911 of ritually murdering a Russian boy. Avowedly antiparliamentarian, the Union nonetheless sent delegates to the second and third Duma to utilize the assembly as a propaganda platform. The tsar and tsarina not only tolerated but publicly commended the Union for its "loyalty." Neither state nor church let the Union's coffers run dry.

What the Union threatened, the Black Hundreds wrought. Reactionary vigilante squads, the Black Hundreds were the storm troopers of a senescent empire. They fomented pogroms and murdered political opponents with a zeal lubricated by surreptitious official handouts.

Vladimir Mitrofanovich Purishkevich (1870–1920), the URP's driving force, has been called the first Russian fascist. The grandson of a Bessarabian village priest, Purishkevich grew up a devout Orthodox in Kishinev, site of a savage pogrom in 1903. He wanted all Jews resettled in Kolyma (northeastern Siberia) but stopped short of his cohorts A. I. Dubrovin and N. E. Markov, who called for physical extermination. To some observers, Purishkevich was a sputtering rabble-rouser. His foulmouthed eruptions in the Duma prompted the Kadet leader Paul Miliukov to dismiss him as a "tragic clown." But bombast and obscenity masked an uncanny talent for organizing men and raising money.

Purishkevich shared the fate of the crumbling edifice that he strove to sustain. During World War I, he broke with his pro-German colleague N. E. Markov and delivered speeches in the Duma that even liberal adversaries roundly applauded. As the old regime tottered on the brink of collapse in December 1916, he joined Grand Duke Dmitry and Prince Felix Yusupov in a plot to kill Rasputin at Yusupov's Moika Palace in Petrograd. When Rasputin failed to succumb to cakes filled with potassium cyanide, Purishkevich dispatched him with a pistol. After the October Revolution, Purishkevich was briefly imprisoned in the Fortress of St. Peter and St. Paul for a quixotic attempt to save the imperial family. He died of typhus in 1920 in Novorossisk, an enclave on the Black Sea temporarily occupied by the Whites.

Purishkevich epitomized the contradictions within Russia's prerevolutionary radical right. While trying to appeal to the bourgeoisie, he, like the Union of Russian People, was unable to jettison his ties to monarchy and the Russian Orthodox Church. The anti-Semitism of both sprang from religious considerations. Burdened with old-

fashioned ideological baggage, these protofascists toyed with new totalitarian methods but ultimately forfeited mass action to the left.

True, a number of URP men such as Markov and V. V. Shulgin
moved to Germany after the October Revolution and sang the praises
of national socialism and fascism. Yet they regarded these movements
not as ends in themselves but as anti-Communist instruments to bring
about a Romanov restoration.

The German Connection

Although the radical right foundered inside Russia, it found apt
students in German exile, particularly among fledgling Nazis in 1919–
23. Berlin and Munich teemed with displaced Russian, Baltic German,
and Ukrainian rightists during these years. Many were former aristocrats, army officers, and politicians who had fought in one of the
White armies or under the banners of General von der Golz's Freikorps along the Baltic. Dazed by events that had stripped them of
family, possessions, and homeland, they grasped at the notion that
Jews and Asiatics had masterminded revolution in Russia and were
about to do the same in western Europe. Some of these émigrés
exerted no little influence over Adolf Hitler. A handful eventually
occupied positions of responsibility in the Third Reich.

Between 1919 and 1923, Baltic Germans, fluent in both Russian
and German, formed an especially strong link between the Russian
diaspora's declining rightist fringe and the rising German national
socialists. As former subjects of the tsar, some felt a residual loyalty
to the Romanov dynasty, but most regarded themselves as the eastern
bulwark of Teutonic civilization, outposts of *Deutschtum* amid a sea
of Slavs. Max Erwin von Scheubner-Richter and Alfred Rosenberg
represented the monarchist and anti-Slav types respectively. The two
had been fraternity brothers at the University of Riga. In different
ways, both personified the "German connection."

Although not an aristocrat by birth (the "von" came from his
wife's family), Scheubner-Richter had what Jimmy Durante called
"class." Handsome, urbane, multilingual, rich and generous, he
dreamed of forging a Russo-German alliance against Bolshevism.
Scheubner-Richter fought in both the Russian (1905) and German
(1918–19) armies against revolutionaries in his native Courland (western Latvia, bordering on the Baltic Sea). In 1920, when he first met

Hitler in Munich, the refugee Balt was on the run from Berlin authorities for involvement in an abortive monarchical coup, the Kapp putsch. But Scheubner-Richter was no mere upstart rowdy. His friends included steel magnate Fritz Thyssen; the hero of Tannenberg, General Erich Ludendorff; and the Coburg tsar, Grand Duke Cyril. Scheubner-Richter's wife, Mathilde, occasionally took Victoria ("Ducky") Romanov to SA exercises outside Munich.

Scheubner-Richter and Hitler felt an immediate mutual attraction. The suave Balt marveled at the ex-lance corporal's hypnotic oratory and was soon extolling him as the "prophet of *völkisch* Deutschland." Hitler shrewdly perceived in Scheubner-Richter an ideal vehicle to gain funds and connections in respectable society.

No sooner had Scheubner-Richter joined the Nazi Party than he started funneling money from wealthy friends into NSDAP coffers. Substantial contributions came from Ducky, who entrusted General Ludendorff with generous sums of her family's cash to distribute among rightist organizations.

Scheubner-Richter's efforts as middleman and fund raiser intensified his desire to build an alliance of German nationalists and Russian monarchists to combat Bolshevism and restore the Romanov dynasty. Late in 1920, he organized a German-Russian popular front called Aufbau (reconstruction), which brought together German rightists and Russian émigrés of similar views. Several Aufbau recruits later served the Third Reich: Balts such as Alfred Rosenberg and Arno Schickedanz, Russians such as Vasily Biskupsky and Pyotr Shabelsky-Bork, and the Cossack hetman Ivan Poltavets-Ostranitsa.

Scheubner-Richter was convinced that only unification of the Russian diaspora's fractured right wing could generate successful collaboration with German nationalists. Determined to bring émigré factions together, he secured funds from sympathetic German businessmen and convened under Aufbau auspices a congress of Russian monarchists in the spring of 1921 at Bad Reichenall, a fairytalelike Bavarian resort not far from Hitler's future Obersaltzberg retreat.

Delegates flocked to Bad Reichenall from throughout Europe. Ataman Semenov sent a representative from Manchuria. Aristocrats, politicians, Ukrainian separatists, Black Hundreds veterans, ex-Okhrana (tsarist secret police) agents, and a former procurator of the Holy Synod mingled in a rare display of fraternity. Rendered euphoric by the alpine scenery, everyone momentarily forgot factional differences and solemnly pledged to rid Russia of Bolshevism. Scheubner-Richter congratulated himself on healing schisms while gently placing the Russian right under German protection. Although their own unity soon dissolved, a number of Russian monarchists thereafter took on a German orientation. And no one left the congress without having heard about an extraordinary man in Munich named Adolf Hitler.

The Bad Reichenall Congress turned out to be Scheubner-Richter's final contribution to Russo-German cooperation. A police slug abruptly ended his life on November 9, 1923, as he marched down Munich's Residenzstrasse arm in arm with Hitler during the beer hall putsch. Falling mortally wounded, he dragged Germany's future Führer to the pavement, probably saving his life from a hail of bullets overhead. Ironically, Scheubner-Richter himself had conceived the idea of a putsch in Munich, although he thought the timing of this one premature.

Had he lived into the 1930s, would Scheubner-Richter have blossomed into a Third Reich luminary? Probably not. Hitler lamented the Balt's passing ("All are replaceable, but not he!") and enshrined him as a martyr in the dedication of *Mein Kampf.* But subsequent Nazi literature ignored him. And no one composed a "Scheubner-Richter Lied" to break the thumping monotony of the Horst Wessel song.

Ultimately, Scheubner-Richter was too tied to the past to become a fully committed Nazi. Like Purishkevich, he remained a conservative who admired storm trooper élan but never embraced national socialism's nihilist and racist core.

If Scheubner-Richter introduced Hitler to money and society, Alfred Rosenberg tutored him in the Russian Revolution. A doltish Balt with an abstruse pen and muddled tongue that spoke better Russian than German, Rosenberg was innocent of intellectual originality. Yet he rose to become—in the ironic words of his archrival, Joseph Goebbels—"the Reich philosopher," and during World War II, he presided over the Ostministerium (Ministry for Occupied Eastern Territories, created in 1941), to the wonder and disgust of Nazi heavyweights. Rosenberg's improbable career prospered thanks solely to Adolf Hitler. During 1919–20, the Balt refugee won the Austrian's confidence as an expert on Russians and Jews, and for a few years, he enjoyed the role of Hitler's ideological mentor. In Rosenberg's turgid pseudoscholarship, Hitler found exhilarating expression for his own inchoate ruminations.

Born in 1893 into a shoemaker's family in Reval (now Tallinn in the Estonian SSR), Rosenberg spent his youth as an awkward, peripatetic bohemian with a strong preference for purple shirts. After wandering around Germany and France before the First World War, he enrolled in the University of Riga to study architecture, joining the same student fraternity as Scheubner-Richter. With the outbreak of hostilities in 1914, Rosenberg evacuated Riga for Moscow. Avoiding conscription and oblivious to the revolutionary upheavals around him, the future "Russian expert" of the Third Reich spent 1917 designing a crematorium embellished with Romanesque vaults and Doric colonnades.

Like many émigrés, Rosenberg stumbled upon politics in exile. After drifting around the Crimea, he gravitated to Munich in 1919, immersing himself in the contagious atmosphere of rightist Russian and German outrage. Suddenly awakening to a new calling, the dreamy architect mutated into a compulsive pamphleteer.

Rosenberg's intellectual contribution to Nazism consisted of blending religiously inspired Russian anti-Semitism with pseudoscientific German racial doctrine. To Houston Stewart Chamberlain and Friedrich Nietzsche, he added Black Hundreds *Zhidomasonstvo* (Jew-Masonism), Baltic-German Russophobia, and dashes of Indian mysticism to produce an apocalyptic vision of the "hidden hand" in history. Rosenberg distilled this brew in *Myth of the Twentieth Century* (1930), which, despite its unreadability, eventually joined *Mein Kampf* as a Third Reich best-seller.

In Rosenberg's phantasmagoric universe, Jews infested the ranks of capitalists, liberals, and revolutionaries alike by camouflaging their identity with Gentile names. Obsessed with Zionism, they had bred every calamity from the fall of Rome to World War I. It was Jewish finance allied with the Asiatic underworld—mainly Armenians and Chinese—that fomented the Russian Revolution as a preparatory step to annihilating the West. Communism was a race conspiracy, not an ideology. Trotsky (Bronstein), Zinoviev (Apfelbaum), Radek, and Kaganovich were collaborators, not enemies, of the Rothschilds, Warburgs, and Schiffs. Brooding, ignorant, indolent, and anarchistic, Russians had failed to resist blood pollution and as a consequence suffered subjection. Only the Germans—disciplined, intelligent, and heroic—could save Europe from the Jewish-Asiatic plague.

Rosenberg owed a special debt to a fellow Balt for devising an efficacious method for handling the Jewish problem. Fyodor Viktorovich Vinberg, a colonel in the Imperial Russian Army who had exiled himself to Berlin, propounded some novel ideas in anti-Semitic periodicals that he published from 1919 until his death in 1927. He introduced to Germany the spurious *Protocols of the Elders of Zion* (an alleged blueprint for global Zionism), which Rosenberg disseminated with epidemic success. But Vinberg's more telling contribution was his insistence that only physical extermination could stop the Jew. He thereby prefigured the "Final Solution" subsequently carried out in the Third Reich.

Rosenberg's demonology appealed to Hitler, confirming the Austrian's views on Jews, Slavs, and Bolsheviks. It elevated his hatreds into a philosophy. By defining Communists in racial rather than in ideological terms, it obviated the need to respond to the intellectual challenge of Marxism. Hitler rewarded the Balt in 1921 by making him editor of the Nazi Party newspaper, *Völkischer Beobachter.*

Toward rightist Russian émigrés Rosenberg felt a mixture of approbation and condescension. On one hand, he appreciated the potential of Black Hundreds doctrine. He scanned émigré newspapers, approvingly noting an occasional swastika or a flattering comparison of Hitler to Peter the Great. On the other hand, Rosenberg nurtured a Baltic German's disdain for Slavs. He regarded Slavs as racially inferior (bastardized by Tartar blood), culturally primitive, and temperamentally chaotic.

Rosenberg conceded that Slavs might become fascists, but not national socialists, this honor being reserved for Germans only. He recoiled from the prospect of a unified fascist Russian state and favored dismemberment of the Soviet Union along ethnic lines into a mosaic of innocuous republics dominated by Germany. Russians, he opined, should seek their destiny in Asia, thereby regaining their "inner balance" and fulfilling their "racial mission." A Ukrainian separatist could tolerate such a scenario, but even the most philo-Nazi Russian patriot choked over the command: "Go East, young man!"

Under Rosenberg's aegis, scores of Baltic Germans joined the Nazi Party in the 1920s and thereafter served the Third Reich as "Russian experts." Their Russophobia reinforced Hitler's own anti-

Slav instincts and stifled any possibility of sympathy for Russian nationalist aspirations.

Rosenberg's chief understudy in the "Baltic Mafia" was Arno Schickedanz. Their friendship dated from student fraternity days at Riga University and ripened through collaboration in Aufbau, *Völkischer Beobachter,* and the NSDAP Foreign Policy Office (of which Rosenberg was appointed director in 1933). Schickedanz carved out for himself a minor reputation as an ideologue, coining the epithet "bastardizing herd" for Jews. For his "mastery" of Russian affairs, he was named *Gauleiter* of the Caucasus in 1942. The Wehrmacht retreat after Stalingrad prevented Schickedanz from reaching his post, and he committed suicide with his whole family in 1945 to avoid capture by erstwhile countrymen.

Not all Baltic Germans who worked for the Third Reich were Rosenberg protégés. Joseph Goebbels collected his own stable of "Russian experts" in Anti-Komintern, a department of the Propaganda Ministry. Rosenberg and Goebbels rarely ceased their jealous feud over whose Russian experts should manage anti-Bolshevik propaganda. The Baltic Mafia had its own share of family quarrels.

With Russophobic Baltic Germans installed as NSDAP advisers on the USSR, Russian émigrés found it increasingly difficult to gain Nazi support for their own anti-Soviet enterprises. Scheubner-Richter's death in 1923 deprived them of a vital link to Hitler. Hitler, for his part, lost interest in wealthy monarchists once Nazism had become a mass movement, and after 1933, Russian émigrés were regarded as expendable nuisances, to be tolerated if they behaved, to be crushed if they showed signs of independence.

Ukrainians, on the other hand, received encouragement not only from Rosenberg but also from Rudolf Hess and Hermann Goering, because Ukrainian separatism fitted neatly into Nazi strategic thinking about eastern Europe. But potential Ukrainian beneficiaries of Nazi largesse fought among themselves incessantly. As their pretensions were sometimes of a magnitude to make even Goebbels blush, their German patrons took them with a grain of salt.

The Russian Nazis

Responding to a deteriorating political and economic situation, the Russian community in Germany declined from 250,000 in 1923 to 50,000 in 1933. Most of the émigrés moved to Paris, Prague, and the Balkans. Of those who remained, some made pathetic attempts to reconcile Russian patriotism with loyalty to the Third Reich. Others abjured their own nationality, became "honorary Germans," and aped their overlords.

General Vasily V. Biskupsky epitomized the combination of sycophancy and self-delusion with which rightist émigrés in Nazi Germany tried to mask their impotence. One of the most universally disliked men of the Russian emigration, Biskupsky compensated for a shattered army career by hatching capers in exile. In 1919, he noisily but unsuccessfully clamored for a command in General von der Golz's Freikorps, boasting that he would personally lead a Russian-German army to Moscow and from there to Versailles. In 1920, he joined the Kapp putsch, organizing sympathetic Russian officers in Berlin. Escaping to Munich when the putsch fizzled, he collaborated with General Ludendorff in a scheme to raise a counterrevolutionary army of Russians, Germans, Hungarians, and Italians to sweep across central Europe restoring monarchies as it went.

Biskupsky shuffled between respectability and crime with blithe insouciance, attracted to action more than to ideology. He slipped into Aufbau and played the portentous impresario at Bad Reichenall. He adopted as protégés two thugs named Sergei Taboritsky and Pyotr Shabelsky-Bork, who in 1922 had fatally shot the liberal journalist Vladimir Nabokov, father of the eminent novelist, in a bungled attempt to assassinate the ex-Kadet leader Paul Miliukov. Biskupsky cultivated the Coburg circle, proclaiming himself Grand Duke Cyril's "prime minister" and lapping up Victoria's subsidies. Unshaken by Cyril's departure from Germany in 1927, Biskupsky continued to sniff out money and concoct quixotic crusades.

Biskupsky hailed the Nazi triumph of 1933, assuming that his old friends "Alfred Voldemarovich" (Rosenberg) and "Arno Gustavovich" (Schickedanz) would repay him for favors rendered in the previous decade. But the Balts turned a deaf ear to his appeals for money and his promise to organize a spy ring within the French General Staff. Biskupsky seems to have annoyed someone with his importunities, because during the summer of 1933 the Gestapo picked him up and let him cool off in prison for a while.

But shameless self-abasement finally earned Biskupsky the prize that had so long eluded him. After pledging eternal loyalty to Hitler, he was in 1936 appointed head of a Nazi agency designed to coordinate émigré affairs: the Bureau for Russian Refugees *(Vertrauenstelle für Russische Flüchtlinge)* on Berlin's Bleibtreustrasse. Assisted by Nabokov's killer, Sergei Taboritsky, Biskupsky presided over the Reich's dwindling Russian community, kept by his masters on a very tight leash. He got nowhere in his attempt to claim 200,000 Reichsmarks deposited at the Mendelsohn Bank before the Revolution in the name of Nicholas II. Nor did he succeed in gaining control of the Nazified émigré paper, *Novoye Slovo.* He ended up a pathetic ornament, decorating sham committees and penning ingratiating invitations to Heinrich Himmler, invitations the Reichsführer SS never bothered to answer.

A few émigrés sought acceptance among Nazis by becoming storm troopers. As early as 1924, some Russian veterans of General von der Golz's Freikorps formed a youth club loosely affiliated with the NSDAP. Called the Russian Auxiliary, its members regularly joined SA (Brownshirt) *Stürme* in training exercises near Zehden, a village about fifty miles northeast of Berlin. On the spacious estate of a Brandenburg Junker (Wilhelm von Flottow), Russian and German youths marched, sang, and practiced the niceties of machine guns, bayonets, clubs, brass knuckles, and jujitsu. Unemployed, impoverished, and action-hungry young émigrés derived a certain satisfaction from these outings, and the NSDAP provided each recruit with hearty food and a small allowance. The Russians even got their own distinctive uniform: white shirt, black trousers, riding boots, and swastika arm bands colored in Imperial Russian red, white, and blue. Brownshirts were apt to smile patronizingly at Whiteshirts. But back in Berlin, everybody fraternized at the Geisbergstrasse Brauhaus where the Slavic storm troopers slaked their thirst on beer laced with vodka. In 1928, the Russian Auxiliary was merged—permanently—with the Schöneberg SA so that its muscle could be employed in rumbles with local Communist *Rotfrontkämpfer.*

Within three weeks of Hitler's appointment as chancellor on January 30, 1933, a small group of émigrés announced the formation of the Russian National Socialist Movement (ROND). ROND revived the sartorial peculiarities of the Russian Auxiliary, and some enthusiasts added the toothbrush mustache in an adulatory if overliteral emulation of their idol. ROND's first *vozhd* (leader) was an obscure figure named A. P. Svetozarov, who bore a certain resemblance to Goebbels. He returned to oblivion before the end of 1933, for reasons that are still unclear.

Svetozarov's successor bore a surname that reminded émigrés of a well-known prerevolutionary vodka brand: Bermondt-Avalov. Born in 1884 in Tiflis, "Prince" Pavel Mikhailovich Bermondt-Avalov reeked of unsavory rumors circulated by his many enemies within and without the diaspora. A mustachioed army officer politicized by revolution, he was popular with his men and brought a number of followers with him into exile. In 1919, Bermondt-Avalov led a detachment of former Russian war prisoners against Bolsheviks in the Baltic area. Like his rival Biskupsky, he hopped in and out of the Weimar Republic as a persona non grata full of questionable schemes.

Bermondt-Avalov stuffed ROND with veterans of the Baltic campaigns and with seedy figures such as Pyotr Shabelsky-Bork, Nabokov's other murderer. But he failed to attract wide support, even among pro-Nazi émigrés. As both Hitler and Himmler were repelled by the spectacle of Slavs aping national socialism, the Gestapo watched ROND closely and periodically broke up its activities. ROND limped along for several years before finally folding in the wake of the Nazi-Soviet Pact in August 1939.

The ultimate step that a collaboration-minded émigré could take was to repudiate his Slavic identity and become an "ethnic German" (*Volksdeutscher*). Only a handful opted for deliberate mutation. One of them, Grigory Bostunich, stands out as a twisted hybrid of Nazi–Black Hundreds psychopathology. Born in Kiev of well-to-do parents, Bostunich grew up fascinated by Jewish sexuality and Judaeo-Masonic symbolism. After serving Denikin and Wrangel as a propagandist during the Civil War, he joined the stream of Russian rightists to Germany. Like Rosenberg, for whom he briefly worked, Bostunich dabbled in the arts, publishing a play that ended with a Jewish Cheka agent crucifying the infant son of a Russian general. But Bostunich found his true avocation as an SS scholar sniffing out Jews and Masons in history books.

Entering the elitist Nazi organization only after changing his name to Schwarz, Bostunich renounced completely his Slavic antecedents. He impressed Himmler with his canine devotion and was appointed "Honorary SS Professor," in which capacity he toured Germany lecturing on Jews and Masons in flawed German, rescued only by his zest as a raconteur. Under Himmler's wing, Schwarz-Bostunich rose through the SS hierarchy to the rank of *Standartenführer* (equivalent to colonel), an achievement unmatched by any Nazi Slav except for a renegade Russian-Pole named Bronislav Vladislavovich Kaminsky.

Kaminsky's brief career as a Nazi coincided with World War II. At the outbreak of hostilities, he was working as an engineer at a liquor distillery in Lokot, a town located about halfway between Moscow and Kiev. Kaminsky bore a grudge against the Soviet regime. Like thousands of other Russians of Polish bourgeois extraction, he had been arrested in 1935 and sent to a concentration camp where he languished until 1940. The arrival of the German invaders not only gave him an opportunity to vent his resentments but prompted him to become a national socialist. In January 1942, with the Wehrmacht's blessing, Kaminsky inherited and consolidated the "Lokot Self-Governing District" into one of the only indigenously administered regions of German-occupied Russia. Dubbed "warlord of the Briansk forest," Kaminsky established a Russian Nazi Party within his midget realm, backed up by a ragged but fierce brigade of Russians, Poles, and Ukrainians. When the eastern front began to fold in 1943, Kaminsky and his followers moved westward through Belorussia to Ratibor on the Polish-Czech frontier. As the SS internationalized itself toward the final months of the war, Kaminsky's brigade emerged as the 29th Division of the Waffen SS, distinguishing itself in savagery during the abortive Warsaw uprising of August–October, 1944.

Kaminsky was spared the fate of falling into the hands of the Soviets or Poles. Even the SS found his rapacity in Warsaw intolerable. While German units mopped up the last pockets of insurgents, Kaminsky was taken into custody, sent to Lodz by car, and shot. His death was officially reported to have been the result of a partisan ambush.

Nazis such as Biskupsky, Bermondt-Avalov, Bostunich, and Kaminsky differed fundamentally from thousands of Soviet citizens who may have worked for the Germans during World War II. Red Army prisoners of war who joined German combat units *(Osttruppen)* or served as auxiliaries *(Hilfswillige)* generally did so to escape slow death in camps. Non-Slavic minorities may have found ethnic gratification in the small Armenian, Azerbaijani, Caucasian, Georgian, Kalmyk, Muslim, and Turkic units formed by the SS. Many collaborators hated Stalin, but virtually none admired Hitler. Andrei Vlasov, a magnetic and able Soviet lieutenant general who in German captivity adorned a "Russian National Committee" and led a chimerical "Russian Liberation Army," was neither a Nazi nor a fascist. The same can be said about the Don Cossack ataman Pyotr Nikolaevich Krasnov, who joined Lieutenant General Hellmuth von Pannwitz's Cossack units operating against partisans in Yugoslavia and Italy. Vlasov and Krasnov, if anything, were symbols of the futility of trying to fight Stalinism without being contaminated with Nazism.

But for all their differences, Russian Nazis and Russian anti-Stalinists shared the same fate. In Soviet eyes, both were traitors and dealt with accordingly. In retrospect, they appear more like creatures ground up in the gears of processes beyond their control or understanding.

The Lure of Fascism

It would be misleading and unfair to assume that Russian émigrés drawn to fascism were indistinguishable from the species that flocked to the NSDAP, Ostministerium, and SS. Fascism as embodied by Benito Mussolini attracted émigrés in all corners of the diaspora during the 1920s, émigrés who were not necessarily anti-Semitic, philo-German, or opportunistic. Exiled youths in particular tended to view the recent Italian experience as relevant to their own needs.

During the 1920s, a new generation of Russian émigrés came to maturity in exile. Its members had outlooks sharply different from those of their parents. Born around the turn of the century, these youthful expatriates had tasted revolution and civil war in childhood or adolescence. Some had fought as beardless cadets in White arms and had seen things that had unhinged older and tougher men.

Detesting Bolshevism, these young exiles nevertheless lacked their elders' nostalgic attachment to prerevolutionary institutions. While they held the monarchy in respect, they largely dismissed monarchists as anachronistic and moribund. While admiring aspects of socialism, they disdained émigré socialists as bickering theorists. They thirsted for action. They scanned the horizon for a dynamic antidote to Bolshevism.

Italian fascism offered many of these young Russian émigrés just what they had been seeking. Mussolini exuded energy, charisma, and idealism during the 1920s. His lieutenants such as Giuseppe Bottai and Gastone Spinetti exalted youth in apocalyptic terms. Fascist youth would transform the world by sweeping away capitalism and communism, twin symptoms of western civilization's decay. Black-shirted *squadristi* had already saved Italy from parliamentary rot and Communist subversion. Europe's nationalist youth, in the words of Bottai and Spinetti, must launch a "fascist international."

Exiled young Russian patriots were susceptible to such rhetoric and impressed by Italy's apparent new sense of national purpose. Craving solidarity, they enthusiastically embraced fascism's repudiation of class conflict and fascism's exaltation of national spirit. Offended by Nazism's racial exclusivity, they welcomed a doctrine that, in the 1920s, was felt to possess a universal character and which contained no humiliating references to Slavs. Convinced that Soviet communism was itself evolving under Stalin into communo-fascism, they felt an urgent need to emulate the Italian model before it was too late.

In perceiving Italian fascism as a key to strength and vitality, Russian émigrés were by no means alone. At various times during the 1920s, and even in the 1930s, some of Europe's leading intellectuals (Pirandello, T. S. Eliot, Yeats, Lawrence, Pound, and Shaw come to mind) expressed admiration for Mussolini. Nor was fascism's appeal confined to Europeans. Chiang Kai-shek declared in 1932 that "fascism is what China now most needs." Seven years later in New York, Harlem black militants founded an overtly fascist Ethiopian Pacific Movement. Sublimely protean, fascism lent itself to radical visionaries of all stripes.

Profascist currents surfaced in several Russian émigré groups that sprouted in Paris, Berlin, and Belgrade during the late 1920s and early 1930s. Members of these organizations often referred to themselves as "solidarists," to signify their rejection of the Marxian notion of class struggle and their conviction that Russians must subordinate their differences to achieve an anti-Soviet national revolution. Solidarists tended to be young and well educated. A high proportion were sons of former tsarist officials. They inherited their fathers' fierce nationalism but not their fathers' monarchist loyalties.

Among the myriad solidarist organizations around the Russian diaspora, the Young Russia movement and the National Toilers' Alliance (*Natsionalno Trudovoi Soyuz*—NTS) probably mobilized the widest support. The Young Russia movement (*Mladorossy*) was founded in Paris around 1930 by Alexander Lvovich Kazem-Bek. The NTS, originally called the National Union of the New Generation, was established in 1932 by M. A. Georgievsky and drew most of its membership from émigrés settled in Yugoslavia and Bulgaria.

The Young Russia group flirted fitfully with the Nazis but formed no lasting relationship with them. Kazem-Bek came to Berlin in September 1933 and signed a friendship pact with Bermondt-Avalov (ROND), but no significant collaboration emerged from this meeting.

Some solidarists responded favorably to "radical" Nazis such as Gregor and Otto Strasser, who stressed the socialist component of national socialism. Viktor Alexandrov, who as a young émigré lived in Berlin under the Weimar Republic, recalled: "For many—and I must confess I was one—the National Socialist movement, as exemplified by Otto Strasser's extremist group which was later liquidated, had a certain attraction."

With Gregor Strasser shot and his brother Otto in exile after the Nazi Party blood purge of June 30, 1934, Russian solidarists found it increasingly unhealthy to operate within the Third Reich. After a series of Gestapo raids, the NTS abolished its German branch in August 1938. While individual NTS members cooperated with Wehrmacht combat units, Rosenberg's Ostministerium, and Kaminsky's Russian Nazi Party during World War II, their actions sprang from opportunistic considerations rather than ideological conviction. Eventually, their Russian patriotism proved incompatible with German requirements, and NTS leaders within German-occupied Europe were arrested and interned by the Gestapo in the summer of 1944.

Europe spawned Russian fascism but gave it no chance to develop into a coherent political movement. Imperial Russia produced proto-fascists who stubbornly clung to monarchy and orthodoxy until their activities were cut short by the October Revolution. Italy offered a model to emulate but lacked a sizable Russian community in which a fascist movement could take root. France and Yugoslavia sheltered semifascist solidarist groups that remained scattered and uninfluential, even within the emigration. Germany attracted the bulk of Russian rightists but after 1933 tolerated them only as Third Reich minions.

Not Europe, as it turned out, but the Far East and the United States provided an environment in which Russian fascism found its fullest expression.

CHAPTER III

White Ghettos in China

You are an Asiatic. So am I.
—JOSEF STALIN (1941)

We are an Asiatic people.
—ALEXANDER SOLZHENITSYN (1973)

The Far East was the Wild West of the Russian diaspora. Some émigrés found an El Dorado there; others stumbled into their graves. No one escaped the shock waves of war and civil war that rocked East Asia after the Russian Revolution. Caught up in a maelstrom of Chinese nationalism, Japanese imperialism, and Soviet communism, Russian expatriates had little choice but to move with the prevailing political currents. Living in turn under warlords, samurai, and commissars, they served each in order to survive.

The uncertainties of Far Eastern exile paled in comparison with the nightmarish exodus from a homeland torn by war and revolution. From European Russia, the shortest routes to asylum led to the west, through Finland, Poland, and the Ukraine. But these were also the obvious routes and were guarded accordingly. Consequently, thousands of refugees elected to risk flight across Siberia toward China and the Pacific.

Siberia from 1918 until 1922 was a scene of bitter struggle between Reds and Whites, exacerbated by the presence of Japanese, British, and American expeditionary forces and some 45,000 armed Czechs (former Austro-Hungarian prisoners of war) trying to get back to their homeland. For a brief period between the autumn of 1918 and the summer of 1919, Admiral Alexander Kolchak, leader of a White government based at Omsk, managed—barely—to maintain order along the central sections of the Trans-Siberian Railroad. As the only means of transportation other than wagons or river boats, the railroad was a vital lifeline for the Whites and an obvious escape route for eastwardbound refugees. The collapse of Kolchak's Ural offensive in the spring of 1919 signaled the beginning of a deluge. As Red Army units erupted into Siberia from the west and Red partisans created terror in the east, the White retreat disintegrated into a frenzied scramble toward the Pacific. A motley throng of troops, peasants, politicians, bureaucrats, merchants, and family dependents surged toward the clogged rails, desperate to get a toehold on any train moving toward Vladivostok. But Czech legionnaires and foreign advisers commandeered all usable rolling stock, and Kolchak himself reached only as far as Irkutsk, where his train was blocked from proceeding further. In an act typical of the Russian Civil War, the Czechs and a French military adviser handed the unfortunate man over to the Bolsheviks in exchange for their own unobstructed passage eastward.

The refugees soon discovered that fellow Whites could act as viciously as the Bolsheviks. Local strongmen along the Trans-Siberian Railroad took advantage of the breakdown of central authority to plunder the helpless stream of humanity passing through their bailiwicks. Carving out sanctuaries in Manchuria and the Maritime Province, Cossacks such as Grigory Mikhailovich Semenov extracted a heavy toll from their fleeing countrymen.

Although there are those who revere his memory, Ataman Semenov was one of the most unsavory characters thrust into prominence by the Revolution. A Cossack leader in eastern Siberia, he was commissioned in 1917 by Kerensky's Provisional Government to recruit a military unit for deployment against Germany on the European front. Semenov responded by raising a private army which he called the "Special Manchurian Detachment." Following the October Revolution, Semenov stepped into a local power vacuum and set himself up at Chita as an independent warlord of Trans-Baikalia. With the Allied Intervention in 1918, Semenov's Detachment suddenly emerged as one of the stronger "native" anti-Bolshevik forces east of Lake Baikal. Despite (or because of) his bad reputation in the American Expeditionary Force, Semenov was generously subsidized by the Japanese. He became a jealous rival of Admiral Kolchak, with whose supplies and communications the ataman wrought havoc. Kolchak's collapse late in 1919 and execution on February 7, 1920, left Semenov virtually alone to face the advancing Red tide, but he managed to prolong his patriotic pillaging for another year before retiring with (reputedly) two railroad carloads of loot to the safety of Dairen in Japan's Kwantung Territory.

Those refugees who tried to avoid Manchuria and reach China through Outer Mongolia risked a grislier fate, here at the hands of a psychopathic Baltic German: Baron Roman Fyodorovich von Ungern-Sternberg. A tsarist officer unstrung by the murder of his wife and children during the Revolution, Ungern sought solace in butchering real or putative Reds. Detaching himself from Semenov in 1920, the red-haired, blue-eyed, cupid-faced sadist prowled the Siberian-Manchurian-Outer Mongolian frontier zone with a cosmopolitan brigade of Mongols, Chinese, Russians, and Japanese. Fancying himself a divine agent destined to purge a decadent Europe by resurrecting the Mongol Empire of Genghis Khan, Ungern drove a Chinese army out of Urga (now Ulan Bator) and prepared for a crusade against the Soviet Union. Backed by a corps of fanatically loyal Mongols, the "Bloody Baron" conscripted anyone imprudent enough to come within his reach. Hundreds of unfortunate Russian refugees found themselves in the clutches of a homicidal maniac; anyone who demurred from joining the baron risked being gibbeted on an Urga rooftop and left to rot.

For those who came out of Siberia and Mongolia alive, China seemed tame—at first.

The Geography of Far Eastern Exile

Of the 250,000 Russians who poured into the Far East during 1918–22, a little over half settled in China, gravitating to Manchuria and to treaty ports such as Shanghai, Tientsin, and Tsingtao. Relatively few went to Japan, in the words of the tsarist diplomat Dmitry Abrikossow, "partly because entry into Japan was more difficult, partly because Russians, though I do not know why, generally feel more at home in China." Some took up residence in Hong Kong, Indochina, and the Philippines. Those who could get visas and could pay the costs of overseas travel continued on to the Americas and Australia. One refugee wound up on Yap, a cluster of reef-ringed rocks in the Caroline Islands, a Micronesian archipelago under Japanese mandate

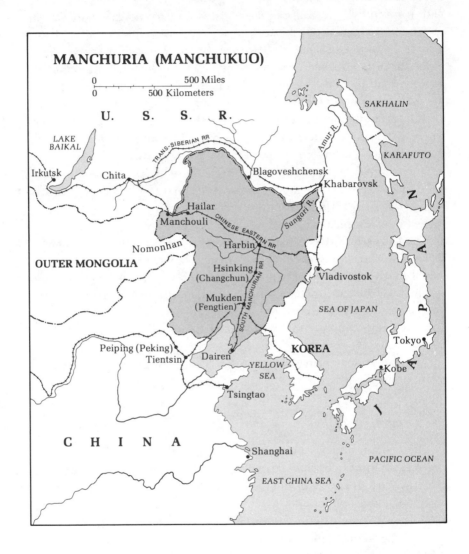

MANCHURIA (MANCHUKUO)

until World War II. He was still living there in 1977, a proud, betel-nut-chewing father of twelve Russian-Yapese.

Located midway along the China coast, Shanghai in the 1920s was undisputably the greatest seaport in the Far East. Connecting the vast Yangtze River basin with the ocean, it served as a trading center for one-eighth of humanity. Most of Shanghai's three million inhabitants lived in huts sprawled out over muddy river flats. Some thirty thousand Europeans, including nineteen thousand White Russians, resided in two extraterritorial enclaves, each of which had its own administration and police force: the International Settlement and the French Concession. A few Russians with means managed to establish residency in the French Concession, but the vast majority clustered north of the Soochow Creek in a corner of the International Settlement called Hongkew. Hongkew, which had a large Japanese population as well, was also known as Little Tokyo.

Life in Shanghai had its share of painful reminders that exile meant downward social mobility. After 1920, the White Russians ceased to enjoy extraterritorial privileges, a loss that set them sharply apart from other Europeans. Hoping to gain a modicum of status, some of the émigrés took Chinese citizenship. Others, with no intention of returning to the USSR, applied for Soviet passports. In general, the Chinese—no strangers to humiliation—showed a sympathetic understanding toward those who had sought refuge in their city. But fellow Europeans rarely concealed their distaste for émigrés who lived and worked in circumstances that tarnished the myth of Caucasian superiority.

Status woes notwithstanding, Shanghai's Russians preferred their adopted city to other Asian alternatives. They even congratulated themselves on not having to haggle with Paris landlords or rusticate on Balkan farms. Besides, Shanghai offered them opportunities to make a living. Lawyers and doctors launched successful practices. Entrepreneurs opened pharmacies, dress shops, and cafes along fashionable Nanking Road. Beefier types joined one of the municipal police forces (such as the International Settlement's Russian Regiment and the French Concession's Russian Volunteer Detachment) or hired themselves out as bodyguards and bouncers. Many women found work as governesses, secretaries, or domestic servants.

To be sure, not all of Shanghai's Russian denizens fared—or behaved—so well. There were those who eked out a living peddling cheap cloth. Others used their impeccable manners and histrionic skills to become genteel con artists, such as the Stanovoi brothers, who posed as French consular officials and sold gambling licenses to unsuspecting Chinese merchants in the French Concession. Shanghai's innumerable dingy bars and noisy carbarets teemed with White Russian "princesses," although, in the uncharitable words of one customer, some had "thick ankles and wrists and the manners of stable peasants." But others gave off a tragic gentility, and a number of Russian bar girls in fact did come from once well-to-do families which, having lived off their jewels until none remained, were forced to sell their pubescent daughters into prostitution. Toughened by the down-and-out life, once fragile virgin blossoms took to Shanghai's alleys, vying for business with the cheapest Chinese streetwalkers.

Regardless of their occupations, the Russian émigrés found that Shanghai had a certain amoral exuberance, an indulgent permissiveness that tranquilized nerves frayed by war and revolution. Former residents of St. Petersburg found that the "Paris of the Far East" offered spiritual (if not material) compensation for what had been left behind in Russia. The Bund promenade along the Huongpu River bustled with cosmopolitan crowds unimaginable even on the Nevsky Prospekt. Where else could one brush shoulders with Frenchmen, Germans, Britishers, Americans, Japanese, Koreans, Indians, Malays, and Annamese, not to mention Chinese? Where else could a drinker drown his sorrow at the longest bar in the world? Besides, Russian newspapers, stores, restaurants, and clubs all invested life in exile with a thread of continuity with a vanished but vivid prerevolutionary past.

Tientsin also attracted a considerable émigré population. Smaller but no less flamboyant than Shanghai, Tientsin served as northern China's main treaty port and as the maritime gateway to Peiping (Peking), which lay about seventy miles to the northwest. A colony of three thousand émigrés nestled in the dilapidated former Russian Concession there, which since the Revolution had reverted to Chinese sovereignty. A few of the wealthier or better-connected families managed to transfer their property to the English and French concessions.

The more affluent Russian residents of Shanghai and Tientsin spent the summer months at Peitaiho, 140 miles northeast of Tientsin, where the Great Wall approaches the Gulf of Chihli, or at Tsingtao and Chefoo, coastal cities on the Shantung peninsula. There they enjoyed the company of British and American naval officers whose squadrons regularly came up from Hong Kong and Manila to avoid the heat. Girls of good breeding came there with their families, dreaming about an emancipating marriage. Tarts flocked there too, drawn by the sailors.

Peiping contained only a handful of White Russians in the 1920s. In the 1930s, however, thousands more moved there from Manchuria to avoid the mixed blessings of Japanese rule.

Manchuria sheltered the greatest concentration of White Russians in the Far East: 155,000 in 1922. Contiguous to eastern Siberia, Manchuria had a historical association with Russia dating from the seventeenth century, when the Cossacks made abortive attempts to occupy the Amur basin. The Russian presence in Manchuria revived in 1896 when China granted the tsarist government the right to construct a railroad that cut across 950 miles of northern Manchuria and linked the Trans-Siberian line with Vladivostok. Called the Chinese Eastern Railway (CER), the line temporarily relieved Russia from having to build a much longer railroad to Vladivostok along the Amur River. In 1898, China awarded Russia permission to construct a CER branch line southward from Harbin to Port Arthur, a leased Russian naval base on the tip of the Liaotung peninsula, southwest of Dairen. Railroad construction brought thousands of Russian laborers, engineers, clerks, guards, and merchants to Manchuria. The new settlers took up residence at various points along the CER tracks, forming Russian enclaves in Chinese territory. Defeat in war with Japan (1904–5) reduced the area of Russian influence to northern Manchuria, while the Japanese took over the southern section of the CER (from Changchun to Port Arthur), renaming it the South Manchurian Railway (SMR) in 1907. A semigovernment enterprise, the SMR became the principal instrument for Japan's economic penetration of Manchuria until 1945.

In the apt words of Owen Lattimore, Manchuria in the 1920s was a "cradle of conflict." By the end of the decade, after heavy immigration from Shantung, about 80 percent—twenty million—of Manchuria's population was Chinese. The indigenous Manchus had become a minority of four million, followed by Koreans (800,000) and Japanese (350,000, including population in the SMR Railway Zone and Kwantung Leased Territory). Manchuria's strategic location and rich natural resources whetted the appetites of both Japan and the

Soviet Union. Legally part of China, Manchuria from 1918 until 1928 was in fact ruled by a colorful warlord named Chang Tso-lin.

Of humble background, Chang Tso-lin rose to become a powerful warlord in the region through a combination of charisma and chicanery. Organizing mounted bandits into guerrilla squads, he hired himself out to the highest bidder, fighting against the Japanese in the Sino-Japanese War (1894–95) and for the Japanese in the Russo-Japanese War. As China sank into a condition of chronic chaos after the fall of the Manchu dynasty in 1911, Chang carved out a satrapy in the Manchu homeland, locating his headquarters at Fengtien* and giving himself the title of "Marshal" (subsequently amended in popular parlance to "Old Marshal" to distinguish him from his son and successor, Chang Hsüeh-liang or "Young Marshal").

A connoisseur of political gamesmanship, the Tiger of Manchuria, as Chang was nicknamed, deftly exploited the rivalries of hungry neighbors to ensure his own survival. He alternately fought and feted the Peiping government, flirted with and put off the Japanese, and propitiated and harassed the Soviets. Like a number of warlords, Chang was obsessed with status and legitimacy. Although his 250,000-man army was paid from his own coffers, the Old Marshal insisted on calling himself a "military governor," thereby preserving the veneer of being appointed by some central Chinese government. Enjoying the comforts consonant with his elevated position, Chang built himself a facsimile French chateau near Fengtien and stocked it with wines, wives, and Confucian classics.

Chang's appearance belied his ruthlessness. He looked like a sedentary scholar, complete with delicate physique, gently sloping shoulders, and mild—almost diffident—manners. But beneath this unassuming exterior lurked a will capable of capricious savagery. On one occasion, he invited nine Chinese bankers suspected of currency manipulation to his headquarters. After listening to his admonitory lecture on ethics, they were decapitated. Executions carried out with imagination and panache satisfied Chang's sense of justice.

Having meted out death so liberally, Chang took elaborate precautions to protect himself. From Detroit, he obtained a custom-made, armor-plated 1921 Packard sedan equipped with steel window blinds, accommodations for six bodyguards, and mounts for two .50-caliber water-cooled machine guns. Whenever he made a sortie from Fengtien

* Also called Mukden. Today the city is named Shenyang.

headquarters, he traveled in one of four armored cars, each of which took off in a different direction to confuse would-be assassins.

Chang Tso-lin deported himself like a gentleman to Russian refugees in his domain, showing not only civility but compassion to those whom fate had put in his hands. He granted extensive territories to some ten thousand Trans-Baikal Cossacks along the Argun River in northern Manchuria. He employed thousands of Russians in his government, army, and police, often giving them preference over Chinese. Sufficiently well financed from the salt tax, railroad revenues, and protection fees, he taxed White Russians lightly. He also tended to leave their own organizations alone, although he did tinker with White Russian representation in the Chinese Eastern Railway administration.

Many White Russians who passed through Manchuria into north China wound up in the service of another warlord, the Old Marshal's junior associate Chang Tsung-ch'ang. In 1922, Chang Tsung-ch'ang disarmed remnants of White military units streaming out of the Russian Maritime Province into Manchuria. Two years later, General Konstantin Nechaev, a popular Imperial Russian Army commander, formed a corps of four thousand Russian volunteers in Chang's service. Called the Nechaev Detachment, it took on warlords such as Wu P'ei-fu and Feng Yu-hsiang and proved its worth by capturing Shanhaikwan, the strategic southern gateway to Manchuria at the eastern extremity of the Great Wall. Traveling in armored trains, Nechaev's troops inspired fear wherever they went. They fought desperately, knowing what fate awaited stateless prisoners. Dubbed "soldiers of misfortune," few men risked so much for causes that concerned them so little.

Cosmopolitan in sexual as well as military procurement, Chang Tsung-ch'ang supplemented his Chinese harem with Russian women. The tribulations undergone by Russian mothers and daughters in Chang's service did not pale in comparison with those of the Nechaev Detachment. When it came to allocating risk, Chang was an equal opportunity employer.

Harbin

A majority of Manchuria's Russians lived in Harbin. Situated in the middle of the central Manchurian plain, Harbin grew up on the right bank of the Sungari River as an agglomeration of Chinese hamlets and a Russian railroad settlement. The city owed its existence to the Chinese Eastern Railway, which radiated out in three directions: northwest to Manchouli and the Trans-Siberian Railway, east to Vladivostok, and south to Changchun, Mukden, Dairen, and Port Arthur. Blessed with excellent rail and river transport, Harbin prospered as a distribution center for grain, cotton, and soybeans after 1900. By 1916, it had a residential Russian population of 34,200.

The October Revolution and its aftermath inundated Harbin with refugees from Siberia, and many decided to settle down in familiar Russian-style surroundings rather than move on to uncertain destinations further afield. In 1922, Russians comprised 120,000 of Harbin's 485,000 inhabitants. Although this figure fell to 55,000 after 1932 as thousands sought refuge from Japanese rule in Peiping, Shanghai, and Tientsin, Harbin remained a major center of the Russian diaspora until the late 1940s.

In addition to Russians, a mosaic of different nationalities lent Harbin a cosmopolitan flavor: Chinese (300,000) predominated, followed by Koreans (34,000) and Japanese (5,000).* There were also pockets of Baltic Germans, Poles, Ukrainians, Armenians, Tartars, Georgians, and Estonians who had fled the Bolsheviks—and about 13,000 Russian Jews, some of them longtime residents and leaders of Harbin's business, religious, and scholarly communities.

Although Harbin was called a city, it came closer to a patchwork of seven towns, each with its own ambience and in some cases with its own administration. Flanking the Sungari River lay Pristan (literally "pier"), a port and commercial hub with the city's principal stores, banks, theaters, and cafes, as well as an Orthodox church, a synagogue, and a mosque. Novy Gorod ("New Town") was perched on a hill to the south and separated from Pristan by a wide network of CER tracks spanned by a single viaduct. In the early 1920s, traffic ran on the left side of the street in Pristan and on the right side in Novy Gorod. Cars and carts adjusted at will along the viaduct connecting the two towns. Novy Gorod exuded a stately atmosphere, its tree-lined avenues such as Bolshoi Prospekt, Novotorgovaya Ulitsa, and Sungari Prospekt sheltering elegant residences, foreign consulates, and the CER Club. Handsome squares opened on vistas of parks

---

* These figures are for the 1920s. After 1932, the Japanese population of Harbin rose to 13,000.

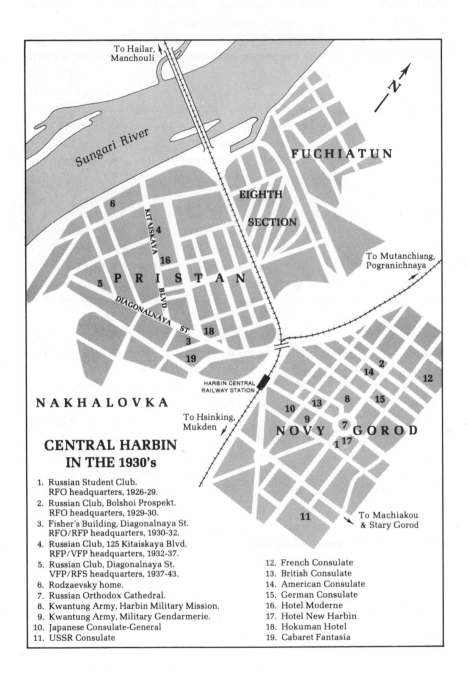

To Hailar, Manchouli

Sungari River

FUCHIATUN

EIGHTH

SECTION

To Mutanchiang, Pogranichnaya

6

KITAISKAYA

4

16

5 P R I S T A N

DIAGONALNAYA ST.

BLVD.

18

3

19

NAKHALOVKA

HARBIN CENTRAL
RAILWAY STATION

To Hsinking, Mukden

2

14

12

10   13   8   15

9

1 17

N O V Y   G O R O D

7

To Machiakou
& Stary Gorod

11

CENTRAL HARBIN IN THE 1930's

1. Russian Student Club.
   RFO headquarters, 1926-29.
2. Russian Club, Bolshoi Prospekt.
   RFO headquarters, 1929-30.
3. Fisher's Building, Diagonalnaya St.
   RFO/RFP headquarters, 1930-32.
4. Russian Club, 125 Kitaiskaya Blvd.
   RFP/VFP headquarters, 1932-37.
5. Russian Club, Diagonalnaya St.
   VFP/RFS headquarters, 1937-43.
6. Rodzaevsky home.
7. Russian Orthodox Cathedral.
8. Kwantung Army, Harbin Military Mission.
9. Kwantung Army, Military Gendarmerie.
10. Japanese Consulate-General
11. USSR Consulate

12. French Consulate
13. British Consulate
14. American Consulate
15. German Consulate
16. Hotel Moderne
17. Hotel New Harbin
18. Hokuman Hotel
19. Cabaret Fantasia

or the Sabul Russian Cathedral. One such square contained the Central Railway Station, in which hung a huge ikon.

Harbin's five remaining sectors were somewhat less picturesque. To the east of Pristan lay the Eighth Section, an industrial morass of bean-oil mills, factories, and rail yards, and beyond that sprawled Fuchiatun, the Chinese quarter, whose river wharves protruded into the Sungari from a labyrinth of cramped dwellings in which nestled the red-light district. Southeast of Novy Gorod lay Stary Gorod ("Old Town") and Machiakou. Stary Gorod was once Harbin's business center but after 1905 lost its preeminence to Pristan, and by the 1920s it consisted mainly of flour mills and garrison barracks. Machiakou had been built largely by Russian émigrés after the October Revolution and continued to serve as a modest residential quarter, its squat wooden houses decorated with ornately carved eaves. To the southwest of Pristan crouched Nakhalovka, locally dubbed "Vagabond Haunt," a cramped, sullen squatters' slum of hovels tacked together with wood scraps, paper, cloth, and discarded boxes. Nakhalovka was Harbin's receptacle for the poorest Russian refugees.

Except for railroad tracks and some huts, the north bank of the Sungari across from Pristan remained undeveloped. Called Sunbei, it served as an execution ground during Chang Tso-lin's heyday. After 1932, the Japanese built a morphine factory there.

Until 1917, Pristan and Novy Gorod enjoyed a privileged position as a foreign concession administered by the Chinese Eastern Railway. Immediately following the Revolution both Reds and Whites claimed to be the legitimate Russian owners of the CER, but in 1924, Chang Tso-lin and the Soviets firmly extended their power over the CER at the expense of the Whites. Thereafter, Pristan and Novy Gorod gradually lost their autonomy, although they continued to be governed separately from the rest of the city.

Pristan looked just like any provincial town on the Volga. The riverside quays and paddle steamers could have been transplanted from Saratov, and onion-shaped cupolas of Orthodox churches rose majestically against the Manchurian sky. Tramcars and droshkies clattered along cobbled streets. In winter, *izvozchiki*—cabbies—solicited business in horse-drawn sleds, and man-propelled icemobiles skimmed across the frozen Sungari, their occupants wrapped in furs and astrakhan hats. Russian children played *lapta,* a ball game, on vacant lots and clustered around every *bakaleinaya,* eyeing sausages and candied crabapples called *takhuli*. Housewives with prams, Cossacks, bearded priests, and uniformed students strolled down the Kitaiskaya, Pristan's main thoroughfare, passing theaters, cabarets, the Hotel Moderne, Tchurin's Department Store, and a tsarist relic called the Russo-Asiatic Bank. Everywhere, advertisements written in Cyrillic letters proclaimed the vitality of bourgeois enterprise that had been all but snuffed out in the Soviet Union.

Harbin offered the Russian exile almost everything to stimulate the intellect and please the senses. Ubiquitous kiosks sold not only local papers such as *Zarya* and *Kharbinskoye Vremya*, but also *Pravda*, *Izvestiya*, and *Krokodil*. There were Russian schools, from kindergartens up to first-rate institutions of higher education, mostly funded by the CER: the Juridical Faculty, the Institute of Oriental and Commercial Sciences, the Pedagogical Institute, and the Polytechnical Institute. Billboard columns called *tumby* carried notices of Borodin, Rimsky-Korsakov, and Tchaikovsky programs performed by the Harbin Symphony Orchestra and the Harbin Opera Troupe, both attached to the CER. Gourmets dined on roast pheasant (at 45¢ each, a poor man's meat in Manchuria) and sturgeon caviar (imported cheaply from the USSR, which in the 1920s had difficulty selling it elsewhere because of Moscow's diplomatic isolation), washed down with locally distilled *Nega* ("Sweet Bliss") vodka at the Unterberger Restaurant or Railway Club. The Mars Cafe served French pastries, and at the Alcazar Restaurant diners reclined amid fountains on balconies supported by Grecian columns while watching shows performed on a revolving stage. At the Cabaret Fantasia, gypsy melodies captured the underlying melancholy of exiles living off the sale of their possessions with no thought for the future. In the Putevaya, Russian harlots labored day and night.

Like excised tissue preserved in formaldehyde long after the parent body has perished, the émigrés of Harbin persisted, a lifelike fragment of the prerevolutionary era.

Harbin teemed with the Russians' organizations. Of course, both monarchist factions maintained local representatives: General Vladimir Alexandrovich Kislitsyn headed the Legitimists, favoring Grand Duke Cyril Vladimirovich; and Lieutenant General Grigory Afanasievich Verzhbitsky led the Manchurian branch of the Armed Services Union, favoring Grand Duke Nikolai Nikolaevich. Cossack groups abounded. Ataman Grigory Semenov, basking under Japanese protection in a Dairen villa, entrusted his Harbin following to Generals Alexei Proklovich Baksheev and Lev Filippovich Vlasevsky. While Trans-Baikal Cossacks generally gave their allegiance to Semenov, local bands of Orenburg and Yenisei Cossacks remained less amenable to his influence. General Vladimir Dmitrievich Kosmin, Manchurian leader of a Berlin-based terrorist organization calling itself the Brotherhood of Russian Truth, presided over a number of suicidally inclined young men who attempted to conduct sabotage operations in eastern Siberia and the Soviet Maritime Province.

Harbin contained more militant White Russian groups than any city in the Far East, and their presence created there an atmosphere of counterrevolutionary urgency that had no parallel in Shanghai or Tientsin. For many Harbiners, "freeing" Russia from Bolshevism was no mere wistful dream but an imminent reality; children too young to remember the Revolution or who had never been in Russia were taught to gird themselves for a war of liberation.

Of course not all Harbin Russians were poised for counterrevolution. Many were tired of violence and accepted Manchuria as a semipermanent home. Some blamed Japan, England, France, and the United States for having raised false hopes by intervening in the Civil War, leaving homeless thousands of Russians who might otherwise have made their peace with the Soviet regime.

Manchuria's strategic location and uncertain status also drew hordes of Soviet officials to Harbin. These diplomats pressed Moscow's claims to the CER, ownership of which had been complicated by the tsarist government's demise, Chang Tso-lin's appetite, and the intransigence of anti-Bolshevik railway employees who refused to yield their posts to Soviet replacements. Kremlin envoys also importuned Chinese authorities to extradite so-called White Guards engaged in hostile acts against the USSR from Manchurian bases.

Soviet agents spared no effort to sow confusion and disunity within the city's White Russian community. A number of ingenious tactics were adopted with notable success. Propagandists wooed exiles with mellifluous appeals to return to the motherland so as to lead "proud," "constructive" lives. Cheka operatives infiltrated émigré organizations, especially groups attempting to dispatch saboteurs into the USSR. Partisans smuggled into Siberia and the Maritime Province rarely returned. Their identities, objectives, and itineraries were known in advance by Soviet security organs, and the intruders were picked up at the frontier. So populous were Moscow's spies that a local Orthodox church was occasionally used to accommodate *in situ* briefing sessions. The priest was a Marxist-Leninist.

There was little the White Russians could do to guard against Soviet infiltration. Congenitally fractious, the émigrés made easy targets, and the "enemy" was a hard one to detect. More than twenty thousand of Harbin's Russians carried Soviet passports. Many of these did so purely for convenience. They were so-called "radishes" (Red outside, White inside) employed by the CER, over which the USSR finally reasserted control in 1924, and it took a sixth sense to distinguish a real from a phony radish.

Ubiquitous Soviet infiltration drove scores of émigrés to chronic suspicion bordering on paranoia. "Red agent" and "Comintern spy" cropped up monotonously in conversations, and nearly every Harbin community leader—socialist, liberal, monarchist, Cossack, or fascist—at one time or another was labeled a Kremlin spy by detractors. Whether justified or not, such accusations rent the social fabric.

The Soviet presence in Harbin increased further in 1929 when the Red Army temporarily occupied parts of north Manchuria in response to an abortive Chinese bid to assume control of the CER. Meanwhile, Moscow's influence in the rest of China appeared, at least in émigré eyes, to be growing as a result of Soviet benevolent noninterference with Chiang Kai-shek's drive to unify the country under the Kuomintang Party. Taken together with mounting nationalist currents among Manchuria's Chinese population, these developments infected the White Russians with a gnawing unease. They felt marked for sacrifice to a pragmatic alliance of Soviet communism and Chinese nationalism, and some began looking expectantly to Japan to check what appeared to them to be the Bolshevization of China.

The combustible blend of Reds and Whites was but one ingredient in Harbin's volatile atmosphere. The city was also an emporium of contraband. Art objects, furs, and jewelry confiscated by the Bolsheviks during the Revolution found their way across Siberia to Harbin for sale. Princess Olga Bodisco came across her mother's porcelain tea set in the window of a Soviet store on Kitaiskaya Street. Narcotics mingled with art. Korean and Japanese smugglers brought opium from the Ussuri region to Chinese and Russian distributors, who serviced a swelling local clientele. *Tairiku rōnin* ("continental adventurers") and the dregs of Japan's underworld prowled about, dripping with the curious admixture of idealism and rapacity that became a hallmark of Japanese rule in Manchuria after 1931.

By the 1930s, Harbin was a near lawless city. Men outnumbered women two to one. Russian deaths exceeded births by the same ratio, thanks to abortions, assaults, and alcohol. Rampant robbery and kidnapping (sometimes with police connivance) obliged affluent citizens to hire bodyguards. George Charles Hanson, Harbin's longtime American consul, kept a loaded pistol on his desk. Prudent golfers equipped their caddies with automatic rifles. Harbiners who emigrated found almost any city beatifically serene by comparison. One survivor who wound up in Los Angeles sighed: "It is such a relief to feel that nobody is lying in ambush to shoot you if you walk out on the streets."

For all its turbulence, Harbin was a pale reflection of the surrounding countryside, which was the province of *hunghutze* or "red beards" (bandits who dyed their beards to look ferocious) who infested Manchuria. Each *hunghutze* band carved out a territorial sphere in which it reigned as an invisible but very palpable government. *Hunghutze* agents could be found among members of Chang Tso-lin's entourage, bank clerks, chamber of commerce functionaries, personal servants, inn owners, cart drivers, and skippers of river junks. The bandits made a regular income from selling "protection" to peasants, merchants, and shopkeepers. Occasionally, they robbed trains, preferably on the CER line, which was less heavily defended than the Japanese-run SMR. *Hunghutze* killed train guards but spared unresisting passengers after relieving them of their belongings. Such mercy stemmed less from chivalry than from foresight; the same passengers would probably be traveling again, with more loot to rob. Veteran passengers accepted *hunghutze* visitations philosophically. Henry W. Kinney emerged from a 1934 encounter with bandits on the SMR Asia Express with only his underpants. But he kept patronizing the railroad as its paid public relations man.

Perhaps sensitive to his own antecedents, Chang Tso-lin treated the *hunghutze* gingerly. He generally left them alone, provided that they did not interfere with his own sources of income. Occasionally, however, the Old Marshal set an example of expeditious justice to remind the bandits of the hazards of excessive ambition. Captured suspects would have their bellies slit, then be kicked from behind, producing an edifyingly florid eruption.

Although Harbin's Russian community included a few affluent families and a small middle class, most of the émigrés lived in modest circumstances. Thousands of less fortunate refugees, who had arrived from Siberia with few possessions and no connections, barely survived in abject poverty. They huddled in Nakhalovka, shunned by their compatriots who had settled and prospered in Harbin before 1917. Unemployment dogged more than half of adult Russian males. Women performed degrading tasks to keep their families together. Refugee children learned how to beg in several languages. Little girls in cotton print dresses could be seen offering themselves at hourly rates.

Émigrés driven to angry desperation by poverty and dislocation did not have to look far for scapegoats.

"Look at those rich Jews! They own the stores, banks, and hotels. They fatten themselves while Russian children beg and sell themselves in the streets!"

"Look at those Reds! They killed our tsar. They desecrated our God. They drove us from our motherland. See how they brazenly molest us even in exile!"

Mixing virulent anti-Semitism and anti-Bolshevism with liberal doses of Russian nationalism, locally brewed fascism exhilarated a number of Manchuria's young émigrés during the 1920s. Under Japanese tutelage in the 1930s, it fermented into a potion that thrilled some and gave nightmares to other White Russians throughout the Far East.

Russian fascism's model was Benito Mussolini.

Its duce—*vozhd* in the Russian parlance—was Konstantin Rodzaevsky.

CHAPTER IV

The Boy from Blagoveshchensk

Oh, give me my freedom
And I shall redeem my shame
I shall save Russia from its enemies!
—"The Song of Igor" FROM ALEXANDER BORODIN'S *Prince Igor*

Blagoveshchensk is a provincial capital on the Amur River about six hundred miles northwest of Vladivostok. The name means literally "good tidings." Those who knew the place in 1900 were more likely to call it "damn tidings."

Outwardly, Blagoveshchensk around the turn of the century was a typical Siberian town. Depending on the season, its wide streets turned to mud or ice. In summer, dust permeated every cranny and left a faint glint on clothing. The "town" as such consisted mainly of *izbas* (peasant huts). In the way of more substantial structures, Blagoveshchensk could boast of several large wooden houses with ornately carved eaves and shutters, an army barracks, two churches, a triumphal arch erected in 1891 to honor the visiting Crown Prince (later tsar) Nicholas Alexandrovich, and a baroque anomaly called the Grand Hotel.

Facing China across the Amur, Blagoveshchensk was a frontier town bypassed by the Trans-Siberian Railway. Until 1900, Chinese residents outnumbered Russians, but on June 28 of that year, the Cossack garrison, nervous about Boxer terrorism against foreigners in China, drove some four thousand Chinese inhabitants into the river.

Blagoveshchensk's reputation for violence continued into the early 1900s. Local gold and cheap contraband liquor from China attracted toughs like flies. Visitors were advised to carry only small currency denominations lest they be garrotted for unwittingly revealing the corner of a ten-ruble note. Nor was the surrounding countryside safe. Fang-toothed tigers roamed about. According to Mary Gaunt, an indomitably peripatetic English spinster who endured Blagoveshchensk for two days in July 1914, one such beast left only the buttons and a butterfly net of an unwary German lepidopterist. He could well have been the Kaiser's first casualty on the Russian front.

Konstantin Vladimirovich Rodzaevsky was born in Blagoveshchensk on August 11, 1907, and throughout his life, the town's reckless spirit flowed in his veins.

The Rodzaevsky family was a member of that small, frail species finally rendered extinct by the Revolution, the Siberian bourgeoisie. Konstantin's father, Vladimir Ivanovich, a pensive, gentle man with a law degree, made a modest living as a notary public. His mother, Nadezhda Mikhailovna, came from an old Blagoveshchensk family and devoted herself to raising him, his younger brother, Vladimir, and two sisters, Nadezhda and Nina.

During the Civil War (1918–22), Reds and Whites turned Blagoveshchensk into a charnel house, but the Rodzaevskys managed to stay intact by keeping a low profile. They might even have made a successful transition to socialism had not Konstantin taken it into his head to run away to Manchuria in 1925.

What led an eighteen-year-old adolescent to abandon home and country for exile? Did he resent—as he wrote Stalin in 1945—not having been admitted to a university despite membership in the Komsomol (the Soviet Communist Party youth organization) and a favorable recommendation from the local soviet? Did his bourgeois class origins poison—as the state prosecutor at his Moscow trial maintained in 1946—his loyalty to the Soviet Union? Or was he—as his rivals and detractors whispered—sent to Manchuria by the OGPU to infiltrate and subvert White Russian organizations? The circumstances behind Rodzaevsky's flight across the Amur are still obscure.

In 1926, Rodzaevsky's mother traced her wayward son to Harbin and even secured an exit visa from Soviet authorities to visit him there. She entreated him to come home, but Konstantin would have none of it. Resigning herself to the youth's intransigence, she returned to the USSR alone, never to see him again.

In 1928, for reasons that remain unclear, Rodzaevsky's father, Vladimir Ivanovich, suddenly fled from Blagoveshchensk to Harbin, taking along his youngest son, Vladimir. Nadezhda and her two daughters, Nadezhda and Nina, were promptly arrested by the OGPU and sent to Turukhansk, a settlement on the Yenisei River one thousand miles northwest of Irkutsk. Skilled at sewing and fitting clothes, she supported herself and her daughters for two years as a seamstress. She contracted typhus in 1930 and died despite the solicitude of a local doctor who had fallen in love with the older daughter, Nadezhda. Nadezhda married the doctor shortly thereafter and eventually moved to Moscow. Nina's fate is uncertain. The two Vladimirs, father and son, found work and continued to live inconspicuously in Harbin. Konstantin, the root of his family's troubles with Soviet authorities, became a fascist.

Once in Harbin, Konstantin Rodzaevsky enrolled in the Juridical Institute. The Institute had a distinguished faculty drawn from different Russian universities and included such illustrious figures as Valentin A. Riasanovsky, a renowned authority on Chinese and Mongol law, and Nikolai V. Ustrialov, leader of the *Smena Vekh* ("changing directions") movement, which promoted émigré reconciliation with the Soviet government during the early 1920s. Rodzaevsky, however, fell under the influence of two outspoken anti-Communist nationalists: Georgy Konstantinovich Gins (sometimes spelled Guins) and Nikolai Ivanovich Nikiforov.

Gins, an official in Admiral Kolchak's short-lived Omsk government (1918–19) and author of a 1921 study of the Siberian Intervention, was a solidarist fascinated with Mussolini. He marveled at the Duce's revitalization of Italy and believed that the corporate state was a viable alternative to class struggle and proletarian dictatorship. In his lectures at the Institute, Gins argued that fascism was universally applicable, even in multiracial Russia. He published these views in 1930 in a book entitled *On the Road to the State of the Future: From Liberalism to Solidarism.*

Whereas Gins was a theoretician, Professor Nikiforov was an activist preoccupied with immediate political realities. He shuddered at the mushrooming Soviet presence in Harbin, and pro-Soviet currents within the Juridical Institute itself struck him as particularly ominous. Financed by the Soviet-dominated CER administration, the Institute depended upon Moscow's goodwill. A majority of the faculty and students, the latter mostly children of CER employees, carried Soviet passports. Stateless White Russian students and faculty, among them Gins and Nikiforov, found themselves a weak and vulnerable minority.

Determined to mobilize stateless students into an anti-Soviet force, Nikiforov organized a Union of the National Syndicate of Russian Workers in 1927.

Gins and Nikiforov were in fact giving expression to inchoate fascist impulses among the students themselves. As early as the summer of 1925, several students of the Institute began meeting to share their excitement about Mussolini and his black-shirted *squadristi.* Disciplined, tough, and dashing, the *squadristi* appealed to the young Russians as models for their own efforts in opposing the dominant pro-Soviet elements on campus. Fascism, moreover, impressed them as a youthful challenge to the older generation of émigré leaders in Harbin.

Three students, Evgeny V. Korablev, Alexander N. Pokrovsky, and Boris S. Rumiantsev, took the initiative in convening informal sessions which soon took the name Russian Fascist Organization (*Rossiiskaya Fashistskaya Organizatsiya* or RFO). Of a retiring, reflective nature, Korablev excelled at formulating platforms and coining slogans. Tall, thin, blond, and bespectacled, Rumiantsev spoke fluent Chinese and was on good terms with Marshal Chang's henchmen. Pokrovsky distilled nervous energy in a frail physique; pale and bushy-haired with a mustache jutting out defiantly above prognathic jaws, he tirelessly canvassed students and CER employees for support.

When the runaway adolescent Rodzaevsky arrived in Harbin in September of 1925, fascist vibrations were just beginning to stir the Juridical Institute. He lost no time in joining the RFO and (in 1927) Professor Nikiforov's National Syndicate. From the outset, the boy from Blagoveshchensk behaved as if he were destined to become *vozhd* of both.

At first glance, Rodzaevsky did not present an imposing sight. At five feet eleven inches and weighing 140 pounds, he looked faintly undernourished. His pallid, concave face framed unblinking blue eyes, and a shock of curly auburn hair cascaded over his high forehead. A pubescent beard awkwardly concealed his receding chin. Delicately sculptured fingers gave his hands an almost effeminate quality.

Rodzaevsky's personal magnetism belied his appearance. He exuded élan. He seemed to live in perpetual motion, running, swimming, pacing, and gesticulating. Caught up by a romantic or exuberant mood, he would burst into the "Song of Igor" in a vibrant baritone, accompanying himself on the piano. When so moved, he flashed broad, spontaneous smiles and surrendered himself to diaphragm-splitting laughter. Anger distorted his voice but left his wide, wondering eyes unaffected. He neither smoked nor drank, aside from a few sips on social occasions.

Rodzaevsky modeled his public behavior on that of Benito Mussolini. He cultivated the Duce's gestures and forensics with considerable success, winning a reputation as a passionate, operatic orator. Even off the rostrum, he spoke in a rapid staccato that made the most trivial matter sound urgent. Like Mussolini, Rodzaevsky read widely in European history and literature.

Rodzaevsky's greatest handicaps were his impulsiveness and credulity. He had a habit of making decisions without reflection. Close friends called him impractical. A consummate but naive demagogue, he hypnotized himself with his own oratory. Utterly sincere, he could not grasp that others took advantage of his gullibility.

Shortly after Rodzaevsky appeared in Harbin, another individual who was to have a profound impact on Russian fascism joined the RFO. Mikhail Alexeevich Matkovsky was the son of a tsarist general who had commanded one of Kolchak's army corps in the Urals only to be routed and imprisoned by the Bolsheviks in 1919. The younger Matkovsky, then barely out of military academy, had served on his father's staff but avoided the old man's fate. After escaping to Manchuria, he briefly studied at Harbin's Polytechnical Institute and then transferred to the Juridical Institute, just in time to fall in with Professor Nikiforov and his young protégés.

Matkovsky presented a sharp contrast to Rodzaevsky. His tall, solid frame supported a broad, open face set off by traces of brown hair around the temples and a tiny, immaculately trimmed mustache. Whereas Rodzaevsky was a visionary, Matkovsky was a realist. The former craved to be seen, while the latter preferred to observe. Whereas Rodzaevsky reveled in flamboyance, Matkovsky never acted without calculating consequences. Noisy, emotional, and impetuous, Rodzaevsky often dismayed his closest friends. Matkovsky's enemies (and, apparently, their wives) succumbed to his tactful gallantry. Rodzaevsky was an ideological fascist, a rabid anti-Semite, an anti-Bolshevik crusader. Matkovsky was a strategic fascist, indifferent to racist dogma, and interested primarily in cultivating advantageous ties with powerful patrons, be they Chinese, Japanese—or Soviet. If Rodzaevsky led the Russian fascist movement, Matkovsky sustained it. Each, sensing a rival, regarded the other with distrust, but neither could succeed alone. For twenty years, they tacitly buried their differences in a tense partnership.

Galvanized by Rodzaevsky's rhetoric and guided by Matkovsky's political acumen, the RFO soon became a visible force within the Institute. It recruited several dozen students, agitated against pro-Soviet groups on campus, and announced in January 1927 its "Theses of Russian Fascism," a heady brew of Italian bombast and anti-Soviet bile. Alert to propaganda opportunities among Harbin's White Russians, RFO cofounder Rumiantsev inaugurated on November 21, 1926 publication of a fascist tabloid called *Nashe Trebovaniya* ("Our Demands"), which circulated well beyond the confines of the Institute.

One of the RFO's earliest allies was an anti-Communist youth group in Harbin called the National Organization of Russian Musketeers *(Natsionalnaya Organizatsiya Russkikh Mushketerov)*, referred to as NORM or Musketeers. Founded around 1924 by one V. S. Barishnikov, NORM presented itself as a sort of teenage knightly order crusading for a "Free Russia" and religious Orthodoxy. Regulation garb consisted of black shirts, black belts with tassels, black trousers with flared legs, and emblematic silver Maltese crosses worn as pendants or armbands. Many Musketeers joined the RFO as they got older, and the two organizations worked closely together.

As the RFO expanded, its activities grew bolder. After graduating from the Institute, Matkovsky joined the CER and began building a network of fascist cells among Russian railroad personnel. Agents were sent to Tientsin and Shanghai to organize fascist clubs in local Russian colonies. Leaflets calling for a "Russian National Revolution" were printed and distributed throughout Manchuria and China. Some literature was smuggled into the Soviet Union. To harass the enemy and call attention to itself, the RFO staged noisy demonstrations outside Harbin's Soviet consulate in Novy Gorod every November 7 and May 1, dubbed respectively "Treason Day" and "Exploitation Day."

Moscow in due course took countermeasures against these irritants. Marshal Chang Tso-lin and his son, Chang Hsüeh-liang—the "Young Marshal"—were sternly reminded that the Peking Agreement of 1924, which had established Sino-Soviet diplomatic relations, prohibited the existence of groups in China seeking to overthrow the

Soviet government. Constant pressure was applied on the Changs to extradite "White Guards" to the USSR. The warlords nodded in sympathy, made gestures of compliance, and looked the other way. They no doubt savored the irony of Soviet officials fretting about revolutionary subversion. Indeed, the RFO by 1930 had become a miniaturized obverse of the Comintern: an international fraternity of radicals working toward a revolution inside the Soviet Union. Harbin's young fascists were grateful to their Chinese protectors. Portraits of both Changs hung at RFO headquarters in Novy Gorod.

Soviet pressure, however, did make itself felt within the Juridical Institute, which was largely financed by the CER. On the eve of his graduation in 1928, Rodzaevsky was called before the Institute's board of directors on a disciplinary charge. Konstantin Vladimirovich had led a demonstration at which the Soviet flag was torn down from the Institute's main building. He declared this act a protest on behalf of stateless White Russian students to whom the hammer and sickle, he claimed, denoted a hateful alien intrusion on campus.

Rodzaevsky appeared before the board of directors, and Harbin gossip recounted the following conversation:

> CHAIRMAN: Identify yourself.
> RODZAEVSKY: I am Konstantin Vladimirovich Rodzaevsky, leader of the Russian fascists.
> CHAIRMAN (with an ironic smile): And just what does that mean?"
> RODZAEVSKY (without blinking): As Benito Mussolini is head of the Italian fascists, so I am head of the Russian fascists.

The interview ended with Rodzaevsky's expulsion from the Institute.

Rodzaevsky, however, had the last word. When Soviet influence within the Institute momentarily lapsed as a result of a collision with Young Marshal Chang in 1929, he was quickly reinstated and graduated. Hostile sources have said that Rodzaevsky intimidated the Institute into granting him a diploma, but there is no corroborating evidence.

According to a close friend, Rodzaevsky felt bitter about the episode but kept his resentment to himself. It did not matter that much anyway, because the career on which he was embarking had little demand for academic credentials.

Birth of the Russian Fascist Party

Outraged by Soviet interference in Manchuria and emboldened by Chinese laxity, a group of RFO activists comprising a faction within Professor Nikiforov's National Syndicate resolved to build a permanent organization broadly based among émigrés throughout the Far East. Accordingly, they planned a congress for the purposes of founding a party and invited young men and women from Russian communities in Manchuria, China, and Japan to participate in the event.

The First Congress of Russian Fascists (as it was called) convened at Fisher's Building on Harbin's Diagonalnaya Street on May 26, 1931. The gathering was ostensibly secret but probably enjoyed Chinese acquiescence. Several dozen delegates, led by Rodzaevsky, Matkovsky, Rumiantsev, Pokrovsky, and Korablev proclaimed the formation of the Russian Fascist Party (*Rossiiskaya Fashistskaya Partiya* or RFP). A former tsarist general and promoter of partisan activities within the Soviet Union, Vladimir Dmitrievich Kosmin, was designated party chairman. But Kosmin merely adorned the RFP as a photogenic figurehead equipped with a sonorous military title. Control was concentrated in the hands of a central committee monopolized by the same young men who had led the RFO (which the RFP superseded). Rodzaevsky, learning from Stalin, saw to it that he was installed as RFP general secretary, a pivotal position among fascists as well as Communists.

Drawn up by Rodzaevsky and Korablev, the RFP's program opened with an assertion of the Soviet regime's impending collapse. Threatening forces (unspecified) were closing in on the USSR from east and west. Kremlin rulers, it was claimed, had isolated themselves from the people, who groaned under despotic collectivization at home and suffered humiliations incurred by "Jewish-Bolshevik internationalism" overseas. A great popular reawakening was sweeping Russia, which would soon erupt into an anti-Communist, anticapitalist National Revolution.

Fascism, the RFP program continued, was uniquely attuned to Russia's current needs. By elevating the nation as the supreme focus of loyalty, fascism could capture the popular imagination and thereby mobilize the masses for the upcoming National Revolution. The old White movement, which had "fought with bayonets, not with ideas," had shown itself incapable of carrying out such a monumental task. It was the sacred duty of Russian fascists, united under the banner of the RFP and its slogan, "God, Nation, Work," to lead the National Revolution.

In formulating the RFP program, Rodzaevsky sought to woo diverse segments of the politically fragmented emigration. He particularly wanted to attract monarchists, still the strongest group in the Russian diaspora, by persuading them that a fascist Russia would conform to their own vision of a Romanov restoration. Rodzaevsky nevertheless avoided specifically committing the RFP on dynastic matters. He had no desire to get involved in monarchist squabbles over rival pretenders to a symbolic throne.

In most other respects, too, aside from its unambiguous opposition to the Soviet regime, the RFP program left the party's ultimate objectives vaguely defined. Class struggle was denounced in favor of class cooperation. Internationalism was called an instrument of Jews and capitalists to be rejected in favor of Russian nationalism. Collective farms were to be abolished and individual ownership of property restored, but vast concentrations of private wealth would be curtailed. A rededication to God and spiritual values would eradicate the corrosive inroads of atheism and materialism, but the revitalized Orthodox Church would be separate from the state. The family was to be strengthened as a procreative pillar of the nation, but the dignity of women would be protected. Rights of ethnic minorities were to be respected, but Jews would find themselves "unwelcome guests." Fascist Russia would achieve such high levels of prosperity and social justice that peripheral nations (Finland, Latvia, Poland, Rumania, Bulgaria, Persia, Afghanistan, and Mongolia) would seek incorporation into what would eventually emerge as a great Eurasian empire.

For all his eclecticism, Rodzaevsky did firmly commit the RFP to the principles of Italian fascism as the basis of Russia's future socioeconomic system. Fascism in this sense meant corporatism: the elimination of class conflict through the reconciliation of labor and capital, of employee and employer, in a corporate state. Rodzaevsky saw his fascist Russia organizing the "creative" forces of the nation into national unions and national corporations. National unions were to be made up of people who shared a common occupation; national corporations were to bring together portions of different national unions collectively concerned with a particular sector of the economy. For example, in a steel factory, metallurgists, engineers, blast furnace operators, and managers would each belong to their own respective national unions; however, all members of the factory would be part of the same national corporation for the steel industry. Elected representatives of the unions and corporations, together with the Fascist Party, were to form the government by staffing a hierarchy of local, regional, and national councils (called "soviets"). At the summit of the state would preside a supreme soviet, called the "All-Russian *Zemsky Sobor,*" a sort of estates assembly consisting of the highest representatives of the nation's corporate units.

The future role of the Russian Fascist Party, a sensitive issue if monarchists were to be recruited, was deliberately left ambiguous. Rodzaevsky spoke of a "federated state" emerging once national unions and corporations had been firmly established. Until then the party would constitute a "temporary dictatorship." Presumably, the chairman of the RFP would lead Russia during this transitional period. Although General Kosmin occupied the RFP's highest office for the time being, there is little doubt that Rodzaevsky thought of himself as a *vozhd* of fascist Russia.

Corporatist jargon notwithstanding, the RFP portrayed itself as a movement largely distinct from Italian fascism and German national socialism. Mussolini and Hitler, asserted Rodzaevsky, were reacting against the chaos and decadence of capitalism and liberalism; their goals were to regiment the individual and centralize the economy. Russian fascists, on the other hand, were combating Bolshevist oppression, and consequently strove to liberate the individual and decentralize the economy. Above all, Russian fascism's deeply religious character distinguished it from Italian and German paganism. Only "Christian fascism" could rescue the displaced Russian soul.

Trying to underscore the native roots of fascism, the RFP's ideologues scoured Russian history for indigenous antecedents. RFP writer Nikolai Ivanov proclaimed that Ivan Kalita, a fourteenth-century Muscovite prince, established the Russian fascist tradition by making Moscow a religious capital. Another party publicist, Gennady Taradanov, professed that the *Zemsky Sobor* (estates assembly) of the sixteenth and seventeenth centuries presaged the modern corporate state. A former tsarist general and RFP ornament, A. I. Spiridovich, pointed out that Mussolini had copied the idea of state-sponsored labor unions conceived of in 1901 by Moscow police chief Serge Zubatov. Some noted that even the swastika, the RFP emblem, had a Russian origin. The last tsarina, Alexandra Feodorovna, it was reported, was captivated by that symbol toward the end of her life and inscribed one on the doorjamb of the house in which she and her family met their deaths.

Anti-Semitism stood out as one of the strongest "native" ingredients of the RFP program. Notwithstanding reservations on Matkovsky's part about the practicality of such a platform, Rodzaevsky zealously proselytized a Black Hundreds' brand of *Zhidomasonstvo*. RFP dogma equated the Soviet system with "Jewish state capitalism," and a party slogan urged: "Against the Jewish fascism of the USSR! For the Russian fascism of the RFP!" Elaborate pedigrees of Soviet leaders were compiled with the same meticulous care exercised by Himmler's SS researchers. Cartoons lifted from Julius Streicher's Jew-baiting *Der Stürmer* and republished in RFP pamphlets depicted Kremlin leaders with exaggerated Semitic features. Special attention was called to Jews within the Soviet Communist Party: Trotsky (Bronstein), Zinoviev (Apfelbaum), Kamenev (Rosenfeld), Kaganovich, and Radek. The OGPU was called a "Zionist nest." Lenin was stigmatized as a "half Jew." Even Stalin, a Georgian who could hardly be accused of philo-Semitism, came off as a "concubine of American capitalists and Jews."

One "Russian connection," to which Rodzaevsky took pains not to call attention, was the RFP's imitation of the organization and rhetoric of the Soviet Communist Party. Lenin's insistence that the party act as vanguard of the revolution was an enthusiastic, if unacknowledged, principle of the Harbin fascists, and RFP terms such as "central committee," "party secretary," "party cell," "supreme soviet," "toiling masses," and "fighting solidarity" were plucked right out of the Communist lexicon. Several Russian fascist songs were in fact Bolshevik tunes sanitized with new lyrics. Russian fascists balked, however, at adopting the Soviet word for "comrade" *(tovarishch)*. Instead they chose *soratnik,* which also means "comrade" but carries military rather than political connotations.

The RFP clarion heralding a fascist Russia sounded thin and unpromising indeed. How were some two hundred students, railroad employees, shopkeepers, and teachers to displace Stalin's two million Communist Party supporters? Rodzaevsky avoided that question, partly because he was reluctant to commit the party to any specific revolutionary strategy and partly because he did not really know the answer. For the time being, RFP propaganda did little more than make hopeful predictions of the USSR's imminent collapse. Yet even the most credulous *soratnik* knew that without massive outside support, the Russian fascist movement would never amount to more than a pathetic charade.

Rodzaevsky did not have to wait long for such support. Before the end of 1931, Japan erupted into Manchuria, opening hitherto unimaginable opportunities for the Russian fascists.

CHAPTER V

The Japanese Connection

Japan's advance, inspired by humanity, should not be confused
with aggression for gain.
—JAPANESE GOVERNMENT OFFICIAL (1938)

Japan's presence in Manchuria dated from its victory in the Russo-
Japanese War of 1904–5. The Portsmouth Peace Treaty, signed on
September 5, 1905, awarded Japan the Russian rights and concessions
in southern Manchuria; leasehold of the Kwantung Territory, comprising 1,300 square miles of the Liaotung peninsula, including Dairen
and Port Arthur; and a narrow railway zone from Port Arthur to
Changchun, about 150 miles south of Harbin. To administer these
acquisitions, Tokyo created a Kwantung Territory governor-general-
ship. Responsibility for economic development in the Kwantung Territory and Railroad Zone was entrusted to a quasi-governmental organization called the South Manchurian Railway Company (SMR).
To defend these possessions and interests, the Japanese Imperial
Army spawned a formidable, at times semiautonomous, offspring:
the Kwantung Army.

During the 1920s, a combination of forces was conditioning Japan
to contemplate unilateral action in Manchuria. For one, a rising tide
of Chinese nationalism had challenged Japan's laboriously accumulated special interests and investments. Further, the Soviet Union
appeared deliberately to be exacerbating the "China problem"
through disruptive diplomacy, Comintern propaganda, and military
preparations in Siberia and Outer Mongolia. And American economic
expansion in the Far East, cloaked in platitudinous Open Door rhetoric, struck the Japanese, who were humiliated by the 1924 Exclusion

Act, barring Japanese immigration to the U.S., as hypocritical and menacing. Domestic crises aggravated Japan's frustration and anxiety, as impetuous industrialization brought about economic dislocation and social tension. The world depression precipitated a collapse of silk exports that devastated many rural communities. Civilian ultranationalists and young military activists, fired by populist impulses, lashed out at "corrupt" business leaders, party politicians, and even senior officers in the Imperial Army and Navy. After 1930, these complex pressures began to resolve themselves in an uncoordinated drive for security and autonomy through continental expansion. When the Kwantung Army took the first steps in Manchuria, its initiative was generally accepted, if not always condoned, by the government, the parties, and by broad sections of the people.

Based in Port Arthur, the Kwantung Army's main responsibility during the 1920s lay in defending the Kwantung Territory and South Manchurian Railway Zone. Yet certain Kwantung Army officers, generally from the middle echelons, nurtured more ambitious plans. Moved by a combination of Pan-Asian idealism, anti-Western and anti-Soviet alarm, and a conviction of Japan's mission in East Asia, these men toyed with the idea of detaching Manchuria from China and building an independent state cleansed of Japan's liberal-capitalist rot.

In the late 1920s, such thoughts began to be translated into actions carried out independently of military superiors in Tokyo. It was a Colonel Kōmoto Daisaku who had Chang Tso-lin blown up in his private rail coach in 1928 after the Old Marshal had shown signs of unmanageable cupidity, and one Colonel Doihara Kenji earned the nickname "Lawrence of Manchuria" for the wild intrigues hatched in the *Tokumu Kikan* ("Special Services Organ"), an ultrasecret department of the Imperial Army General Staff's Second Section (Intelligence).

On September 18, 1931, the chief of Army General Staff's Second Section, Colonel Itagaki Seishirō, and his associate, Lieutenant Colonel Ishiwara Kanji, engineered an incident that signaled the Kwantung Army to take over all of Manchuria. Staging an explosion along the rail tracks outside of Mukden (formerly Fengtien, about 350 miles southwest of Harbin), they manufactured a pretext for Japanese units to attack local Chinese garrison forces.

Although Japanese leaders in Tokyo did seek to contain the fighting around Mukden, they sanctioned reinforcements from Korea, allowing the Kwantung Army to escalate operations throughout Manchuria. Mukden was secured within twenty-four hours. Southern Manchuria came under Japanese control with the occupation of Kirin and Changchun during the next three weeks. Northern Manchuria followed after Kwantung Army columns entered Tsitsihar on November 18. Harbin did not fall until February 5, 1932, although "Lawrence" Doihara and his *Tokumu Kikan* operatives had been softening up the city for two or three months.

With Young Marshal Chang Hsüeh-liang in full retreat southward toward the Great Wall, the Kwantung Army turned its attention to grooming the conquered territory for "independence." Japanese propaganda represented events following the Mukden incident as a spontaneous uprising of "Manchurians" determined to throw off oppressive Chinese rule, a laudable cause which Japan felt bound to assist. On February 18, 1932, Chinese collaborators under Kwantung Army tutelage declared Manchuria's secession from the Republic of China, or more accurately, from Chiang Kai-shek's Nationalist government in Nanking. On March 1, a nominally sovereign state called "Manchukuo" was proclaimed in Changchun (renamed Hsinking, literally "new capital"). To invest Manchukuo with a veneer of legitimacy, the Kwantung Army dredged up a relic from the defunct Manchu dynasty, the last emperor of China, Hsüan-t'ung, also known as Henry P'u-Yi. Since abdicating in 1912 at the age of seven, P'u-Yi had been living comfortably in Tientsin. On November 10, 1931, "Lawrence" Doihara arranged for the former Son of Heaven to be smuggled to a Japanese merchantman in the trunk of a black convertible roadster and transported to Hsinking. After some rudimentary grooming, the somewhat confused young man was formally enthroned, in 1933, as Kang-te, emperor of Manchukuo.

From the moment of its inception, Manchukuo was a clumsily choreographed puppet state. "Manchukuoans" (Chinese) held titular leadership of the government bureaucracy, army, and police, but ubiquitous Japanese "advisers" in fact made the decisions. Harbin's Japanese consul general Ōhashi Chū'ichi, for example, assumed the post of Manchukuo's vice-minister of foreign affairs. The Kwantung Army hovered in the background as the ultimate *éminence grise.* Its commander concurrently held the title of "Special Ambassador Extraordinary and Plenipotentiary," a euphemism for viceroy.

The "Kingly Way"

From the time of the Mukden incident in September 1931 until Harbin's occupation by Kwantung Army units four and a half months later, White Russians in the city, cast in the role of scapegoats, went through purgatory. Angry Chinese heaped vituperation upon them. Pro-Soviet émigrés confidently speculated about how the Red Army would liquidate the Whites when Stalin intervened in Manchuria. Insults and intimidation left them with frayed nerves, frantically seeking protectors.

During this uneasy interregnum, Harbin's Japanese civilians showed the White Russians sympathy and offered them a measure of security. Many of the Japanese residents were armed, and with the breakdown of order, their houses, offices, and stores were transformed into strongholds where grateful White Russians sought refuge.

As it turned out, Chinese violence proved far less than anticipated, and Stalin made no move to block Japan from seizing Manchuria. The army's special operations organ, *Tokumu Kikan,* was therefore obliged to step in and provide palpable evidence that Kwantung Army protection was needed. Accordingly, undercover operatives hired gangs to shoot up Harbin streets and ignite a few fires to leave the impression that Chinese "bandits" were on the rampage. Such staged incidents paid off handsomely in terms of White Russian gratitude toward Japan.

When Kwantung Army formations entered Harbin on February 5, 1932, they met a tumultuous welcome from the White Russian community. Rising Sun flags flew from windows along the Kitaiskaya, and Russian crowds shouted banzais at passing columns. Russian girls along the way flung bouquets and planted kisses on dusty Japanese cheeks. That evening, a procession of ten thousand Russians converged on the Japanese consulate in a sincere outpouring of relief. In France, Grand Duke Cyril publicly rejoiced that a quarter of a million of his subjects had come under the protection of Dai Nippon.

To a certain extent, émigré expectations of justice and benevolence were fulfilled, but for the most part, once the initial exhilaration wore off, they found themselves cruelly disappointed. Too many Japanese behaved with a callous arrogance made all the more mortifying by the ubiquitous slogan epitomizing Manchukuo's credo: *wang tao,* or "kingly way."

Stripped of its Confucian veneer, *wang tao* meant "serve Japan." Manchukuo's Russians began to find themselves depicted in Japanese propaganda as grateful beneficiaries of *wang tao,* rescued from poverty and Chinese misgovernment. Left unsaid was how Manchukuoan *wang tao* operated in practice. It meant learning to bow from the waist before officers of the Imperial Japanese Army. It meant lowering one's eyes when boisterous Japanese sightseers ambled into an Orthodox church during a service. It meant paying protection fees that would have appalled a *hunghutze.* It meant cultivating "sincerity," that is, a cooperative attitude toward Japan's self-conceived mission in East Asia. Above all, it meant fear.

Within days of Harbin's occupation, the newly established Japanese Military Mission, containing the Kwantung Army's local representative, his staff, and the *Tokumu Kikan,* took steps to make all White Russians comprehend the "kingly way." Russian-speaking officers were assigned as "counselors" to each émigré organization. Censorship was clamped on the press. *Stukachi* (informers) were recruited from the Russian community to loiter about railroad stations, hotels, and cafes to pick up snatches of conversations and to report suspicious behavior. Some *stukachi* stood out, like a jaundiced Greek who perennially sat in the Hotel Moderne lobby. Others concealed their identities. Their presence made almost everyone think twice about talking frankly, even with close friends.

A number of Japanese made a mockery of law and order, which their country had avowedly intervened in Manchuria to restore, and some of the Rising Sun's seediest elements soon infested Manchukuo as proprietors of gambling houses, brothels, and opium dens. The shrewder ones remained in the background and operated through Russian, Korean, or Chinese intermediaries.

Paradoxically, one of the reasons crime was flourishing in Harbin as never before was that too many law enforcement agencies were competing for authority. Nine different bodies jostled each other in vague, overlapping jurisdictions: the *Tokumu Kikan,* responsible to the Imperial Army General Staff in Tokyo; the *Kempei,* or military gendarmerie, accountable to the commander of the Kwantung Army, Hsinking; the Harbin Municipal Police, under the Municipal Council; the Harbin Criminal Police, also under the Municipal Council but independent of the Municipal Police; the Japanese Consular Police; the CER Railway Police; and three Manchukuoan agencies (Gendarmerie, Provincial Police, State Intelligence Service). Among all nine organs, the *Tokumu Kikan* and *Kempei* wielded the most power. They were also fierce rivals.

The *Tokumu Kikan* maintained branches throughout Manchukuo, but its Harbin office served as the field headquarters of the Imperial Army's intelligence and counterintelligence work against the Soviet Union. The Harbin branch occupied a squat brick house, formerly owned by a riches-to-rags Pole named Kavalsky, on Bolshoi Prospekt in a stately section of Novy Gorod. A garden connected the house to a building that served as headquarters of the Japanese Military Mission. The Mission's main entrance faced a broad plaza shared by the Sabul Russian Cathedral and the Soviet-owned Hotel New Harbin.

Kempei headquarters were located on Pochtovaya Street near the intersection with Vogzalnaya, a broad avenue that connected Cathedral Plaza with the Central Railroad Station. The *Kempei* distilled some of the less savory aspects of Japanese politics in the 1930s. Nominally responsible for policing army personnel, the *Kempei* extended the scope of its activities to include the investigation and suppression of all forms of military and civilian dissidence. The second floor of Harbin's *Kempei* headquarters housed facilities for "special offenders"—political criminals. So sinister was its reputation that "second floor" became a synonym for a terrible fate among White Russians. Such expressions as "My wife put me on the second floor last night" or "Watch out, or you'll be on the second floor" gave the *Kempei* an arcane currency in local slang.

Both the *Kempei* and the *Tokumu Kikan* used their power for profit. Pecuniary gain was rationalized in the name of Japan's past "sacrifices" for Manchukuo. In the case of the *Tokumu Kikan*, the proceeds did usually make it to Tokyo. But in the *Kempei,* they normally tended to flow into private pockets. Self-enrichment among Japanese police officers in the Kwantung Territory reached scandalous proportions in 1934, when the conservative and nationalistic Tokyo newspaper *Kokumin shimbun* reported that the "take" for a three-year term reached 30,000 yen (about $10,000), or more than triple a policeman's salary. By Harbin standards, that was modest. One Nikolai Nikolaevich Yagi* paid $50,000 to the Military Mission for the privilege of being ap-

---

* A number of Japanese in Manchukuo, particularly soldiers of fortune and intelligence agents, took Russian first names and patronymics.

pointed adviser to the Harbin Municipal Police. He recouped that
investment many times over.

Careful about appearances, the *Kempei* and *Tokumu Kikan* took pains
to invest their pecuniary enterprises with an air of legality. A favorite
device was to institute monopolies and issue licenses for lucrative
businesses such as narcotics, gambling, prostitution, and transport.

Opium became a particularly macabre parody of the "kingly way."
Smuggled into Manchuria before 1931 by Japanese and Koreans who
were protected by extraterritorial privileges, the narcotic blossomed
into a national industry in Manchukuo. Addiction among Chinese
was encouraged to boost revenue and to anesthetize political consciousness. Elaborate promotion schemes were concocted to induce
mass consumption. Airplanes dropped leaflets extolling the pleasures
of the pipe, and Manchukuo's banknotes suggestively flaunted an emblematic poppy in full bloom. Harbin alone boasted several hundred
shops licensed to sell heroin and morphine without prescription. Plush
establishments catering to wealthy clients offered residential deliver-
ies. Bargain hovels featured a hole at the entrance through which
customers could insert their arms with twenty sen (eight cents)
grasped in their hands, and get a quick shot of morphine. Youngsters
could pick up "junior doses" at outlets near schools. In 1934, journalist Edgar Snow estimated that 20 percent of Japanese and Koreans
in Manchukuo were directly involved in narcotics. The Japanese could
freely deal in drugs but were strictly forbidden to sample them.

As the industry expanded, production and distribution of narcotics
devolved upon different agencies. In 1932 and 1933, the *Tokumu Kikan*
made drugs its preserve, but soaring consumption outpaced its regula-
tory capacity. Japan's occupation of Jehol Province in Inner Mongolia
(1933) opened up a vast poppy-growing area and prompted the Kwantung Army to establish the Manchukuo Opium Monopoly Board to
rationalize the industry. Factories were constructed in Hsinking, Mukden, Port Arthur, Kirin, Tsitsihar, and Harbin (at Sunbei) to produce
morphine, heroin, and cocaine. Raw opium output in Korea and Tai-
wan was expanded to accommodate massive Manchukuoan imports.
In 1935, Kwantung Army commander General Minami Jirō invested
the Opium Monopoly Board with complete control of the drug trade.
By that time, official annual production stood at 300,000 pounds yield-
ing $7 million. Actual output was much higher, for the *Tokumu Kikan*
and *Kempei* also maintained their own "private" suppliers.

In addition to an opium business, the *Tokumu Kikan* in Harbin ran a freight racket, selling reduced rates on the CER by labeling consignments "Japanese military supplies." It also managed a prostitution monopoly on Uchastkovaya Street, where an efficient staff sold permits to all wishing to practice the trade and regulated the influx of girls from Japan.

The *Tokumu Kikan* always had to contend with the appetite of the *Kempei.* Jurisdictional disputes chronically erupted into violence between Chinese and Russian henchmen of the two agencies. Usually, however, peace was maintained by compromises. In 1934, the *Tokumu Kikan* agreed that the *Kempei* could "protect" five of Harbin's hundred brothels, five of its four dozen opium dens, and one of its two hundred narcotics shops.

It did not take long for Harbin's White Russians to realize that Japanese rule was at best a mixed blessing. Protest, however, was out of the question. There was nothing to do but adjust or leave. Thousands moved to Peiping, Tientsin, and Shanghai, which remained at least partially out of Japan's reach until the "China Incident" broke out in 1937. Others stayed in Manchukuo, resigning themselves to outward genuflections to the "kingly way" while privately finding solace in cryptic barbs. "They came down from the trees too soon," ran one underground joke that triggered implosions of nervous laughter.

Collaboration

The Kwantung Army was anxious to coordinate Manchukuo's fractured White Russian groups into one manageable entity that could be utilized for anti-Soviet purposes and for administrative convenience. Accordingly, a search was launched for cooperative émigré leaders.

Ataman Grigory Semenov, Japan's Cossack protégé during the Siberian Intervention, looked at first glance like an obvious choice. Semenov was more than willing to collaborate, and he still enjoyed support among Trans-Baikal Cossacks resettled in northern and eastern Manchuria. At the same time, his candidacy posed certain difficulties. Comfortably ensconced in Dairen, he was remote from Harbin, where the White Russian population concentrated. His rampages during the Russian Civil War were still remembered. Most important,

Tokumu Kikan officers who played a key role in "guiding" Manchukuo's White Russians regarded Semenov as impulsive, fanciful, and "behind the times."

On the other hand, the more respected leaders of Harbin's Russian community would have nothing to do with collaboration. Generals Verzhbitsky and Baksheev, representatives of pro-Nikolasha monarchists and Cossacks respectively, politely declined Japanese invitations. Nikolai Lvovich Gondatti, octogenarian former governor of the Maritime Province, flatly refused repeated offers. When four *Kempei* called at his residence to make an offer he could not refuse, Gondatti presented himself wearing a decoration presented personally to him decades previously by the Emperor Meiji. The *Kempei* bowed and withdrew.

The Japanese eventually found a suitable candidate in General Vladimir Alexandrovich Kislitsyn, local leader of the Legitimists (pro-Cyril monarchists). Kislitsyn has been depicted variously as a "cultured . . . honest man" and as an "empty-headed, vainglorious parasite." He always referred to himself as a general, but his detractors sniffed that he was in fact a mere cavalry captain, undeservingly promoted to that exalted rank after the revolution by Grand Duke Cyril. The truth lies somewhere in between. Kislitsyn had fought in the First World War and served under General Miller and Admiral Kolchak in the Civil War. After Kolchak's collapse, he took the rank of general and commanded the First Cavalry Division at Chita, later the First Composite Manchurian Division, and took refuge in Manchuria following the White debacle of 1922. Kislitsyn was dignified and pliable, the latter condition reportedly stemming from fourteen head wounds accumulated during various campaigns, as well, apparently, as from a penchant for vodka.

But the *Tokumu Kikan* and the *Kempei* wanted more than venerable figureheads. They needed young activists who would obey any order without asking questions. There was no objection if such men were anti-Soviet Russian patriots, but most important was that they follow the "kingly way," enforcing the prostitution and narcotics rackets, kidnapping rich Chinese and Russians for ransom, and carrying out occasional assassinations on request. In his florid memoirs, Amleto Vespa, an Italian soldier of fortune who served a succession of Chinese and Japanese employers in Manchuria, quotes a *Tokumu Kikan* officer as follows: "What we want is young men of fair intelligence who

will be proud to accept some sort of rank and who will be disposed
to do what we want. We need Russian names to cover up our activities—men who are not necessarily thinkers."

Among the potential activist collaborators who aroused Japanese
interest was General Vladimir Kosmin, chairman of the Russian Fascist
Party (RFP) and local head of the terrorist Brotherhood of Russian
Truth, whose suicidal forays into the USSR during the 1920s were
public knowledge. From October 1931 until the occupation of Harbin
in February of 1932, Kosmin showed himself eager to win Japanese
confidence, carrying out on behalf of the *Tokumu Kikan* assignments
such as planting discoverable grenades on business premises and staging street fights among local toughs.

Konstantin Rodzaevsky fell into a slightly different category. Only
twenty-four in 1931, the young general secretary of the Russian Fascist
Party was more of a propagandist than a street fighter. Nevertheless,
so enthusiastic was his response to Japanese approaches that the
Tokumu Kikan treated him as a valued if impetuous collaborator who
correctly understood the "kingly way."

Like Kosmin, Rodzaevsky was contacted by the *Tokumu Kikan* in
the fall of 1931. In February 1932, just before the Kwantung Army
occupation of Harbin, Rodzaevsky was instructed to drive a Japanese
journalist in a car bearing a Japanese flag to a spot where Kosmin's
boys had just fomented a brawl. He was warned to expect trouble
but told that the risk was for a good cause. Sure enough, bullets
from an unseen sniper riddled his vehicle, leaving him unscathed
but still quite unnerved. The Japanese consulate duly protested to
Chinese authorities that "Chinese policemen" had deliberately
opened fire on an official car.

Once Harbin was under Kwantung Army control, Rodzaevsky began dealing with two contrasting Japanese, who were to play vital
roles in the White Russian community for the next decade: Major
Akikusa Shun of the *Tokumu Kikan* and Konstantin Ivanovich Nakamura of the *Kempei.*

Thirty-eight years old in 1932, Akikusa Shun was one of the Imperial Japanese Army's Russian specialists, old enough to have served
in the Siberian Intervention but young enough to look forward to
many further years of active duty. After graduation from the military
academy, Akikusa had acquired a practical grasp of Russian language
and politics, working as an interpreter with the Third Division at

Vladivostok and Chita during the Siberian Intervention. He refined these skills later in the 1920s while he was studying Russian at the Tokyo School of Foreign Languages and serving as a Soviet analyst in the Russian Section of the General Staff.

Akikusa already knew Manchukuo well when in 1932 he was assigned to assist Major General Komatsubara Michitarō, chief of the Harbin *Tokumu Kikan*. Major Akikusa quickly familiarized himself with the city's White Russian organizations and before long was counselor to the Russian Fascist Party and liaison officer between the RFP and the Japanese Military Mission. His duties consisted of disbursing advice and subsidies to guide the RFP along "proper" lines. Poised, tactful, and upright, Akikusa won the respect—even the affection— of most émigrés with whom he came in contact.

Rodzaevsky's other contact, Konstantin Ivanovich Nakamura, was a *Manshūgorō* ("Manchurian ruffian") of the first order. A resident of Manchuria for twenty years, he spoke Russian fluently, kept a common-law Russian wife, and, as his name suggests, embraced the Orthodox faith. Well before 1931, "Kostya," as Nakamura was known among his Russian acquaintances, had a record with the Harbin Municipal Police. Ostensibly operating a barbershop in Nakhalovka, he engaged in the narcotics trade and ran a brothel. In 1924, his wife charged him with ravishing her twelve-year-old daughter (by another man), and in 1928 he was investigated by the Chinese authorities for employing prepubescent prostitutes. Yet Nakamura's misdeameanors went unpunished. Aware of his extraterritorial privileges, the Chinese could do nothing but refer complaints to the Japanese Consulate, which took nominal action or none whatever. Kostya's apparent immunity from justice left the impression among émigrés that he had some potent secret connection with Tokyo.

Nakamura's "connection" became apparent on September 19, 1931, one day after the Mukden incident, when he summoned a group of White Russian friends to his shop and announced that Japan was about to "free the people of Manchuria from the Communistic Kuomintang [Chang Kai-shek's Nationalists]" and to help "patriotic" Russians "liberate" their motherland from the Soviets. Noting a sympathetic response, he proceeded to distribute revolvers, rifles, and hand grenades with instructions to defend Japanese and White Russian property until Kwantung Army units could occupy Harbin. He also promised that his listeners would later form the nucleus of a White

Russian army of liberation. Four months later, Kostya openly assumed the title of "secretary-interpreter" in the *Kempei*. Like Major Akikusa, Nakamura acted as an adviser and benefactor of the Russian Fascist Party.

From February 1932, Rodzaevsky made regular visits to Akikusa and Nakamura at the Military Mission and *Kempei* headquarters. He also received modest subsidies, which enabled the RFP to move from confined quarters at Fisher's Building on Diagonalnaya Street to a more imposing brick structure at 125 Kitaiskaya, a few doors down from the Hotel Moderne.

Rodzaevsky's collaboration with the *Tokumu Kikan* and *Kempei* split RFP ranks, and a personnel turnover ensued as all three cofounders of the RFP's precursor, the RFO student organization, dropped out of sight. Evgeny Korablev died of tuberculosis in 1932. Boris Rumiantsev parlayed his fluency in Chinese and Japanese into a position in the Manchukuoan Ministry of Foreign Affairs. Alexander Pokrovsky quit the party in protest over Rodzaevsky's pro-Japanese line and formed a "Fascist-Syndicalist Union," which was soon disbanded by the Japanese authorities. Briefly interned by the *Kempei*, Pokrovsky decided to move to the safer climes of Shanghai. He took along his poetess-wife, Mariana Ivanovna Kolosova, and quietly slipped into obscurity.

General Kosmin clung to nominal leadership of the RFP for several months and even had some discussions with *Tokumu Kikan* chief Komatsubara about forming fighting cadres for a future White Army. But late in 1932, Kosmin succumbed to an ill-conceived plan to enrich himself. The old warrior had for some years dispatched partisans into the Maritime Province from Pogranichnaya, a station on the Harbin-Vladivostok section of the CER, perched just on the Manchukuoan side of the Soviet frontier. In November 1932, Kosmin won RFP approval to raise funds for further guerrilla operations by abducting a wealthy dairyman named Dinitzin and holding him for ransom. Dinitzin lived outside Pogranichnaya, conveniently near Kosmin's commando base. After the general's men had successfully carried out the kidnapping and received the ransom, Kosmin decided to keep the money for himself. He notified RFP headquarters in Harbin that he had been double-crossed and lost all the money. However, a local tough named Boris Shepunov, peeved at not being included in Kosmin's peculations, divulged all to Rodzaevsky, who promptly decided that the photogenic chairman had outlived his usefulness. Convening the RFP Central Executive Committee, he had Kosmin expelled from the party. Shortly thereafter, Kosmin moved on to Shanghai and eventually launched a new political career there.

With the departure of Korablev, Rumiantsev, Pokrovsky, and Kosmin, Konstantin Vladimirovich Rodzaevsky was left *de jure* as well as *de facto* leader of the Russian Fascist Party. He still had to reckon with the other RFP luminary, Mikhail Matkovsky. And he still had to prove to the Japanese his value as a collaborator.

CHAPTER VI

The Manchurian Mafia

[The Russian fascists] are a libel on the good name of Italian Fascism and an insult to all that it represents under Il Duce.
—AMLETO VESPA (1936)

The Japanese seizure of Manchuria in 1931–32 opened breathtaking new vistas for the Russian Fascist Party. Collaboration with Japan held out the prospect of money, patronage, and participation in a preemptive war against the Soviet Union.

Liberating Russia by helping Japan became an *idée fixe* for Konstantin Rodzaevsky, who saw no contradiction whatever between patriotism and service to a potential enemy of his homeland. Trusting Japanese promises and intoxicated by his own rhetoric, the little *führer* raptly embarked on the "kingly way."

The Japanese, however, had their own plans for the Russian fascists. The *Tokumu Kikan* recognized their value as scouts, spies, and saboteurs within the USSR. The *Kempei* envisioned them as puppet racketeers. Consequently, a number of RFP *soratniki* who had been girding for the National Revolution found themselves involved instead in narcotics, prostitution, and extortion. What had started as a political movement began to show signs of turning into a racket as the Russian Fascist Party became part of Japan's Manchurian Mafia.

Brains, Ballads, and Brawn

Rodzaevsky capitalized on his newly acquired Japanese patronage by launching an RFP membership drive throughout the Far East in 1932. With the blessing of Major Akikusa Shun, RFP agents fanned out across China, Korea, and Japan to enlist support in émigré communities. Branches opened in Shanghai, Tientsin, Hsinking, Dairen,

73

Keijo (Seoul), Kobe, Tokyo, and Karafuto (southern Sakhalin). While the number of recruits outside Manchukuo did not exceed several hundred, the RFP was at last able to claim an international constituency.

Keen to spread the fascist gospel, Rodzaevsky gave top priority to formulating and disseminating propaganda. In April 1932, a party theoretical journal named *Natsiya* ("Nation") inaugurated publication from Shanghai RFP headquarters on Avenue Joffre. *Natsiya* contained a heady blend of polemics, pedantry, and poetry. "Professor" V. Nosach-Noskov contributed turgid discourses on tactics and ideology. Nikolai Dozorov and Georgy Semena penned fascist verses that read like parodies of the revolutionary odes of the great Bolshevik poet Vladimir Mayakovsky. Georgy I. Kruchinin serialized quota-fulfilling novels like *Svet s Vostoka* ("Light from the East"), which betrayed an uncanny resemblance to the Soviet literary mode. Foreign contributions were included to add a cosmopolitan touch. Alfred Rosenberg's abstruse fulminations were allocated generous space. *Natsiya's* covers were derivative, borrowing alternately from Mussolini's neoclassical portraiture and *Der Stürmer's* anti-Semitic fare. Occasionally, the editors resorted to some imaginative plagiarism. One cover supported a 1915 French war bond poster of a grinning *poilu* crying *"On les aura"* ("We'll get them"), refitted as a swastika-festooned RFP legionnaire presumably chasing Jewish commissars.

With *Natsiya* aimed only at the "intelligentsia," the RFP still needed a mass organ. Rodzaevsky found just what he wanted in Rumiantsev's tabloid *Nashe Trebovaniya,* which the *vozhd* took over and renamed *Nash Put* ("Our Path") in September 1932. *Nash Put* competed with two other Russian-language Harbin dailies: the pro-Japanese *Kharbinskoye Vremya* and the Jewish-owned *Zarya.* Although *Nash Put's* circulation (4,000) never approached that of *Vremya* (25,000) or *Zarya* (10,000), the paper made itself heard through sheer stridency. Its masthead carried a swastika surmounted by the Imperial Russian double-headed eagle, flanked by RFP slogans "God, Nation, Work," "All Power to the National Revolution," and "Russia for the Russians."

Convinced that the RFP should have its own *Mein Kampf,* Rodzaevsky commissioned Gennady Taradanov and Vladimir Kibardin, both close associates of Matkovsky, to compose suitable scriptures. Published in 1934, *Azbuka Fashizma* went through several editions as it was acquired, if not always read, by all self-respecting

Russian fascists in the Far East. *Azbuka* was arranged in one hundred sections, each consisting of a question and an answer that varied in length from eight lines to two pages. Queries ranged in scope from no. 18, "What is democracy?" to no. 97, "What does the Russian Fascist Party regulation uniform consist of?" Much of the text painted scenarios of Russia after the National Revolution: National unions and national corporations working in harmony and everyone (except Jews) enjoying prosperity and freedom. In general, *Azbuka* recapitulated the RFP's 1931 program, including its vagueness and eclecticism. At the same time, the handbook contained revealing insights into RFP psychology. For example, to the question "Why do Russian fascists call themselves 'fascist'?" came the surprisingly ingenuous reply that Soviet media had identified "fascism" as the main enemy of communism; therefore, fascism had become a popular rallying cry among those within the USSR dissatisfied with the Soviet regime.

Azbuka's title may well have been inspired by Nikolai I. Bukharin's *Azbuka Kommunizma* (1921), a general exposition of Marxist doctrine and Russian revolutionary strategy by the leading Communist theoretician of the 1920s—subsequently a victim of Stalin's purges. If there was any association, Taradanov and Kibardin had no intention of mentioning it. Nor did Rodzaevsky acknowledge indebtedness to either Chernyshevsky* or Lenin** when he chose the title *What Is to Be Done?* for a 1935 booklet criticizing the USSR's Second Five-Year Plan.

Azbuka's concluding sections dealt with RFP symbols, uniforms, songs, and salutes. The party emblem looked at first glance like an incongruous hybrid of Imperial Russia and the Third Reich: a white double-headed eagle (symbol of the Romanov dynasty) superimposed on a black swastika floating on a yellow background. *Azbuka* explained that the double-headed eagle symbolized the Russian nation and that the swastika symbolized solidarity with fascist movements in other countries. The RFP flag dispensed with the eagle and consisted of a black swastika on a yellow-orange background surrounded by a white trim.

The Russian Fascist Party uniform consisted of a rumpled black

* Nikolai Gavrilovich Chernyshevsky (1828–89), radical writer and author of *What Is to Be Done?* (1862–64).

** V. I. Lenin's long pamphlet *What Is to Be Done?* (1902) attacked the "Economists" for abdicating political struggle.

cap with black visor, a black shirt buttoned at the collar, black riding breeches, and knee-length black boots. Lest he be mistaken for a chauffeur, the RFP man wore a Sam Browne belt (girding the shoulder as well as the waist) and an arm band consisting of a black swastika set off against a blazing orange disc enclosed by a thin white circle. The colors matched the Romanov imperial standard.

RFP *soratniki* saluted each other after the Nazi manner, the right arm outstretched slightly above the horizon with imperious rigidity. The gesture was usually accompanied by a hearty *"Slava Rossy!"* ("Hail Russia"), the party's official verbal and epistolary greeting.

No crusade would be complete without music, and Rodzaevsky, a confirmed opera buff, saw to it that the RFP was amply endowed with inspirational songs. Nikolai Dozorov and Nikolai Petlin, party bard laureates, came up with fascist lyrics for a number of tsarist and Communist tunes to produce such Harbin hits as "We're with You, Saint Vladimir!"* "Listen, *Soratnik*!" and "Red Star Blues." The RFP anthem, "Rise Up with Us, Brothers!" was sung to the melody of the Preobrazhensky March, presumably with an eye to the late Tsar Nicholas' honorary membership in the Preobrazhensky Regiment. Each stanza exhorted Russians to join fascists in a march to national regeneration:

> Rise up, brothers, with us
> Russian banners fly
> Over hills and dales
> Russian truth soars
>
> With us all believers in God
> With us Russian soil
> We open the way
> To ancient Kremlin walls
>
> Ever harder our Russian hammer
> Strikes like God's thunder
> Smashing into ashes
> Satanic Sovnarkom**

Rodzaevsky knew that slogans and songs alone could not propel his movement. Émigrés of all ages had to be trained and mobilized

---

* Saint Vladimir (d. 1015), the first Christian ruler of Kiev and the RFP's celestial patron.
** Sovnarkom: an abbreviation for Council of People's Commissars, the Soviet cabinet. Renamed Council of Ministers in 1946.

as shock troops for the approaching National Revolution. To achieve this end, the RFP created peer units in 1932. A Russian Women's Fascist Movement *(Rossiiskoye Zhenskoye Fashistskoye Dvizheniye)* was organized under Rumiantsev's wife, Sheina. Youth groups proliferated: the Vanguard Union *(Soyuz Avangarda)* for boys aged ten to sixteen; the Young Fascist Union *(Soyuz Yunykh Fashistok)* for girls ten to sixteen; and the Union of Fascist Little Ones *(Soyuz Fashistskykh Kroshek)* for demitots five to ten. On August 5, 1932, a secret party school for training *soratniki* in underground activities within the USSR was established in Harbin, financed by Japanese subsidies.

Rodzaevsky did not neglect brawn in building up the RFP. The *vozhd* had never lost his fascination with Mussolini's black-shirted *squadristi,* the RFO idols of the 1920s. "See how they turned little Italy into a powerful state! Think what could be done in Russia!" he declaimed in the July 1932 issue of *Natsiya.* That summer, the party spawned its own version of *squadristi:* the Special Department *(Osoby Otdel).* Officially, the Special Department was charged with protecting party leaders and guarding party meetings. Unofficially, it was a goon squad, which roughed up fellow émigrés, Jews, or whomever their leader wanted mugged. Poverty and boredom rather than ideological conviction swelled the ranks of RFP storm troopers. Restless, beefy adolescents itching for knuckle-bruising action and a satisfying sensation of power found that the Special Department gave them in exile what the NKVD would have offered them in the USSR.

The Special Department was led by a burly youth of twenty-seven: Alexander Alexandrovich Bolotov, known by his friends as "Sasha." Bolotov claimed to have served in the OGPU before escaping from the USSR in 1926. After his arrival in Harbin, he gravitated to the RFP and became a crony of Rodzaevsky's. Bolotov offered a sharp contrast to the *vozhd.* Indifferent to ideology, he warmed to violence, particularly when his craving for morphine was not being satisfied. Bolotov liked to dress in full RFP regalia: high boots, riding breeches, and black shirt. He fondled a revolver as a train conductor fingers his pocket watch. Sasha's official duty was to guard Rodzaevsky and enforce intraparty security, but he also found time to run a gambling den on the second floor of RFP headquarters.

Soratnik Bolotov's specialty was terminating lives. Although he generally killed by contract, he was also known to exceed instructions and act impulsively. Such murderous outbursts made Bolotov somewhat less than an ideal hit-man, especially as he was wont to rhapsodize on the aesthetics of his work—for example the homicidal application of crowbars. Described by Russians and Japanese alike as a sick man (one Japanese diplomatic dispatch called him "kill-crazy"), Sasha nonetheless remained at large through most of the 1930s. His Japanese employers, as well as his Russian *vozhd,* found plenty of work for him.

Patriotic Mobsters

When Rodzaevsky decided to collaborate with the *Tokumu Kikan* and *Kempei,* he had in mind strengthening his own power within the RFP and putting the party in an advantageous position should Japan fight the Soviet Union. Yet it soon became evident that his patrons had their own notions about the RFP's functions. To be sure, Major Akikusa of the *Tokumu Kikan* and Kostya Nakamura of the *Kempei* both encouraged Rodzaevsky to prepare for the day when a great White army built around a nucleus of "Russian patriots" would march shoulder to shoulder with the Imperial Japanese Army to liberate Russia from Bolshevism. But in the meantime, there were practical tasks to be performed, tasks with which Japanese nationals could not afford to be directly associated.

Japanese officials involved in extortion and kidnapping did not directly engage in such enterprises. They retained Chinese and White Russian agents, a convenient arrangement that could be instantly terminated (together with the agents) should there be any threat of exposure. Dozens of White Russians hired themselves out to *Kempei* officers as enforcers, muggers, informers, and hit men. Among these were not only brutes but a number of naive idealists who thought that they were striking blows against "Reds and Jews." Many had no connection with the RFP. Whatever their motives or affiliations, those who performed "special" assignments for the Japanese lost their freedom of movement. They had glimpsed the recesses of the "kingly way," and as such were potentially dangerous to the Japanese, who forbade them to travel outside of Manchukuo without leaving behind family members as hostages.

Starting in 1932, any number of Japanese-employed White Russian gangs prowled the streets of Harbin. Hired by different agencies, they sometimes fought each other over prostitution and narcotics-related "territorial" jurisdictions. At other times, they banded together to carry out a major assignment, such as when the Lytton Commission came to Manchukuo in April of 1932. The Lytton Commission had been dispatched by the League of Nations to investigate the circumstances behind the Mukden incident of September 1931 that triggered Japan's conquest of Manchuria. The French, German, Italian, and American commissioners and their British leader, the Earl of Lytton, spent several days in Harbin at the Hotel Moderne. *Stukachi* and strongmen infested the hotel and its environs on the lookout for "unauthorized" communication with the commissioners, for example, letters, petitions, or whispered entreaties suggesting that Manchukuoans were less than ecstatic about Manchukuo.

The White Russian gangs surely needed no Japanese tutelage when it came to harassing Jews, for anti-Semitism smoldered among former army officers, Cossacks, and monarchists, not to mention the RFP. Anti-Semitism in Harbin fed hungrily upon the myth that the Jews were behind the October Revolution, and upon the reality that a handful of local Jews were rich. It mattered little that thousands of other Jews had fled Bolshevism and shared the desperate poverty and vulnerability of White Russians. What did matter was that a small segment of the local Jewish community was conspicuously affluent. Such affluence kindled a visceral resentment among many less fortunate émigrés. The RFP fanned this resentment, castigating "Jewish Bolshevism" and "Jewish capitalism" in lectures and publications. Words at times spilled over into action, as RFP Blackshirts vandalized Jewish stores, smashed synagogue windows, and waylaid Jewish students. To defend themselves, Harbin's Jews organized a chapter of the paramilitary youth group colloquially called the "Betar." Betar took on not only RFP Blackshirts but squads of Young Pioneers, local recruits of a Soviet youth organization.

In general, Harbin's police agencies showed no special interest in Jews unless they happened to be rich. Wealthy Jews made tempting targets for extortion. Using White Russian hirelings, some *Kempei* and Municipal Police officers also supervised a series of kidnappings during 1932. At first, the victims were Chinese and White Russian merchants or professional men, capable of paying from $5,000 to $100,000 for their lives. Some were abducted more than once after word got around to different gangs that they could afford handsome ransoms.

The first police-engineered abduction of a Jew occurred on March 11, 1932, ten days after the creation of Manchukuo and eleven days after the Lytton Commission arrived in Japan. The victim was a pharmacist named Kofman. The act was organized by Kostya Nakamura and carried out by a half-dozen White Russians, including two thugs named Kirichenko and Galusko, who regularly performed "special" assignments for *Kempei* officers. Kofman was plucked off a Pristan street around ten o'clock at night, held for several hours in a Novy Gorod cellar, then moved to a Chinese hut in the southeastern suburb of Machiakou. On March 12, the Russian language papers announced that Kofman had been kidnapped by *hunghutze* who were demanding $30,000 ransom. During the ensuing month, Kofman's family refused to pay any ransom until authorized to do so by the druggist himself. Eventually, Kofman's wife broke down and disbursed $18,000 with the understanding from the "bandits" that her husband would be released. She never saw him. Three weeks earlier, his diced remains had been dumped into a trench for unidentified corpses found on Harbin's streets. According to one supposed eyewitness, Kofman was tortured and killed by Konstantin Rodzaevsky.

Whether or not the *vozhd* committed murder on behalf of his Japanese patrons is not clear. The Italian mercenary Amleto Vespa graphically recalled being sent by his *Tokumu Kikan* employer to investigate unconfirmed reports of Kofman's murder. Conducted to a house outside of Harbin by *Kempei* trusties, Vespa found Rodzaevsky drinking beer with Kirichenko and Galusko. When questioned, Rodzaevsky allegedly blurted out: "This damned pig of a Jew loved his money more than his skin. That's what he got for not wanting to talk, or write to his wife. I scared him a little and the old fool just died."

"Scared him a little" turned out to mean roasting his face beyond recognition and suffocating him. Asked who had killed the druggist, Rodzaevsky (in Vespa's words) gloated: "I, and this is the way all the dirty Jews, enemies of Russia, should die."

Vespa's portrayal of Rodzaevsky as a sadistic killer was reiterated by an émigré memoir published under the pseudonym Alexandre Pernikoff during World War II. But Vespa's and "Pernikoff's" views do not match the impressions of several people who knew Rodzaevsky well and described him as one who shrank from violence. In an affidavit written and sworn to in Moscow in 1946, Rodzaevsky confessed to a catalogue of crimes, but murder was not among them. No doubt the Harbin *Kempei* files could clarify his role in the Kofman case, but they were destroyed or fell into Soviet hands in 1945.

Kempei officers hushed up the Kofman affair in the Harbin press, but they could not prevent more and more people from suspecting complicity between police and criminals. To protect their lives, some wealthy Jews who had not already done so succeeded in taking out citizenship in countries that enjoyed extraterritoriality in Manchukuo (Britain, France, and the United States were favorites). Foreign flags fluttered like talismans over Jewish homes and stores.

Diplomatic maneuvers, however, did not deter *Kempei* entrepreneurs from even bolder ventures. In the summer of 1933, Kostya Nakamura came to RFP headquarters on the Kitaiskaya with a plan to squeeze one of Harbin's wealthiest Jews: Josef Kaspé. Nakamura enlisted the help of Rodzaevsky because he knew that the *vozhd* had followers who could take orders without asking questions.

The Kaspé Affair

Josef Kaspé had emigrated from Russia to Harbin around the turn of the century, drawn by commercial opportunities attending the construction of the Chinese Eastern Railway. He opened a modest watch repair shop which also dealt in secondhand goods. Gradually his business prospered so that by 1918 he was proprietor of one of the most successful jewelry stores in the Far East. During the 1920s, Kaspé diversified, buying ownership of a theater chain and the Hotel Moderne, Harbin's finest. By 1932, his assets were reputed to run into millions of yuan.

Both *Kempei* operators and the Russian Fascist Party had reasons for taking a special interest in Josef Kaspé. To entrepreneurs in the military police, his obvious wealth presented a tempting target. To RFP hotheads, he personified the blood-sucking Jew, ruthlessly profiteering from the misfortunes of others. To some degree Kaspé's behavior lent itself to such a caricature. He liked to talk about his riches. Worse, his shop on the Kitaiskaya displayed silverware, enamels, diamond necklaces, emerald rings, Fabergé eggs, and Sèvres porcelain obtained at bargain rates from the Soviet government, which had confiscated them from their former owners. Marketing such ware in a fiercely anti-Communist refugee community invited trouble. Starting in 1932, *Nash Put* carried attacks on Kaspé for dealing in "ill-gotten property, stolen and filched from Russian victims." The paper also denounced him as a Comintern agent.

Josef Kaspé was well aware of the hatred that his life-style inspired. A tough and canny man for whom Harbin held few surprises, he knew the risks of getting kidnapped and took elaborate precautions. Thick steel bars laced the windows and doors of his residential section of the Hotel Moderne. Armed Russian guards patrolled the premises and formed a cordon around him whenever he went out. Kaspé also took steps to safeguard his assets. Shortly after Japan occupied Manchuria, he transferred ownership of the Hotel Moderne and theater chain to two sons who lived in Paris and held French citizenship. A tricolor jauntily flapped over each Kaspé establishment, proclaiming it off-limits to "kingly way" depredations. Finally, he instructed the French consul, Reynaud, to take immediate action in the event of threats against his life or property.

But Josef Kaspé left one unprotected flank in the family armor: his youngest son, Semion. Twenty-four years old in 1933, Semion stood on the threshold of a brilliant musical career. Having just finished a course at the Paris Conservatory, he had come to Harbin for his début as a professional pianist. Josef doted on Semion. He declared him to be a maestro superior to Paderewski and spared no expense in arranging recitals at the best theaters in Harbin, Shanghai, and Tokyo.

Josef warned Semion about the hazards of being a rich Jew in Harbin. He advised the young man to be careful about going out unaccompanied, particularly at night. Semion brushed off such talk as typical parental solicitude and reveled in nocturnal excursions. He scoffed at the idea of being intimidated like some stateless refugee. After all, he was a citizen of France, entitled to all the protection proclaimed by his French passport.

It is not clear who gave the order to abduct Semion, but there is reason to suspect that certain *Kempei* officers had their eyes on the Kaspé fortune. Other police agencies, not to mention any number of gangs, also had ample motive and opportunity for the act. In their memoirs, two *Kempei* employees asserted that the agency's Russian interpreter, Kostya Nakamura, conceived the idea of kidnapping Semion to milk Josef. Nakamura enlisted Konstantin Rodzaevsky and a Harbin Municipal Police inspector named Nikolai Martinov to recruit a team that could execute the abduction. During July 1933, the three men met regularly at an inconspicuous house in Novy Gorod rented in Nakamura's name, planning strategy for the project.

As an inspector in the Criminal Investigation Department of the Harbin Municipal Police, Martinov was an ideal instrument for the technical aspects of netting Semion. He possessed a unique knowledge of kidnapping, having both investigated and committed it. He also kept a stable of White Russian underlings who followed orders without asking questions. Martinov's only drawback was a homicidal habit acquired during the Civil War and refined during service in the Brotherhood of Russian Truth. In 1932, he fatally shot a former tsarist army colonel named Argunov. Tried for murder in a Chinese court, he was acquitted on the grounds that his service pistol had discharged accidently as the two men were walking together. How the bullet had managed to pass between Argunov's eyes was not explained. Martinov's impulses were not entirely a disadvantage, however, for they made him beholden to his Japanese patrons, who had intervened in the courts on his behalf.

Nakamura felt reservations about including Rodzaevsky in the Kaspé operation. The RFP *vozhd* saw everything in terms of politics and had exhibitionist tendencies that could jeopardize the secrecy essential to an "inside" kidnapping job. But Nakamura apparently valued Rodzaevsky's RFP contacts and information about Kaspé enough to enlist his cooperation.

As soon as Nakamura had broached the plan to Rodzaevsky, he knew that his initial doubts were justified. Konstantin Vladimirovich wanted Kaspé's blood, not his money. He urged that Semion should not just be kidnapped but be branded a Comintern agent and exterminated in defiance of the "Jewish" French government. Nakamura flatly refused to sanction political murder and made the following stipulations: (1) the operation would have no political overtones; (2) publicity would be kept at a minimum; and (3) the kidnapping would take place only after receiving assurances that French authorities would not intervene. Piqued, Rodzaevsky thereupon withdrew from the operation, and Martinov assumed complete responsibility for the abduction.

Before giving Martinov a free hand, Nakamura made discreet inquiries about relations between Kaspé and French consul Reynaud.

Satisfied by reports that no personal connection existed, he notified Martinov to go ahead and recruit accomplices but under no circumstances to mention his principal. As a professional servant of the "kingly way," Martinov scarcely needed to be reminded that if things went wrong, he would take the blame.

Late in July 1933, Martinov approached a trusty minion, Alexei Shandar, and persuaded him to take charge of the squad that would kidnap Semion Kaspé. He then recruited three veterans of "special assignments": Kirichenko and Galusko, both of the Kofman case, and Zaitsev. Zaitsev was an all-purpose hit man who did much of his work on contract in Shanghai and Tientsin. He referred to killing as "going hunting." For reasons that are unclear, Shandar recommended that two amateurs, Komisarenko and Bezruchko, be included on the team. Martinov reluctantly consented on the condition that neither would be given a sensitive assignment.

Martinov gave each man a specific task. Zaitsev and Kirichenko, led by Shandar, were to snatch Semion Kaspé. Galusko, Komisarenko, and Bezruchko were to guard Semion in a Stary Gorod hideout until the ransom money had been paid. Martinov himself would stay behind the scenes. He could not risk premature contact with the victim, with whom he might later come face to face during the police investigation.

Thanks to *stukachi,* including the Greek in the Hotel Moderne lobby, Martinov was well informed about Semion. He knew the rhythms of the young pianist's life: his male and female companions, his favorite restaurants, his customary routes when making excursions from the Hotel Moderne. He even knew that Semion's chauffeur carried a revolver (Martinov's department had issued the license). Not surprisingly, when the gang struck, it acted with flawless precision.

Semion Kaspé was plucked off the streets of Harbin minutes before midnight on August 24, 1933. He was escorting a girl friend named Lydia Chernetskaya to her home after a late dinner at the Hotel Moderne. As his car came to a halt before her front door, Shandar appeared out of the shadows and slid into the front seat next to the chauffeur, relieving him of his revolver. Kirichenko simultaneously entered through the rear door and ordered Lydia and Semion to remain quiet (they did). Shandar had the chauffeur drive to Novy Gorod, where he and Lydia were released after having been given instructions what to tell Josef Kaspé. Semion was transferred to another car and driven by Zaitsev to a riverbed outside the city. There, Galusko and

Bezruchko assumed custody of him and proceeded in yet another car to a prearranged hideout in Stary Gorod.

Although the kidnapping went smoothly, getting the ransom proved difficult. Nakamura had set the price for Semion's release at $300,000, a sum he considered well within Josef's capacity to pay. But he misjudged the old man's character. As soon as Josef had heard from Lydia about his son's abduction, including the ransom demand and the threat that any attempt to contact the police or French authorities could be fatal to Semion, old Kaspé reacted with a characteristic flourish. He immediately notified all Harbin police agencies of what had happened, called on the French consul to intervene, and announced to the papers that he would pay nothing because no one would dare harm his son.

Semion's abduction electrified Harbin. Nothing like this had befallen such a prominent foreign citizen. Each of the city's police agencies (Municipal, Manchukuoan, *Kempei*, Japanese Consular, CER Railway) opened separate investigations amid a flurry of publicity.

Official and unofficial suspicion fell first upon the Russian Fascist Party. RFP men, with few exceptions, were confirmed anti-Semites, and *Nash Put* had been regularly launching vitriolic attacks on the elder Kaspé. Blackshirt leader Sasha Bolotov was known to dabble in such crimes. The Harbin Municipal Police interrogated several fascists, including a most unlikely suspect, Mikhail Matkovsky, who was detained for three days. Rodzaevsky, however, was not touched.

As he had foreseen, Nikolai Martinov received orders from L. N. Goroshkevich, chief of the Criminal Investigation Department of the Harbin Municipal Police, to look into Kaspé's disappearance. Martinov boldly called upon Josef Kaspé and French consul Reynaud, expressed his regrets, and assured them that he would personally give the case top priority.

Martinov enjoyed little time to savor his dual role. Before the end of August, an unexpected turn of events threatened to render his cover transparent. While French consul Reynaud, true to Nakamura's prognosis, showed only a *pro forma* interest in young Kaspé's fate, the vice-consul, Albert Chambon, sensed that the case had sinister implications and made its solution a personal crusade. Chambon instructed old Kaspé to negotiate with the kidnappers but not to meet their demands. Meanwhile, he hired some Russian free-lance detectives to conduct a private investigation. Within two weeks, Chambon's suspicion that the abduction was an inside job involving the Japanese had become a conviction. It only remained for him to collect proof.

By the middle of September, the kidnappers had grown edgy. Old Kaspé seemed to be stalling for time. Chambon had announced a reward for finding Semion, which even Sasha Bolotov loudly proclaimed he intended to collect. Worst of all, rumor had it that Chambon's agents were picking up hot leads. Fearing that Harbin was no longer safe, the kidnappers removed their prisoner from Stary Gorod to a house near Siaolin, an isolated hamlet some thirty miles from the city.

It has been alleged that in late September, Nakamura grew nervous, dismissed Martinov, and called back Rodzaevsky to finish off Semion. Rodzaevsky's involvement at this stage is neither documented nor probable, but there were plenty of indications that someone was coming to the conclusion that young Kaspé must die.

Although Semion did everything to cooperate with his captors, including writing letters to his father pleading for compliance with their demands, he seems unwittingly to have sealed his own fate. Through weeks of enforced intimacy, he came to know his guards—Bezruchko, Galusko, Kirichenko, and Zaitsev (Komisarenko stayed away from Siaolin). Prolonged inactivity led to boredom and to loose tongues. Zaitsev could not resist talking about his work in the Brotherhood of Russian Truth. In doing so he unveiled details about the planning of Kaspé's own abduction, dropping Martinov's name and hinting at "higher" connections. When Kirichenko heard about this breach of security, he resolved that Kaspé knew too much to live even if the ransom were paid.

On September 28, the kidnappers resorted to a drastic tactic to disgorge money from old Kaspé. They severed Semion's ears, packaged them, and mailed the parcel to the Hotel Moderne with a note that the fingers would soon follow. Beholding his son's bloody flesh, Josef momentarily lost his resolve, but Chambon urged him to hold out a bit longer, saying that Semion's tormentors were about to be exposed.

The vice-consul was right. Several days later, his agents picked up Komisarenko, youngest and least committed member of the gang. Taken to the French consulate and questioned, he broke down and talked. In exchange for his release, Komisarenko signed a written confession implicating six accomplices, including Martinov. Through fear or ignorance, he did not mention Nakamura or Rodzaevsky. Armed with this evidence, Chambon went to the chief of the Harbin Municipal Police and demanded arrests. He also made it clear that he suspected Japanese involvement.

The Harbin Police informed *Kempei* headquarters of Komisarenko's confession and Chambon's suspicions. Nakamura reacted decisively. Komisarenko, he directed, was to be trundled off to lie low in Pogranichnaya, 250 miles east of Harbin on the Soviet-Manchukuo frontier. Chambon's investigators, identified by Komisarenko, were arrested.

Nakamura's countermeasures only reinforced Chambon's resolve to expose the Japanese role in Kaspé's disappearance. He circulated copies of Komisarenko's confession to all foreign consuls. Before long, American, British, and French newspapers were not only publicizing the affair but speculating about Japanese complicity. Possibly on *Kempei* instructions, *Nash Put* and *Kharbinskoye Vremya* launched a scathing attack on Chambon, accusing him of abusing his diplomatic immunity. *Nash Put* called the French vice-consul a "Jewish Communist agent" and urged Russian "patriots" to take direct action against him. Some RFP *soratniki* thereupon challenged Chambon to a duel, but nothing came of the gesture.

Martinov now sensed that a net was closing about him. On October 8, 1933, he discussed with Shandar and Kirichenko what course to take in the light of their imminent exposure. It was decided that Martinov and Shandar would await arrest but thereafter deny any connection with Kaspé. The others (Kirichenko, Zaitsev, Galusko, Bezruchko) would remain at large, guard Semion at Siaolin, and keep trying to extract ransom. Even at this late stage, the kidnappers still believed that they had a chance to succeed. Komisarenko had not divulged the Siaolin hideout to Chambon. And they banked on the chance that Semion's mother, living in Paris, could be approached to put pressure on Josef to relent and pay up.

Martinov and Shandar were duly arrested in their homes by the Harbin Municipal Police on October 9. Interrogated by a Japanese prosecutor from the Harbin District Court, they denied knowing anything about Kaspé's kidnapping or his whereabouts.

At this juncture, Chambon found a potent ally in the person of Colonel Oi Fukashi, chief of the Railway Police, whose jurisdiction comprised the entire CER zone in northern Manchuria. Although he was a Japanese official, Oi had not been briefed by the *Kempei,* and even if he had been, it is unlikely that he would have consented to look the other way. Oi was not one to bend to *Kempei* pressures and tolerated no circumvention of the law within the Railway Zone.

As soon as Oi heard that Komisarenko was about to embark for Pogranichnaya, he ordered his agents to intercept the young Russian at the Imianpo Station (fifty miles east of Harbin) on October 13. Brought back to Harbin, Komisarenko made a fuller confession which gave Colonel Oi important leads. On November 28, Oi learned that two men resembling Zaitsev and Bezruchko were regularly spotted boarding trains from Harbin's Stary Gorod Station. He ordered their arrest.

Contradictory accounts blur the climax of the Kaspé case. According to press reports, Bezruchko turned himself in and Zaitsev, Kirichenko, and Galusko murdered Semion and fled Siaolin. While attempting to reach a sanctuary in a sparsely populated area north of Harbin, the three fugitives were hunted down. Zaitsev and Kirichenko were captured and Galusko was fatally shot "while resisting arrest." Yet sources close to the *Kempei* have related a very different story. After Oi's agents had picked up Bezruchko and Zaitsev at the Stary Gorod Station, *stukachi* who had observed the arrests notified Nakamura, who immediately drove out to Siaolin. Nakamura ordered Kirichenko to kill Semion. Then he drew a pistol and shot Galusko through the head, because, according to one account, Galusko had just made a secret deal with Semion to spring the young man from captivity for a reward. Kostya then ordered Kirichenko to return separately to Harbin, pick up false identity papers from *Kempei* headquarters, and lie low in a remote northern corner of Manchukuo.

In any case, on December 3, 1933, a *Kempei* spokesman announced that Semion's body had been found in a shallow grave near the hamlet of Siaolin. The announcement also said that all of young Kaspé's abductors except Kirichenko* were dead or in custody of the Harbin Municipal Police.

Unable to accept this denouement, Josef Kaspé insisted upon seeing his son's body. The sight of the emaciated, unwashed corpse with its unshaven, earless, gangrene-racked face brought home in one stroke to the old man what his son had endured during ninety-

* Kirichenko was picked up north of Harbin by Colonel Oi's men on December 18.

five days of captivity. Self-controlled until this moment, Josef uttered
a low groan that rose into a howl.

Thousands of Harbin residents from every ethnic group, including
the Japanese, echoed Josef Kaspé's cry of outrage. Semion's cortege
turned into a massive demonstration of indignation. In an impassioned
funeral oration, Dr. Abraham Kaufman denounced not only Kaspé's
killers but those behind them who remained at liberty. The implication
was clear. For his temerity, Kaufman was threatened by *Kempei* toughs
but spared arrest. Evidently Tokyo, concerned about international
opinion, was anxious that the furor die down. Martinov and his associates were not brought to trial until fifteen months later. Final judgment
on the men was not passed until 1936, after a series of judicial traves-
ties that stirred up as much emotion as the crime itself.*

Although Japanese authorities wanted nothing more than to have
the Kaspé affair fade away, their protégé Rodzaevsky made it into a
fascist *cause célèbre*. Oblivious to his patrons' embarrassment, he jubi-
lated about Semion's demise in *Nash Put* and hailed the kidnappers
as Russian patriots. Kostya Nakamura knew all too well that when
Konstantin Vladimirovich got carried away, he had to be muzzled.
Consequently, *Kempei* enforcers made periodic visits to *Nash Put* offices
in order to reinstill there a correct understanding of the "kingly way."

Despite the reverberations from the Kaspé case, Rodzaevsky had
good reason to be proud of himself as the year 1933 drew to a close.
At the age of twenty-six, he stood unchallenged as the head of the
strongest Russian émigré organization in the Far East. RFP membership had soared from 200 in 1931 to 5,000 in 1933, a twenty-five-
fold increase in two years. Throughout the world, fascism gave every
indication of being the wave of the future. Adolf Hitler had just come
to power in Germany. Benito Mussolini sonorously proclaimed the
rebirth of the Roman Empire. Fascist movements were gathering momentum in Spain, France, the Balkans, and South America. Japan
was expanding on the Asian continent and appeared to be on a collision course with the Soviet Union. Japan's Russian-speaking, viscerally
anti-Communist army minister, General Araki Sadao, was sympathetic
to the RFP. A Soviet-Japanese war might precipitate the National
Revolution and leave him—Konstantin Vladimirovich Rodzaevsky—
vozhd of Russian fascists, the *vozhd* of Russia.

* See Chapter XI.

But wait. Was he really *vozhd* of *all* Russian fascists? Faint doubts began to stir as he started picking up echoes of a certain Anastase Vonsiatsky who called himself *vozhd* of Russian fascists in the United States. The boy from Blagoveshchensk decided to investigate. His initial misgivings turned into a ten-year headache as a fake count from Connecticut vaulted dramatically into the rarefied arena of émigré politics.

CHAPTER VII

A Russian Cinderella

I do not mean to say that every Russian who emigrated to the United States is a fake but I am convinced that no other country in the world drew such an imposing quota of Russian fakes.
—GRAND DUKE ALEXANDER (1933)

If Russian fascism looked at times like a cover for organized crime in the Far East, it surfaced in the United States as a theatrical performance. Thanks to a tolerant government, cooperative local police, and liberal private subsidies, a consummate actor named Anastase Andreivich Vonsiatsky gave thousands of Americans an example of showmanship that Hollywood might envy.

Outwardly garrulous and flamboyant, Vonsiatsky was in fact a complex man whose comic antics masked a tragic soul. Rebounding from a shattered adolescence, he pursued a career that skirted teasingly between politics and vaudeville, leaving onlookers guessing whether he was a menace, messiah, or mountebank. His compulsive eccentricities united the disparate strands of Russian fascism, epitomizing at once its futility, absurdity, and pathos.

Vonsiatsky's youth was full of vicissitudinous extremes. He lost a homeland and gained a fortune. Revolution stripped him of family and possessions, leaving him a down-but-not-out refugee. Marriage to an American heiress transformed him into a New England squire envied by thousands as the embodiment of an immigrant's dream. Well before any thought of becoming a fascist *vozhd* had crossed his mind, he had donned the glass slippers of a Russian Cinderella.

Down-But-Not-Out

Anastase Andreivich Vonsiatsky was born on June 12, 1898, in the Citadel of Warsaw, capital of the former Russian province of

Poland. His birthday fell on the same day as that of Peter the Great, a coincidence that Anastase subsequently felt entitled him to claim descent from that erratically enlightened despot. The Vonsiatskys were in fact descended from minor German-Polish nobility of the Holy Roman Empire. Originally, the name had been spelled "von Siatsky," but over the years it became russified.

Generations of service to the tsars had russified the Vonsiatskys in outlook as well as in name. Anastase's great-grandfather had been personally commended by Nicholas I for conspicuous loyalty. His grandfather had helped suppress the Polish uprising of 1863. His father, Colonel Andrei Nikolaevich, commanded Warsaw's gendarmerie.

The Vonsiatskys lived and worked within the Citadel. Andrei Nikolaevich devoted himself to the difficult and often unpopular task of maintaining law and order in a city that seethed with social revolutionaries and Polish nationalists. Andrei's brother-in-law, Anastase Plyshevsky, an Orthodox priest, oversaw the religious needs of the garrison. Andrei's wife, Nina Anastasevna, stoically accepted the spartan surroundings and dedicated herself to raising five children: Maria, Natasha, Tanya, Nikolai, and—the youngest—Anastase.

A robust child with large, inquisitive gray eyes, Anastase grew up in an inexorably military atmosphere. His parents took pride in military service and expected their male children to perpetuate the family tradition with honor.

Young Anastase seems to have accepted his lot with relish. While still an infant, he clambered around the battlements as if they were his own playground. Outfitted in a miniature hussar's uniform, he galloped around the cobblestone courtyards like a toy cavalryman, accompanied by a breathless orderly. A few feet from ,where little Vonsiatsky romped were rows of cells that, between 1900 and 1912, housed a number of subsequently notable prisoners: the Polish statesman Jozef Pilsudski, the German Spartacist martyr Rosa Luxemburg, the ill-fated Comintern wit Karl Radek, and Felix Dzerzhinsky, organizer and chief of the Cheka. In 1908, at the age of ten, Anastase was enrolled in the Moscow Military Preparatory School as the first step toward entering the officer corps of the Imperial Russian Army.

Tragedy struck the Vonsiatskys on June 16, 1910. On the eve of his transfer to Kiev, Andrei Nikolaevich was assassinated in the town of Radom, fifty miles south of Warsaw. Although Anastase later described his father as a martyr to Polish revolutionary terrorists, he was in fact the victim of an irate stool pigeon. Peeved over a private grudge, one of Colonel Vonsiatsky's hired informers walked into Radom's police headquarters and approached his employer who sat unsuspectingly behind a desk. Before aides could intervene, the visitor produced a Browning pistol and drilled the officer between the eyes. The murder precipitated a purge of underground police agents throughout Russian Poland and left a deep psychological scar on Anastase, who bore a lifelong fear of assassination.

Anastase completed the Moscow Military Preparatory School in 1916 and immediately entered the prestigious Emperor Nicholas I Cavalry Academy in St. Petersburg. As a cadet, he was assigned to the Fifth Regiment of the Empress Alexandra Feodorovna Hussars, popularly known as the Black Hussars because they wore black uniforms and rode black horses.

Within a year, revolutionary upheavals closed the Academy and permanently scattered the Vonsiatsky family. Mother Nina died of illness late in 1916. Nikolai died fighting the Bolsheviks in the Civil War. Maria remained in Russia, to vanish in a wave of arrests in 1936. Natasha escaped across Siberia with her husband and opened a cafe in Harbin. Tanya settled down near Moscow. Anastase embarked on a picaresque trail that led to Putnam, Connecticut.

The October Revolution catapulted Anastase Vonsiatsky into the Civil War bloodbath. In late November 1917, he joined several hundred imperial cadets and trekked over a thousand snow-covered miles to Ekaterinodar (now Krasnodar) on the Kuban River in southern Russia, where an anti-Bolshevik Volunteer Army was being formed under General Anton Denikin. For the next two years, Anastase fought Reds in the eastern Ukraine and along the Don under Denikin. Combat turned a pink-cheeked adolescent into a hardened soldier. Promoted from cadet to captain, he shot and bayonetted scores of real or putative Bolsheviks in a savage struggle where neither side cared to verify affiliations before pulling the trigger. Later in life, Vonsiatsky recalled how he and other White soldiers had machine-gunned five hundred Bolshevik prisoners at Rostov on November 27, 1919.

Vonsiatsky had several close brushes with death during this interim. He acquired a triangular scar on his forehead (uncannily congruent with his father's fatal wound) and for the rest of his life carried a Red bullet in his abdominal cavity. Living dangerously taught him a resourceful ingenuity that pulled him through tight spots then and thereafter. On one occasion, he was surprised by a Bolshevik patrol while feasting in a watermelon patch near Rostov in 1919. He took to his heels, only to discover that bowels made unruly by overindulgence jeopardized his flight. Quick action with a bayonet, he reported, ventilated his trousers and ensured a speedy evacuation.

The Russian Civil War marked Vonsiatsky indelibly. It left him with an implacable hatred of communism, which appeared to have filled his homeland with death and destruction. And it created a special bond between Vonsiatsky and other veterans of the Volunteer Army, who were to form the nucleus of his fascist party in the 1930s. Their shared experiences constituted the touchstone of fascist unity, the marrow of the fascist mystique. The icy odyssey to Ekaterinodar, for example, came to be regarded as a sort of Russian fascist Long March, perpetuated in story and song as an immortal symbol of perseverance.

Illness spared Vonsiatsky from being caught in the final White collapse. Contracting typhus near Kharkov in December 1919, he was transported by freight train to the Black Sea port of Novorossisk, from which he took a steamer to the Crimean resort of Yalta, arriving with frostbitten legs and no money on January 3, 1920. At Yalta, a Jewish shopkeeper named Muromsky gave the battered warrior shelter. Muromsky's daughter, Lyuba, nursed his wounds.

Within a few days of his arrival, Vonsiatsky was on intimate terms with Lyuba. On January 31, they became man and wife in a Russian Orthodox ceremony at Yalta's Saint Nicholas Cathedral. The motives for their precipitate marriage are unclear and controversial. Anastase subsequently dismissed the matrimonial contract as a device to protect the Muromskys from pogroms and to expedite their escape from the Crimea, then tottering on the verge of anarchy. He maintained that the marriage had no legal standing because Lyuba had falsified her religion; Russian law prohibited the union of a Jew and a member of the Russian Orthodox Church. But Lyuba, it turned out, was not to let her man off that easily.

The deterioration of the White cause in southern Russia convinced Vonsiatsky to leave Yalta before it was too late. Accompanied by his young wife, he crossed the Black Sea to Constantinople in March 1920 and entered a British hospital in Gallipoli for treatment of the lingering ravages of frostbite. Discharged after a month with only a greatcoat, a tattered uniform, and a pair of hospital slippers to his name, Vonsiatsky decided to set off without Lyuba and look for work in western Europe. In April he managed to reach Marseilles aboard various steamers. In May he moved on to London, via Paris, and found an unexpected benefactor in the person of Prince Felix Yusupov.

Heir to one of Russia's largest industrial fortunes, Felix Yusupov was somewhat of a nabob among exiled royalty. Although the Revolution had deprived him of his Baku oil wells, he had managed to salvage enough portable valuables to live for a while in grand style off the proceeds of their sale. Yusupov liked to give parties at which he regaled guests with the story of how he had helped kill Rasputin in 1916. He also sought an outlet for altruistic impulses by subsidizing a workshop for needy compatriots in an elegant London townhouse. Vonsiatsky became one of his wards.

After spending three months as a "guest of Prince Yusupov," Vonsiatsky counted his alms, said good-bye to the young Romanov princes with whom he would cavort ten years later, and returned to Constantinople in October 1920. What led him to give up a cozy sinecure for the uncertainties of Turkish hospitality is hard to determine. Yusupov may have tired of him. Perhaps he missed Lyuba. Perhaps his English visa had expired.

Whatever his motives for returning there, Vonsiatsky did not tarry in Constantinople for long. The evacuation of General Wrangel and 150,000 troops and civilians from the Crimea in November signaled the collapse of the White cause in southern Russia and flooded the Bosporus with refugees. Having no desire to wind up in a Gallipoli internment camp, the French Foreign Legion, or a Balkan road gang, Vonsiatsky signed up on a freighter bound for Marseilles, took odd jobs in southern France, and finally settled down as a stagehand in Paris' Folies Bergères. Again, Lyuba seems to have been left by the wayside.

Later in life, Vonsiatsky confided to a friend that his ambition as a young man had been to marry money or become a movie star. He achieved the former, thanks to a chance encounter in a Paris dance hall in the spring of 1921 with an American divorcée twice his age and many times richer.

Writing his memoirs on the Côte d'Azur, Grand Duke Alexander sardonically remarked that "nothing is so useful to an exile as his hard-earned ability to recite the Cinderella story in reverse." Vonsiatsky reversed a reversal by becoming a true Cinderella. His Princess Charming turned out to be Mrs. Marion Stephens, *née* Marion Buckingham Ream.

The Ream Connection

One of the wealthiest families in the United States in 1920, the Reams had recently completed the transition from Chicago plutocracy to Connecticut squiredom. In the last quarter of the nineteenth century, clan patriarch Norman Bruce Ream made several fortunes as a livestock and grain operator. Known as one of Chicago's "Big Four" after he cashed in on the Armour pork corner in 1879, Ream was counted with the likes of J. P. Morgan, Marshall Field, George M. Pullman, and E. H. Gray as one of the heroes (or villains) of America's Gilded Age. Toward the turn of the century, Norman Ream branched out into railways, steel, and finance, and at his death in 1915, he was a director of twenty-two corporations, notably National Biscuit Company and United States Steel, both of which he had cofounded. He left an estate worth $40 million to his wife, Caroline Putnam (a descendant of the Pilgrim father William Bradford, second governor of the Plymouth colony), and six grown children: Marion, Frances, Norman, Robert, Edward, and Louis.

After her husband's demise, Caroline continued to live at Carolyn Hall, the family's palatial estate at Thompson, Connecticut. Thompson was and is a picturesque New England village (population in 1975: 300) about three miles from Putnam (population: 7,000), twenty-eight miles from Providence, forty-eight miles from Hartford, and sixty miles from Boston. Nestled in the northeastern corner of the state near the Massachusetts and Rhode Island lines, Thompson missed the Industrial Revolution (unlike neighboring Putnam, which had prospered and later decayed as a textile-mill town).

Although the Ream property in Thompson comprised hundreds of verdant acres, the second generation with one exception eventually took up residence elsewhere. Robert and Norman settled in Greenwich at the antipodal corner of Connecticut. Frances moved to North Carolina, Edward to Kentucky, and Louis to Providence. Only Marion remained in Thompson.

Marion Buckingham Ream was an extraordinary woman. Born on January 9, 1877, in Woodlawn Park, Illinois, she grew up into a petite (five-foot three-inch), brown-eyed, large-headed girl with a broad brow and round chin. Her masculine face, however, could not conceal a grace and compassion that won the hearts of all who knew her. Marion's generosity was almost compulsive. "She couldn't stop giving," recalled a Thompson friend. But Marion's largesse was unsullied by piety or expectation of gratitude, and her sense of integrity never congealed into self-righteous respectability.

Quietly but firmly independent, Marion showed little inclination to play demure spouse, fertile mother, and perennial hostess—all expected of a woman of her economic and social station. Marion had her own ideas about how life should be lived. Without offending her family, she managed to follow her own mildly unconventional inclinations. Had she been a man, she might have taken after her father. Instead, she channeled her energies and money to favorite friends and causes.

Marion's independent streak asserted itself after her betrothal in 1903 at the age of twenty-six to a Chicago attorney, Redmond Stephens. Celebrated as the grandest nuptials of the Chicago season, the marriage gradually foundered on financial and emotional incompatibility. Marion spent some $25,000 a year on dinner parties and travel—thirty-two trips from Chicago to Putnam between 1903 and 1915. Although he enjoyed a successful law practice and received financial support from Norman Bruce Ream during an incapacitating illness, Redmond worried about the drain on his earnings and chafed at his wife's peripatetic habits. He wrote his mother-in-law on May 17, 1915 (Norman Ream had died the previous February), listing his complaints and raising the specter of separation unless Marion spent less money and more time at home.

But Marion, not Redmond, terminated their marriage. Having intercepted letters addressed to her husband from a certain Priscilla—letters that left little doubt about how Redmond consoled himself in his wife's absence—Marion abruptly packed up and returned to Carolyn Hall in 1915. For two years, Redmond apologized abjectly and begged her to forgive him. In a letter dated September 5, 1917, he pleaded:

> As I look back, it seems as though our trouble started because each wanted to make the other a part of one's own family, and I resented, I regret to state, becoming a Ream. Now as I look at it I would become a Ream,

and in addition a slave, an Elk, or a Catholic or a Jew if I could have you, you dear but ungovernable thing.

But Marion remained deaf to all his entreaties. The divorce was made final on April 6, 1918. Devoted to the end, Redmond never remarried. Moreover, he made her a beneficiary in his will. Marion inherited $5,000 when he expired at French Lick Springs, Indiana, on February 13, 1931.

Almost as if to seek distraction from her marital fiasco, Marion threw herself into the idealistic fervor that swept America during World War I. She volunteered for the American Red Cross, qualified as a nurse after receiving training at the Women's Naval Service in Washington, and immediately after the Armistice arrived in France as a relief worker in the YMCA, attached to the American Expeditionary Forces' Army of Occupation. Relief work put her in contact with hundreds of Russian refugees, but she became particularly interested in the welfare of one: Anastase Vonsiatsky.

Marion and Anastase made an odd couple. She was forty-four. He was twenty-two. She spoke no Russian and knew virtually nothing about Russia. He could barely manage a few broken phrases in English and entertained only the dreamiest notions of America. Yet a chance encounter in a Paris dance hall in the spring of 1921 sparked a relationship that was to endure for more than forty years.

To be sure, their mutual attraction sprang from different motives. Marion pitied Anastase as an innocent victim of historical circumstance. His tragic fate cried out to her from expressive gray eyes. His Old World gallantry flattered her self-esteem. She thrilled at the solicitude showered on her by a robust, handsome youth whose fumbling attempts at English could, perhaps, be interpreted as tongue-tied passion. His apparent childlike helplessness appealed to her maternal instincts and reinforced her faith in his sincerity.

For Anastase, on the other hand, it seems to have been love at foresight. Marion's palpable concern for the victims of revolution was immensely gratifying, especially when taken in connection with her financial assets. The combination gave Anastase ideas. Like thousands of other émigrés, he refused to accept the finality of a Bolshevik triumph. He dreamed of returning to Russia, although he was not sure how to do it. Marion's resources and sympathies filled him with confidence that anything was possible. As Edward VIII would later give up an empire for an American divorcée, so Anastase beheld an empire—of possibilities—in the prospect of marrying an American divorcée.

Taking the young Russian under her wing, Marion made up her mind to help him find work in the United States. She began by introducing Anastase to Elliott Bacon, a senior partner in J. P. Morgan & Company, who happened to be visiting Paris. Asked what occupation a patriotic exile might pursue, Bacon advised Vonsiatsky to find work in a harvester or locomotive factory, because knowledge about machinery would be indispensable in Russia. Bacon put Vonsiatsky in touch with another American visitor in Paris, Constance Vauclain, daughter of Samuel M. Vauclain, president of Philadelphia's Baldwin Locomotive Works, which until the Revolution had carried on a brisk business in Russia. Constance in turn supplied the candidate proletarian with a letter of introduction to her father.

Buoyant with bright employment prospects, Vonsiatsky prepared to depart Paris for the United States in June 1921. He bought a boat ticket with a loan from Elliott Bacon and presumably received some money from Marion as well. Before leaving, he could not resist cutting a caper in European émigré circles.

On June 24, 1921, an unusual article appeared in the Paris Russian-language newspaper *Posledniya Novosti,* a liberal organ edited by the Kadet politician and historian Paul Miliukov. Entitled "Memoirs of a Monarchist," it described in graphic detail three torture-murders of Bolshevik suspects in the Crimea in 1920, murders in which the author gave every indication of having been an accessory. In one episode, some White officers pulled out the fingernails and bayonetted the calves of their victim. In another, one of the murderers complained about brain tissue that had spattered on his mackintosh after he had shot a young Jew through the head in front of the latter's horrified parents. The article was signed "A. Vonsiatsky."

Read with a cold eye, "Memoirs" were outpourings of an over-heated imagination. Although he later stated that the material was extracted from his personal diary by a friend who wanted it published, it is unlikely that Vonsiatsky took part in the atrocities that he so floridly evoked. "Memoirs" was set in the Crimea. Yet Anastase's two-month sojourn in Yalta (his only visit to the Crimea) was serenely spent as an invalid and then as a son-in-law in a Jewish household. "Memoirs" might well have been a clumsy didactic tale deploring a tendency among many Whites to equate Jews with Bolsheviks. It probably represented the author's first flight into make-believe.

Whatever Vonsiatsky's intent, readers of "Memoirs" took the revelations literally. The editors of *Posledniya Novosti* printed the item as an antimonarchist barb. Monarchist émigré journals chorused their outrage, protesting that the publication of such material threatened to discredit the entire White cause. It was angrily alleged that the Soviet newspaper *Izvestiya* reprinted a million copies of "Memoirs" for propaganda purposes. "Memoirs" were to haunt Vonsiatsky twenty years later when detractors used the "Crimean torture-killings" to brand him a Russian Himmler. For the time being, however, Vonsiatsky had merely pulled off a stunt and had gained momentary publicity. His departure from Paris came none too soon, as French police notified him that his *permit de séjour* would not be renewed.

Upon reaching New York on the *France* on July 30, 1921, Vonsiatsky was issued a three-month, nonrenewable visa. Residency permits were hard to come by. Congress had just passed (May 19, 1921) the Quota Act, which severely restricted the number of Russian immigrants admitted into the United States. Marion again came to Vonsiatsky's rescue by mobilizing family connections on his behalf.

Circumstantial evidence suggests that a friend of the late Norman Bruce Ream, John R. Gladding, played a key role in bringing Vonsiatsky's case to the attention of proper authorities. Gladding, a Providence stockbroker, had been a college classmate (Brown '81) and correspondent of Charles Evans Hughes, the recently appointed secretary of state. An island of probity in the Harding administration, Hughes leaned over backward to avoid dispensing personal favors inconsistent with his public duty. Vonsiatsky may have been the exception that proved the rule. Gladding's recommendation of the young Russian refugee as a serious young man vouched for by an eminently respectable (and staunchly Republican) family possibly moved Hughes to instruct the United States Immigration and Naturalization Service to grant Vonsiatsky a special dispensation. No written record of such instructions has been seen, since Vonsiatsky's immigration dossier— filed under the heading "Communist"—is still classified. Nevertheless, it is known that a Board of Review granted Vonsiatsky a residency permit on October 29, 1921, one day before his visa expired.

In later years, Thomas Watson, a longtime employee of the Ream family, recalled how John Gladding grumbled that had he (Gladding) known in 1921 what sort of man "that Russian" really was, he would never have interceded with Secretary Hughes on his behalf. Vonsiatsky, for his part, never forgot his gratitude to the "Long-Legged Bulldog." He became a lifelong Republican and upon several occasions spoke and wrote about Hughes with deep respect and affection for helping him remain in the United States.

Vonsiatsky spent the summer and autumn of 1921 at Carolyn Hall. Marion showed affection for him but made no open allusions to marriage. One of her Thompson friends recalled many years later that Marion treated the young Russian as a protégé rather than as a potential spouse. She tutored him in English, introduced him to family and friends, and quietly asked everyone to be nice to him—in short, spared no effort to win him social acceptance among Thompson's gentry.

It is difficult to determine exactly when the idea of marriage crept into Marion's philanthropic project. In view of their characters, Vonsiatsky most likely proposed and Marion accepted, possibly in the fall of 1921 when his residency status was clarified.

Whatever the staunchly conventional Ream family felt about an exotic houseguest, it undoubtedly had reservations about an impoverished Russian refugee of questionable background marrying Norman's most independent and unpredictable offspring. Unfortunately for clan discipline, Norman was no longer alive to keep wayward hearts in line, as he had done when Marion's younger brother, Louis Marshall Ream, eloped with an actress to Hoboken, New Jersey, in 1911. Faced with filial disobedience on that occasion, Norman gave his son the choice of leaving the girl or being disinherited. Louis caved in and came home. His father pacified the actress with a $210,000 wedding-annulment gift. But 1911 and 1921 were worlds apart. Norman had passed on. Marion possessed a stronger will than Louis, and in 1921 was nearly double the age that Louis had been in 1911. She also enjoyed financial independence, having inherited one-seventh of her father's estate. Whatever their misgivings, the Reams had little choice but to defer to Marion's choice and pray that the wedding would pass with a minimum of publicity. No one counted on the affair's assuming the proportions of an international soap opera.

On Vonsiatsky's insistence, Marion agreed to be married at the Russian Cathedral of Saint Nicholas on 97th Street in New York. Marion also converted to the Orthodox faith for the occasion. A private wedding ceremony was scheduled for 4:00 P.M. on February 4, 1922. It was to be a small affair. The Reams did not plan to attend, and Vonsiatsky had no relatives in the United States.

Late in January, the New York press suddenly learned of the approaching nuptials. Within days, the story leapt into international prominence. By February 1, newspapers throughout the United States, England, France, and Germany were carrying bulletins of the event. Ladies' magazine covers carried cameos of Marion. The prospect of an American millionairess marrying a penniless Russian refugee caught the popular imagination. It was not simply romantic; it epitomized the American dream. Thousands looked on with vicarious excitement, wistful envy, or wry cynicism.

Hardly had Anastase and Marion moved into the Chatham Hotel on Vanderbilt Avenue and 48th Street two days prior to the ceremony, when they were besieged by reporters. The Reams hired private detectives to insulate the couple from intruders, but interviews took place nonetheless. To her family's dismay, Marion was artlessly candid with the press. When asked about the discrepancy of age and wealth between herself and her fiancé, she responded: "He is older than his years. And happiness is not a matter of money." Vonsiatsky, for his part, launched into a Walter Mitty routine that was fast becoming a trademark. He identified himself as "Count von Siatskoi-Vonsiatsky" (which columnists reduced to "VV"). VV had once owned vast estates in southern Russia. VV's father was the former "Governor of Warsaw." VV's grandfather was the "suppressor of the Polish Uprising of 1863." VV fought on every front in the Russian Civil War. VV came to the United States on the invitation of the president of the Baldwin Locomotive Works, a personal friend of his. VV met his fiancée in Connecticut while staying as a guest of the Ream family at Carolyn Hall. The papers took such fare with a grain of salt, but they wildly overestimated Marion's dowry, citing figures from $40 million to $600 million.

Anastase and Marion outwitted reporters and celebrity mongers by getting married a day earlier than announced. To cover their honeymoon tracks, they feinted a return to Carolyn Hall, then bolted for Quebec, where they registered under assumed names at the Château Frontenac. Such deviousness only fanned the publicity, which caught up with them when someone recognized them walking along the St. Lawrence River.

Although it was obvious that with Marion's resources the newly-weds could easily embark on a life of gracious leisure, neither of them favored such an option. Anastase wanted to prepare himself for a useful role in Russia's future and had already followed Elliott Bacon's advice to learn something about machinery.

In January 1922, a chauffeur-driven limousine pulled up to the main gate of the Baldwin Locomotive Works' Eddystone plant along the Delaware River in Philadelphia's southwestern suburbs. The passenger asked to meet the company president, Samuel M. Vauclain, saying that he had a letter of introduction from Mr. Vauclain's daughter recommending him for a job. After recovering his composure, the Eddystone plant manager asked the visitor about his qualifications. It quickly became apparent that he knew nothing about locomotives. The manager did not know what to do until a sympathetic foreman offered to take the visitor into the plant's chemical laboratory as a junior apprentice at $8.50 a week.

Vonsiatsky had already started work at Eddystone when he married Marion in February. He requested and received time off for the wedding and honeymoon while fellow laborers (who nicknamed him "Annie") looked on in disbelief.

Back from Quebec, Anastase and Marion moved into a modest house at 505 Swarthmore Avenue in the Ridley Park section of Chester, Pennsylvania. From Monday through Friday, the "Eddystone apprentice" commuted to a laboratory bench while his wife bustled about doing household chores. On weekends, he frequented the Ridley Fire Department poker games as a volunteer fireman. The press gleefully lampooned the incongruous spectacle of plutocrats playing proletarians. In a cartoon entitled "Wash Day at the Cabin" carried in the *New York Record,* Marion was depicted as hanging jewelry on a clothesline while "Hubby" gaily trotted off to a factory with his lunch pail. For the entertainment of thousands if not millions of readers, the nationally syndicated Hearst magazine, *American Weekly,* featured an illustrated story of how Marion "Nearly Lost Her Enthusiasm for 'Love in a Cottage' When She First Saw Her Humble New Home." Pulp magazines dubbed their house a "love nest." When Anastase won a wage raise to $22.50 a week, the media greeted the event with tongue-in-cheek acclaim.

This proletarian idyll was suddenly interrupted in April 1922 by a ghost from the past. Lyuba Muromsky surfaced to stake her matrimonial claim—plus interest. Once again, Vonsiatsky appeared in the public limelight, this time as a bigamist and adulterer. The Reams found themselves not only singed by scandal but saddled with a half-million-dollar lawsuit.

Mystery still shrouds the relationship between Anastase and Lyuba. They had left Constantinople separately in 1920 but lived together as man and wife in Paris early in 1921. When Anastase met Marion, he started to shed Lyuba. Just how much Marion and Lyuba knew about each other can only be surmised. Lyuba probably suspected what lay behind Vonsiatsky's abrupt departure for the United States. But Marion seems to have remained ignorant of her betrothed's other woman until Lyuba announced herself.

Lyuba, living in Paris, waited until two months after Vonsiatsky's marriage to Marion before taking action. Her method of operation suggests that she was interested in pecuniary rather than emotional compensation. On April 6, 1922, Lyuba's attorney, Edouard de Braz, wrote the Ream family lawyer, Clarence Mitchell (of Choate, Larocque, and Mitchell), and simultaneously filed a complaint against Vonsiatsky with Myron Herrick, American ambassador in Paris. Herrick forwarded the complaint to Washington, where, after passing through several agencies, it wound up at the desk of the New York district attorney. The district attorney advised Lyuba that her presence in New York was required before any proceedings could be inaugurated. Meanwhile, Anastase and Marion offered Lyuba an out-of-court financial settlement.

Lyuba decided to play it both ways. She accepted hush money. And she bought a steamship ticket to New York.

Sensing Lyuba's intentions, Vonsiatsky appealed to the Russian Orthodox Church to reconfirm the legitimacy of his second marriage. On November 22, 1922, an ecclesiastical court presided over by Metropolitan Platon of New York duly decreed that the Vonsiatsky-Ream marriage was valid and that the Vonsiatsky-Muromsky union was void on the grounds that it had been procured for temporary purposes through the use of false documents. The court's ruling followed precedent. Marriages contracted in areas occupied by White armies during the Civil War were generally regarded as illegal when contested. Vonsiatsky was off the hook with the church. He still had to reckon with the state.

Amid wide publicity, Lyuba Muromsky and Edouard de Braz arrived in New York on January 27, 1923. De Braz made a statement to the press that his client was suing Marion Ream for $500,000 for alienation of Anastase's affections and was also seeking alimony payments from Vonsiatsky. With the princess-and-pauper romance still fresh in the public memory, Lyuba's dramatic appearance added a twist to a good story. RUSSIAN WOMAN ARRIVES TO MAR MECHANIC'S BLISS announced the St. Paul (Minnesota) *Pioneer Press* in a headline that Midwestern readers instantly understood. Lyuba adroitly fanned up sympathy for herself as a trusting waif callously abandoned by an ambitious lover for a jaded moneybags. In July, the plaintiff gave the press an alleged letter from Vonsiatsky offering her a lifetime pension of $40 a month for keeping quiet. Adding a new convolution to the eternal triangle, Lyuba quoted her husband as beseeching her to write him in care of the Chester YMCA "because Marion is taking Russian lessons."

Lyuba may have aroused public sympathy, but the New York Supreme Court threw out her suit on August 3, 1923. The judge dismissed charges of bigamy, citing the ecclesiastical court's ruling and reminding Lyuba that she had written Vonsiatsky in January 1922 expressing pleasure at his betrothal to Marion Ream. Apparently, the jilted lady had consented to the bigamous marriage for a price, but after learning more about Marion's worth decided to raise the ante.

Worn down by abrasive publicity, the Vonsiatskys sensed that their proletarian experiment had begun to pall. Carolyn Hall beckoned, luring them with promises of soothing privacy, gracious leisure, and congenial friends. Besides, Marion's mother Caroline, entering her seventy-second year, showed signs of failing health.

Disposing of their Ridley Park "love nest," Anastase and Marion moved to Thompson in January 1924. Baldwin Locomotive lost a junior apprentice. Connecticut gained a nascent folk hero.

Grooming

In transplanting Anastase to Thompson, Marion launched his re-education as a New England squire. For the next decade, she gently tried to groom her Russian boy as a fixture of the Windham County gentry. But Vonsiatsky turned out to be more than she could cope with. Before long, he was transforming Thompson and its stalwart citizens into stage props for his own theatrical pretensions.

Anastase and Marion lived at Carolyn Hall until Caroline Putnam Ream died in December 1924. Caroline's passing signaled the end of a grand life-style that Norman Bruce Ream had planned for his descendants. In 1926, Carolyn Hall was sold to a Lithuanian Marian order which renamed the estate Marianopolis College.

On June 12, 1925, Marion bought for $25,000 a 224-acre dairy farm called Larnard Place, located a mile south of Thompson on County Home Road (now Connecticut Route 21), which connected state routes 193 and 101 (now U.S. Route 44). The farm's structures consisted of a three-story white frame house, a large dairy barn, hen coops, and sheds. Shaded by oaks, blue spruce, and chestnuts, it lay along a ridge overlooking gently rolling fields and copses to the west. To the east, across County Home Road, it faced a golf course built by Norman Bruce Ream at the turn of the century.*

Marion renamed Larnard Place "Quinnatisset Farm" after the Quinnatisset Brook, which ran through the property and under County Home Road into Ream's Pond. Anastase preferred to call his new home "Nineteenth Hole" because it was so close to the golf course.

Vonsiatsky had acquired a taste for golf during his first visit to Thompson in 1921. By 1925, he had outfitted himself with a tweed cap, knickerbockers, cleated brogans, clubs, and a basket of balls. Anastase like to drive more than to putt, and he expended balls like ammunition. His flailing form soon became a familiar sight on the Quinnatisset links, launching white missiles which arched gracefully out of sight, far wide of the fairway. The Russian's ballistics provided ample employment for local youths willing to retrieve balls under fire. But prudent golfers learned to keep their distance.

Golf alone could not absorb Vonsiatsky's attention for long. His energies demanded ever new outlets or they degenerated into mischief. Marion recognized this and deftly encouraged her husband to become involved in community activities.

From the outset of his life in Thompson, Vonsiatsky had demonstrated an aptitude for theatrical and entrepreneurial pursuits. In January 1924, he organized a musical soirée at Carolyn Hall for émigré

* Now the Quinnatisset Country Club.

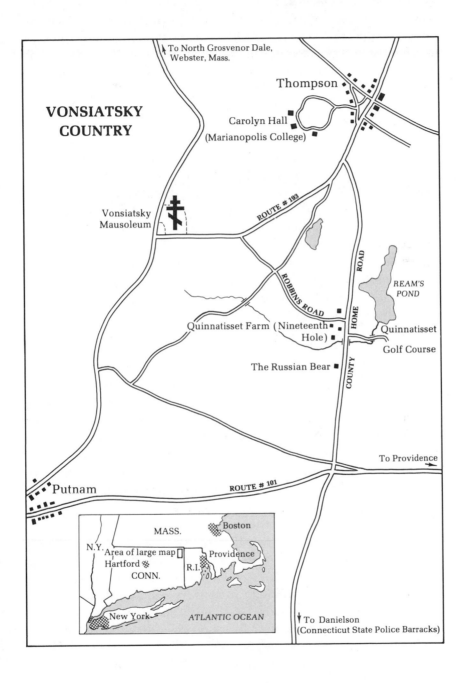

To North Grosvenor Dale, Webster, Mass.

Thompson

VONSIATSKY COUNTRY

Carolyn Hall
(Marianopolis College)

Vonsiatsky Mausoleum

ROUTE # 193

ROBBINS ROAD

COUNTY HOME ROAD

REAM'S POND

Quinnatisset Farm (Nineteenth Hole)

Quinnatisset Golf Course

The Russian Bear

To Providence

Putnam   ROUTE # 101

MASS.   Boston

N.Y. Area of large map
Hartford   Providence
CONN.   R.I.

New York   ATLANTIC OCEAN

To Danielson
(Connecticut State Police Barracks)

friends and local citizens. Entitled "An Evening of Fun," the printed program featured snatches of opera, ballet, and vaudeville. Anastase and several fellow Volunteer Army veterans stomped out some Cossack numbers. Andre Roosevelt, a distant cousin of Franklin Delano and producer of cinematic thrillers at his Vitagraph Studios, put on slapstick skits. Roosevelt's daughter Leila (billed as "Leila Andreivna Rooseveltskaya") capped the evening with Russian songs and dances.

Emboldened by success, Vonsiatsky tried his hand at writing, producing, and acting in musical comedies. Recruiting local talent, he put on shows in a converted stable at Carolyn Hall. If the *Putnam Patriot's* drama critic is to be believed, Vonsiatsky's *The Arrival of Kitty* (1925) and *Ain't It the Truth?* (1929) won solid acclaim.

Encouraged by the favorable reception of his theatrical ventures, Anastase diversified into other forms of entertainment, always capitalizing on his unique position as Putnam's resident Russian. He staged annual Fourth of July costume balls at Carolyn Hall until 1926, wrote an unpublished romantic novel called "Russian Love," and toured Windham County delivering lectures on "Old Russia" to Elks clubmen and American Legionnaires.

Affluence inevitably affected the former Eddystone apprentice's tastes. Shedding vestiges of whatever asceticism he had acquired in the Warsaw Citadel, he soon took on the trappings of a dandy. He collected French phonograph records, practically bathed in eau de cologne, smoked expensive cigarettes with an amber holder, and wore only the best clothes. Enthralled by Charles Lindbergh's transatlantic flight in the *Spirit of St. Louis,* Anastase persuaded "Mama" (as he called Marion) to buy him a single-engined plane in 1927 so that he could play Lone Eagle around northeastern Connecticut.

The automobile also claimed Vonsiatsky's devotion. He reacted to sports cars as if they were ravishing women. Marion catered to these vehicular crushes, perhaps as an innocuous surrogate, and in 1928 presented "Alex" (as she called Anastase) with a yellow Mercer coupe as an incentive to enroll in Brown University in Providence.

Brown educated Vonsiatsky in different ways than Marion had envisioned. She had wanted him to improve his English and acquire an Ivy League cultural veneer. Alex did actually register in English 1 (Rhetoric and Composition) for one semester but did not show up for the final exam. College football, not academics, captivated him. He fell in love with football not only as a sport but as a vicarious war game. By the end of Brown's successful 1928 season (eight wins, one loss—to Yale, 14–32), he was rhapsodizing about his alma mater's gridiron forays as if they were Denikin's campaigns. He also began chipping off a piece of the goalpost after the end of each Brown-Yale game. The fragments were reverently enshrined in a glass display case at Nineteenth Hole.

More than football attracted Vonsiatsky to Providence. He liked to have his head shaved each spring, and only a few barbers were up to the task, one being a certain Orlando, who practiced near the Brown campus. Even Orlando complained that he dulled five razors on Alex's head. After his annual shearing, Vonsiatsky felt a bit self-conscious about his pink scalp. According to Jimmy Bakker, one of his caddies, whenever some comely female golfers approached him after he had visited Orlando, Anastase would blurt out: "Jimmy, give me hat!"

Taking permanent leave from academe after one semester, Alex graduated to an olive-green twelve-cylinder Pierce-Arrow, by means of which he augmented an already extensive collection of speeding tickets. For football weekends, he ordered a Prince Albert coat specially tailored to accommodate three pint-sized flasks of vodka.

Such behavior may have been typical of any number of wealthy, exuberant college males in the 1920s, but Alex's expenses mounted to atypical heights. Despite her family's disapproval, Marion showed no inclination to curtail her husband's spending. On the contrary, she saw to it that his needs were generously taken care of through a combination of revenue sharing and a personal allowance. Marion made arrangements through her younger brother, Robert Clarke Ream, for Anastase to receive an annual income of $20,000, disbursed in $5,000 quarterly instalments by Ream, Wrightson & Company (99 John Street, New York), which handled her trusts and of which Robert was president. Anastase used approximately $12,000 of this income to pay household expenses, which included the purchase and upkeep of four automobiles, fuel for heating the houses, wages for gardeners and handymen, and sundry repairs. The balance Alex spent in whatever way he pleased.

Robert Ream disapproved of Vonsiatsky. "Robert Ream has never considered him a gentleman," remarked the family caretaker, Richard Barton, who was instructed to keep an eye on his employer's brother-in-law. Robert had reason to be concerned. Since Marion had plucked

Vonsiatsky from the Folies Bergères, the Russian had brought nothing but annoyances to the Ream family. For all their wealth, the Reams preferred to remain inconspicuous. Vonsiatsky stood out in Thompson, in the words of one resident, "like a Hottentot at a meeting of the D.A.R." First came the unwanted publicity surrounding the marriage, then a bigamy scandal, then speeding tickets, and then—worst of all—wild parties.

As an extrovert twenty-one years his spouse's junior, Vonsiatsky naturally sought out companions his own age who shared his appetite for alcohol and jazz. Ever eager that Alex feel at home in his adopted country, Marion raised no objections to members of Thompson's younger set occasionally gathering at Nineteenth Hole for a little fun. Alex loved to dance and could give a forceful interpretation of the tango, although he had a disconcerting habit of abandoning his partner on the floor when his eye caught another prospect. He also liked to steer the ladies from fruit punch to stronger concoctions. By and large, the girls found him exotic and charming. One admirer rhapsodized about his "lavender eyes" and military bearing. Even his mischievous streak exerted an appeal, judging from entries in the Quinnatisset Farm (Nineteenth Hole) guestbook:

> Alec be good
> Or be careful!
>
> Y. S. H.
> February, 1925

> Here lives that nice man Vonsiatsky
> Whose parties are all very hotsky
> Though he never does boast
> He's a real Russian host
> And the best of them all by farsky
>
> Peter van der Bennet
> April 4, 1927

This one was apparently addressed to Marion:

> How did you get him?
> And how do you keep him?
>
> Margary C. Taylor
> September 25, 1928

One of Alex's flings may actually have helped unhinge his brother-in-law Louis Marshall Ream's second marriage. In October of 1924, Louis walked into a Vonsiatsky party to find his wife, Mary Weaver, enjoying herself under the influence of alcohol. A shot was fired—one account says by a panicked Mary—but it is not clear at whom. Five months later, Mary sued Louis for divorce on grounds of "intolerable cruelty." The Hartford *Times* linked the separation with Vonsiatsky's party. Alex did his best to make up for the unfortunate affair by introducing Mary to a fellow Russian émigré, a New York florist, whom she eventually married. Nevertheless, the episode did not endear Alex to the Reams. Only Marion seems to have taken it in stride.

Ream family disapproval did not deter Alex from sinking roots into his adopted soil. On September 30, 1927, he became a naturalized American citizen, thereby escaping an alien's uncertain status. By that time, he had already invited his older sister Natasha (born in 1892) and her husband, Lev Beck Mamedov, to come live in Thompson.

Born in 1886 in Central Asia, Mamedov had been a Muslim until his conversion to Orthodoxy at the Moscow Military Preparatory School. As a young army officer assigned to the Caucasus, he allegedly led a squad that in 1908 apprehended a Georgian Bolshevik named Iosif Dzhugashvili (later known as Stalin) for subversive activities. Lev married Natasha Vonsiatsky in 1910 and during World War I rose to the rank of colonel in the artillery. Revolution sent the Mamedovs fleeing across Siberia to Harbin, where they opened a cafe. But Harbin proved too hazardous for their tastes. Encouraged by Anastase, they came to the United States in 1924.

In the course of their visits to Thompson during 1924–26, the Mamedovs grew attached to its verdant serenity. Marion in turn took an immediate liking to her Russian in-laws. Hefty Natasha radiated wholesome cheerfulness. Short, swarthy, curly-haired, and rotund, Lev mirrored his wife's affability. Their young son Andy won the childless Marion's heart.

Marion decided to give her Russian relatives a new start in life. Early in 1927, she bought a 150-year-old farmhouse (locally known as Flint House) located about four hundred feet down County Home Road from Nineteenth Hole. On March 3, she presented the house and surrounding property to Natasha as a birthday present. The Mamedovs gratefully accepted this extraordinary largesse and lost no time sprucing up the house and gardens. By the end of the year, they had transformed Flint House into a restaurant named after an establishment in old St. Petersburg: The Russian Bear.

The Russian Bear prospered. First it won over Windham County diners. Then it attracted a clientele from Hartford, Providence, and Boston. During the 1930s, its guests included such entertainment celebrities as Edward Everett Horton, Alan Ladd, and Tom Mix.

The secret of the Russian Bear's success lay in its special food and atmosphere. Lev and Natasha enlivened the American colonial setting by outfitting locally hired waitresses in Russian peasant costumes and by supplying Russian gypsy music for dancing on an outdoor terrace. "Madame Mamedova's" (as a brochure called her) cooking had no peer between New York and Boston. Her specialties included homemade borscht, *pirozhki, shashlik,* beef stroganoff, *blini* with sturgeon caviar and sour cream, mocha rum cake, and *paskha* (a rich mixture of sweetened curds, butter, and raisins).

As an added attraction, the Mamedovs worked out a weekend vacation plan with local entrepreneurs and the Ream family. For twelve dollars, a visitor received food, drinks, "tea-dancing," and bridge games at the Russian Bear, one night's accommodation at Thompson's historic Vernon Stiles Inn, swimming at Webster Lake, and golf privileges at the Quinnatisset links.

Encouraged by their success in Thompson, Lev and Natasha in 1932 opened a second Russian Bear at 11 Newbury Street in Boston, practically next door to the Ritz Hotel and within a stone's throw of the Public Garden. The Boston Bear's kitchen was presided over by Vasily Kovan, billed in a brochure as "former chef to the Shah of Persia." Kovan's culinary feats were appraised as follows by the Boston *Herald* on April 7, 1933: "There is a thing he does with the breast of a chicken that makes strong men weep."

Natasha apparently interpreted that remark as a compliment, because it was reprinted in a Russian Bear brochure.

The arrival of the Mamedovs signaled the demise of Marion's noble experiment to groom Alex as a New England squire. Surrounded by genial Russian in-laws, she gradually surrendered herself to his life-style. Almost daily, she accompanied him to the Russian Bear for some *zakuski,* drinks, cards, and conviviality. She was soon chatting a hybrid of Russian and English that served as a makeshift private language among the Vonsiatskys and Mamedovs.

What had started as the Americanization of Anastase came to entail the Russification of Marion.

The Romanov Connection

Vonsiatsky was no stranger to royalty. On the eve of the revolution, he had rubbed shoulders with adolescent Romanovs, Trubetskoys, and Oldenburgs at the elite Emperor Nicholas I Cavalry Academy in St. Petersburg. Four years later in London, he had enjoyed the hospitality of Prince Felix Yusupov. In 1925, Vonsiatsky entertained Prince (later King) Paul of Greece at Nineteenth Hole when the latter came to dedicate Saint Constantine's Church at Webster, Massachusetts.

Repeated encounters with aristocrats whetted Vonsiatsky's appetite for titles. Since first coming to Thompson in 1921, he had referred to himself as a count. Marion went along with this appellation and may even have believed it. Before long, Anastase was being called "the count" as well as "Alex" by local residents, but he never used that title for himself in the company of bona fide aristocrats such as Grand Duke Alexander Mikhailovich.

Grand Duke Alexander, one of the handful of Romanovs to survive the Revolution, watched the empire's collapse with avian detachment as commander of the short-lived Imperial Russian Air Force. Shortly after his evacuation from Sevastopol on the British cruiser *Forsythe,* Alexander succumbed to an archly elusive Englishwoman at Biarritz and sought to terminate his marriage to Xenia, Tsar Nicholas' younger sister. Refusing to grant her wayward spouse a divorce, Xenia moved with their six sons to England and settled in Windsor at Wilderness House, a cottage thoughtfully provided by her first cousin King George V. Barred from the British Isles, probably because of his Germanophilia, Alexander spent the rest of his life traveling, lecturing, writing memoirs, and putting up with phony relatives and status-hungry millionaires.

Notwithstanding Alexander's distaste for poseurs, he did succumb to Vonsiatsky's charm and spent several days at Nineteenth Hole during the summer of 1931, just two years before his death. Wearing a white suit and panama hat with a turned-up front brim, the aging grand duke cast an imposing figure, strolling alone under a panoply of majestic oaks, maples, and chestnut trees. What brought this proud, wise Romanov to Thompson? Not money. More likely, it was the area's beauty and serenity, accented by his host's uncomplicated hospitality. Moreover, two of Alexander's sons, Princes Theodore and Nikita, were Vonsiatsky's contemporaries and personal friends.

At six feet six inches, Prince Theodore Alexandrovich possessed a truly Romanov physique. Theodore was born in the same year and attended the same military academy as Vonsiatsky. How and when the two men became reacquainted after the Revolution is unclear. Theodore passed most of his time at Windsor with his mother, studied architecture, and designed model homes. In the summer of 1930, he spent three months as a guest at Nineteenth Hole, and from then until the outbreak of World War II, he made frequent visits to the Vonsiatskys, who always treated him as an esteemed friend. In the summer of 1932, the "count" and the prince took a lighthearted tour of the southwestern United States in Alex's four-door blue Packard convertible. It was a carefree fling marred only by periodic speeding tickets and a squabble with an El Paso border guard who failed to show proper respect to the two gentlemen.

While Prince Theodore enjoyed his classmate's company, he evinced little interest in politics throughout the 1930s and apparently nurtured no dreams of a Romanov restoration. Completely reconciled to what history had wrought, he was quite content to design houses rather than empires.

Prince Nikita, Theodore's younger brother, was less immune to the undertow of émigré causes. Tall, handsome, and shy, Nikita had escaped from Russia on the British cruiser *Marlborough,* moved with his mother to Windsor, and studied at Oxford. He later found work as a bank clerk in Paris, where he became known as "Monsieur Romanoff" who commuted on the Métro. This quiet routine was interrupted suddenly in January 1929, when upon the death of Grand Duke Nikolai Nikolaevich, a monarchist faction, refusing to support the imperial pretensions of Grand Duke Cyril, "elected" Nikita "Tsar of Russia." The young prince neither accepted nor rejected the honor but maintained a discreet silence. At this juncture, Vonsiatsky appeared and tried to lure Nikita into sponsoring a military academy for Russian émigré youth.

As a former cavalry cadet with a deep attachment to his St. Petersburg alma mater, Vonsiatsky had sentimental as well as patriotic reasons for concerning himself with the education of young exiles. He keenly felt the absence of institutions that would instill patriotism and martial discipline into the diaspora's youngest generation before time eroded all ties with the Russian motherland. An opportunity to rectify this situation arose in 1930 when a group of émigrés established the Nicholas II Military Academy in Paris. Vonsiatsky contributed a substantial sum to the project and, according to an émigré newspaper, was instrumental in convincing Prince Nikita to act as the academy's official patron. The school opened its gates in the fall of 1930 with an enrollment of thirty-seven boys.

Nikita's friendship with Vonsiatsky ripened in 1931 when he came to the United States and spent June through September as a guest at Nineteenth Hole. Nikita brought along his wife, the Countess Marie Vorontsov, and their two young sons, Nikita and Alexander.

Although the Hartford *Courant* described Prince Nikita as an "ardent fascist" in 1934, his relationship with Vonsiatsky in 1931 rested more upon bonhommie and perhaps nostalgia than upon shared political convictions. Like his brother Theodore, Nikita was neither a dreamer nor a crusader, even if some exiles regarded him as their tsar.

For Vonsiatsky, however, the princes Theodore and Nikita became more than just congenial houseguests. They were destined to adorn the early stages of his political career.

CHAPTER VIII

New England's Russian Duce

This year, next year, five years hence or even fifty years from now some unknown man will arise who will become dictator of Russia and deliver my people from their oppressors.
—ANASTASE A. VONSIATSKY (1927)

As the 1920s drew to a close, Anastase Vonsiatsky began flirting with the idea of going into politics. The transition from musical comedy came effortlessly. Politics struck the count as a natural extension of theater, and confident of his abilities in the latter, he expected to succeed in the former as a matter of course. The difference between the two was simply one of scale. Politics offered the world, not just Windham County, as a stage.

But politics for Vonsiatsky went deeper than an outlet for histrionic impulses. The attitudes instilled during his Warsaw childhood persisted in Thompson, and, however much he frolicked about as a Connecticut squire, he could not shed a visceral devotion to Russia. "Russia" to Vonsiatsky distilled all that he had lost in the Revolution: family, friends, home, a way of life. His patriotism focused not on an existing polity but on a dream. He sought no less than the resurrection of the past. Beneath Alex, the hyperactive playboy, lurked Anastase Andreivich, the quixotic counterrevolutionary. By plunging into politics, he gave expression to both sides of his character.

At first Vonsiatsky did not even have a clear idea of precisely what ideology best suited his aspirations. Communism was of course out of the question; the Revolution and Civil War had filled him with hatred for the Bolsheviks. As a Russian patriot, he gravitated to monarchist ideals but at the same time he was disgusted with the decrepitude and factionalism afflicting monarchist organizations. Vonsiatsky's emergence as a self-proclaimed fascist in 1933 emanated

116

from his perception of fascism as a youthful, dynamic, universally ascendant movement that held out the best hope to reclaim Russia from the clutch of Stalin. Moreover, the living incarnation of *Homo fascistus,* Benito Mussolini, struck an empathetic chord with the count's own behavioral idiosyncrasies.

Exactly when Vonsiatsky began to fancy himself destined to star in a counterrevolutionary drama is difficult to say. His heroic dreams may have been sparked in 1930 by the publication in Riga of Nikolai Nikolaevich Breshko-Breshkovsky's *Goluboi Mundir* ("Blue Uniform"), a laudatory biography of Alex's assassinated father, Andrei Nikolaevich Vonsiatsky. Or perhaps something was afoot as early as November 1927 when the *Windham County Observer* announced that Anastase and Marion, "weary of picking apples and planting bulbs," had boarded the SS *President Harding* bound for Europe. While Mama relaxed at Monte Carlo, Alex went straight to Paris to make contact with an assortment of émigré activists, notably General Kutepov.

General Alexander Pavlovich Kutepov was one of the most dashing figures of the exiled Volunteer Army. Formerly commander of the élite Preobrazhensky Regiment, in which Tsar Nicholas II had held the honorary rank of colonel, Kutepov rose to prominence as General Denikin's most able lieutenant during the anti-Bolshevik campaigns in southern Russia (1918–20). Moving to Paris after the White collapse, Kutepov formed in 1923 a militant faction within General Wrangel's Russian Armed Services Union, advocating sabotage operations within the USSR. Kutepov's penchant for action appealed to Vonsiatsky, who contributed ten thousand francs to the Union as soon as he reached Paris late in 1927. When Kutepov assumed leadership of the Union after Wrangel's death in 1928, he appointed Vonsiatsky coeditor of *Chasovoi* ("Sentinel"), the Union's official organ. Vonsiatsky continued to subsidize Kutepov until the general's abduction, and presumed liquidation, by the OGPU on January 26, 1930. Although Kutepov, a monarchist, may not have taken it well had he been alive to hear it, Vonsiatsky later eulogized him as "one of the founders of Russian fascism."

During his sojourn in Paris in the winter of 1927–28, Vonsiatsky joined a supposedly secret organization calling itself the Brotherhood of Russian Truth. Founded in 1923 by a Don Cossack ataman (General Pyotr Nikolaevich Krasnov), a minor aristocrat (Duke Georg Leuchtenberg), and a nebulous denizen of the Berlin Russian colony (one

Sokolov), the Brotherhood pledged to overthrow the Soviet regime by violence and to restore the tsar (it did not specify which pretender). Most of the Brotherhood's members were former White officers living in Paris, Berlin, Belgrade, and Harbin. The Brotherhood claimed that it conducted sabotage operations within the USSR, although such claims were probably inflated, with the exception of the Harbin— Far Eastern—branch, headed by General Kosmin, chairman of the Russian Fascist Party during 1931–32. In exchange for a $25,000 contribution, Vonsiatsky was made head of one of the Brotherhood's nine American branches. The count snared his first recruit upon returning to Thompson in April 1928: brother-in-law Lev Mamedov.

Dabbling in émigré fringe groups did not sate Vonsiatsky's growing interest in politics. The fall of 1928 saw him campaigning (between Brown football games) for the election of Herbert Hoover. Attending a Republican rally at Putnam in September, he proudly shared the speakers' platform with Robert T. Hurley, commissioner of the Connecticut State Police. Traffic tickets notwithstanding, Vonsiatsky welcomed the opportunity to become personally acquainted with the chief of Connecticut's law enforcement agency.

With Hoover safely elected, the football season over, and a college education terminated after one semester, Vonsiatsky occupied himself by representing the Brotherhood, subsidizing émigré organizations,* and producing another musical comedy. Then, in 1930, he threw himself into a new passion: gun collecting. Years later, Vonsiatsky recalled that around 1930 he had grown "interested in making a collection of Russian military souvenirs." Coming from the count, that was a rare understatement.

Vonsiatsky liked guns. They catered to his nostalgia for a Warsaw fortress childhood and a combat-filled adolescence. They allayed the anxiety about being assassinated, which undoubtedly had come about as a result of his father's murder. Guns were cheap and easily available in 1930. Yet before starting his collection, Anastase deemed it natural and appropriate to equip himself with proper credentials.

Accordingly, parlaying his apprenticeship at the Baldwin Locomotive Works into a scientific skill, Vonsiatsky obtained, on March 17,

---

* Vonsiatsky wrote in 1941: "Between 1922 and 1933 I contributed approximately $40,000 to Russian churches, Russian hospitals, Russian schools, Russian disabled war veterans, and so forth through the world." These contributions came from the $20,000 annual allowance provided by Marion.

1930, a commission in the United States Army Reserve as a first lieutenant, Chemical Warfare Division. Nine days later, he walked into New York's Abercrombie & Fitch and purchased a 1921 model (#8349) .45-caliber Thompson submachine gun. He brought the weapon back to Nineteenth Hole and installed it on a stairway landing overlooking the front hall of the main house. Guests who had just passed through the entrance found themselves welcomed by a host gleefully peering down at them along an aerated barrel.

Vonsiatsky lost little time in filling out his firearm collection. On October 18, 1930, after returning from a chemical warfare course near Baltimore, he placed the first of a series of orders for rifles with Francis Bannerman & Sons, a New York gun dealer at 501 Broadway. Bannerman's stocks provided him with a tidy inventory of weapons: fourteen Westinghouse 30/06-caliber rifles and forty-five Remington rifles made for the Imperial Russian Army during the World War but never delivered. The Remingtons were in fact unusable, for they had been specially calibrated for Russian ammunition not available in the United States.

Aware that the rifles were more decorative than functional, Vonsiatsky supplemented his arsenal with devices designed to defend him from unfriendly intruders. On September 2, 1931, he purchased from Federal Laboratories, Inc. two tear gas riot guns, three tear gas billies, and six Protecto guns—objects looking like fountain pens but also emitting tear gas.

To create a suitable repository for this collection, Anastase engaged masons late in 1930 to construct a stone annex on the south side of Nineteenth Hole's main house. The annex took shape around an open pavilion (called the "Clubhouse") that Marion and Alex had used as a rain shelter when entertaining outdoors. Directly beneath the pavilion had been a room used for storing milk brought from the cow barn, thirty feet away. When it was completed, the annex's sixteen-inch granite walls contrasted dramatically with the white clapboard of surrounding structures. Nineteenth Hole came to encapsulate Vonsiatsky's own checkered background: a bit of Warsaw fortress transplanted among New England country houses.

Within the stone annex, Vonsiatsky set up a Military Room (as he called it), a meticulously decorated, fifteen-by-twenty-foot den that looked like a gun worshiper's Sistine Chapel. The room was furnished with an amber oriental rug and green wicker furniture covered with chintz cushions. Lamps fashioned from rifle stocks and empty shell casings illuminated racks of firearms along the walls. Inverted helmets suspended from a cathedral ceiling floated at waist level, serving as cherubic ashtrays. An array of daggers, sabers, hand grenades, knuckle dusters, and revolvers adorned an altarlike table.

In addition to weapons, usable and decorative, Vonsiatsky filled the Military Room with personal mementos. A clock set in an airplane propeller recalled his fleeting emulation of Charles Lindbergh. Six-inch goalpost fragments made off with at the conclusion of Brown-Yale games were reverently arranged in a velvet-lined glass display case. The count's fascination for goalpost trophies went deeper than a fondness for football. The chunks of wood demonstrated, in Alex's words, "what great things can be accomplished by a small group" (securing a piece of goalpost in a chaotic postgame crowd, leading a counterrevolution against the demonic Soviet regime).

In one corner of the Military Room stood a life-sized human mannequin, cloaked in an Imperial Russian Army greatcoat and wearing a military cap. The greatcoat was the very one that Vonsiatsky had worn during the Civil War. A tag called attention to two holes (each neatly darned with gold thread) through which "Bolshevik bullets" had passed. One, of course, still resided in the owner's abdomen.

From the Military Room's vaulted ceiling hung flags and shields of Imperial Russia's military academies, including Vonsiatsky's alma mater, the Emperor Nicholas I Cavalry School. A broad archway was cut through the south wall of the room, leading to an alcove containing an open stone fireplace and an ikon of the Virgin and Child before which burned a devotional flame in a wine-colored cup. Photographs of cadets and cavalry officers lined the alcove's walls.

To the left of the stone fireplace was a narrow door leading to a five-foot by twelve-foot closet formerly used to store wood until the advent of central heating. Vonsiatsky furnished this nook with a cot, rifle racks, and swastika-studded wastepaper basket, making it a nostalgic near facsimile of his cadet quarters in St. Petersburg. He called it his "Gun Room."

Amid all the military paraphernalia, Vonsiatsky reserved a table for portraits of Russian royalty. A photograph of the late imperial family showed Nicholas, tightly clasping his hemophilic son, Alexis, surrounded by Empress Alexandra and their four daughters. There were also pictures of Grand Duke Cyril, Grand Duke Alexander, Xenia, and Princes Theodore and Nikita (the last two autographed). The supreme place of honor was reserved for a large portrait of Nicholas, which Alex told guests had once hung in the Imperial Russian Embassy in Paris.

The Military Room and Gun Room gave their owner pleasure and pride throughout the 1930s. Marion rarely set foot inside, but Alex brought all his friends there to chat, drink, and play records on a phonograph.

The Military Room's pungently tsarist ambience did not prevent Vonsiatsky from growing progressively impatient with monarchism. In 1931, he terminated his contributions to the Russian Armed Services Union, finding Kutepov's successor, General Evgeny Miller, lackluster and uninspiring. When Anastase and Marion toured Europe that year, they bypassed Paris in favor of Berlin and Belgrade, twin headquarters of the action-oriented Brotherhood of Russian Truth. But even the Brotherhood eventually lost Vonsiatsky's confidence. Peeved over its refusal to include him in negotiations with "wealthy Americans connected with Standard Oil" who wanted to blow up Soviet oil pipelines, Vonsiatsky handed in his resignation in July 1932. He quit just in time. The "wealthy Americans" turned out to be on the payroll of Amtorg, the Soviet corporation handling trade with the United States. The Brotherhood contact, moreover, was an OGPU agent. Shaken to its foundations by the scandal, the Brotherhood dissolved shortly thereafter.

Disillusioned by his misplaced faith in existing émigré organizations, Vonsiatsky began contemplating the possibility of creating his own anti-Soviet group. Years later, he recalled:

> Upon breaking with the Brotherhood of Russian Truth in 1932 I decided that I would form a political party myself to carry on my ideas and aims in attempting to overthrow the Soviet Government and establish a free government for the Russian people.

Just what the count's "ideas and aims" were in 1932 is hard to determine. He may not have been too sure of them himself. Whatever bold initiatives he may have considered, he took no visible steps to form a party for the duration of the year.

After resigning from the Brotherhood, Vonsiatsky spent the remainder of the summer with Prince Theodore on a motor safari around the American Southwest. With the approach of autumn, he threw himself into Herbert Hoover's reelection campaign.

The presidential election of 1932 had an intensely personal meaning for Vonsiatsky. He deeply respected Hoover, not only for his domestic policies but for his having fed millions of Russians during the 1922 Volga famine. Anastase made these views known by writing an article for the San Francisco Russian newspaper *Novaya Zarya* entitled "Hoover: Friend of the Russian People." Franklin Delano Roosevelt, on the other hand, struck Vonsiatsky as an opportunist who was not beneath working with Stalin for political expediency. Wondering aloud why any Russian émigré would vote for the Democratic candidate, he asked in the New York Russian newspaper, *Novoye Russkoye Slovo,* a question echoing Paul Miliukov's famous words to the Fourth Duma in 1916: "Is this stupidity or treason to our Russian cause?" Roosevelt's prompt recognition of the Soviet regime after his election victory confirmed Vonsiatsky's worst suspicions and triggered a lifelong antipathy for the President.

Although Vonsiatsky never admitted to having been influenced by Hitler, the national socialist triumph in Germany no doubt opened his eyes to a potent brand of anticommunism. Hitler's suppression of German Reds and mobilization of Teutonic energies convinced Vonsiatsky that a similar mass movement, properly tailored to Slavic sensibilities, could destroy Bolshevism and revive Russia's latent grandeur. He also began to see himself as the only man with the brains, charisma, and money to lead such a movement.

After February 1933, Vonsiatsky was no longer alone with his dreams. A fellow émigré took up residence at Nineteenth Hole and for the next seven years faithfully served as the count's secretary.

Donat Yosifovich Kunle was born in Russia in 1900 and, like Vonsiatsky, had fought with Denikin in the Ukraine. Evacuated to Constantinople in 1920, he made his way to the United States with the help of the American Red Cross and in 1921 found work as a mechanic at the Vought-Sikorsky aircraft plant in Stratford, Connecticut. Of medium height, Kunle had an athletic physique. The childlike expression conveyed by his curly auburn hair and pouting lips was belied by a pair of sorrowful eyes that had seen too much during the Revolution and Civil War.

It is not clear whether Kunle and Vonsiatsky met each other before

the Revolution or during the Civil War when both served under Denikin. During the mid-1920s, the Quinnatisset Farm guestbook shows
that Kunle visited Nineteenth Hole a number of times. Early in 1933,
Kunle's wife, Paula, left him and went to live with a certain Prince
Demidov on Long Island. Donat Yosifovich simultaneously quit his
job at Sikorsky and came to live at Nineteenth Hole, occupying a
bedroom in the main house. Kunle anglicized his name to "Coonley."
Locals dubbed him "Coontz." Before long, the inseparables, Count
and Coontz, had won a colorful niche for themselves in Putnam gossip.

Kunle's addition to the Nineteenth Hole menage gave Vonsiatsky
a sounding board for his dreams. The two men spent hours talking
in the Military Room, on the Quinnatisset links, and at the Russian
Bear. They ruminated about the bankruptcy of the White cause, deplored the lack of young leaders, and marveled at the effectiveness
with which Italy and Germany were dealing with domestic Communists. They agreed that Stalin could be destroyed only from within
Russia, not from without, as the Whites had tried and failed to do.
What was needed was a militant nucleus of propagandists and storm
troopers that would catalyze an anti-Communist National Revolution
within the Soviet Union. The more Vonsiatsky and Kunle talked, the
more convinced they became that they were the anointed instruments
for Russia's regeneration.

The All-Russian Fascist Organization

On May 10, 1933, Vonsiatsky and Kunle formally resolved to establish a party. Accordingly, they composed an "open letter" in the name
of the "Russian Fascist Supreme Staff" calling for the formation of
a fascist united front of activist émigrés throughout the world. In a
burst of inspired prolixity, they christened their creation the All-
Russian National Revolutionary Toilers and Worker-Peasant Fascist
Party. For the sake of convenience, this was reduced for general
use to the All-Russian Fascist Organization (*Vserossiiskaya Fashistskaya
Organizatsiya*) or VFO.

The VFO was a family affair from the outset. Vonsiatsky took
the title of *vozhd*. Kunle became party secretary. Mamedov was given
the title "president of the Central Executive Committee," but, anxious
to protect his relatives still in the Soviet Union, he adopted the pseudonym "Illarion Suvorov." Marion played no active role in the VFO,

regarding it as Alex's patriotic hobby, but Vonsiatsky subsequently saw to it that she was given such honorary appellations as "First Lady" and "Countess Vonsiatskaya." In their enthusiasm to please the *vozhd*, party troubadours later added "Cleopatra," "Lady Hamilton," and "Empress Eugénie" to Marion's titles.

Vonsiatsky paid little attention to dogma. Unlike the Russian fascists in Manchuria who talked endlessly about corporatism, anti-Semitism, and fascist five-year plans, the count preferred to let ideas take care of themselves. Fond of improvisation, he was quite willing to play his platforms by ear. The most important thing was to get the show on the road.

The *vozhd* quickly realized that if the VFO were to expand beyond Windham County, it must publicize itself. A newspaper was the obvious answer. Drawing upon his annual allowance from Marion—now up to $25,000—he hired carpenters to renovate some hen coops beyond the barn so that they could accommodate printing presses. Meanwhile, he retained two New York firms to print his newspaper until the hen coops were ready.

Vonsiatsky called his newspaper *Fashist*. Although in newspaper format, *Fashist* was printed on high-quality glossy paper that made it feel like *National Geographic*. The first issue of two thousand copies appeared in August 1933. Thereafter, *Fashist* came out at roughly monthly intervals with about ten thousand copies of each issue. It cost $4,000 a year to operate, $2,400 of which went into postage.

To handle *Fashist*'s clerical details, Vonsiatsky hired a twenty-one-year-old Thompson lad named Norman B. Watson. His father, Thomas Watson, worked as a caretaker on the Quinnatisset golf course, and Norman had caddied for the count on and off since 1921. The Watson house was conveniently located just across Robbins Road from Nineteenth Hole, well within shouting distance. Anastase commissioned his new assistant "foreign adjutant." In addition to filling subscription orders and carting bundles of *Fashist* down to the Thompson or Putnam post office for mailing, Norman typed the *vozhd*'s English-language correspondence.

Fashist gave Vonsiatsky ample scope to exercise his imagination. Articles written by himself and Kunle floridly recounted exploits of chimerical VFO agents throughout the world and even within the USSR. Actual names were "withheld" to "protect" these agents from Soviet security organs. All operators were instead identified by the acronym *fashkor* ("fascist correspondent"), followed by a party membership number and the geographical location of the post (e.g., *Fashkor* 18337, Smolensk). In this way, Vonsiatsky could create as many agents in as many parts of the globe as he wanted.

While about half of *Fashist* dealt with current VFO activities, the other half cultivated nostalgia. Richly illustrated pages resurrected paternal tsars, fearless generals, and loyal peasants. *Fashist* abounded in photos of the Civil War. Campaigns in the Baltic, Siberia, and Ukraine were recalled in vivid detail, illustrated with regimental portraits and cameos of White heroes (Kornilov, Kolchak, Denikin, and Wrangel). The VFO was made to look like the inheritor of Russia's great military and monarchical traditions, and portraits of Nicholas II were artfully interspersed with those of Vonsiatsky. To underscore the Romanov connection, a letter from ten-year-old Nikita Nikitivich (son of Prince Nikita Alexandrovich) to Vonsiatsky dated December 3, 1933, was reproduced on page one of the December 1933 issue of *Fashist.* The boy wrote: "I'm so happy to become a Russian fascist."

Aside from fantasy and nostalgia, *Fashist* advertised Vonsiatsky's recipe for counterrevolution: cease ideological quibbling and try to reach the Russian masses. Only by using the anger of Russia's workers and peasants could the National Revolution become a reality. Convinced that Russia was still basically an agrarian country, Vonsiatsky argued that the VFO must first seek support among the peasants and turn their antipathy to the kolkhoz (collective farm) into a "national popular movement." To woo the peasant, he adopted a three-point propaganda scheme: restoration and protection of private property, distribution of all collectivized lands to the peasants, and abolition of all restrictions on trade in agricultural products.

Vonsiatsky's own conception of fascism was pragmatic; fascism meant effective anticommunism. Late in 1933, the *vozhd* remarked to a reporter: "Why, the Reds gave us our name. They called us Russian Fascists and we adopted the title." Like Rodzaevsky, Vonsiatsky regarded "fascist" as the most stirring anti-Communist rallying cry within the USSR. As long as the Soviets labeled everything hostile to their regime as "fascist," they were unwittingly creating a symbol of resistance in the eyes of the masses.

Fascism did not connote association with Hitler or Mussolini except insofar as they opposed communism. In later years, Vonsiatsky was to be accused of being a Nazi. He vehemently denied that Russian fascism and national socialism were similar in structure or congruent in aims:

> To my mind the word Fascist means 100 per cent anti-Communist and not necessarily what it means in Germany and other countries.

Or again:

> The German, Italian, and Russian fascisms are different in many respects. The Russian Fascist Party is just a united movement of Russians against communism, and fascism is the only political system on the earth at the present time that can wipe out communism.

Vonsiatsky insisted that the adoption of the swastika as the VFO emblem was not an imitation of the Third Reich. Whenever someone asked him, usually in a disapproving tone, why he used "Nazi symbols," he would launch into a long explanation that the swastika was neither a Nazi invention nor a Nazi monopoly. He pointed out that swastikas had been used in ancient India and by the early Greeks. The first Christians also drew swastikas on the walls of the catacombs in Rome. Empress Alexandra had inscribed them on the doorjamb of the house in Ekaterinburg in which she and her family were shot by the Bolsheviks in 1918. While touring the Southwest in 1932 with Prince Theodore, Vonsiatsky had noticed that Arizona state highway markers used swastikas. (The practice was discontinued in 1937.) "Why should I change it just because Hitler adopted it?" complained the *vozhd*. In fact, Vonsiatsky did experiment on a number of occasions with reversed (arms extended counterclockwise) swastikas.

For all his disclaimers about the swastika, Vonsiatsky could not explain away his adoption of the Nazi salute (accompanied by a shouted "Slava Rossy!"), titles such as *Shturmovik Smerty* ("Death Storm Trooper"), and a personal oath of allegiance to the *vozhd* redolent of the one required by *Der Führer*. More tellingly, Vonsiatsky used the Horst Wessel song as the VFO anthem ("Raise the Banner!"). Kunle composed new lyrics which—among other things—substituted Russian Blackshirts for German Brownshirts and Vonsiatsky for Hitler:

> Comrades! Our native land awaits us!
> All under the banner!
> Our motherland calls!
> Despising treason and cowardice

Vozhd Vonsiatsky
Leads us fascists to great deeds

The day of victory draws near
Scattering kolkhoz, Stalin, and GPU
Over the Kremlin
A swastika brightly shines
As our black legions
March through Moscow

Not content merely to publish his anthem, Vonsiatsky recorded "Raise the Banner." He purchased sound equipment that could cut 78 rpm records and, with Kunle and Mamedov, formed a vocal trio. He then engaged the services of a local band for accompaniment. With double bass and saxophone substituted for drums and trumpets, "Raise the Banner!" possessed a jazziness that, if heard in Berlin, would have made Hitler live up to his nickname: *Teppichfresser*—"carpet chewer."

Vonsiatsky borrowed more than regalia and songs from the Nazis. Acting in musical comedies had given him a rudimentary stage presence, but a fascist *vozhd* by definition needed to project a personality capable of mesmerizing mass audiences. Adolf Hitler unquestionably possessed such charisma, and his oratorical style struck the count as an ideal model to emulate. Vonsiatsky lost no time in recording Hitler's performances at the Sportpalast from the radio. Their content interested him only parenthetically. He concentrated on tones, modulations, rhythms, and crescendos. He then hit upon the idea of recording his own speeches, partly for critical evaluation and partly for the pleasure of hearing himself (with dubbed-in applause). On one of his first discs (probably recorded in 1934), the *vozhd* sounded somewhat like a dyspeptic Boris Godunov. Worse, the applause crackled suspiciously like a dozen frenzied hands and feet rather than a stadium full of rapt followers. But this could not be helped. There was only so much noise that Kunle and Mamedov could make, given their limit of four extremities each.

Sometime in 1933, the exact date is not known, Anastase Vonsiatsky and Konstantin Rodzaevsky became aware of each other's existence. Compared with the Far Eastern *vozhd*, Vonsiatsky looked at first glance like a lightweight. He was a latecomer on the fascist bandwagon, possessing neither experience nor a following worth the name. No government patronized him. But the Connecticut count made up for these handicaps with a fertile imagination, infectious panache, and money.

Two ambitious young expatriates eyed each other across half the globe separating Thompson and Harbin. Would they pool their resources to build a united movement throughout the Russian diaspora? Or would each claim exclusive leadership? Their relationship to a great extent colored the character and development of Russian fascism after 1933.

CHAPTER IX

Toward a Fascist United Front

When war is a game,
how can peace be serious?
—RUSSIAN PROVERB

The year 1933 brought an escalation of tension on both flanks of the Soviet Union. In Europe, the rise of Adolf Hitler left Germany in the hands of a man who not only detested communism—hardly something uncommon among Western leaders—but who had publicly urged that Germans seek *Lebensraum* in the East. On the Asian front, Japan followed up her seizure of Manchuria by probing the Siberian and Outer Mongolian frontiers, and as diplomats exchanged recriminations in Moscow and Tokyo, the Red and Kwantung armies girded for a showdown. Journalists speculated on what form the collision would take: a Soviet-German war, a Soviet-Japanese war, or a German-Japanese crusade against the USSR.

Alarmed by what he perceived as a lethal mutation of capitalist encirclement, Josef Stalin set aside proletarian revolutionary goals and began to court France, Great Britain, and the United States with collective security proposals. In 1935, the Seventh Congress of the Comintern coined the slogan "anti-fascist Popular Front," which for the next four years reverberated through Soviet propaganda like a Wagnerian leitmotif.

What bred apprehension in the Kremlin stirred anticipation in the Russian diaspora. Émigrés in Europe, the Far East, and the Americas excitedly scanned the war clouds for harbingers of the long-awaited counterrevolution. Old dreams and discarded scenarios came to life again. As war had unseated the Romanovs, so war would topple the Bolsheviks and give the Russian people a chance to show their will. Peasants groaning under collectivization would withhold crops.

129

The Red Army would refuse to fight. National minorities would secede. Unable to cope with the confluence of foreign and domestic pressures, Stalin and his henchmen would flee, leaving Russia headless. A new government would arise around a core of anti-Communist exiles assisted by Germany and Japan. Of course, Germany and Japan, according to these inspired visions, would withdraw their armies from Russian soil after the counterrevolution had taken root.

The emergence of Germany and Japan as imminent antagonists of the Soviet Union also jarred activist émigrés into an awareness of their own disarray. Confronted with opportunity, they were seized with a sense of urgency.

Fascist and other rightist émigré groups were woefully ill-equipped in 1933 to take advantage of a Soviet-German or Soviet-Japanese war. Ensconced in expatriate enclaves scattered about the world, they were isolated from and suspicious of each other. In Manchuria, Konstantin Rodzaevsky commanded the Russian Fascist Party under Japanese auspices, but he lacked followers outside the Far East. Pavel Bermondt-Avalov's Russian National Socialist Movement (ROND) limped along on a lilliputian scale in Germany under the jaundiced eye of the Gestapo. Alexander Lvovich Kazem-Bek's Young Russians *(Mladorossy)* were getting older and still wielded little influence outside of Paris.

It gradually dawned upon some of the more perspicacious rightists that their disparate groups would have to cooperate in order to exploit the providential opportunities created by a German or Japanese attack on the USSR. Some saw that the best way to prepare for such opportunities was to establish a global organization. The form and structure of such an organization was only dimly perceived, yet it was more apparent with each passing day that only by coalescing could émigrés avoid debilitating and ultimately self-defeating factionalism, maximize their stature in the eyes of Russia's masses, and impress potential German and Japanese patrons with their utility.

At first glance, Anastase Vonsiatsky looked like the most improbable candidate to be charged with the unification of the diaspora's rightist fringe. Life as an Ivy League playboy and Connecticut squire had insulated him from those tribulations that molded the psychology of many of his fellow exiles. Worse, his windfall wealth (greatly exaggerated in the press) aroused jealousy and envy. He knew next to nothing about the Far East. He lacked political savoir faire. Immodest and tactless, he ruffled sensitivities. And Russian, not to mention Ukrainian, émigrés had notoriously thin skins.

On the other hand, Vonsiatsky was uniquely well placed to pollinate a global constituency with a plan of action. Unlike Rodzaevsky or Bermondt-Avalov, he was beholden to no government. Based in the United States, he enjoyed freedom of speech and freedom to organize, amenities unthinkable in Manchuria or Germany. American citizenship enabled him to travel at will in any part of the world except the Soviet Union. Thanks to Marion, he had plenty of cash to open doors, mollify rivals, and recruit followers.

But what was ultimately most significant in launching Vonsiatsky on his far-flung bid to mount a global fascist united front was his own indomitable self-confidence. After 1933, he never doubted that he could exploit the approaching holocaust for Russia's advantage. That swelling collection of goalpost fragments in Nineteenth Hole's Military Room assured him that he, and only he, could possibly snatch victory from the jaws of chaos.

Rendezvous in Berlin

Shortly after establishing the All-Russian Fascist Organization (VFO) in May 1933, Vonsiatsky came to the conclusion that his first strategic task was to incorporate rightist émigré groups around the world into a united fascist front. As an incentive to join, tractable émigré leaders would be accorded positions on the "general staff" of the "National Revolution." Vonsiatsky used military titles as bait, hoping to attract White army veterans who might not otherwise have fascist proclivities.

Europe struck Vonsiatsky as the logical place to start building his front. His trips with Marion in 1927 and 1931 had put him in touch with monarchist generals such as Kutepov. In 1933, he intended to seek out and tap a younger generation. Needless to say, he was also curious, in his own words, "to see what was going on" in Hitler's Germany.

Late in September, Vonsiatsky crossed the Atlantic and made straight for Berlin, where he registered at the swank Hotel Adlon on the corner of Unter den Linden and Wilhelmstrasse. He timed his arrival to coincide with the opening of a conference of the Paris-based Young Russians *(Mladorossy)* and the local Russian National Socialists (ROND).

Reflecting the centripetal impulses already beginning to suffuse the diaspora's right wing, the Young Russians and the Russian Nazis were meeting to discuss closer cooperation. Alexander Kazem-Bek, head of the Young Russians, brought along two associates from Paris, Count Sergei Obolensky and a Ukrainian named Gleb Baletsky. ROND führer Pavel Bermondt-Avalov was accompanied by ROND general secretary A. V. Meller-Zakomelsky and a bevy of ROND trusties. Vonsiatsky showed up alone at the conference to represent the VFO. Kunle and Mamedov had stayed behind in Connecticut to bring out *Fashist* and run the Russian Bear. The tripartite discussions took place at swastika-bedecked ROND headquarters on Bleibtreustrasse just off the Kurfürstendamm.

The main achievement of the Berlin conference was that it managed to take place in an atmosphere of comparative decorum. ROND troopers diplomatically removed their jackboots. The Gestapo did not interfere. On the other hand, little was accomplished, because no consensus could be reached on substantive issues. To be sure, everyone expressed confidence in the inevitability of the Russian National Revolution and gave lip service to solidarity in the anti-Soviet struggle. But solidarity dissolved on the question of national minorities, particularly whether Ukrainians should or should not be granted autonomy in Russia after the National Revolution. The touchiest issue was not even broached: Who would be *vozhd* of an anti-Soviet front? As a Germanized denizen of the Third Reich with presumed access to Hitler, Bermondt-Avalov regarded himself as a natural choice. Vonsiatsky modestly waited for himself to be nominated by acclamation. Kazem-Bek had little use for either man; he balked at subordinating the Young Russians to a Nazi, and could not tolerate an upstart *alfons* (gigolo) from America. With the leadership question unresolved, there was little left to do except exchange platitudinous pledges that all parties would work together more closely in the future.

Aside from a flattering article about him in the ROND organ, *Probuzhdeniye Rossy* ("Awakening of Russia"), Vonsiatsky achieved little in Berlin. Certainly his cherished dream of a united front came no closer to realization.

During his stay in Berlin, Vonsiatsky made no effort to seek interviews with Nazi leaders, although some friends urged him to do so, enumerating all sorts of advantages that would supposedly accrue from striking up personal friendships with Rosenberg, Goebbels, or Goering. For the time being, he preferred to observe the Reich as a tourist and stay clear of Nazi patrons.

Returning to New York in October, Vonsiatsky was pleased to discover himself—once again—in the international limelight. Émigré papers in Europe, the United States, and the Far East gave prominent coverage to the Berlin conference, hailing or denouncing it according to editorial politics. Capitalizing on the free publicity, Vonsiatsky made the December 1933 issue of *Fashist* a paean to his European tour. For good measure, he added an ecclesiastical touch, reprinting a letter from Metropolitan Anthony of Sremski Karlovci (in northeastern Yugoslavia) blessing the young American *vozhd.*

Courting Notoriety

Vonsiatsky's self-advertisement was bound to provoke a reaction. For a while, he was merely castigated in the liberal and pro-Soviet press. But it was not long before his detractors took more active steps to rally public opposition to his activities.

On November 11, 1933, members of Harlem's Russian community staged an Armistice Day demonstration denouncing Vonsiatsky as a fascist. Elated by such attention—he carefully saved newspaper clippings of the incident in a scrapbook—the count responded by filling the next issue of *Fashist* with "bulletins" of VFO terrorism within the USSR:

MILITANT WORK IN WESTERN RUSSIA!

On October 7 [1933], Fascist trio no. A-5 caused the crash of a military train. According to information received here about 100 people were killed.

In the village of Bresin, district of Mozyr, a group of *soratniki* shot five Communists.

In the Starobinsk district, thanks to the work of *soratniki,* the sowing campaign was completely sabotaged. Several Communists in charge of the sowing campaign mysteriously disappeared.

On September 3, in the district of Ozera Kniaz, the Communist chairman of a collective farm was killed by *Fashkor* nos. 167 and 168.

Nor did Vonsiatsky stop at fabricating sabotage. In a gesture calculated to raise pulses immediately after U.S. recognition of the USSR
in late 1933, *Fashist* announced the creation of a 1,500 zloty ($300)
fund to be awarded to Boris Koverda upon his release from prison
in Warsaw. In 1927, Koverda had assassinated the Soviet ambassador
to Poland, Pyotr Lavarevich Voikov. As a member of the Ural Soviet
in July 1918, Voikov had requisitioned the gasoline and sulphuric
acid to dispose of the corpses of the murdered imperial family. Vonsiatsky made no secret of considering the assassination of Voikov—
and by implication of other Soviet diplomats as well—worth a reward.

Encouraged by expressions of outrage in the *Daily Worker,*
Vonsiatsky filled *Fashist* in 1934 with yet more lurid fantasies. Among
the more notorious and widely quoted examples were his murderous
instructions to a chimerical VFO underground within the USSR:

> Arrange the assassinations of military instructors, military correspondents,
> political commissars, as well as the most stalwart Communists.

> Assassinate Chekists, members of the GPU, responsible workers, Party
> members, and generally all who unequivocally favor Red power. Smash
> state Red banks, treasuries, and safes. Use the money for the Brotherhood
> [VFO] work.

> By every means shatter the Red apparatus of power. Set fire to or explode
> the buildings of the GPU, of all Party committees, and all clubs,

> Assassinate, first of all, the Party secretaries, the true dogs of the power
> of the commissars.

> Hamper communication of Red power. Hack down telegraph poles, smash
> the porcelain insulators, cut wires, interrupt and destroy all telephone
> communication.

> Do not allow exports of the people's goods. Seize whatever you can and
> distribute it. Whatever you cannot seize, destroy. If this is impossible,
> then damage in every way the goods which are being exported. For each
> commodity adopt that method of damage which is best suited to it. Into
> the food products add all sorts of rubbish and garbage. Put in dead rats,
> throw in lice, cockroaches, and bedbugs.

Such antics seem to have been taken at face value in quarters
that should have known better—and perhaps did. The *Daily Worker,*
for example, had attacked Vonsiatsky since 1931 when it exposed
Nineteenth Hole as a "cover address" for an anti-Soviet conspiracy

RUSSIAN FASCISTS IN THE FAR EAST

Konstantin Vladimirovich Rodzaevsky, fiery young *vozhd* of the Manchurian-based Russian Fascist Party and its off-shoots from 1932 until 1943.

General Vladimir Dmitrievich Kosmin, White partisan leader in the Far East and chairman of the Russian Fascist Party (RFP) from 1931 until he was replaced by Konstantin Rodzaevsky in 1932. (*Nash Put*)

RUSSIAN FASCISTS IN GERMANY

Russian Nazi A. P. Svetozarov in 1933, during his brief tenure as führer of the Russian National Socialist Movement (ROND) in the Third Reich. (*Fashist*)

ROND storm troopers wearing Hitlerian toothbrush mustaches and celebrating May Day in Berlin in 1933. (*Fashist*)

Anastase Andreivich Vonsiatsky, Connecticut-based *vozhd* of the All-Russian Fascist Party. (*Fashist*)

Marion Ream Stephens, American heiress who in 1921 picked up a penniless Russian refugee named Anastase ("Alex") Vonsiatsky in Paris, brought him to New York, married him, and financed his antics for more than four decades.

A June 1922 *American Weekly* cartoon of "The Troubled Dream of the Multi-Millionairess and her Lover in Overalls" shows the "Accusing Finger of the Discarded First Wife"—Lyuba Muromsky—reaching from Paris across the Atlantic to claim her husband Anastase Vonsiatsky, from "Very Rich Mrs. Ream."

A February 1922 cartoon from the *New York Record* poking fun at Anastase and Marion Vonsiatsky for their attempt to live like proletarians in a Philadelphia suburb. Despite his bride's immense wealth, Anastase insisted on working—for a little while—as an $8.50-a-week junior apprentice at the Baldwin Locomotive Works in Eddystone.

Connecticut squire Vonsiatsky with his friend and classmate Prince Theodore Alexandrovich Romanov, nephew of Tsar Nicholas II, during their auto safari around the American Southwest in 1932. (*courtesy of Andre A. Vonsiatsky*)

A general view of Quinnatisset Farm, dubbed "Nineteenth Hole" by Vonsiatsky because of its proximity to the golf course in the foreground. On the right is the farmhouse. In the center, dark and partially hidden by trees, is the stone annex, which housed a Military Room and offices. The white structure on the left, originally a barn, was converted into a shooting gallery. (*photo by the author*)

The Russian Bear restaurant located about four hundred feet down County Home Road from Nineteenth Hole. Run by Lev and Natasha Mamedov from 1927 until 1947, it provided a convenient venue for Vonsiatsky's entertainments during the 1930s.

Participants in the tripartite conference of rightist émigrés in Berlin in 1933. The meeting marked Vonsiatsky's debut into international politics as leader of the All-Russian Fascist Organization (VFO). Seated at the center with a bow tie and mustache is Russian Nazi (ROND) *vozhd* "Prince" Bermondt-Avalov. On his left is the head of the Paris-based Young Russia (*Mladorossy*) Party, Alexander Lvovich Kazem-Bek. On Bermondt-Avalov's right is Vonsiatsky. (*Fashist*)

financed by "New York and Hartford capitalists." In 1932, the organ of the American Communist Party credited the count with plotting to liquidate American engineers working in the USSR and implicated him in the assassination of Inukai Tsuyoshi, the Japanese prime minister shot in Tokyo by naval cadets on May 15, 1932. The *Daily Worker* traced Vonsiatsky's connections to the Department of State, asserting that a sister-in-law of Secretary of State Henry Stimson (a certain "Mrs. Loomis") was a Vonsiatsky supporter.

Indeed, the State Department had been aware of Vonsiatsky ever since 1922 when Lyuba Muromsky filed bigamy charges against him with the U.S. ambassador in Paris. In 1933, Washington opened a new file on Vonsiatsky as a result of a stunt in which the count invented a *soratnik* named "Ivanoff-Krivkoff" to dramatize the VFO's international exploits. The caper began in July when Donat Kunle sent the following cable to the Polish Ministry of Interior:

> IVANOFF KRIVKOFF IS OUR MAN   WILL APPRECIATE HIS FREEDOM
> FINANCIAL ASSISTANCE WILL BE GIVEN BY US   (SIGNED)   DONALD
> COONLBEY   LIEUTENANT CHIEF OF STAFF

The ministry checked every prison in the country but could find no inmate named "Ivanoff-Krivkoff." Rather than answer the cable, a Polish official brought it over to the American consul general in Warsaw on August 7 and asked for an explanation. The consul general referred the matter to Washington, and within a few weeks the State Department's Eastern European Affairs Division was conducting inquiries in the War Department about the identity of the "lieutenant chief of staff." Although the cable was traced to Thompson, there is no record of whether Vonsiatsky was called to account. Meanwhile, "Ivanoff-Krivkoff" performed valiant feats in the pages of *Fashist:*

> Captain Ivanoff-Krivkoff, member of the All-Russian Fascist Organization, has crossed the Polish-Soviet border in the district of Temashevich. He is an active member of the Organization and went there several months ago to carry on fascist propaganda. He was, however, spotted by the GPU and forced to escape from the Soviet Union. He is now detained by Polish authorities, but the Central Headquarters of the All-Russian Fascist Organization has already taken measures to secure his release.

The "Ivanoff-Krivkoff" caper succeeded not only in bringing Vonsiatsky to the attention of the United States government but reinforced his notoriety throughout the émigré community. It epitomized the mixture of showmanship and public credulity on which the count's political ambitions thrived.

The Yacheika Drive

Not all VFO agents were chimerical. During the latter half of 1933, Vonsiatsky assiduously set out to establish party cells *(yacheiki)* in North and South America, Europe, and the Middle East. The task was not as difficult as it sounds, for recruitment focused only on those cities with Russian émigré enclaves. Vonsiatsky maintained contact with many Civil War veterans, a number of whom formed the skeleton of his international network. Subscription lists of *Fashist* provided another source of agents. Finally, subsidies from the $25,000 annual allowance that Marion gave him (about $10,000 of which went into the VFO) enabled Vonsiatsky to attract supporters. Some VFO agents never met Vonsiatsky. They just accepted his money and called themselves *soratniki*. With such a geographically scattered constituency, the VFO by necessity became a mail-order party with Thompson as "The Center" (Vonsiatsky's expression).

In order to expand membership as rapidly as possible, Vonsiatsky defined criteria for joining the VFO in broad terms:

> The only requirement for membership in my party was an interest exhibited on the part of individuals to join the organization and to help in promoting its principles. The principles of the party were to give help to the Russians to overthrow communism and to establish a government which the Russian people themselves desired.

Recruitment by mail yielded one man who eventually became the VFO ideologue: Mikhail Mikhailovich Grott. Little is known about Grott except that he lived in Königsberg, East Prussia, and wrote regularly for *Fashist,* sometimes under the pseudonym Spassovsky. Grott authored most of the party's propaganda pamphlets ("About Our Secret Work," "I Serve Russia," "Tactics of Russian Fascists"), which were printed at Nineteenth Hole and bound in brown paper stamped with the VFO emblem: the Romanov double-headed eagle behind a swastika. Grott made no secret of his rabid anti-Semitism and his adoration of Adolf Hitler, and from 1934 until 1940, *Fashist* serialized his Russian translation of *Mein Kampf.* Grott was described in *Fashist* as the "great ideologist of the Russian fascist movement."

In fact, Vonsiatsky disagreed with Grott over the Jewish question but let him expound freely on ideological matters. Anastase displayed neither interest nor aptitude for the fine points of theory and seemed content to let the correspondent in East Prussia be the party philosopher.

Vonsiatsky's first party cell outside of Thompson sprang up in New York City. The downtown Manhattan *yacheika* was led by Alexander Plyshnov, an émigré of uncertain avocation, who shared dilapidated offices at 480 Canal Street with Nikolai Rybakov, publisher of the rightist Russian daily *Rossiya.* Rybakov does not appear to have been a VFO member, but his presses brought out several issues of *Fashist* until Vonsiatsky was able to set up his own print shop in the converted hen coop at Nineteenth Hole in 1936.

Plyshnov reluctantly shared his authority with an uptown *yacheika* consisting of Evgeny Bogoslovsky and his wife. Of Goeringesque proportions, Bogoslovsky wore a thick mustache to compensate for a bald pate; his small eyes poised like black droplets at the end of inwardly sloping eyebrows. Bogoslovsky's physiognomy did not do justice to his good nature and sportsmanship, both of which endeared him to Vonsiatsky. Mrs. Bogoslovsky became something of a VFO Betsy Ross by embroidering party flags and arm bands.

The Boston *yacheika* was represented by Ivan Novozhilov. Little is known about Novozhilov except that his wife, Valentina, helped run the Newberry Street Russian Bear and his daughter Natasha was a favorite of Marion's.

On the west coast, some fifty VFO members came under the local supervision of a Hollywood fixture named George Doombadze. However, in 1936, Doombadze gravitated into the German-American Bund and was replaced by Feodor Semens of Los Angeles, who concurrently lent his services to the Silver Shirts of self-proclaimed North Carolina fascist William Dudley Pelley. In San Francisco, the VFO boasted several activists, all of obscure background: Valerian von Meier, Christ Latsgalv and his daughter Marina, and Mr. and Mrs. Herbert G. Vantz. Being an "activist" in San Francisco apparently meant giving away copies of *Fashist* to potential recruits. In Seattle, Vonsiatsky subsidized a certain Prokopy Vasiliev (*"Fashkor* no. 293") to run off mimeographed sheets called *Rassvet* ("Dawn") and *Put* ("Path") from 911 Lakeview Boulevard.

Outside the United States, Vonsiatsky's representatives tended to be émigrés on the party dole. In return for a $600 annual subsidy, Nikolai Trofimovich Dakhov joined the VFO in 1933 and sang the *vozhd*'s praises in his São Paulo newspaper, *Russkaya Gazeta.* Near East VFO "headquarters" were located in Cairo, first in the person of a certain Stalbetzov and later by "Baron" Georgy Taube, a former White officer who had fought under Denikin. Vonsiatsky founded a *yacheika* in Bulgaria by remitting $600 annually to a man called Butov, who published a weekly called *Rus* in Sofia. Vonsiatsky also paid $600 a year to a certain Rklitsky to publish favorable articles in the Belgrade weekly *Saktzarsky Vestnik,* but Yugoslav government regulations forbade Rklitsky actually to join the VFO. *Fashist* also mentioned a number of other overseas VFO representatives: Alexander Leiburg in Belgrade (not actually a member), Vladimir Kishinsky and Trofim Loviagin in Canada, Rzbinsky in Prague, Vladimir Prutkovsky in Sydney, and Petrashevsky in Berlin. Whether these individuals were full-time agents, fellow travelers, or "Ivanoff-Krivkoffs" can only be surmised.

Real or fancied, VFO members paid no dues. In 1941, Vonsiatsky recalled that contributions to the party had been "infinitesimal." In 1935, when someone actually sent $5.65 from Edmonton, Canada, *Fashist* wrote up the contribution as if it were a major event.

For all his international contacts, Vonsiatsky had no followers in the Far East. And the Far East in 1933, as nearly every politically cognizant Russian émigré knew, was the most likely spot for the USSR to become embroiled in war. Not surprisingly, the Connecticut *vozhd* jumped at the opportunity when he received an offer of collaboration from his counterpart in Harbin, Konstantin Rodzaevsky.

An Invitation from Harbin

Sooner or later, Vonsiatsky was bound to come to the attention of the other self-proclaimed Russian fascist *vozhd,* Rodzaevsky. It is not clear how or when the two men, separated by half the globe, became aware of each other. In a 1934 interview with the Hartford *Courant,* Vonsiatsky stated that he and Rodzaevsky had "simultaneously" discovered fascism, but that they had learned about each other only in the fall of 1933. Anastase was stretching the duration of "simultaneous," for while Rodzaevsky was organizing fascist cells throughout Manchuria in the late 1920s, Vonsiatsky was writing musical comedies and dreaming of the next Brown-Yale game. Yet it is conceivable that the two men woke up to each other only in 1933. Rodzaevsky made the first gesture toward getting acquainted.

On October 28, 1933, Rodzaevsky wrote Vonsiatsky, inviting him to Harbin and suggesting that they amalgamate their two parties into a global organization representing all Russian fascists. Despite the letter's fraternal rhetoric, the proposal to unite sprang neither from belief in VFO exploits nor from admiration of Vonsiatsky. Rodzaevsky's motives were strictly pecuniary. Vonsiatsky's money—Marion's, more accurately—held tantalizing prospects for impecunious Harbin *soratniki* living off capricious and niggardly Japanese handouts. Regardless of his objectives, Konstantin Vladimirovich doubtless found some reason to justify the invitation to his Kwantung Army patrons. After all, Vonsiatsky could not set foot in Manchukuo without their acquiescence.

Vonsiatsky quickly accepted Rodzaevsky's offer "in the name of 2,000 VFO members" and set about preparing for a world tour that would take him to Japan, Manchukuo, China, the Near East, and Europe. He sensed that the moment had come for decisive action. Soviet-Japanese relations, exacerbated by border clashes and friction over the Chinese Eastern Railway, seemed on the verge of a rupture. Army Minister General Araki Sadao was publicly intoning the inevitability of a Soviet-Japanese war and cryptically calling for a preemptive attack against Siberia. There was no time to lose. As Vonsiatsky told a reporter, if Japan and Russia were going to fight, he wanted "to be there at the start." Here was also a chance to meet Japanese leaders, particularly Araki, and discuss collaboration. This was the propitious moment to mobilize global émigré support for a fascist united front. Above all, this was a providential chance to show himself to the world.

From December 1933 until February 1934, the *vozhd* ensconced himself with Kunle and Mamedov in Nineteenth Hole's Military Room planning every detail of the upcoming world tour. The Berlin conference had taught Vonsiatsky the importance of looking important. First, he needed an immaculate, obsequious attendant (he had made a mistake by going to Berlin alone to face Kazem-Bek and Bermondt-Avalov with all their flunkeys). Donat Kunle fit the specifications admirably. Alex outfitted his "adjutant" with a U.S. Army surplus uniform and a briefcase. Second, he required tangible proof of affluence. Marion, a gentle personification of the American plutocracy, provided that.

Third, he needed to make the trip look momentous. This Alex did by publicizing the tour in *Fashist* (and any other papers that would write about him) as a grand recruiting campaign to raise an army of 150,000 White Russians in the Far East for an eventual assault on the Soviet Union—with Japanese assistance.

The world tour got under way on March 1, 1934 with a gala gathering at the Vanderbilt Hotel in New York. Anastase, Marion, and Kunle drove down from Connecticut, accompanied by Lev Mamedov. Although Mamedov knew Harbin well (having briefly run a cafe there after the Revolution), he was to stay behind and fulfill responsibilities at the Center. At the Vanderbilt, the Connecticut contingent was joined by some New York *soratniki*, led by Plyshnov and Bogoslovsky, who managed momentarily to endure each other's presence. John Eoghan Kelly, New York representative of Pelley's Silver Shirts, was also on hand to wish the *vozhd* well. Pelley had approached Vonsiatsky in January 1934 with an offer to get together, but Alex preferred to postpone any meeting until after his global peregrinations. Kelly's appearance at the Vanderbilt probably reflected his chief's desire to be remembered as a friend—and beneficiary.

From New York, the trio set out by train for San Francisco, where on March 6 they boarded the Dollar Line's SS *President Van Buren* bound for Honolulu, Kobe, and Shanghai. The *Van Buren*'s passenger list described the party as "Count and Countess A. A. Vonsiatsky and Lieutenant D. I. Coonley of Thompson, Connecticut."

Before leaving San Francisco, Vonsiatsky gave a few reporters a florid description of his mission, including his prediction of Japanese aid for a Russian fascist invasion of the USSR. Published, among other places, in the *Morning Oregonian* on March 7, the story was spotted by Nakamura Yutaka, Japanese consul in Portland, who promptly forwarded the clipping to Foreign Minister Hirota Kōki. Nakamura's communication is the earliest known item in what soon became a bulging Japanese Foreign Ministry file on the count from Connecticut.

No sooner had the *President Van Buren* docked at Kobe on March 22 than Vonsiatsky started expounding to an Osaka *Mainichi* reporter about his plans to hurl 150,000 Russian troops against the USSR. Pleased with the next day's news coverage, Alex proceeded with Marion and Kunle by train to Tokyo, 350 miles to the northeast. His arrival was awaited by Konstantin Rodzaevsky, who had come from Harbin to greet him.

CHAPTER X

Harbin Summit

The tactical unity of Russian fascism has been achieved.
—ANASTASE A. VONSIATSKY (1934)

Sugar attracts flies.
—RUSSIAN PROVERB

Rodzaevsky had not come to Tokyo alone either. The Harbin *vozhd* brought along with him Mikhail Matkovsky, chief of Agitburo, *Nash Put'*'s propaganda department. A shrewd strategist, Matkovsky commanded a personal following within the RFP and posed a latent challenge to Rodzaevsky's party leadership. But Rodzaevsky needed Matkovsky's political acumen for the crucial first encounter with Vonsiatsky.

Rodzaevsky planned to meet Vonsiatsky in Tokyo rather than in Harbin, because he wanted to work out the multitude of practical questions raised by an RFP-VFO merger. Their "summit" in Harbin, scheduled for the end of April, was to be a grand but essentially ceremonial affair. In the meantime, he was eager to size up the man whose career was verging uncomfortably close to his own.

From March 24 until April 2, the Manchurian and Connecticut *soratniki* got to know each other in a series of meetings at RFP Tokyo headquarters. The local RFP representative, Vasily Petrovich Balykov, acted as official host. After a very few hours of talks, it became obvious that the two parties had differences which, if left unattended, would preclude unity. Rodzaevsky insisted on retaining RFP corporatist and anti-Semitic dogma intact in the new party. Vonsiatsky cared little about corporatist theories and felt uncomfortable committing himself publicly to anti-Semitism. Besides, he wanted to discuss anti-Soviet tactics, not "program mongering." Rodzaevsky, thoroughly coached

141

by the *Tokumu Kikan,* urged Vonsiatsky to work closely with the Japanese and with their favorite protégé, Ataman Grigory Semenov. Vonsiatsky responded that for the time being he was willing to attune Russian fascist tactics to Japanese strategic requirements, but under no circumstances would he have anything to do with that Cossack scoundrel Semenov. Balancing such differences, pragmatic considerations drew Rodzaevsky and Vonsiatsky together. The RFP had muscle which the VFO, *Fashist* fantasies notwithstanding, utterly lacked. The VFO had money which the RFP, despite Japanese subsidies, urgently needed.

Vonsiatsky took the initiative in resolving the deadlock by proposing a global organization to be called the All-Russian Fascist Party (*Vserossiiskaya Fashistskaya Partiya,* hereafter VFP). The VFP would harmonize its Far Eastern and American components by blending RFP theory and VFO tactics. Rodzaevsky gave his consent to this innocuous abstraction after being promised $500,000 as an initial VFO dowry for the amalgamation.

The VFP was structured so as to give Vonsiatsky a lofty title while leaving Rodzaevsky and his associates firmly in control of Far Eastern activities. The new party was to be directed by an eight-man central executive committee with Vonsiatsky as chairman and Rodzaevsky as general secretary. Party headquarters would be in Harbin.

On April 3, 1934, the results of the negotiations were drawn up and signed at Yokohama's New Grand Hotel. Called "Protokoll Number 1," the document sealed the RFP-VFO merger and created the VFP, which was described as an "anti-Communist front" destined to "replace the Communist Party of the Soviet Union."

Protokoll Number 1 left two issues unresolved: whether or not to cooperate with Ataman Semenov and how to deal with the Jewish question. For the time being, everyone surrendered to a heady exhilaration that a global Russian fascist party existed. The stage was set for Vonsiatsky's triumphant entry into Harbin to preside over what *Nash Put* touted as a World Congress of Russian Fascists.

Moscow did not even wait for Protokoll Number 1 to be announced before denouncing its authors. In an article entitled "White Guard Nest in Tokyo" published on March 30, *Pravda* lashed out at Vonsiatsky, accusing him of trying to bring Far Eastern White Guards into the Nazi orbit, an allegation that must have provoked wry smiles in Berlin. However wide of the mark, this was not the first time that Vonsiatsky would be called a German agent.

Eschewing the caution that had constrained him from seeking out Nazi leaders during his Berlin visit the previous September, Vonsiatsky took advantage of being in Tokyo to meet a Japanese notable on whom some Russian émigrés pinned their hopes for a crusade against the Soviet Union: General Araki Sadao. How their meeting was arranged, exactly where and when it took place, and whether Rodzaevsky accompanied Vonsiatsky is not recorded. However, the Connecticut *vozhd* made several references to his interview with Araki in later months, an interview that evidently marked a highlight of his Tokyo sojourn.

Aged fifty-seven in 1934, Araki Sadao had just passed the peak of his career as an influential force in the Imperial Japanese army, having resigned as army minister that January. A short but erect soldier with close-cropped hair and a handlebar mustache, Araki was fond of extolling the Japanese "spirit" and periodically preached about the inevitability of war with the Soviet Union. Such rhetoric won Araki popularity among line officers, military cadets, and civilian ultranationalists, but technocrats in the Army Ministry and Central Headquarters found his preoccupation with spiritual matters unrealistic and his advocacy of attack on the USSR alarmingly premature.

The prophet of an anti-Soviet war had considerable experience in Russian affairs. Before the Revolution, he had spent eight years in Russia, five as a language officer and military attaché in St. Petersburg and three as a liaison officer with the Russian Army General Staff during World War I. During the Siberian Intervention (1918–22), he had headed the army's field intelligence unit for Russia, the Harbin *Tokumu Kikan.* These experiences left Araki with many Russian friends and a good command of the Russian language. After returning to Japan, the general continued to drink tea from a samovar. It was even whispered that the apostle of Japanese spirit had secretly embraced the Orthodox faith. Araki loathed Bolshevism to a great extent because in his eyes it had destroyed the Russia that he had known and loved. Yet he got along quite well on a personal basis with the Soviet ambassador to Japan, Alexander Troyanovsky.

Araki felt more than a casual interest in White Russians, particularly those who were actively anti-Communist. He sympathized with their predicament and appreciated their potential utility to Japan. The general regretted that party politicians had lacked the nerve to take over eastern Siberia during the Allied Intervention. By doing so, Japan could have permanently safeguarded her northern frontier while creating, in the form of a puppet state, a beachhead for counterrevolution.

Such thoughts may explain Araki's willingness to meet Vonsiatsky early in April 1934. What transpired between the count and the general can only be inferred from Vonsiatsky's subsequent pronouncements. The *vozhd* recalled that Araki pledged to help his anti-Soviet front (the VFP) but remained noncommittal on specifics. Apparently, Vonsiatsky did most of the talking, no mean achievement in view of the general's well-known loquaciousness. He promised that Russian fascists would assist Japan in the approaching war with the USSR. Such assistance would take the form of propaganda work among the Siberian population prior to the Japanese invasion and during the ensuing occupation. VFP "shock troopers" would infiltrate Siberia and convince the "peasants and workers" to welcome the Japanese as harbingers of the National Revolution. After driving the Soviets out of eastern Siberia, the Japanese could establish a "White Russian buffer state" stretching from Vladivostok to Lake Baikal. In Vonsiatsky's words, "Japan would govern and police the captured territory until the National Party [VFP] announced the time appropriate for transfer of title and authority to its own organization." In response to this scenario Araki said little, but Vonsiatsky went away convinced that the general was sympathetic.

If Vonsiatsky concluded that Araki would help him, he was mistaken. Just as Anastase was about to embark for Dairen, en route to Harbin, he learned that the government of Manchukuo would not give him a visa. He was thunderstruck. Were not the Japanese, and their puppets the Manchukuoans, his allies? Unfortunately, Japanese sources do not explain this development. It is possible that Tokyo advised the Manchukuoan Ministry of Foreign Affairs to withhold Vonsiatsky's visa because his presence in Harbin, broadcasting Japan's support of an anti-Soviet crusade, would constitute a grave provocation at a time when Soviet-Japanese relations were already on thin ice. It is also conceivable that intragovernmental rivalries were responsible. The Kwantung Army and Ministry of Colonization had a running jurisdictional squabble about their spheres of authority in Manchukuo. Or the problem could simply have been a case of bureaucratic red tape.

Whatever the reason was for his being denied a visa, Vonsiatsky was peeved and decided to make a show of forgoing the Harbin summit. On April 7, with Marion and Kunle in tow, he boarded the SS *President Hoover* bound for Shanghai. The *vozhd* calculated that his going off in a huff would put pressure on Rodzaevsky to do something.

In this instance, Vonsiatsky was right. On April 8, Rodzaevsky called upon Araki Sadao at the general's private residence to plead for his intervention on Vonsiatsky's behalf. He took the opportunity to brief Araki on the importance of the RFP-VFO merger and the Harbin summit in the anti-Soviet struggle. Without referring directly to Vonsiatsky, Araki replied that he fully approved of the Russian fascist movement and promised to help it. The general added that Japan must someday fight the Soviet Union and hoped that as a result of this contest a "National Russia" friendly to Japan might emerge.

Hoping that Araki would follow through, Rodzaevsky and Matkovsky departed for Dairen on April 9. At the Yokohama Railroad Station, Konstantin Vladimirovich gave a platform address to assorted *soratniki*, passersby, and plainclothesmen, declaring that the Tokyo conference with Vonsiatsky had been a "great success," that a global Russian fascist party had come into existence, and that Japan had pledged its help to free Russia of communism.

Arriving in Dairen on April 12, Rodzaevsky called on Ataman Semenov. Like Vonsiatsky, Rodzaevsky bristled at the idea of collaborating with the Cossack whom he regarded as an anachronism. But the *Tokumu Kikan* thought otherwise, and he could not afford to deviate from the "kingly way." He consoled himself that Semenov might after all be useful in the short run, for the ataman wielded a certain influence in Tokyo and in Hsinking, Manchukuo's capital and headquarters of the Kwantung Army.

Rodzaevsky took the opportunity to test Semenov's utility by asking his good offices on Vonsiatsky's visa problem. Semenov agreed to help and cabled the Manchukuoan Ministry of Foreign Affairs, urging that a special dispensation be given to a distinguished American visitor.

Semenov's and/or Araki's intervention paid unexpected dividends. Not only did the Manchukuoan government promptly issue Vonsiatsky a visa, but the Kwantung Army took steps to designate the *vozhd* as a VIP.

Meanwhile, unaware of these moves on his behalf, Vonsiatsky arrived in Shanghai on April 10 and registered at the Cathay Hotel. That night he came down with acute stomach pains. A Jewish physician attended the *vozhd* and oversaw his recovery during the next few days. Vonsiatsky recalled in later years that the experience left him profoundly affected. He grew suspicious of Rodzaevsky, who he guessed had tried to poison him, and hardened his resolve to oppose anti-Semitism in the VFP program.

Informed now that they could proceed to Manchukuo, the trio left Shanghai on April 20 on the *Tsingtao maru,* arriving in Dairen, the southern terminus of the South Manchurian Railway, on April 22. If Vonsiatsky had intended to proceed directly to Harbin, he discovered upon his arrival in Dairen that Rodzaevsky had made other plans for him. A delegation of RFP *soratniki* led by Dairen branch leader Konstantin Saraev met Vonsiatsky at the pier and informed him that he would attend a special reception in his honor at the local Russian Club that evening. Then a *soratnik* named Sergei Dolov stepped forward and handed Anastase a letter from Rodzaevsky. If authentic, this letter is the only extant personal communication between the two men, moreover one that elucidates their complex relationship with Ataman Semenov and the Kwantung Army.

General Secretary
Russian Fascist Party
20 April 1934

To: Chairman of the Central Executive Committee, VFP
     A. A. Vonsiatsky

CONFIDENTIAL

Slava Rossy,

Dear Soratnik!
We greet you and D. I. Kunle on your arrival in Dairen. I wish to inform you of a few developments, and express certain possibilities with which you will undoubtedly agree.

Upon my arrival in Dairen, I was assured that the words given by Ataman Semenov in his telegram sent to you prior to my arrival in Tokyo have a solid basis. It is evident that Ataman Semenov has far more connections with Japanese military circles, to whom a decisive role in coming developments belongs, than I had assumed. In particular, it was through Ataman Semenov that:

a)   the government of Manchukuo officially permitted you to enter Manchukuo and informed its Tokyo representatives (unfortunately, by that time I had already left [Tokyo]).

b) Dairen authorities have received instructions to issue a visa to you without delay, and also to issue a special document for traveling to any part of Manchukuo without a visa.

c) an official of the government of Manchukuo in Dairen will offer you an unofficial apology.

d) to assist you, a responsible member of the Japanese Gendarmerie [*Kempei*] will accompany you.

e) the entire line of the Dairen-Harbin railroad will be placed under a special guard during your transit.

f) the police department, as well as the Gendarmerie, will take special measures for your safety.

g) finally in Hsinking, you are to be waited on by representatives of the general staff of the Kwantung Army for very special and extremely important, absolutely secret, negotiations.

As you see, Ataman Semenov has accomplished a great deal. For some unknown reason, you did not reply to his telegram, sent to you from Dairen on April 12. In the interests of our cause, say that you did not receive his telegram or that your reply did not reach its destination.

At any rate, in view of considerations enumerated above, you cannot go to Harbin directly, for that would be interpreted as ignoring General Semenov. Therefore, I beg you, as a friend, to talk to General Semenov prior to your departure, and then proceed to Hsinking where you will stay two days. General Semenov will immediately arrive there by plane and I will subsequently join you if necessary. You are to devote those two days to a detailed conversation with Semenov and, subsequently, you are to work out a secret plan together with the staff of the Kwantung Army. Then, on Wednesday, you are to arrive in Harbin.

In view of all the circumstances so closely connected with events which we anticipate, and realizing the tremendous significance of the conferences to be attended by you, we have decided to give you a grand reception at the railroad station, as well as at the Russian Club on Wednesday.

For these very reasons, it is desirable that you should reach an agreement with Ataman Semenov whereby he is to join the All-Russian Fascist Party with all his Cossack organizations and to assume the leadership of the future Fascist army.

While visiting Dairen, we discussed with Semenov the text of a special act of incorporating his organization with the All-Russian Fascist Party. Two copies of this act are now in possession of Ataman Semenov. It is understood that it is subject to revision, correction, and detailed rewriting, subject to your approval.

This letter will be delivered to you by assistant chief of the Far Eastern section, and a member of the Supreme Soviet of the R.F.P., S. E. Dolov. In my and Matkovsky's absence from Harbin, he functioned as acting general secretary. He carries out his work diligently, and I recommend him to your trust with full confidence. I ask you to burn this letter immediately.

> Slava Rossy!
>
> With fascist greetings
>
> General Secretary RFP   K. V. Rodzaevsky

Vonsiatsky obviously ignored Rodzaevsky's final instruction, in all likelihood because he wanted to preserve such an ego-gratifying letter. He did assure Dolov, however, that he would meet Semenov and address local *soratniki* that evening.

At 8:30 P.M. on April 22, the Russian Club on Rokoton Road was packed as never before. Local RFP members, reporters, and on-lookers drawn by curiosity mingled in an atmosphere of expectation. Those unable to squeeze into the main hall stood in the corridors, craning their necks at every door to catch a glimpse of the *vozhd* and his wealthy American consort.

When Anastase Andreivich rose to speak after being introduced by *Soratnik* Saraev, his hands trembled. This was not the Military Room at Nineteenth Hole but the real thing, a Far Eastern debut, a dress rehearsal for Harbin. The impressions made here could make or break his reputation. Alex did his best to rise to the occasion. In an operatic bass punctuated by pregnant pauses, he spelled out the fascist formula for counterrevolution.

Vonsiatsky's Dairen speech contained the basic arguments that he repeated again and again at each stage of the world tour. Communism had degraded and pauperized Russia to the brink of revolution, but "White" attempts to overthrow Bolshevism had failed because they were ideologically anachronistic and tactically uncoordinated. The National Revolution must find Russian patriots "within and without their homeland" ready to act in perfect concert for a final show-down with communism. Only fascists, embodying the best traditions of Old Russia and harmonizing with modern trends, could lead the National Revolution. He concluded with a call to arms.

We want all local emigrant Russians, all patriots of the Russian race, to join a Fascist organization here, so that when the decisive day comes, you will be ready to carry out your assignments in order to overthrow the Communists.

Under the headline "Fascists Plan Wholesome Russia," the *Manchurian Daily News* called Vonsiatsky's April 22 address "stirring." It did not mention how many new recruits had flocked to the VFP banner.

Vonsiatsky, it turns out, may or may not have met Semenov while he was in Dairen. A Japanese police report submitted to the Home Ministry on April 10 noted that such a meeting was projected so that VFP leaders could discuss with Semenov the affiliation of their party with the Far Eastern Cossack Union. But there are no further references to a Semenov-Vonsiatsky encounter in Japanese sources. Anastase, usually loquacious about contacts with celebrities, remained uncharacteristically silent about this meeting. In the unlikely instance that the two men actually met face to face, it must have been a cold affair. Semenov deplored the attraction of some young émigrés to fascism. Vonsiatsky's public disparagement of White failures could hardly please a man who had been a major anti-Bolshevik leader during the Civil War and who regarded himself as the *vozhd* of the White cause in the Far East. For appearances' sake, both men kept their differences to themselves.

On April 24, Anastase, Marion, and Kunle boarded a South Manchurian Railway express for Hsinking. Their route led from the hilly Kwantung Territory through Liao River lowlands to the central Manchurian plain. At Hsinking, where the SMR line ended, the party changed to a CER train for the final 150-mile run to Harbin.

Did Vonsiatsky linger in Hsinking for what Rodzaevsky's letter had forecasted would be "extremely important, absolutely secret negotiations" with representatives of the Kwantung Army general staff? Both Japanese and White Russian sources are silent on this matter. Even Vonsiatsky never made a single reference to such negotiations. It is somehow difficult to imagine Kwantung Army commander General Hishikari Takeshi sitting down at general headquarters to talk with an American tourist (regardless of the latter's pretensions) about anti-Soviet strategy. More likely, some local *Tokumu Kikan* Russian specialists looked him over before passing him on to their Harbin colleagues.

Rodzaevsky was not exaggerating, however, when he promised that the Dairen-Harbin line would be well guarded. Sure enough, soldiers clustered behind sandbags on flatcars and patrolled through the coaches. What Konstantin Vladimirovich failed to tell his guest was that SMR trains commonly carried such guards to ward off ubiquitous *hunghutze*.

Vonsiatsky did have a personal escort of sorts in *Nash Put* reporter I. G. Kurbsky. As they traveled northward, Kurbsky tried to pin the *vozhd* down on his plans, goals, and opinions. Although often prone to loose talk, Anastase on this occasion showed a politician's knack for sidestepping sensitive issues:

> KURBSKY: How do you look upon the Ukrainian question?
> VON: This question can only be settled at a Congress of the All-Russian Fascists since it demands particular attention.
> KURBSKY: What is your relationship with the Musketeers [a White Russian nationalist youth organization]?
> VON: I am well acquainted with the Musketeer organization in San Francisco. Our work is in common, and in San Francisco many Musketeers have entered our organization.
> KURBSKY: How long do you think that you will be in Harbin?
> VON: This depends on how long our work takes to complete.

Vonsiatsky's dreams seemed close to realization when on April 26, 1934, he entered Harbin. Rodzaevsky had made elaborate preparations for the visitor to be accorded a triumphal reception at the Central Railway Station. He ordered Sasha Bolotov to flush out all available Blackshirts to form an honor guard along the platform. He mobilized local units of the Fascist Women's Movement, the Fascist Vanguard, the Young Fascist Union, and the Fascist Little Ones. Delegations of Musketeers, Cossacks, and Legitimists also lent their presence. This colorful host arrayed itself along the station platforms, ready to cheer a man few had ever heard of a few weeks previously.

When the Hsinking-Harbin express pulled in at 2:10 P.M., the crowd pressed forward toward the tracks, eager to catch a glimpse of the American visitors. Cries of *"Slava!"* greeted Anastase when he appeared at the door of a first-class coach. Descending gingerly onto the platform, he looked more like an Ivy League football fan than a fascist *vozhd*. Dapperly outfitted in tweed sport coat, wool vest, four-in-hand, and a cocked fedora, he made only a nominal concession to military garb—a khaki shirt. Kunle looked more orthodox in his army surplus uniform, swastika arm band, and briefcase. Marion modestly remained in the background as her husband and Rodzaevsky exchanged *Slavas* and salutes. The host gave a short speech of welcome and introduced Anastase to members of the RFP (now VFP) Central Executive Committee. Vonsiatsky had already met Matkovsky, Balykov, and Dolov. He now also came face to face with Sasha Bolotov.

Flanked by Blackshirts, Rodzaevsky and his guests proceeded by taxi along the Vogzalnaya to the Sabul Russian Cathedral in Novy Gorod. There had been plans for a brass band, but Japanese authorities had demurred. At the Sabul Cathedral, Vonsiatsky entered the Chapel of the Siberian Virgin and lit several tapers. The procession then retraced its steps along the Vogzalnaya, crossed the CER tracks into Pristan, and made for the Hokuman Hotel on Novogorodnaya Street.

The Hokuman was a far cry from being Harbin's finest hostelry, but Rodzaevsky had compelling reasons for not quartering his guest in the town's two leading establishments. The elegant Hotel Moderne at 177 Kitaiskaya (right down the block from RFP headquarters at no. 125) was out of the question, being Jewish-owned. Moreover, its proprietor Josef Kaspé had only four months earlier learned of his son's murder by kidnappers with RFP links, and could hardly be expected to welcome a fascist jubilee. The Hotel New Harbin, being Soviet-owned, was also taboo, despite its fine view of the Sabul Cathedral and the Japanese Military Mission. That left the Hokuman, a Japanese hotel whose lack of class was only partially redeemed by its proximity to Harbin's most fashionable night spot, Cabaret Fantasia.

Vonsiatsky had little time for frivolity during his first day in Harbin. Rodzaevsky called a press conference at the Hokuman for 5:20 P.M., leaving his guest to field questions about the RFP-VFO merger. Asked what his purpose was in Harbin, he replied: "To draw up a general tactical program for our struggle with the Bolshevik regime."

At eight that evening, Vonsiatsky attended a gala reception in his honor at the Russian Club. *Nash Put* had printed instructions for party faithful to gather one hour in advance. Crowds filled a large auditorium well before that. On the stage was a lectern, a long table with chairs, and an enormous double-headed eagle surrounded by red, black, and yellow banners. Upon the appearance of Vonsiatsky,

Rodzaevsky, Kunle, Matkovsky, and Bolotov, a band struck up the RFP and VFO anthems. Rodzaevsky then spoke some words of introduction, and the audience settled down to hear what the new *vozhd* had to say.

Vonsiatsky started by reiterating themes that he had dwelt on in Dairen: failure of the White movement to appeal to the Russian masses, Soviet exploitation of peasants and workers, deepening crisis within the USSR, and the urgent need for a united front of anti-Communist émigrés to prepare for the National Revolution. Then he spelled out the major propaganda points designed to win over the peasantry: disbanding of collective farms, distribution of land to individual cultivators, and use of state funds to assist poor peasants. Fascist propaganda, Vonsiatsky continued, should eschew abstractions and address itself to the "daily needs" of Russia's "worker-peasant masses." Such propaganda, he predicted:

> . . . will enable us to take advantage of all the potential revolutionary energy of the oppressed peasant masses for a general struggle with Soviet power, transforming the population of Russia . . . from a reserve of Communist reaction into a true ally of the fascist revolution.

Mindful of those sharing the stage with him, Vonsiatsky expressed the hope that his visit to Harbin would remove "certain slight friction" among newly united Russian fascists. He closed the speech by calling for a "sacrifice of personal ambitions" in order to achieve fighting unity in the showdown with communism. According to an eyewitness employed by the American consul in Harbin, Vonsiatsky's speech produced a "deep impression" on the audience.

Although the speaker did not elaborate on "certain slight friction," his listeners knew that he was referring to the Jewish issue. With the exception of a few like Matkovsky, RFP *soratniki* were viscerally anti-Semitic. Vonsiatsky refused to follow that line, partly for pragmatic and partly for personal reasons. Vonsiatsky's reticence was a hard pill for Rodzaevsky to swallow. But the pill went down, sweetened by promises of financial largesse. *Nash Put* even suspended Jew-baiting while Vonsiatsky was in Harbin.

Only a few onlookers realized that there was another source of "certain slight friction" that posed a more immediate obstacle to VFP unity than Jews: Ataman Grigory Semenov. Supported by Rodzaevsky (under Japanese advice) as commander of a future White Russian army, Semenov struck Vonsiatsky as nothing but a Japanese tool with a bad reputation.

After the tumultuous welcome of April 26, what followed seemed anticlimactic. While Marion went shopping, Rodzaevsky took Anastase and Kunle about Harbin, showing them the *Nash Put* offices, a school for party agitators and organizers, and the exterior of the Soviet consulate. On May 4, Vonsiatsky spoke to an audience of two thousand at the Ves Mir Theater, and on the following day reviewed formations of Fascist Youth, Fascist Vanguard, and Fascist Little Ones parading in his honor. At nine thirty on the morning of May 6, the three visitors boarded an express for Hsinking and Dairen, from where on May 8 they embarked on the *Tsingtao maru* for Shanghai.

Vonsiatsky derived a childlike pleasure from the publicity attending his trip and culled local newspapers in search of his name. Even hostile articles gratified him. The *vozhd,* given to melodrama, never doubted that Soviet and Japanese agents had been shadowing him from the moment he left Nineteenth Hole. Extant Japanese records show a moderate but not extraordinary interest in him. Vonsiatsky attracted more attention in Tokyo than the average American tourist but far less than had Charlie Chaplin when he visited Japan in 1932. Soviet agents undoubtedly attended Vonsiatsky's speeches in Dairen and Harbin, and Tass duly lambasted the VFP as a tool of Germany, but it is far from clear how seriously the Kremlin took him. Vonsiatsky did not realize it, but the government keeping the closest watch on him was probably his own.

Official American concern about Vonsiatsky dated from 1922, when Lyuba Muromsky's transatlantic bigamy charges prompted some brisk paper shuffling between the State and Justice departments. Dormant for a decade while Anastase underwent grooming in Thompson, this concern revived in August 1933 when the "Ivanoff-Krivkoff" caper came to the attention of the State Department's Division of Eastern European Affairs.

Until November 16, 1933, Vonsiatsky had been merely an annoyance to the State Department. But on that date, when the United States and the Union of Soviet Socialist Republics established diplomatic relations, he suddenly became a problem. According to an exchange of letters on that day between President Franklin D. Roosevelt and Commissar for Foreign Affairs Maxim Litvinov, each country pledged not to permit the formation or residence on its territory of any organization aiming to overthrow the other's government. According to *Fashist,* Vonsiatsky's VFO was not just aiming but was actually *engaged* in overthrowing Stalin. Nevertheless, at first neither the State nor Justice department took immediate action to muzzle or even to investigate Vonsiatsky. Robert F. Kelley, chief of the State Department's Division of Eastern European Affairs, was accused in pro-Soviet circles of turning a blind eye to White Guard activities, but it is just as likely that Kelley simply discounted *Fashist*'s claims as nonsense.

In April 1934, however, press reports emanating from Tokyo and Shanghai finally obliged the Department to act. The primary concern was with ascertaining whether Vonsiatsky—a naturalized American citizen—was enlisting Japanese aid for his anti-Soviet campaign.

On May 3, while Anastase was basking in Harbin's adulation, Division of Far Eastern Affairs chief Stanley K. Hornbeck sent a "strictly confidential" wire to the American legation in Peiping asking for a "discreet investigation and report on the activities and movements of Anastase Andre von Siatsky, bearer of Department passport No. 53198 issued July 14, 1933 and Marion Ream von Siatsky, bearer of Department passport No. 74421 issued January 11, 1934." Edwin S. Cunningham, consul general in Peiping, forwarded these instructions to the Tokyo embassy and Harbin consulate. After conducting inquiries with the Kobe Water Police, the Tokyo Metropolitan Police, shipping lines, and leading hotels in Kobe, Yokohama, and Tokyo, U.S. Ambassador Joseph C. Grew could only report to Secretary of State Cordell Hull that "the von Siatskys were rumored to be traveling in the interest of some White Russian or Japanese organization." Harbin consul Cabot Coville had more success. Assisted by a "reliable Russian émigré," he was able to provide Washington with detailed information about the VFP "summit," including discord over the Jewish question between Vonsiatsky and Rodzaevsky.

Grew and Coville had received the Department's instructions only after Vonsiatsky had passed through Tokyo and Harbin respectively. Cunningham, in contrast, was fully prepared when the Connecticut travelers arrived for the second time in Shanghai aboard the *Tsingtao maru* on May 10. He assigned M. S. Nicholson, an attaché from the Treasury Department, to keep an eye on them.

After the exhilarating atmosphere of Harbin, Shanghai turned out to be a disappointment for Vonsiatsky. He had counted on whipping up the local White Russian community into a frenzy of enthusiasm for his united front. But Shanghai was a world apart from Harbin. Most of its Russian colony was more cosmopolitan and less obsessed with counterrevolution. Nor did Japan—yet—control the city. In fact, those Japanese authorities who were in Shanghai, mainly diplomats, were, in contrast with the Kwantung Army in Manchukuo, not inclined to give open support to anti-Soviet activities.

Vonsiatsky's host in Shanghai was one P. M. Zaitsev, an RFP fellow traveler who edited a staunchly rightist, pro-Japanese newspaper called *Slovo*. Zaitsev made arrangements for the *vozhd* to deliver a lecture entitled "The Crisis of Communism in the USSR and the Rise of Russian Fascism" at a 1,500-seat hall owned by the Mainichi Newspaper Company. Invitations were printed and distributed to all Russian organizations and prominent émigrés. On the eve of the lecture, however, Japanese consular officers brought pressure on the management to deny Vonsiatsky use of the hall, reportedly because they wished to avoid provoking local Soviet officials. Instead of cancelling his speech, Vonsiatsky rescheduled it for the following day at the Embassy Theater. Meanwhile, he invited those who showed up at the Mainichi Hall to tea at the Cathay Hotel ballroom.

According to Nicholson, the impression created by Vonsiatsky's Embassy Theater address on May 21 was "nil." The audience had expected to be told how fascism would succeed where the White movement had failed. Instead, he reported, the speaker gave them a "rehash" of hackneyed rhetoric. Even panache failed to camouflage the speech's triteness. The audience listened in silence for fifty minutes and applauded politely. Thereafter, the only thing about Vonsiatsky that interested Shanghai Russians was his money.

Vonsiatsky's exertions in Shanghai were not entirely in vain. He struck up an acquaintance with a young man named Konstantin Steklov, who was attracted to the ideal of a global Russian fascist movement and, like Vonsiatsky, felt reservations about subordinating it completely to Japanese interests. The two men became friends, and for the next seven years Steklov acted as Vonsiatsky's chief (indeed almost only) bona fide follower in the Far East. As editor of the newspaper *Russky Avangard* (1936–42), Steklov did his best to give Vonsiatsky good exposure. It was a lonely assignment, only slightly alleviated by a $600 annual subsidy from Connecticut.

On May 22, the visiting trio left Shanghai aboard the SS *President*

Harrison bound for Europe. Information about the last half of Vonsiatsky's world tour is scarce, partially because the State Department kept looser tabs on him and partially because he later talked about it less. It is clear that he hoped to rally support for a united front among White Russians in the Near East and Europe. He also wanted to get to know his own agents, some of whom he had yet to meet personally, and to appoint new representatives where necessary.

At Alexandria, Anastase paid his respects to "Baron" Georgy Taube, the VFO (now VFP) man in Cairo. He then proceeded to Naples.

Although only a handful of White Russians lived there, Italy held a special attraction for Vonsiatsky: Benito Mussolini. The *vozhd* made straight for Rome but did not succeed in gaining an audience with *Il Duce*. He contented himself with a not entirely cordial interview with Carlo Bossi, a "Russian expert" in the Italian Intelligence Service. Bossi, whose only discernible connection with Russia was being the son-in-law of a Bordeaux wine merchant who had once purveyed clarets in St. Petersburg, was suspicious of Vonsiatsky's Japanese connections (the Anti-Comintern Pact, which linked Germany, Japan, and Italy, was still more than two years away) and treated him coldly. Disappointed but not dejected, Anastase moved in early July to Paris, where he felt he had friends.

Paris occupied a special niche in Vonsiatsky's affections. He had met a woman there who had changed the course of his life, enabling him to rise in thirteen years from a Folies Bergères curtain puller to the wealthy leader of a global movement to liberate Russia. It was in Paris that he had first won notoriety with his "Memoirs of a Monarchist" and had first tasted the sweet fulfillment of philanthropic endeavor, the Emperor Nicholas II Military Academy.

For all these fond associations, Vonsiatsky could claim few political supporters in Paris. He no longer wielded influence in the Russian Armed Services Union since his friend General Alexander Kutepov, kidnapped by the OGPU in 1930, had been replaced by a comparative stranger, General Evgeny Miller. Alexander Kazem-Bek, head of the Paris-based Young Russians (*Mladorossy*), had disliked Vonsiatsky ever since the two had met the year before in Berlin.

Anastase's chief object in coming to Paris in July 1934 was to relax and catch up with the fluid profile of émigré politics in Europe. He had a number of aristocratic friends there who shared his taste for the good life: Prince Felix Yusupov, Prince Theodore Romanov, Daniele Volkonsky, and Prince Alexis Sherbatoff. Prince Theodore, an architect who had spent the summers of 1930 and 1932 with Vonsiatsky, happened to be in Paris in the summer of 1934. Anastase half jestingly offered to hire him for two weeks as a chauffeur and guide. Theodore, for reasons known best to himself, gamely accepted. Shortly afterward Anastase invited Daniele Volkonsky and Prince Sherbatoff to lunch at Maxim's. After dining, the guests were asked if they would care to go for a drive in Anastase's private limousine. They never recovered from the sight of a liveried Romanov holding the door open for them with a gracious, slightly self-deprecating smile. Alex enjoyed the scene immensely, but he was not insensitive to its pathos.

Refreshed by Paris, Vonsiatsky resumed stumping for a united front. His itinerary took in the major Russian communities in Central Europe and the Balkans: Berlin, Prague, Budapest, Sofia, and Belgrade. He tarried only a few days at each stopover, just long enough to make contact with local VFP *soratniki* and to deliver a speech or two. He repeated more or less what had been said at Dairen, Harbin, and Shanghai, and his appearances met a mixed reception. After addressing two thousand listeners (mainly ROND members) at Berlin's Landwehr Casino, he felt elated by the enthusiastic applause. Yet in Belgrade, Yugoslav authorities prohibited him from mentioning Japan. Moreover, the audience remained cool. In a cable to Washington, the American chargé d'affaires in Belgrade reported that a number of listeners had felt that Vonsiatsky had "made a fool of himself" and looked "tipsy."

Did Vonsiatsky mix with top Nazis during his 1934 visit to Berlin? Anastase subsequently spoke inconsistently on this question. To Putnam cronies, he boasted about being received by Hitler. To the FBI, he alluded to no contacts with Nazi officials. His New York Police Department file, swollen with letters from informants, mentioned meetings with Hitler, Goering, Hess, and Rosenberg.

Amid such contradictory evidence, there is little that can be said with certainty about the *vozhd*'s Berlin connections. If Vonsiatsky did meet any ranking figure in the Third Reich, it was most likely Alfred Rosenberg. Chief of the NSDAP Foreign Policy Office throughout 1934, Rosenberg nurtured a special interest in Russian and Ukrainian affairs, and it is not unreasonable to assume that had Alfred Voldemarovich heard about Vonsiatsky (whose travels and speeches were well publicized), he would have entertained at least a mild curiosity about a rich former countryman who was trying to mount a crusade against the USSR. If the two men did get together in Berlin for a cup of tea, as Vonsiatsky told a reporter in 1939, nothing very concrete resulted from their encounter. Anastase was too flamboyant and too self-willed for even those Nazis, such as Rosenberg, who deigned to deal with Slavs. Had he been more malleable, Vonsiatsky might have become Rosenberg's protégé or a flunkey such as General Biskupsky. As it turned out, the Gestapo barely tolerated Vonsiatsky's speech at the Landwehr Casino. One year later, his party was to be banned within the Third Reich.

On August 1, 1934, Anastase, Marion, and Kunle sailed from Marseilles for New York on the SS *President Johnson*. Anastase could afford to look back on the five-month odyssey with a certain satisfaction. The first global fascist organization, the All-Russian Fascist Party, had been born with him as its *vozhd*. He had visited the Russian diaspora's most populous communities, had met dozens of émigré leaders, and had recruited hundreds of followers (to be sure, with the help of money). He had spoken to thousands about how fascists formed the vanguard of Russia's National Revolution. He had become a celebrity. Kunle's briefcase bulged with clippings testifying to that. Henri Rollin, a well-known French commentator on Russian affairs, had proclaimed him a "Russian Hitler" in *Le Temps*. Never before had his dream of a fascist united front seemed closer to realization.

Entranced by publicity, Vonsiatsky was oblivious to the fragility of his triumph. But before the year 1934 had ended, his cherished united front lay in shambles, dashing his hopes for émigré unity and propelling him ever deeper into a world of make-believe.

CHAPTER XI

Schism

Opposition is not necessary for the proper working of a healthy political regime. We Fascists carry out opposition inside ourselves.
—BENITO MUSSOLINI

It is hardly surprising that the All-Russian Fascist Party came apart so soon after its birth. Considering the social diversity and geographical dispersion of VFP membership, unresolved contradictions within the VFP program, and the volatile egos of VFP *vozhd* Anastase Vonsiatsky and VFP general secretary Konstantin Rodzaevsky, it is remarkable that the party endured for as long as it did after the Harbin summit. Indeed, poor communications between Harbin and Putnam may have delayed the schism by keeping Manchurian and Connecticut *soratniki* ignorant of each other's aspersions.

During the summer of 1934, the VFP gave every appearance of being a happy family. *Fashist* and *Nash Put* rhapsodized about global unity. In August, in Harbin there opened a new Higher Party School, also known as the St. Vladimir Academy, or the Stolypin Academy. Interviewed in mid-September at Nineteenth Hole by Hartford *Courant* reporter Wesley Griswold, Vonsiatsky exulted about how the VFO-RFP betrothal had welded twenty thousand Russian fascists "from Alaska to Buenos Aires and from Manchuria to Berlin" into a monolithic force, had spawned new fascist cells "springing to life like dandelions on a spring lawn," and had put at his disposal "an army of 150,000" in Manchuria, ready for infiltration and propaganda work inside the USSR.

Yet beneath the comradely facade, Vonsiatsky and Rodzaevsky disliked and disrespected each other. Both knew that their collaboration was essentially pragmatic and would endure only as long as both stood to gain from it. Poor and dependent upon Japanese largesse,

159

Rodzaevsky resented Vonsiatsky for the independence that had accrued from wealth and American citizenship. He bridled at having to play the underling to an amateur, an interloper, an *alfons* lucky enough to have latched onto an American heiress. For his part, Vonsiatsky found his younger colleague crude and intemperate. Sensing Rodzaevsky's bile and envy, he became all the more determined to show everyone that he, Anastase Andreivich, was boss. Hostility to Rodzaevsky hardened under the influence of Lev Beck Mamedov, Vonsiatsky's brother-in-law. Mamedov had once operated a cafe in Harbin and knew the city's seamier side well. When asked by Vonsiatsky what he thought about Rodzaevsky, Mamedov answered without a moment's hesitation: "He's a crook." Mamedov had never met Konstantin Vladimirovich, for he had left Harbin a year before the runaway adolescent arrived from Blagoveshchensk. Nevertheless, as far as Vonsiatsky was concerned, Mamedov's word was final.

The clash of personalities was one of several divisive forces undermining VFP unity. Vonsiatsky and Rodzaevsky disagreed fundamentally over several issues. In an immediate way, the most important of these was Semenov.

Semenov and Rodzaevsky were essentially rivals. They competed for supporters throughout Manchuria, the Cossack hetman generally getting the upper hand in rural areas (where his people predominated) and Rodzaevsky prevailing in Harbin. Albeit anti-Communists, they disagreed sharply over ideology. Semenov deplored the appeal of Italian fascism and German national socialism among Russian émigré youth. Rodzaevsky disparaged Cossack pride as anachronistic. The two men also differed in their ultimate political objectives. Rodzaevsky sought to build a Russian fascist empire. Semenov's regional loyalties conditioned him to think in terms of an autonomous Siberian state.

The *Tokumu Kikan* had little patience with squabbles among its protégés and took steps to compel fascists and Cossacks to resolve their differences. Early in 1934, Major Akikusa Shun, *Tokumu Kikan* liaison officer with White Russian groups in Harbin, had advised Rodzaevsky that he should henceforth cooperate with Semenov. Dependent upon Japanese subsidies and sanctions, he had no choice but to comply.

This had put Rodzaevsky into an awkward position when Vonsiatsky came to Tokyo in April. Konstantin Vladimirovich found himself playing the distasteful game of trying to convince one of his rivals to come to terms with another. As we have already seen, the Connecticut *vozhd* balked at this. A veneer of unity was preserved by omitting any mention of Semenov in Protokoll No. 1 and at the Harbin summit. Vonsiatsky, however, had no intention of letting the matter drop there. And Rodzaevsky knew that he could not compromise without jeopardizing Japanese patronage.

Divergent orientations toward Jews also inhibited cooperation between Vonsiatsky and Rodzaevsky. Rodzaevsky was a confirmed anti-Semite. Although hardly innocent of such impulses, Vonsiatsky did not want to alienate anti-Communist Jews who might support the Russian fascist movement. By and large, he regarded Jews pragmatically. Shortly after returning from Harbin, he remarked to a reporter: "If the Jews want to be our friends and helpers we shall welcome them gladly." Five years later, in another interview with a journalist, he made this view more explicit:

> Well, our attitude toward the Jews depends on their attitude toward us. If they want to go along with us, O.K. If not, we fight them. If they want to fight the common enemy that is all right with us. Russia has too many tribes and kinds of people to start fighting with one kind. It is not like Germany where they have only one race.

This pragmatism did not stop at words. Like the British fascist Oswald Mosley who hired a Jewish boxer ("Kid" Lewis) to train his Biff Boys, Vonsiatsky retained a Jewish firm in New York to design and tailor his party uniforms. In 1934, Mark Weinbaum, Jewish editor-in-chief of the New York Russian daily *Novoye Russkoye Slovo,* spent a night with Vonsiatsky at Nineteenth Hole discussing the possibility of his newspaper's being used as a medium for VFO propaganda. According to Vonsiatsky, Weinbaum left Thompson hopeful that some form of cooperation could be worked out, but a few days later he wrote the count saying that collaboration was impossible. Anastase deduced that Weinbaum had changed his mind under the influence of colleagues. The *vozhd* continued to feel "quite friendly" toward the editor for years afterward.

Personal as well as pragmatic considerations left Vonsiatsky cool to anti-Semitism. His first wife, Lyuba Muromsky, was Jewish. A Jewish physician had attended him in Shanghai (and in Vonsiatsky's opinion saved his life). Marion and Kunle had been called Jews at various stages of the world tour. These experiences reinforced Vonsiatsky's conviction that ethnic hatreds had nothing to do with true Russian fascism.

Vonsiatsky and Rodzaevsky shelved the Jewish question at the Harbin summit for the sake of party unity. *Nash Put* and *Natsiya* momentarily suspended anti-Semitic diatribes. Some of the frustration felt by Rodzaevsky under these constraints can be gauged from a passage in the July 1934 issue of *Natsiya:*

> Our enemies never miss an opportunity to sow dissension in our ranks. Having found out that there are minor differences between us and *soratnik* Vonsiatsky concerning the Jewish question, they choose to provoke us on this matter.
>
> The truth is, however, that having taken into consideration the fact that the All Russian Fascist Party is operating in the United States, a country governed by Jews and Masons, we decided that it is as yet premature to raise the Jewish question . . ."

As in the case of Semenov, suspending discussion did not solve the basic incompatibility of views. Neither man was prepared to compromise, making it only a matter of time before mute disagreement burst into open polemics.

Japan constituted yet another schismatic force within the VFP. Rodzaevsky of necessity worked closely with Japanese Army officers. Rarely did he make any political decision without consulting Major Akikusa or Kostya Nakamura. Living in a comparatively tolerant society, Vonsiatsky could follow his own instincts without fear of state intervention. Although Anastase did not object to subordinating Russian fascist tactics temporarily to Japanese requirements, he differed fundamentally with Rodzaevsky over the degree and duration of that subordination. The Connecticut *vozhd* was not about to take arbitrary orders from *Tokumu Kikan* or *Kempei* advisers, as Rodzaevsky was doing. As he indicated to a reporter in September 1934, he was willing to concede that Russian fascists would support Japan *after* the outbreak of a Soviet-Japanese war:

> In case of war between the Reds and the Japs, we, the Russian Fascists, will fight shoulder to shoulder with the latter, for Japan is the only country in the world that can provide us with sufficient arms and ammunition for our army, which is going to cut the Bolsheviks to pieces from Vladivostok to Moscow.

Vonsiatsky favored a limited, practical alliance with Japan but stayed clear of any commitment to the "kingly way."

The question of Japan's relationship to the Russian fascist movement also came into sharp focus over Vonsiatsky's and Rodzaevsky's conflicting scenarios of the National Revolution. Rodzaevsky envisioned the National Revolution's being brought to Russia on foreign bayonets. Vonsiatsky, in contrast, insisted that Russia's masses must be won over to the National Revolution before a foreign invasion. In Vonsiatsky's opinion, the primary responsibility of Russian fascists was not to work for Japan in Manchukuo but to propagandize among workers and peasants throughout the USSR. As he told a Hartford *Courant* reporter in September 1934:

> I have learned the ABC of the technique of revolt from Lenin and Trotsky. We shall adopt the identical tactics of the Communists and their subjugation of Russia. . . . We shall invade Russia, but not with arms. Our weapons shall be words which shall penetrate the head and the heart of workman and peasant.

Vonsiatsky insisted that the National Revolution must come from within Russia and could not be imposed from outside or "waged according to the instructions of the government of a foreign power." The implication was clear. Japan's material assistance would be welcome, Japan's political manipulation would not. Rodzaevsky may have agreed with this view privately, but he could not afford to say so publicly. The *Tokumu Kikan* would simply replace him with a more pliant protégé if he dared refer to Japan as a "foreign power."

A final source of division between Vonsiatsky and Rodzaevsky lay in the treatment of aristocrats in fascist Russia. Recognizing monarchist strength in the Far Eastern Russian diaspora, Rodzaevsky carefully tailored the VFP program to woo monarchist support. While stopping short of pledging to restore the Romanov dynasty, he left that possibility open (at least in the minds of those who wanted to see it open) by adopting vague and eclectic slogans. Notwithstanding his aristocratic friends, Vonsiatsky entertained no thoughts of an imperial restoration and made his position abundantly clear. "There will be no titles, no special privileges in Fascist Russia," he declared to a reporter in September 1934. Asked by the reporter how Russia's exiled royalty would take to such a statement, the *vozhd* answered in a manner that showed that his nostalgia went no further than Nineteenth Hole's Military Room and *Fashist*'s misty photogravures:

> We have not asked them [exiled Russian royalty]. Some of them have joined us of their own accord. The others we shall be glad to receive

within our party if they are so disposed. For them, however, there can never be a return of the old order.

Vonsiatsky saw Russia after the National Revolution being ruled by a charismatic fascist dictator such as Mussolini. Although modesty prevented him from mentioning names, few who knew Vonsiatsky doubted whom he had in mind for the post. That point alone precluded lasting cooperation between the count from Connecticut and the boy from Blagoveshchensk.

Open Breach

After simmering beneath a veneer of VFP harmony during the summer and autumn of 1934, the Vonsiatsky-Rodzaevsky schism surfaced with dramatic suddenness in December. The "Sarajevo" for an all-out breach was an article on Semenov published in issue no. 13 (October–November 1934) of *Fashist,* entitled "He Should Be Shot." On December 11, *Nash Put* came back by denouncing and excommunicating Vonsiatsky in the name of the VFP Central Executive Committee.

The *Nash Put* salvo opened on a portentous note, announcing that the Central Executive Committee of the All-Russian Fascist Party had convened an "urgent and extraordinary" session on December 8 to discuss *Fashist*'s slander of Semenov and to review Vonsiatsky's activities since he had left Harbin the previous May. There followed a catalogue of the *vozhd*'s sins: failure to intensify the national revolutionary struggle in accordance with decisions reached at the Second Congress of Russian Fascists (i.e., the Harbin summit); failure to keep the Central Executive Committee informed of his contacts with European and North American fascist groups; paying "more attention to the popularization of himself than to serious propaganda"; misrepresenting the party program and usurping Central Executive Committee privileges by publishing an unauthorized attack on Semenov in *Fashist;* attempting to "force the party as a whole and even the Central Executive Committee to reject their anti-Jewish principles"; and "lack of appreciation of the importance of his responsible position and of the greatness of the party's aims in an epoch-making period." The *Nash Put* announcement concluded with a Central Executive Committee resolution to strip Vonsiatsky of his title of *vozhd,* drop him from the Central Executive Committee, expel him from the VFP, and to instruct *soratniki* throughout the world to deal henceforth only with Harbin. This resolution was placed on the agenda of the Third Congress of Russian Fascists (scheduled to convene in Harbin in June 1935) for approval by the general VFP membership.

Vonsiatsky reacted to the *Nash Put* offensive by publishing an "open letter" to Rodzaevsky, dated December 31, 1934, in the January 1935 issue of *Fashist*. Ignoring the *Nash Put* charges, he assailed Rodzaevsky's "deviations" from policies agreed upon at Yokohama and Harbin, notably those concerning Semenov and Jews. Cooperation with Semenov not only contravened Harbin summit agreements but threatened the National Revolution. If, as Rodzaevsky planned, Semenov were placed in command of Russian forces attached to the Imperial Japanese Army, he would only repeat errors committed by the Whites in 1918–22. Russian fascists, Vonsiatsky continued, must concentrate on revolutionary struggles within the USSR and at all costs avoid looking like interventionist Japanese puppets. On the Jewish question, Vonsiatsky called attention to the Harbin summit's moratorium on anti-Semitic propaganda and warned that its revival would "only weaken the national revolutionary struggle against the one chief enemy, Soviet communism."

Vonsiatsky followed up the "open letter" with a vigorous campaign in *Fashist* against Manchurian "deviationists." He simultaneously terminated remittances to Harbin (which never amounted to more than a tiny fraction of the $500,000 promised in Tokyo). He appointed a new Central Executive Committee, consisting of Mamedov, Kunle, and some of his New York cronies (Evgeny Bogoslovsky, Dmitry Sidorov), and proceeded to act as if Thompson, Connecticut, had inherited the mantle of capital of the Russian fascist movement.

None of the above measures spared Vonsiatsky from being upstaged in Harbin. The Third Congress of Russian Fascists, held between June 28 and July 7, 1935, turned into an unqualified personal triumph for Konstantin Rodzaevsky. In the absence of Vonsiatsky and his supporters, the congress quickly approved the Central Executive Committee's recommendations without a murmur. Two hundred delegates (including Rodzaevsky's aunt, representing Tientsin) from Manchukuo, China, Japan, the United States, Germany, Australia, Yugoslavia, Finland, Estonia, and Syria voted to strip Vonsiatsky of his titles and VFP membership and to elect Rodzaevsky as *vozhd*. Under the watchful eyes of Major Akikusa, the congress dutifully endorsed VFP cooperation with Ataman Semenov and his Far Eastern Cossack Union.

The Third Congress completed the break but did not end the vituperation between Vonsiatsky and Rodzaevsky. Starting in the fall of 1935, *Fashist* lumped Rodzaevsky with Kazem-Bek, head of the Young Russians, and General Miller, head of the Russian Armed Services Union, as vestiges of the bankrupt old White cause. By 1936, Vonsiatsky was openly accusing Rodzaevsky of betraying Russia by subordinating the National Revolution to Japan's "Pan Asiatic" ambitions. In February 1937, *Fashist* escalated the invective still further by identifying Blackshirt leader Alexander ("Sasha") Bolotov as the murderer of Semion Kaspé and describing the act as personally ordered by Rodzaevsky.

By implicating Rodzaevsky in the Kaspé case, Vonsiatsky was obviously trying to capitalize on the affair's international notoriety. Since Nikolai Martinov and his five surviving associates were arrested for the act in October 1934, the matter had transmuted from a sordid criminal case into a political *cause célèbre*. Fearful of their involvement being exposed, Japanese authorities had kept the kidnappers incommunicado and showed no inclination to bring them to trial. Albert Chambon, the French vice-consul in Harbin almost singlehandedly responsible for tracking down Kaspé's abductors, was declared *persona non grata* and forced to leave Manchukuo. Unfavorable publicity in the European and American press, combined with strong remonstrations from Jewish leaders in Shanghai and New York, eventually induced Tokyo to expedite judicial proceedings. The first trial (June 7–December 25, 1935) was suspended upon the transfer of the presiding judge. The second (March 23–June 14, 1936), held in the Harbin District Court, saw a Japanese prosecutor passionately arguing on behalf of the defendants. Their crime was depicted as being politically motivated—to raise money for the Brotherhood of Russian Truth. Martinov and his associates were characterized as patriots "who had raised the flag against a world danger—communism." But to everyone's surprise, the supposedly subservient Chinese judges passed out death sentences for Martinov, Kirichenko, Shandar, and Zaitsev, and life sentences with hard labor for Komisarenko and Bezruchko. *Nash Put* denounced the verdict, hailed the condemned men as "martyrs of Holy Russia," and collected thousands of signatures for a petition of clemency to Manchukuo's puppet emperor Henry P'u-Yi.

As it turned out, *Nash Put*'s campaign was unnecessary. Japanese authorities promptly appealed the case to the Hsinking Supreme Court, whose Japanese judges reversed the verdict of the Harbin District Court in July 1936. In February 1937, all six kidnappers were set at liberty. Martinov resumed his duties with the Harbin Municipal Police. Meanwhile, newspapers from *Pravda* to *The New York Times* chorused their outrage. It was this widespread indignation at a miscarriage of justice that Vonsiatsky hoped to utilize against Rodzaevsky. The tactic backfired. Most *soratniki* felt little remorse for the murder of a wealthy Jew and regarded Rodzaevsky's involvement as a regrettable but pardonable excess of zeal. Vonsiatsky, in contrast, came across as philo-Semitic, which hardly won him any support from within the VFP.

Rodzaevsky clearly emerged as the victor of the schism. A vast majority of *soratniki* around the world declared their support for Harbin and broke off contact with Thompson. The Far Eastern fascists retained the official party name—VFP. However distasteful, gestures of cooperation with Semenov paid immediate dividends in terms of Japanese subsidies. The Third Congress of Russian Fascists left Rodzaevsky confident enough of his leadership to ignore *Fashist*'s fulminations. Rodzaevsky also learned that his rival feared neglect more than infamy. He therefore deliberately refrained from responding to Vonsiatsky's attacks. The August 1935 issue of *Natsiya* dismissed Vonsiatsky as a self-promoter full of talk but incapable of action. Thereafter, published references to him dwindled to occasional jokes.

Although bested by Rodzaevsky for leadership of the VFP, Vonsiatsky still held two trump cards—money and imagination—that could create the image if not the substance of a *vozhd*. He determined to use both of these to the best of his ability.

Compensatory Fantasies

To counter stories disseminated from Harbin that he was all talk and no action, Vonsiatsky devised special issues of *Fashist,* starting in January 1935, that were made to look as if they had been clandestinely printed in the bowels of the Kremlin. Above a stylized logo (the name *Fashist* was written so as to form a triangle) ran the slogan:

RED ARMY SOLDIERS!
IN THE EVENT OF WAR,
STICK YOUR BAYONETS IN THE GROUND!

The paper was identified as the underground organ of the Central Executive Committee, All-Russian Fascist National Revolutionary Party of Workers and Peasants, Moscow. The Moscow *Fashist* was smaller than its American counterpart, almost devoid of photographs, and printed on pulp paper (to give it a certain verisimilitude to published material in the USSR). Its first issue contained two articles, both by Vonsiatsky, entitled "What Have Communists Given Russia's People?" (answer: slavery, oppression, famine) and "What Will Fascists Give Russia?" (answer: security, prosperity, justice, pride). The final page of the first issue consisted of a manifesto to the Russian people urging them to disbelieve "Bolshevik lies" about conditions in foreign countries, to prepare for the National Revolution, to form fascist cells, and to read *Fashist.* The manifesto was signed "Kronstadt Fascists," an artful reference to the naval base near Leningrad where sailors had played prominent roles in the revolutions of 1905 and 1917 but had risen against the Bolsheviks in 1921.

Printed at Nineteenth Hole, Moscow *Fashist* was mailed out to subscribers of the regular *Fashist* to demonstrate how active Vonsiatsky was inside the USSR. It is doubtful whether a single copy reached Moscow, unless it was brought there by Soviet authorities for analysis.

Alert to any chance to prove that his agents were indeed active inside the Soviet Union, Vonsiatsky claimed responsibility for what Robert Conquest has called "the crime of the century": the murder of Sergei Kirov, first secretary of the Leningrad Communist Party organization, Politburo member, and rumored chosen heir of Stalin. Kirov was shot in the back around four-thirty in the afternoon of December 1, 1934, moments after he had walked out of party headquarters at Leningrad's Smolny Institute. According to the official Soviet story of the time, Kirov's assassin, Leonid Nikolaev, was acting on behalf of the "leftist" opposition to Stalin led by the fallen party leaders Zinoviev and Kamenev. Trotsky, then living in exile, was named as coconspirator. There were also rumors, publicly expressed only outside the USSR, that Stalin himself had instigated the crime to remove a popular and potentially competitive comrade and to fabricate a pretext for a massive purge of real and imagined enemies within the party.

To Vonsiatsky, the Kirov affair offered a providential opportunity to gain stature throughout the Russian diaspora and particularly vis-à-vis his archrival, Rodzaevsky. Why not appropriate Leonid Nikolaev as his own agent? Accordingly, Anastase hailed Nikolaev's feat in the pages of *Fashist,* leaving the impression that Kirov's death had been decided in Thompson, Connecticut. The gesture did not impress Rodzaevsky, but it did serve Stalin's objectives admirably. At last the Kremlin had grist for its allegations that foreign-supported agents in league with party traitors were assassinating Soviet officials and sabotaging social construction. On December 19, 1934, the *Daily Worker* headlined: WHITE GUARDS ADMIT ASSASSINATION PLOTS AGAINST USSR CHIEFS. *Fashist*'s claims about murder and sabotage within the USSR were accorded prominent attention. Quoting *Izvestiya,* the organ of the American Communist Party predicted that "the shots fired at Comrade Kirov" would result in "the most rapid extermination of fascist terrorists."

But Soviet editors, presumably with approval of the Politburo, evinced more interest in exhibiting than in exterminating Vonsiatsky. On December 25, *Pravda* published a lurid portrait of the Connecticut *vozhd,* calling attention to his reactionary class roots ("son of a gendarmerie colonel"), his counterrevolutionary exploits ("fought in the White Guard army during the Civil War"), his plutocratic in-laws ("married to the daughter of the American steel magnate Norman Rhys [*sic*]"), his Wall Street associations ("has important connections with American capitalists"), and his links with the Rising Sun ("closely tied up with Japanese militarists"). Stalin himself could not have invented a more serviceable bogey. Vonsiatsky was endowed with just the right class, political, and national configuration to personify what the Kremlin was trying with only mixed success to concoct: a credible conspiracy against the Soviet Union.

Führerbunker

Vonsiatsky knew better than anyone that his own terrorist agents were chimerical. Yet that knowledge did not comfort him when it came to worrying about his own safety. Alex regarded himself as a prime target for hit men coming from any number of camps. Surely the NKVD had marked him down for liquidation. Rodzaevsky was perfectly capable of sending Sasha Bolotov on a hunting trip to Thompson. And the Muromsky clan might come over from Europe at any moment to do him in for cheating Lyuba out of an alimony El Dorado.

In public, Vonsiatsky put up a brave front. When Hartford *Courant* reporter Wesley Griswold told him in September 1934, "You undoubtedly realize that your open declaration of war against Communists everywhere involves you in considerable personal danger. You may even be assassinated," the count replied: "What does one life in 20,000 matter? So long as the party moves forward to success, what happens to me is of little concern."

In private, however, Alex was very much concerned about what happened to himself. For all his craving for public exposure, memories of his murdered father haunted him. He ruminated about falling ill in Shanghai, becoming more and more convinced that it had been caused by a deliberately administered dose of poison.

Shortly after returning from the world tour, Anastase decided that it was time to take concrete steps to protect himself. At first, he requested special protection by the Connecticut State Police, but this measure proved unfeasible. He then bought a bulletproof vest, but this too turned out to be an unsatisfactory expedient. The vest was hot, uncomfortable, and hampered his golf swing. It also crimped his gallantry and elicited sly smiles. He finally settled on the idea of making Nineteenth Hole absolutely secure from prowlers.

Vonsiatsky conceived of the Quinnatisset Farm as having an outer and an inner defense line. According to a plan that he and Kunle evolved late in 1934, dogs would guard the perimeter. Subterfuge would take care of the central redoubt.

Early in 1935, a litter of German shepherd pups took up residence in a newly constructed pen south of the main barn. Vonsiatsky trained them as attack watchdogs, occasionally unleashing them against neighborhood strays to test their proficiency. Anastase doted on his canine cohort, supplementing their bone meal with succulent leftovers that Mamedov carried up daily from the Russian Bear. Alex christened each dog with the name of someone whom he admired. The queen of the kennel was a gray bitch called Lady Astor.

To foil would-be assassins who succeeded in breaching Nineteenth Hole's outer defenses, Vonsiatsky came up with an architectural device worthy of a pharaoh's tomb. At the northern end of the Military Room, closest to the main house and farthest from the Gun Room, workmen tore up the floor, leaving a gaping hole that revealed a dark cavity called the milk room (once used to store milk from cows inhabiting the nearby dairy barn). A false wall was built along the north side of the Military Room to conceal the hole but affording access to it through a doorway. Steps were constructed to the milk room below, steps so steep that they could be negotiated only by grasping a handrail. Over these steps was suspended a false staircase made of papier-mâché, which Vonsiatsky could lift up and pass under when he wanted to go below. Any intruder attempting to descend the Potemkin staircase, however, would noisily and painfully crash through the camouflage.

At the foot of the stairs, Vonsiatsky had carpenters convert the milk room into two small offices, accessible only from the Military Room above. The office closest to the base of the stairs was furnished with a desk surmounted by a plaque inscribed A. A. VONSIATSKY. That desk belonged to Kunle, who manfully volunteered to be a decoy. The room beyond, which could be reached only through Kunle's office, was the *sanctum sanctorum*. It contained a desk (with no identifying plaque), a swastika-studded wastebasket, and a red banner set off by a white swastika. Anastase referred to the latter as his "Good Luck John," presumably because it served as his innermost ring of defense, like a guardian deity of a temple.

If not quite as impregnable as Berchtesgaden or as ornate as Palazzo Venezia, Nineteenth Hole could not be surpassed as a castle of quixotic dreams. It was an ideal setting for a man who, shunted aside for leadership of the Russian fascist movement, realized that the semblance of power and glory agreed with him as much as its substance. In this bucolic country retreat, Vonsiatsky steeped himself in a private vision of Russia's liberation from Bolshevism and in the process confounded Nazis, Communists, and the American government alike.

Meanwhile, Konstantin Rodzaevsky was sinking ever deeper into a fatal embrace with the Imperial Japanese Army.

CHAPTER XII

Metastasis

A remarkable expansion of Russian fascist groups is occurring throughout Manchukuo.

JAPANESE CONSUL, MANCHOULI
(November 6, 1936)

Few decades in recent history evoke more ominous images than the 1930s. Americans, staggering under the Depression, wondered increasingly whether the capitalist system could (or even should) survive, and found themselves listening to prophets ranging from radio saint Father Charles Coughlin to Communist presidential candidate Earl Browder. The European democracies, sapped by economic woes, rent by political bickering, and hypnotized by false hopes raised by appeasement stood aside as Mussolini crushed Ethiopia, Franco destroyed the Spanish Republic, and Hitler absorbed the Rhineland, Austria, and most of Czechoslovakia into a rearmed Third Reich. In the USSR, Stalin presided inscrutably over the evisceration of his own party and army while quota-fulfilling judges and NKVD *apparatchiki* herded millions to death in labor camps. Japan, gripped by a security complex and dazzled by messianic visions of a "New Order" in Asia, plunged into a protracted war in China and girded itself for a showdown with the United States and the Soviet Union.

As the world slid toward a brink no less terrible because of its indistinctness, the All-Russian Fascist Party continued to grow. Membership doubled between 1934 and 1938. Branches sprouted in the Americas, Europe, and Africa, far outdistancing the rival network of Vonsiatsky. Newspapers, books, journals, and pamphlets rolled off party presses as never before, flowing along postal arteries to the remotest corners of the Russian diaspora. In Manchukuo, party schools from kindergartens through a higher academy indoctrinated

172

young Russians to be militant fascists. The party won a mandate to wield a degree of authority over the White Russian community.

Yet the growth of the All-Russian Fascist Party did not ensure its independence. Party branches overseas lacked viability. Within Manchukuo, in exchange for subsidies and patronage, the party developed from a small band of outraged youth into a Japanese pawn. Most *soratniki* believed their own slogans about being the nucleus of a White Army and the vanguard of the National Revolution that would liberate Russia, but more astute minds realized that the Russian fascists were in effect Japanese puppets, albeit puppets with the capacity to do a good deal of damage.

Extending the Party Reach: BREM

Although the All-Russian Fascist Party (VFP) could use Blackshirts in the early 1930s to intimidate fellow émigrés, it lacked a "legal" administrative hold over Manchukuo's eighty thousand Russian residents. This situation did not last for long. A few months after the Second Party Congress in April 1934, the Kwantung Army came up with an offer that Konstantin Rodzaevsky could hardly refuse.

Since 1932, the Japanese Military Mission in Harbin, which contained the *Tokumu Kikan* or "Special Services Organ," had been groping for a means to exert more effective control over Manchukuo's Russian population. The task was complicated by the fact that nearly half of the Russians (36,500 out of 80,000 in 1934) carried Soviet passports and were thus outside Manchukuoan (Japanese) jurisdiction. Of course some of these were "radishes" employed by the Soviet-owned Chinese Eastern Railway (CER). Others, however, were fiercely loyal to the USSR and intensely antagonistic to Japan. That left somewhat more than forty thousand "White" Russians (mostly citizens of Manchukuo but including stateless refugees) whom the Japanese wanted to organize into an obedient, anti-Soviet entity.

From 1932 until 1934, *Tokumu Kikan* chief Major General Komatsubara Michitarō and his staff handled the White Russians, more than half of whom lived in Harbin, through Japanese advisers attached to each émigré organization. Major Akikusa Shun fulfilled this function as liaison officer between the *Tokumu Kikan* and the Russian Fascist Party.

Late in 1934, the *Tokumu Kikan* developed plans to create a single organ staffed by Russians invested with broad powers to regulate Manchukuo's White Russians. The organ would of course have a Japanese "adviser," who would guide its operations. Major Akikusa approached Rodzaevsky and Mikhail Matkovsky about the idea, easily persuading both men to support it.

On the evening of December 28, 1934, an extraordinary assemblage convened at the Russian Club (VFP headquarters) at 125 Kitaiskaya. Present were representatives from the major émigré organizations—Legitimists, Armed Services Union, Cossack League—the Harbin Municipal Council, the Manchukuoan government, the Japanese consulate, several newspapers, and local police agencies including the *Kempei*. The meeting had been convened under the pretext of discussing a Japanese offer to build a Russian library. Once assembled, however, the émigré attendants suspected that something far more momentous was in the air.

Speaking in fluent Russian and pausing intermittently to translate his own statements for the benefit of Japanese listeners, Major Akikusa explained that all patriotic émigrés must realize the importance of unity if they really wanted to free their motherland from Bolshevism. In Manchukuo, such unity was to be achieved by the creation of the Bureau of Russian Émigré Affairs (*Biuro po delam Rossiiskikh Emigrantov*, hereafter BREM).

Akikusa paused to take in the effect of his words. No one stirred. He proceeded expansively. Members of all existing societies—political, social, religious—were to be automatically under BREM's purview. BREM, however, was not to become the preserve of any faction. It was to be a truly supraparty organization, run by émigrés for all émigrés. BREM would have its own medical clinics, dining rooms, libraries, and clubs. It would help émigrés materially, give them a sense of mutual solidarity, teach them how to combat Bolshevism within Manchukuo, instruct them in the "kingly way," and prepare them for the epochal task of regenerating their homeland.

Akikusa then turned to an elderly man seated nearby and announced that he would like to introduce BREM's first director: Lieutenant General Veniamin Veniaminovich Rychkov. Rychkov was an old subordinate of Semenov's, who had recently been awarded the honorary post of chief of the "Military Division" of the All-Russian Fascist Party. Like the photogenic onetime RFP *vozhd* General Kosmin, Rychkov was clearly intended to play an ornamental role in BREM. After his death in 1937, Rychkov was followed by a succession of three equally pliable figureheads as directors of BREM, all of them "generals": Alexei Proklovich Baksheev (1937–38), Vladimir Alexandrovich Kislitsyn (1938–44), and Lev Filippovich Vlasevsky (1944–45).

Having completed his presentation, Major Akikusa sat down amid polite applause. The meeting adjourned without further discussion. By this time, nearly three years after Japanese troops had occupied Harbin, seasoned émigrés winced at the major's mellifluous phrases, guessing there was always a great deal that was unstated. But few listeners comprehended at that moment just how much the establishment of BREM would affect their lives.

BREM's administrative structure consisted of seven departments: (1) agricultural settlement, (2) cultural affairs, including public relations, education, physical training, (3) administration and planning, including the issuance of passports, permits, and personal documents, (4) finance, (5) welfare, (6) legal affairs, and (7) military affairs, including veterans' activities and military training for White Russian youth. True to Akikusa's promise, officials were recruited from different émigré groups so as to prevent BREM from falling into the hands of any single faction. Yet fascists and their allies held most of the key positions. Rodzaevsky served concurrently as adviser to successive BREM directors and headed the Second Department (cultural affairs). Matkovsky directed the key Third Department, which issued residence permits, employment cards, and passports required of all White Russians in Manchukuo. Mikhail Nikolaevich Gordeev and Leonid Lvovich Chernykh, chiefs of the Fourth (finance) and Fifth (welfare) departments respectively, were not members of the VFP but came under Matkovsky's influence. The Seventh Department (military affairs) was led by a succession of aging tsarist officers such as General Verzhbitsky.

All BREM officials were responsible to Major Akikusa, who met with them at regular intervals. Also influential was a Russian employee of the Japanese Military Mission in Harbin, Ivan Adrianovich Mikhailov. Mikhailov had formerly served as minister of finance in Admiral Kolchak's short-lived Omsk government of 1919.

By the middle of 1935, BREM was operating in White Russian communities throughout Manchukuo. Branches sprang up in Mukden, Hsinking, Manchouli, Hailar, Aigun, and Pogranichinaya. When Japanese forces occupied north and coastal China in 1937–38, BREM-like organizations were set up under local Japanese military commanders to administer White Russian affairs in Tientsin and Shanghai. Needless to say, VFP *soratniki* were prominently represented in these bodies.

BREM wielded jurisdiction not only over ethnic Russians but over other nationalities who had lived within the old Russian Empire: Ukrainians, Poles, Estonians, Latvians, Lithuanians, Georgians, Armenians, Tartars, and Baltic Germans. Collectively, these non-Russians comprised about 10 percent of Manchukuo's "White Russian" population.

BREM exercised no authority over the 36,000-odd Soviet citizens residing in Manchukuo in 1934. But in 1935 when Japan, using Manchukuo as a front, purchased the Chinese Eastern Railway, the number of Soviet citizens dropped precipitously. More than 25,000 returned to the USSR in the summer of 1935 alone. Only five thousand remained in Manchukuo at the end of 1936 and fewer than a thousand in 1939. Many radishes greeted the CER sale by switching to "White" status, thereby falling within BREM's purview. At the same time, thousands of Whites left Manchukuo for Shanghai, Tientsin, and Peiping. Throughout these demographic ebbs and flows, BREM recorded a slight increase in registrants: from 42,581 in 1935 to 45,295 in 1939.*

Using the authority it wielded in BREM, the VFP quietly expanded its power over White Russians in Manchukuo and to a lesser degree in China. Although Rodzaevsky could exert some influence on Russian schools through the Second Department, it was Mikhail Matkovsky in the Third Department (administration) who could affect the fate of every émigré. Matkovsky took advantage of his position to gather extensive information on every White Russian individual and enterprise in Manchukuo. All émigrés over the age of eighteen were required to register with his department. No one was permitted to move, change jobs, or travel without his department's knowledge and approval. After the Chinese Eastern Railway became a Japanese enterprise (called the North Manchurian Railway or NMR) in 1935, Matkovsky, concurrently an NMR official, screened all prospective employees. Thousands desperate to get out of Manchukuo had no choice but to apply for passports and travel documents from Matkovsky. In her autobiographical novel *Vozvrashcheniye* (Return), Natalya Ilina vividly evoked the dilemma of stateless Russians trapped in Manchukuo. These double refugees (first from Bolshevism, then from

---

* The actual number of White Russians under BREM was in fact greater, because the above figures included only registrants over eighteen years of age.

fascism) knew that only by currying favor with BREM and tearfully protesting their fidelity to the "kingly way" could they secure a chance to escape.

Matkovsky's colleague Gordeev, head of the Fourth Department (finance), instituted a licensing system for émigré commercial ventures from banks to kiosks. To make sure that this regulation was obeyed, BREM inspectors hovered about business establishments.

By 1936, BREM functioned at the heart of a symbiotic relationship between the Military Mission and the All-Russian Fascist Party. The Japanese gained recruits for "antibandit" campaigns and rested secure in the knowledge that Manchukuo's White Russians were following the "kingly way" under their own leaders. The VFP acquired sanctions to impose its will over virtually the entire White Russian community.

BREM also provided a framework for cooperation between the VFP and Japanese businessmen eager for a larger share of the Harbin market. In September 1936, for example, BREM directed all Russian textile and dry goods merchants to obtain their supplies exclusively through the Hiroshimaya concern. In November of the same year, BREM assisted the Japanese in taking over the oldest and most influential retail firm in Manchukuo, E. Y. Tchurin & Company. Rodzaevsky lent his talents to the operation by running articles in *Nash Put* denouncing Tchurin's president, N. A. Kassianov, as a Comintern agent.

However much BREM enhanced VFP power, it contributed little to VFP solvency. Until 1937, BREM's income came from licensing receipts and a lottery. The Harbin Military Mission provided BREM with a 10,000 yen ($3,300) monthly subsidy. This barely sufficed to cover staff salaries and to fund a library, a publishing house, and some water sports facilities along the Sungari. Unable to siphon BREM revenues into the party, the VFP made do by collecting membership dues (one Manchukuoan yuan monthly), holding benefit dances, selling "Anti-Communist Struggle Stamps"—the VFP version of Christmas seals—and hoping for Japanese subsidies. Just how much the Military Mission paid to the VFP is not known. The amount probably varied from year to year but cannot have been very much. Rodzaevsky lived in spartan circumtances in a tiny apartment and wore the same clothes interminably.

In addition to serving in BREM, the All-Russian Fascist Party joined a Japanese-sponsored behemoth called the *Kyōwakai* (Concordia Association). Founded in July 1932 at the behest of Kwantung

Army and civilian idealists, the Concordia Association was orginally designed to mobilize loyalty to Manchukuo and to counteract ethnic particularism under the slogan "harmony among five races" (Manchus, Chinese, Japanese, Koreans, Mongols). Upon its creation, the Concordia Association absorbed all political, social, economic, and cultural organizations in Manchukuo, attaching to each a Japanese adviser, often a Kwantung Army officer. Contrary to the hopes of its founders, however, the Association gradually degenerated into a propaganda and intelligence machine manipulated by Kwantung Army bureaucrats. This mattered little to Rodzaevsky, who welcomed any chance to carve out a VFP niche in the Association's Harbin-based Russian section.

The Russian section was headed by a dignified ornament named Ayunuma Mutsumi. Vice-director Katō Ren'ichi performed the practical liaison work with émigré groups, including the VFP. Rodzaevsky seems to have won Katō's confidence, for he succeeded in having *soratnik* Viktor Abramov installed as a Concordia Association functionary. Meanwhile, the *vozhd* pointedly referred to "VFP-*Kyōwakai* brotherhood" on speaking tours throughout Manchukuo, calculating to magnify the party's stature at the expense of rival émigré organizations. In fact, monarchist and Cossack groups were also represented within the Concordia Association, but that did not deter Konstantin Vladimirovich from verbally appropriating their membership.

Recruitment and VFP-Cossack Friction

A determination to build up VFP membership constantly preoccupied Rodzaevsky. On May 22, 1935, the fourth anniversary of the party's birth, the *vozhd* claimed that he commanded twenty thousand *soratniki*. This figure probably exaggerated VFP strength by a factor of three, but within a year of that boast party membership did actually reach around ten thousand.

Part of this growth accrued from railway employees who joined the VFP after the Soviet-owned CER was sold to Manchukuo in 1935. With Matkovsky issuing work permits and interviewing job applicants for the NMR, very few railway workers felt secure enough to decline an invitation to join the VFP.

During the mid-1930s a demographic shift occurred in Manchukuo's White Russian population, resulting in an increasing proportion living in rural areas. The shift was due mainly to higher birth rates in the countryside and to the exodus of Harbin merchants and professional people to Peiping, Tientsin, and Shanghai. Noting this trend, Rodzaevsky sought to take advantage of it to bolster VFP membership. Using his leverage as head of BREM's Second Department, he solicited schoolteachers throughout Manchukuo's scattered Russian communities to adopt fascist material in their curricula. He also stepped up efforts to recruit youngsters in rural areas. Both of these measures soon brought the VFP into a confrontation with the Cossacks.

Several thousand Trans-Baikal Cossacks lived in small settlements in a broad arc along the Soviet frontier region from Manchouli to Pogranichnaya. Most of them had sought refuge in Manchuria after retreating from Siberia and the Maritime Province in the wake of the White collapse in 1922. Coming with their families and livestock, they preserved their cohesiveness and kept apart from other émigrés. Fiercely independent and generally anti-Communist, they stayed out of politics and—except for one brief but bloody local uprising against the Japanese in 1935—peacefully tended their farms. If they looked upon anyone as a natural leader, it was most likely to be Ataman Grigory Semenov. Living in Dairen, Semenov kept in touch with his followers through the Far Eastern Cossack Union, based in Harbin, and led by General Baksheev.

Historical circumstance seemed repeatedly to throw Rodzaevsky and Semenov together, forcing them into an association that neither man wanted. Other than hatred of communism, they shared very little. Semenov dreamed of dismembering the USSR and setting up an independent Cossack republic in Trans-Baikalia. He distrusted Rodzaevsky as a Russian chauvinist and deprecated his fascism as an unhealthy infatuation with Italy and Germany. Rodzaevsky regarded the ataman as a symbol of the defeated White cause, a hopelessly outdated and parochial boor. Ideologically incompatible and personally antagonistic, the two *vozhds* were obliged by their Japanese patrons to put up a united front. Since 1934, Rodzaevsky had been repeatedly instructed to compose his differences with Semenov. This advice was hard to swallow, especially with Vonsiatsky loudly denouncing Semenov in the very words that Rodzaevsky would have liked to be using himself.

Saddled with constraints, Rodzaevsky resorted to cunning. At the Third Congress of Russian Fascists (June 28–July 7, 1935), he pledged, for the benefit of Japanese monitors in attendance, full cooperation with Semenov, but to his lieutenants he confided that the ataman must be undermined at every opportunity.

Just what the *vozhd* meant soon became apparent as VFP recruiters began appearing in Cossack settlements along the Argun River, appealing to local youth to join the Fascist Vanguard. Before long, Blackshirts and young Cossacks were brawling in Harbin, Hailar, Tsitsihar, and Manchouli while VFP and Semenovite officials traded insults and recriminations in BREM.

Convinced that internal dissension among White Russians violated the spirit of the "kingly way" and jeopardized anti-Soviet projects, the Kwantung Army put its foot down and ordered a permanent reconciliation. On November 22, 1937, under the watchful gaze of several Japanese liaison officers, VFP and Cossack Union leaders met at BREM offices in Harbin. General Kislitsyn, gently anesthetized by old head wounds and vodka, presided over the meeting. Semenov himself came up from Dairen. The ataman sat down with Rodzaevsky and, seconded by Baksheev and Matkovsky respectively, signed a protocol which provided that both sides would henceforth refrain from provocations, coordinate their anti-Soviet activities, pledge not to form alliances with third parties without mutual consent, and work harmoniously within BREM. A Japanese observer described this agreement as a "Fascist-Cossack Alliance."

The 1937 Fascist-Cossack alliance was a palliative. Outwardly, the VFP paid lavish respects to Semenov. *Nash Put* hailed the ataman as a pillar of the "White International" and ranked him with Mussolini, Hitler, and General Araki Sadao as "leaders of new mankind." In January 1938, the All-Russian Fascist Party even changed its name to the Russian Fascist Union (*Rossiisky Fashistsky Soyuz,* or RFS) in an oblique gesture toward the party's new catholicity.

But by this time, fascists and Cossacks alike had learned from their Japanese patrons how to put up a harmonious public front. Beneath the surface, the old feud flourished unabated. Well-behaved as long as they felt themselves under observation, fascists and Cossacks invariably reverted to squabbling as soon as they thought no one was watching.

Exporting Russian Fascism, Manchurian Style

When it came to extending party activities overseas, Rodzaevsky suffered serious disadvantages compared with his American rival,

Anastase Vonsiatsky. Vonsiatsky enjoyed the freedom and mobility accorded by a wealthy wife and an American passport. Rodzaevsky was barely able to feed and clothe himself on capricious Japanese subsidies and could not leave Harbin, let alone cross an international frontier, without Japanese permission. Yet these handicaps did not prevent the Far Eastern *vozhd* from building up an international constituency which by 1938 far surpassed that of his Connecticut counterpart.

When Rodzaevsky began giving serious thought to establishing party branches outside Manchuria in 1931, his eyes fell first upon Tientsin and Shanghai because both cities contained large émigré colonies. But Tientsin and Shanghai presented special problems. Their White Russian denizens were more cosmopolitan and less susceptible to fascist rhetoric than Harbiners. And British and French extraterritorial enclaves, not to mention Chinese sovereignty, restricted the Japanese power upon which Rodzaevsky had been relying to put pressure on fellow émigrés.

In Shanghai, two émigré bureaus claimed to represent local White Russians: the Russian Émigré Committee, led by the former tsarist vice-consul K. E. Metzler, and the Soviet of United Russian Organizations, headed by General F. L. Glebov. Maneuvering between these two, the fascists had managed in 1932 to carve out for themselves a tiny niche in the form of a journal (*Natsiya*) published at Shanghai RFP headquarters on Avenue Joffre. Whatever *Natsiya* might have achieved in propaganda, it produced few flesh and blood *soratniki*. Local conditions were anything but congenial for Rodzaevsky's Shanghai lieutenants, Perminov and Spassky. In 1935, a rival fascist organization materialized, led by Konstantin Steklov, Vonsiatsky's Far Eastern representative. Steklov used his newspaper, *Russky Avangard,* to pillory the VFP as much as to attack the USSR. Then, to compound Rodzaevsky's problems, the dethroned ex-RFP *vozhd* General Kosmin turned up in Shanghai, won a seat on the Russian Émigré Committee, and lost no time in making trouble for his erstwhile *soratniki.* But what really crippled Rodzaevsky in Shanghai was the uncompromising hostility of the thousands of White Russian and Jewish refugees from the "kingly way" in Manchukuo. Their antifascism could not be as easily muffled in Shanghai as it had been in Harbin by the threat of Japanese-sanctioned reprisals.

Rodzaevsky fared better in Tientsin, where local conditions came closer to those of Harbin, particularly after Japan's North China Army occupied the city in August 1937. Under Japanese rule, Tientsin's White Russian colony was administered by the Anti-Communist Committee, a facsimile of BREM. The ACC was entrusted to a hard-drinking Cossack named E. N. Pastukhin. Pastukhin described himself as a journalist and indeed edited a pro-Japanese newspaper called *Vozrozhdeniye Azii* ("Rebirth of Asia"). His coeditor, Ushakov, concurrently led the Tientsin branch of the VFP. Ushakov and his assistant, Karamishev, were able to use their friendship with Pastukhin to wield influence on the ACC. As no émigré living in Tientsin could obtain a passport without first securing a certificate from the ACC, there was ample opportunity for intimidation and forced contributions. Rodzaevsky's aunt, a certain Petrova, lived in Tientsin and seems to have been active in party affairs, although in what capacity is not clear.

In addition to its Chinese branches, the VFP maintained representatives throughout Japan, from Karafuto (southern Sakhalin) in the north to Kagoshima in the south. The Karafuto VFP branch, run by a haberdasher named Sergei Rekonzev, was nothing much to speak of, because there were only six dozen Russians in all of Karafuto. Kobe's VFP unit, under K. V. Shabukhin, claimed several dozen *soratniki* from the city's relatively populous Russian colony. The Tokyo branch was rightfully regarded as the most important next to Harbin itself by virtue of its proximity to the Army Ministry and Imperial Headquarters. Offices were located in Hongō (Yushima 4-chome) near the Nikolai Orthodox Cathedral. From 1932 until 1936, Vasily Petrovich Balykov represented the party in Tokyo, maintaining contact with Japanese patrons such as General Araki Sadao and the ultranationalist Black Dragon Society. The high point of Balykov's career came in April 1934, when he supervised local arrangements for the Rodzaevsky-Vonsiatsky meeting. In 1936, Balykov was succeeded by Nikolai Kipkaev, an enigmatic figure who concurrently worked for the Russian Section of the Imperial Army General Staff.

Rodzaevsky wanted to extend party operations to Europe and America from as early as 1932, and it was partially this desire that led him to write Vonsiatsky in 1933 suggesting that they join forces. Upon expelling Vonsiatsky from the VFP in December 1934, Rodzaevsky made a bold bid to inherit his European and American representatives by issuing a proclamation ordering all overseas branches to terminate ties with Connecticut and deal exclusively with Harbin.

Personal friendship with Vonsiatsky and expectations of his largesse caused a number of VFP branch leaders to hesitate before complying with Rodzaevsky's command. But once the drift of opinion and the limits of Vonsiatsky's pocketbook had become apparent, a majority of *soratniki* opted for the Far Eastern over the American *vozhd*. At the Third Congress of Russian Fascists (June–July 1935), VFP representatives in Germany, Australia, Syria, Yugoslavia, Estonia, and Finland acknowledged—by mail—Rodzaevsky's authority.

Prevented by poverty and Japanese restrictions from traveling abroad, Rodzaevsky used the mail to establish party branches on every continent and in almost every city containing a Russian colony. Finding appropriate local leaders posed a nagging problem, for rarely was it possible to meet the candidate personally. Anyone willing to peddle *Nash Put* qualified for ordinary membership, but for the post of branch leader Konstantin Vladimirovich looked for enterprising, articulate propagandists who could give lectures and recruit followers. Most émigré communities managed to provide at least one candidate. In 1938, party representatives outside the Far East included I. P. Rozhestvensky (Brisbane), T. D. Yanovsky (the Bronx, New York), Dr. Sergei Zolotnitsky (São Paulo), Boris Ern (Asunción, Paraguay), Mikhail Lezhnev (Buenos Aires), I. V. Rychkov (Belgrade), K. P. Kondreev (Sofia), A. S. Mikhailov (Bucharest), Vladimir Shelikhov (Warsaw), and Madame E. Sialskaya (Paris). In the Middle East, the party maintained an "ambassador-at large," who moved between Istanbul and Cairo dispatching articles to *Nash Put* denouncing Zionism under the slogan: "Palestine for the Palestinians!" (VFP policy supported Palestinian Arabs on the premise that they and White Russians shared a common fate of having been driven out of their homelands by "international Jewry").

Rodzaevsky assigned great importance to establishing party representation in Italy and Germany. He regarded Rome and Berlin as fascist meccas and felt that even a nominal VFP presence there conferred spiritual vitality and political legitimacy. Konstantin Vladimirovich dreamed of the day when Hitler and Mussolini would join Japan in overthrowing the Soviets. He would never forgive himself if *soratniki* were not stationed in Berlin and Rome when that momentous day arrived. And he shuddered at the thought that Vonsiatsky might, simply by being on hand, secure some sort of official status as spokesman for all Russian fascists.

It took several years of patient preparation before Rodzaevsky could establish a VFP branch in Italy. Although not unfriendly with

Japan, Mussolini deferred granting recognition to Manchukuo pending the resolution of other issues. Rodzaevsky, meanwhile, tailored party propaganda in a manner that could not fail to please Italians, presuming any of them ever saw it. *Nash Put* and *Natsiya* lauded the Duce as a great ideologist, statesman, and national leader. In 1935–36, both publications hailed the Ethiopian campaign and condemned the League of Nations for interfering in Italy's "national destiny."

Rodzaevsky's goodwill efforts bore fruit shortly after Rome joined the Anti-Comintern Pact (November 6, 1937) and established diplomatic relations with Manchukuo (November 29, 1937). A group of Italian Fascist Party officials visited Manchukuo in the spring of 1938, and Rodzaevsky took advantage of their presence to arrange a gala reception in Harbin. The affair took place on April 29, Emperor Hirohito's birthday, making the occasion doubly festive. The *vozhd* gave the fascist salute to each dignitary, starting with Italian ambassador to Manchukuo Marquis Giacomo Paolucci di Calboli Barone. Within two months, the VFP (by then renamed the RFS) had a representative in Rome: Dmitry Rodionov, president of the "Circolo Russo" on Via delle Colonetti. The "Russian Circle" had a tiny membership, but even a symbolic connection with the Eternal City gratified the boy from Blagoveshchensk.

Although Germany was listed among those countries from which letters of support reached the Third Congress of Russian Fascists, the VFP did not yet have a representative in the Third Reich. Inaugurating operations there posed a severe challenge to Rodzaevsky's ingenuity during the mid-1930s. Nazi racial doctrine defined Slavs as *Untermenschen,* biologically incapable of becoming national socialists. Hitler despised Slavic nationalism, asserting in *Mein Kampf* that Russia's erstwhile greatness rested upon German elements in the prerevolutionary ruling class. Even Alfred Rosenberg, the Russian-born chief of the NSDAP Foreign Policy Office, whom émigrés looked upon as a potential patron, favored Baltic Germans and Ukrainian separatists rather than Russians, for the aspirations of the former fit in with his vision of a dismembered USSR. In addition to Nazi indifference and hostility, the VFP faced established rightist émigré groups in Germany such as the Russian Nazis (ROND) and National Toilers' Alliance (NTS), who could be expected to resent the intrusion of yet another supplicant for the Führer's favors.

The SS, however, did exhibit an interest in Manchukuo's Russian fascists. On October 18, 1935, SS Ministerialdirigenten Dr. Otto Bräutigam, an expert on Russian affairs, presented a report to Heinrich Himmler on émigré political groups around the world. Bräutigam's analysis of the VFP betrayed a curious mixture of acuteness and misinformatión. The party was described as "openly" led by Rodzaevsky but "secretly" commanded by Ataman Semenov. Bräutigam was quite accurate, however, in characterizing it as a "tool of the Japanese General Staff."

Meanwhile, the Gestapo and SD apparently saw no immediately subversive potential in the VFP, for in 1936 Rodzaevsky was finally permitted to open a "Deutsche Sektion" of the "Allrussische Faschische Partei" on Berlin's Würzburger Strasse. G. A. Kozlovsky was appointed local representative and was succeeded in 1937 by A. A. Averkiev, a former ROND member, who moved the party's quarters to Hohenzollerndam.

Nazi tolerance of the VFP may have stemmed from practical considerations. During June 1936, an NSDAP official identified in Japanese documents as Erwin von Schultz visited Dairen, Hsinking, and Harbin, meeting with émigré leaders such as Rodzaevsky and Semenov to determine the anti-Soviet potential of White Russians in Manchukuo. Schultz may have put in a good word in Berlin for the VFP. It is also conceivable that the Stuttgart-based Deutsches Ausland-Institut (DAI) had something to do with the VFP's being allowed to operate within the Reich. Dedicated to maintaining contact with ethnic Germans (*Volksdeutschen*) abroad, the DAI served as an adjunct of the NSDAP Foreign Organization. Of the 197,000 ethnic Germans living in Asia in 1939, 306 resided in Manchukuo (152 of these in Harbin). Almost all of Manchukuo's *Volksdeutschen* came from Imperial Russia's former Baltic provinces and consequently they fell under the jurisdiction of BREM. Given the Russian fascists' power within BREM, the DAI may well have sought their goodwill on behalf of the ethnic Germans by influencing proper authorities in the Reich to acquiesce to a VFP branch in Berlin. Although this connection is conjectural, *Izvestiya* tried to convey such an impression in June 1937 when it accused the Stuttgart Institute of abetting Russian fascists.

In addition to appointing local representatives in each capital, Rodzaevsky wanted a peripatetic factotum who could act on his behalf anywhere in Europe as the need arose. He finally found an eager candidate for such a role in the person of Boris Petrovich Tedli (or Tödtli in German sources).

Of Russian-German extraction, Tedli was born in Kiev in 1901 and harbored ambitions to study medicine until the October Revolution intruded, leaving him eking out a living as a journalist in Bern, Switzerland. During the 1920s, Tedli nursed his shock and anger at what had befallen Russia—and himself—by wallowing in anti-Semitic *Weltschmerz*. He quickly adopted the view fashionable in rightist émigré circles that Jews had been behind the Revolution. In the process, he became an avid devotee of *The Protocols of the Elders of Zion* and of Alfred Rosenberg's *Myth of the Twentieth Century*. He approvingly watched Hitler's rise and, in June 1933, declared himself leader of Russian national socialists in Switzerland. There were, in fact, only two of them: Tedli himself and Rurik von Kotzebue, a thirty-year-old Manchurian-born Baltic German living in Lausanne. From 1933 until 1936, the pair consoled their loneliness by making pilgrimages to the Third Reich to attend anti-Semitic congresses in Erfurt and Nazi Party rallies at Nuremberg.

One can only speculate on how Rodzaevsky and Tedli made contact, but it is clear that their needs were complementary. Each sought to create the image of a puissant Russian fascist organization girdling Europe, although in reality the "organization" consisted of several dingy offices, cartons of pamphlets, and a few sheets of postage stamps.

In April 1936, Tedli began his service for the VFP as its "European leader" and promptly demonstrated his utility by promising Rodzaevsky to supply the Gestapo with incriminating material on Vonsiatsky. Whether Tedli in fact had anything to do with the Gestapo's suppression of Vonsiatsky's handful of followers in the Reich is doubtful, but Harbin seemed to be pleased. In January 1938, Rodzaevsky promoted Tedli to "European and African" leader of the RFS or, as it was known in Germany, the *Bund Russischer Faschisten.*

Tedli took advantage of his grandiose title by moving from Bern to Berlin, leaving von Kotzebue to carry on alone in Switzerland. In Berlin, Boris Petrovich busied himself by trying to upstage ROND führer Bermondt-Avalov and presided hopefully over a gossamer constituency stretching from Cairo to Copenhagen.

CHAPTER XIII

National Revolution
Far Eastern Style

The All-Russian Fascist Party has announced a fascist Three-Year
Plan. This means that towards May 1, 1938—no later and possibly
much earlier—from either external or internal blows, the Soviet
Communist Party will cease to exist.

—NASH PUT, *November 7, 1935*

By the mid-1930s, the All-Russian Fascist Party was operating on
four different levels. On one level, it was a propaganda machine publishing a newspaper, a theoretical journal, and pamphlets, running
schools and clubs, sponsoring lectures, broadcasting radio programs,
and maintaining overseas branches for maximum visibility throughout
the Russian diaspora. On a second level, it was an administrative
body assisting Japanese authorities, through BREM, to control Manchukuo's White Russian minority. On a third level, it was a "Manchurian Mafia," engaged in the narcotics, prostitution, and kidnapping rackets on behalf of certain individuals in the *Kempei*. Finally,
on a fourth level, it was an agency that, with Japanese help, recruited, trained, and dispatched spies and saboteurs into the Soviet
Union.

Operating on the fourth level cost the party most in terms of
human lives. Just how many youthful *soratniki*, burning with Russian
patriotism and loathing of communism, failed to return from missions
into Trans-Baikalia and the Maritime Province will probably never
be known. Only after 1939 did some of the survivors begin to realize
that they were not shock troopers of the National Revolution but
expendable guinea pigs for Japanese Army Intelligence.

187

White Partisans

White partisans began making forays into the Amur and Maritime provinces from Manchurian bases shortly after the Russian Civil War ended in a Bolshevik victory in 1922. These bands were small, each numbering about two or three dozen men. Some consisted of peasants from around Vladivostok who after the Revolution had resettled just inside Manchuria near towns such as Pogranichnaya, located only a few miles from their former homes. Others were made up of veterans—soldiers and Cossacks—who had served under Kolchak or Semenov. Lacking supplies and coordination, the partisans operated haphazardly in sparsely populated areas close to the Manchurian frontier: around Lake Khanka (just north of Vladivostok), along the Ussuri River at Iman, along the Amur River between Khabarovsk and Blagoveshchensk, and beyond the Argun River toward Nerchinsk and Sretensk. Rarely did White partisans do more than momentarily occupy isolated hamlets and kill a few "commissars." Their activities suffered at the hands of increasingly efficient GPU border troops, called *pogranichniki,* and GPU agents who infiltrated Manchuria to assassinate White partisan leaders. The high mortality rate reduced, but did not eliminate, young volunteers ready to risk any odds for a chance to return to their homeland and strike a blow at the hated Bolsheviks.

During the 1920s, any number of individuals attempted to weld these disparate bands into a single partisan movement under a unified command. Harbin crawled with would-be unifiers, each claiming that he alone possessed the ability and credentials for the task. From Paris came K. K. Shubert, dispatched by the Supreme Monarchist Council. General N. P. Sakharov insisted that he represented the personal will of ex-Russian Army commander and tsarist pretender Grand Duke Nikolai Nikolaevich. The Berlin-based Brotherhood of Russian Truth had its local activist on hand, General Dmitry Kosmin. The Far Eastern branch of the Russian Armed Services Union, led by Generals M. K. Diterikhs (Dietrichs) and G. A. Verzhbitsky, asserted that it was their exclusive prerogative to organize a White partisan front. None of these claimants succeeded, first because they refused to cooperate with each other, and secondly because local partisan leaders did not trust them. Ironically, it was the Kwantung Army rather than any Russian leader that eventually imposed its will over all White partisans in the Far East and transformed them into instruments of Japanese continental strategy.

The Japanese Army had begun conducting intelligence operations in Siberia as early as the 1890s, when spies masquerading as Chinese and Korean workers collected information on the progress of the Trans-Siberian Railway, then under construction. There were also agents among Japanese prostitutes plying their trade in railroad camps and Amur River ports. Siberia had had its own Mata Hari—O Kiku, the siren of Blagoveshchensk. At this time, a certain heroic and exotic aura attached itself to Japanese intelligence missions in Siberia, particularly that of Captain Fukushima Yasumasa, who rode solo on horseback from Berlin to Vladivostok (1892–93), passing through the Urals and Outer Mongolia and then following the Amur and Ussuri rivers to the Sea of Japan. Before and after the Russo-Japanese War, *shishi* ("men of spirit") and *tairiku rōnin* ("continental adventurers"), many of them members of the ultranationalist Black Dragon Society* made forays into the Russian Far East, sometimes sharing their discoveries with army authorities. The Siberian Intervention (1918–22) provided Japanese military personnel with a rare opportunity to reconnoiter, without hindrance, Trans-Baikalia, Amuria, and the Maritime Province. Although the Intervention turned out to be domestically unpopular and diplomatically damaging for Japan, it bequeathed a generation of Siberian experts who for the next quarter-century served in the Russian Section of the Second Department (Intelligence) of the Imperial Army General Staff and its field arm, the Harbin *Tokumu Kikan.* Japanese troops may have evacuated Vladivostok in 1922, but *Tokumu Kikan* agents (some of them Chinese and White Russians) continued to operate on Soviet soil.

The Harbin *Tokumu Kikan* recruited émigrés for intelligence assignments virtually from the time of its inception in 1918. Toward the end of the 1920s, White Russians came to be seen as having a greater potential than as merely gatherers of information. In 1928, Major Kanda Masatane drew up plans for White Russian-conducted sabotage in the Soviet Far East. Yet the *Tokumu Kikan* was not in a position to recruit Russians on a large scale until the Kwantung Army occupied Harbin in 1932.

In 1932, the Harbin *Tokumu Kikan* was made field headquarters for Imperial Army intelligence and counterintelligence operations against the Soviet Union. Newly appointed *Tokumu Kikan* chief Major

---

* Popular but misleading English name for the *Kokuryūkai* (literally Amur River Society), founded in 1901 by Uchida Ryōhei and Kuzuu Tōkai. As its name implies, the *Kokuryūkai* promoted Japanese expansion to the Amur River.

General Komatsubara Michitarō, who had been a military attaché in Moscow from 1927 to 1929, lost no time in approaching General Verzhbitsky with a proposition to unify all White partisan bands under Japanese guidance. The scheme foundered for several reasons. Essentially, the *Tokumu Kikan* wanted to transform partisans into spies, something that a combatant like Verzhbitsky could not countenance. Nor did Verzhbitsky, at least at this stage, relish forfeiting his independence to some Japanese commander. Finally, General Komatsubara soon realized the difficulty of coordinating the fiercely autonomous formations of peasants, Cossacks, and tsarist army veterans scattered around Manchukuo's perimeter. For the time being, the *Tokumu Kikan* limited itself to recruiting and training White Russians on a piecemeal basis.

The recruitment of White Russians by Japanese Army Intelligence coincided with an intensification of Soviet espionage in Manchuria. Agents of the OGPU (NKVD after 1934) packed Harbin's Beaumonde and Yara cafes, secure in their diplomatic immunity. This is not to say, however, that all Soviet citizens escaped harassment. Until the Chinese Eastern Railway was sold to Manchukuo in 1935, CER personnel (who carried Soviet passports) were chronically detained as "Comintern agents."* In 1936, an employee of the Soviet-owned Far Eastern Bank *(Dalbank)* succumbed under suspicious circumstances in Japanese custody. When such incidents occurred, they inevitably sparked loud protests from Moscow and critical publicity in the United States. But no one raised an eyebrow if some White Russian stopped a GPU bullet or vanished into the "second floor" of Harbin's *Kempei* building.

White Russians bore the brunt of Soviet-Japanese intelligence sparring. As stateless refugees or as citizens of Manchukuo (which was practically the same thing), they were utterly vulnerable. No government protected them. No consuls remonstrated on their behalf. Their precarious status made them even more suspect. Soviet authorities suspected them of being Japanese minions. Japanese authorities were quick to see reverse radishes (white outside, red inside) among them. Cossacks settled in frontier areas were particularly liable to double jeopardy. Hardly had Argun Cossacks recovered from Soviet

---

* After being repatriated to the USSR in 1935, ex-CER employees found themselves under suspicion of being Japanese agents. Untold numbers were arrested and sent to labor camps.

commando raids in the 1920s when they reeled under Japanese pacification campaigns in the 1930s. Even while oppressing White Russians, Soviet and Japanese security organs adeptly exploited their economic destitution and outraged patriotism for strategic purposes. The émigré was everybody's cat's-paw, and the Russian fascists were no exception.

National Revolution by 1938

On May 22, 1935, in a speech commemorating the fourth anniversary of the RFP (VFP since 1934), Konstantin Rodzaevsky made a portentous prediction: that the National Revolution would occur in the USSR by May 1, 1938. His speech started out by asserting that the VFP had "20,000 activists" in Manchukuo alone, an achievement that marked the end of the fascist movement's first stage: "the preparation and rallying of forces." The second stage, he continued, was to be a "Fascist Three-Year Plan" to "liquidate Jewish rule over the Russian land" and to bring the VFP to power no later than May 1, 1938.

The *vozhd* spelled out his formula for taking over the USSR at the Third Congress of Russian Fascists, which took place one month later. It entailed five points: (1) intensification of fascist propaganda activities; (2) coordination of Manchukuo's White Russians under the VFP; (3) closer cooperation with Germany and Italy; (4) closer ties with Japan; and (5) infiltration into the Soviet Union to make contact with "anti-Stalinist elements." The fulfillment of these five points, coinciding with the failure of the "Jewish" Soviet Second Five-Year Plan (1932–37), would enable the VFP to assume leadership of a spontaneous Russian National Revolution estimated to erupt early in 1938.

In the summer of 1935, the party seemed to be making fair progress toward attaining four of the five goals. Propaganda was being turned out at a high pitch in VFP schools, publications, and even VFP radio braodcasts beamed to the USSR from a station in Tsitsihar. Through BREM and the Concordia Association, the VFP was "coordinating" Manchukuo's White Russians. The party did not yet have a representative in Berlin, but prospects looked good for opening a branch in Rome. Relations with Major General Andō Rinzō, General Komatsubara's successor as chief of the Harbin *Tokumu Kikan,* were civil, and Rodzaevsky's friendly mentor Major Akikusa Shun continued to act as party counselor. Konstantin Vladimirovich, moreover, enjoyed the personal friendship of General Araki Sadao, the idol of idealistic young army officers and leading figure of the Japanese Army's "Imperial Way Faction," which sought a showdown with the USSR. The *vozhd* also basked in the favor of Japan's godfather of godfathers, the ultranationalist *kuromaku* (wirepuller), Tōyama Mitsuru. In 1935, Tōyama sent a Black Dragon Society trusty named Tomita to Harbin with a samurai sword to present to Rodzaevsky as a token of his esteem, and with a message that he sympathized with the Russian fascist movement and hoped that it would succeed in its anti-Soviet struggle.

However well the VFP was doing on points one through four, point five—infiltration into the USSR and contact with anti-Stalinist elements—proved to be a major stumbling block. Rodzaevsky's brave words notwithstanding, the party did virtually nothing to penetrate the USSR during the remainder of 1935 and the first half of 1936.

VFP inactivity inside the USSR resulted not from any lack of will or courage but rather from a Japanese veto. For the time being, the *Tokumu Kikan* wanted information, not sedition. Although the party was barred from sending its own propaganda and sabotage teams into the USSR, the *Tokumu Kikan* did recruit individual VFP members, usually youngsters just out of high school, and trained them to slip across the frontier to gather data on Red Army troop deployments. These *soratniki* found themselves part of a composite group of Koreans and White Russians working as professional scouts for Japanese Army Intelligence, not for the National Revolution.

However nonrevolutionary, this illicit penetration angered Moscow. In April 1936, Ambassador Konstantin Yurenev lodged a strong protest in Tokyo about Japanese sponsorship of White Russian "terrorism" inside the USSR. A Foreign Ministry spokesman, Horinouchi Kensuke, blandly replied that Moscow should seek satisfaction from the Manchukuoan government, because Japan had nothing to do with such activities and was "greatly embarrassed to intervene in Manchukuoan affairs." This answer, as can be imagined, did not satisfy Moscow. Tension mounted along the Manchukuo-Soviet frontier as diplomats traded ever more strongly worded notes.

Sometime during the summer of 1936, the *Tokumu Kikan* seems to have changed its policy about what type of operations could or could not be conducted within the USSR. It now took a broader view of "intelligence" so as to encompass propaganda and sabotage as well as information gathering. What caused this departure from the *Tokumu Kikan*'s strict adherence to "pure" intelligence can only be surmised. Whatever the stimulus, the new orientation gave the Russian fascists a chance to test their strength within their motherland.

In September 1936, a *Tokumu Kikan* officer named Major Suzuki* approached Rodzaevsky with a proposition to form a VFP commando unit trained and equipped by Japanese experts for propaganda and sabotage assignments in eastern Siberia. The unit would also establish a "fascist underground" wherever it operated. Rodzaevsky leapt at the offer and appointed one of his aides, Matvei Platonovich Maslakov, to work with Suzuki on the project.

By the end of October, Suzuki and Maslakov had enlisted several dozen young *soratniki* and had given them rudimentary training in marksmanship, shortwave radio transmission, and explosives. Early in November, the unit divided into several teams and crossed the Manchukuo-Soviet frontier at widely scattered points. Their mission: to create a disturbance on November 7, the nineteenth anniversary of the October Revolution.

Half of the teams were intercepted and annihilated at the frontier by *pogranichniki*. One team managed to cross the Amur not far from Blagoveshchensk and spent some time roaming the Zeya (an Amur tributary) district, cutting telephone lines and shooting at people. Only one team reached its assigned destination. After slipping into Trans-Baikalia near Junction 86 (a border station where the North Manchurian Railway from Harbin met a spur from the Trans-Siberian), a half-dozen VFP commandos made their way along the tracks for 250 miles to Chita, a fair-sized (102,555 population in 1939) provincial capital and army base which during the Civil War had served as Ataman Semenov's headquarters.

Mixing inconspicuously with holiday throngs that had gathered to watch the November 7 parade and to hear local party leaders commemorate the anniversary of the Revolution by eulogizing Stalin, the commandos noiselessly passed out handbills denouncing the leader as a criminal. For a few moments, recipients of the handbills were

---

* Major Suzuki seems to have succeeded Major Akikusa as counselor to the VFP after Akikusa's promotion to lieutenant colonel and transfer to the General Staff's Second Department (Intelligence) in Tokyo early in 1936.

too incredulous, confused, and scared to do anything. Within minutes, word reached security officials that someone was spreading seditious material. NKVD squads, reinforced with soldiers, swooped down on the crowds, arresting anyone found with an incriminating pamphlet. Before long, downtown Chita resembled an ant colony reacting to an intrusive termite, but by this time, the commandos had scurried from the scene and were making their way overland toward Manchukuo.

Determined not to be left out of the action, Rodzaevsky had alerted his *soratniki* in Harbin to prepare for an assault on the Soviet consulate timed to coincide with commando operations on November 7. The *Tokumu Kikan,* in a venturesome mood, not only gave its approval but coached the *vozhd* on where to deploy his Blackshirts for a breakthrough into the consulate compound. But local Japanese consular officers learned what was in the air and set about trying to squelch it. The Foreign Ministry had no desire to be handed another crisis just because some Army "Lawrences" wanted to provoke the USSR. In this case, unlike many others, Foreign Ministry intervention proved effective. On November 7, Harbin Municipal Police ringed the consulate precincts so densely that VFP Blackshirts could not even approach them.

Although not quite an overture to the National Revolution, the events of November 7, 1936, gave Rodzaevsky considerable satisfaction. He could now assert, with little exaggeration, that Russian fascists had disrupted the most hallowed Communist ritual right under the nose of the NKVD. He could read fulminations in *Amurskaya Pravda,* published right in his home town, Blagoveshchensk, about "fascist terror bands" ravaging the Zeya hinterland. He could listen to reports of massive detentions in Chita as NKVD henchmen hunted for fifth columnists among the local inhabitants. Yet Rodzaevsky's satisfaction came at a high price. Half of the VFP commandos did not return.

Harbin itself was already in the midst of a mini war scare on the eve of the raids. On November 7, Shanghai's *China Weekly Review* speculated, with tongue firmly in cheek, that a run on gas masks in Harbin was boosting the Japanese rubber industry. What brought about the scare is not clear, but the raids no doubt added to it.

When Tokyo announced on November 26, 1936, that Japan and Germany had concluded an Anti-Comintern Pact, pledging their cooperation against international communism, Rodzaevsky could practically hear the drums of the National Revolution summoning him to immortality.

But the drums that Rodzaevsky thought he heard portended a destiny rather different from the one he had in mind. For one thing, contrary to losing his grip over Russia, Stalin tightened it as the NKVD purged real and imaginary opponents and intimidated the entire population into fawning credulity or terrified submission. For another, the General Staff and Kwantung Army gradually revised their thinking about how to employ Manchukuo's White Russian militants. Specifically, the *Tokumu Kikan* came to envision a purely military role for its fascist protégés, a role calculated exclusively to fulfill Japanese strategic objectives rather than White Russian visions.

These currents took place against a background of deepening Japanese involvement in China south of the Great Wall during 1937–38. After full-scale hostilities had erupted with Chiang Kai-shek on July 7, 1937, few Japanese military planners saw any possibility of action against the Soviet Far East until the "China Incident" was solved. At the same time, Soviet-Japanese relations deteriorated in the wake of the Anti-Comintern Pact. The Nationalist-Communist anti-Japanese united front, coupled with Soviet military aid to Chiang, reinforced convictions among Kwantung Army officers that the USSR was still Japan's ultimate enemy. Unable to launch a full-scale strike northward yet keen to test Soviet strength, the Kwantung Army resorted to probing selected points along the Soviet-Manchukuo and Manchukuo-Outer Mongolia frontiers. For this exercise, White Russians came in handy, particularly if they were willing to face death.

The Asano Brigade

Of the thousands of White Russian soldiers who sought refuge in China following their defeat in the Civil War, a number had become mercenaries. Shantung warlord Chang Tsung-chang hired a Russian detachment under General Nechaev for campaigns against his rivals in North China. After seizing Manchuria in 1931–32, the Kwantung Army followed this precedent and recruited both White Russian units and individuals. But the terms of employment differed in one important respect. Under the Chinese, White Russians fought for pay and knew it. Under the Japanese, White Russians believed they were fighting for a National Revolution that would destroy Bolshevism and let them return to their homeland. Herein lay a tragic illusion which neither the Kwantung Army nor the General Staff did anything to dispel.

At first, the Kwantung Army tried to tap the White Russian military potential by enlisting émigré leaders as recruiters. In the summer of 1932, *Tokumu Kikan* chief Major General Komatsubara Michitarō requested RFP *vozhd* General Kosmin to raise an armed detachment. Komatsubara assured Kosmin that the detachment would constitute a nucleus of a "White Army" in Manchukuo and would someday play an important role in a Soviet-Japanese war. Kosmin gladly consented and formed two units of several hundred men each. These were assigned to guard duty on the Mukden-Shanhaikwan and Kirin-Lafachan railroads. Shortly afterward, Komatsubara asked Kosmin to recruit additional units. The general again complied, dreaming of that "White Army." The newly raised levies wound up hunting Chinese and Korean guerrillas around Hailin and Muling, roughly midway between Harbin and Vladivostok. Kosmin's formations were duplicated by monarchist and Cossack units, employed by the Japanese for similar purposes.

Toward the end of 1936, Colonel Kawabe Torashirō, a Kwantung Army staff officer, conceived of the idea of uniting disparate émigré detachments into a single White Russian combat unit. Such a unit would be drawn from the population as a whole, and its rank and file would take orders from Japanese officers or their appointees, rather than from existing émigré leaders. Toughened and disciplined by Kwantung Army officers, the new unit could make valuable contributions in espionage and sabotage. After securing the approval of his superiors, Kawabe took the idea to Harbin *Tokumu Kikan* chief Major General Andō Rinzō, who agreed to cooperate. During 1937, a *Tokumu Kikan* Russian specialist took charge of making Kawabe's idea a reality. Early in 1938 the new unit came to life. It was called the Asano Brigade, named after its Japanese adviser, Colonel Asano Takashi.

The Asano Brigade was based at Erchan ("second station"), a hamlet on the Sungari River sixty miles upstream from Harbin. Russians called the place Sungari Two. Originally composed of two hundred men, the brigade soon expanded into five companies totaling seven hundred soldiers.

As with all White Russian groups since 1931, the Asano Brigade was advised by a Japanese officer. But here all similarity to precedent ended. Colonel Asano was responsible to Kwantung Army headquarters in Hsinking rather than to the Harbin *Tokumu Kikan.* This arrangement reflected the brigade's official status as a unit in the Manchukuoan Army. Although under direct Kwantung Army control, the brigade was designed to look like a Manchukuoan affair. Pay came from the Manchukuoan Ministry of War, and the brigadiers wore Manchukuoan uniforms, except when they were on special missions.

Determined to prevent any single White Russian faction from dominating the Asano Brigade, the Kwantung Army selected an Armenian to lead it. Gurgen Nagolen was as tough as his short, swarthy appearance suggested. He had dropped out of Harbin's Juridical Institute in the late 1920s to work with the CER Railway Police. Sensing opportunity in the political winds of 1932, Nagolen enlisted in the newly formed puppet Manchukuoan Army and was quickly promoted to major on the instructions of Japanese advisers impressed with his understanding of the "kingly way." In the Asano Brigade, he held the rank of colonel.

A Russian nationalist like Konstantin Rodzaevsky had no desire to see his *soratniki* serving under some Armenian, but the Japanese knew how to make him discover that desire. In March 1938, *Tokumu Kikan* chief Major General Higuchi Kiichirō invited the *vozhd* to his private residence for (in Rodzaevsky's words) a "heart to heart talk" about burying petty differences with other émigré groups in order to undertake the great task of destroying communism. Higuchi expertly plucked the strings of Rodzaevsky's ambitions and anxieties. Japan planned, he confided, to turn the Soviet Far East into a White Russian buffer state in which the fascists could play an important role. But that role depended upon how well the fascists functioned within the Asano Brigade. Higuchi's successor, Major General Hata Hikosaburō, reiterated this double-edged message in 1939, as did envoys from General Araki, then minister of education, and General Itagaki Seishirō, coarchitect of the 1931 Mukden incident, appointed Army minister on June 3, 1938.

Rodzaevsky took his patrons' advice without quibbling. He had little choice but to accede to recommendations that emanated from people who could ensure—or foreclose—his future. Accordingly, he publicly hailed the Asano Brigade and visited Sungari Two to pay respects to its commander. Inwardly, he gritted his teeth and prayed for better times. It was bad enough to work with Semenov. Now there was also an Armenian gendarme. Who would be next?

To funnel Russian Fascist Union youngsters into the Asano Brigade, Rodzaevsky appointed Lev Okhotin to take charge of recruitment within the party. Okhotin was a burly, two-hundred-pound lad of twenty-seven who had only just joined the RFS himself. His zeal and efficiency had caught the *vozhd*'s eye, and Rodzaevsky made Okhotin his personal secretary. He also saw to it that Okhotin's wife, Nina Grigorevna, succeeded Sheina Rumiantseva* as first lady of the All-Russian Women's Fascist Movement.

The Kwantung Army lost no time in putting the Asano Brigade to work on hazardous assignments that, because of their secrecy, brought not even posthumous glory. Members of the Brigade donned Red Army uniforms and slipped across the frontier to reconnoiter Soviet positions. Occasionally, they staged a "Soviet provocation" by opening fire on Manchukuoan territory, a ruse to which the Red Army was no stranger. Lacking advanced training and identification papers, these infiltrators were extremely vulnerable within the USSR. If apprehended, they were shot as traitors, even though some of the younger brigadiers had been born in Manchuria.

With the *Kempei* watching its members in Manchukuo, the NKVD hunting them down in the USSR, and an Armenian giving them orders, it is hardly surprising that the Asano Brigade suffered a high attrition rate. But there seemed always a fresh supply of Russian youths to fill in the decimated ranks.

Escalating tension along the Manchukuo-Outer Mongolia and Manchukuo-Soviet frontiers during 1938–39 gave Asano Brigade members ample opportunity to prove themselves under fire. Their most spectacular ordeal came in fighting at a place called Nomonhan (or Khalkin Gol) on the Mongolian-Manchurian plain, from May to September 1939. Prominent among the Japanese forces participating was the Kwantung Army's 23d Infantry Division, commanded by former Harbin *Tokumu Kikan* chief General Komatsubara Michitarō, and an unrecorded number of Asano troops served under General Komatsubara as scouts, infiltrators, and interpreters. They found themselves in the midst of a slaughter. Outmaneuvered and encircled by Soviet heavy tanks with flame throwers, entrenched Japanese infantry were

---

* Wife of Boris Rumiantsev, cofounder of the RFO (1925), who quit the RFP in 1932.

exterminated like gophers on the flat, treeless steppe. The 23d Division took the heaviest losses of any Japanese unit: 11,124 of its 15,140 men fell in ten days of combat. It is not recorded how many, if any, White Russian auxiliaries survived.

Japanese censorship kept the Nomonhan disaster a secret until after World War II. At the time of the battle, thousands of Manchukuo's White Russians, hearing bulletins of Kwantung Army victories over Red forces at Nomonhan, leapt with anticipation of a Soviet-Japanese war. But these hopes were to be cruelly disappointed.

Seeds of Disillusion

By 1939, Konstantin Rodzaevsky was beginning to have doubts about the future of the Russian fascist movement. Part of his discouragement came from sheer fatigue. Only thirty-two, he was aging prematurely. Incessant demands from multiple Japanese patrons, chronic rivalry with other émigré groups, and factionalism within his own party, not to mention the ever present possibility of assassination, were taking a toll on his nerves. External events further eroded his once unshakable optimism. Despite all his efforts, the Russian Fascist Union was no closer to taking over the USSR in 1939 than had been the Russian Fascist Party in 1931. The deadline for Russia's delivery from communism, May 1, 1938, had come and gone without the slightest sign of a National Revolution. Of course in public Rodzaevsky explained the nonoccurrence of the National Revolution as a consequence of Stalin's purges, which had eliminated Marshal Tukhashevsky and other senior Red Army officers "who had been planning the end of the Comintern." Yet specious arguments could not blot out the now humiliating memory of all those confident predictions made back in 1935.

Nearly the only putative achievement of which Rodzaevsky could boast was the defection of the Far Eastern NKVD chief, General G. S. Lyushkov, in June 1938. Lyushkov had walked into Manchukuo after staging a bogus inspection of the frontier area near Vladivostok. His defection was a prize plum for the *Tokumu Kikan,* and *Nash Put* tried to propagandize it as an anti-Communist ideological victory. But Lyushkov had bolted to save his skin, not to express any ideological convictions. He had smelled danger when notified by Moscow that a new man was coming to replace him as head of the NKVD in the Far East. Since Lyushkov had liquidated his own predecessor upon arriving in Khabarovsk a year before, his premonitions were perhaps justified.

The failure of the National Revolution to occur in 1938 reinforced Rodzaevsky's long-standing belief that an external blow was imperative to topple the Soviet regime. By external blow, Rodzaevsky had in mind a simultaneous attack on the USSR by Japan and Germany. This line of thinking grew ever more insistent in the *vozhd*'s calculations until by 1939 he regarded a German-Japanese military alliance as essential to ultimate victory.

Soviet-Japanese and Soviet-German relations in early 1939 were indeed strained, but prospects for a German-Japanese military alliance looked uncertain, largely as a result of disagreements within the Japanese leadership. Kwantung Army and some General Staff officers, civilian ultranationalists, and some factions within the bureaucracy, including the Foreign Ministry, favored an alignment with the Reich. But the Navy, dominant factions in the Foreign Ministry, business and financial circles, and the influential elder statesman Prince Saionji Kinmochi all had deep reservations about tying Japan to Adolf Hitler. These divisions were mirrored inside the Russian Fascist Union.

Rodzaevsky's pro-Nazi orientation brought him into conflict with Mikhail Matkovsky. Suave and soft-spoken, Matkovsky commanded increasing respect among Russians and Japanese alike for his tactful realism and efficient management of BREM's Third Department. Although not an ideologist, he attracted a personal following among party intellectuals such as Vladimir Kibardin, a short, scholarly blond who worked in BREM; Sergei Razhev, a *Nash Put* editor; and Gennady Taradanov, an instructor at the Higher Party School and author of *Azbuka Fashizma*. Shortly after the Third Party Congress in 1935, these men formed the core of what came to be known as the "Matkovsky group" within the VFP/RFS. The Matkovsky group regarded itself as more literate and more practical than the party mainstream. It doubted the value of anti-Semitism, deplored Blackshirt excesses, and shunned collaboration with seedier Japanese patrons such as *Kempei* operator Kostya Nakamura. The group's relations with Rodzaevsky, never intimate, grew strained in 1939 over the issue of whether to pursue closer ties with Nazi Germany.

The Rodzaevsky-Matkovsky split surfaced at the Fourth (and last) Congress of Russian Fascists, held in Harbin during January 21–23,

1939. Compared with its predecessors, this assemblage was poorly attended and acrimoniously conducted. Only three dozen delegates from Manchukuo, Shanghai, Tientsin, Korea, and Japan gathered at a building on Diagonalnaya Street* under the watchful eyes of a *Tokumu Kikan* adviser. The Congress had little to celebrate. RFS membership had fallen off since 1938 when the National Revolution had failed to occur, and party ranks had been further depleted by an exodus of White Russians from Harbin to Tientsin and Shanghai. Such unfavorable developments prompted the Matkovsky group to speak out boldly.

Describing Hitler as an enemy of Russia and of all Slavs, Matkovsky and his followers proposed that the RFS could recoup its dwindling constituency in the emigration only by severing ties with the Nazis and by dropping the swastika from the party emblem. They appealed to the assembled delegates to seek alliances with other anti-Communist Russian organizations throughout the diaspora, such as the National Toilers' Alliance (NTS). They criticized the party's financial management and concluded with a direct slap at the *vozhd* by calling for "new leadership."

While most of the delegates granted these motions a cold reception, Rodzaevsky, nonetheless, did not succeed in persuading the Congress to adopt an openly pro-German platform. The Fourth Party Congress adjourned without taking any noteworthy action except to pass a resolution protesting to Manchukuoan authorities for assisting Jewish refugees arriving from Europe via the Trans-Siberian Railway. A pall of disappointment hung over the delegates as they dispersed. Both Rodzaevsky and Matkovsky had lost stature within the party. And neither trusted the other thereafter.

Shaken by party morbundity and internal disaffection, Rodzaevsky resolved to get a new mandate for his leadership from Tokyo. Taking advantage of his position in BREM—chief of the Second Department—he organized a tour of Japan for White Russians. Between April 17 and May 2, 1939, while his charges were sightseeing about Tokyo, Rodzaevsky called on influential figures actually or potentially sympathetic to his cause.

He first looked up Akikusa Shun. As a Russian specialist in the Harbin *Tokumu Kikan* from 1932 to 1935, Major Akikusa had been attached to the RFP/VFP as counselor. By 1939, he had been trans-

* Party headquarters had moved from 125 Kitaiskaya to the Diagonalnaya in 1937.

ferred to Tokyo, promoted to full colonel, and appointed director of the Reconnaissance Officers' Training School, a cover name for what later became known as the "Nakano School" for spies and saboteurs. Colonel Akikusa agreed to help Rodzaevsky tell selected Japanese officials about the Russian Fascist Union. For the next ten days, the two men visited a veritable who's who among proponents of an "active" policy toward the Soviet Union: Army Minister General Itagaki Seishirō, leading member of the so-called "Manchurian faction" within the Imperial Japanese Army; General Hayashi Senjūrō, former Army minister and prime minister then living in retirement; Matsuoka Yōsuke, the mercurial, American-educated president of the South Manchurian Railway Company; Miyata Mitsuo, ex-superintendent of the Metropolitan Police and famous hunter of domestic Communists; and two members of Prime Minister Hiranuma's cabinet: Colonization Minister General Koiso Kuniaki and Education Minister General Araki Sadao. Rodzaevsky had never met Koiso before, but the general had known about Russian fascists since serving as Kwantung Army chief of staff in 1932–34. A proponent of Japanese penetration of Manchuria and Mongolia since 1913, Koiso appreciated Rodzaevsky's collaboration and promised to support RFS anti-Soviet activities to the best of his ability. Araki, of course, could almost be counted as a personal friend of Rodzaevsky's. The two had first met in 1934 and had corresponded ever since. Araki, like Koiso, pledged his support for the RFS.

Finally, Rodzaevsky had the privilege of a personal interview with Tōyama Mitsuru, venerable head of the ultranationalist Black Dragon Society. Rarely seen in public, Tōyama's influence was hard to measure but widely felt. For nearly six decades, he had been threatening politicians, milking businessmen, and mobilizing superpatriots, yet was reputed to be a man of modesty and simplicity. At eighty-four, he was almost a living legend. Tōyama, after expressing sympathy and support for the RFS, posed with the *vozhd* for a photograph.

Rodzaevsky returned to Harbin in May, full of Japanese promises but with not a single concrete commitment. Hardly had he unpacked when reports of fighting between Kwantung Army and Outer Mongolian units at a place called Nomonhan began appearing in the press. By mid-June, the Nomonhan affair had escalated into a pocket war involving Soviet air and armored units.

Reading about the fighting at Nomonhan, Rodzaevsky sensed that this was not simply another border fracas. The commitment of such heavy forces by both sides could only indicate that Japan and the USSR were on the verge of all-out war. If that were the case, the day of Russia's delivery from Bolshevism was at hand.

Starting in July, *Nash Put* predicted the imminent formation of a German-Italian-Japanese alliance against the USSR and called for a "Far Eastern National Front" under RFS guidance to prepare White Russians for the National Revolution. On August 20, the day of a massive Red Army attack that left the Nomonhan plain dotted with burning tanks and rotting corpses, a Soviet-Japanese war appeared to be only a matter of days, if not hours, away.

Such prospects evaporated overnight in one of the most dramatic political realignments in history. On August 21, 1939, Germany and the Soviet Union announced that they had agreed to conclude a non-aggression pact. Signed on August 23, the pact provided not only for the abstention of either party from attacking the other, but for neutrality of either party should the other come under attack from a third country. Moreover, each signatory pledged not to join any group of powers "which is directly or indirectly aimed at the other party." The logic of this extraordinary arrangement between Hitler and Stalin became apparent a week later when Germany and the USSR divided Poland between them, precipitating the outbreak of World War II.

The Nazi-Soviet pact struck Japan with stunning force and left her diplomatically isolated. Engaged in a showdown with the Red Army at Nomonhan, Japan had been negotiating with Berlin for an anti-Soviet alliance. The German announcement of August 21 produced more than surprise and shock in Tokyo. It unleashed a sense of anti-German outrage. Taking upon itself responsibility for a major diplomatic reversal, the Hiranuma cabinet resigned on August 30. Hiranuma's successor, General Abe Nobuyuki, took a dim view of a German alliance and steered clear of involvement in the European war. Military and civilian advocates of a pro-German orientation suffered a severe setback and had little choice but to remain quiet for the time being.

Manchukuo quickly felt the shock waves released by Nazi-Soviet collaboration. On September 7, Umezu Yoshijirō replaced Ueda Kenkichi as commander of the Kwantung Army. Transferred from North China, Umezu had long opposed General Araki's call for a preemptive attack on the USSR. Although he was anything but pro-Soviet, Umezu believed that Japan should take care of one problem at a time. And the current problem was China. A stern disciplinarian, Umezu was one of the few senior army officers equipped to make the Kwantung Army, furious about its humiliation at Nomonhan, disengage from Soviet forces during September of 1939.

The Nazi-Soviet pact shattered those Russian fascists who had placed their faith in Adolf Hitler as an anti-Communist messiah. Rodzaevsky stood amid the shambles of his own propaganda, wondering how to face Matkovsky. For perhaps the first time in his life, the boy from Blagoveshchensk was at a loss for what to say.

Rodzaevsky's shock was shared by Russians of all political persuasions throughout the diaspora. In the immediate aftermath of the announcement, few grasped the full significance of Hitler and Stalin's working together. But after the annihilation of Poland, émigrés throughout the world rallied to support England and France, who, in the winter of 1939–40, were not only fighting Hitler but stood on the verge of hostilities with Stalin (over the Soviet attack on Finland).

These rapid developments caused a precipitous drop in the Russian Fascist Union's already depleted membership. Resignations of *soratniki* in Manchukuo created an exodus that threatened to turn into a stampede. In Germany, the Gestapo cracked down on all anti-Soviet émigrés, fascist or otherwise. Despite hailing the Nazi-Soviet pact as a brilliant Reich coup to neutralize the Western plutocracies, European RFS representative Boris Tedli was deported to Switzerland in November. For neither the first nor the last time, Russian fascists discovered themselves to be expendable pawns of big-power maneuvers. But it was particularly galling to be Hitler's doormat for welcoming Stalin.

Konstantin Rodzaevsky's public reaction to the Nazi-Soviet pact appeared in *Natsiya* on September 3. He deplored the pact as Germany's "fatal error" in the struggle against Jewry and communism. Perhaps hoping to keep doors open for future collaboration with the Reich, he did not mention Hitler by name. Recent events, he lamely asserted, had proven Japan to be Russia's true savior. "An alliance of Japan and the Russian people," he wistfully concluded, would someday topple the Soviet regime without any help from fickle friends in Europe.

The Imperial Japanese Army, however, cared nothing about a Russian National Revolution unless it served Japanese national interests. And Japanese national interests were generally perceived in both Tokyo and Hsinking after August 1939 as being the rapid resolution of the China incident and the building of a "New Order in East Asia." In the wake of the outbreak of war in Europe, the key to these twin goals seemed to lie in Southeast Asia. In Japan's eyes, Chiang Kai-shek's resistance was made possible by supplies reaching him overland from Burma and Indochina. Moreover, British Malaya and the Dutch East Indies possessed the rubber and petroleum vital to the Japanese war machine in the face of mounting American embargoes. The German *Blitzkrieg* in April–June 1940, overrunning Belgium and Holland, knocking France out of the war, and driving English forces from the Continent, turned the Dutch, French, and British colonies in Southeast Asia into so much ripe fruit ready to be plucked without fear of retaliation.

As Southeast Asia loomed up in Japanese perceptions, the USSR lost its allure as a target. Moscow, still neutral in the European conflict, was free to concentrate its forces in the Far East, and Soviet air bases in the Maritime Province were well within striking distance of Tokyo. Further, at Nomonhan, the Red Army had demonstrated its mobility and technical superiority, filling Kwantung Army commanders with a new sense of caution.

Such conditions combined to deflate whatever enthusiasm for Siberian adventures had remained in the post-Araki Japanese Army. However hotly the Kwantung Army burned to avenge battlefield disgraces, larger strategic considerations hobbled revanchist impulses. The phrase *hokushu-nanshin,* "defend the north, advance to the south," reverberated through ministries, headquarters, and barracks, signaling an entire new stance.

This new stance was visible in Manchukuo within days of the Nazi-Soviet pact. On September 16, a truce ended hostilities at Nomonhan and provided for a Mongol-Manchu (in fact Soviet-Japanese) boundary commission to demarcated the disputed frontier. The commission met at Chita in December. Meanwhile Moscow and Tokyo moved to improve relations by releasing each other's confiscated fishing boats. Trade resumed, and the Trans-Siberian Railway started handling a heavy volume of shipments between Germany, which was landlocked by the British fleet, and Japan.

Disturbed by signs of a Soviet-Japanese rapprochement, Rodzaevsky made a flying visit to Tokyo in October to gain clarification of Japan's intentions and to impress upon Japanese leaders the utility of the RFS. His chief Army patrons, Araki and Koiso, had not fared well in recent political realignments. Both generals had lost their cabinet seats when the Hiranuma government fell in August. Rodzaevsky called upon Koiso, but about all that the retired general could offer was affirmation of his feeling that "Japan should drive the Soviet Union from the Pacific Ocean." These were thrilling words but carried no authority. Once again, Konstantin Vladimirovich returned from Tokyo empty-handed.

Rodzaevsky was soon disabused of whatever confidence he may have acquired in Tokyo about Japanese intentions. On January 5, 1940, the Mongol-Manchu Boundary Commission moved its deliberations from Chita to Harbin. Anxious to avoid untoward incidents, the Harbin Military Mission decreed that all White Russian leaders must leave town for the duration of the Commission's presence.

To mollify ruffled feelings among White Russian collaborators, *Tokumu Kikan* chief Major General Yanagita Genzō hosted a banquet for BREM officials on January 26. Rodzaevsky, Matkovsky, and other RFS *soratniki* were present. The guest of honor and principal speaker for the occasion was Kwantung Army chief of staff General Imamura Hitoshi. Imamura shrugged off the thought that the Kwantung Army would ever make a "deal" with the Soviets and disavowed any intention to disband "loyal" White Russian organizations. He concluded with some words of advice coated with compliments:

> Watching the activities of your organizations, I note with the greatest pleasure that you leaders of the Russian emigrants are correctly understanding the ideas emanating from the Japanese Army. The principles laid as a basis for the guidance of the White Russians are without change. Taking into account the political situation, I am deeply confident in you and ask you not to believe rumors. Trust the Japanese Army.

Trust the Japanese Army. Did Rodzaevsky, or any émigré in Manchukuo, have any choice?

Trust the Japanese Army. Within days after these words were uttered at the BREM banquet, Manchukuo's White Russians were discovering—or rediscovering—their implications. In March of 1940, the Kwantung Army instructed Ataman Semenov to organize Russian units for deployment in central China as a "nucleus" of an army for Wang Ching-wei, a former Kuomintang official who had become Japan's chief collaborator south of the Great Wall. By the end of March, three Russian regiments of one thousand men each were on their way to Nanking to serve under Wang's newly created puppet government.

Trust the Japanese Army. In Manchukuo, the Kwantung Army proclaimed a goal of thirty thousand White Russians under arms by 1941. Russian males aged seventeen to forty-five were declared eligible for compulsory military service.

Trust the Japanese Army. In March 1940, Twenty-four RFS *soratniki* were arrested by the *Kempei* at Mutanchiang, a town on the rail line between Harbin and Vladivostok. Mutanchiang fell within the bailiwick of Boris Nikolaevich Shepunov, a pint-sized Pogranichnaya-based strongman who enjoyed local *Kempei* patronage. Shepunov resented RFS men encroaching upon his "territory" and decided to get rid of them in one stroke. He therefore denounced all local Russian fascists to the *Kempei* as Soviet spies who were spreading the plague among cattle and typhus among people. The *Kempei* not only arrested the twenty-four *soratniki,* they also abducted an RFS Central Executive Committee member, Konstantin Arseniev, from Harbin for questioning. Arseniev underwent a brutal interrogation at Mutanchiang's *Kempei* headquarters, including water torture.

Apprised of Arseniev's disappearance by the latter's distraught wife, Rodzaevsky sought an explanation from *Tokumu Kikan* chief General Yanagita. Yanagita denied any knowledge of Arseniev's whereabouts but promised to investigate.

After two days of torture, Arseniev signed a "confession" implicating himself and the twenty-four *soratniki* in espionage and germ warfare on behalf of the NKVD. They were thereupon taken to Hsinking and imprisoned to await trial.

Several weeks later, at the trial, the prosecution produced an old radio receiver and some glass jars as evidence of the charges and demanded the death penalty. Under examination by Japanese experts, the radio proved unworkable and the jars contained no trace of bacteria. The accused, moreover, bore ample traces of physical abuse. A Japanese judge acquitted them. Arseniev returned to Harbin, and the other twenty-four made their way back to Mutanchiang.

Two days later, Rodzaevsky received a telegram from Mutanchiang informing him that all twenty-four *soratniki* had been shot upon arrival by the *Kempei*. Barely able to control himself, the *vozhd* stormed into General Yanagita's office for an explanation. Yanagita was quoted as saying: "They were executed, it is true. It was a mistake. The act leaves a dark spot upon the uniform of the Imperial Japanese Army. I sincerely apologize."

Relatives of the victims poured into Harbin. Yanagita declined to see them and instead directed BREM's Finance Department to distribute 1,000 yen ($330) to each bereaved family as "consolation" from the Harbin Military Mission. Beyond that gesture, the Mutan-chiang affair was considered closed.

Spellbound by the mirage of a National Revolution, thousands of Russians worked for the Japanese Army during the 1930s. Yet very few saw themselves as expendable tools of their employers and patrons. They could not afford to open their eyes to that reality, because they had nowhere else to turn.

CHAPTER XIV

Connecticut Capers

"Russian Hospitality in a New England Setting."
—ADVERTISEMENT FOR THE RUSSIAN BEAR (1934)

As with Shakespearean tragedy the Russian fascist movement had its moments of comic relief—some might say more than its share. The tragic and comic ingredients were epitomized by Konstantin Rodzaevsky and Anastase Vonsiatsky respectively. After converging briefly at Harbin in 1934, the two leaders parted, never to meet again, except through acrimonious exchanges in their own newspapers. Having wrested control of the All-Russian Fascist Party (VFP) away from Vonsiatsky in December 1934, Rodzaevsky plunged ever deeper into collaboration with the Imperial Japanese Army in Manchukuo. Vonsiatsky, by contrast, nursed his bruised ego by reverting to showmanship and, through his rechristened party (All-Russian National Revolutionary Party, abbreviated VNRP) and its newspaper, *Fashist,* indulged himself in a great burst of flamboyant political fantasies that reverberated around northeastern Connecticut.

Except for a quick trip to Europe in 1938 and world tours in 1936 and 1939, Vonsiatsky spent the years between 1934 and 1941 ensconced comfortably at Nineteenth Hole. He met few foreigners, and aside from a few émigré friends who dropped by periodically from New York, Boston, or Providence, he lived mainly among local gentry, house servants, storekeepers, farmers, and assorted companions.

During the mid-1930s, an entourage of sorts coalesced around Vonsiatsky, attracted variously by his money, his pretensions, and by his love of fun. A blend of Russian exiles and local stalwarts, the entourage exuded a peculiar combination of tsarist nostalgia, Yankee ingenuity, and adolescent exuberance. Its members, whether they

209

realized it or not, were the *dramatis personae* of an imaginatively engineered theatrical production.

Family

As early as 1934, Anastase was well established as a Ream family albatross. Not only had he helped scuttle the marriage of his youngest brother-in-law, Louis Marshall Ream, but he had turned into an eccentric who collected guns as well as gridiron goalposts, and his newfound political pretensions were a source of profound embarrassment. Rakish dandies were a common affliction of rich, self-respecting families, but how many proud scions of the *National Cyclopedia of American Biography,* such as Marion's younger brother Robert Clarke Ream, had to contend with a would-be fascist field marshal for an in-law? Of course it was permissible in polite society to credit Hitler with solving Germany's unemployment problems and to admire Mussolini for making Italian trains run on time. But Vonsiatsky clearly went beyond the bounds of good taste. He whistled the Horst Wessel song on the Quinnatisset links, barked out commands to servants as if there were *Arbeitsdienst* recruits, and boasted about how his legions would someday march through Red Square. On one occasion when brother-in-law Robert, who was a New York insurance executive with staunch Republican-Episcopalian affiliations, held a black-tie dinner, Vonsiatsky showed up in khakis, a Sam Browne belt, black riding boots, and a red-white-and-blue swastika arm band.

Marion did not fully recognize how seriously Alex's behavior disturbed her family. Partially blinded by a streak of romantic philanthropy that back in 1921 had propelled her toward a Folies Bergères curtain puller, Marion treated her Alex as a helpless foundling, a tragic orphan of the Revolution, a waif who needed to be mothered and educated. She saw nothing wrong whatever with Alex having his little fascist party as a hobby. As she remarked to a friend, it was wiser to have her husband occupied than always at loose ends.

Marion also overlooked Anastase's idiosyncrasies because she did not entirely comprehend what was going on around her. Although only in her fifties, she was beginning to show signs of age. Her sense of hearing was faltering in the early 1930s and thereafter degenerated seriously, despite three operations. Much of what Vonsiatsky was saying and doing simply escaped her attention. Much—but not all. She had no trouble divining the nature of his words if she could observe the faces of his listeners. One friend recalled that when guests blanched or flushed, Marion would sometimes turn to her husband and trill: "Alex, whatever you are saying, stop it."

As Vonsiatsky grew more involved in politics, Marion made certain adjustments in their relationship. She continued to pay him a $25,000 annual allowance, about $10,000 of which he could spend on his "hobby." But realizing that he embarrassed her friends, Marion began entertaining separately. As they developed different circles of friends, they came to see each other only sporadically.

The domestic arrangement posed delicate problems for Nineteenth Hole's servants, most of whom felt sympathetic toward Marion and cool toward Anastase. Richard Barton, an elderly gardener who had worked for the Reams since 1903, kept tabs on Vonsiatsky on behalf of Marion's brother Robert. Two chauffeurs, James Morgan and Warren Towne, found the count overbearing. Mrs. Elliott, the chambermaid, also stood squarely in Marion's corner. Emil Lajeunesse, a caretaker, felt well disposed to master and mistress alike but resigned in 1932 to take a new job. Perhaps it was Lajeunesse's successor, Steve Roshak, who came closest to maintaining a balanced relationship with Marion and Anastase. Adopted by Lajeunesse at the age of seven from a New Haven orphanage, Steve had grown up around Nineteenth Hole and continued to work there as a handyman after his foster father had moved elsewhere. When Steve married, his wife Helen waited on tables at the Russian Bear for Lev and Natasha Mamedov.

The Mamedovs were Anastase's only relatives to have escaped from Russia. A former colonel in the artillery, Lev Mamedov shared his brother-in-law's fancy for military hardware and tsarist nostalgia. In general, he went along with Alex's political ventures, and he accepted membership in the VFO (1933) and VNRP (1935). He refused, however, to have anything to do with Rodzaevsky, even during Alex's brief honeymoon with the Manchurian fascists in 1934. Natasha Mamedov was one of the few who could deflate Anastase without giving offense. Whenever her brother got out of hand, she told him to come to the Russian Bear and eat something. The Mamedov son, Andy, was a thoroughly Americanized teenager who captivated his uncle and aunt's hearts and may have filled a void created by their childlessness.

Cronies

To create a suitable ambience for his grand pretensions, Vonsiatsky surrounded himself with a number of assistants and companions. Some of his aides were politically naive local youngsters with only the vaguest conception of Russia. Sadie Locke, for example, an Irish girl from New Hampshire, did the *vozhd's* stenographic work. Norman Watson, son of a caretaker of the Ream-owned Quinnatisset Golf Club, graduated from caddying for Vonsiatsky to lugging bundles of *Fashist* from Nineteenth Hole to the Thompson Post Office. Michael Kapral, a blond teenager whom everybody called Misha, did odd jobs such as posing for publicity photos in full party uniform.

However, Vonsiatsky did not rely entirely on local talent. Donat Yosifovich ("Coontz") Kunle served as the *vozhd's* amanuensis and editor of *Fashist.* Comely, modest, and soft-spoken, Coontz was probably the best-liked fascist in Windham County. He was rumored to be Jewish, but unfortunately he was not; the count would have welcomed the opportunity to underscore the party's stated position that a Jew could make a perfectly good *soratnik.*

Alex had a soft spot in his heart for journalists, who, after all, held out the promise of publicity. Although fear of assassination made Vonsiatsky generally suspicious of strangers, bona fide newsmen were welcome at Nineteenth Hole, and in some cases, they were invited to spend the night. After the count returned from his 1934 world tour, dozens of enterprising reporters made the trip to Thompson looking for a colorful story. They were usually successful.

Vonsiatsky choreographed his hospitality for maximum dramatic effect. Kunle, decked out in storm trooper trappings, would greet guests at the outer gate. Watson, Kapral, and brother-in-law Mamedov hovered nearby, one of them holding the attack dog Lady Astor on a tightly drawn leash as if to remind the visitor that he was alive only by grace of his host. The guest would then be ushered into the main house, past the machine-gun-defended stairwell and into the stone annex where the *vozhd* himself waited in enigmatic majesty. Once inside the Military Room, the visitor found himself facing a six-foot mass of khaki and swastikas advancing toward him with arms outstretched in hearty cordiality. "It's like being admitted to an audience with the Führer," marveled a reporter in 1937.

Whether he asked for it or not, the guest was invariably taken on an extended tour of the Military Room. Vonsiatsky proudly identified flags, rifles, portraits, goalpost bits, and a perforated Russian Army greatcoat draped over a human mannequin. He never failed to dwell on the greatcoat, relating how a bullet responsible for one of the holes was still lodged in his stomach.

After the tour, the guest was initiated into the arcanum of VNRP operations. Pacing up and down, gesticulating in a well-rehearsed imitation of Italian newsreels, Vonsiatsky spelled out the aims of his party, recited statistics about sabotage and assassination inside the USSR, and name-dropped his way through a who's who of Japan and the Third Reich. As the reporter hurriedly jotted down notes, the *vozhd* would occasionally pause, wait for his listener to catch up, and then deliberately offer some particularly graphic metaphor, knowing that it would probably be quoted.

"The Russian Fascist Party is the automobile for the ride to the Kremlin. All it needs is a push," he declaimed to Garrett Byrnes of the Providence *Journal* in 1935.

Asked how many followers he commanded, Anastase responded according to his mood:

"Twenty thousand." (1935)

"One million." (1937)

"Can one count the kernels of corn after they have started to pop?" (1934)

"We agreed never to reveal how many people we have. You know the OGPU would love to find out." (1939)

Hostile reporters were as welcome as friendly ones. Harry Raymond of the *Daily Worker* was entertained at Nineteenth Hole in 1937, gathering material to keep the paper filled with stories about the "fascist fortress." Far from resenting attacks against him, Vonsiatsky lapped them up. He collected and circulated *Daily Worker* clippings about himself to friends and *Fashist* subscribers. The count regarded publicity in the *Daily Worker*—which he thought was sure to be seen in the USSR—as an ideal way to make his name a household word among the Russian masses.

Of the newsmen who visited Nineteenth Hole, three became what might almost be called cronies of Vonsiatsky: Richard McCauley, George Connell, and James Richard Bakker.

McCauley, a resident of Putnam, wrote articles and did photos for several papers, including the Worcester *Gazette*, the Norwich

Bulletin, the Hartford *Times,* and the Hartford *Courant.* He first met the count in 1933 and saw him frequently thereafter, both professionally and socially. They liked to disport themselves in the Military Room, listening to recordings of German marching bands and Hitler's speeches.

George Connell, editor of the Putnam *Patriot,* made Vonsiatsky's acquaintance in 1935 and got together with him about once a month until 1942. Each autumn, the count invited him to the Brown-Yale game, to which they went as a foursome with Kunle and Mamedov. Connell appreciated having such a colorful character within his bailiwick. It enlivened the local news and offered him opportunities to write for national magazines. In 1937, Connell wrote a lurid story about Vonsiatsky which was published in *True* magazine.

James Richard Bakker, described by a friend as "bright, brash, and a constant joker," was Thompson's village intellectual. He liked to carry around a copy of Will Durant's *Story of Philosophy,* and after skimming Nietzsche referred to himself as the "blond roving beast." Bakker had caddied for Vonsiatsky in the 1920s. Later, as a stringer for the Putnam *Patriot* and Webster *Times,* he wrote features about Vonsiatsky's putative Civil War exploits, such as how he had saved Kolchak after the admiral's horse had been shot out from under him. In 1937, Bakker started a weekly newspaper called the Putnam *Democrat.* Although George Connell, as editor of the Putnam *Patriot,* was Bakker's competitor, the two men collaborated on the *True* magazine story about their mutual friend.

The friendship between Bakker and Vonsiatsky thrived upon a shared taste for fantasy. The two liked to get together in the Military Room, have a few drinks, and make recordings of their own mockpretentious speeches—Alex was an accomplished mimic—with dubbed-in applause. They then sat back on the chintz sofa to listen to themselves, roaring with laughter at the absurdity of their illusory grandeur. Bakker never wrote about these sessions. That would have dispelled the *True* magazine image of the count as a Russian Fu Manchu, an image that both men wanted to perpetuate.

Law and Order

Although he plotted insurgency vis-à-vis the USSR, Anastase Vonsiatsky considered himself a friend of law and order within the United States. As the son of a gendarme, he felt a certain professional empathy for policemen. Moreover, knowing that their lot was not always a happy one, he did his best to lighten their constabulary duties by offering, from time to time, entertainment and a helping hand.

By the time Vonsiatsky moved to Thompson in 1924, he had already accumulated considerable firsthand knowledge of American policemen. His exuberant driving habits had made him a familiar figure in Philadelphia precincts and courthouses during 1922 and 1923. Alex continued to collect tickets after moving to Thompson, especially during his dashes to and from football games in Boston, Providence, and New Haven. This did not prevent him from forming personal friendships with Connecticut State Police officers stationed at the Danielson barracks twelve miles south of Nineteenth Hole. One of the earliest of these friendships was with Sergeant Elton Thomas Nolan.

Sergeant Nolan first met the count in 1927, when Vonsiatsky asked the police to investigate the disappearance of a large stone from a wall in front of the main house. The stone was never found, but its owner gained a crony. By 1930, Nolan was dropping by Nineteenth Hole during off-duty hours for drinks and a round of golf, sometimes bringing along a girl friend. Nolan enjoyed Alex's company but took him with a grain of salt. It did not take long for the sergeant's practiced eye to perceive that most of the guns in the Military Room were unusable.

In 1933, Vonsiatsky also befriended Nolan's superior, Lieutenant Ross B. Urquhart, officer in charge of the Connecticut State Police barracks at Danielson. Like Nolan, Urquhart came up to Nineteenth Hole for drinks and golf. Unlike Nolan, he also borrowed money. Alex was always ready to cultivate camaraderie with cash.

Vonsiatsky's relations with the Connecticut State Police matured in time to embrace practical collaboration in maintaining law and order in Windham County. In 1934, when mill workers went on strike in North Grosvenor Dale, three miles northwest of Thompson, the *vozhd* sprang into action, remembering all too well how proletarian unrest in Russia had foreshadowed revolution. How the count lent his peculiar talents to the cause of law enforcement is related in his own words in a letter to the commissioner of State Police, Edward J. Hickey:

> On September 4, 1934 two State Police officers came to me and asked if I could loan them some of my tear gas hand grenades, as they expected trouble the following day, owing to a strike at the North Grosvenordale [*sic*] Mills. I told the officers that I would gladly loan them not only all

of my tear gas hand grenades, but also two 1½ inch caliber tear gas riot guns, together with 1½ inch caliber tear gas long range projectiles, and a few billies.

Owing to the fact that at the time State Police officers in Danielson had had very little experience with tear gas riot guns, I told these two officers that I felt it was my duty as a citizen to give all possible assistance to them and that I, together with my secretary Mr. Kunle (a former White Russian Army officer), would be present to help them use the guns, if occasion required.

On the following morning, September 5, at 6 A.M., Mr. Kunle and I delivered the equipment personally to Lt. Urquhart, who was in charge of the police operations in North Grosvernordale. Mr. Kunle and I stayed with the State Police force nearly all that day, ready to give assistance at any moment. Fortunately, things quieted down at North Grosvernordale and it was not necessary to use my supplies. However, they were used later in another mill locality.

Vonsiatsky received no official commendation for his services, but the police did reimburse him for the expended gas grenades, replacing them with equivalent ordnance from a Connecticut National Guard arsenal.

In subsequent years, Anastase Andreivich made periodic gestures calculated to curry favor with law enforcement agencies. In the summer of 1939, for example, he offered to give the Connecticut State Police thirty-five acres of Nineteenth Hole for target practice. The offer was apparently declined, but Commissioner Hickey did come up to Nineteenth Hole for a visit and subsequently thanked Alex in writing for his hospitality.

Political Charades

Throughout its existence, the All-Russian National Revolutionary Party amounted to little more than a soap bubble. After his break with Rodzaevsky late in 1934, Vonsiatsky exerted virtually no influence on émigrés in China and Manchuria, the only areas where Russian fascists mustered any muscle. Anastase nonetheless continued to claim anywhere from 20,000 to 1,000,000 followers in forty-three countries and asserted that he could mobilize an army of 150,000 White Russians to march on Moscow. During the last half of the 1930s, some three million copies of *Fashist* and countless leaflets and postcards were disgorged throughout the world from the Putnam and Thompson post offices. According to this literature, the VNRP was waging an unceasing struggle within the USSR, sabotaging installations and assassinating commissars.

Rarely has any political movement betrayed such a discrepancy between image and reality. The VNRP in fact consisted of a dozen members in New England and a dozen mail order "cells" whose activities oscillated according to monetary remittances from Thompson. Aside from Vonsiatsky, Kunle, and Mamedov, there were only three active Russian fascists on the east coast. Evgeny Bogoslovsky and Alexander Plyshnov divided Manhattan between them—uptown and downtown respectively. Ivan Novozhilov reported in from Boston, where he helped run a branch of the Russian Bear.

In 1935, however, the VNRP dramatically expanded its membership by recruiting a *soratnik* of the cloth: Reverend Alexander Tzuglevich, a Russian Orthodox priest in charge of St. George's Church in Bayside (Queens), Long Island. A short, bespectacled man with close-cropped hair and a beard and mustache, Tzuglevich had been buffeted through most of his adult life by political upheavals and ecclesiastical squabbles. A student in St. Petersburg when the October Revolution erupted, Tzuglevich had joined the southern exodus and taught briefly at a Russian school in Constantinople. He later drifted to Prague and in 1924 was ordained a priest in the Russian Orthodox Church. Five years later, he was expelled from Czechoslovakia for trying to lure a Greek Catholic congregation from its prelates in a Slovakian village. Surfacing in New York's Russian Cathedral, he parlayed his Slovakian expertise into a mission on behalf of Metropolitan Vitaly to the Carpathians in 1933.

Reverend Tzuglevich brought more than a spiritual touch to the VNRP. His missionary zeal so impressed Vonsiatsky that in April 1936 the *vozhd* put him in charge of the party's first educational enterprise: the Russian Fascist Bible School of New York. Despite its imposing name, the Bible School was a modest affair. Its "campus" consisted of Bogoslovsky's apartment at 507 West 144th Street. The student body, two dozen boys and girls aged eight to fourteen, was drawn from Harlem's Russian colony. Tzuglevich shared instructional responsibilities with Bogoslovsky. The former intoned prayers and taught the Russian language. The latter lectured on Russian history—in full VNRP uniform. Portraits of Vonsiatsky and Nicholas II graced the walls, interspersed with paper swastika pendants.

Neither licensed nor accredited, the Bible School rested on shaky foundations. Its students came late in the afternoon after attending regular schools. Tzuglevich and Bogoslovsky added to the aura of instability by loudly disputing the boundary between ecclesiastical and secular prerogatives. When Bogoslovsky died in 1939, the Bible School lost its campus. Tzuglevich was not about to bus little Harlem *soratniki* to his midtown apartment, so the whole enterprise quietly folded.

The Bible School had also given Vonsiatsky the idea of starting a summer camp for the children of New York's Russian community. Windham County's bucolic surroundings seemed to offer an ideal setting for outdoor activities. Accordingly, in June 1936, the *vozhd* opened a "Young Avantgarde Camp" at Nineteenth Hole. Tzuglevich and Bogoslovsky came up from New York to help out, but the main burden of looking after a dozen "Russian boy scouts," as Vonsiatsky called them, fell to Misha Kapral. Each summer between 1936 and 1938, the boys descended upon Nineteenth Hole for hiking, swimming, and singing. On weekends, Lev Mamedov often treated the young avantgardists to a movie in Providence. Mamedov's occasional female impersonations sparked much hilarity and, except for his mustache, were utterly convincing.

For all his entrepreneurial feats in New York and Connecticut, Vonsiatsky was notably unsuccessful in finding foreign patrons. German and Italian officials regarded him as a nuisance. For a while in 1934, it looked as if the Japanese might be his guardian angels. During his world tour that year, he had voiced high hopes of Japanese support, telling an American reporter that "Japan is the only country in the world that can provide us with sufficient arms and ammunition." Asked in Belgrade if he ever doubted Japan's ultimate motives, Alex replied confidently: "They [the Japanese] do not seek a single foot of Russian territory. They know that their best interest is to have a strong nationalist Russia as a neighbor."

After splitting with Rodzaevsky, however, Vonsiatsky turned sharply against Japan. He publicly decried Kwantung Army mistreatment of White Russians in Manchukuo and warned that Russian patriots must never rely on Japan to help overthrow Stalin.

Nor did Vonsiatsky cultivate ties with European fascists. He apparently neither met nor corresponded with France's Charles Maurras, England's Oswald Mosley, Norway's Vidkun Quisling, Holland's Adriaan Anton Mussert, Hungary's Ferenc Szalasi, or Rumania's Cornelius Zelia Codreanu. He did not attend the International Fascist Congress at Montreux, Switzerland in 1934. Although detractors linked Vonsiatsky with the philo-Nazi Dutch oil magnate Sir Henri Deterding, there is no evidence that the two men had anything to do with each other.

The *vozhd* also kept his distance from right-wing groups in the United States. Henry D. Allen, creator of the American White Guard, tried unsuccessfully in 1936 to persuade Vonsiatsky to collaborate on anti-Jewish propaganda. Major Frank Pease, head of the American Defenders of Coral Gables (Florida), managed to establish epistolary contact with Thompson but got no further than securing a franchise to distribute *Fashist* south of the Mason-Dixon Line. Anastase did correspond with William Dudley Pelley, leader of the Silver Shirts, and the Catholic radio personality Father Charles E. Coughlin, but their relationship never went beyond *Fashist*'s occasionally reprinting articles from *Pelley's Weekly* and *Social Justice.*

Vonsiatsky remained aloof from the American far right for several reasons. He was not at all comfortable with their hostility to Washington, never forgetting that the United States government had given him refuge and citizenship. "Our status obliges us to be especially careful not to violate our position as guests," he remarked to a reporter in 1938. Nor, in fact, did the prospect of a fascist America particularly appeal to him. As he candidly put it to a newsman in 1939: "I would not like to see the United States become fascist. In fascist countries we [Russian fascists] are not allowed to carry out our work." In general, the count had little confidence that America's rightist fringe would offer significant help in the struggle against Stalin. Ironically, it was in the left rather than the right that Vonsiatsky perceived the richest opportunities for propaganda, as we have already seen with his symbiotic relationship with the *Daily Worker* on publicizing the VNRP within the USSR.

The purges that racked the Soviet Union during 1937 and 1938 provided Vonsiatsky with ample grist for *Fashist.* Yet Anastase Andreivich was not content simply to attack Stalin's ruthlessness or paranoia. Rather, he employed imagination and humor to attract attention to himself. For example, on December 21, 1937, the Boston *Evening Transcript* published a telegram sent by Vonsiatsky to Alexander Troyanovsky, the Soviet ambassador in Washington, with a transparently allusive invitation:

IF STALIN IS GOING TO RECALL YOU TO MOSCOW,
I SUGGEST YOU AND YOUR WIFE COME TO THOMPSON
AND STAY WITH ME. MY COMPLIMENTS AND HOPE TO
SEE YOU SOON.

Troyanovsky passed up Vonsiatsky's invitation when he was recalled to Moscow in 1939, and he lived not to regret his decision.

In teasing the left, Vonsiatsky savored the double-edged compliment, such as the one he paid Stalin in the New York émigré newspaper, *Novoye Russkoye Slovo,* in 1938: "Stalin is the best fascist of them all. No one has killed more Communists than he, not even I!"

The count was not being facetious, however, when he told a reporter in 1939 that "Trotsky is my automatic ally." Alex appreciated the exiled Bolshevik revolutionary and military strategist as a devastating critic of Stalin and praised him as a "100 percent sincere socialist." Vonsiatsky is said to have written Trotsky shortly before the latter's assassination near Mexico City on August 20, 1940. If sent, the letter was not answered.

Throughout the 1930s, Vonsiatsky's political oratory bristled with contradictions. As George Connell understated it: "He is very frank, but not always consistent." Alex raved enthusiastically about Japan one day and denounced it the next. He welcomed a Communist reporter to Nineteenth Hole, then drove down to New York to disrupt a lecture by a former tsarist army officer. He admired Trotsky as a socialist and denounced Stalin as a fascist.

These political charades were in part the product of Vonsiatsky's thirst for quick fame and his indifference to conventional labels and categories. At a deeper level, though, one cannot help but sense that Alex remained an exile, unreconciled to present reality and searching through illusion for the key to a lost past.

Thompson Follies

The Russian National Revolutionary Fascist Party is moving on Thompson, Connecticut, but there is no need to be alarmed—at least no need for the United States to be alarmed. The Union of Socialist Soviet Republics [sic] had better look out, though.

Providence *Evening Bulletin*
July 2, 1937

By the mid-1930s, Anastase Vonsiatsky was hitting his stride in Thompson. The town had become his stage for enacting on a small scale what he dreamed of doing someday in all of Russia.

It would be surprising to learn that anyone in Windham County had not heard of "the count" by 1937, thanks to extensive coverage by the local press. By then Alex was no longer simply a character; he was becoming an institution. To be sure, opinions about him varied widely. Self-consciously respectable citizens, including Marion's more frumpish friends, regarded him as a social embarrassment. More people than would admit it today took the count's aristocratic claims at face value. Yet even gullible bumpkins dismissed his political pretensions as those of a slightly deranged poseur. Not a few locals appreciated him for injecting some excitement into an otherwise soporific New England village. After all, while millions of Americans were seeking to escape the grim realities of the Depression by going to the movies, Anastase Vonsiatsky provided thousands of Putnamites and Thompsonites with free, live entertainment.

Anyone who glimpsed Vonsiatsky in his prime was unlikely to forget him. His khaki-clad form was a familiar sight on the Quinnatisset golf course, at parties, and on the road, driving about in an olive-green Pierce Arrow with swastika pennants on each front fender. Putnam storekeepers still remember how he tossed coins onto the counter, as if he were playing horseshoes. Sometimes, he would sport a monocle and swagger stick, which together with his military posture, *en brosse* hairstyle, and black riding boots produced a more than successful impression of Erich von Stroheim. Children and a few timid souls kept their distance, scared off by Vonsiatsky's size and booming voice, but most locals saw through his bluster, knowing him to be an incorrigible ham.

Vonsiatsky did not let what other people might think interfere with his fantasies. He liked to call himself a "man of destiny" and tirelessly repeated how his birthday providentially coincided with that of Peter the Great. He compared himself favorably with Mussolini and Hitler, grudgingly including them in the "world trio" who were molding the twentieth century. In lighter moments, he referred to this trio as the "Three Musketeers." If pressed, he would concede that Franco might qualify as D'Artagnan.

Totally confident of ultimate success, Alex relished drawing up elaborate plans for a glorious future. He drafted blueprints for a racetrack in Russia, reserving for himself a stable to house fifty-two horses. Not one to neglect details, he ordained the name and sex of each steed. He declared that the life-size mannequin wearing his perforated army greatcoat in the Military Room would someday be a national shrine in Moscow. He also printed postage stamps bearing his own portrait, but, mindful of U.S. postal laws, contented himself with using them as Christmas seals until such time as they might be needed in the new Russia.

Nor was Anastase to be caught short of cash after the National Revolution had restored Russia's old currency. In 1936, he purchased tsarist ruble notes with a face value of $7,500,000, calculating that after the National Revolution he would reap a financial windfall.

Vonsiatsky devised a number of ingenious stratagems to draw the locals into his fantasy world. It was reported that he included cronies and domestic servants in his roster of Russia's future governorships and ministerial portfolios. He showed himself particularly adept at turning sports to political ends—and vice versa. Shortly after General Alexander Kutepov, head of the Russian Armed Services Union, was kidnapped in Paris by the OGPU in 1930, Alex raised a Kutepov Relief Fund by sponsoring an exhibition boxing match in Putnam between world lightweight champ Al Singer and the former champ Benny Leonard. When General Evgeny Miller, Kutepov's successor, vanished into Soviet hands seven years later, Vonsiatsky offered a $25,000 bounty for the general's abductor.

Early in 1937, as the purges entered a climactic stage in the USSR, Vonsiatsky converted the cow barn at Nineteenth Hole into a shooting gallery. On one wall, he tacked up portraits of the Soviet Communist Party Politburo, and guests were invited to test their marksmanship with BB guns. Just how many reporters, policemen, farmers, and school children took pot shots at Stalin, Kaganovich, Voroshilov, Zhdanov, and Yezhov will never be known. It is known, however, that in 1939 a reporter named David Karr visited Nineteenth Hole to gather material on subversive elements in the United States for a newsletter called *The Hour,* organ of the American Council Against Nazi Propaganda. After interviewing Vonsiatsky, Karr took a tour of the estate with Kunle, who asked him if he would care to take a few shots at the Soviet Politburo. Karr blazed away at the targets until he ran out of BB's, managing to hit Stalin several times on the nose. That particular episode did not get into *The Hour.*

As a living counterpart to the shooting gallery, Vonsiatsky announced the inauguration of a "Murder Sweepstakes" on July 18, 1938. Visitors were invited to place bets, for cash prizes, on which Soviet leaders would be liquidated in the ongoing purges. That day, the count posted his own list of Stalin's next victims: General Vasily Blücher (commander of the Far Eastern Military District), Lazar Kaganovich (Politburo member), Maxim Litvinov (commissar of foreign affairs), Kliment Voroshilov (defense commissar and Politburo member), Pavel Postyshev (member of the Politburo and high-ranking party official in the Ukraine), and Nikolai Yezhov (head of the NKVD). Alex scored 50 percent, guessing correctly about the fates of Blücher, Postyshev, and Yezhov.

One year later, the *vozhd* composed a second sweepstakes list but, as he complained to a reporter: ". . . the pickings are very thin. It's getting hard. Most of the good birds are gone."

The second list started with Viacheslav Molotov (who had succeeded Litvinov as foreign commissar the previous May) and included Kaganovich, Ivan Maisky (ambassador to England), General G. M. Shtern (Blücher's successor in the Far East), and Lavrenty Beria (Yezhov's successor as NKVD chief). "They will all be gone before another year is out," announced the count happily. This time, he proved wrong on all except Shtern.

The more remote his chances grew of exercising any political influence within the Russian diaspora, the more determined Vonsiatsky became to have the trappings of power. Nothing better illustrates this than the birth of Alex's private armed forces.

Since 1930, the count had collected various types of usable and unusable arms, partly from nostalgia, partly out of fear of assassination, and partly for show. But after his U.S. Army reserve officer's commission expired on March 16, 1935, he no longer enjoyed the privilege of being able to pick up a Thompson submachine gun at Abercrombie & Fitch. And, needless to say, heavy ordnance—artillery, tanks, warships—was not something that Alex could buy, even with an officer's commission. Besides, neighbors could not be expected to put up with cannon fire, and Marion would never stand for tank treads churning up her flower beds. As for warships, the Quinebaug River, which flowed through Putnam, could not even accommodate an ordinary yacht.

Vonsiatsky overcame all of these obstacles in one swoop by building his military establishment with toys and pets. Possibly the idea came to him in the bathtub, where he was wont to linger and practice his speeches. Every tub lounger knows that given the proper angle of vision, judicious squinting, and a little imagination, bathwater can look like the open sea. Why not fill that sea with a navy?

In 1937, Alex requisitioned seven hundred model battleship kits from Woolworth's, an order that emptied the company's New England inventories and had finally to be filled by a special shipment from Chicago. As the crates arrived, the *vozhd* and Kunle set about unpacking and assembling the kits. Each battleship was christened after an actual vessel in the old Imperial Russian Navy. The tsar's great dreadnoughts were the first to take shape, their names proudly emblazoned in Cyrillic letters: *Petropavlovsk, Gangut, Sevastopol,* and *Poltava.* Others followed, each conjuring up memories of a glorious past: *Admiral Ushakov, Imperatritsa Maria, Imperator Nikolai I, Andrei Pervozvanny, Borodino,* etc. Seven hundred proved to be more than Alex and Coontz could handle, so they halted construction at three dozen. The unopened kits were kept in reserve, ready for use in the event of a naval armaments race.

The Russian Fascist Navy had its inaugural cruise on Ream's Pond, located across County Home Road from Nineteenth Hole just north of the Quinnatisset Golf Club. Those vessels that did not capsize and sink were retrieved, divided into four fleets (Baltic, Black, White, Pacific), and deployed on windowsills around the main house and stone annex.

With between twenty thousand and one million chimerical *soratniki* around the world, Alex felt no need to recruit toy soldiers, but he did feel the absence of armor. Rather than pursue the Woolworth option, however, he decided to look into animate ordnance. Scouring local ponds, Alex, Kunle, Mamedov, and Jimmy Bakker managed to collect a dozen or so snapping turtles. On the shell of each turtle, they painted the VNRP insignia: a white swastika on a red background ringed with blue trim. Instead of confining his tank turtles, the *vozhd* let them waddle back into the woods so that, according to one source, they could convert their fellows. Although he never succeeded in imbuing the VNRP reptilian corps with quite the operational dash of Heinz Guderian's panzers, the count derived no little satisfaction from watching their testudinal forms purposefully advancing across the lawn toward imaginary Soviet defenses lining the Quinnatisset stream.

In 1927, inspired by Charles Lindbergh, Alex had briefly piloted a single engine plane around Windham County, but ten years later, all that remained of his aeronautical days was a propellor clock in the Military Room. Grand Duke Alexander, chief of the Imperial Russian Air Force during World War I, had visited Nineteenth Hole in 1931, but his death in 1933 deprived the count of advice from that quarter. Kunle had only a rudimentary knowledge of aircraft mechanics, which he had acquired at the Sikorsky works at Stratford. Dmitry Olshevsky, a Vonsiatsky acquaintance who worked at the Eclipse Aviation Corporation in East Orange, New Jersey, knew a good deal more about planes, but the *vozhd* presumably lost his goodwill after he called him a "secret agent of the GPU" in the November 1935 issue of *Fashist.* For lack of anything better, Vonsiatsky settled on carrier pigeons for his air force and built a loft for them in the cow barn. Eagles would have been more imposing (not to mention consistent with the VNRP emblem), but pigeons, if nothing else, were readily available.

If local gossip is to be believed, Anastase's increasing interest in procurement also had a sexual dimension. To be sure, he had always been something of a flirt, but by the mid-1930s flirting may not have been enough. As Marion grew older and as her hearing difficulties left her more and more out of touch with her surroundings, Alex found himself in a position to give his libidinous impulses freer reign.

While gossip is rife, details are murky. "Alex was not very discriminating about his choice of companions," discreetly recalled a former headmaster of Pomfret School. Other Thompsonites reminisced about how the count would drive into New York and have a fling with some lady (never identified) at the Vanderbilt Hotel, then send Marion the bill. According to local lore, Vonsiatsky had an eye for pubescent students of the Howe-Marot Schools for Girls, an exclusive finishing academy located on Thompson's southwestern fringe. One longtime resident admitted that some of the bolder Howe-Marot girls did provoke the *vozhd* by parading suggestively up and down County Home Road in front of Nineteenth Hole, but it took very little to launch Alex on a nymphet chase.

Despite her infirmities, Marion seems to have been aware of her husband's indiscretions. One night (the exact date is unclear), the elderly lady returned home early from a shopping trip to Boston to find Alex in the middle of a "wild party." As her Cadillac touring car pulled up the driveway, its headlights caught a flurry of females running around the house in various stages of dishabille.

Marion's reaction to that particular incident is not recorded, but she apparently neither called Alex to account nor threatened to divorce him. Asked in 1942 why Marion put up with such flagrant misbehavior, one of her closest friends replied: "She finally realized she was stuck, but she is poise to the core."

Marion surely was "poise to the core" when it came to tolerating Alex's Fourth of July parties. These festivities took considerable forbearance on her part, for by the mid-1930s they had begun to assume the character if not the scale of a Nuremberg rally. In 1937, July 4 fell on a Sunday. It so happened that on Monday, July 5, Alex's friend Prince Theodore Alexandrovich Romanov was arriving in New York from England. Accordingly, Vonsiatsky decided to put on a festive weekend show for his *soratniki,* the highlight of which would be the personal appearance of a nephew of Nicholas II.

To guarantee a good turnout, Anastase provided travel funds for all *soratniki* within a two-hundred-mile radius, and he instructed Reverend Tzuglevich and Evgeny Bogoslovsky to round up a hefty contingent from New York's Russian colony. To ensure maximum publicity, he also alerted newspapers ranging from the Putnam *Patriot* to the *Daily Worker.*

The weekend got under way late Friday evening, July 2, when Vonsiatsky, Kunle, Mamedov, and Kapral drove to the Putnam railroad station to greet about thirty *soratniki* and their families arriving from New York. It took a half-dozen taxis to get everyone to Nineteenth Hole after a midnight welcoming ceremony on the station platform.

As the sun rose on Saturday, July 3, about thirty-five *soratniki,* having changed from business suits and dresses into brown shirts with swastika arm bands, stood at attention while Kunle hoisted the VNRP red, white, and blue flag over the stone annex. A half-dozen newsmen buzzed about with cameras and note pads, recording what the Hartford *Courant* would soon headline: GRIM GROUP OF RUSSIAN FASCISTS AT CONCLAVE IN THOMPSON PONDER INDEPENDENCE FOR NATIVE COUNTRY.

Saturday was devoted to speeches and business matters. Lev Mamedov, president of the VNRP Central Executive Committee, convened the general assembly in the cow barn, where BB-riddled portraits of Soviet leaders shared the walls with swastika-studded emblems. Three dozen brownshirts sat on folding chairs and listened to their *vozhd.* Vonsiatsky welcomed everyone to the Center, congratulating all the *soratniki* on their political work and expressing confidence that if the purge of Soviet Communist Party leaders and Red Army generals were to continue, the VNRP would be in Russia by Christmas.* Then each VNRP branch leader stood up to say a few words about the state of affairs in his bailiwick. Plyshnov, Bogoslovsky, and Tzuglevich glared at each other throughout but kept their tempers. After lunch, the *vozhd* met with each *soratnik* to offer encouragement. That evening, Natasha Mamedov served a gala dinner at the Russian Bear.

Sunday morning, July 4, belonged to the VNRP ecclesiastic, Reverend Tzuglevich, who conducted religious services in the Military Room at eleven. Instead of a full mass, he celebrated an abbreviated "combat mass," which he claimed to have performed in the trenches for White troops during the Civil War. From the Military Room's cathedral ceiling hung swastika banners and regimental emblems of the Imperial Russian Army. Everyone knelt before a votive altar consisting of an ikon of the Virgin and Child overlooking a wine-colored cup in which burned a flame. The assembled prayed aloud for their relatives and countrymen living under Stalin.

Sunday afternoon was given over to festivities after Tzuglevich had blessed the converted hen coop that housed *Fashist*'s printing press. Alex led his guests across the Country Home Road to Ream's Pond, where the servants had prepared a picnic. Someone started singing, and the melody, mixed with happy shouts of the children splashing in the pond, drifted across the Quinnatisset golf course until finally it was lost in the faint din of holiday firecrackers.

Throughout this pastoral scene, brown-shirted guards with Lady Astor and other German shepherds kept curiosity seekers away. Only reporters who identified themselves were permitted to circulate among the picnickers. Asked by a newsman if he felt safe from Communist attacks in Thompson, one *soratnik* replied:

> The Communists, like many other people, have heard a report that we have a button, a secret button, in the building [stone annex?] which we may push and so blow up the whole of Thompson, and that we have machine guns all about, but we haven't. The publicity, however, is our best protection.

* An unidentified *soratnik* later complained to a reporter that there might not be any Stalinists left to punish by the time that the VNRP took over Russia.

For a moment, it did look as if the Communists were at hand. Two airplanes circled low over the estate, releasing bundles of shredded red tissue paper which fluttered down like confetti. In the words of Hartford *Courant* reporter Frank Quinlan: "Whether the dropping of red tissue was meant as a Communist warning or merely was a holiday prank, no one knows, for the planes left at once and the identity of their owners was not available."

The weekend ended on Monday, July 5—anticlimactically. The guest of honor, Prince Theodore, was scheduled to arrive at Nineteenth Hole in the afternoon, having disembarked in New York from the liner *Europa* that same morning. As it developed, however, his progress was impeded by an unforeseen development centering around Thompson's Marianopolis College. Marianopolis (formerly Carolyn Hall, the Ream family estate) was a religious academy operated by Marist Fathers. Most of its students were boys of Lithuanian descent being trained for the priesthood. It so happened that on July 4, 1937, Marianopolis had been celebrating Lithuanian Day, and some ten thousand Lithuanian immigrants and their families had descended upon Thompson from all over New England and eastern Canada. On July 5, thousands of cars were clogging routes 101 and 193 leaving the area as the Lithuanians started home. Theodore's limousine became entangled in the general exodus and did not reach Nineteenth Hole until 11:30 P.M., by which time most of the *soratniki* had already departed for Harlem and Back Bay, some unknowingly passing him in the traffic jam.

It was probably just as well that Theodore had missed the reception that Vonsiatsky had prepared for him. The tall Romanov scion liked Alex well enough but smiled wryly at any mention of the VNRP. Although too polite to say so, the prince was probably relieved to have been spared an encounter with three dozen overexcited fellow countrymen. Living quietly in England, he now had no desire to return to Russia, whatever its form of government. For the benefit of reporters gathered at Nineteenth Hole, he remarked that "the present form of government in Russia can be easily changed into a fascist state." Whether he meant that the National Revolution was at hand or merely that Stalinism was moving toward fascism was left unclear.

The remainder of Theodore's visit passed uneventfully, at least as far as the press was concerned. Preoccupied with the flood of Lithuanians, Thompson residents paid little attention to his arrival or to the previous day's festivities at Nineteenth Hole. After all, local folk were by now accustomed to Alex's exotic guest lists and Fourth of July jubilees. But unbeknownst to Vonsiatsky, this particular week- end set in motion forces that would someday get him into serious difficulties. His antics, it seemed, were beginning to win him notoriety in New York and Washington, where unlike Thompson, there were people who took him seriously.

CHAPTER XV

Mounting Storm

> Then there are the White Russian Fascists in Connecticut. I can
> take you out there and show you an arsenal as big as this building
> with powder, guns, and ammunition with an army of 50,000 Fas-
> cists right in the state of Connecticut. Why does not the governor
> of Connecticut do something?
>
> —CONGRESSMAN SAMUEL DICKSTEIN (D–N.Y.), in a speech before
> the House of Representatives. July 27, 1937.

Anastase Vonsiatsky possessed a Midas touch with notoriety. Again
and again, through a disarming combination of imagination and gall,
he succeeded in transforming the most banal happening into a colorful
news story. As early as 1921, he had stumbled into infamy by "confess-
ing" to a half-dozen fanciful murders in "Memoirs of a Monarchist."
Then in 1922, by going to the altar with Marion, he had captured
international attention as a sort of marital jackpot winner, then had
soared to even loftier heights of publicity when Lyuba Muromsky
showed up and charged him with bigamy. Throughout the 1920s,
his seemingly endless succession of speeding tickets, wild parties,
and musical comedies ensured that the count from Connecticut was
never far from the public eye.

In the 1930s, however, the nature of Vonsiatsky's notoriety underwent a fundamental change. Until then, his critics—mainly his in-
laws—had regarded him primarily as a nuisance. But by the end of
the 1930s, he was being depicted as a serious threat to both the
United States and the Soviet Union. Noisy accusations aimed at him
in the press and in Congress obliged Washington to make an effort
to ascertain just what Vonsiatsky was. At least twenty government
and private investigations of Vonsiatsky were conducted between 1933
and 1941. The time spent by officials in the State, War, Navy, Justice,
and Treasury departments on these investigations, not to mention

230

БОГ, НАЦІЯ, ТРУДЪ.

К ОБЪЕДИНЕНІЮ! К ОЗДОРОВЛЕНІЮ! К ПРОБУЖДЕНІЮ!   РУССКІЙ РУССКОМУ ДРУГ И БРАТ

НАШ ПУТЬ

ЕЖЕДНЕВНЫЙ ОРГАН РУССКОЙ НАЦІОНАЛЬНОЙ МЫСЛИ ЗА РУБЕЖОМ.
РЕДАКТОР: К. В. Родзаевскій.

Год изданія II.   № 101 (198)

Харбин   Четверг 26 апрѣля 1934 г.   Цѣна 10 цент.

„Наш Путь" привѣтствует Вождя!

ДА ЗДРАВСТВУЕТ АНАСТАСІЙ АНДРЕЕВИЧ ВОНСЯЦКІЙ!

Да здравствует Русская Національная Фашистская Партія!

ДА ЗДРАВСТВУЕТ РУССКАЯ НАЦІОНАЛЬНАЯ РЕВОЛЮЦІЯ!

Да здравствует грядущая Фашистская Національная-Трудовая Россія!

ПРИВѢТ! СЛАВА РОССІИ!

Сегодня в 2 ч. 10 м. дня А. А. ВОНСЯЦКІЙ приѣзжает в Харбин.

"НАШЪ ПУТЬ" — ВЪ ДЕНЬ ПРІѢЗДА А. А. ВОНСЯЦКАГО ВЪ ХАРБИНЪ.

A special issue of the newspaper *Nash Put* for April 26, 1934, welcoming Anastase Vonsiatsky to Harbin for a celebration of the union of his All-Russian Fascist Organization (VFO) with Konstantin Rodzaevsky's Russian Fascist Party (RFP) to form the All-Russian Fascist Party (VFP). Slogans in the headlines include: "Long Live Anastase Andreivich Vonsiatsky!" "Greetings to the *Vozhd*!" and "Hail Russia!"

Rodzaevsky, beardless and hands clasped, waiting with a squad of Blackshirts for Vonsiatsky's arrival at the Harbin Railroad Station. (*Nash Put*)

Members of the All-Russian Women's Fascist Movement also line up in honor of Vonsiatsky at the Station in Harbin. (*Nash Put*)

A moment of triumph for Anastase Vonsiatsky as *vozhd* of all Russian fascists. The count from Connecticut, wearing a sport coat, accepts salutes as he disembarks at the Harbin Railroad Station. On his left, Donat ("Coontz") Kunle, carries the mandatory bulging briefcase. (*Nash Put*)

Vonsiatsky addressing a gala reception in his honor at Harbin's Russian Club on April 26, 1934. From left to right: Donat Kunle; Mikhail Matkovsky, VFP Central Committee member; Alexander ("Sasha") Bolotov, chief of the strong-arm VFP Special Detachment; and Vonsiatsky. (*Nash Put*)

Konstantin Steklov, Vonsiatsky's representative in Shanghai after the schism with Rodzaevsky in 1935. Subsidized by his Connecticut patron, Steklov published an intermittently anti-Japanese newspaper called *Russky Avangard* from 1936 until 1941. (*Fashist*)

Mikhail Mikhailovich Grott (also known as Grott-Spassovsky). A Hitler fan who translated *Mein Kampf* into Russian, Grott was hailed by both Rodzaevsky and Vonsiatsky as a "great ideologue of Russian fascism." In the summer of 1941, Rodzaevsky recommended him to the Germans for a cabinet ministry in the future "Russian National Government." (*Fashist*)

Vonsiatsky at ease amid racks of old rifles and mementos of cadet days in the White armies in his small chamber next to the Military Room at Nineteenth Hole. Note the swastika on the wastebasket. (*Fashist*)

Portrait of an unidentified Japanese woman found among Vonsiatsky's papers. On the back is written, in Japanese: "On the occasion of our parting in Paris, I give [you] thanks from my heart. I pray that our friendship will continue forever." The woman seems to have been Nakamura Fusako, daughter of a Tokyo businessman whom Vonsiatsky met in 1934 and subsequently saw in Connecticut. Their friendship aroused suspicion in the Justice Department that Vonsiatsky might be an agent for Japan. (*courtesy of Andre A. Vonsiatsky*)

A portrait of Marion Ream Vonsiatsky at the age of sixty-two, painted by V. Podgursky when she and Alex visited Shanghai in 1939.

Three *soratniki* (comrades) take time out at Nineteenth Hole during the notorious Fourth of July weekend of 1937. From the left: Donat ("Coontz") Kunle, the VNRP secretary; Anastase Vonsiatsky, *vozhd* of the VNRP; and Reverend Alexander Tzuglevich of St. George's Church in Bayside, Long Island, and principal of the Russian Fascist Bible School in Harlem.

КРАСНОАРМЕЕЦ, в случае войны, - в т ы к а й
штык в землю!

Орган Ц. И. К. ВСЕРОССИЙСКОЙ ФАШИСТСКОЙ (национал-революцион-
ной трудовой и рабоче-крестьянской) ПАРТИИ и Организации

The masthead for *Fashist*, organ of Vonsiatsky's All-Russian Fascist Party. Above the stylized triangle forming the word "*Fashist*," a slogan exhorts Red Army soldiers to stick their bayonets into the ground in time of war.

Staff and students of New York's Russian Fascist Bible School. Financed by Vonsiatsky, the school operated from 1936 until 1939 in the apartment of VNRP uptown Manhattan leader Evgeny Bogoslovsky (upper right, with mustache) and was directed by Reverend Alexander Tzuglevich (center, with glasses and priestly garb). Note the portraits of Tsar Nicholas II (upper left), Vonsiatsky (upper right), and the liberal use of swastikas, including what appears to be a Christmas tree ornament on the extreme left. (*Fashist*)

the cost to the American taxpayer, can only be imagined. Yet even in 1941, the Federal Bureau of Investigation was still not sure whether it was dealing with a German-Japanese superspy or with an innocuous poseur.

How could Anastase Andreivich have created such nationwide agitation when practically everyone in Thompson knew him to be little more than a showman? For one thing, the farther away one got from Thompson, the easier it was to inflate the count's power and importance. For another, a number of people, particularly newspaper reporters, were more than willing to make Vonsiatsky look important. The *Daily Worker* obviously found him an ideally constituted bogeyman, but even apolitical reporters discovered that Vonsiatsky made good copy. He was colorful, dynamic, outrageous, exotic, and veiled himself in just the right amount of mystery. At the same time, he made himself available to all newsmen, regardless of their politics.

In addition to those consciously building up Vonsiatsky, there were others predisposed to take his claims at face value. These included many liberals who were alarmed and revolted by the rise of fascism in Europe and tended to regard the USSR as the main bulwark against its spread (at least until the Nazi-Soviet Pact in 1939). In the eyes of these people, it was natural to link Vonsiatsky with Hitler. Vonsiatsky called himself a fascist, wore a swastika arm band, sang the Horst Wessel song (albeit with different words), and made no secret of being anti-Soviet. Therefore, he must be a Nazi. And once the label "Nazi" had been applied to the count, all the associations conjured up by that word attached themselves to him.

Finally, there were a few politicians who, regardless of whether or not they considered him a threat to American security, made Vonsiatsky a steppingstone for their own careers. It was from this last group that the *vozhd* eventually met his nemesis.

The national storm over Vonsiatsky brewed for about ten years, a decade punctuated by four outbursts separated by lulls. Although each outburst showed Alex where his antics would ultimately lead, he took no notice—until it was too late.

Breeze, 1931–35

Public attacks on Anastase Vonsiatsky began in 1931–32 when the *Daily Worker* linked him with capitalist conspiracies against the

USSR, with a plot to murder American engineers in Russia, and with the assassination of Japanese prime minister Inukai Tsuyoshi. Then, in 1933, when Vonsiatsky established the VFO and launched *Fashist,* consulted with Russian rightists in Berlin, and mounted a propaganda campaign against American diplomatic recognition of the USSR, criticism of him in the *Daily Worker* and liberal émigré newspapers escalated. But what provoked a far wider reaction was his bid in 1934 to become *vozhd* of Russian fascists throughout the world.

As a publicity stunt, Vonsiatsky's world tour of 1934 was an unqualified success. He joined his soap-bubble VFO with Rodzaevsky's relatively powerful Manchurian organization and was thought to have met with Japanese generals, Hitler, Goering, Goebbels, and Rosenberg—a misapprehension that he deliberately left uncorrected. He also established his own visibility in Russian colonies between Shanghai and Paris. *Fashist* chronicled his peregrinations as those of a Roman conqueror. Even the normally restrained French newspaper *Le Temps* proclaimed him a "Russian Hitler."

The 1934 world tour caused a flurry of concern in Washington. Alerted to the *vozhd*'s forthcoming visit to Japan in March 1934, Secretary of State Cordell Hull took no chances and notified legations in China, Japan, the Middle East, the Balkans, and France to prepare reports of Vonsiatsky's movements and utterances. Military intelligence at Fort Shafter, Territory of Hawaii, was apprised that the count's itinerary would take him through Honolulu.

Between April and August 1934, Washington received reports on Vonsiatsky from Tokyo, Harbin, Shanghai, Sofia, Belgrade, and Paris. These were often accompanied by newspaper clippings and texts of Vonsiatsky's speeches, jotted down and translated by émigré informants. From all this material, Secretary Hull learned (1) that while holding a commission as first lieutenant in the United States Army Reserve, Vonsiatsky had held discussions with Japanese military personnel, and (2) that the VFP, of which Vonsiatsky had just been named leader, sought to overthrow the Soviet government. The secretary of state was thereupon faced with the problem of determining whether Vonsiatsky's activities constituted a violation of the 1933 Roosevelt-Litvinov agreement establishing U.S.-U.S.S.R. diplomatic relations, in which both sides promised not to permit the formation or residence on its territory of any organization or group "which has as an aim the overthrow or the preparation for the overthrow of, or the bringing about by force of a change in, the political or social order of" their respective countries. To answer this question for the Department, Assistant Chief of Eastern European Affairs Earl L. Packer was instructed to investigate Vonsiatsky. Packer promptly dispatched Special Agent R. C. Bannerman to Thompson.

Bannerman called Vonsiatsky from New York on November 7, 1934, identifying himself and frankly stating his assignment. The count told him that such sensitive matters could not be discussed over the phone and invited him to come up to Nineteenth Hole for a four-thirty appointment that afternoon. When Bannerman arrived, he was subjected to "very careful scrutiny" by a male secretary, ushered into the Military Room, and interrogated by Donat Kunle. Kunle then took Bannerman's identification papers downstairs. A moment later, a tall, erect man in civilian dress strode into the Military Room and courteously asked how he could be of help.

For the next hour and a half, Bannerman listened to the *vozhd* describe his party and objectives. The count assured his visitor that Russian fascists in America engaged only in propaganda and were not involved in plans for military intervention. Of course at some time in the future, the USSR would be confronted simultaneously with internal upheaval and foreign invasion. At that moment, American VFP "shock troopers" would join their comrades in the Far East. Their task would be to win over Russian peasants and laborers in advance of, and in territory occupied by, the Japanese army. Japanese forces, following the creation of a "national" Russia, would withdraw or face "a second Ireland" on their hands. Alex said that he had discussed this plan with Japanese leaders who, however, had remained noncommittal. While conceding that some of his shock troopers were anti-Semitic, Vonsiatsky insisted that the VFP as a whole was not. In fact, Mark Weinbaum, Jewish editor of the *Novoye Russkoye Slovo,* had recently spent a night at Nineteenth Hole, discussing the possibility of collaboration with *Fashist.* Vonsiatsky then handed Bannerman some newspaper clippings about himself and assured the agent of his willingness to hold further interviews upon request.

Bannerman submitted a report on his conversation with Vonsiatsky to Packer on November 10. It professed to see nothing harmful in the count and concluded:

> . . . here is a White Russian of the old aristocracy intent on doing as much harm as possible to the Soviets and, by a fortunate and apparently happy marriage supplemented by his own attractive personality, able to translate his desires into action in a big way.

Anastase concluded that he had made a good impression on Bannerman. Six weeks later in an interview with the Washington *Star*, he asserted that State Department investigators (he used the plural) had given him a "clean bill of health."

Vonsiatsky's remark to the Washington *Star* triggered an indignant reaction from pro-Soviet quarters which quickly lambasted the State Department for complicity in Vonsiatsky's misdeeds. In a series of articles on Vonsiatsky published in *Soviet Russia Today*, monthly organ of the New York-based Friends of the Soviet Union (FSU), Leon Dennen identified Packer's superior, Robert F. Kelley, chief of the State Department's Division of Eastern European Affairs, as the culprit. Kelley, according to Dennen, was a "notoriously anti-Soviet" tool of Wall Street who got "most of his information from White Guard papers published in Paris and the United States." Kelley supposedly accepted Vonsiatsky "with open arms" as an instrument to undermine Soviet-American relations.

Dennen's articles, republished in 1935 as a thirty-page FSU booklet entitled *White Guard Terrorists in the USA*, became a prototype of "Vonsiatskiana": a species of imaginatively alarmist literature that built up the count as a menace to the USSR and the United States. Anastase was introduced as "a murderer of the Russian workers and the son of a murderer." His aim was to take over the USSR "through terror, through the assassination of Soviet leaders, and through plotting war on the Soviet Union." Behind him stood an "aged heiress, Marion Ream, and what is more important, her connections with Wall Street bankers," not to mention William Randolph Hearst, Sir Henri Deterding, Japanese militarists, and Adolf Hitler. Alfred Rosenberg had personally "acclaimed and feted" Vonsiatsky in Berlin in 1934, hoping to enlist the court's services in a planned German-Japanese invasion of the Soviet Union. Vonsiatsky, according to the booklet, was more than ready to oblige. In fact, Dennen warned, he was building up a global army:

> There are at least a million White Guards all over the world who are plotting to destroy the Soviet Union. In New York alone there are more than 3,000 of them. . . . In Mexico, Argentina, United States, Germany, Poland, Japan, China, Manchuria—all over the world—the agents of Vonsiatsky and his like are recruiting the army of the counterrevolution.

Anastase was so pleased with Dennen's booklet that he used it as a model for a commissioned biography of himself three years later.

Dennen and Vonsiatsky alike were incorrect in assuming that the State Department had given the count a "clean bill of health." On March 13, 1935, Secretary Hull wrote to Secretary of the Army George H. Dern, outlining Vonsiatsky's activities and asking if his officer's commission should not be revoked. Dern passed the letter on to the Army Chief of Staff, General Douglas MacArthur, who assured Hull on March 26 that Vonsiatsky's commission had expired ten days earlier and would not be renewed.

Hull did not let the matter drop there. On May 18, he sent Attorney General Homer S. Cummings a bundle of newspaper clippings and confidential reports on Vonsiatsky and asked whether the count's anti-Soviet activities violated any provision of the law. Cummings replied on June 17: "An examination of the facts disclosed fails to indicate that the activities of Mr. Vonsiatsky, at least up to the present time, are in violation of any provisions of Federal law."

Was the attorney general deliberately turning a blind eye to a movement that professed the overthrow of a foreign government? This question was soon to become a live issue in Soviet-American relations. When American Communists attended the All-World Congress of the Communist International (Comintern) in Moscow during July and August of 1935, Hull considered their attendance a "flagrant violation of the pledge of noninterference given us on November 16, 1933" and promptly sent off a strongly worded protest. In rejecting the protest, Moscow called attention to "White Guard" activities in the United States—an elliptical reference to Vonsiatsky.

There is, in fact, no evidence that the State Department or any American government agency approved the count's antics. Most likely, the government left Vonsiatsky alone for the time being because he looked ineffective. And at least he could no longer parade about in a U.S. Army uniform.

Gust, 1937

Two years after the first series of outbursts over his political behavior, Vonsiatsky again found himself the object of public outrage. Although the immediate cause of the furor was trivial (the Fourth of July weekend spectacular described in the previous chapter), the outcry assumed grander dimensions.

Tremors began more than a month before the weekend as a result of a picture story about Vonsiatsky appearing on May 21, 1937, in the Pittsburgh *Press* under the headline:

REVOLT AGAINST RUSSIA!
U.S. HEIRESS DEVOTES FORTUNE
TO HUSBAND'S ANTI-SOVIET PARTY

The article was illustrated by portraits of Anastase in full uniform, a sunbonneted Marion ("devoting her 50 million dollar fortune to her husband's cause"), the stone annex ("a veritable fortress . . . capable of withstanding a siege"), the Military Room ikon ("amidst a bristling display of rifles and war helmets"), and Misha Kapral giving "the familiar Nazi salute beside the familiar Nazi banner." Under a photo of two dozen antiquated rifles was the caption: "These rifles are used to drill his private army of White Russians whom he transports from New York City by motor bus." The unsigned article concluded on an upbeat note: "Connecticut state police find Mr. Vonsiatsky a handy neighbor. They occasionally borrow his rifles and tear gas to quell strike disorders."

One reader of the Pittsburgh *Press* was upset enough to write the secretary of state asking whether it was legal for anyone to raise a "private army" inside the United States. The State Department passed the query on to the attorney general, who informed the Pittsburgh *Press* reader that: "The Attorney General is authorized by law to give opinions only to the President and heads of the Executive Departments." That answer would not suffice for dealing with the aftermath of Vonsiatsky's Fourth of July weekend.

Hardly had the last *soratnik* pushed home through the Lithuanian traffic jam around Thompson on July 5 when angry letters began pouring into Washington. One of the first, written to Rhode Island Congressman Aime J. Forand, fulminated:

> . . . a motley crew of fascists, subversive elements, and malcontents are using the comparative freedom of our country to plot the overthrow of a friendly country, namely the Soviet Union. I also note that this band of criminals and cut-throats is apparently in possession of deadly weapons.

The writer demanded an immediate investigation by the FBI and Secret Service. Forand forwarded the letter to the secretary of state who, in what was becoming a reflex, sent it on to the attorney general to decide what action should be taken.

In addition to notes from individual citizens, there were letters and telegrams from three Communist-front organizations: the American League Against War and Fascism (ALAWAF), Friends of the Soviet Union (FSU), and the International Workers Order (IWO). Hester Huntington, secretary for ALAWAF's Norwalk, Connecticut branch, wired Connecticut Congressman William M. Citron, Connecticut Senator Francis T. Maloney, and Secretary of State Hull on July 19 protesting the existence of Vonsiatsky's party as violating the Roosevelt-Litvinov Agreement. Stanley Randolph, FSU New York district secretary, conveyed similar views to Maloney, Hull, Connecticut Governor Wilbur Cross, and Attorney General Cummings in a series of letters dated July 12 to July 29. The New York-based IWO mounted a write-in campaign through July and August. Letters from IWO locals in Hartford, Providence, New York, and Chicago descended upon Hull and President Roosevelt. Chicago IWO leader Nicholas Kutzko charged that Vonsiatsky "uses his home for the purpose of an arsenal for storing war munitions for use against the Soviet Union and its friends at home or abroad." IWO president William Weiner asserted that:

> The Russian National Revolutionary Fascist Party is a menace and a threat both to our good relations with the Soviet Union and to our democratic form of government in the United States. It must be liquidated and forbidden to operate any further.

Nor were letters and telegrams the only form of Vonsiatskiana provoked by the Fourth of July weekend. Anastase Andreivich's name was soon reverberating through Congress. Congressional attention came not from Connecticut or Rhode Island representatives but from a New York City Democrat, Samuel Dickstein. Born near Vilna, Russia, in 1885, Dickstein had emigrated to America in 1891 and grew up on New York's Lower East Side. Elected to the House of Representatives in 1922, he specialized in immigration affairs. With the rise of Hitler and persecution of Jews in Germany, Dickstein became an avid hunter of extreme rightists within the United States, serving from March 1934 to February 1935 as vice-chairman of John W. McCormack's Special Committee on Nazi Propaganda. In January 1937, as chairman of the House Committee on Immigration and Naturalization, Dickstein introduced a bill to deport "undesirable aliens" who had contracted marriages to expedite admission into the United States. Perhaps Vonsiatsky was one of those whom he had in mind.

Dickstein launched his first public attack on Vonsiatsky over the radio on July 9, 1937. He had the broadcast appended to the Congressional Record. In the broadcast, the congressman dropped mysterious hints that made Vonsiatsky look like a formidable adversary: "In the state of Connecticut today there is an organization controlling 50,000 Fascists in the United States. They are conspiring with the other subversive foreign groups in this country."

Seventeen days later, in a speech before the House of Representatives, Dickstein identified "the other subversive foreign groups" as German Nazis and Italian Blackshirts:

> The Nazis, the Black Shirts, the Fascists, and the White Dirty Shirts have formed an organization. The leader of the White Russians who has combined with the Nazis and the Black Shirts, is Anastase A. Vonsiatsky, and if I do not pronounce his name properly I think the best thing to do is to whistle it. Some woman who had a lot of money, running into the millions, was crazy enough to marry this so-called ex-prince or ex-somebody, and this whole fortune is being spent to build up a White Russian organization in this country. This organization is combining with the Nazis to overthrow the Russian Government.

The very next day, July 27, Dickstein continued his exposé of Vonsiatsky. This time, he located all "50,000 Fascists" within the state of Connecticut and credited Nineteenth Hole with an arsenal "as big as this building" (presumably the U.S. Capitol). Furthermore, he demanded to know what Connecticut Governor Wilbur Cross was doing about the situation.

Where Dickstein obtained his figure of fifty thousand Connecticut fascists remains unclear. Even with turtles and pigeons, the number far exceeded all but Vonsiatsky's most whimsical claims. Such details did not deter the congressman from confidently hammering away at the "White Dirty Shirts" throughout the remainder of July and well into August.

Under such a barrage of indignation, the State Department could not help but—in Dickstein's words—"do something." At just about the same time as Dickstein's speech Special Agent Bannerman was ordered by Division of European Affairs chief Jay Pierrepont Moffat to look in on Vonsiatsky again and find out what he was up to this time. Before driving up to Thompson, Bannerman called on the Connecticut State attorney general's office in Hartford to see what was being done about Vonsiatsky. Apparently nothing was being done. No one had brought the count's antics to the attorney general's attention. Bannerman then drove on to Putnam and talked with the local postmaster about the notorious Fourth of July weekend. He learned that:

> . . . there had been no recent publicity about the Vonsiatsky situation other than a local item copied from a Bridgeport, Connecticut, paper with reference to a Fourth of July meeting on the Vonsiatsky estate of a number of delegates affiliated with that movement. There was no local interest in the gathering, as over the same week-end there had been a large gathering of priests of the Marist Fathers on an estate adjoining Vonsiatsky, and this was given considerable prominence in the Putnam paper. There was no local gossip about the County Attorney being requested to take any action. There had been no disturbance of the peace, and there was no intimation that the Vonsiatsky delegates had uniforms or participated in any military drills or parades. In fact, the meeting would have passed without notice in Putnam if the Bridgeport news item had not been quoted in the local paper.

Concluding that under the circumstances it was unnecessary to see the county attorney, Bannerman phoned Vonsiatsky from Putnam and asked for an appointment. The count invited him to come directly. Fifteen minutes later, at three o'clock in the afternoon on July 26, the two men met on the lawn in front of Nineteenth Hole and adjourned to the Military Room.

Asked if the recent newspaper publicity meant a change in his activities, the count replied that he remained essentially a propagandist. Propaganda, he continued, was his "best weapon against Soviet Russia and really the only one available for the relatively small number of White Russians now living in the United States." Consequently, he welcomed any publicity about himself.

As to the Fourth of July weekend, Vonsiatsky explained that he had invited about thirty-five party members and their families to be his guests and to meet the nephew of Nicholas II. True, there had been political discussions, but no drilling. Several days after the Fourth, Harry Raymond of the *Daily Worker* had phoned from New York asking about the weekend. Knowing that Raymond would use any material at hand to denounce the VNRP, Vonsiatsky had invited him up for a personal interview. Raymond had accepted and, true to expectation, the *Daily Worker* made much of the "Fascist camp" and its "huge arsenal." Alex expressed himself as quite satisfied with such publicity. No matter how adverse, it would make him and his cause known inside the Soviet Union.

Asked by Bannerman about his foreign connections, Vonsiatsky spoke bitterly about Japan. Japan's callous treatment of White Russians in Manchuria precluded any VNRP cooperation with Tokyo. As to Germany, Alex declared himself neither a supporter nor an enemy of Hitler. The *vozhd*'s attitude to Hitler would depend upon the Führer's understanding of and policies toward White Russian aspirations.

Vonsiatsky then conducted Bannerman on a tour of the Military Room, explaining where he had bought the rifles and reciting stories of each regimental flag and autographed portrait. Of course he did not fail to dwell upon the bullet-ridden greatcoat draped over a human mannequin. He asserted that concern for personal security, not subversive intentions, dictated the basement office, German shepherds, and tear gas bombs, which, he reminded Bannerman, had not been used by the state police since September 1934—press reports notwithstanding.

When Special Agent Bannerman left Nineteenth Hole later that afternoon, his mind was made up:

> To describe the annex to the Vonsiatsky residence as an arsenal is a complete perversion of the facts. . . . There is no evidence of any military activity. . . . For an active anti-Soviet propagandist residing in a rather remote section, the presence of the dogs and the bombs on the property must be reassuring. Evidence of the possession of aggressive military equipment or the pursuit of any military purpose is entirely lacking.

On July 28, before drafting his report to Moffat, Bannerman dispatched two subordinates to 501 Broadway to check out Francis Bannerman & Sons (no relation), where Vonsiatsky had purchased five dozen rifles starting in 1930. The clerk, C. J. Scott, could not locate the invoice for these transactions but vividly remembered the purchaser because of his "striking appearance and aristocratic deportment." The rifles, manufactured by Remington Arms and the Westinghouse Company for the tsarist government, were calibrated for Russian ammunition and sights (paces rather than feet). Undelivered because of the February Revolution, they wound up in a downtown Manhattan gun dealer's storeroom, priced at $14 each. Scott recalled that Vonsiatsky had explained he was organizing a local gun club in Connecticut and, being Russian, wanted equipment associated with his motherland. The clerk attached no special significance to the sale, for "it was not unusual for gun clubs, American Legion posts and similar organizations to purchase a number of rifles for the reasons given by the Thompson customer."

By the time Bannerman's report, dated July 29, reached the State Department, Secretary Hull had also received a legal opinion on Vonsiatsky's activities from Assistant Attorney General Brien McMahon. After scrutinizing all the complaints, McMahon concluded that the count had not violated any federal criminal statute. However, whether Vonsiatsky had contravened the Roosevelt-Litvinov agreement was another matter. McMahon deferred judgment on the latter question, asking Hull to request a formal investigation should he want an answer.

Apparently reluctant to request a formal investigation of Vonsiatsky, the State Department nudged the attorney general to issue an informal opinion on the legality of the *vozhd*'s activities in the light of the Roosevelt-Litvinov agreement. On August 12, one of Secretary Hull's assistants sent McMahon copies of Bannerman's 1934 and 1937 reports, together with transcripts of the Roosevelt-Litvinov correspondence. The covering letter asked: Did Vonsiatsky violate "any undertaking embodied in the President's letter of November 16, 1933" to Litvinov? A faint echo of bureaucratic ping-pong can be detected in McMahon's reply, dated August 17:

> While I have given consideration to the statements contained in the enclosures transmitted with your letter, it occurs to me that this Department is not in a position to express its views on the question propounded, for the reason that it appears to be entirely a diplomatic question to be decided from an administrative standpoint by your Department.

Thrust back on its own resources, the State Department took no further action.

Vonsiatsky might have fallen into bureaucratic limbo had not McMahon notified the Commissioner of Internal Revenue and the Federal Bureau of Investigation about his activities. As a result, Treasury Department and FBI agents prowled around Thompson during August and September. FBI agent George J. Starr interviewed Vonsiatsky at Nineteenth Hole on September 24. His findings—twenty-six typewritten pages, together with photos and copies of *Fashist*—were submitted to J. Edgar Hoover, who forwarded them to Attorney General Cummings on January 4, 1938. From this time onward, the FBI maintained a general surveillance of Vonsiatsky.

Lull, 1938–39

The public outcry and governmental deliberations that swirled around Vonsiatsky following his Fourth of July weekend gradually dissipated toward the end of 1937, ushering in a comparatively placid interim that lasted almost two years. Such unwonted serenity resulted in part from Alex's being overseas more often.

In the spring of 1938, Alex and Marion toured Europe. Early in March, they tarried in the Third Reich long enough to feel unwelcome. Moving on to Austria, they stood among thousands of onlookers as Adolf Hitler entered Vienna on March 14 to consummate *Anschluss*. Continuing on to Yugoslavia, they stopped in Belgrade to meet a White hero of the Civil War, General Andrei Shkuro, leader of the Kuban Cossacks, who invited Vonsiatsky to a banquet of about 150 Cossack veterans. Vonsiatsky gave a speech ("heartily applauded," he later recalled) and was made an honorary member of the Kuban Cossacks. That episode marked the high point of his trip.

Returning to Thompson in May, Anastase discovered that his fame had dwindled precipitously. No papers mentioned his trip. The State, Justice, and Treasury departments, so it seemed, were ignoring him. Congressman Dickstein appeared to have forgotten him. The House Special Committee on Un-American Activities, also known as the Dies Committee, paid no attention to him. Alex's name did crop up once (November 21, 1938) during the Committee's hearings when someone said that "he has an arsenal and a little army of his own," but the statement aroused no visible interest. According to the Bridgeport *Sunday Herald*, Vonsiatsky actually felt slighted about being overlooked by the Dies Committee.

Oblivion seems to have made Alex restless. Late in 1938, he and Marion agreed to go on another world tour, their third in five years.* Despite (or perhaps because of) the schism with Rodzaevsky, Anastase wanted to check on his handful of followers in the Far East, most

---

* Their second world tour was an uneventful world cruise on the SS *President Adams* in 1936.

of whom lived in Shanghai. He also was concerned about the German government's unfriendly attitude toward him and felt that a little lobbying in the Reich might help. Finally, he was planning to commission a biography of himself and was looking for a pliant author and cheap press.

Embarking on the Dollar Line's SS *President Polk* from New York shortly before Christmas of 1938, Alex and Marion (this time without Kunle) proceeded via Panama to Los Angeles, where they arrived on January 16 and were greeted by California VNRP branch leader Feodor Semens. During a brief stopover, Vonsiatsky met some members of the local German-American Bund, a pro-Nazi organization with whom Semens enjoyed good relations, and gave an interview to the Los Angeles *Times* predicting a Soviet-German war over Rumania. The couple then continued on the *Polk* up the coast to San Francisco, arriving on January 18. Registering at the St. Francis Hotel, Vonsiatsky spent the next three days meeting local VNRP representatives and some prominent members of San Francisco's Russian community, including Grigory Timofeevich Suhoff, editor of the Russian newspaper *Novaya Zarya,* and Prince Vasily Alexandrovich Romanov, youngest son of Grand Duke Alexander and brother of Princes Theodore and Nikita. On January 21, Marion and Alex reboarded the *Polk* and headed across the Pacific.

During a ten-hour stopover in Honolulu on January 28, "Count and Countess Vonsiatsky" (as the *Polk*'s passenger list identified them) gave Honolulu *Advertiser* and Honolulu *Star Bulletin* reporters an interview in the couple's first-class cabin. Nicholas II gazed down at the proceedings from a frame hung on the bulkhead.

The count shrugged when asked about his mission. "Spies will know anyway. Why should I not tell the world about my plan? After all, it concerns the world."

In a conspiratorial murmur, Vonsiatsky confided that he was en route to rendezvous with party leaders in the Far East.

> I have scheduled my trip for strategic reasons. An army of propagandists is waiting in Russia to launch an attack within. Thousands of my party members are on the outside waiting to help those within. Events this year will be important. Stalin's rule is weakening all the time.

Anticipating a question about a swastika pin on his lapel, Vonsiatsky explained: "No, this is not a Nazi swastika. Hitler's swastika is black on red. Ours is white on blue. We adopted this symbol long before Hitler came to power."

As usual, Anastase added a dash of color for the reporters' benefit by describing Nineteenth Hole as "a castle made into an attack-proof fortress." Perhaps carried away by images of a rocky redoubt, both Honolulu papers substituted Plymouth for Thompson.

Arriving in Shanghai on February 17—Vonsiatsky did not even get off the boat when it stopped at Yokohama and Kobe—Alex and Marion registered at the Park Hotel. They were welcomed by Konstantin Steklov and a dozen local *soratniki.* Steklov, who liked to be called "colonel," had been bringing out a pro-Vonsiatsky newspaper *(Russky Avangard),* subsidized from Thompson. He also held the exalted but largely ornamental title of Far Eastern chief of the VNRP.

Vonsiatsky's 1939 visit to Shanghai has been described in grandiloquent terms by Natalya Ilina, an émigré who returned to the USSR in 1947 and subsequently published two volumes of fictionalized memoirs. Ilina assessed Marion's worth at $50 million, hinted at sinister ties between Vonsiatsky and Tokyo, and depicted RFS *vozhd* Rodzaevsky making a special trip from Harbin to confer with Vonsiatsky at the Park Hotel.

Alex would have been flattered by Ilina's scenario, but Japanese diplomatic and army files paint a somewhat less intriguing picture. They make no mention of a Vonsiatsky-Rodzaevsky meeting, nor did either *vozhd* ever allude to a Shanghai encounter in 1939 or any other year. Japanese Army Intelligence considered Steklov's newspaper to be anti-Japanese, and Consul Miura Yoshiaki thought that Vonsiatsky might try to stir up anti-Japanese sentiment among Shanghai's White Russians. Accordingly, he warned Tokyo that the American merited "strict surveillance."

The Japanese need not have been concerned. Vonsiatsky left Shanghai on February 21 after only a four-day stopover, boarding a liner bound for Europe. His only achievement in the city had been to find an author for his biography: N. N. Grozin.

Grozin's subsidized product, *Protective Shirts,* was brought out by a Russian-language press in Shanghai later in 1939. The rapidity of the book's completion was due to the fact that much of it was lifted from Leon Dennen's 1935 pamphlet by Friends of the Soviet Union: *White Guard Terrorists in the USA.*

The rest of the tour proved disappointing. No reporters flocked to interview him in the Middle East and Balkans as in 1934. No Cossack general entertained him as in 1938. When he arrived in Berlin and registered at the Adlon, he learned that the VNRP and *Fashist* were banned throughout the Reich.

Vonsiatsky fell afoul of German authorities for a number of reasons. Local Russian Nazis such as Bermondt-Avalov regarded him as an interloper and spared no effort to discredit him. Vonsiatsky's lack of anti-Semitic ardor made him vulnerable in ways that his rivals hastened to exploit, and rumors circulated that Kunle was Jewish, that Marion's Aryan ancestry was suspect, and that the VNRP was financed by American Jews. Boris Tedli, Rodzaevsky's Berlin-based agent, assiduously brought such rumors to the attention of the Gestapo, which needed no prodding. Around this time, a young VNRP *soratnik,* perhaps Vonsiatsky's only follower in the Reich, was summoned to Gestapo headquarters in Berlin and asked if he would prefer to finish his education in school or in a concentration camp. Quickly indicating that he preferred the former option, the terrified lad was told to sever connections with Vonsiatsky. In this atmosphere, the VNRP stood no chance of gaining even a modest constituency in Berlin's White Russian community.

Returning to Thompson on April 20 after an absence of four months, Anastase surveyed the political horizons. The international scene looked promising. The Soviet Union appeared to be on a collision course with Japan and Germany. Stalin's purges had seemingly eviscerated the Red Army and the Communist Party, leaving the regime—in Vonsiatsky's perception—gravely weakened. The *vozhd* sensed that the call of destiny could come at any moment. But was he ready to respond? His party still lacked foreign patrons. Banned in both Germany and Japan, it stood little chance of taking advantage of a Soviet-German or Soviet-Japanese war. Anxious lest the coming cataclysm leave him out in the cold, Vonsiatsky made a fateful decision. He would ingratiate himself with the German-American Bund and thereby establish his credentials in Berlin.

Gale, 1939

Vonsiatsky was not entirely a stranger to the Bund or to its belligerent, blue-eyed leader, Fritz Julius Kuhn. Born in Munich in 1896, Kuhn spent four years in the trenches during World War I and one year fighting Bolsheviks along the Baltic as a Freikorps volunteer. He joined the Nazi Party in 1921 and allegedly participated in the Munich beer hall putsch two years later. He came to the United States via Mexico in 1928, took out citizenship papers, and found employment as a chemist with the Ford Motor Company in Dearborn, Michigan. In 1933, Kuhn joined the Friends of New Germany, a Nazi organization of Germans and German-Americans with close ties to Goebbels' Propaganda Ministry, and quickly rose to head its Middle West department. When a "purely American" German-American Bund *(Amerikadeutscher Volksbund)* was formed in 1936, Kuhn emerged as its führer. Kuhn shared with Vonsiatsky a military background, immigrant status, and a penchant for showmanship. He strutted about in a custommade uniform (which he claimed was modeled on that of the American Legion), delivered blustery orations, and struck extravagant poses. But unlike Vonsiatsky, Kuhn hated Jews, worshiped Adolf Hitler, and had neither imagination nor humor.

Appropriately, Kuhn and Vonsiatsky became acquainted at a theatrical performance. In January 1937, the *Bundführer* wrote the count asking if he would like some complimentary tickets to a rally at the New York Hippodrome scheduled for Friday, February 12. The occasion was designed to bring together Bundists and representatives of Italian-Americans, Spanish monarchists, and Imperial Russia for a massive denunciation of communism, antifascism, Spanish loyalists, and the anti-Nazi boycott. Curious to hear Kuhn's oratory and eager to represent "Imperial Russia," Vonsiatsky decided to accept the invitation. But then it occurred to him that he certainly could not afford to show up at the Hippodrome alone. After all, he was a führer in his own right with a reputation to uphold. Accordingly, the *vozhd* instructed Donat Kunle to order fifty tickets in the name of the VNRP. When the packet of tickets arrived at Nineteenth Hole, Vonsiatsky forwarded it to uptown Manhattan VNRP chief Bogoslovsky with orders to scrape together sufficient bodies to occupy the entire reserved bloc of seats.

On February 12, Anastase, Kunle, and Mamedov turned up in full uniform at the Hippodrome. Looking at the endless rows of seats in the cavernous hall, Vonsiatsky momentarily felt a twinge of nerves. But his apprehension eased at the sight of Bogoslovsky's corpulent face, wearing a triumphant smile, as he strode through an entrance. Behind him shuffled a motley, bewildered herd of drab overcoats and crushed fedoras. Evgeny Mikhailovich had fulfilled his assignment admirably, having pressed nearly fifty tickets on assorted members of Harlem's Russian colony.

His flock safely seated, Vonsiatsky glanced at the program and emitted a snort of indignation. Another Russian name appeared in addition to his own: Nikolai Melnikov, identified as head of the "Russian National Union." The count instantly recognized an enemy in the arcane pantheon of émigré factions. He knew that the RNU had just established friendly ties with Rodzaevsky.

At this moment, Kuhn came over, introduced himself, and asked Vonsiatsky if he cared to say a few words to the assembly. Miffed by a pro-Rodzaevsky Slavic intruder's sharing the spotlight, Anastase truculently replied that he had a sore throat and could not speak. Kuhn nodded and walked off to the speakers' platform. After everyone had sung the "Star-Spangled Banner" standing at attention with arms outstretched in a Nazi salute, the speeches began. By the time Melnikov's turn came, Vonsiatsky was highly agitated. A Melnikov associate approached the podium and began to introduce the RNU. When he intoned that "Hitler is our leader" and "the Russian National Union is participating in actual warfare against Communist military forces," Vonsiatsky could stand it no longer:

> I signaled Kunle to leave and both of us rose, at which time the entire group which Bogoslovsky had drawn in got up and walked out with us. It gave the distinct impression of a mass walkout, and Fritz Kuhn hurried out and asked me what was the matter. I told him nothing was wrong but Kunle and I had to catch a train.

That episode dampened Bund-VNRP relations for the next two years.

Shortly after Vonsiatsky had returned to Thompson from his second world tour in April 1939, he received an invitation from Kuhn to attend the opening of Camp Siegfried, a Bund training and recreational ground adjacent to Camp Upton, a U.S. Army base, at Yaphank, Long Island. After discussing the matter with Kunle, Anastase decided that this was a good opportunity to reestablish friendly relations with the Bund. A reconciliation, he hoped, might eventually bring about the VNRP's reinstatement inside the Third Reich. He also relished the prospect of being photographed with Kuhn. That would make good material for *Fashist*.

On Sunday, May 21, Vonsiatsky, Kunle, and Mamedov drove into

Camp Siegfried in Marion's Cadillac touring car. They wore ceremonial garb: khaki shirts, riding slacks, black boots, and Sam Browne belts. Kuhn greeted the trio warmly and introduced them to his Russian-born secretary, James Wheeler-Hill, and to his national publicity director, Wilhelm Gerhard Kunze. As a band struck up the Horst Wessel song, Kuhn motioned Vonsiatsky to his side, and the two set off marching around the field, followed by about three thousand Bundists, including two hundred boys and girls of the *Jugendschaft* and three hundred storm troopers of the *Ordnungsdienst* (which journalists dubbed the "Bund SS"). Much to Alex's satisfaction, photographers abounded.

Exhilarated by all the fanfare, Vonsiatsky impetuously extended an open invitation to Kuhn and other Bund officers to drop by Nineteenth Hole whenever they found themselves in the vicinity. During June and July, Bund publicity director Kunze availed himself of the *vozhd*'s hospitality several times. Before long, Alex was calling him "Wilhelm Gerhardavich." Sooner or later, such fraternization was bound to reach the press, making Nineteenth Hole appear all the more sinister. But neither the *Daily Worker* nor the Bridgeport *Sunday Herald* could have devised a more improbable scenario than the incident that in one stroke brought the Bund-Vonsiatsky connection to the nation's attention.

On the afternoon of Saturday, July 15, 1939, after presiding over a Bund meeting in New Britain, Connecticut, Kuhn and three lieutenants (Wilhelm Kunze, James Wheeler-Hill, and Bund treasurer Gustav Elmer) headed by car toward Boston. Recalling Vonsiatsky's standing invitation, Kunze suggested, "Let's drop in on Alex. It's on the way."

Two hours later the Bundists, announced by Lady Astor, pulled up the driveway of Nineteenth Hole. Although not expecting guests, Anastase seemed delighted to see them and phoned Natasha Mamedov at the Russian Bear to prepare four extra settings for dinner. Donat Kunle, who found Kuhn offensive, suppressed his displeasure behind a noncommittal greeting. Marion, as was her custom when Alex entertained, excused herself. Her brother Louis Marshall Ream happened to be playing golf at the Quinnatisset Club with Frank Decker, an old family friend. Catching sight of them across County Home Road, Alex shouted an invitation to come over for a drink with some visitors. Louis whispered to Decker that he did not wish to accept, whereupon Decker called back to Alex that they were sorry but had another engagement. Decker later recalled that had he known that "some visitors" included Fritz Kuhn, he would have accepted Alex's invitation for curiosity's sake. Louis Marshall Ream, however, had been singed too many times by his brother-in-law to have any curiosity left.

Kuhn was in a bad mood that night. Even Natasha's chicken cutlets and mocha rum cake failed to distract him from his own problems. Kuhn was convinced that the press and the Roosevelt administration were persecuting him. Two months previously, a New York grand jury had indicted him for larceny after $14,548 had disappeared from Bund offices in Manhattan. New York District Attorney Thomas E. Dewey was pestering him with subpoenas. He had been in and out of jail, and was currently out on $5,000 bail. Half-reclining on a chintz sofa in the Military Room, Kuhn surrendered himself to self-pity. He drank everything offered, morosely half-listening to his host's prattle about grand dukes and greatcoats.

Around midnight, Kuhn suddenly blurted out: "Anyone want to go for a ride?" The *Bundführer* felt a restlessness that animates some drinkers when they are no longer sober but not quite besotted. Kunze, Wheeler-Hill, and Elmer dutifully nodded in agreement. Anastase, Kunle, and Mamedov did not look enthusiastic. As the visitors were unfamiliar with local roads, however, it was decided that Andy Mamedov, Vonsiatsky's nineteen-year-old nephew, would accompany them.

As Wheeler-Hill took the car up the County Home Road toward Thompson, Andy pointed out barely discernible landmarks: the Howe-Marot School for Girls, Marianopolis College, Vernon Stiles Inn. Thompson offered little in the way of night life, so Wheeler-Hill drove toward Route 12, turned north, and entered Webster, a town lying just across the Massachusetts state line. The night riders were now eight miles from Nineteenth Hole.

Just after one o'clock on the morning of Sunday, July 16, Andy took the Bundists to a cafe on Webster's Main Street, but upon entering they were told that Massachusetts law did not permit the sale of liquor after midnight Saturday. Disgruntled, the men sauntered over to another cafe for some coffee and pie. Meanwhile, Andy waited outside on the sidewalk, chatting with Webster's nocturnal guardian, Patrolman Henry Plasse.

Around one thirty, Kuhn, Wheeler-Hill, Kunze, and Elmer emerged from the cafe and headed toward their car. Noticing that Kuhn seemed unsteady on his feet, Officer Plasse remarked that he'd better not drive in that condition. Kuhn wheeled about and snarled: "Do you know who I am? Do you think you can talk to me like that?" Plasse, his own temperature rising, retorted that he did not care who Kuhn was. No one was going to drive around Webster under the influence of alcohol.

What followed is still difficult to disentangle. According to the Bundists, Kuhn then said: "Let's get the hell out of here." But Plasse recalled Kuhn's saying: "Go to hell." Whatever the exact wording, Plasse took Kuhn to the police station and booked him for drunkenness and profanity.

Four hours later, after Alex had been awakened and come over to the Webster police station to pay $54 bail, Kuhn and his companions were back at Nineteenth Hole. As the sun rose, word of the incident spread. Local reporters descended on Webster and besieged Plasse for a statement. By Sunday night, word of the affair had reached major networks and papers around the country. On Monday morning, July 17, *The New York Times* carried it on the front page.

Initial media reports garbled and sensationalized the events of July 15–16. Kuhn was described as having threatened the local police. One paper talked of an "attempted putsch." Officer Plasse was hailed as a hero for saving a defenseless New England village from a Nazi takeover. In several newspaper accounts, Vonsiatsky was said to have been present at, or even implicated in, the imbroglio.

On July 20, Vonsiatsky appeared at Webster's courthouse together with a throng of reporters and spectators for a hearing of *The People of Western Massachusetts* v. *Fritz Kuhn*. The *vozhd* did not come just to see the *Bundführer* plead guilty ("to avoid a theatrical performance," insisted Kuhn) and pay a $5 fine, the maximum statutory penalty for profanity, there being no fine for drunkenness. Alex was there to deny his involvement in the incident, and he brought along a Boston attorney, John H. Devine. Devine made a statement to the press, verbally confirmed by Kuhn, that his client had taken no part in the Webster affair and had not even been in Webster when it happened.

Alex was angry at the press for linking him with a local "putsch." He did not mind being accused of trying to overthrow Stalin, but to be associated with drunkenness and profanity in a neighboring town struck him as a smear on his good name. To show the press that he was serious, Vonsiatsky filed libel suits against several newspapers. The suits never reached court, for the newspapers published corrections or issued apologies. But such retractions came only after months of delay. *The New York Times,* for example, printed a statement of regret (on page 52) on June 5, 1940. By that time, the Webster affair had already triggered yet another major outburst of Vonsiatskiana.

This time, the opening salvo was fired by the American Council Against Nazi Propaganda (ACANP), headed by former American ambassador to Germany William Edward Dodd. One vehicle for the ACANP attack was its newsletter, *The Hour,* edited by Albert E. Kahn. Through the good offices of Richard McCauley, a Putnam free-lance journalist and friend of Alex's, a reporter for *The Hour* named David Karr interviewed Vonsiatsky three times at Nineteenth Hole shortly after the Webster affair. Karr used the occasion to gather considerable information about the VNRP and to take photographs of the count and his Military Room. After the third interview on August 2, Karr and McCauley drew up a notarized affidavit testifying that Vonsiatsky had acknowledged to them authorship of "Memoirs of a Monarchist." This material formed the basis for a fat file on Vonsiatsky at *The Hour's* Forty-second Street offices in New York. Starting with the July 30 issue, *The Hour* featured Vonsiatsky stories designed to arouse public alarm at, and catalyze government action against, the *vozhd.* Thirty-seven years later, editor Kahn recalled that:

> To the best of my knowledge, the first public information about Vonsiatsky's fifth column activities and murky past appeared in *The Hour* and was publicized in other news media as a consequence. It was also, I think, *The Hour* stories which resulted in government action being initiated against Vonsiatsky.

On August 3, following the first exposé in *The Hour,* the ACANP telegraphed Secretary of Labor Frances Perkins that it possessed documentary material proving that when Vonsiatsky had petitioned for U.S. citizenship in 1927, he had concealed "torture murders" committed in Yalta in 1920. The ACANP requested an immediate investigation of the charges and forwarded the "supporting documentary evidence" (presumably the August 2 Karr-McCauley affidavit on Vonsiatsky's authorship of "Memoirs of a Monarchist"). On August 18, ACANP chairman Dodd wired Congressman Martin Dies urging that Vonsiatsky be subpoenaed to testify before the Un-American Activities Committee about his connections with the German-American Bund and the Third Reich.

The ACANP campaign soon began to yield dividends. More and

more newspapers around the country took up the lurid "torture murders" and demanded that the Dies Committee take action. Some insisted that the "Russian Nazi" be deported.

Not surprisingly, Congressman Dickstein added his voice to the
clamor. On August 21, Dickstein wrote Secretary of State Hull that
"Vonsiatsky is a person who is seeking to ferment [sic] trouble on
the soil of this country" and whose activities were "un-American"
and "should be stamped out." He asked Hull to "let me have any
information you possibly can furnish me." Hull answered Dickstein
on August 30, suggesting that the representative from New York provide evidence "which tends to support the charges contained in your
letter." The secretary also forwarded a copy of Dickstein's letter to
Attorney General Frank Murphy for "such action as you may deem
appropriate."

Hull was well advised to route such material to the attorney general, for the Justice Department was without doubt the best-informed
government agency when it came to Vonsiatsky. The FBI had been
keeping the count under surveillance since 1937 and had conducted
two special investigations of him, the results of which were submitted
to the attorney general in January 1938 and May 1939 respectively.
FBI sources of information included interviews with Vonsiatsky himself, with Vonsiatsky's friends, with Putnam and Thompson residents,
and reams of unsolicited letters from informants. One FBI agent was
assigned exclusively to watch Vonsiatsky and lived in Putnam for two
years posing as a soap salesman. On one occasion, while out driving,
Alex unwittingly almost ran his shadow off the road. The attorney
general also collected information on Vonsiatsky from the Immigration and Naturalization Service and from the Treasury Department,
which in March 1939 provided him with Alex's income tax returns
for every year after 1933. What did all these data reveal?

Nothing—and everything. A Treasury Department investigation
established that Vonsiatsky's only operable firearm, the Thompson
submachine gun bought at Abercrombie & Fitch in 1930, had been
properly registered with the Connecticut State Police and the Internal
Revenue Service. Perhaps more to the point, it had no ammunition
drum. Exhaustive FBI investigations "failed to disclose any information which would indicate that Vonsiatsky is receiving any financial
or other support from any foreign country or group." As to oft-re-
peated allegations of drilling and military maneuvers on the "fortress-

estate," the FBI agent stationed for two years in Putnam to watch Vonsiatsky reported that:

> . . . any such drilling would be visible from the highway and would become a matter of public knowledge. No information was obtained to indicate that any retainer, follower, or other individuals who might constitute any type of trained force of men reside on the premises [of Nineteenth Hole], and it is noted that interviews in this connection were conducted with numerous persons at Putnam and Thompson, with a view toward verifying this information which appears to be groundless.

After poring over the FBI files, Justice Department official Alexander Holtzoff notified Attorney General Murphy on May 31, 1939, that in his opinion Vonsiatsky was not an agent of a foreign principal. After investigating charges of "torture murders," the Immigration and Naturalization Service reported that its files indicated "no apparent fraud or other illegality in the securing of his naturalization as an American citizen." On September 13, after examining all this evidence, Assistant Attorney General O. John Rogge informed Congressman Dickstein that Vonsiatsky had not violated any federal criminal statute.

The Justice Department findings silenced Dickstein for the time being. But *The Hour,* fed with ammunition by Vonsiatsky himself, continued its assaults well into 1940.

The Eye of the Storm, September 1939–June 1941

On August 23, 1939, a diplomatic *volte-face* shook the world when Germany and the Soviet Union, supposedly implacable enemies, joined hands in a nonaggression pact. The pact's significance became apparent a week later when Hitler invaded Poland, and Stalin stood by as a benevolent neutral while England and France declared war on Germany. The Nazi-Soviet pact had curious repercussions within the United States. American Communists (at least those who weathered the shock and remained in the party) and German-American Bundists found themselves bleating the same slogans. Russian émigrés throughout the diaspora who had put their faith in Hitler as an uncompromising anti-Bolshevik suffered a stunning blow. Inside the Reich, Russian Nazis had no choice but to look inconspicuous.

Vonsiatsky reacted to the Nazi-Soviet pact with the insouciance of one who choreographs reality to suit private illusion. *Fashist* welcomed the pact, comparing it with the (temporary) accommodation between Napoleon and Tsar Alexander I in 1807. Vonsiatsky's attitude confused some people. For example, one of his detractors, Reverend Joskin V. Tkoch, a Russian Orthodox priest from Willimantic, Connecticut, told an FBI agent that Vonsiatsky had "made peace with Stalin" and was working for the Communists.

At the same time, the Nazi-Soviet pact created considerable strain on Vonsiatsky's relations with the German-American Bund. The count attended no more Bund rallies, and, except for "Wilhelm Gerhardavich" Kunze, the Bundists stopped visiting Nineteenth Hole. The Bund was having its own problems during this interlude. On November 28, Fritz Kuhn was found guilty of larceny and sentenced to five years' imprisonment. When he went to Sing Sing, the New York *Daily News* dubbed it the "Drang nach Ossining."* Kunze took over as *Bundführer.*

The Nazi-Soviet pact dealt the VNRP a more damaging blow than all the assaults of the *Daily Worker,* Friends of the Soviet Union, the International Workers Order, Dickstein, and *The Hour* combined. The never-too-congested ranks of *soratniki* had already been thinned by the death of Evgeny Bogoslovsky on February 11, 1939. But the most painful defections came when Hitler and Stalin joined hands.

Lev Beck Mamedov, the *vozhd*'s brother-in-law and president of the VNRP Central Executive Committee, quit the party in October 1939. Mamedov was so discouraged about the prospects of a Russian National Revolution that he decided his time would be better spent attending to culinary responsibilities at the Russian Bear.

Donat Yosifovich Kunle, *Fashist* editor, VNRP secretary, and Alex's faithful companion since "Count and Coontz" had cofounded the VFO in 1933, also left the party shortly after the Nazi-Soviet pact. Kunle lingered on for a while at Nineteenth Hole, but in June 1940 he departed Connecticut and Alex's life and headed for California to study flying.

Interviewed by an FBI agent in July 1940, Vonsiatsky confessed that many VNRP members were resigning and canceling their subscriptions to *Fashist.* He was once again almost all alone, except for Lady Astor, turtles, and pigeons.

As his party disintegrated around him, Vonsiatsky shed some of

* Sing Sing Penitentiary is located in Ossining, New York.

the props of his dream world. On June 7, 1940, he gave Sergeant Nolan the .45-caliber Thompson submachine gun, explaining that he wanted the Connecticut State Police to have it "in case of need."

On July 4, 1940, usually an occasion to bring *soratniki* together at Nineteenth Hole, Alex issued a manifesto that suggested a modification of his political activities:

> The Russian National Revolutionary Party, of which I am a leader, does not support either Germany's or Japan's ambition for hegemony in Europe or the Far East.
>
> The Germans and the Japanese have never made clear their attitude toward a replacement of the present Stalinist rule by a Russian National Government.
>
> The sole aim of our organization is to return Russia to a free people with a Government elected by the people, of the people, and for the people.
>
> Our intention is to form in Russia a truly democratic government.
>
> Our party is not anti-Semitic.
>
> Our party has no membership dues; it is financed solely by voluntary contributions from its members and sympathizers. It is not subsidized by any foreign power or foreign individuals.
>
> Our organization is banned in Germany and Japan.
>
> Only in the United States can we enjoy freedom of action and thought within the laws of the country.
>
> I herewith state emphatically that the activities of our organization are against the present Soviet government alone and that in no way whatsoever does it act against the Constitution of the United States or violate its laws which we loyally support.
>
> Anastase A. Vonsiatsky
>
> Thompson, Conn.
> July 4, 1940

The July 4 manifesto reflected Vonsiatsky's desire to disassociate himself from anything "Un-American." By 1940, the count knew that he was under investigation by the FBI. Moreover, he had a premonition, particularly after Roosevelt's reelection in November, that the United States was inching toward involvement in the European war.

When Congress passed the Lend-Lease Act on March 11, 1941, Vonsiatsky became convinced that war with Germany was only a matter of months. The *vozhd* also suspected that although Germany and the Soviet Union were, for the moment, still adhering to their non-aggression pact, Roosevelt and Churchill would eventually count on an alliance with Stalin to defeat Hitler. Such a development would preclude the VNRP from operating in the United States.

Passage of the Lend-Lease Act convinced Vonsiatsky to transfer VNRP headquarters from the United States to the Far East and to resign his office as *vozhd*. Besides, there was little left of the VNRP in the United States to lead. On March 17, 1941, the count wrote Konstantin Steklov (VNRP Far Eastern representative, living in Shanghai) asking him to assume leadership of the VNRP and informing him that *Fashist* would cease publication after its July 1941 issue.

Ironically, while Vonsiatsky was gradually withdrawing from politics during 1940 and early 1941, Vonsiatskiana flourished as never before. *The Hour* was busy depicting the count as a menace to America. *Liberty* magazine joined the campaign late in 1939, telling readers that Vonsiatsky had turned his wife's estate into a camp to train Bund storm troopers in military tactics and target practice. In 1940, Harold Lavine's *Fifth Column in America* devoted a chapter to Vonsiatsky, declaring that he ran arms to Franco during the Spanish Civil War and drilled uniformed men with guns at Thompson.

Vonsiatskiana also had a private dimension: communications from "concerned citizens" to the FBI and other law-enforcement agencies. The New York City Police Department started a file on Vonsiatsky after it received a letter saying that he fraternized with Hitler, Goering, Rosenberg, and Hess. The Naval Intelligence Division of the 12th Naval District in California was told in 1940 by a Youngstown, Ohio, informant that Vonsiatsky was a German agent and "one of the principal leaders of 5th Column activities in the United States" who had tried to forge a conspiracy between the Friends of New Germany and the Irish Republican Party to sabotage airplane factories in California. The Youngstown informant even confided that he had been present at a secret meeting of the conspirators on March 22, 1940, at the All-Ireland Cafe on Third Avenue, New York. A Rochester, New York, woman wrote the New York City FBI office on August 13, 1940, that Vonsiatsky was a "very dangerous man" who hoped to overthrow the United States government and bring in Adolf Hitler.

Perhaps more influential with the Justice Department than either published attacks or denunciatory letters were the actions of an editor, a reporter, and a government official. Albert E. Kahn, editor of *The Hour,* opened his files on Vonsiatsky to Justice Department investigators. A certain air of melodrama attached itself to some of the documents in these files. As Kahn recalled in 1976: "You see, in those bygone days I acquired documents and other data by all sorts of means, some official, some unofficial—and some not exactly like but with certain qualities of those of the Plumbers of Watergate." One wonders whether these included the documents sent to *The Hour* by Vonsiatsky himself. The *vozhd* was rarely able to resist free publicity.

In addition, Kenneth Watson of the New York *World-Telegram* sent the Justice Department a number of "confidential reports" during 1940–41, based on his interviews with named and unnamed informants. One of the former, a certain John C. Metcalfe, had been the witness who brought up Vonsiatsky's "little army" before the Dies Committee in 1938.

Mordecai Ezekiel, an economic adviser to the secretary of agriculture, may also have influenced the Justice Department's attitude toward Vonsiatsky in 1940–41. In late 1940 or early 1941, Ezekiel wrote the attorney general asking whether cause existed for the revocation of Vonsiatsky's American citizenship. He enclosed "exhibits," the content of which is not known with certainty but which presumably concerned the alleged "torture murders" of 1920. On January 15, 1941, Acting Assistant Attorney General Wendell Berge forwarded Ezekiel's exhibits to the Commissioner of the Immigration and Naturalization Service, who on January 31 sent them to the INS New York office for a thorough investigation.

During February and March, INS Special Inspector Mitchell Solomon combed through files of the New York FBI office, the New York City Police Department, Naval Intelligence, and *The Hour* for incriminating material on Vonsiatsky. Solomon of course encountered information provided by informants (such as the Rochester woman and Youngstown man) that portrayed Vonsiatsky in the most sinister terms. This information was duly incorporated into Solomon's report of April 1, a report that subsequently found its way into any number of Justice Department dossiers on Vonsiatsky. At each stage, hearsay evidence took on a slightly higher level of legitimacy.

In this way, public and private varieties of Vonsiatskiana finally succeeded in generating a degree of bureaucratic momentum in 1941, despite the fact that State, Justice, and Treasury department investigations of him between 1934 and 1940 had uncovered no evidence of any violation of federal statutes.

Had Vonsiatsky maintained a low profile as he had done during 1940 and early 1941, he probably would have stayed out of trouble throughout World War II, Vonsiatskiana notwithstanding. But Hitler's invasion of the Soviet Union on June 22, 1941, reignited an old spark in the count and propelled him back into politics, this time with fateful consequences.

CHAPTER XVI

Year of the Apocalypse

Soratniki! The Russian National Revolution has started! There is no turning back. Russia will either perish or be ours!
—KONSTANTIN RODZAEVSKY, June 27, 1941

As soon as the Nazi flag flies over Moscow, I shall within twenty hours inform the State Department that I am representing the Russian National Government in America.
—ANASTASE VONSIATSKY, July 25, 1941

Adolf Hitler's invasion of the Soviet Union took the Russian diaspora as much by surprise as had his nonaggression pact with Stalin twenty-two months earlier. Once the initial shock had worn off, émigrés reacted in widely different ways. Pro-Soviet elements instantly rallied to Stalin. Some anti-Communists found themselves torn between their hatred of Stalin and a visceral Slavic patriotism that drew them to the defense of their motherland. Others succumbed, in the words of Marie Avinov, to "that blind naïveté which let one misconceive of Hitler as a potential liberator." Among the latter were not only fascists but monarchists. From Paris, Prince Trubetskoi petitioned Berlin for permission to form a White Russian Freikorps that would fight side by side with the Wehrmacht inside the USSR.

Russian fascists in Europe hailed the invasion as a harbinger of the long-awaited National Revolution and jumped to get on the German juggernaut. In Berlin, Biskupsky and Bermondt-Avalov sent the Führer pledges of unconditional support. Rodzaevsky's European representative, Boris Tedli, deported from the Reich to Switzerland in the wake of the Nazi-Soviet pact, besieged the German embassy in Bern with entreaties to let the RFS contribute to the war effort and "participate in the reconstruction of Russia." Tedli avowed that the RFS regarded Adolf Hitler as its "spiritual leader and teacher" and generously conceded Germany a "leading role in the New Europe." Lest anyone think that the RFS supported the Reich in words alone, Tedli proudly pointed out that his son Albert was serving with distinction in the SS division Deutschland.

Even before the invasion of the Soviet Union on June 22, Konstantin Rodzaevsky had felt confident that a German-Soviet clash would occur sooner or later, regardless of the nonaggression pact. By coincidence, he wrote an editorial for *Natsiya* on the morning of June 22 predicting that war was "near." Later that day, when word of the German attack reached him while he was at a christening, his first reaction was to propose a prayer and lead those present in singing the Russian fascist anthem. That night, the *vozhd* held an emergency session of the RFS Central Executive Committee. Meanwhile, his assistants worked feverishly to bring out a special edition of *Nash Put,* which Japanese censors promptly suppressed on the grounds that it might create undue excitement and provoke anti-Soviet incidents.*

Within a few days, Rodzaevsky was acting as if the war were already won. He occupied himself by mailing out a series of orders to RFS representatives in Warsaw, Sofia, Paris, and Bern. Order no. 3 (June 27, 1941) created "Detachments of Liberation" which were to form the nucleus of the "Russian National Army." "Wealthier Russian emigrants" were to fund party military expenditures or face punishment as traitors. Order no. 15 (June 3) appointed RFS regional leaders in European Russia, the Ukraine, the Caucasus, Central Asia, Siberia, and the Far East. All *soratniki* were advised "to study urgently the territory and population of their districts" and "keep in readiness sufficient cash to enable them to reach their appointed destinations in Russia."

Rodzaevsky cabled Berlin that the RFS would recognize "the first National Government formed on liberated Russian soil." He did not forget to recommend to the Germans suitable candidates for the National Government, starting with himself and including the Duke of Leuchtenberg, divorced husband of Nicholas II's sister Olga; Boris Tedli; Vladimir Shelikhov, RFS representative in Warsaw; Vladimir

---

* The Japanese government (with the exception of Foreign Minister Matsuoka Yōsuke, who was clamoring for an attack on the USSR) was undecided at first about how to react to the German invasion, but both Tokyo and the Kwantung Army preferred to avoid friction with the Soviet Union until the situation in the West clarified. Shortly after June 22, *Nash Put* editorial offices moved from Harbin to Shanghai, presumably at the request of the *Tokumu Kikan.*

Mikhailovich Despotuli, editor of the Berlin Russian daily *Novoye Slovo;* General A. V. Turkul, Russian National Union, United States; and Mikhail Mikhailovich Grott, anti-Semitic publicist living in Königsberg, East Prussia.

Mailed from Harbin in late June and early July 1941, few of Rodzaevsky's directives reached their destinations. Intercepted by British and Canadian postal censorship, they wound up in Foreign Office or Military Intelligence files.

During the summer of 1941, Rodzaevsky did not for a moment doubt that the Red Army would disintegrate, that peasants and workers would turn against the political commissars, and that swastika flags would soon flutter over the Kremlin. His preoccupation with postwar details calls to mind Hitler's order for invitations to be printed for a 1941 Christmas banquet at Leningrad's Astoria Hotel, or Wehrmacht planners ruminating over whether to divide up the USSR with Japan at the seventieth degree of longitude or along the Yenisei River. Rodzaevsky's naiveté went beyond faith in a quick German victory. He implicitly believed that Hitler would not only establish a Russian National Government but also staff it with Manchurian fascists. Like scores of other émigrés swept up by apocalyptic visions in 1941, he was unable to grasp that Slavs played no part in Nazi plans for how conquered Russia would be ruled.

At the other end of the world, Anastase Vonsiatsky also sprang back to life upon hearing of the German invasion. Since the Nazi-Soviet pact, Vonsiatsky had gradually withdrawn from political activity, discouraged by trends in American foreign policy, VNRP defections, and the seeming hopelessness of the anti-Stalinist cause. During this interim, Alex had detached himself from the European war, regarding it as a sports event. On June 13, 1940, with German units approaching Paris, he had rushed into the living room at Nineteenth Hole, clutching a copy of the New York *Herald Tribune,* and exclaimed: "Hurrah! Third down and five yards to go!" That remark had emptied the room of Marion's friends and left the impression that Vonsiatsky was an avid Hitler fan. Such was far from the case. Despite his emulation of Hitler's oratory, he regarded the German leader pragmatically:

> If Hitler comes out against Russia, the Fascist Party of Russia [VNRP] will come out against him. But if he opposes the enslavers of Russia— the Bolsheviks—then the tactical interests of Russian fascism and German national socialism will coincide.

Consequently, when Vonsiatsky heard about Operation Barbarossa on June 22, he perceived a chance to fulfill his cherished hopes and resolved to return to the political arena.

Vonsiatsky's first response to the German invasion was a characteristic piece of showmanship. He sent a telegram to Stalin offering "bloodless and peaceful" surrender terms to the Soviet government on behalf of the VNRP. As published in Konstantin Steklov's Shanghai newspaper *Russky Avangard* (*Fashist* no longer appeared) on July 22, the cable outlined six conditions for a Soviet capitulation:

1. a promise of full amnesty and no reprisals against members of the Soviet government.
2. a guarantee of life and possessions to all members of the government, Communist Party, and NKVD.
3. a guarantee of job security to all government employees.
4. immunity of all Red Army officers, excepting political commissars.
5. guarantee to all members of the Communist Party to a full share in the national life of Russia.
6. guarantee of free passage out of Russia to all members of the Communist Party, if so granted by the people.

The cable concluded:

> The above conditions may be revised by arbitration from the side of neutral countries. Acceptance of this proposal will prevent a civil war in Russia and automatically put an end to the war between Russia and Germany. Any counterproposal from the present Russian Government can be transmitted to the All-Russian Revolutionary Party headquarters through mediation of any Russian Embassy or Consulate in the following countries: Sweden, Bulgaria, Portugal, Brazil, or China.

Listening to war bulletins during the first few days after June 22, Vonsiatsky let himself indulge in heroic reveries. One of his favorite scenarios had been given an inspired expression by Donat Kunle in the VNRP anthem: "swastikas shining over the Kremlin as black [fascist] legions march through Moscow." Just before its demise *Fashist* had carried a doctored aerial photo of a military parade in Red Square in which dubbed-in swastika banners fluttered over Kremlin towers, walls, and Lenin's mausoleum. Ambling across the Quinnatisset links with a number five iron thrown over his shoulder like a rifle, Anastase could feel in the summer air the imminence of his triumphal return home. Perhaps Hitler would appoint him to some position of responsibility. Of course, he would have to acquiesce to territorial concessions to Germany, and perhaps Japan as well. But once Russia had regained its former power, he would settle accounts with eastern and western neighbors.

Such musings were interrupted on June 26 by a personal tragedy. Donat Kunle, word came, had been killed the previous day when an airplane in which he was learning to fly exploded over San Diego. His scattered remains, charred beyond recognition, were identified by dental charts. Together with Marion and the Mamedovs, "Coontz" had been Alex's closest companion. They had fought in the Civil War together, shared the bitterness of defeat and the loneliness of exile, and had devoted themselves since 1933 to restoring the Russia that they remembered and loved. Kunle had quit the VNRP in 1939 and left Thompson in 1940, discouraged at the Nazi-Soviet pact. His sudden and violent end, coming only three days after a dramatic German *volte-face* had opened apocalyptic vistas, dealt Alex a staggering blow.

Indignant upon learning that his dearest *soratnik* was scheduled to be cremated in San Diego "like garbage," Alex ordered the remains brought to Thompson for a dignified interment. The count had already prepared a place of repose fit for heroes, having the previous year invested $20,000 for the construction of a crypt at the West Thompson Cemetery, located not quite two miles from Nineteenth Hole. It was an impressive structure: an exterior of granite blocks, an interior of Italian marble, a lancet arch entry facing a stained-glass window in which the Virgin Mary cradled the holy child in her arms amid elaborate tracery, and six capacious sarcophagi stacked three on a side. Above the crypt's sloped roof rose an Orthodox cross. Surrounded by cypress trees, the mausoleum towered incongruously over the modest tombstones that made up an otherwise typical New England burial ground. Vonsiatsky's Gothic-Byzantine edifice was completed just in time to accommodate what was left of Donat Yosifovich early in July.

The Berlin-Tokyo-Putnam Axis

Although Bund-VNRP relations remained officially cool during the Nazi-Soviet Pact interim, the *Bundführer,* Wilhelm Kunze, continued to drop by Nineteenth Hole for drinks and handouts whenever his travels took him through northeastern Connecticut. Late in February 1941, Kunze brought along a bricklayer named August Klapprott, who edited the Bund's newspaper, *Free American,* and managed Camp Nordland in Andover, New Jersey. Kunze and Klapprott had been among nine Bund leaders sentenced by a Sussex County court on January 31, 1941, for violating New Jersey's 1935 "race hatred" law by giving anti-Semitic speeches at a Camp Nordland rally in June 1940. Freed on bail on February 4 while Bund attorney Wilbur Keegan appealed the sentences, Kunze was looking for money to pay a $2,000 fine to the state of New Jersey. He knew that Vonsiatsky was a potential source of cash but decided to wait for the right moment to ask.

Donat Kunle's funeral on July 3 provided Kunze with just the opportunity he had been looking for. What better occasion for a public Bund-VNRP reconciliation (and private solicitation) than a ceremony to honor a fallen anti-Communist soldier? Kunze brought along Bund national secretary Hugo "Willi" Lutke, but made sure that he was alone when he asked Anastase for a special favor.

Kunze wanted money for more than one purpose. In addition to the fine due the state of New Jersey, he needed cash so as to be able to travel to Germany at a moment's notice. Kunze did not like the idea of being in the United States during a German-American war, which seemed more likely with each passing day. The son of German immigrant parents, Kunze had been born in Camden, N.J., but bore bitter memories of being beaten up almost daily by classmates in a Pennsylvania public school during World War I. Wanting no repetition of that experience, he had sent his wife and son to Germany in January 1941 and planned to follow them. Kunze did not at this time reveal his plans to Bund associates. On the contrary, early in July he assured Klapprott (now Eastern Department head) and Otto Albert Willumeit (Midwestern Department head) that he would remain in the United States if reelected Bund chairman at the next national convention scheduled to meet in Chicago on Labor Day. But Kunze decided to hint to Vonsiatsky about his plan to return to Germany, because that would be the lure to snare the count's largesse.

Kunze did not have to convince Vonsiatsky of his utility. The *vozhd* was already thinking along the same lines, as he later related to an FBI agent:

> . . . after the outbreak of the war between Germany and Russia, I realized that Germany more than ever could help my party and its purposes, and when it appeared in the summer of 1941 that the Germans were

going through to Moscow I felt that undoubtedly the Germans would set up in Russia a government similiar to the governments set up by them in Norway and occupied France, and would probably want to have a government with a Russian at the head of it. For this reason when Kunze came to my home in July, 1941 [for Kunle's funeral], I asked him when he was returning to Germany. He stated he did not know, but planned to go as soon as he could, and I asked him if he would care to be my representative and put me in contact with whomever formed the new government in Russia. . . . My idea was to avoid U.S. departmental red tape and to deal directly with Kunze and have him get in touch with the representatives of the new government, on the theory that perhaps eventually the U.S. might recognize this new government and recognize me as its representative in the U.S.

Conferring privately after Kunle's funeral, the two men quickly reached an oral agreement. Vonsiatsky would give Kunze $2,800 ($2,000 to pay off the New Jersey fine, $800 for traveling expenses to Germany). In return, Kunze would use his influence to lobby for the VNRP within the Reich. Whether Kunze actually intended to carry out his end of the bargain is questionable.

Despite his reputation as a man of means, Anastase did not have enough cash on hand for the transaction. He therefore told Wilhelm Gerhardavich to return about ten days later. In the meantime, he would sell some shares of AT&T common stock and deposit the proceeds in his Putnam bank account, ready for distribution.

Kunze left Nineteenth Hole quite satisfied with himself. Perhaps to demonstrate his good intentions, he published an effusive eulogy to the late Kunle on the front page of *Free American* of July 10. In words that would have provoked a wry smile from Donat Yosifovich, a confirmed anti-Bundist, Kunze hailed the deceased as "instinctively the friend and brother-in-arms of the German and other National elements within the citizenry of the United States." For good measure, he added that Vonsiatsky was a "great Russian."

On July 12, Kunze drove up to Nineteenth Hole from New York, alone. Vonsiatsky was waiting with a check for $2,800. Asked about his intentions, Kunze replied that he was still uncertain about his German travel plans but promised to keep Anastase informed. In the meantime, Kunze added, he was going to take a vacation at a Bund camp in Michigan and then spend some time in Chicago. Alex thereupon said that he happened to be planning a trip to the west coast and would probably be coming back through Chicago late in

July. That being the case, why not get together there? Vonsiatsky proposed the meeting for more than casual purposes. He wanted to keep track of Kunze, in whom he had invested funds and hopes. Kunze agreed to meet in Chicago and suggested July 30 at Bund headquarters, Haus Vaterland.

Two days later, back in New York, Kunze wrote Vonsiatsky thanking him for the money and assuring him that the count had not misplaced his trust. Two passages in particular must have flattered the count's ego:

> I admire and honor the Russian character which you and your *soratniki* embody and shall be happy to be of assistance in making you and your work known at the place where the new, free Russia is being created. . . . I shall bend every effort to make available to you the place in which you can best serve in the reconstruction of your great country, receiving as my great reward the opportunity to actively serve a holy cause instead of remaining condemned to practical inactivity at this crucial hour. Should conditions not permit me to leave within a reasonable time, please be assured that all of the above mentioned money, except as to amounts necessarily expended in preparing and beginning the voyage, will be returned to you. I am indescribably honored that you place such great trust in me and shall prove worthy of it. We both are serving a common cause to which I pray God the power of an awakened United States may also yet be lent!
>
> *Slava Rossiya!   Heil Hitler!   Do Svidaniya!*

About a week later, Anastase set off for San Francisco. Marion did not accompany him, for a good reason. He was planning to meet a young Japanese woman named Takita Momoyo, a passenger on the linear *Tatsuta maru,* scheduled to arive in San Francisco from Yokohama on July 24. Takita's identity and relationship to the count remain nebulous. Fragmentary evidence suggests that she was a mutual acquaintance of another Japanese woman upon whom Vonsiatsky had bestowed his most tender affections: Nakamura Fusako.

Sometime during his 1934 world tour, Vonsiatsky had made the acquaintance of a wealthy, cosmopolitan businessman from Tokyo named Nakamura Hitoshi. Nakamura's daughter Fusako and Alex soon became, in the count's own words, "especially friendly." During his second world tour in 1936, he saw Fusako again in Tokyo. As Nakamura's business brought him to the United States, Vonsiatsky extended an open invitation to the family to visit Thompson. In the fall of 1936, the Nakamuras, including Fusako, did spend a month and a half at Nineteenth Hole. Alex took Fusako to some football matches in New Haven and to the Army-Navy game at Philadelphia's Municipal Stadium on November 28. Subsequently, Fusako went to study in Paris, where Alex met her in 1938 and 1939 when he passed through with Marion. Possibly with Marion in mind, Alex and Fusako always spoke to each other in French. In Paris, Fusako gave Alex a photograph of herself, inscribed in Japanese,* which he kept for the rest of his life.

In the fall of 1940, Fusako came to Nineteenth Hole and spent three weeks with Alex. The arrangement disturbed Marion's friends. They disapproved of such a "young and clever" woman being around Alex. Marion, who was now sixty-three, as usual maintained her composure and made no move to interfere with her husband's choice of companions. She even allowed Alex and Fusako to go to the Brown-Yale game in New Haven on November 2 and to attend a postgame party at the Taft Hotel.

Takita Momoyo, described on the *Tatsuta maru*'s passenger list as twenty-seven years old, single, and bound for Montebello, California, could have been a friend of Fusako's, for according to Vonsiatsky, she had mailed him a bowl as a present from the Nakamuras. There is a possibility that Fusako herself was also on board the *Tatsuta maru*, for Vonsiatsky later told some friends that Takita Momoyo was not the only woman he was hoping to meet at the pier.

For practical purposes, it mattered little who was on board, because Vonsiatsky never saw the *Tatsuta maru*. Scheduled to arrive in San Francisco on July 24, it remained at sea for six extra days because of the international uncertainty attending Japan's announcement of her intention to occupy French (Vichy) bases in southern Indochina and President Roosevelt's retaliatory executive order freezing Japanese assets in the United States.

Vonsiatsky had arrived in San Francisco on July 23 and registered at the Mark Hopkins Hotel under the name of Albert Vohn. His presence in town was no secret, however, either to the FBI or to Evgeny Serebrennikov, a reporter for the local Russian daily, *Novaya Zarya*. When Serebrennikov called Vonsiatsky at the Mark Hopkins on July 25, the count could not resist the lure of free publicity and acceded

---

* "On the occasion of our parting in Paris, I give [you] thanks from my heart. I pray that our friendship will continue forever."

to an interview published in *Novaya Zarya* on July 26. Blissfully unaware of possible consequences, Alex unfolded his grandest pretensions for all to see:

Q. What are the plans for liquidation of the Russian Fascist Party in America?

A. None. . . . I am getting ready to represent here the Russian National Government, which will have its seat in Moscow.

Q. How soon will it function?

A. In the nearest future. As soon as the German armies occupy Moscow.

Q. And how soon may this happen?

A. In about two weeks.

Q. In that case, the government is already formed and you, perhaps, know the names of the members of the cabinet?

A. Oh yes, it is already formed, but of course you will understand that I cannot give you the names either officially or unofficially.

Q. All this is known to Hitler?

A. Certainly.

Q. And with his blessing?

A. Of course!

Q. Thus, you have established communications with the members of the government in Berlin?

A. Certainly, only on account of the present situation and circumstances, this is being done secretly and in a conspiratorial manner.

Q. What are you going to do if the U.S.A., as it is believed, will eventually enter the war against Germany?

A. I shall represent the Russian National Government.

Q. But, what if the U.S.A. were not to recognize that government?

A. I still will inform the State Department that I am representing the Russian National Government.

Q. But is it not possible that the U.S.A. will not recognize the Russian National Government?

A. In that case it will not be the business of the U.S.A. to bother about as to who represents the Russian government.

The *Novaya Zarya* interview was about all that Vonsiatsky accomplished in San Francisco. Inquiries at local offices of the Japan Mail

Line revealed that the *Tatsuta maru* was being diverted to Mexico.*
Resigning himself to missing his rendezvous, Alex set out for Chicago
on July 26.

As soon as he reached Chicago on Tuesday, July 29, Alex looked
up Kunze at Haus Vaterland. The Bund chairman greeted him warmly
and asked whether he would like to meet a fellow Russian anti-Bolshevik from South America who now lived in Chicago and was a friend
of the Bund's Midwestern leader, Willumeit. Anastase answered af-
firmatively, saying that they might have some friends in common in
South American Russian communities. Kunze thereupon told Willumeit to get in touch with the Russian and bring him that evening at
nine o'clock to the Bismarck Hotel cocktail lounge.

The "Russian" turned out to be a Ukrainian priest and FBI undercover agent named Alexius Pelypenko. Pelypenko combined a sense
of imagination with a flair for melodrama to a degree that rivaled
that of the count. Alex was not only about to meet his match, he
was about to get into serious trouble.

Born in 1893 in the Carpatho-Ukraine, Pelypenko was shaped by
the political and religious uncertainties that plagued a region chronically buffeted by the shifting frontiers of Russia, Poland, and Austro-
Hungary. After being consecrated as an Orthodox priest in 1915 and
serving in the Imperial Russian Army, Pelypenko moved to Warsaw
and in 1925 converted to the Ruthenian rite of the Uniate (Byzantine-
Roman) Church. He subsequently taught Catholic theology in Munich
and in 1937 came to Buenos Aires as a missionary to Argentina's
Ukrainian colony. Obsessed with the goal of freeing the Ukraine from
Soviet Russia, Pelypenko fell under the spell of promises of assistance
emanating from the German Embassy in Buenos Aires. Under the
guidance of an embassy adviser named Prince Stephan zu Schaumburg-Lippe, onetime adjutant to Propaganda Minister Goebbels, Pelypenko undertook to spread pro-German propaganda among Argentina's Ukrainians. After a while, Pelypenko began to suspect that the
Germans were not living up to their promises. He accordingly turned
to the British and became an undercover agent for them, preserving
all the while his good relations with the Germans. Late in 1940, Pelypenko was approached by American Embassy officials and asked if

---

* The *Tatsuta maru* eventually docked in San Francisco on July 30. If Fusako was
on board, she did not come east. Takita Momoyo sent Vonsiatsky a present from
the Nakamuras and then disappeared from Alex's life (and Alex's FBI file).

he would work for the United States government (without specifying which agency). Around the same time, Pelypenko agreed with Prince Stephan to work on behalf of Germany among Ukrainians in the United States. On March 24, 1941, Pelypenko arrived in New York, where he was met and hired on the spot by an agent of the FBI. The FBI sent Pelypenko to Chicago where in April he made the acquaintance of Otto Willumeit at a restaurant.* Pelypenko assured Willumeit of his pro-German sympathies, and the latter took him over to Haus Vaterland and introduced him to Kunze. When Vonsiatsky arrived in Chicago on July 29, it was only natural for the two Bundists to bring the two Slavs together.

The four men gathered just after nine on the evening of July 29 at the Bismarck Hotel cocktail lounge. Pelypenko came in priestly garb: a black cassock that touched his shoes, and a black, broad-brimmed hat with a low crown. The others wore coats and ties. As Pelypenko was fluent in German, but not English, and Vonsiatsky spoke no German, communications among the four turned out to be unwieldy. Pelypenko addressed Kunze and Willumeit in German and Vonsiatsky in Russian. Vonsiatsky and the Bundists talked to each other in English. Consequently, anything said by anybody had to be translated before it could be universally understood. Such complicated linguistic crosscurrents may partly explain why the content of that night's discussions later became the subject of controversy.

All four participants in the Bismarck Hotel meeting subsequently agreed that the discussion concerned means by which Kunze could return to Germany. By this time, Kunze had confided to Willumeit that he might return and even mentioned Mexico as an intermediate sanctuary should German-American relations break. Willumeit had tried to dissuade Kunze on the grounds that leaving the United States at such a critical juncture would endanger the Bund. But Kunze refused to make any promises except that he would not depart before the Bund's national convention on Labor Day (September 1). Kunze was worried about how to travel. Although he had Vonsiatsky's $2,800, he doubted that he could get a U.S. passport let alone run the British naval blockade that ringed continental Europe. Pelypenko remarked that he could secure "immigration papers" from the Polish Consulate in Philadelphia that would enable Kunze to enter Argentina. Kunze seemed interested but took no action that evening.

* Willumeit recalled that it was a Russian restaurant. Not surprisingly, Pelypenko insisted that it was Ukrainian.

According to Willumeit, much of the discussion took place between Pelypenko and Vonsiatsky. Although he could not understand the details, Willumeit gathered that Vonsiatsky was bragging to the Ukrainian about his party and agents throughout the world. Unfortunately for Alex, his listener took him seriously.

Before they parted that night, Pelypenko told Vonsiatsky that he was planning a trip to New York and would like to visit the count in Thompson. Anastase replied that he would be welcome there at any time.

Four days later, two days after returning to Nineteenth Hole, Vonsiatsky received a telegram from Pelypenko saying that he was coming to Thompson on August 6. Hardly had the Ukrainian settled down on a sofa in the Military Room after his arrival when he blurted out: "Do you know anybody at the Japanese Embassy?" Instantly suspicious, Vonsiatsky replied that he did not. But then the *vozhd* decided to test Pelypenko:

> . . . I was curious as to his reasons [for asking] and remembering that I had a calling card which had been given me by some of the Nakamura's [*sic*] or their acquaintances while I was visiting in Japan, I said I may have a name that will help you, got the calling card and gave it to him saying again that perhaps that would help him.

Vonsiatsky also asked Pelypenko to inquire at the Japanese Embassy about the whereabouts of Takita Momoyo "in order to determine whether Pelypenko was on the level."

On August 13, Pelypenko visited Nineteenth Hole again and told Alex that the Japanese Embassy would need time to locate Takita but in the meanwhile the military attaché wondered if Vonsiatsky had any contacts in Alaska who would act as espionage agents. Anastase, now extremely suspicious, described his reaction as follows:

> I became incensed at Pelypenko and thereupon decided to get rid of him at once. I took him to the Russian Bear Inn, paid for his supper, and requested [Lev] Beck Mamedov, my brother-in-law, to feed him and then take him to the railroad station so that we would be rid of him.

Vonsiatsky and Pelypenko never saw each other again. On August 18, the FBI terminated its employment of Pelypenko, but not before the Ukrainian had submitted an extraordinary account of what had transpired during the previous three weeks.

Pelypenko reported on separate occasions—and in different versions—to the FBI and to a confidential informant of the Immigration

and Naturalization Service during mid-August that Anastase Vonsiatsky was both a German *and* a Japanese espionage agent, engaged in
a massive conspiracy against the United States. He had collected top
secret data on American army, navy, and air bases, which he had
intended to deliver to a female Japanese agent named "Madame Takita," who had been due to arrive in San Francisco on the *Tatsuta
maru*. In addition to traveling incognito to San Francisco to meet
Madame Takita, Vonsiatsky had planned to contact "military agents
and saboteurs" along the west coast. When the *Tatsuta maru* did not
call at San Francisco as scheduled, Vonsiatsky, Pelypenko reported,
rushed to Chicago in order to hand over the military secrets to Wilhelm Kunze, who would carry them to Germany via Mexico and
Argentina.

At the Bismarck Hotel, Pelypenko continued, five men* had gathered to discuss how to smuggle Kunze and the secrets out of the
United States. Vonsiatsky pressed Pelypenko to equip Kunze with
travel documents. Kunze told Pelypenko that such documents could
be obtained with the help of a Lutheran pastor in Philadelphia named
Kurt Molzahn. Part of the evening's discussion was devoted to "how
to do away with Roosevelt and his Jewish servants." "Very often,"
according to Pelypenko, the three exchanged "Heil Hitlers." The
meeting concluded on the understanding that there would be another
session at Vonsiatsky's Connecticut estate to finalize "what was to
be done in the United States."

On August 6, according to Pelypenko, he came to Nineteenth
Hole, where Vonsiatsky instructed him to get in touch with the Japanese military attaché in Washington and to tell him that (in Pelypenko's words): ". . . his [Vonsiatsky's] espionage system is so well organized that within a few hours of his order he can—within a few hours
he can give full information about [American] forces to Tokyo and
Berlin." Vonsiatsky then handed Pelypenko a calling card upon which
was written the name of the "commander of the Japanese Army in
Manchukuo."** Vonsiatsky also instructed the Ukrainian priest to

---

* In his August 1941 reports to the FBI, Pelypenko said that George Froboese,
Chicago Bund leader, was also at the Bismarck Hotel meeting. However, under oath
at the trial of Kurt Molzahn on July 30, 1942, he testified that there were only four
(Kunze, Willumeit, Vonsiatsky, and himself).
** The calling card was inscribed: "G. Kobayashi, Commandant d'Artillerie de
l'Armée Japonaise." Under questioning, Vonsiatsky identified him as a Japanese military
attaché in Paris. Japanese Army Ministry records reveal no such name among military
attachés but list a colonel of the artillery, Kobayashi Gunji, in the Bureau of Supplies
and Equipment during 1939–40.

find out from Japanese Embassy officials the whereabouts of "a very important espionage agent of the Japanese staff" known as "Madame Takita."

In Washington, Pelypenko allegedly visited the Japanese Embassy and talked with the military attaché. The officer, whom Pelypenko never named, purportedly said that he wanted to meet Vonsiatsky personally in order to learn how many airplanes were being sent from the United States to the USSR via Alaska. When Pelypenko brought this message back to Nineteenth Hole on August 13, Vonsiatsky allegedly said that his trove of military secrets included details of trans-Alaska flights and that he was eager to establish contact with the Japanese military attaché.

Pelypenko's version of events between the Bismarck Hotel meeting (July 29) and his second visit to Nineteenth Hole (August 13) possesses a thread of internal consistency. But the Ukrainian's imagination seems to have gotten out of hand shortly thereafter, probably because he was acting on behalf of so many different principals, including German diplomats, Bundists, a White Russian, the FBI, and an increasing number of fellow Ukrainians. Sensing that he was surrounded by double agents, Pelypenko began telling different things to different people, probably becoming hopelessly confused in the process. To the INS informant, he revealed that Vonsiatsky had returned to Chicago in August to meet Kunze and Willumeit. To the FBI, he reported that Kunze and Willumeit had come to Thompson in August to meet Vonsiatsky there.

Unaware that the Immigration and Naturalization Service was part of the same Justice Department bureaucracy as the FBI, Pelypenko confided to the INS informant that he was withholding key information* from the FBI, because he knew that the FBI had been infiltrated by a Ukrainian double agent who leaked his (Pelypenko's) revelations back to the Bund.

As shadows multiplied about him, Pelypenko paid less attention to his original FBI assignment—to inform on Bundists—and became absorbed in ferreting out crypto-Nazis among the FBI's Ukrainian stool pigeons. Inevitably, such irregularities came to the attention of J. Edgar Hoover, who promptly terminated Pelypenko's services.

---

* The "key information" (which eventually reached the FBI via the INS) consisted of the allegation that on August 13 Vonsiatsky had shown Pelypenko (1) the names and addresses of seven agents in Alaska who sent him military information which he forwarded to the Japanese military attaché in Washington, and (2) the name of a Brazilian censor in São Paulo who relayed orders to Vonsiatsky from Berlin.

But Pelypenko was by no means rendered inactive. If the FBI failed to appreciate him, there were others who could use his services.

While Pelypenko was spinning tales about him, Vonsiatsky spent the last half of August and all of September in Thompson, luxuriating in the deceptive calm that followed his jaunt to San Francisco and Chicago. With *Fashist* no longer in operation, the count had time on his hands. Things were unusually quiet at Nineteenth Hole. Lev Mamedov had quit the party. Kunle was dead. Marion, dear thing, heard less and less. Andy Mamedov, eager to fly a Spitfire, had run off and joined the RAF without even telling Lev and Natasha, who learned of their son's enlistment only after he had reached England.

Bucolic serenity did not fit Anastase's temperament, particularly when a war was going on that promised to rid his motherland of Stalin. He carefully followed German-Soviet war bulletins in the press and was heartened by almost daily reports of Wehrmacht victories along a front stretching from the Baltic to the Black Sea. In an interview with the Bridgeport *Sunday Herald* on August 16, he slipped into a particularly euphoric mood. The next issue of *Fashist,* he declared, would be published in Moscow (apparently forgetting that special issues of *Fashist* had purportedly been published surreptitiously in the bowels of the Kremlin since 1935). By spring, he predicted, the Germans would push what was left of the Red Army beyond the Volga and Urals, leaving the job of mopping up to White Russian units.

In addition to playing the armchair strategist, Vonsiatsky spent his energies, in the words of the Putnam *Patriot,* "improving the Quinnatisset Country Club." No longer subsidizing VNRP branches and newspapers around the world, Alex used his allowance from Marion on planting, fertilizing, and landscaping the fairways and putting greens across County Home Road.

One particle of uncertainty clouded the count's mind during this placid interim: Wilhelm Kunze. Alex had invested $2,800 in the Bund leader and had been counting on him to lobby for the VNRP in Germany. But Kunze was showing no signs of returning to the Reich, and Vonsiatsky began to sense that his chances of participating in the future Russian National Government were slipping away with each passing day.

Kunze was playing a delicate balancing act with the Bund, the FBI, and his own enigmatic impulses. During August, when his thoughts about leaving the United States became known to other Bund leaders, heated arguments erupted about whether he deserved to be retained as chairman. During August, Kunze was obliged to remain in Chicago, closely watched by the *Ordnungsdienst* as well as the FBI, both of whom were concerned about his bolting the country while still under indictment in New Jersey. After much debate, Kunze was reelected chairman at the Bund's national convention at Haus Vaterland, but only after promising his supporters that he would remain in the United States and return the $2,800 to Vonsiatsky. Nonetheless, Kunze kept Alex's money, and contributions from the Bund membership paid the $2,000 New Jersey fine.

The Ring Closes

Anastase Vonsiatsky blithely, almost unconsciously, had weathered three assaults against him during the 1930s. Each assault was triggered by one of his extravagant, even outrageous, pieces of showmanship. In 1934, the count's world tour and whimsical claims in *Fashist* aroused the *Daily Worker* and Friends of the Soviet Union to an ostensible fury, but State and Justice department investigations had revealed no violations of federal law. In 1937, a sensationalized Fourth of July weekend get-together at Nineteenth Hole had galvanized Communist organizations to launch a letter campaign and provoked some hyperbolic oratory in Congress, but, on investigation, this too turned out to be a storm in a teacup. In 1939, after marching in a Camp Siegfried Bund rally and being erroneously implicated in Fritz Kuhn's Webster "putsch," Vonsiatsky incurred the combined opprobrium of progressive organizations, liberal intellectuals, and a congressman, but again, after intensive probes by several government agencies, was found to have acted within the law. As late as July 15, 1941, a Justice Department official wrote that Vonsiatsky was neither a criminal nor a foreign agent. He was simply a damn nuisance.

Vonsiatsky failed to weather the fourth assault, which gathered force late in July 1941 and peaked in June 1942. What made the difference in 1941–42 was, broadly speaking, the climate of opinion prevailing in the United States. Antics that rational observers had dismissed as farcical in 1934 and 1937 looked sinister in the charged national atmosphere following Pearl Harbor. In addition, by some unwritten law of legitimacy-through-age, all of the rumors and denunciations considered unreliable when received and filed away by the Justice Department began to take on a cumulative weight that was far greater than the sum of the parts.

Had Anastase been even dimly aware of the rapids toward which his showboat was hurtling, he might have put to shore and avoided disaster. He had made a move in that direction after the Nazi-Soviet Pact. But the German invasion of the USSR twenty-two months later swept away all scruples, so excited was he at the seeming imminence of Stalin's downfall. When Alex finally did see the waterfall ahead in December 1941, it was already too late.

Although Vonsiatsky did not know it, he was already in trouble in September 1941 as a result of Pelypenko's inspired revelations. Although the FBI had dismissed Pelypenko his reports were still incorporated into Vonsiatsky's file. And instead of containing a cautionary note on Pelypenko's questionable credibility, the files referred to him, incredibly, as "someone prominent in the National Councils of the Bund." Consequently, anyone unfamiliar with Pelypenko and reading his reports on Vonsiatsky would be struck by the former's fact-finding skills and the latter's criminality.

Early in September, a section within the Justice Department called the Special Defense Unit, headed by Lawrence M. C. Smith, inaugurated an investigation to determine whether Vonsiatsky had violated Public Act No. 583, commonly known as the Voorhis Act, passed by Congress in 1938 and requiring the registration of all agents of foreign principals. Smith's assistant, R. Keith Kane, assigned responsibility for the probe to Samuel S. Bisgyer, who in turn utilized the services of Justice Department analyst Louis Nemzer. Nemzer began collating material on Vonsiatsky from the FBI, INS, State Department, Naval Intelligence, *Fashist,* letters from plaintiffs, and reports from informants. Nemzer and Bisgyer completed a preliminary investigation of the material late in September.

On October 6, Bisgyer drafted a letter to Vonsiatsky stating that the Justice Department requested that the Russian National Revolutionary Party register in accordance with the Voorhis Act.

Meanwhile, on October 4, the Treasury Department, without warning, blocked Alex's and Marion's bank accounts at the New York Trust Company and Cargill Trust Company (Putnam), and sealed their joint safe deposit box at the Citizens National Bank in Putnam. Marion managed shortly thereafter to obtain a license enabling her to withdraw not more than $1,500 monthly for their living expenses.

As the government closed in on Vonsiatsky, tragedy again struck Nineteenth Hole, barely four months after Kunle's plane crash. On October 14, Lev and Natasha Mamedov were informed that their only son, Andy, had been killed in action five days earlier while piloting a Spitfire in the RAF's Eagle Squadron. Mamedov was buried in a special plot reserved for American volunteers in the RAF. Although desolate at his nephew's loss, Anastase thoughtlessly told a Norwich *Bulletin* reporter on October 15 that Andrew's death was "unnecessary." That remark, in conjunction with Anastase's reputation of being pro-German, created a bad impression and hastened the count's isolation within the community.

After receiving the Justice Department letter of October 6, Vonsiatsky sought legal counsel with the New York firm of Choate, Mitchell and Ely. On October 27, senior partner Clarence V. S. Mitchell wrote the Justice Department on behalf of his client expressing the opinion that the VNRP was only "more or less a one-man affair" and hence should not be subject to the provisions of the Voorhis Act. R. Keith Kane, assistant chief of the Department's Special Defense Unit, replied to Mitchell's letter on November 14, reiterating that Vonsiatsky should register the VNRP and suggesting that an attorney come to Washington to discuss the matter. Mitchell thereupon went to Thompson and obtained from Vonsiatsky a nine-page affidavit detailing the count's family background, career, and current status. The attorney then called upon Kane in Washington at eleven o'clock on Friday morning, December 6. Kane took the affidavit and handed Mitchell a thirty-two-page registration questionnaire for Vonsiatsky to complete.

On the same day (December 6), the New Jersey Supreme Court, holding the 1935 "race hatred" law unconstitutional, reversed the conviction of Kunze and eight other Bundists for anti-Semitic speeches delivered at Camp Nordland. But Kunze was not around to celebrate his legal vindication. He had fled to Mexico on November 6. In mid-November he had written Anastase a postcard from Mexico City cheerily reporting (for all to see) that he was on his way to Germany.

As soon as Mitchell returned to New York from Washington on Saturday, December 6, he assured Kane by letter that he would get hold of Vonsiatsky "next week" and have him fill out the registration form. By the next week, the United States was at war with Japan.

America's entry into World War II jolted Vonsiatsky into an aware-

ness of his own jeopardy. Nazis and fascists were now national enemies. Stalin was an ally. As an outspoken anti-Communist dripping
with German and Japanese connections, Alex suddenly realized that
he stood out like a sore thumb as nervous and angry Americans looked
around for spies and fifth columnists. He quickly burned Kunze's
postcard and other documents.

But Kunze, like a mistress who refused to be jilted, wrote to Vonsiatsky on December 8:

> My dear Anastase Andreivich!
>
> Roosevelt finally has what he thinks he wants, but before long he will
> have it "in the neck." If the Japanese war had waited a few weeks more
> I would have been in Japan. As it is, I shall have gone on in another
> direction by the time this letter reaches you.
>
> The Atlantic crossing by air which I originally had in mind would cost
> *$2,600 more than I have now* and would require months of waiting. Another
> method of travel, *the only one left open*, will require about $1,000 more
> than I have.
>
> There can be *no going back* for me any more, and the farther away I go
> the more difficult it will become to send me money. Please send what
> you can to: Dr. Wolfgang Ebell, 111 Mesa, El Paso, Texas. He is my
> very good friend, and I have asked him to forward money or mail intended
> for me to another address. Now, please do not use my name on money
> orders or letters but *only his.* Do not write much, as his mail is censored.
>
> I am being very careful with my money and still have about two-thirds
> of the travel sum ($800) I originally took along. I shall certainly save
> what I can for you of whatever money you send me.
>
> *Do vstrechi v Moskve, Slava Rossii, H.H.**
>
> > Yours
> > Wilhelm Gerhardavich

Such a letter was the last thing that a chastened, jittery Vonsiatsky
wanted to receive. If read by censors, it could get him into serious
trouble for aiding a fugitive Nazi—or worse. Alex would have been
even more on edge had he known that the letter, together with Pelypenko's stories, was already in his FBI file.

For the first time in his life, Vonsiatsky tried to be inconspicuous.
Filling out the registration questionnaire that Mitchell had given him,

---

*[Until (we) meet in Moscow. Hail Russia. Heil Hitler.]

he made the VNRP look like a pen-pal club. The party was said to have "no officers." Its activities consisted of "correspondence with Russians of similar ideas" and the publication of *Fashist* ("now discontinued"). In a supplementary affidavit, Anastase identified his "four main correspondents" as Konstantin Steklov (Shanghai), Baron Georgy Taube (Cairo), Evdokim Matzikov (Subotica, Yugoslavia), and Feodor Semens (Los Angeles). The aim of such correspondence was "to keep White Russians throughout the world in touch with the others so that when the Soviet government was finally overthrown they might take their proper places in their home country and endeavor to establish good relations with the United States." Of course, the VNRP did not espouse violence: ". . . while I would naturally be delighted to see the Soviet government overthrown, I have never in this country advocated this by force."

By the time that this angelic disclaimer was filed with the Justice Department on December 30, 1941, other forces had been at work building up Vonsiatsky as a spy and criminal. A certain Belgian journalist of Russian extraction named Mr. Akivisson, described by a Justice Department official as "well and favorably known to our office," wrote the Department on December 9 that the Japanese government was employing Vonsiatsky as an agent. Arnold Foster and Miles Goldberg of the Anti-Defamation League were in direct contact with Bisgyer of the Special Defense Unit, supplying information derived from a certain informant named Constantine Kaledin. And *The Hour*'s Albert E. Kahn made available his "cabinet full" of Vonsiatskiana to the Special Defense Unit, including Alex's "confession to the commission of seven murders."

Bisgyer passed these and other data to analyst Louis Nemzer, who was left with the awesome task of making sense out of it. During November and December, Nemzer pored over documents ranging from bigamy charges in 1922 to allegations of treason in 1941. In a thirty-four-page memorandum submitted to Bisgyer on December 19, Nemzer outlined three possible areas in which Vonsiatsky might be prosecuted: (1) violation of the Voorhis Act, (2) violation of the McCormack Act (working for a foreign principal against American interests), and (3) revocation of citizenship on the grounds that he had misrepresented his marital status, concealed "torture killings," and had "mental reservations" while taking the oath of allegiance to the United States.

Pearl Harbor succeeded in doing what a decade of public outrage and private denunciations had failed to accomplish: to convince the Justice Department that Anastase Vonsiatsky *might* not be a joke. As Nemzer cautiously noted in his December 19 memorandum to Bisgyer: ". . . it may well be that this very resemblance to a comic opera character has permitted Vonsiatsky to indulge in unspectacular but nonetheless illegal activities."

It still remained for a prosecutor to demonstrate in a court of law that Anastase Vonsiatsky was in fact a German-Japanese spy and a menace to American security. To get an indictment from a grand jury, a prosecutor would have to put the stamp of reality on Pelypenko's revelations, for they would constitute the most damaging (and in some areas the only) evidence. More important, a prosecutor would have to keep a straight face as he became more familiar with the suspect's actual character and activities.

The man for the job turned out to be a young assistant to the attorney general. His name was Thomas J. Dodd.

CHAPTER XVII

Mime and Punishment

It is not just a marching chowder club, we don't think.
—THOMAS J. DODD, May 14, 1942

During the first four months of 1942, Anastase Vonsiatsky took pains to be on his best behavior. He scrupulously avoided outrageous gestures or even colorful remarks and tried to look patriotic and inconspicuous. His forty-three years put him beyond the draft. But to show that he was contributing to the war effort, he lent fifty-four of his vintage rifles to the Putnam Civil Defense Company.

Meanwhile, the wheels of the Justice Department bureaucracy kept turning in Washington. The Special Defense Unit completed its probe of Vonsiatsky in April and, with the approval of Attorney General Francis Biddle, handed all the findings over to the Criminal Division for prosecution. The Criminal Division formulated the charge, which turned out to be far more serious than infractions of the Voorhis and McCormack acts. Vonsiatsky, it turned out, was to be prosecuted for having violated section 32 of the Espionage Act of 1917: namely, for delivering information injurious to the United States to a foreign agent or power.

Of course a federal grand jury had to indict Vonsiatsky for conspiracy before he could be tried and sentenced. And for the government to get an indictment, it would have to convince a grand jury that reasonable evidence of his guilt existed. The Special Defense Unit had collected a massive volume of material on the suspect. Much of it, however, was circumstantial and based upon hearsay. The most incriminating evidence, if it still existed, would probably be in Vonsiatsky's private files.

Clearly, an FBI raid on Nineteenth Hole was in order.

Blitzkrieg

When Anastase devised Nineteenth Hole's elaborate architectural and canine defenses in 1934–35, he never dreamed that they would be put to the test not by Soviet agents or Rodzaevsky's hit men but by federal law-enforcement officers. But by 1942, the count should have expected such a visitation. In Congress, Representative Dickstein was calling him a "dangerous element in this country." Connecticut State Police Lieutenant Ross Urquhart even came up to Nineteenth Hole early in the spring to warn his friend Alex about the likelihood of an FBI raid. Nevertheless, when the raid came, the count was taken completely by surprise.

Armed with a federal search warrant, thirteen G-men swooped down on Nineteenth Hole shortly after noon on Saturday, May 9, 1942. They were led by FBI New Haven branch director Richard H. Simons and accompanied by Lieutenant J. Victor Clark, commanding officer of the Connecticut State Police barracks at Danielson (Urquhart had been transferred to another post). When a caravan of cars pulled up the driveway, only Marion and the servants were at home. Alex was in Boston doing some weekend shopping.

The agents lost no time in going through the premises. They scoured the fourteen-room farmhouse, the stone annex containing the Military Room and offices, the cow barn, and the converted hen coops which still sheltered *Fashist*'s printing presses. Within two hours, they had collected six khaki uniforms, a dozen swastika arm bands, a box of swastika pins, six 1916 vintage rifles, a recording machine with some 78 rpm discs, four cannisters of tear gas, two dozen toy boats, and what looked like a moth-eaten overcoat draped over a human mannequin. Some agents went over to the West Thompson Cemetery, entered the Vonsiatsky crypt, and peered at the sarcophagi. Only Kunle was there. The agents focused their attention on eleven steel filing cabinets bulging with correspondence, scrapbooks, office ledgers, copies of *Fashist,* and several varieties of pamphlets. As almost everything was written in Russian, the agents were not sure what they were looking at. So they waited for their man to come home.

It was after ten o'clock that evening when Vonsiatsky returned from Boston. Upon seeing the driveway full of cars, he concluded that Marion must be entertaining some of her own friends. But as soon as it became apparent that he was the object of attention, Anastase warmed to the occasion. He eagerly led the agents from room to room, opening locked drawers and closets with a set of keys. He took them into the Military Room and recited the same stories to which Nazis, Communists, and cronies had been treated since 1930. He insisted that the government take all eleven filing cabinets, so that their contents would remain intact.

Shortly before eleven o'clock, Vonsiatsky sat down with agents Meunier and Mahan and talked without interruption until four thirty the next (Sunday) morning. He told them about his life from Warsaw to Windham County, dwelling on his relations with Wilhelm Kunze, because his listeners seemed particularly interested. Meunier took copious notes.

On Sunday, newspapers from coast to coast gave prominent coverage to the raid on Nineteenth Hole, although it was but one of the nationwide strokes carried out by the FBI against fascist suspects over the weekend. Among VNRP *soratniki* visited were Reverend Alexander Tzuglevich in Manhattan, T. Savin in Queens, Feodor Semens and George Doombadze in Los Angeles, and Herbert G. Vantz and Princess Anne Gantamoura in San Francisco. Neither they nor Vonsiatsky was immediately taken into custody. The raids were designed to gather evidence for possible prosecution. Robert P. Butler, U.S. district attorney for Connecticut, announced that material collected at the Vonsiatsky estate was being brought to Hartford for presentation to a federal grand jury scheduled to convene at the United States District Court on Tuesday, May 12.

After staying up all night with FBI agents, Vonsiatsky felt listless on Sunday. Yet he had little opportunity to sleep. The phone rang constantly as newsmen asked him for statements. Contrary to his usual loquaciousness, Anastase responded to their queries by saying that he knew only what he read in the press. Apparently his attorney, Clarence Mitchell, had advised him to say little and sign nothing. Indeed, three days later, Alex avoided signing an affidavit summarizing his Saturday night monologue to Mahan and Meunier which the latter brought back to Nineteenth Hole for his signature.

On Monday afternoon, May 11, a truck arrived at Nineteenth Hole to pick up the filing cabinets, rifles, trinkets, and what the Hartford *Courant* termed "an elaborate wardrobe of fascist uniforms." The Military Room was left bare except for a naked mannequin. Its alabaster sheen made the waxy figure literally a "white guard." Not able to bear the sight of it, Vonsiatsky packed the thing away in a coffinlike wooden trunk.

Written in Russian, the VNRP documents befuddled local officers in Hartford, so it was decided to call in three linguists from Washington to sift through everything and translate whatever looked significant.

Monday's papers followed up the raid story by reviving Vonsiatskiana with a few embellishments for wartime readers. Nineteenth Hole was no longer just a "fortress" but had graduated to "an armed camp, where followers drilled rigorously." Anastase emerged as a "collaborator" with Rodzaevsky, Ataman Semenov, and the Kwantung Army. *PM's Daily Picture Magazine* magnified Alex's age as well as his connections, calling Marion twenty-two years his junior.

On Monday, the newspapers also announced the name of the man assigned by the Justice Department to prosecute Vonsiatsky before a Hartford grand jury: Thomas J. Dodd.

Indictment

Born in Norwich, Connecticut, on May 17, 1907, Thomas Joseph Dodd was not quite thirty-five when assigned by the Justice Department to prosecute Vonsiatsky. His youth, however, belied a toughness and acumen gained from a rigorous apprenticeship and a powerful inner drive to succeed. Dodd had grown up in a devout middle-class Irish Catholic family. He had wanted to become an actor, but his father refused to countenance such frivolity and directed him toward the law. During the late 1920s, while Vonsiatsky was commuting to Brown football games in a yellow Mercer sports coupe, Dodd was studying Thomas Aquinas at nearby Providence College, an austere fortress of Dominican theology. Dodd's interest in politics germinated at Yale Law School, where he was elected president of the Yale Democratic Club and took time out to act as frontman for major candidates on the campaign trail. The job, which involved warming up impatient and sometimes hostile Depression crowds in union halls, on courthouse steps, and at open-air rallies without microphones, taught Dodd practical oratory and forensic tactics. A longtime aide later recalled:

> Dodd learned, in a sort of trial by combat, to project and conserve his voice, to bully hecklers in an authoritative manner, to take quickly the

measure of a crowd, divining the touchstone of its reaction and the jugular vein of its discontent.

Dodd's promotional efforts attracted the attention of Homer S. Cummings, a powerful Connecticut Democrat. Shortly after Franklin Roosevelt made Cummings his attorney general in 1933, Cummings recommended Dodd to J. Edgar Hoover, who offered him the job of an FBI special agent. However, Hoover's harsh discipline did not sit well with Dodd's restless ambition. He resigned from the FBI in 1935 to join the campaign staff of a Connecticut politician, Francis T. Maloney. When Maloney was elected to the United States Senate in 1936, he rewarded Dodd by appointing him deputy director of Connecticut's WPA. Dodd soon rose to become state director of another New Deal program, the National Youth Administration. In 1938, Dodd returned to the Justice Department as a special assistant to his old mentor, Homer Cummings. After Cummings resigned in 1939, Dodd continued to serve under Frank Murphy, Robert H. Jackson, and Francis Biddle. When America entered World War II, Dodd found himself disqualified for military service by high blood pressure and five children. So he specialized in prosecuting draft dodgers—until he was assigned to Anastase Vonsiatsky.

Vonsiatsky was Dodd's first big case. He had three reasons to accord it extraordinary importance. Nazis aroused his moral indignation. Vonsiatsky seemed to be a key figure in a German-Japanese spy network, a scenario that fit neatly into his readiness to perceive international conspiracies. Finally, given the wide publicity about Vonsiatsky in the press, the case could not help but put anyone who prosecuted it in the national limelight. Here was a providential opportunity which, if properly handled, could dramatically boost Dodd's political fortunes. But success, Dodd knew, depended upon Vonsiatsky's being made to look like a clever and dangerous masterspy. No one would be grateful to him for saving America from a clown.

Dodd threw himself into the Vonsiatsky case determined to secure an indictment and conviction. His biggest handicap was lack of time for preparation (only three days elapsed between the removal of documents from Nineteenth Hole and the opening of grand jury hearings). But this handicap was overcome to some extent by the help of Albert E. Kahn, who shared with Dodd *The Hour*'s massive file on Vonsiatsky. Besides, Dodd was not that concerned about being unprepared, because he viewed the case as one of straightforward, self-evident espionage. Intricacies and contradictions in the evidence came to his attention only after the hearings had begun and did not at first interest him. Dodd's approach to the case was deeply influenced by the wartime atmosphere. The United States was fighting fascism, as embodied in Germany and Japan. Vonsiatsky, a self-professed fascist, maintained connections with Japanese and Germans, connections that in themselves pointed to an anti-American conspiracy. Such questions as the genesis and nature of Vonsiatsky's anticommunism, Vonsiatsky's actual relations with German and Japanese authorities, Vonsiatsky's relations with other émigré groups, and above all, Vonsiatsky's penchant for exaggeration, showmanship, and fantasy all struck the young prosecutor as unimportant. In fact, he seemed to feel that they obscured the simple truth—that Vonsiatsky was just what *The Hour* and Pelypenko said he was.

Formal judicial proceedings opened on Thursday morning, May 14, at the Federal Building in Hartford. At ten o'clock, United States District Court Judge J. Joseph Smith swore in twenty-three members of the grand jury, eleven women and twelve men, including foreman John J. Scott, a retired agency superintendent of the Connecticut Mutual Life Insurance Company. Representing the government were Dodd, U.S. District Attorney Robert P. Butler, and two assistant district attorneys, Joseph E. Cooney and Valentine J. Sacco. Neither Vonsiatsky nor his legal counsel appeared at this or any subsequent grand jury session, all of which were held *in camera*.

Butler made some opening remarks. He emphasized that everything said in the courtroom must be kept secret, because "it is a matter that we believe very gravely concerns the safety of this government and this country and the safety of certain of our allies in this war." He went on to stress the case's importance: "I have been acting almost eight years now as United States Attorney in this district and I think that this is the most serious investigation that has ever been conducted by a grand jury in this district in that time." Butler concluded by indicating that a special assistant to the United States attorney general would be in charge of the proceedings. He then handed the floor to Dodd.

Dodd gave a final glance at his notes, rose with deliberation, and slowly surveyed the twenty-three members of the grand jury. Despite a short, chunky build, he projected an impressive presence. His face, except for its ruddiness, was that of a Roman patrician: full-bodied cheeks, straight lips, a sturdy nose, piercing eyes set off by thick black brows, and a touch of premature gray around the temples. But Dodd's most striking features were kinetic. He radiated energy and willpower with every movement. And his speech, if not always grammatically phrased, carried a hammering conviction that never betrayed a moment of doubt.

Dodd began by giving the grand jury a summary of Vonsiatsky's background, "not in any attempt to present evidence to you, or in any wise to prejudice your mind . . . but in order that you will have some intelligent idea at least of what this thing is all about." The prosecutor started with Anastase's youth, upbringing, military service, meeting with Marion in Paris, and immigration to the United States "through the influence of the Ream family . . . who were in that time in rather important places in governmental circles." Dodd described the count's participation in the Brotherhood of Russian Truth, his fascist party, and his presence in Manchukuo in 1934 "apparently in the uniform of a Japanese army officer." Next covered were VNRP worldwide activities, Bund connections, the Webster putsch, the $2,800 check to Kunze, the San Francisco jaunt and Chicago rendezvous, the Military Room with its "very usable rifles" and submachine gun ("and ammunition"), military drilling at Nineteenth Hole, the fascist school in New York, and Alex's plan "to take over the new Russian government when the Germans had conquered Russia." As his narrative drew to a close, Dodd put heavy emphasis on Vonsiatsky's ties with Kunze, his possession of a calling card of a Japanese army officer, and certain alleged correspondence with people unknown in Alaska:

> Vonsiatsky, not so long ago, gave a Russian priest a card of introduction to the Japanese Embassy, which he admits he gave himself, and the card had on it the name of a Japanese Army officer, a colonel. The individual who got the card brought it to the Japanese Embassy, and the Japs told him to go back and ask Vonsiatsky for the names of some contacts for Alaska. We know that Vonsiatsky has been sending registered mail to Alaska until very recently. In that way you are beginning to see the significance of this thing. It is not just a marching chowder club, we don't think.

Following Dodd's opening statement came the examination of witnesses.

Thirty-nine individuals received subpoenas to appear before the grand jury. They all showed up at Hartford and gave testimony during the course of eight day-long sessions between May 14 and June 9. Collectively, they represented a good many facets of Vonsiatsky's life. There was a relative and Russian Civil War veteran: Lev Mamedov. Then there were current and former VNRP *soratniki:* Reverend Tzuglevich, Norman B. Watson, "Misha" Kapral. Alex's cronies showed up in force: George Connell of the Putnam *Patriot;* freelance reporter and photographer Richard McCauley; ex-caddy, ex-newspaper editor, ex-insurance salesman and current U.S. Army private Jimmy Bakker; and Connecticut State Police officers Ross Urquhart and Elton Nolan. Domestic servants had their day in court: Ream handyman Richard Barton; Ramiro Sisson, a Filippino cook; Nicolina Johnson, a Norwegian maid; Emil LaJeunesse, an ex-caretaker of Nineteenth Hole; and former chauffeurs James Morgan and Warren Towne. Two close friends of Marion's were also called in: Frank Decker and Marion de Floresz.

The rest of the witnesses came from outside the Thompson-Putnam community but had known or done business with Vonsiatsky. These included reporters Wesley Griswold of the Hartford *Courant,* who had interviewed Vonsiatsky in September 1934 after his first world tour; Francis Quinlan, who covered the 1937 Fourth of July weekend for the Hartford *Courant;* and David Karr, who interviewed Vonsiatsky after the 1939 Webster putsch for *The Hour.* There were also salesmen: Charles J. Scott and Lloyd Curtiss of Francis Bannerman & Sons, where Vonsiatsky had purchased his rifles; Geoffrey Oberdick of Federal Laboratories, Inc., where he had replenished his tear gas supply; and Marcus Graham, a Providence photographer who had taken Vonsiatsky's portrait (in full uniform). Also called in were several Russian émigrés: Alexander Egorovsky and Vladimir Illyn, whose presses had once printed *Fashist;* Boris Brasol, a former tsarist prosecuting attorney, criminologist, anti-Soviet publicist, reputed anti-Semite, and avid monarchist member of the New York-based Russian National Committee; and Mooza Pookhir, a young Russian-born interior decorator from Washington, D.C., who had met Vonsiatsky casually three times since September 1941. Philip King, a retired headwaiter from the Taft Hotel in New Haven, testified that he saw Vonsiatsky entertaining *two* Japanese girls after the Yale-Brown game in 1940. A Boston attorney, Paul Killiam, and his wife,

Mary, were questioned on why they had rented their Kirkland Place house in Cambridge to a group calling itself "The Russian Club." FBI special agent Lionel Meunier presented an affidavit of his six-hour conversation with Alex at Nineteenth Hole on the night of May 9–10 following the raid.

Finally came the key witnesses who were crucial to establishing Vonsiatsky's involvement in a German-Japanese espionage ring. These included Bundists Otto Willumeit and August Klapprott, and the Lutheran pastor from Philadelphia, Reverend Kurt Molzahn, all accused of abetting Kunze's escape from the United States to Mexico. But the star of the proceedings was Alexius Pelypenko. Since February, Pelypenko had been vegetating in an alien detention center at Fort Howard, Maryland, while the Immigration and Naturalization Service tried to figure out what to do with him. Dodd, however, quickly perceived Pelypenko as an invaluable witness, yanked the bewildered man out of Fort Howard, and installed him in Hartford's Bond Hotel.

Missing from the procession of witnesses was a person who perhaps knew Vonsiatsky better than anyone: Marion. Marion had lived with Anastase for twenty years. Marion had accompanied him on all of his foreign travels since 1928, travels during which he allegedly entered into a conspiracy with the German and Japanese governments. Why didn't Marion testify? The reasons can only be inferred. It is possible that the Ream family tried to prevent her from taking the stand; moreover, in grand jury hearings, an individual could not be compelled to testify against a spouse. It is also possible, but unprovable, that when Dodd learned about Marion's age (sixty-five), physical condition, popularity in the local community, and insulation from her husband's political activities, he decided to spare her the pain and humiliation of testifying about her husband. Moreover, Dodd probably had discovered by this time that Vonsiatsky's "Japanese connection" contained a sexual ingredient, and he may have concluded that it would be gratuitous cruelty to confront an innocent old lady with her husband's amatory dalliances.

Dodd's courtroom strategy called for eliciting from each witness evidence that would give credibility to the government's charge that Vonsiatsky had conspired to convey American military secrets to Japan (via Madame Takita) and to Germany (via Wilhelm Kunze). Of all thirty-nine witnesses, Alexius Pelypenko tried hardest to help Dodd substantiate this charge.

Pelypenko testified twice (on May 20 and 21), speaking volubly if sometimes incoherently through an interpreter. The priest not only repeated what he had told the FBI about Vonsiatsky, he improvised embellishments. For example, he assured the grand jury that during his visit to Nineteenth Hole on August 6, 1941, Vonsiatsky had given him the name of Prince Stephan zu Schaumburg-Lippe as his agent in Brazil. Now Pelypenko had reported to an INS informant that Vonsiatsky had given him the name of a Brazilian censor in São Paulo who was an agent of sorts. But never before had Pelypenko mentioned Prince Stephan. The prince, of course, was none other than the German Embassy official in Buenos Aires who had sent Pelypenko to the United States to conduct pro-Nazi propaganda. That the priest should have cited his own contact as Vonsiatsky's was astonishing and even a bit daring. Dodd jumped on the sinister-sounding Germanic name, and for the rest of the hearing, Prince Stephan zu Schaumburg-Lippe was Vonsiatsky's man in Brazil.

But Pelypenko had still bigger stories to spin. At one point he described Vonsiatsky as "the director of the German—of the Japanese—spy ring in this country." Later, he added that Anastase was also "in charge of German espionage in Canada." Pelypenko quoted the count as saying that he maintained agents on Kodiak Island and Sitka in Alaska. The information that Vonsiatsky had tried to hand over to Madame Takita in San Francisco and eventually gave to Kunze consisted of "the complete placement of the American army and fleet." Lest his listeners think that Vonsiatsky retained any vestigial loyalty to the United States, Pelypenko quoted the count as saying: "I spit upon American citizenship."

Despite his eagerness to help Dodd, Pelypenko was at times as much of a liability as an asset. His buildup of Vonsiatsky at times became so overblown that it bordered on caricature. For Dodd, that type of testimony was distinctly undesirable. The jurors might get skeptical. Indeed, one jurywoman who evidently had grown suspicious of Pelypenko asked why he was under detention. The question triggered an outburst from the Ukrainian priest, who began to rant about "the Polacks" being responsible for his incarceration at Fort Howard. When it was learned that Pelypenko had a son, a juryman asked how he could do so as a priest. This question too touched a sore spot, for Pelypenko immediately launched into a tirade against his former FBI supervisor, who had allegedly shown more interest in the legitimacy of the priest's son than in catching spies.

By this time, Dodd saw that his prize witness was beginning to become a problem. While motioning to the interpreter to take Pelypenko away, Dodd intoned: "Anything else? That is all. [to Pelypenko] Thank you very much. We don't need you anymore."

Pelypenko was not needed anymore. He went back to Fort Howard.

For all the problems Pelypenko may have caused for Dodd, he at least tried valiantly to put flesh on the government's charges against Vonsiatsky. Other witnesses proved less cooperative. Willumeit, Klapprott, and Molzahn stubbornly rejected the notion of a conspiracy. Willumeit contradicted Pelypenko's version of the Bismarck Hotel meeting. Klapprott admitted only to drinking liquor and listening to records of marches at Nineteenth Hole. Molzahn testified that he had never met or corresponded with Vonsiatsky. The anti-Soviet writer Boris Brasol also denied ever meeting Vonsiatsky, although he admitted that the count had asked him by letter in 1930 to take over leadership of the Brotherhood of Russian Truth in the United States. Even under intense prodding from Dodd, Reverend Tzuglevich could not recall any priestly contacts in Alaska.

Dodd was handicapped throughout the hearings by a lack of historical background in general and an understanding of the Russian diaspora in particular. He persisted in treating Rodzaevsky and Semenov as members of Vonsiatsky's party who led a "branch" in Harbin. When Mamedov mispronounced Nakamura Hitoshi's first name as "Hiroshita," Dodd linked him with Hirohito, the emperor of Japan. As soon as Boston attorney Paul Killiam mentioned that Harvard historian Michael Karpovich had lectured at the Russian Club—an informal group of academics, artists, and professionals of Russian ancestry—in Cambridge, Dodd wondered aloud whether Karpovich was not a fascist too.

Dodd encountered more difficulties when witness after witness from Windham County came to the stand and claimed that Vonsiatsky was a dreamer and poseur but neither a German nor a Japanese spy. Sergeant Nolan of the Connecticut State Police, who had known the count since 1927, remarked: "I knew he was a great man for publicity and always liked to be in the public eye. I daresay, in none of his conversations was there anything that was detrimental to anybody connected with this country." Lieutenant Urquhart echoed Nolan: "Well, he [Vonsiatsky] is a darn fool for one thing. He certainly sought all the publicity he could get."

Asked by Dodd what he thought when Vonsiatsky talked about

taking over the Russian government with German help in the summer of 1941, George Connell answered: "I didn't take these things seriously."

Jimmy Bakker, appearing in the Hartford courtroom in a U.S. Army uniform, had caddied for Vonsiatsky in the early 1930s, had caroused with him in the mid-1930s, and since 1941 had carried the insurance on the stained-glass window of the Vonsiatsky crypt. He had this to say about the count:

> The impression that I have makes it difficult for me to conceive of his [Vonsiatsky's] movement as being serious . . . that is, sufficiently effective to worry anyone. I mean, I think that when I speak in that sense I am speaking perhaps on behalf of most of the people that are residents near his estate. I don't think that the movement is taken too seriously.

Other witnesses spoke warmly of Vonsiatsky. Norman B. Watson, a turret lathe operator of the Colt Firearms Company in Hartford who had caddied for Vonsiatsky in the 1920s and had done secretarial chores for him between 1933 and 1937, testified that his former employer was kind, fair, and a good American citizen. Ramiro Sisson, a Philippine-born naturalized American citizen who had served in the U.S. Navy during World War I and since 1940 had worked as a cook at Nineteenth Hole, reaffirmed Watson's positive estimation of Vonsiatsky.

The most hostile testimony from a local source was that of Marion de Floresz, a crisply respectable grande dame from Pomfret who was one of Marion's oldest friends. De Floresz had known Vonsiatsky since 1921 when he had first visited Thompson as a houseguest at Carolyn Hall. She had always found him boorish and impudent and avoided his company. In the summer of 1941, Alex had outraged her by boasting: "If Mr. Hitler wishes me to represent Germany in Russia, I am willing to go." She had retorted: "Well, I doubt very much if Mr. Hitler even knows you are alive." Despite her dislike for Vonsiatsky, Marion de Floresz could not bring herself to testify under oath that she thought him to be a spy. Under questioning, she could not recall a single occasion when she had seen Germans or Japanese at Nineteenth Hole (she probably overlooked Nakamura Fusako). And she finally echoed other witnesses by saying that "everybody looked on him as more or less a joke."

Mooza Pookhir, a pert twenty-four-year-old interior decorator from Washington, had gone up to Nineteenth Hole the previous summer out of curiosity whetted by stories she had heard about the man who lived there. Incorrigibly gallant when it came to pretty young women, Vonsiatsky had invited her to spend the night and entertained her with relish. They subsequently dined in New York and went to a Brown-Yale game in New Haven. While they were together, he boasted about his agents around the world and about his grand plans for Russia. But Mooza's instinct told her that "it was just a lot of soap bubbles."

Faced with the prospect of his case being undermined by levity, Dodd began to show signs of touchiness. George Connell was the first to feel the bite of his frustration when the prosecutor grumbled: "Is there anything the matter with your memory?" Upon hearing that Lieutenant Urquhart had socialized with and borrowed money from the suspect, yet could offer the grand jury no more information than that Alex's guns were probably unusable, Dodd ruefully commented that "it seems as though there might be some other information which your men should have obtained." When Sergeant Nolan failed to produce incriminating evidence about Vonsiatsky, Dodd could barely contain his irritation:

> All these conversations you had with him [Vonsiatsky] over the years, and the close association with him, it would seem that you might have picked up some association that would be of value other than to just believe that he was, as I suppose I assume you did, a sort of a buffoon? . . . Isn't it a fact that you know him too well for your own official contact up there, and don't you know some other things about him that you haven't told us here?

When Jimmy Bakker testified that he had not taken the FBI raid too seriously, Dodd asked peevishly:

> You are a United States citizen and a soldier and you necessarily knew that some of the German representatives were up there [at Nineteenth Hole]. Didn't it ever occur to you that there was something serious about this individual [Vonsiatsky]?

Bakker, however, was not to be intimidated: "I would like to correct you, sir. I had no knowledge at any time that any German representatives were in attendance at his estate." Dodd finished with Bakker by warning him not to see Vonsiatsky again: "It might mean your head."

Norman Watson bore the full brunt of Dodd's anger. Because Watson had worked as Vonsiatsky's secretary (1933–37), the prosecutor felt that he should be able to tell the grand jury about his employer's conspiratorial connections with Germany and Japan. But Watson could only recall writing letters, paying bills, going with Vonsiatsky to New York for dental work, entertaining state policemen, and mailing bundles of *Fashist* at the Thompson and Putnam post offices. This was about all that Dodd could take, as the following extracts from his interrogation of Watson suggest:

> Don't you think it might be some part of your responsibility to tell the grand jury in this country anything that you might know honestly and truthfully and rightly and without equivocating about this situation? Has that ever dawned on you?

> And you sit here and pretend you don't know what we are talking about and generally you are as reluctant and as difficult to question as anybody could be.

> I don't know whether you are dumb or don't want to answer the questions.

> You get out of here and sit down somewhere and think about it. Go ahead. Get out. [after Watson had left the courtroom] He is a liar, that fellow.

Dodd need not have become so upset. War had conditioned ordinary citizens such as the twenty-three grand jury members to accept readily the plausibility of plots against national security, even from the most unlikely candidates. On the afternoon of Tuesday, June 9, after deliberating for thirty minutes, the grand jury made its decision. Foreman Scott announced the decision to Judge Smith: that the jurors had returned an indictment against Vonsiatsky for violating section 32 of the 1917 Espionage Act by participating in a conspiracy between January 1 and December 6, 1941, to transmit national defense secrets* to Germany and Japan. Named as coconspirators with the count were Kunze, Willumeit, and two German-Americans who had forwarded Kunze's mail, Reverend Kurt Molzahn of Philadelphia and Dr. Wolfgang Ebell of El Paso, Texas.

---

* The secrets transmitted included: "documents, writings, code books, signal books, sketches, photographs, photographic negatives, blueprints, plans, maps, models, notes, instruments, appliances, and information relating to the national defense of the United States . . ."

The bill of indictment listed twelve "overt acts" committed by the conspirators. Vonsiatsky figured in five:

1. meeting Kunze at Thompson on July 12, 1941
2. handing Kunze a check for $2,800 on July 12, 1941
3. traveling to San Francisco "in or about the month of July, 1941"
4. meeting Kunze and Willumeit at the Bismarck Hotel "in or about the month of July, 1941"
5. receiving "certain letters" written by Kunze "in or about the month of November, 1941"

Vonsiatsky now faced the choice of pleading guilty or standing trial.

Vonsiatsky did not remain inactive while a federal grand jury inquired into his activities. Perhaps it would be more accurate to say that Vonsiatsky's attorneys were not inactive. Late in 1941, Bund counsel Wilbur V. Keegan told an FBI agent that Marion "has her own lawyers" working on Anastase's behalf. One of these was Clarence Mitchell, who, between October and December 1941, corresponded with the Justice Department about registration requirements for the VNRP under the Voorhis Act. After the FBI raid on Nineteenth Hole on May 9, 1942, however, it became apparent that Anastase might need a first-class trial lawyer. Marion (or possibly her brother Robert Clarke Ream, who was far more practiced in these matters) procured one of the most noted defense attorneys in the country: Martin W. Littleton, Jr.

Littleton was an appropriate choice. His father, Martin Sr., had successfully defended Harry K. Thaw, the millionaire playboy who had murdered the famed architect Stanford White at the Madison Square Garden Roof at 11:05 on the evening of June 25, 1906, during the closing minutes of a musical comedy, *Mam'zelle Champagne*. In one of the most publicized murder trials of the century, Littleton won his client a "not guilty" verdict from the jury by showing that insanity ran in Thaw's family. During the trial, Thaw bridled at being called deranged, but the defense's tactic worked.

Martin Jr. inherited his father's flair for vivid presentation and moving oratory. A partner wistfully remarked that "he would have made a great dramatic actor." During the mid-1930s, Littleton briefly served as Nassau County district attorney but switched to private practice, finding it more remunerative to save people from, rather than send them to, the electric chair.

Littleton's plans for Vonsiatsky followed the pattern of his father's strategy with Thaw. The defendant would be certified insane and thus held not responsible for his acts.

Littleton was by no means the first person to label Vonsiatsky abnormal. A 1939 FBI report noted that "he is considered somewhat deranged in his revolutionary party activities." Any number of friends and enemies had called Anastase erratic, outlandish, megalomaniac, and obsessed. Littleton's innovation was to magnify these eccentricities to such an extent that his client would be committed to an asylum rather than a penitentiary.

Did Vonsiatsky go along with Littleton's plan? He probably had some doubts. Incarceration in an asylum could be as unpleasant as imprisonment in a penitentiary. Moreover, the option for Vonsiatsky was not between insanity and execution as it had been for Thaw. Anastase knew that at worst he would get a stiff prison term, with the possibility of parole. Incarceration in an asylum could be permanent.

The Ream family, on the other hand, had good reason to welcome Alex's commitment to an institution and may have had a role in Littleton's plan. The family had never approved Marion's marriage to a penniless refugee half her age. Alex's sexual and political forays embarrassed and irritated the Reams. Certification would be a humane and inconspicuous way to remove Alex from sight and to detach him from Marion. Insanity, after all, was grounds for divorce.

Efforts to brand the count an "ill-balanced, hysterical teuto-polack" (as Ezra Pound described Nietzsche) began early in June when Littleton took Vonsiatsky to New York's Bellevue Hospital for an examination by the chief neurologist, Dr. Foster Kennedy. The attorney also engaged three eminent physicians (Dr. Richard H. Hoffman of New York, and Drs. Daniel Griffin and Harold Ribner of Bridgeport) to declare Vonsiatsky "paranoiac—dangerous both to himself and to the community." Armed with such weighty medical opinion, Littleton phoned Dodd, then conducting the grand jury hearings, at the latter's Lebanon, Connecticut home on Thursday, June 4, saying that his client was "dangerous to himself and others." Without telling Dodd, Littleton had already made arrangements through Dr. Griffin to place Vonsiatsky in the Fairfield State Hospital on the next day, Friday, June 5.

Littleton's tactic backfired. Quickly perceiving that Vonsiatsky's hospitalization would help the defense establish his insanity in court, Dodd found out where Anastase was headed and telephoned the Fairfield State Hospital superintendent, who told him about Griffin's arrangement. Griffin himself phoned Dodd a few minutes later and acknowledged responsibility for plans to admit Vonsiatsky. After talking with Dodd, however, Griffin changed his mind. When Vonsiatsky appeared at the hospital on June 5, he was denied admission.

Littleton's hospitalization ploy prompted Dodd to seek a bench warrant at Hartford on Friday, June 5, for Vonsiatsky's arrest. The warrant was issued on Saturday, June 6. Two FBI agents descended on Nineteenth Hole to take the count into custody. Alex happened to be in Providence getting a haircut from his favorite barber, Orlando. The agents drove to Providence, picked him up, and put him in the Providence County Jail. Bail was set at $25,000.

If Alex thought that anyone would come to his aid, he was mistaken. Marion's bank accounts were blocked. Her brothers would have been the last to bail him out. Having contended that Vonsiatsky was a dangerous lunatic, Littleton knew that pressing for bail could jeopardize his court case. As a result, the count spent the weekend in Providence getting to know his cell. Dodd came over to Providence at this time, but there is no record of the two men's meeting. According to U.S. Marshal Neal Murphy, Vonsiatsky passed the weekend restlessly pacing up and down, arms akimbo, chain-smoking cigarettes from an amber holder.

On Monday, June 8, after waiving an extradition hearing, the prisoner was delivered to Hartford by a U.S. marshal and placed in the Hartford County Jail to await the grand jury's decision. When the grand jury returned an indictment for conspiracy the next day, it was suddenly clear that the count would not be at liberty for some time to come.

On June 10, war bulletins from Europe and the Pacific, including accounts of the battle of Midway, were shunted aside as the Hartford, *Times* proclaimed in banner headlines:

BIG SPY CASE BREAKS HERE WHEN U.S. INDICTS VONSIATSKY
4 OTHERS IN AXIS CONSPIRACY PLOT

The story described how "one of the biggest spy cases in America" had just broken with the exposure of a Russian fascist "führer" who had been plotting with Bundists to "transmit military information to the Axis."

At his arraignment at three o'clock in the afternoon on June 10, Vonsiatsky, dressed in "natty sports clothes," clicked his heels smartly before Judge Smith while his attorney entered a plea of not guilty.

Minutes after his client strode out of the courtroom, Littleton filed a petition with Judge Smith for a pretrial sanity hearing on the grounds that an examination by four eminent physicians had demonstrated that Vonsiatsky was incapable of understanding the proceedings against him and suffered from paranoia and "colossal delusions of grandeur." Littleton characterized Vonsiatsky as "secretive, verbose, and given to babbling along on delusive and fantastic conceptions."

Outside the courtroom, Littleton gave reporters details about what he had until then referred to only in generalities. Marion was supposedly living behind locked doors at Nineteenth Hole to protect herself from him. Vonsiatsky had vowed to kill Hitler and Tojo prior to incorporating Germany and Japan into Fascist Russia. Vonsiatsky was planning to make football the national sport in Russia and would personally lead All-Russian gridiron teams on U.S. tours, trouncing West Point and Wisconsin by scores of 60 to 0. Vonsiatsky had promised to award Littleton a medal of honor if he won an acquittal.

Littleton's comments to the press made colorful copy but did not deter Dodd from seeking an early trial. "Whether or not he was insane during the time of the acts alleged in the indictment is not an issue until the trial," asserted the prosecutor. Nor did Dodd believe that Vonsiatsky was insane: "We think he is guilty of what we charge him with and that he knew what he was doing when he did it." Dodd did not overlook that there were other possible charges against Vonsiatsky not mentioned in the indictment: that the count had withheld information about the Crimean "torture killings" and about his marriage to Lyuba Muromsky when entering the United States in 1921, and had mental reservations when taking out American citizenship in 1927. In view of these additional crimes, Dodd announced on June 12 that he was preparing a petition to cancel Vonsiatsky's citizenship.

The statements by Littleton and Dodd gave the impression that a long, drawn-out legal battle was shaping up over Vonsiatsky. Writing in the New York *World-Telegram* on June 15, Kenneth Watson posed the issue: "Either Anastase Vonsiatsky is one of the most curious lunatics in the country, with almost incredibly fantastic delusions of grandeur, or he is a dangerous and clever conspirator against the government of the United States."

The anticipated showdown never materialized. After what appears to have been some quiet bargaining between Dodd and Littleton, Vonsiatsky reappeared before Judge Smith on June 22 and changed his plea to guilty. In contrast to the dapper confidence he had displayed twelve days earlier, the count looked drawn and haggard. At the rear of the courtroom sat Marion, comforted by Natasha Mamedov.

Speaking for the government, Dodd gave a diluted version of Pelypenko's account of Vonsiatsky, the Bund, and Japan. Seemingly unaware that Vonsiatsky had been *persona non grata* in Japan and Germany since 1934, Dodd came up with contacts that even Pelypenko had overlooked: that in 1939 Anastase had conferred with the Japanese "War Office"* in Tokyo and with "high Nazi officials" in Berlin. But, continued the prosecutor, in a stunning understatement, Vonsiatsky was not necessarily "the central figure" of the conspiracy. "We believe that there were others who occupied more important roles." Moreover, by changing his plea to guilty, Vonsiatsky had saved the government time and expense. Dodd concluded by recommending the imposition of a five-year prison sentence to be served in an institution designated by the attorney general, and a $5,000 fine.

Littleton then told the court that Vonsiatsky "was flung into the turmoil" of the Bolshevik Revolution at the young age of seventeen (he was actually nineteen) that he had been "lugged through Russia, half frozen, in cattle cars," and that he still carried a bullet within him as a reminder of those horrors. Vonsiatsky had "flirted" with the Bund and Japan only because he thought they could be used against Stalin. The attorney stumbled a bit in trying to explain why he had dropped the insanity plea, but recaptured his eloquence in defending the "unimpeachable integrity" of the four physicians who had declared Vonsiatsky incurably insane. In conclusion, Littleton turned toward Marion and said that "it would be a horribly cruel and most uncalled-for thing if there were any recriminations against

---

* Presumably a reference to the Army Ministry or the Imperial General Staff. It will be recalled that Vonsiatsky did not get off the boat when the SS *Polk* called at Yokohama and Kobe during February 1939. It is unlikely that senior Japanese military officers would have boarded the liner to talk with him.

Vonsiatsky's wife," who was a "splendid citizen," knew nothing about her husband's transgressions, and deserved everybody's sympathy.

Following statements from the prosecution and the defense, Judge Smith noted that Vonsiatsky had "abused the hospitality of this country" by allowing his anticommunism to lead him to work against the United States. Smith acknowledged that Vonsiatsky carried an obsession "which had so warped him that he has taken this course" but added that "he apparently knew what he was doing" and as such deserved "substantial punishment." Nevertheless, because Vonsiatsky was not the leader of the conspiracy, and because he had saved the government time and money by pleading guilty, the maximum penalty would not be imposed. Following Dodd's recommendation, Smith pronounced a sentence of five years' imprisonment and a $5,000 fine.

Anastase sat through the entire proceeding in silence. At times he stared intently at Dodd. At times, he seemed on the verge of tears, particularly when Judge Smith censured him for abusing American hospitality. After the session adjourned, Alex was led out of the courtroom by a guard. Marion and Natasha silently watched him leave. They then drove back, alone, to Nineteenth Hole.

The events of May and June were not easy for Marion. It was little consolation that Littleton exonerated her in the courtroom, that the Hartford *Times* gushed about her local popularity ("They hate him and love her"), or that twenty-four hours after the sentencing Judge Smith revoked the $5,000 fine after learning that the amended Espionage Act did not provide for monetary penalties. Marion was shaken but not shattered. She possessed far more resilience, determination, and devotion than most people suspected. Whatever her relatives and friends advised, she would neither divorce nor desert Alex simply because it was easy to do so with him in prison. She would see him through prison, just as she had seen him through pranks, politics, and promiscuity.

Vonsiatsky was lucky to receive a sentence when he did, for had he been judged a week later, there is a possibility that he would have been implicated in "Operation Pastorius," an Abwehr plan to cripple American aircraft production by blowing up cryolite and aluminum plants in the East and Midwest. Unknown to the court when it sentenced Vonsiatsky on June 22, eight German saboteurs had just landed from U-boats near Amagansett, Long Island, and Jacksonville, Florida. All eight had lived in the United States and spoke English with flawless Midwestern accents. The Amagansett group was immediately apprehended after being spotted by a young coast guardsman on the beach. One of them confessed all, enabling the FBI to track down the Florida group within days. When J. Edgar Hoover announced the capture of the saboteurs on June 27, he provided biographical data on each man. Published on June 28, these revelations indicated that one member of the Florida group, Hermann Neubauer, had worked at a Hartford hotel in 1931 and at Chicago's Bismarck Hotel from 1936 until 1939. Dodd seized upon the Hartford-Bismarck connection as something that could implicate Vonsiatsky with Neubauer. In an interview with the Hartford *Times* on June 29, Dodd remarked that Neubauer "might be very important" in the Vonsiatsky conspiracy case. Had Anastase not already been safely convicted and sentenced, he might have been credited with yet more subversion. There is no telling what could have happened to the count, given the charged atmosphere of that summer. Neubauer, who had carried the American flag for the United States team at the 1936 Berlin Olympics, was executed in July.

The four German-Americans with whom Vonsiatsky had allegedly conspired to transmit American military secrets to Berlin and Tokyo were indicted in June or July and sentenced on August 21. Otto Willumeit, Midwest Bund leader who had been at the Bismarck Hotel meeting, pleaded guilty and received a five-year sentence. Dr. Wolfgang Ebell, the El Paso physician who had forwarded Kunze's mail after the latter had bolted to Mexico, changed his original plea of not guilty to guilty and got seven years. Wilhelm Kunze, arrested on July 3 outside Mexico City while working as a ranch hand under the alias Alfonso Gratt-Cabedes, was extradited to the United States, pleaded guilty, and received a fifteen-year sentence. The Reverend Kurt Molzahn, pastor of the Old Zion Lutheran Church in Philadelphia, who had received passport photos of Kunze from Pelypenko, pleaded not guilty. He was the only member of the conspiracy to stand trial.

The Molzahn trial (formally called *U.S.* v. *Anastase Vonsiatsky et al.*), held at the United States District Court in Hartford between July 28 and August 20, looked like a rerun of the grand jury hearings on Vonsiatsky. The government's case, led by Dodd, rested upon Pelypenko, who was again released from Fort Howard to testify. Lacking solid evidence linking Molzahn to Japan, Dodd brought in Yale orientalist George A. Kennedy to read aloud from *Who's Who in Japan* about General Araki Sadao, whom Vonsiatsky had met once in 1934. Dodd made maximum, and apparently effective, use of the jurors' sensitivities by accusing Ebell during cross-examination of having advance knowledge of the Pearl Harbor attack.

Molzahn was found guilty on August 20 and sentenced to ten years in prison. An appeal to the United States Circuit Court of Appeals in 1943 was unsuccessful. Throughout the proceedings, Molzahn was strongly supported by members of his congregation, who paid his legal expenses, and by several ministers of the Lutheran Church. T. Henry Walnut, one of Molzahn's attorneys and a former Justice Department official, later called the judgment "a great injustice" on the grounds that it was based upon "the uncorroborated version of a conversation with him [Molzahn] as related by a priest [Pelypenko] acting as an undercover agent." Walnut also asserted that "the prosecution stooped to deceit in its efforts to secure a conviction." Published in 1943, that was probably the first public criticism of Thomas Dodd.

VNRP *soratniki* fared better than their *vozhd* and his Bundist associates. Mamedov, Reverend Tzuglevich, Feodor Semens, T. Savin, and Herbert G. Vantz were questioned by the FBI but neither detained nor indicted. Some of Vonsiatsky's draft-age friends recall being inducted into the army with unusual dispatch. But no one tried to deport émigré *soratniki* back to the USSR, a possibility to which Vonsiatsky found himself exposed in December 1942 when U.S. District Attorney for Connecticut Joseph Cooney filed a petition in the United States District Court at Hartford to strip the count of his citizenship.

Prison

Vonsiatsky remained in the Hartford County Jail until July 14, when he was allowed, under escort, to visit a downtown dentist to have an infected tooth pulled. The following day, accompanied by a United States marshal, he boarded a train for the first leg of a trip to "a penitentiary selected by the Attorney General." Anastase had no idea of his destination. After a change of trains in New York and an overnight trip, he found himself in Chicago, only to embark on yet another train. At 10:15 P.M. on July 17, the count was admitted to his new domicile: the Medical Center for Federal Prisoners in Springfield, Missouri.

On the evening of his arrival, Vonsiatsky was given a registration number (3775-H) and a physical examination. Since his arrest early in June, Alex had lost twenty-one pounds (200 to 179) and had contracted a gum infection. All other signs were normal. The doctor noted, regarding his mental condition at the time of registration, "patient is perfectly rational but states that he was told that he was paranoid."

During his first weeks at Springfield, Vonsiatsky underwent intensive observation. Prison psychiatrists conducted frequent interviews and compiled voluminous reports. These reports included intimate details ranging from childhood fantasies in Warsaw to sexual promiscuity in Thompson. When not being questioned, he was watched through a peephole in his cell.

Springfield physicians quickly saw that no. 3775-H was unhappy:

> He appears to be somewhat depressed. He rarely smiles and frequently tears come to his eyes when he speaks of his difficulty and especially when his wife is mentioned. . . . He shows much anxiety. He continues to bite his fingernails and to move about in his chair and to keep picking at his fingers.

Marion's name moved Alex to tears because he felt that, in the words of a prison report, "he had brought disgrace upon her and had done things that will probably cause her death."

Vonsiatsky admitted to his medical guardians that he had been a "sucker" to give Kunze $2,800, but he could not see how that act constituted a conspiracy against the United States. He was disappointed that such a famous (and expensive) lawyer as Littleton had put up such a poor defense. The insanity plea had shocked him, and the last-minute switch to a guilty plea, to which Alex had acquiesced on Littleton's advice, struck the count as a pragmatic compromise rather than an admission of guilt. According to a prison report:

> While he is not bitter toward the defending attorney and toward the psychiatrists who examined him, he feels that they placed him in an unfavorable light, but, no doubt, making him look so silly and grandiose probably lightened his sentence. Nevertheless he would have preferred to have the Court understand that he had no intention to commit espionage against this Government and that he did not know anything about the plans that Kunze took out of the country.

After listening to Vonsiatsky talk about himself, a Springfield psychiatrist made the following remarks on August 11, 1942:

> He speaks English fairly well with a marked Russian accent. . . . He is cooperative in every way and speaks frankly and coherently. He does not act suspicious or evasive. . . . His fund of general knowledge is good, especially when it comes to history and geography. In regard to international developments, he is keenly interested in them and shows a good knowledge of what is going on. . . . While this patient is rational and rather logical in his thinking and is a very likeable person, it is probably abnormal to set oneself apart from the group and to say, "I have a great cause and plan for 180,000,000 people; follow me and we will put this plan into operation." Great leaders have been successful by this method but still they may be different from the common herd.

Although Alex felt uncomfortable at Springfield and petitioned for a transfer to a regular penitentiary within a month of his arrival, he eventually grew accustomed to his surroundings. Early in 1943, he assumed the duties of prison librarian. He read for hours (mostly history) and often prayed when alone in his cell.

A dispute over the length of Alex's hair led to a minor crisis between Vonsiatsky and the prison administration in September 1942. Alex insisted that his hair be cut very short, because (here he was following an old Russian superstition) it "made the roots grow" and helped him to think clearly. Told by a guard that prison regulations did not permit shaven heads, Alex wrote petitions to the associate warden, the warden, and the Hospital Committee. When his petitions were rejected, he managed to get his hair cut short "in defiance of the rules." The Hospital Committee summoned Vonsiatsky to appear, and the following scene ensued (as recorded by a committee member):

> Upon being called before the Committee to answer this charge, inmate seemed quite agitated, became emotionally upset, crying, shaking violently, begging that we overlook that or give him that permission, that he would do anything else necessary towards a good adjustment and good work in this institution. He was told that we believe it is not necessary to have his hair cut short and that if he persisted in this action, it would be necessary to place him in the psychotic building with psychotic inmates (Ward 2–2). Inmate stated that rather than live in other parts of the institution and let his hair grow, he would prefer living in Ward 2–2 if he could cut his hair.

Apparently, Vonsiatsky won his case. He kept his hair *en brosse* yet managed to stay out of Ward 2–2.

Hair problems notwithstanding, Vonsiatsky impressed his guardians more and more favorably as the months passed. A ward surgeon's progress report dated February 3, 1943, noted: "The diagnosis of paranoia prior to being transferred to this institution seems quite doubtful at the present time. His insight and judgment appear fairly good, and he is well oriented. There are no delusions or hallucinations."

A progress reported dated January 4, 1944, gave an even more positive appraisal of the prisoner:

> This patient has continued to make an excellent adjustment in this institution. He is very polite, cooperative, and appreciative. He is careful in his selection of friends and is seldom seen congregating with other inmates. He spends most of his time reading, while not at work. Each time he has been approached on the subject of his trial and experiences in his past life . . . he does not demonstrate any evidence of gross delusions or hallucinations. He appears to be emotionally stable and is fairly cheerful.

Vonsiatsky's successful adjustment to prison life was to a great extent made possible by Marion's extraordinary devotion. In her late sixties, "Mama" showed a surge of renewed interest in her husband now that he was in trouble. It was almost as if her humanitarian instincts, so vigorous more than twenty years earlier when as a Red Cross nurse she had "rescued" a Russian refugee half her age from the Folies Bergères, were resurrected on behalf of the same Russian, now middle-aged but still, in her view, a helpless child. Marion wrote Alex constantly, enfolding him in love and encouragement. Twice, she made the 1,400-mile trip from Thompson to Springfield, speeding across half of America in a Cadillac touring car driven by handyman Steve Roshak and lubricated with fifty-dollar notes to mollify traffic policemen. Marion's letters and visits meant more than anything else to Alex, who otherwise received little good news (Stalin was winning the war) and certainly had no friends.

Indeed, judging from what was written about him during the war, Anastase Vonsiatsky ranked somewhere between Hitler and Hirohito in America's affections.

Wartime Brouhaha

In prison, Vonsiatsky achieved more notoriety than he had ever been able to stir up while at liberty. As usual, such notoriety sprang from the eyes of beholders rather than from anything that Alex had done before his arrest or was capable of doing in Springfield. Certain politicians, writers, editors, and a novelist consciously or unconsciously used him as an Axis bogey in 1942–45, just as the *Daily Worker* had used him as an anti-Soviet bogey in 1934–37.

Samuel Dickstein set the tone for what was to come when, on July 1, 1942, in a speech before the House of Representatives, he congratulated himself for exposing Vonsiatsky as a spy "four or five years ago" and chided fellow congressmen and the Dies Committee for having been so unappreciative of his vigilance:

> Mr. Speaker, Vonsiatsky was finally indicted [*sic*] a week ago. He pleaded guilty as a spy against this country and was sentenced to 5 years and a fine of $2,000 [*sic*]. A great number of the people I have named on the floor of this House years ago have been picked up as spies, and God knows how many more are floating around.

Dickstein's rhetoric sounded like a self-effacing understatement compared with what later rolled off the presses. In *Passport to Treason: The Inside Story of Spies in America* (1943), Alan Hynd described Nineteenth Hole as a massive structure on a promontory affording a view for miles around, surmounted by a turret with a machine gun on a swivel and steel compartments for storing grenades. In the Military Room were hung maps of England and the United States studded with swastikas at strategic points. Vonsiatsky employed Bundists as his agents. Kunze offered his home for subversive planning sessions (something never thought of by Pelypenko or Dodd):

> G-men looking into the Kunze home through powerful glasses could see Vonsiatsky-Vonsiatsky pacing up and down the Bundsman's living room, gesturing and pointing to a map of Europe that was unfolded on a table. It was the same kind of map that the Count had in his fabulous study.

Hynd also came up with a scenario of peripatetic espionage: Anastase driving around the country in a limousine, visiting defense factories and collecting secrets from worker-agents:

> He [Vonsiatsky] made a telephone call from a paystation right outside of the shipyard. In about ten minutes, a man in workmen's clothes came

out of the yard and stepped into the Count's fancy limousine. They made a strange pair, these two, the grimy workman and the elegant Count.

Arthur Derounian, a onetime FBI informer who wrote *Under Cover* in 1943 under the alias John Roy Carlson, repeated the now common tale that Vonsiatsky had shipped arms to Franco and had built up a global "Nazi espionage ring." Derounian could not resist inserting a few interpolations of his own. The Russian Bear cropped up as a "nightclub" and Anastase stalked the pages as a "legendary figure in the Nazi underworld. . . . His name was spoken in awe and his deeds whispered in secrecy."

Someone who should have known better was Albert E. Kahn, editor of *The Hour*. Kahn had collected a thick file on the count which included material sent to *The Hour* by Vonsiatsky himself. Kahn was in a position to separate fact from fancy. The result of his judgment was *Sabotage! The Secret War Against America* (1942), coauthored with Michael Sayers.

In *Sabotage!*, Kahn devoted a section to Vonsiatsky under the heading "Millionaire Saboteur." By a bold stroke of historical sleight-of-hand, he had Vonsiatsky "actively conspiring with the German American Bund and other Axis agencies to bring about a fascist coup in the United States" in 1934—two years before the Bund was established.

Kahn put Vonsiatsky in places and with people with whom the Count had doubtful, if any, connections. He "addressed large meetings of Bund Storm Troopers at Camp Nordland" (there is no record of Vonsiatsky ever having been at Nordland). In 1934, he "conferred with Alfred Rosenberg, Dr. Goebbels, and representatives of the Military Intelligence of the German High Command" (Vonsiatsky boasted that he had sipped tea with Rosenberg, but there is no evidence of any conferences with Goebbels or the Abwehr). "His last visit to Tokyo was in 1941; he returned to the United States shortly before the Japanese attacked Pearl Harbor" (Vonsiatsky did not go abroad after 1939).

Kahn's treatment of the July 29, 1941, Bismarck Hotel meeting went beyond the inspired visions of Pelypenko:

Shortly before Japan attacked the United States, a clandestine meeting was held in a room at the Hotel Bismarck in Chicago. . . . Future plans for espionage-sabotage activity in America were discussed. Kunze stressed the growing difficulties of getting funds from abroad. He asked Vonsiatsky to help finance the work of Nazi agents in the United States. Vonsiatsky handed the Bund leader $2,800 in cash, as a down payment.

Kahn apparently overlooked the fact that Vonsiatsky had given Kunze $2,800 in the form of a check on July 12 at Thompson. Even Pelypenko made no mention of money changing hands at the Bismarck meeting. Even Pelypenko said nothing about Vonsiatsky being asked to help fund Nazi espionage and sabotage in the United States. Even Pelypenko did not insinuate that the Bismarck Hotel meeting had taken place anywhere but in a public lounge.

The only significant difference between Kahn's account of Vonsiatsky and Vonsiatsky's fantasies about himself was that the former interpolated a plot against the United States:

> Scarcely a week passed without important Japanese, German, or Italian functionaries visiting Thompson, Connecticut. Sitting in comfortable chairs within Vonsiatsky's luxuriously furnished house or outside on the spacious lawn, they discussed with the White Russian Fuehrer ways and means of expediting the victory of World Fascism and, particularly, of bringing about a fascist coup in the United States.

Asked in 1976 about the sources for his exposé of Vonsiatsky, Kahn wrote: "I was fighting Nazis, and I didn't bother too much about amenities."

Fictional journalism blended into journalistic fiction. In 1944, Upton Sinclair put Vonsiatsky—using his actual name—in *Presidential Agent,* a novel in the popular Lanny Budd series. Anastase appeared as a fixture at a Fifth Avenue soirée hosted by a New York millionairess. Sinclair populated the scene with real and fictional rightist or conservative goblins: a fictional fascist publisher, a real fascist intellectual (Lawrence Dennis), a real ex-undersecretary of state (William R. Castle), and two fictional high-ranking military officers. As hero Lanny Budd entered this sinister assemblage (as an undercover agent), he heard Vonsiatsky boasting "in loud bellows" about his arms shipments to the Mexican Gold Shirts. After leaving the soirée, Budd wrote his chief, FDR: "America has everything that Germany had during the period that Hitlerism was in the egg."

Surpassing Dickstein, Pelypenko, Hynd, Derounian, and Kahn as practitioners of Vonsiatskiana were Walter Winchell and Tom Foley. In an article entitled "Americans We Can Do Without" (*Liberty* magazine, August 1, 1942), Winchell called Vonsiatsky "a key man in the Nazi plan in the USA" who led "a secret army in 46 countries" from "fortress-headquarters" guarded by "hundreds of machine guns." When the count visited Tokyo (the date was not given), he allegedly greeted high-ranking Japanese officials with: "When ice box party please?" "Ice box party" was, Winchell explained, their code word for an American revolution.

In "Cracking Down on the Screwball" (*Liberty* magazine, November 28, 1942), Tom Foley revealed that Vonsiatsky's well-known eccentricities were but a cloak for epochal cruelty and subversion. The count's true nature, according to Foley, was apparent as early as 1922, when he beat a reporter with brass knuckles. He was also a slippery character, throwing off FBI shadows by leaving a decoy in a New York taxicab. But Vonsiatsky periodically betrayed himself, such as when he read aloud to some local workman in Thompson a letter from his friend "Jake" Ribbentrop promising him a high position in Nazi Russia. Paid $50,000 by Japanese Intelligence, Vonsiatsky had headed a spy network that gravely threatened America. In Foley's words:

> From certain data confiscated in Von's fortress near the Rhode Island border, J. Edgar Hoover laid hands on some of the most important information seized since the beginning of the war. It was of potential danger to every man, woman, and child on the Atlantic seaboard.

With such extraordinary revelations emanating from the "experts," who could blame the anonymous reporter writing, in the Springfield, Missouri *Sunday News & Leader* (March 23, 1943), that the FBI had found plans at a "Putnam fort" to divide up the United States between Japan and Germany at the Rocky Mountains?

Vonsiatsky was a lucky man. Pranks, fantasies, and misdemeanors got him into trouble. For his mimes, he was punished with a short prison term. Konstantin Rodzaevsky was not that fortunate.

CHAPTER XVIII

Last Tango in Harbin

It does not help the mouse
to say "miaou" to cats
—RUSSIAN PROVERB

The apocalyptic sense of expectation felt by Konstantin Rodzaevsky following Germany's invasion of the Soviet Union on June 22, 1941, did not last long. Although German victories over the Red Army continued throughout the summer, prospects of the Russian Fascist Union's achieving a political role on Soviet soil soon faded, and the RFS *vozhd* suspected that his dreams of leading a Russian National Revolution were far from being realized.

For one thing, the Soviet-German war actually weakened rather than strengthened party unity. *Soratniki* who had barely recovered from their shock at the Nazi-Soviet Pact of 1939 found new reasons to feel ambivalent about Hitler when they heard reports of the barbaric treatment of Red Army prisoners, forced labor in Germany by thousands of Russian civilians, savage occupation policies, and Nazi proclamations about "colonizing the East" with Germans. However much they hated Stalin, they could not help but feel for their motherland in its terrible ordeal. Even hardened *soratniki* began asking themselves whether it was possible to defend Russia without helping Stalin, whether it was possible to oppose Stalin without destroying Russia.

To Rodzaevsky, the choice was simple. Again and again he repeated the slogan: "Even with the devil, always against Bolsheviks!" However callous and destructive, Hitler was Russia's only hope. Russian fascists had no choice but to go along with any foreign power that was destroying communism.

Rodzaevsky's arguments convinced few *soratniki*. Matkovsky and his faction, who had been opposed to RFS cooperation with Germany since 1939, remained silent and bided their time, cultivating good relations with Japanese military authorities and carrying out their duties in BREM (Bureau of Russian Émigré Affairs). Some *soratniki* left the party after June 22, 1941. Among these was the composer and onetime head of the RFS Political Division, Nikolai Petlin, who felt he could simply not tolerate collaboration with Hitler when the Führer was trying to annihilate Russia. Petlin argued about this issue with Rodzaevsky until July, then resigned. With him, he took the *vozhd*'s first wife, an attractive brunette named Lydia Malkova.*

Despite his outspoken enthusiasm for close collaboration with the Nazis, Rodzaevsky failed to arouse discernible German interest in the RFS. Early in 1942, when German consular officials began wooing Manchukuo's White Russians, they channeled subsidies through Ataman Grigory Semenov in Dairen. The RFS was ignored, possibly because Berlin was under the impression that Rodzaevsky was, in any case, Semenov's flunky.

Nor did Rodzaevsky's representative in Europe, Boris Tedli, have much success in enlisting German patronage. Deported to Switzerland after the Nazi-Soviet Pact, Tedli vegetated in Zurich until Germany attacked the Soviet Union. The summer of 1941 saw him in Bern pestering German Ambassador von Nostitz for permission to reenter the Reich. Abject professions of loyalty to Hitler and glowing reports of his son's SS exploits failed to make an impression, until, finally, Tedli received a visa after being vouched for by Erwin von Schultz, a Nazi official who had become acquainted with Rodzaevsky in Harbin in 1936. Tedli made straight for Berlin in September but failed to catch the ear of Alfred Rosenberg, then head of the Reich Ministry for Eastern Occupied Territories, or his adviser on Russian émigrés, Dr. Otto Bräutigam. When Bräutigam arranged a conference of pro-Nazi émigrés in Berlin in June 1942 to rally White Russian support behind the war effort, neither Tedli nor any other RFS representative was invited. Boris Petrovich consoled himself by indulging in anti-Semitic reveries at the Institute for Research on the Jewish Question at Frankfurt am Main.

Rodzaevsky just could not grasp the brutal fact that Russian fascists, no matter how philo-Nazi, had no place in German plans for

---

* Lydia Georgievna Malkova was the daughter of a Social Revolutionary who committed suicide shortly after the Bolsheviks came to power. She married Rodzaevsky in 1929 and divorced him in 1936. They had two children, both of whom died in infancy. Petlin subsequently married Lydia.

Russia. None of the major Nazi leaders envisioned a "Russian" entity following a German victory in Operation Barbarossa. "The Russians can never have their national state," wrote Heinrich Himmler to SS General Walter Schellenberg in 1942. Rosenberg's blueprint for post-Soviet Russia, drawn up in May 1941, called for the partition of the USSR into "independent states" (Ukraine) and "protectorates" (Baltic republics, eastern Poland, the Caucasus), ruled or manipulated by Germans. Hitler was unwilling to announce any specific plans for postwar Russia, but he hinted at the general direction of his thinking at a July 16, 1941, conference with Rosenberg, Goering, Keitel, and Bormann at his Rastenburg headquarters in East Prussia. Germany would control Russian territory to the Urals* in three *Reichskommissariats* (Moscow, Ukraine, Caucasus) each under a *Gauleiter*. The Kola peninsula (rich in nickel deposits), Crimea, and areas hitherto populated by *Volksdeutschen,* such as the Volga Germans, would be incorporated into the Reich. The Baku oil fields would become German "concessions." Leningrad would be razed and handed over to the Finns. The Führer made no mention of using Russian collaborators, although on another occasion, according to Albert Speer, he joked about entrusting Russia's postwar administration to Stalin, because that Georgian surely knew how to handle Russians.

In addition to misreading Germany's political plans for Russia, Rodzaevsky apparently could not comprehend the implications of Nazi racial doctrine, which defined all Slavs as *Untermenschen.* In 1942, the Reich prohibited translations into Russian of writings on national socialism. The idea of Russian émigrés aping Nazi dogma and regalia must have repelled Hitler and his henchmen. Small wonder that the RFS was ignored in Berlin.

However, the immediate obstacle to Rodzaevsky's dream of using the German-Soviet war to advance RFS fortunes was neither party disunity nor German indifference but, rather, Japanese priorities. Since 1932, Manchukuo's Russian fascists had been depending upon Japanese patronage for whatever power they wielded over fellow émigrés and for whatever hopes they entertained about coming to power in their homeland. Japanese "guidance" constituted the ultimate authority for political and military action. No matter how much

---

* The range of German territorial claims in the USSR seems to have expanded subsequently. In May 1942, Wehrmacht strategists were demarcating the eastward limits of projected German control along the Yenisei River, over one thousand miles east of the Urals.

Rodzaevsky thirsted to hit the USSR while it was reeling from a German attack, nothing could be done without Japan's approval. And
Japanese priorities in the summer of 1941 pointed south—not north.

Japan's southern orientation had gained impetus during the spring
of 1940, when German victories in western Europe suddenly exposed
the vulnerability of resource-rich French, British, and Dutch colonies
in Southeast Asia. Eager to terminate the "China Incident" (which
had dragged on since 1937) and to build a "New Order in East Asia,"
Japan capitalized on the European war by joining Germany and Italy
in the Tripartite Pact (September 27, 1940) and concluding a Neutrality Pact with the Soviet Union (April 13, 1941). These diplomatic
maneuvers were calculated to discourage American intervention and
to protect Japan's northern flank, leaving Tokyo a free hand in Southeast Asia.

The Soviet-Japanese Neutrality Pact of 1941 had much the same
effect on Russian émigrés in Manchukuo as the Nazi-Soviet Pact of
1939 had had on Russian émigrés in the Third Reich. Overnight,
anti-Soviet views became taboo. Supervision of the RFS and censorship of *Nash Put* were carried out with unprecedented strictness. Rodzaevsky, of course, had no choice but to bend with every shift in
the winds.

Hitler's attack on the Soviet Union caught Japan off guard. A series
of high-level conferences of cabinet ministers and army and navy
commanders met in Tokyo during late June and early July to determine Japan's response. At a June 27 conference, Foreign Minister
Matsuoka Yōsuke urged that Japan immediately strike the USSR in
order to solve the "northern problem" once and for all. A former
president of the South Manchurian Railway, Matsuoka was a "conti-
nentalist" who had allegedly declared in 1936 that he hoped to hoist
Japanese flags over the Urals. But Matsuoka was also impulsive, mercurial, and erratic. He had engineered the Soviet-Japanese Neutrality
Pact and only just come back from signing it in Moscow, where Stalin
had hugged him at the railroad station. Consequently, his exhortation
to march on Siberia fell upon skeptical ears. Not that his listeners
were opposed to his proposal in principal. They felt the timing to
be premature.

The Japanese leadership came to a decision about its options at
an imperial conference on July 2. Expansion into Indochina would
proceed. Intervention in the German-Soviet war would be deferred

until Wehrmacht advances created a favorable opportunity. Matsuoka not only failed to persuade his colleagues, he was dropped as foreign minister when Prime Minister Konoye formed a new cabinet on July 18.

Japan's decision to move south in the summer of 1941 provoked a confrontation with the United States that led to war before the year's end. Pearl Harbor extinguished any possibility for an attack on the USSR, for Japan found itself in a total war with the greatest industrial power in the world. Even as Japanese planes made their way toward Hawaii on December 7, outside Moscow the Red Army was dealing the Wehrmacht its first serious reverse.

The Pacific war was immediately felt by Manchukuo's White Russians. Émigrés who had been eagerly anticipating a Japanese strike against the Soviet Union woke up on December 8 to find themselves engaged in a crusade against Britain and the United States. There was no choice but to follow the "kingly way." Aging BREM figureheads Vladimir Kislitsyn and Lev Vlasevsky—a Semenov henchman—made obligatory speeches in Harbin under the watchful eyes of Japanese advisers, pledging total support for Japan's "holy war" against "Anglo-Saxons" and promising White Russian cooperation for building a New Order in East Asia. Rodzaevsky repeated the same slogans in *Nash Put* and *Natsiya*. Inwardly, he must have felt discouraged. A chance of a lifetime had come that summer, only to fade away. Now Japan was marching off in another direction against a formidable adversary that no Russian émigré had any desire to fight.

The "Otsu" Plan

Tokyo's diplomatic accommodation with Moscow in April 1941 did not keep the Kwantung Army from preparing for hostilities with the USSR. Anti-Soviet feeling ran deep among Kwantung Army officers; no one had forgotten the humiliation suffered in the pocket war at Nomonhan in 1939. Even after the outbreak of the Pacific war, Japan's soldiers in Manchukuo continued to regard the USSR as the principal enemy. Whatever happened in the South Pacific, the Kwantung Army kept its eyes on the Amur, the Ussuri, and the Outer Mongolian steppe.

The Kwantung Army possessed a contingency plan, code-named

"Otsu,"* for offensive operations against the Soviet Union. Formulated by the Imperial General Staff in 1934, the Otsu plan envisioned a surgical strike detaching Eastern Siberia and the Soviet Far East from the USSR. While some units were defending the western approaches to Manchukuo from Outer Mongolia, the main forces would drive into Soviet territory in two thrusts. One thrust, launched from the lower Sungari River and Pogranichnaya, would capture Khabarovsk and isolate the Maritime Province, including Vladivostok, principal base for the Soviet Pacific Fleet. Another thrust, moving northwest from Manchouli toward Chita, would take Irkutsk, thereby cutting off Siberia east of Lake Baikal from the rest of the USSR. The Otsu plan exploited the Red Army's logistic vulnerability in the Far East by aiming at key points on the Trans-Siberian Railroad. Soviet forces were strung out along the railway and heavily dependent upon it for supplies and reinforcements. With the railroad cut at Irkutsk and Khabarovsk, Kwantung Army strategists calculated that isolated Red Army units could be destroyed before help could arrive from European Russia.

Activation of the Otsu plan was predicated upon the Kwantung Army's enjoying a two-to-one superiority in infantry, armor, artillery, and air power over Far Eastern units of the Red Army. This superiority did not materialize at any time between 1934 and 1945, although that fact was a tightly kept secret.

As originally conceived, the Otsu plan made no provisions for utilizing White Russians, except insofar as individual field commanders chose to enlist them as scouts or interpreters. However, the Asano Brigade, an all-Russian unit in the Manchukuoan Army which had taken shape in 1938, offered a potential nucleus for White Russian combat units.

Early in 1940, military planners began giving thought to how the White Russians might contribute to the Otsu plan. On February 16, operations officers from Kwantung Army headquarters in Hsinking joined *Tokumu Kikan* chief Major General Hata Hikosaburō in Harbin to discuss the employment of White Russians as shock troops in operations against the USSR. Although the initiative for these discussions came from the Kwantung Army, there was support for the idea from

*The Chinese ideograph "otsu" can mean variously "second," "latter," "queer," "fanciful."

two retired generals in Tokyo who had recently held cabinet posts: Araki Sadao and Koiso Kuniaki. At Harbin, it was decided that White Russians should not only be trained as combat troops but be groomed as functionaries for a puppet administration on occupied Soviet territory (provisionally dubbed the "Far Eastern Anti-Comintern Self-Government"). All émigré groups friendly to Japan would be eligible for participation in the administration, but preference would be given the RFS and Ataman Semenov.

Hata's successor as head of the Harbin *Tokumu Kikan,* Major General Yanagita Genzō, began to implement the military aspects of the 1940 discussions in mid-1941 in preparation for massive Kwantung Army maneuvers (code-named *Kantokuen**) along the Manchukuo-Soviet frontier. Carried out in August 1941, *Kantokuen* was not simply a military exercise. It was a show of force designed to intimidate the USSR while the Red Army was fighting to survive in the West. In conjunction with *Kantokuen,* some two thousand White Russians were recruited and trained in infiltration and sabotage, and Rodzaevsky was called up and ordered to supervise a half-dozen émigré writers who were drafting anti-Soviet leaflets for distribution within the USSR.

Kantokuen, however, did not develop into actual hostilities against the USSR, and by September, Rodzaevsky's summer euphoria was flagging. To sustain their protégé's morale, Japanese advisers titillated Konstantin Vladimirovich with rosy visions. In October, a Colonel Niimura confided to Rodzaevsky that all was ready for Japan to invade Siberia "after the German troops take Moscow." Somewhat later, Major General Doi Akio, Yanagita's successor, promised Rodzaevsky that BREM, in which the RFS played a prominent role, was going to be the new Russian government.

Japanese promises may have propped up Rodzaevsky's flagging morale during 1942, but they did little to sustain his standard of living under the crunch of total war. The Pacific war soon reduced life for most White Russians in Harbin to subsistence levels, as the Japanese requisitioned all supplies of meat, grain, and fuel and blocked Red Cross shipments of food and medicine. During the winter of 1942–43, it was not uncommon for White Russians to burn their furniture to keep warm and to barter their few possessions for food.

Harbin's wartime ambience was vividly captured by an anthropologist named Fukuda Shinsei who visited the city late in 1942. In a

* An acronym for "Kwantung Army Special Maneuvers."

book that, remarkably, passed the Japanese censorship, he described how pre-pubescent girls suggestively lifted up their skirts to strangers from shadowy recesses along the Kitaiskaya. Seeking relief from this depressing scene, Fukuda ventured into the Fantasia, one of two cabarets that remained open in what had once been the "Paris of Asia." As his eyes adjusted to the darkened interior, Fukuda beheld a fat Russian woman clad in a cotton print dress, lurching through a tango with a Japanese partner on a near-empty dance floor. Her jerky dips and sweaty amplitude at first struck Fukuda as grotesque. But then he noticed her eyes, caverns of hopelessness beneath a glaze of make-up. The pathos of this spectacle struck him so forcefully that he immediately got up and left.

Amid such trying conditions, Rodzaevsky had to support, on meager subsidies, an aging father, a pregnant wife,* and a daughter. The *vozhd* of the Russian Fascist Union lived in a small flat in Pristan, facing the Sungari, and he wore the same threadbare overcoat that had covered him as a student in the Juridical Institute fourteen years previously. But economics became the least of Rodzaevsky's worries late in 1942 when, improbably, he fell under suspicion of being a Soviet agent.

Crackdown

No White Russian who worked for Japanese Army Intelligence or the *Kempei* (military gendarmerie) forgot for a moment his or her occupational hazards. Once a collaborator, one was always a hostage. Anyone who had glimpsed the seamier sides of "the kingly way" was watched with special vigilance and not allowed to leave Manchukuo except under escort. The slightest suspicion of disloyalty meant imprisonment—or worse.

By 1942, most RFS *soratniki* realized that their intimate ties with the *Tokumu Kikan* and the *Kempei* were a mixed blessing. To be sure, Japanese patronage gave them status and power vis-à-vis other émigrés, but it also took a toll. Conspicuous in their black uniforms, the transparently nationalistic *soratniki* were tempting targets for *Kempei* thugs, particularly when the latter had been drinking and were

---

* Rodzaevsky married for the second time in 1937. His bride, Neonilla Yalisheva, bore him a daughter, Olga, in 1938 and, in 1941, a son who died in infancy. Another son, Vladimir Konstantinovich, was born in 1943.

looking for a little excitement. If a *soratnik* fought back when mugged on the street by Japanese, he was in deep trouble. Blackshirt leader and hit man Sasha Bolotov apparently met his end that way, winding up a corpse on the notorious second floor of Harbin's *Kempei* headquarters shortly before the Pacific war.

Except for an occasional anti-Semitic excess, Rodzaevsky was such a faithful and accommodating collaborator that he would have seemed to be the last person to arouse Japanese doubts. But the seeds of suspicion can sprout on fabrication as well as substance.

Japanese doubts about Rodzaevsky apparently originated in Germany. In late 1942, the Japanese Foreign Ministry learned through diplomatic channels that Boris Tedli and other RFS members in the Reich had just been arrested by the Gestapo as Soviet spies. Unfortunately, German documents do not throw light on Tedli's innocence or guilt—or fate. But the news of his arrest had an immediate impact in Tokyo and Manchukuo.

Japanese authorities were already hypersensitive to Soviet agents posing as fascists or Nazis. Just over a year earlier, a German journalist named Richard Sorge had been exposed as an agent of Red Army intelligence. Camouflaging himself with impeccable Nazi credentials and urbane continental manners, Sorge had for several years been successfully cultivating a wide variety of Japanese contacts. As the full scope of Sorge's activities gradually unfolded under investigation, the Home Ministry conceived an exaggerated respect for Soviet espionage.

Rodzaevsky's exemplary pro-Japanese record did not put him above suspicion. Informed about Tedli's arrest, a Japanese diplomat in Manchukuo wrote the foreign minister in early 1943 that it was not only plausible but quite natural that a Kremlin spy should pose as a fascist. Could there be a better cover? Conceivably the entire Russian Fascist Union was nothing but a Soviet front cunningly designed to divide the White Russian community on one hand and to alienate it from Japan on the other.

Apprised of possible traitors among its protégés, the *Kempei* conducted investigations of the RFS, apparently between February and May 1943. Certain incriminating evidence, all of it circumstantial, about Rodzaevsky and the RFS came to light during these inquests. Two of the three cofounders of the Russian Fascist Organization (RFO) in 1925 (Alexander Pokrovsky and Boris Rumiantsev) were

said to have returned voluntarily to the Soviet Union.* Inquiries about
Rodzaevsky's early years in Manchuria raised a number of questions.
First, the circumstances behind his escape from Blagoveshchensk in
1925 could not be verified. Also, émigré informants alleged that in
1927 and again in 1931, Rodzaevsky had been temporarily expelled
from the RFO, on both occasions in connection with the disappearance
of personnel files. Some of these informants, according to Japanese
documents, stated that these files had been sent to the Soviet Union
and that Rodzaevsky still maintained secret links with the Soviet consulate in Harbin.

In May 1943, Rodzaevsky was detained by the *Kempei* and subjected
to intensive interrogation. Also questioned were Matkovsky, Kibardin,
Nikolai Kipkaev (former RFS representative in Tokyo), and Gennady
Taradanov (RFS branch leader in Shanghai). Rodzaevsky seems to
have exonerated himself, for he was released in June and instructed
to resume his duties as chief of BREM's Second Department. Matkovsky and the others were also set at liberty.

While Rodzaevsky was undergoing questioning in Harbin, another
Kwantung Army protégé, Ataman Semenov, committed a gaffe that
sent shudders through Hsinking and Tokyo alike. Early in May, without consulting the Japanese, Semenov sent an open letter to General
Andrei Vlasov, a Red Army officer in German captivity who had raised
an anti-Soviet force from among fellow Russian POWs, praising him
for striking a blow against Stalin. Somehow, Semenov's letter passed
Japanese censors and was published in the Harbin newspaper,
Kharbinskoye Vremya, on May 7, and shortly thereafter it was broadcast
over a Rumanian radio station. Informed about the incident, Foreign
Minister Shigemitsu Mamoru issued an urgent notice to all Japanese
diplomatic officials in Manchukuo and China, including the commander of the Kwantung Army, warning about the dangers of untimely
White Russian pronouncements.

Japanese doubts about Rodzaevsky and Semenov grew quickly as
World War II reached a turning point in 1943. Japan's early advances
in the Pacific had been followed by reverses on Guadalcanal and in
the Aleutians. In Europe, the initiative had shifted from Germany
to Russia. The Red Army was maintaining the initiative won at Stalingrad and reaped a crushing summer victory at Kursk. As Japanese

* Pokrovsky actually spent his last years in Shanghai after breaking with Rodzaevsky
in 1932. Rumiantsev returned to the Soviet Union only in 1947.

setbacks and Soviet triumphs multiplied, even the Kwantung Army grew solicitous about honoring the 1941 Neutrality Pact. Anxious to avoid friction with Moscow, the Kwantung Army took drastic measures in the summer of 1943 to curtail anti-Soviet organizations. The Russian Fascist Union was the first victim of this new policy.

The end of the RFS came with dramatic suddenness and without any official explanation. On July 1, the Harbin Military Mission ordered its abolition throughout Manchukuo, Japan, and China. *Nash Put* and *Natsiya* were closed down the same day. Meetings among former RFS *soratniki,* wearing of the RFS uniform, singing RFS songs, and displaying the RFS emblem were strictly forbidden. Rodzaevsky, stripped of his party, had no choice but to keep quiet and continue working in BREM.

By the summer of 1943, therefore, the Russian fascist movement had ceased to exist. In the United States, it had sputtered out after Pearl Harbor. In Europe, its few members had been arrested by the Gestapo. In the Far East, it was terminated by its own patrons.

Red Star Ascendant

The years 1943 and 1944 witnessed a surge of popularity of the Soviet Union among White Russians in Manchukuo and China. A Japanese diplomat in Shanghai glumly reported in 1944 that 90 percent of White Russians in East Asia were pro-Soviet. In addition to Red Army victories, changes within the USSR since 1941, some real, some only apparent, evoked a favorable response from émigrés. Stalin's wartime tolerance of the Orthodox Church struck a responsive chord among the religious. The restoration of rank insignias to Red Army officers appealed to exiled tsarist commanders. The creation of foreign and defense ministries for each constituent Soviet republic inspired visions of decentralization and democracy. The Comintern's dissolution in May 1943 suggested an abandonment of world revolution and proletarian internationalism.

Pro-Soviet feelings among the émigrés found a number of public expressions. Soviet consulates in Harbin, Hsinking, Dairen, Tientsin, Peiping, and Shanghai were deluged with applicants for Soviet citizenship. Émigré youths petitioned to be allowed to enlist in the Red Army. Bearers of Soviet passports, including former "radishes," talked of repatriation. Merchants solicited the patronage of Soviet diplomats.

Bankers suddenly discovered the virtues of socialism. Thousands who had cheered Japan in 1932 and Hitler in 1941 applauded Stalin in 1944. This time, the enthusiasm had a more genuine ring, for it was based on patriotism as well as on a desire to survive.

At first, Soviet officials in Manchukuo, suspecting opportunism, responded warily to the USSR's newfound popularity, and, at least until late 1944, they were probably under instructions from Moscow not to give Japan undue cause for offense. Only in 1945, with Germany and Japan facing certain defeat, did the Soviets begin to launch direct appeals for émigré support in Manchuria. In February, Radio *Otchizna* ("Fatherland") started broadcasting to Manchukuo's White Russians from somewhere in Siberia. In March, copies of an underground pro-Soviet newspaper, *Kharbinskaya Pravda,* appeared in Harbin. On April 20, Kwantung Army commander General Yamada Otozō sent a top secret cable to Foreign Minister Tōgō Shigenori, admitting that Soviet propaganda had made deep inroads into the White Russian population, causing widespread disaffection and even desertions.

As a Japanese-sponsored instrument to administer Manchukuo's White Russians, BREM came under considerable strain at this time. General Kislitsyn, BREM's figurehead chief since 1938, died of illness in 1944 and was succeeded by an only slightly less senile General Lev Vlasevsky. Heading BREM's cultural affairs and administration departments, Rodzaevsky and Matkovsky bore the responsibility for implementing Japanese policy over an increasingly restive constituency. Their task was made somewhat easier by the reappearance of an old friend: Akikusa Shun. During 1932–35, Major Akikusa, a Russian specialist in the *Tokumu Kikan,* had served as adviser to the Russian Fascist Party and its successor, the All-Russian Fascist Party. Promoted to major general after tours of duty in the Army Ministry, General Staff, and with a Ussuri River frontier garrison, Akikusa returned to Harbin in February 1945 as chief of Kwantung Army Intelligence. Akikusa not only enjoyed good rapport with Rodzaevsky and Matkovsky, he was widely respected and trusted as a man of honor in Harbin's Russian community.

The cataclysmic end of the Third Reich in late April and early May 1945 threw Manchukuo's White Russians into a maelstrom of conflicting emotions. On one hand, there was reason to rejoice. Adolf Hitler was dead and his juggernaut destroyed. Russian soldiers bestrode Berlin as their forefathers had Paris one hundred and thirty years before. As peace returned to a battered Europe, it seemed a time for mending wounds, for reconstruction, and for forgiveness. On the other hand, anxiety gnawed at this vision. A war still raged in the Pacific, China, and Southeast Asia. Would the Soviet Union, emboldened by its spectacular victory over Germany, enter the Far Eastern war and attempt to settle some old scores with Japan? If so, what would become of the Russian émigrés living in Manchukuo, the most likely arena for a Soviet-Japanese showdown? Rumors crackled through White Russian communities like wildfire, spreading fear along the dry grass of uncertainty: The Japanese would force everyone to fight the Red Army or be shot. NKVD squads were waiting to ship all Whites to Kolyma camps, after executing community leaders. Something like this had occurred in 1942 when the Red Army invaded northern Iran; Russian émigrés caught there were rounded up en masse and sent—so it was said—to camps in Central Asia.

As spring gave way to summer in 1945, omens of an approaching deluge multiplied. Formations of B-29s began bombing Dairen and Anshan with impunity. Radio *Otchizna* announced that Japan was going to mobilize all White Russian males for combat duty. Hundreds of émigrés panicked and tried to get out of Manchukuo. But their efforts got them nowhere. Under Japanese orders, BREM withheld travel documents. With the day of reckoning drawing near, Manchukuo was becoming one enormous trap.

Unknown to either Japanese or White Russians, Manchukuo's fate had already been decided at Yalta on February 8, 1945. In a secret agreement signed by Stalin, Roosevelt, and Churchill, the United States and Great Britain sanctioned Soviet territorial and other gains in the Far East and undertook to secure Chiang Kai-shek's acquiescence to these gains. In return, Stalin vowed to strike Japan three months after Germany's capitulation. The diplomatic stage was now set for a military drama, although some of the actors were still unaware of their intended roles.

Starting in February 1945, a mammoth logistical operation unfolded throughout the entire length of the USSR, as a portion of the Red Army shifted from European battlefronts to the Far East. During the next six months, train after train crawled across Siberia, hauling thirty-nine divisions over five thousand miles to bolster the nineteen divisions that had been guarding the Soviet-Manchukuo border since 1941. Tanks, planes, fuel, ammunition, and food were all transported by rail across Siberia's endless expanses and deployed in a vast arc from Outer Mongolia along the Argun, Amur, and Ussuri rivers to Vladivostok. By August, an awesome host of over 1,500,000 officers and men, 26,000 guns and mortars, 5,500 tanks, and 3,800 combat aircraft were ringing three sides of Manchukuo in a vise. Marshal of the Soviet Union A. M. Vasilevsky, a tough former chief of the General Staff, assumed command of what was to be the final great campaign of World War II: the destruction of the Kwantung Army and the occupation of Manchukuo, Korea north of the thirty-eighth parallel, southern Sakhalin, and the Kurile Islands.

The Soviet vise consisted of three army groups, each entrusted with specific objectives in what was expected to be a *blitzkrieg* operation. The strongest group, assembled along the Outer Mongolia–Manchukuo frontier, was the Trans-Baikal Front under Marshal Rodion Malinovsky. Largely mechanized, Malinovsky's force was to sweep across the Mongol desert into western Manchukuo, breach the Hsingan Range, and descend on Hsinking and Mukden. Malinovsky also planned to cut rail lines leading to Peiping, Tientsin, and Dairen, thereby sealing off escape routes. The vise's opposite jaw was the First Far Eastern Front under Marshal K. A. Meretskov. Arrayed along the Ussuri River and the southwestern edges of the Maritime Province, Meretskov was to stab into eastern Manchuria, seize Kirin, and cut rail communications to Korea. The Second Far Eastern Front, under General M. A. Purkayev, was poised along the Amur River for two strikes: one from Blagoveshchensk into northern Manchukuo and another up the Sungari River toward Harbin. Amphibious operations were planned against Korean ports and, pending success in Manchurian operations, against southern Sakhalin and the Kurile Islands.

Within the Soviet vise lay Japan's vaunted Kwantung Army, consisting in early August 1945 of 787,600 men, 1,215 tanks, 1,800 aircraft, and 6,700 heavy guns and mortars. In addition, there were about 200,000 Manchukuoan and Inner Mongolian puppet troops of doubtful reliability. Like pips in a watermelon, about four thousand White Russians and Cossacks of the Asano Brigade huddled outside Harbin and Hailar. At their head was the Japanese-appointed Armenian colonel, Gurgen Nagolen.

Japan's military position in Manchukuo that August was even weaker than the figures indicate. Maritime communications with the home islands had been reduced to a trickle by American submarines.

Gasoline was in such short supply that some planes were burning fuel made from pine cones. The Kwantung Army was but a shell of its former self. Once a crack corps with some of the Imperial Army's toughest officers and men, the Kwantung Army had been sapped of trained troops and first-rate equipment by transfers to crumbling battlefronts in the Marianas and Philippines. The most seasoned unit had been formed only in the spring of 1944. One quarter of the Kwantung Army's rank and file had been mobilized in July 1945. Its tanks were, by Soviet standards, light and antiquated. Its artillery was small, obsolete, and thinly distributed; one division had no artillery whatever. Nearly all of the emperor's best pilots and planes were at the bottom of the Pacific, in the jungles of the Solomons, or among the volcanic cinders of Iwo Jima.

Although woefully manned and equipped, the Kwantung Army had no lack of advance warning of a Soviet attack. In February, Kwantung Army Intelligence had picked up signs of Soviet troop transfers from Europe to the Far East. By March, it had learned about Stalin's promise at Yalta to attack Japan three months after Germany's capitulation. On April 5, Foreign Commissar Viacheslav Molotov publicly denounced the Soviet-Japanese Neutrality Pact, due to expire on April 13, 1946. By May, there was no doubt about the Red Army's buildup around Manchukuo. Equally ominous was the number of departures of Soviet diplomats and their families from Japan and Manchukuo.

Despite such omens, Kwantung Army Intelligence persistently underestimated the Soviet timetable for offensive operations. In April, Kwantung Army strategists placed Soviet entry into the war at April 1946, assuming that Moscow would give Japan a one-year grace period after denouncing the Neutrality Pact. In May, Imperial Headquarters in Tokyo warned Hsinking that a Soviet invasion could come as early as August or September, but Kwantung Army Intelligence disagreed, arguing that given the Trans-Siberian Railway's logistical limitations, a major campaign could not be launched in 1945. However, after the Potsdam Conference had produced a declaration on July 26 calling for Japan's unconditional surrender, the Kwantung Army revised its estimates, moving D day up to late August. Indeed, late August was the date given by Stalin to Truman at Potsdam. But when, on August 6, the United States dropped an atomic bomb on Hiroshima, Stalin advanced his schedule, anxious lest the war end before the USSR could, in the words of Marshal Malinovsky, "honor its commitments to the Allies under the Yalta Agreements."

At 5:00 P.M. on August 8, Ambassador Satō Naotake was handed a note from Molotov in the latter's Kremlin office, announcing that a state of war would exist between Japan and the USSR starting August 9. At that moment, it was exactly midnight in Khabarovsk, where Marshal Vasilevsky had just ordered his vise to start closing. Ten minutes later, the first units from the Trans-Baikal Front slipped silently into Manchukuo. Within an hour, elements from the First and Second Far Eastern Fronts had crossed the frontier, some of them preceded by an artillery barrage, others moving quietly under the cover of a thunderstorm.

The Japanese were taken completely by surprise. Just as a blitzkrieg had opened World War II in September 1939, so a blitzkrieg finished it, six years later and six thousand miles away.

In Manchukuo immediately preceding the Soviet invasion, some White Russians had an instinctive feeling that the Red Army would attack. But few knew what it would bring: enslavement or liberation, punishment or amnesty, exile or repatriation. Some émigrés expected the worst—with good reason. Ataman Semenov, a ruthless anti-Bolshevik leader during the Russian Civil War and a major Japanese collaborator since 1918, knew what lay in store for him. So did ex-NKVD General G. S. Lyushkov, who had defected to Manchukuo in 1938 and, having told the Japanese everything he knew, was now alone and unprotected in Mukden with no illusions about what his former colleagues would do with him.

But what about Konstantin Rodzaevsky, the ex-*vozhd* of Russian fascists? He had taken no part in the Civil War. His party had dissolved, under Japanese orders, in 1943. Would the Soviets really want to punish him? What should have been obvious somehow eluded Konstantin Vladimirovich as he made a dizzying series of life-and-death decisions during the next few weeks.

CHAPTER XIX

Fatal Conversion

Stalinism is exactly what we mistakenly called "Russian Fascism." It is our Russian Fascism cleansed of extremes, illusions, and errors.

—KONSTANTIN RODZAEVSKY (1945)

Although just about every White Russian in Manchukuo had heard rumors since the beginning of 1945 about an impending Soviet intervention in the Pacific war, most were taken completely by surprise when they woke up on August 9 to learn that the USSR and Japan were at war and that the Red Army had already crossed the Amur, Ussuri, and Outer Mongolian frontiers. After hearing a Tass war announcement on Radio *Otchizna,* BREM chief General Lev Vlasevsky rushed to the Harbin Military Mission to ask Akikusa Shun for information and instructions. Akikusa was too preoccupied to see his protégé. Told to come back later, Vlasevsky trudged forlornly over to the BREM offices without the slightest idea of what to do. The old Cossack was so conditioned to following Japanese orders that independent action simply did not occur to him. He assembled the BREM department heads, including Rodzaevsky and Matkovsky, and told them that no decisions would be taken until he had consulted with Akikusa, hopefully the next day.

On that same day, the BREM offices were besieged by crowds of excited émigrés trying to find out what was happening and whether or not to flee Harbin. Rodzaevsky urged them not to act precipitously, for the military situation was still far from clear. Unsatisfied by such vague assurances, a number of people turned to Matkovsky and demanded to know whether the Red Army would reach Harbin and if so, did the Japanese plan to evacuate White Russians who wished

All-Russian Fascist Party branch headquarters in Manchouli, northwestern Manchuria. A brilliantly lit swastika tauntingly faces the Soviet frontier, just two miles away.

БОГ, НАЦІЯ, ТРУД.

К ОБЪЕДИНЕНІЮ! К ОЗДОРОВЛЕНІЮ! К ПРОБУЖДЕНІЮ! — РУССКІЙ РУССКОМУ ДРУГ И БРАТ!

НАШ ПУТЬ

Год изданія III. | Ежедневный орган Русской Національной мысли за рубежом. Главный Редактор К. В. Родзаевскій. | № 283 (711)

Registered at the Manchu-Di-Kuo Post office as a news paper.

Редакція, главн. Контора и Типографія — Харбин, Китайская 125 угол Японской тел. № 38-13 почт. ящик № 402 Контора открыта с 9 до 1 ч. и с 3-х до 7 ч. в. Редактор принимает по вторникам и пятницам с 4-х до 5 ч. Рукописи обратно не возвращаются.

УСЛОВІЯ ПОДПИСКИ: на один мѣсяц для всѣх пунктов Маньчжу-Ди-Го 1.80 гоби. В Ниппон (включая линію ЮМжд) 2.50 іен. В Китаѣ 2.50 сер. дол. В других странах 1.20 ам. дол.

Харбин — Четверг 7 Ноября 1935 г. — Цѣна 20 фен го-би.

7-XI 1917 — СЕГОДНЯ - 18-ая годовщина КРОВАВАГО „ОКТЯБРЯ“ — 7-XI 1935

18 лѣт тому назад с карты міра исчезла РОССІЯ

18 лѣт тому назад началось Еврейское Царство на РУССКОЙ ЗЕМЛѢ.

18 лѣт идет хищническая эксплоатація, угнетеніе и уничтоженіе РУССКАГО НАРОДА.

Долой Кагановичей!

На смѣну - Еврейскому октябрю --

Владимир Ильич Ульянов (ЛЕНИН) сын русскаго отца и еврейской—матери. Главная декорація кроваваго октября без ретушовки услужливаго панегириста.

18 лѣт тому назад русскій народ попал в страшную кабалу.

18 лѣт тому назад началось убіеніе РУССКОЙ НАЦІИ.

18 лѣт, обращенным в рабство русским народом правит Міровой Еврей.

Долой компартію!

-- да придет Фашистскій Май!

Красный Октябрь

Крушеніе Великой Россійской Имперія было спровоцировано масонами. И масонскій февраль принес к власти масонское Временное Правительство.

В самом дѣлѣ,—кто же эти дворянчики и интеллигенты, эти Львовы, Милюковы, Гучковы, Керенскіе, как не наиболѣе выдающіеся представители россійскаго масонства? И если мы вспомним—кто стоит за спиной масонства и тайно им руководит — и если мы вспомним—кто стоит за спиной соціализма и тайно руководит им—нам понятным станет то подлѣйшее непротивленіе, с которым взирало Временное Правительство на разрушительную работу большевиков.

В теченіи всего 17-аго года, с марта по октябрь, совершенно свободно шла по всей Россіи формированія совѣтов и красной гвардіи и совершенно открыто назначался день финальнаго выступленія — 25 октября стараго стиля — 7 ноября новаго стиля.

В свѣтѣ фактов исторія — „октябрьская революція“ выступает, как откровенная передача власти из одной еврейской инстанціи в другую —от одних агентов евреев — масонов к другим агентам евреев,—к болѣе откровенным агентам—большевикам.

Еврейскій „октябрь“ пришел на смѣну масонскому „февралю“ с вѣдома и попустительства послѣдняго; Керенскій эволюціонным порядком передал власть Ленину--и только героическое сопротивленіе вѣрных сынов Націи окрасило эволюцію в цвѣта крови и сдѣлало ее революціей, послѣ которой началось откровенное истребленіе русскаго народа.

18 лѣт, прошедших с тѣх страшных и подлых дней, убѣдили русскій народ и должны были бы убѣдить весь мір:

— Марксистскій соціализм есть вернѣйшій способ захвата власти еврейством.

— Под флагом „совѣтской власти“ и „диктатуры пролетаріата“, Россией правит международное еврейство.

— Міровой еврейскій капитал сдѣлал Россію своей хищнически - эксплоатируемой колоніей.

— В СССР идет систематическое убійство Россійской Націи и и планомѣрное уничтоженіе, закабаленнаго в страшное рабство, русскаго народа.

— Через коллективизацію и индустріализацію — еврейская власть пятилѣтками укрѣпляет свое владычество над Россіей и обезсиливает подвластный народ, создавая для себя крѣпкую базу для дальнѣйшаго наступленія на остальное человѣчество, в первую очередь—на пробуждающіеся народы Азіи.

— Завоевав Россію, ненасытная „избранная“ „интернація“ готовится к дальнѣйшим завоеваніям во имя „міровой соціальной революціи“—еврейскаго господства над всей землей.

Вот они достиженія кроваваго „октября“ к 18-ой годовщинѣ самой кровавой, самой жестокой, самой подлой, самой грабительской в мірѣ революціи!

Вот она — страшная правда современной россійской дѣйствительности, властно диктующая каждому русскому человѣку, каждому вѣрному сыну своей Націи, необходимость напрячь всѣ силы для обузданія міровых хищников—для побѣды над вѣковѣчным врагом Бога, Истины и Красоты, всѣх Націй и свободнаго творческаго труда!

К БОРЬБѢ!

К. РОДЗАЕВСКІЙ

Подлинный лик чудовища — Октября

СЕГОДНЯ — ДЕНЬ ОБЩЕРУССКАГО ТРАУРА по милліонам убитых, по милліонам замученных, по милліонам задыхающихся в красном плѣну

ВСѢ НА ПАНИХИДУ ПО ЖЕРТВАМ ІУДО-КРАСНЫХ ЛЮДОѢДОВ!

ВСѢ НА ОБЩЕРУССКІЯ СОБРАНІЯ — НЕПРИМИРИМОСТИ.

Фашистскій Май

Мрак и ужас царит над Россіей, но близится час освобожденія и возрожденія!

Уже нѣт в СССР ни одной соціальной группы, которая искренне поддерживала-бы диктатуру ВКП (б), остается полицейскій аппарат ГПУ— или как его теперь называют Наркомвнудѣл и Красная Армія, насквозь охваченная проклятым ПУР-ом-сѣтью политуправленій и политруков.

Власть сильна—своей системой всеобщаго шпіонажа и террора — борьба будет трудной, потребует многих жертв, но уже есть бойцы, есть идея, есть организація.

Всероссійская Фашистская Партія объявила фашистскую трехлѣтку. Это значит что к 1-го мая 1938 г. — не позже, а может быть гораздо раньше если будет внѣшній или внутренній толчок — диктатура ВКП перестанет существовать.

Но для этого необходимо напряженнѣйшее усиліе Россіи Подъяремной и Россіи Зарубежной.

Нужны четкія цѣли, способные поднять на борьбу — актив — Цвѣт Націи.

Такія цѣли ставит программа ВФП, утвержденная III-м Съѣздом Россійских Фашистов в текущем году.

Она рисует не утопическія картинки, не политиканствующую демагогію, а реальныя, достижимыя задачи, — которыя принесут родному народу счастливую, красивую сытую, привольную жизнь.

Программа В.Ф.П. несет русскому народу фактическое самоуправленіе, русским трудящимся — дѣйствительную защиту их профессіональных интересов, а русским крестьянам — землю.

Программа В.Ф.П. путем подчиненія промышленности и сельскаго хозяйства интересам и потребностям всего населенія обезпечивает полный достаток всѣх необходимых продуктов широкаго потребленія и продуктов сельско-хозяйственной дѣятельности страны.

— Не трудящійся для промышленности, а промышленность для трудящихся!

Не народ для власти, а власть для народа!

Вот что значит наш лозунг — кромѣ Программы — Россія для Россіян.

Россія для Россіян — это Національно -- Трудовая Россія, общій отчій дом, в котором нѣт сыновей и пасынков, а есть Русская Власть—Первый слуга и страж Націи и сыны Націи опора власти— весь народ.

Всероссійская Фашистская Партія взяла на себя смѣлую задачу дать закабаленному цѣпями коммунистическаго рабства русскому народу план и цѣли его борьбы во имя освобожденія и возрожденія -- и эту задачу выполнила.

Теперь заканчивается період подготовки и с планом національной революціи и с планом національнаго фашистскаго устроенія Россіи в руках — мы, Россійскіе фашисты, — может смѣло двинуться в бой с красной гадрой — с еврейским коммунистическим спрутом.

Фашистскій май в огнѣ и бури Національной Революціи грядет на смѣну еще не исчезнувшему из практической дѣйствительности Россіи сегодняшняго дня еврейск. октябрю.

Фашистскій май несет русским трудящимся пробужденіе освобожденіе и возрожденіе!

Фашистскій май даст нам новую Великую Россію — Россію свободную и счастливую, Россію крѣпкую и могучую!

Отдадим же всѣ силы, всѣ средства и даже жизни наши на борьбу за счастье и свободу русскаго народа!

С. РАЖЕВ.

Цѣна настоящаго №-ра 20 фен или 10 ам. цент.
Весь сбор в Фонд Противокоммунистической Борьбы.

November 7, 1935, issue of *Nash Put*, marking the eighteenth anniversary of the October Revolution ("Jewish October") and hailing the advent of "Fascist May," which *vozhd* Konstantin Rodzaevsky predicted would occur by May 1, 1938. Lenin, in the center, is described as having a Jewish mother. The anti-Semitic cartoon directly below was lifted from Julius Streicher's *Der Stürmer*.

НАЦІЯ

Natsiya cover depicting a Russian fascist soldier advancing in the anti-Soviet struggle. Compare with the 1915 French war-bond poster, shown right.

НАЦІЯ

Cover of the All-Russian Fascist Party's theoretical organ, *Natsiya*, a monthly journal published in Shanghai between 1932 and 1943. Under a swastika sun, a Russian worker smashes the serpent of "Judo-communism."

General Araki Sadao, hero of many young Japanese army officers as a proponent of national spirit. A man of considerable experience in Russian affairs, Araki was a respected patron of Russian fascists in the Far East.

Nash Put issue of September 13, 1936, hailing Mussolini, Hitler, General Araki Sadao, and Cossack hetman Grigory Semenov as *vozhds* of "new mankind." The article calls for a "White International" and predicts the alliance of Japan, Germany, and Fascist Russia. Semenov, a bitter rival of Russian fascists, was no doubt included on the advice of Japanese authorities.

Konstantin Rodzaevsky, bearded, at center, poses with his followers at Russian Fascist Union headquarters in 1940. The Japanese to his right is Konstantin Ivanovich ("Kostya") Nakamura, an interpreter for the Military Police (*Kempei*). To Rodzaevsky's left, wearing black shirts, stand Special Detachment chief Alexander ("Sasha") Bolotov and the *vozhd*'s personal secretary, Lev Okhotin. The men in khaki are members of the party's military unit, under the command of Sergei Dolov, the short man on Nakamura's right.

Admiral Ushakov, flagship of the Russian Fascist Navy. Constructed at the Wool-
worth shipyards, circa 1937. Displacement: approximately 160,000 milligrams.
Home port: windowsill at Nineteenth Hole, Thompson, Connecticut. (*New York
World-Telegram*)

A Christmas party of Vonsiatsky's supporters in Shanghai in 1939. The long banner declares: "Long Live VNRP *Vozhd* A. A. Vonsiatsky!" Note swastikas on the
ceiling lamp shade and on the Santa Claus figure. (*Fashist*)

Weather Forecast
Warmer Tonight.
United States Official Report

The Hartford Times.

Average Daily Circulation
Week Ending
June 6, 1942   82,053

VOL. CII. NO. 138.   34 PAGES   HARTFORD, CONN., WEDNESDAY, JUNE 10, 1942.   ★   FOUR CENTS

Big Spy Case Breaks Here When U.S. Indicts Vonsiatsky, 4 Others on Axis Conspiracy Plot

Hartford *Times* headlines on June 10, 1942, the day after Vonsiatsky was indicted for espionage by a federal grand jury in Hartford, Connecticut.

Grand Jury Reveals Probe Of Group's Activities; Kunze Named As 'Emissary'

One of the biggest spy cases in America broke here today in indictments linking four German-American Bundists, including its national leader and the midwest leader, with a self-styled "fuehrer" of Russian Fascists, in a plot to transmit military information to the Axis.

Three alleged conspirators already were in custody or fugitives from the United States. A fourth was expected to be arrested in Hartford today. The federal grand jury returned the indictments to Judge J. Joseph Smith in United States District Court after deliberating only 30 minutes.

Those Indicted for Conspiracy

Indicted for conspiracy to violate the Espionage Act of 1917 by transmitting national defense information to Germany and Japan, under penalty of 20 years in prison, are:

Anastase A. Vonsiatsky of Thompson, leader of the All-Russian Revolutionary Fascist Party, who, according to the Department of Justice, has been active in various organizations having Nazi and Fascist objectives.

Gerhard Wilhelm Kunze of New York, national leader of the German-American Bund.

Dr. Otto Willumeit of Chicago, leader of the Midwest division of the bund.

Dr. Wolfgang Ebell, El Paso, Tex., now interned as an enemy alien.

The Rev. Kurt N. Molzahn, pastor of a Lutheran church in Philadelphia.

The arraignment of Vonsiatsky and Willumeit was set for 2:30 today, after Thomas J. Dodd, special assistant to the attorney general, asked for bench warrants for all the accused except Vonsiatsky, who already was in custody today.

Face 20-Year Terms

The indictment is based on conspiracy to violate Section 32 of Title 50 of the United States Code, known as the Espionage Act. It provides that:

Whoever with intent or reason to believe that it is to be used to the injury of the United State or to the advantage of a foreign nation communicates, delivers or transmits to any foreign government . . . any document, code, book, writing . . . . for information relating to the national defense shall be

only one of its kind and magnitude in the 150-year history of federal courts in Connecticut, was handled for the government by Thomas J. Dodd, special assistant to the attorney general; Robert P. Butler, U. S. attorney for the district; Joseph P. Cooney, assistant U. S. attorney, and George F. Kneip, attorney from the Department of Justice at Washington.

The case is considered one of the three most important spy cases since Dec. 7, owing to its nationwide ramifications.

In the so-called Ludwig Case in New York, nine persons were indicted and given sentences ranging from five to 20 years. The third big espionage prosecution was in Brooklyn where 33 defendants received sentences ranging from one to 18 years.

Thomas J. Dodd, special assistant to the U.S. attorney general, who in May and June 1942 represented the government before the grand jury.

Twilight companionship. Anastase and Marion Vonsiatsky sipping champagne in 1962 at Marion's winter home in Tucson, Arizona. (*courtesy of Andre A. Vonsiatsky*)

The Vonsiatsky crypt at the West Thompson Cemetery, just north of Putnam, Connecticut. Built in 1940, the vault can accommodate six bodies. The remains of Donat ("Coontz") Kunle rested there alone from 1941 until 1964, when they were removed on Vonsiatsky's instructions to an adjacent site. As of 1975, the crypt contained the bodies of Vonsiatsky, his wife, Marion, and his companion of later years, Priscilla. Shortly after this photograph was taken by the author in 1973, vandals destroyed the stained glass window depicting the Virgin Mary and Christ child.

to leave? Matkovsky, visibly nervous, repeated that such questions could be answered only after Vlasevsky had talked with Akikusa. When somebody suddenly asked Matkovsky whether he planned to get out of Harbin, the normally urbane Mikhail Alexeevich flushed and mumbled that it was too early for idle speculations.

On August 9, the Japanese were almost as much in the dark about Soviet movements as were the White Russians. The Kwantung Army Staff at first failed to grasp the full magnitude of the invasion. Accustomed to border incidents, General Yamada Otozō, and his chief of staff, Lieutenant General Hata Hikosaburō, at first thought that they were dealing with a local provocation. Their misapprehension was reinforced by the absence of Soviet air strikes (prevented by bad weather). But by day's end, the gravity of Manchukuo's crisis began to reveal itself.

During the next three days, the Kwantung Army buckled like twigs under a steamroller. Three Soviet army groups smashed through frontier defenses and converged on Hsinking and Mukden from the east, west, and north. In some localities, Red Army units slipped across the border and overran Japanese positions before their occupants could fire a shot. Where resistance proved intractable, such as in the Halun-Arshan fortified area near Nomonhan, the Soviets bypassed the obstacles and pushed onward into the central Manchurian plain. Individual Japanese units fought fiercely but succumbed one by one to pulverizing firepower. Japanese infantrymen tied grenades to their belts and hurled themselves under Soviet tanks. No less sacrificial, individual Red Army soldiers covered bunker embrasures with their bodies, absorbing bullets, while comrades passed by.

As a conflagration engulfed Manchukuo's perimeter, an eerie silence descended on Harbin. The city was far from the battlegrounds, and overcast skies continued to preclude air strikes. Yet beneath the placid exterior lurked fear, for Harbin was isolated from the rest of Manchukuo. The Military Mission lost radio contact with Kwantung Army headquarters in Hsinking. Rumors ran rampant in the Russian community, and word spread that Japan was about to surrender. Refugees from surrounding villages brought harrowing stories of mutinies among Manchukuoan troops and savage reprisals against Japanese civilians and soldiers alike by Chinese and Koreans. People whispered that the Red Army would reach Harbin within days, perhaps within hours.

Flight

As soon as a Soviet conquest of Manchukuo appeared imminent, knots of émigrés met behind locked doors and closed shutters to debate what to do. Opinions were divided on whether to remain in Harbin or to flee south to China or Korea, the only visible sanctuaries. The choice was not easy, for each option involved risks and sacrifices. Older émigrés remembered their bitter experiences as refugees after the Revolution and were reluctant to repeat them. Moreover, running away meant abandoning painfully accumulated property and possessions. Proponents of evacuation warned that even if the Red Army refrained from rape and pillage, NKVD squads followed close behind with long lists of people to be picked up. Others rejected such dark views, arguing that having just won a great victory over Germany, Stalin would not stoop to wreaking vengeance on exiled compatriots. This optimistic prognosis was reinforced by Soviet consular officials in Harbin, who declared at every opportunity that there were no longer "Soviets" and "émigrés" but only "Russians." The Red Army was liberating fellow Russians from a Japanese yoke and had not the slightest intention of harming them.

While thousands of émigrés vacillated between inaction and flight, Vlasevsky finally succeeded in getting an interview with Akikusa on August 10. The Japanese officer seemed as much in the dark as everyone else. Haggard from lack of sleep, he confessed that communications with Kwantung Army headquarters had broken down, making the general situation in Manchukuo impossible to grasp. He promised to do everything within his power to help any White Russians who wished to evacuate Harbin and proceed to China and Korea. He handed Vlasevsky some notes outlining what Kwantung Army Intelligence knew about the Soviet declaration of war and asked that Rodzaevsky put them into an announcement to be issued in the name of the Harbin Military Mission to the local Russian community. Vlasevsky noticed that Akikusa showed signs of nervous strain and barely held back tears when their conversation momentarily touched on the possibility of a Japanese surrender.

As soon as Vlasevsky had finished briefing BREM department heads about Akikusa's remarks, arguments erupted about whether or not to take advantage of a Japanese offer to evacuate. Rodzaevsky sat through these exchanges with uncharacteristic detachment. He had his own plans.

Rodzaevsky intended to head for Tientsin at the first sign that Soviet forces were approaching Harbin. He confided this on August 10 to three young *soratniki*—Vladimir Migunov and two others, Goltzev and Senzhin—and to his mistress, Vera Yanshina. They quickly pledged to follow him. He then gave them instructions to collect valuables and a few clothes in readiness for an immediate departure. The Military Mission, he asserted, would supply them with false passports, arms, food, and horses for an overland trek toward the Great Wall. Asked what would happen to his family, Konstantin Vladimirovich replied that his father, his wife Neonilla, and two children, Olga and Vladimir, would remain in Harbin. He was apparently not on speaking terms with Neonilla at this time, and his infant son was too ill to travel.

Rodzaevsky forgot all about his plans for an overland trek early on August 12 when Major Akaki, a liaison officer from the Military Mission attached to BREM, notified Vlasevsky that a special train was scheduled to leave Harbin Central Railway Station at eight o'clock that same evening, carrying White Russian collaborators. The train's destination was not given but was assumed to be Tientsin or Dairen. Akaki's announcement sent half a dozen BREM officials scurrying home to alert their families, and others began burning BREM archives. But then someone came in and said that he had heard a rumor about a Japanese plan to liquidate all collaborators on a death train. Hearing this, some expressed second thoughts about taking up Akaki's offer. Matkovsky, whose customary self-assurance had wilted since August 9, mumbled that he would like to join the evacuees but "unforeseen circumstances" required that he stay in Harbin a bit longer. He added, unconvincingly, that American forces were supposed to occupy Manchukuo and would guarantee the security of its inhabitants.

That evening, only twenty-odd White Russians showed up at the Harbin Central Railway Station. The waiting rooms and platforms were spilling over with Japanese civilians, mainly dependents of businessmen, merchants, and SMR workers. Mothers carried babies on their backs, their older children toddling alongside, bewildered at the nervous bustle. Japanese families were desperately trying to get out of Manchukuo before it was too late. Most sensed that available rolling stock could accommodate only a small proportion of them. But they waited nonetheless, for it was their only hope.

On one platform stood an incongruous sight: an empty train consisting of a second-class coach, two third-class coaches, and an anti-

quated locomotive. White Russians arriving at the station were guided
to this train by Japanese conductors. Police guarded all approaches
to make sure that no one from the crowds slipped on board.

When Major Akaki arrived shortly before eight and saw how few
Russians had shown up, he ordered the departure postponed for
several hours and set off to inquire about some prominent absentees.
Around midnight, Akaki returned with General Vlasevky, his wife,
and son. At the last moment, Vlasevsky had decided to stay in Harbin,
but Akaki had now persuaded him to reconsider—according to one
account, with a revolver. Matkovsky put in an appearance at the station
but told Akaki that he must remain at his BREM post to relay instructions from the Military Mission to the émigré community. Rodzaevsky
and his four traveling companions needed no prodding. They had
arrived at the station early. Also among the special evacuees were
ex-police inspector Nikolai Martinov (ringleader of the Kaspé kidnappers), ex-*Nash Put* reporter Iliodor Karnaukh, BREM Fourth Department director Mikhail Gordeev, and two Japanese: a commandant
and a train conductor.

Shortly before dawn on August 13, the old locomotive gave a
shrill whistle and belched smoke. Three coaches lurched forward out
of Harbin Central Station under the numb gaze of stranded Japanese
lining the platforms. Minutes later, the train was rumbling out of
Harbin's southwestern suburbs. Darkness denied the forty Russian
passengers a last look at what had been their home in exile.

Moving south along the SMR mail line, the train paused briefly
in Hsinking to pick up local BREM officials whom Rodzaevsky had
telegraphed the previous night. No one showed up at the station,
presumably because the cable had not arrived. Mukden, about 175
miles farther south, was reached early in the evening of August 13.

The Mukden railroad station seethed with refugees and rumors.
Soviet pincers were said to be approaching the city from the east
and west. Red airborne troops had reportedly landed at Dairen and
Port Arthur, cutting off the hope of reaching ships in the Kwantung
Territory. The rail line along Liaotung Bay toward the Great Wall
and Tientsin was still open, but Soviet armored columns were dashing
across Inner Mongolia and could close that route at any moment.
Only the tracks leading southeast to the Korean frontier seemed relatively safe, for the time being.

Leaving Mukden at eight in the evening, the special train headed into the mountains and soon began passing through tunnels. At dawn the next day, August 14, the passengers caught sight of a broad river. It was the Yalu, dividing Manchukuo from Korea. Suddenly the locomotive braked and the entire train screeched to a halt. Ahead on the tracks clustered a group of Japanese soldiers, barring their way. The commandant and conductor got off and went over to speak with the soldiers. The engine, meanwhile, backed up and pulled the coaches over to a siding. For what seemed like an eternity, the passengers waited and listened, convinced that they were being abandoned. After what could not have been more than an hour, the commandant and conductor returned, and the train started moving again. Everyone was about to heave a sigh of relief until someone noticed that they were going backwards—to the north.

Rodzaevsky cursed himself for having left Harbin. Here he was on a train full of collaborators while his wife and children remained in Harbin to face the Red Army, alone and unprotected. Marital problems faded into insignificance as he thought of what could happen to Neonilla at the hands of NKVD interrogators. Unable to sit still, he jumped up and strode up and down the aisle, babbling to himself about someday rebuilding the Russian Fascist Party and showing Stalin once and for all who was who. His mouth suddenly contorted in the middle of a word. Hiding his face, Rodzaevsky slumped into a seat, his whole body shaking with sobs. No one paid much attention to the ex-*vozhd*, everyone being too preoccupied with his own problems.

The afternoon of August 14 found the train back in Mukden, where it picked up additional coaches full of Russian refugees from Harbin and departed again, this time to the southwest along the shores of Liaotung Bay. Tension suffused the train. Everyone knew that they were racing against time. If those Soviet armored columns converging from the north reached the tracks before the evacuation train could pass by, the passengers were finished. To make matters worse, the commandant ordered that blinds be drawn over all the windows. The air grew unbearably hot and stuffy as the train inched its way, hour after hour, toward the Great Wall.

About twenty hours after leaving Mukden, the train abruptly halted. A Japanese army officer boarded and said something to the commandant in a barely audible voice. The commandant covered his face. Every Russian passenger who saw him guessed immediately what had happened. The war was over. No matter how much resentment had accumulated during fourteen years of "the kingly way," many on that train felt a pang of sympathy for the vanquished. Now they were all veterans of defeat and humiliation.

Several hours later, the train stopped again. A now subdued commandant walked up the aisles, murmuring that the window blinds could be raised. As light flooded the coaches, eyes blinked and peered outside. Someone exclaimed: "We're in China!" A chorus of sighs and congratulations rippled from one end of the train to the other. Indeed, the station sign said Peitaiho, a Chinese coastal city and fashionable summer resort for Europeans and Americans about 120 miles from Tientsin.

The atmosphere in China contrasted starkly with that of Manchukuo. Here, the White Russian evacuees from Harbin felt safe for the first time. Here they could almost inhale serenity, for Peitaiho had hardly been touched by the war. Behind them lay a nightmare, ahead— a new lease on life.

Konstantin Rodzaevsky, however, did not share in the rejoicing. He knew that the past could not be shed so easily. His family was still in Harbin. And a voice from the depths of his consciousness whispered that sooner or later he would have to come to terms with his homeland.

Conversion

After a brief stop at Peitaiho the train resumed its progress toward Tientsin, arriving on August 16. At the station, its passengers were met by representatives of the local Émigré Bureau and Japanese Military Mission, who found temporary lodgings for most of them at hastily outfitted offices of a local Russian newspaper.

Tientsin's White Russians did not rush out to welcome the new arrivals, who appeared at a time of overcrowding and shortages. All prominent collaborators, they were tainted with Japanese associations, something that everyone was trying to shed. Nationalist Chinese forces were taking over Tientsin's administration from the Japanese, but the Red Army was too close for local White Russians to feel at ease. Would not the presence of such notorious anti-Soviet elements tempt Stalin to attack Tientsin? The locals wanted the Harbiners to move on to Shanghai, and said so. It took several weeks for this alarm and hostility to subside, by which time most of the Harbiners had melted into the community, sometimes by concealing their backgrounds.

Rodzaevsky, however, remained a conspicuous pariah, as Tientsin's White Russian society ostracized him. The Émigré Bureau refused to house him, although it took in his mistress, Vera Yanshina, and his three young followers. Rodzaevsky wound up sharing an apartment with seven Red Army deserters, two of them NKVD border guards, who had fled to China via Manchukuo at various times during the 1930s.

Rodzaevsky had escaped Manchukuo none too soon. On August 17, the day that the Kwantung Army received a ceasefire order from Imperial General Headquarters in Tokyo, Soviet pincers closed on Hsinking and Mukden. Red Army units, led by Major General G. A. Shelakhov, entered Harbin on August 18, five days after Rodzaevsky had entrained for points south. Kwantung Army Chief of Staff Lieutenant General Hata Hikosaburō was waiting for them at the airport, having made arrangements the previous day through Akikusa and Harbin's Soviet consul. By dawn of August 19, Soviet troops had occupied the city's railway stations, the Sungari bridge, and major roads. That day, Hata flew to Marshal Vasilevsky's headquarters to conclude a formal surrender. At the Mukden airport, Manchukuo's puppet emperor, Henry P'u-Yi, was snatched by a Soviet detachment just as he was about to board a plane for Japan.

Manchukuo's end came remorselessly and with dire consequences for the Japanese who lived, worked, and served there. Some 563,000 Kwantung Army POWs faced up to eleven years of "corrective labor" in camps from Kharkov to Kamchatka. Senior officers, among them Yamada, Hata, and Akikusa, were flown to Khabarovsk for trial and imprisonment as "war criminals." Over a million Japanese civilians—agrarian colonists, clerks, factory workers, businessmen, merchants, doctors, teachers, and gangsters—remained in Soviet hands for at least a year. About 83,000 soldiers and 15,000 civilians died in battle or were killed by vengeful Chinese and Koreans; 91,000 more succumbed before 1946 from disease, hunger, and exposure. Thousands simply vanished without leaving a trace.

In escaping Manchukuo, Rodzaevsky avoided the fate of Ataman Semenov and other prominent Whites who stoically awaited the NKVD. According to an official Soviet source, Semenov, the "butcher of the workers and peasants," was arrested by "security organs" and "made a clean breast of all his activities with an expression of submission and humiliation." Émigré accounts of Semenov's encounter with the NKVD are more explicit and possibly more imaginative. According to one source, a SMERSH detachment parachuted near Semenov's Dairen house on the night of August 19 and, by prearrangement with the local Soviet consulate, whisked him by air to Moscow. Another account states that NKVD troops kept him and his family under house arrest for three weeks and then removed him to Moscow without allowing him to say good-bye to his wife and daughters. One romantic version depicted the Cossack as having prepared a sumptuous repast for his captors. When a squad of heavily armed NKVD *osobisti* showed up early one morning, he introduced himself, pointed out his carefully arranged private archives, and invited everyone to breakfast. After a thorough search, the colonel in charge accepted and ordered his men to sit down around a table heaped with food and vodka. Semenov toasted Russia's victory over Germany and expressed himself prepared to submit to Stalin's judgment, but declared that he had always acted out of patriotism. After feeding himself, the NKVD colonel stood up, announced that his host was under arrest, and escorted him to the airfield for shipment to Moscow.

Instead of congratulating himself for having escaped the Manchurian maelstrom, Rodzaevsky felt depressed in Tientsin. He missed his family and worried about their safety in Harbin. He smarted at the way former friends shunned him. Above all, he was dumbfounded at reports of pro-Soviet euphoria in Manchuria. Cossacks, once the staunchest anti-Communists, welcomed the Red Army with open arms. On August 19, thousands of White Russians crowded Novy Gorod's Sabul Cathedral plaza, cheering Soviet troops and waving red flags. The Asano Brigade melted away without firing a shot. Its commander, Colonel Gurgen Nagolen, turned out to be a Red Army Intelligence officer.

Even ex-*soratniki* shamelessly joined the pro-Soviet stampede. Tientsin's RFS branch leader, one Ushakov, brazenly paraded about with a Soviet passport, as did RFS Shanghai branch leader Gennady Taradanov, who only ten years earlier had vilified Stalin in *Azbuka Fashizma*. Boris Rumiantsev, RFO cofounder in 1927, resurfaced as vice-president of the Shanghai Association of Soviet Citizens.

But the greatest shock of all was Mikhail Matkovsky. Rodzaevsky could hardly believe his ears when he heard that this suave RFS leader was working for the USSR. Suddenly, Matkovsky's strange behavior earlier in August, his reluctance to be evacuated from Harbin, his nervous evasiveness all became clear. Now he openly served the Red Army just as efficiently as he had served the Japanese, registering émigrés and issuing residence permits. The thought of Matkovsky supplying the NKVD with BREM personnel files filled Rodzaevsky with impotent rage. The boy from Blagoveshchensk had been aware of Soviet infiltration, but its actual scope, fully revealed after Japan's defeat, staggered him. And that he, Konstantin Rodzaevsky, should have been suspected by the Japanese as a Red! Matkovsky had no doubt planted that idea in the Military Mission.

Rodzaevsky's world was collapsing around him. Nothing seemed certain any longer. It seemed as if everyone had betrayed him. He felt terribly alone and insecure.

At the nadir of his dejection, sometime early in September, Konstantin Vladimirovich began to undergo an extraordinary psychological metamorphosis. The process unfolded gradually, with subtle reinforcement from outside.

Meanwhile, two of his young followers, Goltzev and Migunov, had struck up an acquaintance with a pair of loquacious and free-spending émigrés: Nikolai Korobkov and a certain Demianovsky. Korobkov, a Matkovsky crony, had formerly worked for the *Kempei* in Harbin as a minion of Konstantin Ivanovich ("Kostya") Nakamura. He had occasionally run errands for Nakamura in Peiping and Kalgan until Japan's surrender. Demianovsky, a onetime stalwart of Tientsin's Anti-Communist Committee, switched to a Soviet passport after V-J Day and was out to prove his devotion to Stalin.

Korobkov and Demianovsky regaled Goltzev and Migunov with rosy descriptions of Harbin under Soviet occupation. Complete harmony prevailed between the Red Army and the White Russian community. Past differences were forgotten amid a surge of fraternal solidarity. What now mattered was to be a true Russian. And what did it mean to be a true Russian? It meant to love one's *Rodina* (mother country) and to demonstrate that love by returning to the Soviet Union as a Soviet citizen. The days of lonely exile were over. Now was the time for the younger generation—Soviet and émigré—to clasp hands and rebuild Russia from the ravages of war, restoring her former greatness. To achieve this epochal goal, exiles, particularly young exiles, must show their sincerity by voluntarily returning home and taking part in the great tasks that lay ahead.

Rodzaevsky, Demianovsky argued, was just the sort of fine young man whom Stalin could really use at such times. He was intelligent, energetic, a stirring orator, and an experienced propagandist. People with his qualifications and dedication were vitally needed by the *Rodina.* Konstantin Vladimirovich would have no trouble establishing his credentials with Soviet authorities. Why, Matkovsky himself, now happily working in a responsible capacity for the Red Army in Harbin, would vouch for him.

Goltzev and Migunov excitedly repeated to Rodzaevsky what they had heard. Although he may have sensed danger, the ex-*vozhd* could not help listening. He began to see that his self-imposed isolation ill suited him. He craved belonging to a nation, *his* nation, and the idea that the Soviets would accept, even welcome, him stimulated his imagination. His vanity swelled further upon hearing that Stalin wanted such men as himself for "the great tasks that lie ahead."

Rodzaevsky's credulity was reinforced by his ignorance. As yet he knew nothing about Semenov and other White leaders apprehended in Manchuria, except that they had been taken to Moscow. *Pravda* carried no notices of trials. News from Harbin was fragmentary and largely hearsay. Finally, Rodzaevsky worked himself up into a state of wanting to be convinced by Demianovsky's promises. He now saw the pro-Soviet euphoria around him in different light. Perhaps the "prodigal sons" of Russia were truly returning to the maternal fold. If so, he did not want to be left out.

Rodzaevsky instructed Goltzev and Migunov to keep seeing Korobkov and Demianovsky and to find out as much as possible from them about conditions in Harbin. During the next few days, the two followers came back repeatedly to Rodzaevsky's lodgings with ever more tantalizing stories: Demianovsky had described Archbishop Nestor, once an honorary RFS *soratnik,* conducting an Orthodox mass at Harbin's Sabul Cathedral attended by hatless Red Army officers and men. Demianovsky had offered to deliver personally a letter from Rodzaevsky to Matkovsky so that steps could be taken toward reestablishing communication with his family. Korobkov had lamented that Rodzaevsky's absence from Harbin was widely felt, because his talents were much needed there. Both men had urged Rodzaevsky not to take too long making up his mind. Moscow might construe hesitation as a lack of sincerity.

Rodzaevsky mulled over these propositions. Recent experiences had eroded his trust in others. Yet at thirty-eight, he desperately wanted to "be somebody." A decade as *vozhd* of a political movement had left him hungry for action, for teamwork, for involvement in the "great tasks that lie ahead."

After several days of intense introspection, Rodzaevsky started writing feverishly. He poured himself out without reserve, shedding past faiths and allegiances in a dramatic *volte face* that took on the character of a religious conversion. First, he drafted an apologia entitled "One Week Resurrecting the Soul." Then he wrote two letters: one to Marshal Rodion Malinovsky, commander of the Trans-Baikal Front, and another to Stalin.

In "One Week Resurrecting the Soul," Rodzaevsky described his own "spiritual crisis" as having just been resolved by an awakening to the continuities underlying Russian history. In an inspired vision, he saw that national expansion linked the tsarist and Soviet periods. The Soviet victory over Germany and Japan confirmed a glorious tradition and opened his eyes to the fact that his loyalties had been misplaced. By perpetuating the hallowed tradition of "gathering Muscovite lands" (Soviet territorial gains in eastern Europe and the Far East in 1940–45), Stalin had shown himself to be a "new Ivan Kalita."*

Rodzaevsky's letter to Marshal Malinovsky has not survived, but the likely drift of its contents can be inferred from the remarkable missive that he wrote to Stalin. The authenticity of this letter is hotly denied by Rodzaevsky's family, but a number of qualified observers have treated it as genuine or regard it as plausible given his state of mind at the time.

Konstantin Vladimirovich opened by stating his purpose:

> Every worker, every collective farmer may address a letter to the *vozhd* of the Russian people, the *vozhd* of the people of the Soviet Union, Comrade I. V. Stalin. Perhaps this will be granted me, a Russian emigrant, who has wasted twenty years of my life in a struggle which seemed to me, and for those who followed me, a struggle for the liberation and rebirth of our motherland—Russia.
>
> I want to explain the causes underlying the existence and activities of the Russian Fascist Union and to reach an understanding about the

* Ivan Kalita ("Moneybags"), who reigned from 1328 to 1341, increased Muscovite lands by purchase rather than conquest. Perhaps Rodzaevsky's comparison of Ivan Kalita with Stalin sprang from wishful thinking. Kalita ransomed a number of Russian prisoners from the Mongols.

poignant drama of the Russian emigration. Therefore, this letter is not so much a personal document as it is an attempt to map a way out of a cul-de-sac for more and more Russian people trying to do all they can for their motherland.

Avowedly "not so much a personal document," the letter took on an intensely personal tone as Rodzaevsky launched into an intimate confession of his own life and activities. He related why he had run away from the Soviet Union and had thrown himself into a militantly anti-Communist movement. He recalled his disappointment and anger at not being admitted to a university despite the favorable recommendation of the local soviet. Personal grievances, he continued, coalesced into hatred of communism once he had enrolled in the Harbin Juridical Institute and had come under the spell of Italian fascism. Fascism struck him as an effective antidote for the ills sapping Russia's strength: class struggle, internationalism, Jews, and the cold imperatives of dialectical materialism. Fascism, he felt, could instill a new sense of creative nationalism among Russians while at the same time providing a foundation for social justice. His greatest mistake, Rodzaevsky confided, was his failure to recognize that the USSR was, in any event, evolving naturally toward fascism.

Jews, he continued, still constituted Russia's most insidious internal threat, for their intense racial consciousness gnawed at national roots. Stalin, and only Stalin, could solve Russia's Jewish problem by "exhuming Jews from Talmudic surroundings and making them into Soviet people." Russian fascism and Soviet communism, he asserted, shared basically the same aims. Although RFS *soratniki* had failed to realize it, Stalin was their true *vozhd:*

> Not all at once, but step by step, we came to this conclusion. We decided that: Stalinism is exactly what we mistakenly called "Russian Fascism." It is our Russian Fascism cleansed of extremes, illusions, and errors.

Turning to his activities since 1931, Rodzaevsky blended apologies with excuses. He admitted that the party had mistakenly indulged in anti-Soviet activities, but these were "acts against the motherland out of love for the motherland." Supporting Germany had been wrong, but *soratniki* had sincerely believed that Hitler could help Russia by ridding it of Jews. Accused at various times of being Soviet, American, German, or Japanese agents, the Russian fascists, Rodzaevsky conceded, worked mainly for Japan. Nevertheless, he had always refused to obey Japanese orders whenever he perceived them as harmful to Russia. In 1937, he had terminated RFS espionage and sabotage inside the USSR, a decision that ultimately led to the party's being banned. Semenov, by contrast, was no more than a tool who did anything to curry Japanese favor. Semenovites had dominated BREM and were therefore responsible for BREM's oppressive management of émigré affairs. Rodzaevsky explained that his flight from Harbin on August 13, 1945, had been motivated by a determination not to fight the USSR: "Once having made the terrible mistake [of supporting] Germany's war against the USSR, we did not want to repeat it in the USSR's war against Japan, [which was] started by the USSR clearly for Russian national interests."

As the letter proceeded, the tone grew more emotional. After lugubriously describing his life in Tientsin, Rodzaevsky announced that he and his *soratniki* (not mentioning that there were three of them all told) thirsted to be reunited with their motherland. He begged "Iosif Vissarionovich" to forgive his followers on the grounds that they should not be held accountable for propaganda and acts that he, the RFS *vozhd,* had formulated and ordered:

> I am prepared to take upon myself responsibility for all RFS work, prepared to appear before any court, prepared to die if necessary. If this is necessary for Soviet power, you may kill me, kill me with or without a trial.

Lest Stalin take him at his word, however, Rodzaevsky promptly added that "I want to start a new life" as a "national Communist and convinced Stalinist," and to make it worthwhile for Stalin to spare him, Rodzaevsky promised to work for a Soviet administration in Manchuria. Better yet, he would mobilize the RFS's worldwide organization to bring back émigrés to the USSR "under Stalinist banners" from Asia, the Americas, and Australia.

The letter concluded with an impassioned appeal for clemency and an exile's *cri de coeur:*

> In the interest of the motherland and the revolution, I beg you, Great Stalin, and the Supreme Soviet of the USSR, to promulgate a humane act of amnesty for all emigrants. . . . Death without the motherland, life without the motherland, or work against the motherland, ah! We want to die by order of the motherland or in any place fulfilling any

work for the motherland. We want to give all our strength to our people and to the holiest thing in all the world—the victory of radiant Stalinist ideas.

Long Live Stalin, the People's *Vozhd!*

Your unworthy slave,
Konstantin Vladimirovich Rodzaevsky

P.S. There is no time [for me] to think this over and refine it. Everything here has been poured from the heart onto the paper.

Rodzaevsky took "One Week Resurrecting the Soul," together with his letters to Stalin and Malinovsky, and gave them to Goltzev to hand over to Demianovsky. Demianovsky in turn took them to Peking and gave them to an attaché of the Soviet consulate, Ivan Timofeevich Patrikeev. Rodzaevsky's case deeply interested Patrikeev who was in China on a special mission—to hunt émigré souls.

The Hunt

At the end of World War II, millions of displaced Soviet citizens were scattered around Europe, mostly in Germany, Czechoslovakia, Yugoslavia, and Austria, but also in Italy, France, Holland, Denmark, and Norway. A vast majority were Red Army POW's who had managed to survive Nazi death camps. Of these, just under a million Russians, Ukrainians, Georgians, Turkestanis, Azerbaijanis, Uzbeks, Tatars, Cossacks, and Armenians had opted for, or been coerced into, serving as noncombat *Wehrmacht* auxiliaries or had joined special military formations such as General Andrei Vlasov's Russian Liberation Army, Lieutenant General Hellmuth von Pannwitz's Cossack Division, or General Ralph von Heygendorff's Turkestani and Caucasian detachments. In addition to military personnel, there were many thousands of Soviet men and women whom the Germans had rounded up in the Ukraine and Belorussia and sent to the Reich as laborers *(Ostarbeiter)*. Finally, there were untold numbers of civilian collaborators, fellow travelers, and their dependents who had retreated westward with the Wehrmacht, fleeing the advancing Red Army, or more accurately, the NKVD squads that followed in its wake.

Stalin wanted all of these people returned to the USSR, by force if necessary. Collaborators were to be punished. But Stalin's definition of a collaborator encompassed far more than those Soviet citizens who had put on German uniforms or served the enemy in some political capacity. Capture by the enemy constituted grounds for suspected collaboration, and survival of prison camps carried a stigma of guilt. Prisoners who had left POW camps to work in factories as an alternative to almost certain death by starvation fell within the category of "collaborator," as did Russian women who had served as domestic servants in Germany.

But Stalin was interested in more than the collaborators. He also wanted to repatriate even the most uncompromisingly loyal soldiers and civilians, because their exposure to different social systems and standards of living may have contaminated them too and made them potentially dangerous. Upon their repatriation, they would have to be questioned carefully, and where necessary be given an opportunity to contribute to socialist construction under the auspices of GULAG.

As Stalin had surmised, there were many Soviet citizens (estimated by Western sources at anywhere from tens of thousands to two million) who preferred to remain permanently outside the USSR, no doubt because they foresaw what fate awaited them in the motherland. If they had been allowed their own choice, there might have been another Russian diaspora, equaling that generated in 1917–22. Stalin managed, however, to extract a written pledge from the British and Americans at Yalta that "all Soviet citizens" liberated by Allied armies would be speedily handed over to Soviet authorities. The text of the Yalta Agreement made no reference to employing force against recalcitrant repatriates, but that was, in fact, its legal meaning, and such was the tacit understanding among the cosignatories. However repulsive the idea of forced repatriation, the British and Americans complied with Stalin's wishes for reasons of political expediency. They were also anxious about the safety of British and American POWs liberated by the Red Army from German camps in eastern Europe and awaiting repatriation from Soviet occupation zones.

Acting on the basis of the Yalta Agreement, British and American forces rounded up and delivered some two million Russian men, women, and children to Soviet authorities between 1945 and 1947. Force was rarely necessary, because deception generally proved more effective. Prospective repatriates were carried in lorries to transfer camps along the perimeters of Soviet zones and lulled into a false sense of security by banners welcoming them to the *Rodina,* festive music over loudspeakers, and generous food rations. The game continued until they were securely in Soviet hands.

Occasionally, however, blood flowed. Between May 28 and June 1, 1945, some 50,000 Cossacks and their families were forcibly deported by British units at Judenburg, a small town 120 miles southwest of Vienna on the Mur River which separated the British and Soviet armies. At the sight of waiting Red Army guards, some of the Cossacks killed themselves by leaping from a bridge into a deep gorge over which they were being herded into the Soviet zone. Others tried to escape into the Austrian Alps, only to be hunted down by Anglo-Soviet patrols. Once over the Mur bridge, the bulk were loaded into trucks and driven to railheads for transshipment to the USSR where they faced (depending upon rank and record) anything from a labor camp sojourn to the firing squad.

Among those handed over at Judenburg were émigrés who had left Russia during the Civil War some twenty-five years earlier and could by no stretch of the imagination be construed as Soviet citizens. Their deportation constituted a violation of the Yalta Agreement, but such infractions were overlooked in the confused aftermath of the war.

Needless to say, Stalin was particularly eager to get his hands on old White leaders, many of whom he and fellow Bolsheviks had bitterly fought in 1918–22. Although not many Old Bolsheviks were still around in 1945 to witness the occasion, Stalin presumably derived a certain satisfaction from putting these battered but defiant tsarist relics on trial and then hanging them—denying them even a soldier's death by firing squad. One such plum turned up among the Judenburg deportees: Cossack hetman Andrei Shkuro, who had entertained Vonsiatsky in 1938.

In the Far East, a very different situation prevailed from that in Europe. Stalin could do much as he wished inside Soviet-occupied Manchuria. The NKVD squads that closely followed the Red Army carried detailed lists of émigrés to be picked up, repatriated, and tried under Article 58 of the Criminal Code of 1926, which provided penalties for treason, aiding capitalist countries, conspiracy against the Soviet Union, and sundry anti-Communist activities. High priority was given to the apprehension of BREM officials, members of monarchist and Cossack organizations, the Russian Armed Services Union, the Musketeers, and of course, the Russian Fascist Union. Assisted by agents operating in these organizations, such as Matkovsky in the RFS and Nagolen in the Asano Brigade, the NKVD quickly picked up their quarries and transported them to Voroshilov, Khabarovsk, and Chita prisons to await trial. Luminaries such as Ataman Semenov and Generals Verzhbitsky and Baksheev were flown directly to Moscow for more publicized judicial proceedings.

In China south of the Great Wall, however, Soviet authorities enjoyed no such freedom of action. Chiang Kai-shek had not taken part in the Yalta Agreement. Nor did the Generalissimo, in fact, show any inclination to hand over Russian émigrés or Soviet defectors within his jurisdiction. Consequently, Moscow was obliged to adopt a soft approach in China. The strategy consisted of luring exiles "home" by appealing to their national pride and manipulating their loneliness.

The soft approach harvested a rich crop of wayward souls throughout Chinese centers of the Russian diaspora in the fall of 1945. In October, a Soviet plenipotentiary arrived in Shanghai and announced that the Presidium of the Supreme Soviet had extended forgiveness to all émigrés. Soviet diplomats promised that all expatriates would meet a warm welcome in the motherland. Nor would their standard of living suffer. Émigrés could bring back all their possessions, including pianos and cars, and could settle wherever they pleased. Steamships would be available to transport homebound citizens to a port near Vladivostok, whence repatriates could entrain for points west.

Although such promises persuaded thousands of ordinary Russians living in China, something more alluring was needed to bring back "difficult cases," namely "White Guards" who had good reason to stay away from the USSR. "Difficult cases" were, of course, the people most keenly sought by the NKVD. To snare them required a special type of agent. He could not simply be a kidnapper, for that would provoke bad publicity and scare off other émigrés. Rather, he had to be a consummately skilled salesman for the "new Russia." Ivan Patrikeev filled the role admirably.

Stationed at the Soviet consulate in Peiping, Patrikeev, only thirty-five years old, was a soft-spoken diplomat with a broad, pleasant face. Unlike his colleagues, he enjoyed socializing with émigrés. Not only was he affable, but he took a sympathetic interest in their problems. Not infrequently, he offered them help. But Patrikeev's concern for White Russian welfare was no personal idiosyncrasy. He had been specifically instructed in Moscow to expedite the repatriation of "difficult cases."

Patrikeev went about his task with the aplomb of a practiced connoisseur. He first familiarized himself thoroughly with the background and character of each prospective case. He then got to know the person in question and won his confidence. Never one to rush, he acted with utmost discretion so as not to arouse the suspicions of the White Russians, the Chinese government, or the quarry.

Patrikeev's first big catch turned out to be General Lev Vlasevsky, the sixty-two-year-old Semenovite and last chief of BREM. Five days before Soviet troops occupied Harbin, Vlasevsky and his family had escaped on the special evacuation train to Tientsin. Rumor had it that he had been reluctant to evacuate Harbin, where he had left behind a house full of possessions, not to mention friends and memories. As soon as Patrikeev heard this, he made discreet inquiries among émigré friends of the Vlasevskys and discovered that the general's wife and son were even more dissatisfied with life in Tientsin. Before long, Patrikeev had established indirect contact with Mrs. Vlasevsky, who was soon urging the Soviet diplomat to meet her husband and son. Patrikeev readily agreed, vowing that he would talk with them "as a Russian man to Russian men."

The meeting took place one evening in the apartment of an ex-BREM official who had become active in the Tientsin Society of Soviet Citizens. Upon being introduced to the general, Patrikeev dispensed with formalities and proceeded to the central point without, however, betraying the slightest awkwardness. Obliquely referring to the Stalinist purges of the 1930s, Patrikeev remarked that life in the Soviet Union had recently reached a new stage where ordinary citizens could live in peace and security. He then expounded on the harmonious atmosphere that reigned in Harbin. Diplomatically touching upon Vlasevsky's flight, he expressed himself convinced that the general had been forced to evacuate "under the muzzle of a Japanese revolver." Moreover, he could guess how much the whole family must miss their Harbin home. Certainly, he could understand their qualms about returning, but such anxieties were really quite baseless. In fact, Patrikeev continued expansively, he could prove how baseless they were if the general cared to visit Harbin for a few days as a guest of the Soviet Foreign Ministry. His safety, of course, would be unconditionally assured. He could come to Peiping and discuss the matter at any time with the Soviet consul.

Vlasevsky may have been tempted, but he was not yet ready to bite the bait. It took several more friendly encounters with Patrikeev and pro-Soviet émigrés, together with his wife's prodding, before the general began to drop his guard. A key catalyst for his conversion appears to have been one of Patrikeev's émigré assistants, Gennady Levitin, who deftly cultivated Vlasevsky's nostalgia. Levitin assured the general that were he to return to the USSR, the people of his home town, Chita, would elect him honorary mayor. Ultimately, however, Vlasevsky deceived himself. He knew that his two closest associates, Semenov and Baksheev, had been picked up and sent to Moscow. Common sense should have told him what they were undergoing, but he kept clinging to the illusion that they were at liberty serving the motherland. He apparently never dared to ask Patrikeev what had become of them.

After several weeks, Vlasevsky finally succumbed and took up Patrikeev's offer. The two men drove to Peiping and from there flew in a Soviet plane to Hsinking (renamed Changchun in 1945), where Vlasevsky had the unexpected privilege of being introduced to Marshal Malinovsky himself. Although he did not reach Harbin, Vlasevsky was so deeply impressed by the hospitality extended to him in Changchun that he became an eloquent spokesman for repatriation upon his return to Tientsin.

A few weeks later, in mid-October, Vlasevsky and his family bade an emotional farewell to Patrikeev as they prepared to entrain for Peiping. They thanked him effusively for his solicitude, which had given them a new lease on life. In Peiping, they boarded a Soviet plane that was to take them to Harbin for a gala reunion with home and friends. Instead, the plane flew to Chita. No popular delegation awaited Vlasevsky at Chita to acclaim him honorary mayor. Instead efficient NKVD personnel were there to separate him from his wife and son and put him on another plane. Vlasevsky was then flown to Moscow, where he was soon accommodated with Semenov and Baksheev at the Lubyanka, a prison conveniently within the Police Ministry headquarters and only a few minutes stroll from the Bolshoi Ballet and Red Square.

Patrikeev had had his eye on Rodzaevsky well before disposing of Vlasevsky. Rodzaevsky presented a more important target. Whereas the general merely represented the old "White Guards," Rodzaevsky vividly symbolized a more immediate object of popular hatred: fascism. As such he would make good material for a Moscow show trial, linking the White movement with German fascism and Japanese imperialism. As a preliminary ploy, Patrikeev instructed some minor employees of the newly reopened Soviet consulate in Tientsin to take Rodzaevsky out to dinner so as to put him at ease.

Meanwhile, Rodzaevsky was having second thoughts about his conversion. He wavered between visions of himself as a Soviet journalist and a clammy fear of what might happen to him once Stalin had him in his grasp. However, Demianovsky and Korobkov, whom Rodzaevsky had by this time met personally, kept urging him to act and offered to introduce him to a helpful contact named Patrikeev. At the same time, Nikolai Martinov (former police inspector, Kaspé abductor, and fellow fugitive from Harbin) warned him not to believe Demianovsky or the Soviet promises. A policeman's instinct told Martinov that Rodzaevsky was being set up for a trap. But he had no proof. Semenov's and Baksheev's fates remained unclear. And by this time, Vlasevsky was going around Tientsin rhapsodizing about his reception by Marshal Malinovsky in Changchun. Rodzaevsky eventually promised Martinov that before meeting Patrikeev he would go to Peiping and seek the advice of a man whom he trusted implicitly: Archbishop Viktor, head of the Orthodox mission in China.

Viktor quite simply advised Rodzaevsky to get as far away from North China as possible, because of rumors that Chinese authorities were rounding up anyone connected with the RFS and turning their catches over to the Soviet government.

While Rodzaevsky was ruminating over Viktor's warning, Goltzev, the ex-*vozhd*'s youthful follower, went alone to Peiping and met Patrikeev. So charmed was he by the Soviet diplomat that he begged Konstantin Vladimirovich to talk with him personally. Goltzev's enthusiasm prevailed, and the two men returned to Peiping late in September to meet the man whom Vlasevsky was extolling as an angel of grace.

Patrikeev apparently made a good initial impression, for Rodzaevsky soon broached the subject of repatriation, declaring himself willing to return to the USSR under certain conditions. Patrikeev ignored "certain phrases" and stroked Rodzaevsky's ego. Looking his quarry over appreciatively, Patrikeev remarked that such a man needed a motherland. Moreover, it was "criminal" (he chose the word carefully) that Rodzaevsky's manifold talents be wasted abroad. Russia was facing new and graver challenges. Its erstwhile Anglo-American allies were taking advantage of Soviet war losses and economic dislocation to hatch imperialist plans. At such times, a true Russian patriot could walk but one path: to the *Rodina*. Rodzaevsky was admirably equipped to serve his people as a journalist and propagandist. If he returned to the USSR, he could edit a journal aimed at overseas émigrés. His repatriation, and that of followers who wished to accompany him, could be arranged in gradual stages; first would come an interim at the Soviet consulate in Peiping, then a sojourn with his family in Harbin, and finally—homecoming.

Patrikeev adroitly fashioned his offer to fit Rodzaevsky's self-interest. He correctly identified his quarry's passions (nationalist propaganda), ambitions (global fame), and anxieties (family) and then made repatriation appear to fulfill all of them.

Thrilled and flattered by Patrikeev's words, Rodzaevsky spent the next few days discussing them with his friends. Goltzev and Migunov took them at face value. Senzhin and Vera Yanshina remained unconvinced. So did Martinov.

Early in October, Rodzaevsky indicated to Patrikeev his readiness to proceed with stage one of repatriation, namely, taking up residence in Peiping's Soviet consulate. Patrikeev promptly issued instructions. Rodzaevsky, Goltzev, and Migunov should wait at a certain point on Tientsin's Victoria Road where at five o'clock in the morning on a certain day they would be picked up in an automobile driven by Levitin and driven to Peiping. Other than the three of them, no one should know about these plans.

Committed to a specific course of action, Rodzaevsky relapsed into indecision. The night before his scheduled rendezvous, his nerves were too frayed for sleep. At one in the morning, he phoned Martinov, revealed what was happening, and confessed to a gnawing anxiety. Half fearfully, half angrily, the ex-*vozhd* complained that he felt like a cog in some vast Soviet plot.

Yet at five o'clock on the appointed morning, the three men were waiting as instructed on Victoria Road with their portable belongings. Levitin drove up and motioned them into the car. Without exchanging a word, they obeyed. No one saw them leave.

For the next three weeks, Rodzaevsky, Goltzev, and Migunov lived in the Soviet diplomatic compound in Peiping, a large, slightly run-down stone house with bars on every window. Goltzev and Migunov were permitted to go outside upon request, but Patrikeev persuaded

Rodzaevsky to remain inside for his own safety. As a consolation, the ex-*vozhd* was given a spacious, well-lit room furnished with a bed, desk, and dining table. Attentive to his guest's needs, Patrikeev saw to it that a piano was installed in Rodzaevsky's quarters.

Goltzev and Migunov freely availed themselves of their privileged mobility and spent considerable time about the city. Occasionally, Patrikeev sent them on errands. He asked them to urge Archbishop Viktor to reunite the Peiping Orthodox Mission with the Moscow patriarchate. He dispatched them back to Tientsin to fetch Nikolai Martinov, whom Rodzaevsky wanted to see again before returning to Harbin. Martinov came, after receiving assurances of his personal safety.

Rodzaevsky, meanwhile, with time on his hands, took advantage of the desk and writing materials to begin a more detailed version of his confessions, elaborating upon the letter to Stalin. Patrikeev seemed pleased and asked that he be as specific as possible about his collaboration with the Kwantung Army. During the evening when he was often alone, Rodzaevsky practiced on the piano.

On the evening of October 24, Rodzaevsky took a respite from the piano and entertained three guests in his room: Goltzev, Migunov, and Martinov. Around nine o'clock, the door swung open and in walked Patrikeev, unannounced, followed by three heavyset men wearing jackboots and uniforms with blue shoulder boards and collar tabs that instantly identified them as *osobisti*. Rodzaevsky and his companions shot to their feet. Without a word, Patrikeev installed himself at the desk, upon which were piled notes and drafts of Rodzaevsky's latest confessions. One of the NKVD officers, a blond major in his late thirties, sat heavily on a chair opposite Patrikeev. The other two officers remained standing, flanking their superior.

After a silence of several seconds, Martinov asked, in a voice that sounded steadier than he felt, how the newcomers wished to be addressed.

"Call us what you want. It makes no difference to us," replied the blond officer with a slightly tipsy shrug. His answers triggered guffaws from the other two *osobisti*. It was apparent that the visitors had been drinking, but their manner portended more than a social call. Goltzev and Migunov stared mutely at the floor. Rodzaevsky, visibly trembling, looked around the room like a cornered animal. The NKVD officers surveyed him with amused smiles. Patrikeev, apparently oblivious to the charged atmosphere, gazed meditatively into the distance.

Martinov felt in no mood for games. He addressed the blond major, asking under what conditions Rodzaevsky was returning to the USSR. The major answered that Marshal Malinovsky had already announced that all émigrés, regardless of their past, could return to the motherland. Unsatisfied, Martinov inquired why the Supreme Soviet did not issue an official amnesty. The major retorted that an amnesty implied the pardon of a criminal, and émigrés were not criminals; moreover émigrés did not need "conditions" for returning home. The door was open for all.

At this point, the major stood up, sauntered over to Rodzaevsky, and began questioning him about Manchukuo, about White Russians living under Japanese rule, about the Kwantung Army and the Asano Brigade. Rodzaevsky mumbled answers in a barely audible voice until Goltzev broke in and spoke on his leader's behalf. The major listened for a while to Goltzev but then turned again to Rodzaevsky. This time, however, he spoke in a polite, almost solicitous voice, inquiring about his career. This line of questioning brought Rodzaevsky to life, and he gradually grew more confident as he described organization work, oratorical achievements, and the editorship of *Nash Put.* At the mention of *Nash Put,* the major interrupted:

"There will be a lot of work for you in the motherland. Our demand for such work is big. You're probably well acquainted with all sorts of social and political affairs in Manchuria?"

"Oh yes, very much so. I know all about them."

"That's especially valuable for us, because right now it's all such a muddle. It's hard to make any headway without having people who really know the situation. You could help us in this, reducing the mistakes in appraising people and in determining their utility and shortcomings."

The major obviously had struck a chord, for Rodzaevsky was beaming in spite of his fear. Martinov took advantage of this congenial interlude to ask about Semenov. The major took the question in stride.

"Oh, Semenov? Of course, I took him by airplane to Chita where he was doing absolutely fine. As a matter of fact, when we occupied Dairen, he came to us. Until I picked him up, he had been left completely at liberty. Why should anything have happened to him? After all, he wanted to come home."

The other two NKVD officers looked at each other and laughed at the thought of anything happening to Semenov.

Still unsatisfied, Martinov started to ask the major about Nechaev's fate, but Patrikeev cut him short, abruptly standing up and announcing that it was late and everyone should get some sleep. Then, without changing his expression, he casually asked the blond NKVD officer: "Major Gusev, will you be ready to fly tomorrow?"

At that instant, the truth exploded noiselessly within the room. The four émigrés stared at each other, speechless at the suddenness with which the future of three of them had been revealed. Pretending not to notice the remark's effects, Gusev nonchalantly answered Patrikeev's question, saying that he would fly if the weather was good. Then, turning to Rodzaevsky, he smiled wryly and added:

"I'm glad that we've talked together so openly tonight. It will help us understand each other better and will contribute to our work against enemies of the Soviet Union."

As soon as Patrikeev and the *osobisti* had left the room, Rodzaevsky dissolved in self-recriminations. He had spoken tactlessly. He had put himself in a bad light. Goltzev and Migunov trooped off to bed, wrapped in their own thoughts. Martinov stayed behind. Alone with the ex-*vozhd,* he urged him not to go back to the USSR. There was still time to relent. He could leave the compound tonight. Konstantin Vladimirovich looked at his friend mournfully:

"No, the door is closed. My family would pay for it. I couldn't let that happen."

Dawn on October 25, 1945 revealed a cloudless sky, perfect weather for flying. Martinov, who had spent the night in the compound, found Rodzaevsky praying in front of a small ikon. The ex-police inspector again tried to persuade him to change his mind about going, saying that this was his last chance to reconsider and perhaps his last chance to stay alive. Rodzaevsky, his face lined with sleeplessness and wet with tears, shook his head. Then he abruptly stood up and embraced Martinov.

At that moment, Major Gusev reappeared, looked disapprovingly at the two men, and asked Rodzaevsky if he had finished packing. It was time to go to the airport. They were flying to Changchun. Gusev handed Rodzaevsky some papers which identified him as a Soviet lieutenant, for the benefit of Chinese immigration officials. Goltzev and Migunov were similarly equipped, as was Senzhin, who showed up that morning after changing his mind a second time and opting to accompany his *vozhd* and *soratniki.*

Asked by Martinov about Rodzaevsky's ultimate destination, Major Gusev replied that from Changchun he would fly to Khabarovsk or Vladivostok for "familiarization with Soviet journalistic matters." After a period of orientation he would be given a newspaper or radio assignment, probably in whatever part of the country he preferred to live.

When they stepped outside, two automobiles were waiting at the entrance to the compound. Rodzaevsky, Goltzev, and Migunov were told to join Gusev in the lead car. Senzhin and two *osobisti* climbed into the second.

Patrikeev said hearty good-byes to the repatriates. Shaking hands with each, he wished them a happy journey and successful careers in the motherland. Martinov stood mutely apart, taking in what he was sure would be his last look at a man who once had predicted that he would return to Russia as a liberator.

As the cars pulled away, Patrikeev waved cheerfully. The diplomat looked pleased with himself. He had good reason to feel a certain professional pride. Without even a hint of force, he had netted another dangerous enemy of the Soviet Union.

Martinov hastily excused himself and returned alone to Tientsin. A few days later, he heard a rumor that Rodzaevsky had been flown from Changchun, via Chita, to Moscow and placed in the Lubyanka with Semenov, Vlasevsky, and Baksheev. Martinov generally discounted rumors emanating from the USSR. But something told him that this one was true.

Trial

On the evening of August 26, 1946, Colonel General Vasily Vasilievich Ulrikh called to order a special session of the Military Collegium of the USSR Supreme Court, At fifty-six, Ulrikh was a veteran executor of Stalin's orders. For twenty years, he had presided over major show trials of traitors and anti-Party groups, including those of Kamenev and Zinoviev, Tukhachevsky, Radek and Pyatakov, and Bukharin. His pudgy face, perpetually contorted with sarcasm during the 1930s, had congealed into an impish grin that uninitiated observers mistook for good humor. Albeit eventful, Ulrikh's judicial career had been devoted to dispatching Communists: old Bolsheviks, Red Army generals, and other internal enemies. A few months earlier, to be sure, he had processed some Poles for resisting liberation. But now he and his colleagues faced a novel set of criminals: bona fide anti-Communists, or at least ex-anti-Communists. *Pravda* labeled them "leaders of anti-Soviet White Guard organizations and Japanese spies."

That evening, and for the next three days, the small courtroom was filled to capacity with privileged spectators who had come to see an extraordinary and unusual trial. Aside from Soviet and foreign news correspondents, there were dozens of bemedaled generals and *apparatchiki.* Their attention focused on eight pale, shabbily dressed men seated in two rows of chairs ringed by elite guards with fixed bayonets. The defendants ranged in age from thirty-five to seventy-three. Some were almost legendary figures. Others nobody recognized. State Prosecutor Lieutenant General A. P. Vavilov referred to them as "Semenovites," but only three fell into that category: the ataman himself and two deputies, Lieutenant General Alexei Proklovich Baksheev and Major General Lev Filippovich Vlasevsky. Of the remaining five, two were self-proclaimed fascists: Konstantin Vladimirovich Rodzaevsky, *vozhd* of the Russian Fascist Union, and his secretary, Lev Pavlovich Okhotin. Boris Nikolaevich Shepunov, a monarchist mafioso from eastern Manchuria, had been Rodzaevsky's mortal enemy since 1940, when he had engineered the execution of twenty-four RFS *soratniki* in Mutanchiang. Ivan Adrianovich Mikhailov, former minister of finance in Admiral Kolchak's Omsk government (1919), had been an adviser to Japanese Military Intelligence in Manchuria. Finally, Prince Nikolai Alexandrovich Ukhtomsky, a cavalry officer who had fought the Bolsheviks with spectacular success at Kazan during the Civil War, had since been a roving newspaper reporter in Europe and East Asia.

One by one, all eight defendants pleaded guilty to anti-Soviet crimes; espionage, sabotage, terrorism, and armed struggle against the Soviet state. To a man, they confessed to being Japanese spies. Some volunteered that they had also acted as German agents.

Semenov, star of the trial, took the witness stand first. His broad head now fringed with gray hair, his proverbial handlebar mustache turned white, the ataman told the court what it wanted to hear. He recalled how before World War I he had led Cossack cavalry in saber charges against helpless strikers, how in 1917 he had attempted to assassinate Lenin in Petrograd, how with Japanese support during the Civil War he had raised an army of fifty thousand which burned villages and shot suspected Bolsheviks throughout Trans-Baikalia. Moving to more recent crimes, he testified how Japan had offered him 20 million yen to lead an uprising within the USSR (he had turned it down as too little). During World War II, he had established spy schools and had plotted with the Kwantung Army to seize Asiatic Russia. He concluded by expressing pleasure at the Soviet victory over Germany.

Baksheev and Vlasevsky testified in much the same vein. Baksheev pushed back his anti-Soviet crimes to 1906, when he had used violence to suppress revolutionaries in Harbin. Both men admitted to forming White Guard units. Shepunov confessed to the court-prescribed crimes, but not to those crimes against fellow émigrés. Mikhailov told how he had assisted the Japanese in sending spies into the USSR on the eve of a projected Japanese invasion of Siberia in 1941.

Prince Ukhtomsky made the most eager witness, volubly describing how he "manufactured anti-Soviet rumors" for German and Japanese intelligence agencies. Not satisfied with the defendant's implicating only two employers (and perhaps with an eye on the Anglo-Americans), Ulrikh interrupted Ukhtomsky's testimony with a parenthetical comment that no one in the courtroom could fail to appreciate:

"You of course received money from other secret services besides the Japanese and German, but we are interested only in the Japanese and German—for now."

The prince nodded penitently, then added, as reporters scribbled in their notebooks:

"The happiest day of my life was the day I was arrested by the Soviet authorities in Dairen."

Rodzaevsky at thirty-nine and Okhotin at thirty-five were by far the youngest defendants, both being too young to have taken part in the Civil War. But Rodzaevsky made up for this shortcoming by the intensity of his anti-Soviet activities in more recent years. He confessed to having become a Japanese spy upon entering Manchuria in 1925 at the age of eighteen, and described the RFO as intimately linked with Generals Araki Sadao and Koiso Kuniaki. Calling himself an "ideological fascist," the ex-*vozhd* described the party's uniforms, swastika emblems, songs, and salutes. He told the court how he had participated in the Manchurian Incident, staged border incidents, and operated a spy school. He detailed how *Nash Put* and *Natsiya* had vilified the USSR and announced that he had served Germany as well as Japan. However, he said nothing about his letters to Stalin and Malinovsky, let alone about regarding Stalin as the greatest Russian fascist. He did, however, describe Anastase Vonsiatsky as an American collaborator, without mentioning the bitterness of their association.

Lest the court or the spectators think that the accused were exaggerating their own crimes, State Prosecutor Vavilov produced seven ranking Kwantung Army officers as witnesses, notably Major General Akikusa Shun, who confirmed that Rodzaevsky had been a "very active Japanese agent."

On August 29, Assistant State Prosecutor Colonel of Justice Kulchitsky summed up the prosecution's case. Defense counsel then spoke for the first time, conceding the guilt of the accused but asking that sentences be mitigated in view of their willingness to confess their crimes. Each defendant then said a few words. All reaffirmed their guilt. Only Semenov asked for clemency.

After deliberating with his colleagues, Ulrikh announced the verdicts. All defendants were found guilty of violating multiple sections of Article 58 of the Criminal Code of the RSFSR (Russian Republic). Semenov, "a most vicious enemy of the Soviet people," was condemned to death by hanging, with confiscation of his entire property. Rodzaevsky, Baksheev, Vlasevsky, Shepunov, and Mikhailov were sentenced to be shot, with confiscation of their entire property. Prince Ukhtomsky and Okhotin, "in consideration of their comparatively lesser part in anti-Soviet activities," were sentenced respectively to serve twenty and fifteen years at hard labor, with confiscation of their entire property.

On August 30, 1946, Konstantin Rodzaevsky finally tasted "the great tasks that lie ahead." Together with five codefendants, including two rivals and a bitter personal enemy, he was executed in a Lubyanka cellar, just a few hundred yards away from the headquarters of his last hero, his true *vozhd,* Josef Stalin.

CHAPTER XX

Transmutation

Castles in the air cost a vast deal to keep up.
—EDWARD GEORGE BULWER-LYTTON

The Russian fascist movement died well before the end of World War II, liquidated by the Gestapo in Germany, suppressed by the Japanese in Manchuria, and hounded out of existence by an ambitious prosecutor in the United States. Branches in the Middle East, Australia, and South America quickly withered for lack of sustenance and direction. A few prominent Russian fascists—Konstantin Rodzaevsky, Alexander Bolotov, and presumably Boris Tedli—met violent ends. Most *soratniki* and one *vozhd,* however, continued to live and even thrive in the postwar world. Their experiences offer eloquent testimony to human resilience and adaptability in the face of life's most improbable vicissitudes.

Homecoming

In 1937, Anastase Vonsiatsky had remarked to an FBI agent interviewing him at Nineteenth Hole that after the National Revolution had toppled the Soviet regime, he would probably not stay in Russia long but come back to Thompson and play golf. Fate met Alex halfway, denying him the National Revolution but granting him, in the end, Thompson and the Quinnatisset links.

Although his five-year sentence at Springfield was to have run until June 21, 1947, Vonsiatsky won a conditional release for good behavior on February 26, 1946. A final entry in his prison file noted that during three years and seven months under observation, the patient had shown no signs of paranoia or other psychological disorders. His afflictions were physical: fibrosis of the lung, influenza, in-

355

fected gums, and (in his own opinion) long hair. Overall, he had made an "excellent adjustment" during his confinement.

On the day of Vonsiatsky's discharge, the warden handed him a train ticket and offered some parting advice. Being on parole, Vonsiatsky should observe certain rules. He was not to leave the state of Connecticut. He was to report regularly to a parole officer. He must refrain from political activities. All three strictures were applicable until the natural expiration of his term. The last restriction was hardly necessary. Soviet military victories had disabused Alex of any illusions about a National Revolution and, at least for the time being, dulled his taste for politics.

Two days later, Alex arrived at the Union Station in Providence. Dressed in a loose-fitting tan suit, he looked thinner and older. The pallor and hollowness of his cheeks contrasted sharply with their pre-war ruddy amplitude. He smiled wanly as Marion and Natasha rushed toward him along the station platform. After tearful embraces, they walked arm in arm over to the Biltmore Hotel for a hot meal. A Providence *Evening Bulletin* reporter tagged along, asking Anastase about his plans. "I plan to stay on my estate and mind my own business," replied the count wearily. Clearly this was not the same character whom reporters remembered.

After a few days of rest at Nineteenth Hole, Anastase began to regain some of his old zest. One of his first projects was to collect newspaper clippings about his release from prison.

Alex still faced a legal problem with potentially serious overtones. In 1942, Connecticut District Attorney Joseph Cooney had filed a petition with the U.S. Circuit Court at Hartford to strip Vonsiatsky of his American citizenship. W. Arthur Countryman, an attorney retained by Marion, had pleaded with the court that the petition not be granted. The case was still under consideration by Federal Judge Carroll C. Hincks when Vonsiatsky was released on parole. Only on April 3, 1946, the day that Hincks fully ruled in favor of Vonsiatsky, could Alex breathe freely, knowing that he no longer ran a risk of being deported to the USSR and sharing the fate of Shkuro, Semenov, and Rodzaevsky.

Other than being home again and retaining his citizenship, Vonsiatsky had little to be happy about. He found himself ostracized in Thompson and Putnam. Even onetime cronies shunned him, ducking his invitations to play golf. The count's solitary figure became a common sight on the Quinnatisset links. Aside from Marion, Natasha, and Lev Beck, only his old barber Orlando did not let disgrace come between friendship. But Orlando's shop was in Providence and thus off limits for the time being.

Vonsiatsky greeted the expiration of his term on June 21, 1947, like a caged wild bird suddenly facing open air. He flew first to Hollywood, then to San Francisco. Whether or not the mysterious "Madame Takita" awaited him in California is not known, but the count's pent-up energies, denied a political outlet, soon flowed into amatory channels. Interviewed in San Francisco for the *Novoye Russkoye Slovo,* Alex sighed "I bore the cross for Russian émigrés." Left unsaid was how Marion had borne—and was continuing to bear—the cross for Alex while he played Russian roué.

Fact and legend blend inextricably in the stories people in Thompson still tell about Voniatsky. After World War II, a new variety of Vonsiatskiana materialized, depicting the count as a sexual rather than a fascist threat to American security. When the Howe-Marot School for Girls closed down shortly after the war, apparently as a result of a crippling fire, local gossip ascribed it to the count's satyric depredations. People whispered about how Alex ran off with loose women and then wrote Marion saying, "Send me money and I'll come home," or how he bedded tarts in New York hotels and sent Marion the bills. There was talk, too, that Marion not only did not object to such promiscuity but actually paid the bills, provided her husband a cottage for local trysts, and supported his illegitimate offspring. No doubt, most of these stories were vaporous discharges from over-wrought imaginations. Nevertheless, even discounting the more extravagant scenarios, Anastase continued to show an unflagging interest in the fair sex. And Marion, in her seventies, could provide him with little that he was looking for except money and understanding.

Early in 1948, Anastase finally found a woman whose unpredictable passion matched his own. He met her not in New York or San Francisco, but in a city whose name alone surely made his heart beat faster—St. Petersburg.

Florida Twilight

Late in 1947, Lev and Natasha Mamedov closed down the Russian Bear and moved to St. Petersburg Florida. Both were attracted by the climate and, as Natasha admitted, by the name. While visiting the Mamedovs early in 1948, Alex encountered a restaurant hostess from North Carolina named Edith Priscilla Royster. Priscilla, five feet seven inches tall, and 133 pounds, was a well-endowed beauty with auburn hair and gray eyes. The difference in their ages (she was twenty-four, he was just short of fifty) exceeded that between Alex and Marion but did not prevent their acquaintance from blossoming into intimacy. He nicknamed her "Sweetsky." She called him—probably in all innocence—"Natsiya."

That autumn, Alex brought Priscilla north and lodged her not far from Nineteenth Hole at Webster, Massachusetts (the scene of Fritz Kuhn's 1939 "putsch"). Before long, Thompson tongues were wagging about "that redhead from Webster," but Marion maintained a stiff upper lip. Perhaps she savored the irony that both her first and second husbands had taken mistresses named Priscilla.

The eternal triangle lost its geographical cohesiveness late in 1949 when Priscilla discovered that she was pregnant. Alex promptly moved her back to St. Petersburg, where, on July 2, 1950, she gave birth to a boy: Andre Anastase Vonsiatsky. Little Andre inherited more than his grandfather's first name. His forehead bore a birthmark where, Alex said, Colonel Andrei Nikolaevich had been shot forty years earlier.

Andre's arrival constituted grounds for divorce and may have complicated Alex's relationship with Marion. Whether a legal separation ever took place is a question obscured by conflicting evidence. John Wrightson Ream, Marion's nephew, has claimed that his aunt's divorce from Anastase "became effective" on May 22, 1952. Yet Irving Myron, a Putnam attorney who handled many of Marion's legal affairs, asserts that no divorce ever took place. Myron's opinion was substantiated by a former domestic servant at Nineteenth Hole and by a Thompson resident who knew both Anastase and Marion well.

It is known that Priscilla did eventually take Alex's surname, although it is not at all clear whether they in fact ever married. Had Alex wedded Priscilla without divorcing Marion, he could well have been plagued by visions of Lyuba Muromsky resurfacing to sue him not just for bigamy but for full-scale polygamy.

Legal niceties aside, Vonsiatsky continued to feel a deep affection for both Marion and Priscilla throughout the remainder of his life. Marion characteristically refused to let the presence of another woman diminish her own attachment to the charming Russian she had rescued from the Folies Bergères. And she adored little Andre. Whenever Anastase and his son came to Nineteenth Hole during the 1950s and early 1960s (their visits appear to have been regular and frequent), they always received a warm welcome from "Aunt Marion."

Although he spent his twilight years in a city known as a mecca for the elderly, Alex was anything but sedentary. He always had some project in the works and was ever vigilant for any opportunity to make a *grande geste*. In 1949, he garnered publicity by challenging the professional cardplayer Oswald Jacoby to a $5,000 canasta match (it never took place). Two years later, he was written up in the St. Petersburg *Independent* for having entertained Prince and Princess Dadiani, Georgian royalty related to Grand Duchess Leonida Bagration, wife of tsarist pretender Grand Duke Vladimir (son of the late St. Briac tsar, Grand Duke Cyril). In 1956, standing on a pier, Vonsiatsky lectured at the crew of a docked Soviet vessel. Asked by the St. Petersburg *Independent* whether he thought that he was making any impression, Alex showed that he still retained his old touch: "They pretend not to listen, but I've seen crewmen applaud me silently through the portholes."

In 1953, Vonsiatsky unveiled his most ambitious postwar enterprise: The Tsar Nicholas II Museum of St. Petersburg. "Museum" sounded a bit grandiose for a few mementos from Nineteenth Hole's Military Room exhibited in a small house on 5th Avenue North, but Vonsiatsky was never one to deny himself a little exaggeration. The museum's opening was timed to coincide with the two hundred and fiftieth anniversary of the founding of St. Petersburg by Tsar Peter the Great, and to Alex's delight, the local press gave the affair good coverage. In the place of honor hung a portrait of Nicholas II, which purportedly had once graced the walls of the Imperial Russian Embassy in Paris. Also displayed were papier-mâché regimental epaulettes cut out and painted in their original colors, portraits of aristocrats and generals, and a framed letter from the last tsar to his military cadets. Aligned on racks stood forty-five antiquated Remington and Westinghouse rifles, the same weapons that had decorated the Military Room at Nineteenth Hole two decades earlier.

Vonsiatsky also took up the pen in St. Petersburg. A voracious reader of anything about Russia, he contributed articles on historical and religious subjects to émigré newspapers and journals such as

Novaya Zarya, Nashe Vremya, and *Bich* ("Whip"). Occasionally, his letters, including one comparing the NKVD to the Gestapo, were published in the St. Petersburg *Independent.* Now an ardent monarchist, Vonsiatsky never alluded to having once been a self-proclaimed fascist *vozhd.*

In 1960, Anastase distilled a number of his reminiscences in a book entitled *Rasplata* ("Retribution") which he had published in São Paulo. A good part of *Rasplata* was devoted to cataloguing those individuals and groups who had undermined the anti-Soviet cause between the wars. One of these was the Japanese government. By treating the White Russians in Manchuria so callously, Vonsiatsky claimed, Japan had deprived herself of valuable human resources.

Rasplata's principal targets, however, were Franklin D. Roosevelt and Thomas J. Dodd. Vonsiatsky bluntly called Roosevelt a Communist.* Why else would the late President have done so much for Stalin? Dodd aroused even stronger passions, for by 1960 the onetime prosecutor had become a United States senator from Connecticut with a reputation as a vociferous anti-Communist who lectured to right-wing groups and incessantly inveighed against the Soviet Union. On July 17, 1959, Dodd had introduced a resolution in the Senate calling the Russian people "enslaved" and urging American support for separatist movements within the USSR. This pronouncement, and Dodd's anticommunism in general, struck Vonsiatsky as opportunistic posturing. In *Rasplata,* he asked why Dodd had said nothing in 1940 when Stalin had absorbed the Baltic republics. Why did Dodd, who had so assiduously prosecuted anti-Communists during the Roosevelt administration, then parrot Joseph McCarthy in the 1950s? Alex answered his own question: Political ambition, not principles, determined Dodd's behavior. Vonsiatsky never forgave Dodd, not just for sending him to prison, but for using him for self-advancement.

However much Russia preoccupied Vonsiatsky in public, his private life centered around family and mundane pleasures. A sign hung on the wall of his Park Street North home: "We will not talk politics or religion in this house." Under that banner, Alex basked in the warm companionship of Lev and Natasha Mamedov. His love for little Andre knew no bounds. Having his own son filled him with pride. Lev and Natasha also doted on Andre, whose presence filled

---

* So strong were Vonsiatsky's feelings about Roosevelt that he refused to use dimes that bore the President's cameo.

a vacuum created by their own son's death in the RAF in 1941. Vonsiatsky was with Andre almost constantly, for Priscilla, a restless spirit, spent little time at home. Father and son slept in the same room, shared the same friends, and built up a fund of common enthusiasms. When Andre wanted his father to come to bed, Anastase would feign compliance and pretend to go to sleep. Then, as soon as the boy had dozed off, he would tiptoe out of the bedroom, install himself behind a desk on the porch, and write articles or paste newspaper clippings about himself in albums.* On July 2, 1961, Andre's eleventh birthday, his father gave him a .22-caliber rifle, a bottle of whiskey, and a carton of cigarettes, and told his son that it was time to sample them all—under supervision—so as not to become addicted to any.

As with millions of other Americans, television made inroads into Vonsiatsky's leisure time during the 1950s. He detested war movies, which brought back painful memories of the Russian Civil War, and baseball, which he had been obliged to listen to at Springfield. Football, however, never relinquished its hold on him. Even Andre, otherwise indulged, was sternly instructed never to pass before a TV screen during a football game except on all fours. Alex followed his alma mater's (Brown University) gridiron forays with the same old enthusiasm, but goalpost trophies no longer interested him. Gina Lollobrigida entranced Vonsiatsky almost as much as football. When she appeared with Tony Curtis and Burt Lancaster in *Trapeze*, he practically commuted to the theater.

Anastase continued to see Marion, either at Nineteenth Hole or at her winter home in Tucson at 250 Cottonwood Boulevard (where she spent more and more time after her eightieth birthday in 1957). Crippled by arthritis and practically deaf, Marion was cared for by several servants. Although neither the Ream family nor most of its employees seem to have approved Vonsiatsky's visits, Marion apparently continued to hold Alex in her affections.

Did pecuniary considerations figure in Anastase's sustained attach-

---

* Vonsiatsky had accumulated an extensive collection of clippings about himself, which he arranged chronologically and pasted into twenty-eight bound volumes of approximately 110 pages each. The clippings date from 1910 (Warsaw papers announcing his father's assassination) and proceed through "Memoirs of a Monarchist," marriage to Marion, Lyuba Muromsky's bigamy suit, proletarian idylls in Pennsylvania, speeding tickets, Romanov visits, world travels, VFO and VNRP activities, Thompson follies, assorted Vonsiatskiana, the Hartford indictment, imprisonment, release, and postwar activities. Newspapers from around the United States and the world are represented, but there are no clippings from *Fashist*, *Nash Put*, or *Natsiya*.

ment to Marion? There is no doubt but that he felt deep affection for the woman who for upward of forty years had been his faithful spouse and supporter. Yet Alex did not let his love for Marion prevent him from asking her for money. In a letter dated March 22, 1960, Anastase addressed Marion as "My beloved, I press you to my heart," and went on to say that he needed funds to take care of Andre's flu infection. Marion does not seem to have refused these requests. To do so would have been out of character. Moreover, her own income easily permitted such disbursements.*

As Marion grew older and more frail, Anastase had reason to give thought to inheritance. Most of her income apparently came from trusts, but Marion owned a substantial fortune in her own right.** In 1958, Marion drew up a will in which she bequeathed $5,000 to the Mamedovs and created a $12,000 trust for Andre, but the will contained no bequest for Anastase. However, on April 10, 1963 (some say after Alex visited her in Arizona), she had a codicil to the 1958 will prepared, leaving Vonsiatsky a bequest of $25,000.

Death came to Marion in Tucson on November 11, 1963. She was eighty-six. Among her papers was an unsigned Chemical Bank New York Trust Company check for $222.49 dated June 12, 1963, made out to the Hilton Credit Corporation. The amount was exactly one half the sum for which the Hilton Corporation was about to sue Alex—for unpaid debts incurred by Priscilla Vonsiatsky on a Carte Blanche credit card.

Marion's remains were brought from Tucson to Putnam and taken to the West Thompson Cemetery for interment in the Vonsiatsky mausoleum. Alex, Lev, and Natasha came up from St. Petersburg for the funeral. As "Mama's" coffin was gently carried into the crypt and slid into place opposite the coffin of Donat Kunle, the count wept unabashedly.

On April 24, 1964, Marion's possessions were auctioned off at Nineteenth Hole. Alex sat alone and unnoticed among the bidders,

---

* According to statements from Ream, Wrightson & Company discovered beneath the chicken coop at Nineteenth Hole and now deposited at Providence College, Marion's income from one account between December 1958 and April 1959 alone totaled $134,327.52.

** Her fortune was not so substantial as many people thought. Probate court records put her estate's worth at $1,258,695. This was comprised of $1,042,949 in securities, $122,150 in real estate, $52,154 in cash, $39,242 in auctioned property, and $2,200 for two automobiles. Property in trusts, of course, was not included. The American press at various times estimated Marion's worth at $7 to $600 million.

watching one memory-filled object after another being sold and carted off: paintings, American colonial furniture, Chinese bronzes, jewelry, and an old airplane propeller clock that had once adorned the Military Room. *Fashist*'s presses were also up for sale, but nobody would take them, so they remained in the hen coop to rust. Alex lacked cash (Marion's pecuniary bequests were not distributed until five months later) or he might have bid. Instead he simply sat and mused, a solitary sixty-five-year-old man contemplating relics of brighter times.

On April 28, four days after the auction, Donat Kunle's remains were removed from the Vonsiatsky mausoleum after having rested there for twenty-three years. An undertaker buried them fifty feet away, marking the spot with a small flat slab that was quickly overgrown by vegetation. Alex, it is said, ordered the eviction, but no one really knows why, although there is no shortage of speculations. The old Quinnatisset Club caretaker, Tom Watson, opined that Kunle was taken out "to make way for Priscilla." But Priscilla was a young, healthy woman in 1964. Besides, the crypt contained slots for six occupants. Could Vonsiatsky, the eternal lady's man, have begrudged Coontz and Mama being in there together, alone and unchaperoned?

Upon receiving his $25,000 share of Marion's estate in September 1964, Alex started making plans for a trip to Europe. He would take Andre along to London, Rome, and Paris. How proud he would be, introducing his son to friends whom he had not seen since the 1930s, such as Prince Nikita and Prince Theodore. Father and son would depart as soon as Andre had finished the spring term at Admiral Farragut Academy.

Vonsiatsky never took that trip. On the evening of February 4, 1965, he invited Lev and Natasha over to his Gulfport cottage on the southern fringe of St. Petersburg, overlooking Tampa Bay. They all consumed a pork roast for dinner. After going to bed, Alex suddenly felt a stabbing pain in his chest. It was a coronary thrombosis. Rushed to Mound Park Hospital, he died at 8:45 A.M. the next day. He was sixty-six. The Florida state death certificate identified him as a "free-lance writer" who had served in the U.S. armed forces from 1920 until 1937. The body was shipped up to Thompson on February 7 and placed in the mausoleum, directly beneath that of Marion.

Vonsiatsky would have been truly disappointed had he known what little notice his death attracted. No obituary appeared in *The New*

York Times. Only the *Connecticut Herald* (Norwalk) announced his passing with an error-filled headline calling to mind the Vonsiatskiana
of the 1930s: WORLD WAR II SPY DIES AT HIS HOME IN THOMPSON.

Alex's death was soon followed by that of most of his household.
Lev Mamedov suffered a fatal heart attack on February 12, 1966.
Priscilla succumbed to pancreatitis on March 25, 1966, joining Marion
and Alex in the Vonsiatsky mausoleum. Natasha died of heart failure
on September 9, 1968.

Left alone, Andre was placed in the care of foster parents. From
his father he inherited several mementos: a wooden swastika shield,
a framed portrait of Nicholas II, twenty-eight volumes of newspaper
clippings, and a diary.* Andre discovered the diary in a St. Petersburg
bank safety deposit box. Upon opening it, he saw written across the
front page: *"La Vie en Rose, La Vie en Rouge."* Andre also found a
note in his father's hand instructing him to destroy the diary. He
did.

Where Are They Now?

Rodzaevsky was shot in 1946, and Vonsiatsky succumbed to a
coronary in 1965, but what about their followers, patrons, and friends?
Ex-*soratniki* have understandably covered their tracks and are hard
to find.

Most of Rodzaevsky's followers in the Far East returned voluntarily
or involuntarily to the Soviet Union. Lev Okhotin died in 1948 after
serving two years of a fifteen-year term. Mikhail Matkovsky left Manchuria in 1946 and has not been seen or heard of since. Matkovsky's
associates all received prison terms. Sergei Razhev and Vladimir Kibardin vanished into a labor camp in the Khabarovsk territory after
being sentenced under Article 58. After returning to the motherland
aboard the Soviet repatriation ship *Gogol* in November 1947, Boris
Rumiantsev and Gennady Taradanov also headed for camps. Taradanov, however, was released in 1949 in order to contribute his journalistic talents to *Golos Rodini* ("Voice of the Motherland"), a Soviet magazine aimed at émigrés who still remained abroad. Vladimir Migunov,
a bitter anti-Semite who followed Rodzaevsky back to the USSR,

---

* This may have been the diary that Anastase told a reporter in 1939 that he
was planning to have published posthumously.

wound up sharing GULAG barracks with the former head of Harbin's Jewish community, Dr. Abraham Yosifovich Kaufman.

A handful of *soratniki* managed, after many vicissitudes, to reach the United States. *Nash Put* reporter Iliodor Karnaukh and RFS trooper Anatoly Skripkin live in San Francisco. Party poet Nikolai Petlin moved to Tokyo in 1943 and worked for the Japanese as an announcer for Russian language broadcasts. After the war, Petlin served as an interpreter for the U.S. Army and from 1950 until 1963 managed a branch of a shipping firm on Okinawa. In 1963, Nikolai (now Nicholas) and his wife, the former Mrs. Rodzaevsky, settled in San Francisco, where they still live.

Of the handful of European RFS *soratniki*, all are either dead or untraceable. Boris Tedli was heard from no more after his arrest by the Gestapo in 1942. Tedli's associates were rounded up as Soviet spies at the same time and presumably were also executed. Mikhail Mikhailovich Grott was last heard from in 1941 in Königsberg, East Prussia. If still alive, it is doubtful that he is there.

Rodzaevsky's family is divided between the United States and the Soviet Union. His younger brother, Vladimir Vladimirovich, returned to the USSR in 1945, was briefly interned (despite his having taken no part in the fascist movement), and today is approaching retirement from his position in a cosmetics factory. His sister, Nadezhda, reportedly still lives near Moscow.

Rodzaevsky's second wife, Neonilla, came to the United States with her two children after a number of vicissitudes. When Konstantin Vladimirovich fled from Harbin on August 13, 1945, she was left alone with little Olga and Vladimir. She remained there until 1952, protecting herself and her children by reverting to her maiden name: Yalisheva. She not only lived through the Soviet occupation, which lasted until April 1946, but also the Chinese Civil War, which raged around Harbin in 1946 and 1947, as the Nationalists tried unsuccessfully to seize the Sungari's north bank from the Communists. In 1952, Neonilla managed to secure emigration papers to Brazil. After ten years in South America, she and the children, by then young adults, moved to San Francisco and acquired American citizenship. Once in the United States, they felt safe enough to go again by the name Rodzaevsky. Neonilla operated a Russian restaurant called The Opera on Hayes Street near the Opera House. In 1974, she left San Francisco and founded another restaurant, Cossack, in Sacramento. Olga and Vladimir still live in San Francisco.

Of Vonsiatsky's *soratniki,* only Reverend Alexander Tzuglevich can be accounted for. Critically ill in 1977, Tzuglevich was clinging to life in a Manhattan nursing home. Other VNRP lieutenants who might still be alive (Semens, Vantz, Novozhilov, Doombadze, Savin, Gantamoura) are untraceable—and probably grateful to be so.

Vonsiatsky's aristocratic friends nearly all outlived him. Prince Theodore Romanov died at Biarritz in 1968 after a career as an architect. Prince Nikita taught Russian at the U.S. Army Language School in Monterey, California, retired to a Park Avenue apartment, and died at Cannes in 1974. His son, Nikita Nikitivich, who as a boy had written Vonsiatsky how happy he was to become a Russian fascist, instead became a Berkeley-trained Russian historian and coauthor (with Robert Payne) of a popular biography of Ivan the Terrible published in 1975. Prince Vasily, the youngest of Grand Duke Alexander's sons, resides in San Francisco.

Andre Anastase Vonsiatsky grew up into a tall, handsome young man with a striking facial resemblance to his father. He graduated from the University of South Florida in 1976, married, and went on to do graduate work at Wake Forest University.

Marion's brothers are all deceased. Robert Clarke Ream passed away in 1957, leaving his son John Wrightson Ream to act as executor of Marion's will. Louis Marshall Ream died in 1970.

Death has also decimated the count's Thompson cronies. George Connell, Richard McCauley, Steve Roshak, James Bakker, and David Sherry are all gone. Their tombstones, like Kunle's, dot the grass around the Vonsiatsky mausoleum. Norman Watson, the *vozhd*'s former secretary, now lives in Hartford, a retired insurance salesman. Connecticut State Police officers Ross Urquhart and Elton Nolan are also retired. Watson, Urquhart, and Nolan will probably never forget being cross-examined by Thomas Dodd at the grand jury hearing on Vonsiatsky in 1942. Even after the war, Dodd used Urquhart's friendship with Vonsiatsky for political ammunition, attacking Connecticut State Police Commissioner Edward J. Hickey in 1949 for failing to discipline his subordinate for borrowing money from a fascist.

Dodd, however, reaped his own crop of scandal. In January 1966, citing documents given them by Dodd's aides, columnists Drew Pearson and Jack Anderson charged the U.S. senator from Connecticut with using campaign funds for private purposes, double-billing the government, accepting questionable payments from corporations, and using a European junket* to perform favors for Julius Klein, a West German public relations agent. On June 23, 1967, after an investigation by the Senate Ethics Committee, the United States Senate voted 92–4 to censure Dodd, a condemnation visited upon only five senators in the nation's history. Vonsiatsky did not live to witness the disgrace of his nemesis, but he probably would have felt a pang of sympathy. In 1971 Thomas Dodd died, a broken man.

What has happened to Harbin, one of the rival centers of the Russian fascist movement? In 1973, fewer than one hundred White Russians remained in Harbin out of a 1945 population of 50,000. About half returned to the USSR, and the rest emigrated to Australia and Brazil, leaving only those who were too frail to travel or who preferred to live out their days along the Sungari River. There are still physical vestiges of Russian influence: the green-domed Sabul Orthodox Cathedral (now used to store furniture), wooden houses with ornately carved eaves, cobblestone streets, and borscht on a local hotel's menu. A number of Russian buildings, including churches, have reportedly been destroyed in the wake of deteriorating Sino-Soviet relations. According to one unverified account, Harbin's Russian cemetery, which once separated Pristan and Novy Gorod, was plowed under by bulldozers and turned into a park. The human and physical ingredients that once made Harbin one of the most colorful spots in Asia are no more. Harbin today is a drab industrial center. But one element remains unchanged since the 1930s: the looming proximity of Soviet power.

On the opposite side of the world, continuity and change sublimely intermingle in Windham County. Interstate Route 52, a four-lane highway destined to link the Connecticut and Massachusetts turnpikes, runs up a gently sloping valley between Putnam and Thompson. Perhaps because it has no direct access to Route 52, Thompson is still a quiet New England village, possibly quieter now that Vonsiatsky is no longer around. The Reams are also gone, but a Dodd, Thomas' son Christopher, represents Putnam and Thompson in Congress.

---

* The official business on which Dodd visited Germany in April 1964 was to interview a Soviet defector, convicted murderer, and self-confessed ex-member of a KGB émigré-killer squad: Bogdan N. Stashynsky.

What used to be the Russian Bear is now an empty, run-down homestead. Weeds choke the once immaculate rose garden, and poison ivy nestles around the handsome stone walls. Architectural accretions reveal that the property has changed hands several times since Lev and Natasha closed down the restaurant in 1947. The Russian Bear's most recent incarnations have been as a gift shop and a day camp. Yet here and there, telltale signs recall a grander past. The window shutters still contain the carved-out forms of bears. A wooden placard of a prancing bear turned up under the wreck of a piano in a nearby barn. In 1974, when the property went up for sale, the realtors contacted Andre Vonsiatsky in the hope that he might follow in his uncle's and aunt's footsteps. He did not.

Just up County Home Road, the golf course is now the Quinnatisset Country Club. Across the road, Quinnatisset Farm (Nineteenth Hole) has been subdivided. The central structures have become a lavishly appointed athletic camp for teenagers, called the Koinonia School of Sports. The main farmhouse has been partitioned into rental units. The stone annex looks much as it did in the 1930s, but its interior has been renovated. What used to be the Military Room is now a recreation area. Alex's former office is a bedroom; Kunle's—a bathroom. The converted hen coop which housed printing presses for *Fashist* has been reconverted into a girls' dormitory. An enclosed grassy expanse, around which Lady Astor and other four-legged fascists once cavorted, is now a parking lot. The dairy barn where the count and his guests took potshots at portraits of Stalin and Beria has been transformed into an Olympic-sized indoor swimming pool and gymnasium, complete with showers and lockers.

Amid all the changes, Vonsiatsky's presence lingers on, cropping up in unexpected ways and places. During renovation of the stone annex, workmen tearing out a ceiling were suddenly deluged by ammunition clips, assorted cartridges, and a bayonet. Later, four guano-encrusted crates were unearthed from under the hen coop as it was being remodeled. One crate contained a selection of Marion's private papers. A second crate yielded photographs of Nicholas II and various White military units. A third crate was stuffed with maps of the USSR on which had been drawn colored arrows and circles that looked like invasion routes. The fourth crate consisted of VNRP pamphlets and 78 rpm recordings of Herbert Hoover's acceptance speech of the 1928 Republican presidential nomination, Eleanor Roosevelt talking about ham sandwiches (undated), and a trio of Vonsiatsky, Kunle, and Mamedov singing a russified Horst Wessel song, briskly accompanied by clarinets, muted trombones, and a gamely strummed double bass.

Such discoveries alerted the new owners of Quinnatisset Farm to the unusual background of their property. Yet nothing prepared them for what they found in a derelict wooden trunk buried in a tool shed. As they pried open the lid, their eyes beheld a perfectly preserved nude human body. It took them a few electrified seconds to realize that they were not looking at a cadaver but at a mannequin. Stripped of its perforated greatcoat by the FBI on May 9, 1942, it had been hiding its shame in darkness for thirty years.

A more enduring memorial to the count stands in the West Thompson Cemetery: a solid granite structure shaded by cypress trees. There, surrounded by his cronies, faithfully attended by Kunle, and cradled next to Marion and Priscilla, Anastase Andreivich Vonsiatsky floats in eternity. From a stained glass window at the far end of the crypt, the Virgin Mary and Christ child hover beatifically over a stone inscription that both Moscow and Washington would heartily endorse:

REQUIESCANT IN PACE

Postmortem

Now that the Russian fascist movement has been dead and buried for a generation, it is a good time to take stock of it with the benefit of historical hindsight.

Amid a burgeoning literature about fascism, the Russian variant is conspicuously absent. Does it follow that the Russian fascist experience has little or no significance? Hardly. Russian fascism has been overlooked because of both the apparent lack of written sources and personal constraints among those who knew the subject firsthand. Following the contours of the Russian diaspora, the Russian fascist movement requires a global approach that poses problems not encountered in fascist movements restricted to a single nation's frontiers. Moreover, source materials are geographically dispersed, linguistically diverse, and, in the case of the Soviet archives, inaccessible. Finally, there has been a reluctance among both émigrés and Soviets—obviously for different reasons—to call attention to a fascist mutation of Russian nationalism.

The absence of comprehensive, systematic studies on the Russian fascists* has led to misunderstandings and misrepresentations in both Soviet and Western literature since World War II. Konstantin Rodzaevsky and Anastase Vonsiatsky have been branded creatures of Germany and Japan. This may be partially true in the case of Rodzaevsky and Japan, but is a gross distortion when applied to Vonsiatsky.

Thirty-odd years after World War II, Vonsiatskiana flourishes in the United States almost as much as it did under the magic touch of Alexius Pelypenko in 1942. In a piece of popular nonfiction called

---

* A notable exception is an excellent article by Erwin Oberländer, "The All-Russian Fascist Party," *Journal of Contemporary History,* I (1966), 158–73.

The Battle Against Disloyalty (1951), Nathaniel Weyl improved upon Pelypenko by depicting Vonsiatsky's agents smuggling U.S. military secrets to a Japanese submarine off the coast of Mexico. Spy-buff Ladislas Farago somehow managed to make Vonsiatsky the head of a Nazi-manipulated "global Ukrainian conspiracy" in *The Game of the Foxes,* his 1971 best-seller on German espionage in the United States. Farago implies that Vonsiatsky's "Ukrainian underground group" shared responsibility for forty "mysterious accidents and disasters" occurring throughout the United States between January and December 1941, including an explosion that "shattered" a new naval air base on Japonski Island, Alaska (echoes of Pelypenko?). Even a sober work such as Sheldon Marcus' *Father Coughlin* (1973) labels the count a "Nazi agent" (perhaps because Pelypenko lurks in the footnotes).

Stripped of myths, Rodzaevsky and Vonsiatsky were egoistic dreamers, comic in their posturing, pathetic in their vulnerability, and tragic in their commitment to the impossible. In 1974, Neonilla Yalisheva described her late husband as a patriot. No doubt Rodzaevsky and Vonsiatsky perceived themselves as such. But their patriotism grew out of private visions based upon anachronisms and wishful thinking. Blind to the USSR's ethnic diversity, Rodzaevsky saw only Russians who supposedly shared his own Orthodox faith, his own hatred of internationalism, his own repugnance to class struggle, and his own anti-Semitism. Vonsiatsky assumed that some mystic popular will would well up of its own accord and, with the aid of foreign invaders, sweep away the commissars and enshrine fascist exiles as national leaders. As such scenarios sounded improbable even to fellow émigrés, neither *vozhd* attracted many followers by ideology alone. Rodzaevsky built up a party by playing upon the loneliness, poverty, and restlessness of White Russian youth in Manchuria, and by promising advantages that would supposedly accrue from Japanese patronage. Vonsiatsky recruited a handful of Civil War veterans and hangers-on through a combination of personal flair, nostalgia, and subsidies—mostly subsidies.

Some of the most accurate characterizations of Rodzaevsky and Vonsiatsky have come from fellow Russian émigrés. Nicholas Slobodchikoff, a former Harbin resident and current director of the Museum of Russian Culture in San Francisco, aptly described Rodzaevsky as "vain, gullible, and stupid—but not criminal." If Rodzaevsky's misdirected patriotism is added, such a characterization carries a more authentic ring than such hackneyed labels as "Japanese spy," "bandit," and "murderer," which are commonly found in both Western and Soviet literature.

Prince Alexis Sherbatoff, director of the Russian Nobility Association of America and a friend of Vonsiatsky's, captured Anastase Andreivich's essential nature when he remarked that "Alex would have made a brilliantly successful condottiere in fifteenth-century Italy. He possessed just the right combination of bravura and bluff."

In retrospect, it seems that Vonsiatsky's "bravura and bluff" made some contribution to human happiness by affording others opportunities to indulge in their own fantasies. Where else could the *Daily Worker* have found a more appropriate bogey? Who else could have provided Thomas J. Dodd with a German-Japanese masterspy or Congressman Dickstein with fifty thousand Russian fascists right in the state of Connecticut, enabling both men to rise heroically to America's defense? And who could have so enlivened Putnam and Thompson that old-timers still reminisce wistfully about "the count"?

And yet for all his amusing antics, Vonsiatsky was by no means an entirely sympathetic character. Preoccupied with self-promotion, he showed little consideration for family or friends until relatively late in life after the birth of his son. He never matched and probably did not comprehend Marion's selflessness. Marion remained devoted to him for forty years, uncomplainingly putting up with his social gaffes, political notoriety, financial whims, and multiple infidelities. Without Marion, Alex might have grown old hacking cabs, lugging trunks, or bouncing drunks like thousands of his peers.

However comic or pathetic Rodzaevsky and Vonsiatsky look as quixotic failures, they could well have wrought terrible harm had they been successful in building a Russian fascist state. More than one buffoon has roasted his former audience. How many people lived to regret laughing at the Austrian with a Charlie Chaplin mustache who tried to seize a Munich beer hall? Russian fascists differed not markedly from the Stalinists, Nazis, and Italian *fascisti* who were their contemporaries. Vonsiatsky's showmanship had its counterpart in Mussolini. Rodzaevsky's oratory resembled that of Hitler. Mikhail Grott's anti-Semitic fulminations echoed those of Rosenberg and Streicher. Given an opportunity, Sasha Bolotov could probably have filled in for Himmler or Beria.

Unlike the Nazi and Italian *fascisti*, however, the Russian fascists lacked the external conditions for success. They were not up against a calcified monarchy or a floundering republic but a totalitarian state policed by ubiquitous security organs and guarded by the largest standing army in the world. And Stalin was surely no Hindenburg. Second, being members of a global disapora (like the Jews whom they scorned), the Russian fascists lacked an independent, geographically cohesive base of operations. Rootlessness made them dependent upon foreign governments, notably Germany and Japan. When it became clear that they could not overthrow the Soviet regime without German or Japanese help, the Russian fascists found themselves in an insoluble moral dilemma: They were nationalists pinning their hopes on a foreign invasion of their own homeland. Their predicament ultimately took yet another ironic twist: Russian fascists were destroyed or deactivated by their own patrons.

Was the Russian fascist movement a Soviet front? The Gestapo thought so. The Japanese Military Gendarmerie and Foreign Ministry half agreed. Yet the question, however tantalizing, cannot be answered without access to Soviet archives. It is known that a number of Rodzaevsky's closest lieutenants were Soviet agents. But it is hard to imagine Vonsiatsky operating in that capacity, although he was certainly willing to play bogey in return for free publicity.

If not Soviet agents, both leaders of the Russian fascist movement nevertheless eventually adopted the view that Stalin was the ultimate fascist. Vonsiatsky came to this conclusion in 1939 when he computed that Stalin had killed more Communists than Mussolini, Hitler, and Chiang Kai-shek combined. Rodzaevsky followed suit in 1945, praising Stalin for resurrecting Russian national power through internal regimentation and external expansion.

Therein could lie the Russian fascist movement's significance: that it patterned itself after, and wound up worshiping, its archenemy.

Glossary of Abbreviations
and Selected Terms

BREM *(Biuro po delam Rossiiskikh Emigrantov)*. Bureau of Russian Émigré Affairs. An administrative body created by the Japanese Military Mission in Harbin in 1934 to coordinate and regulate the political, economic, social, and cultural activities of White Russian communities in Manchuria. Headed by a succession of senescent tsarist army officers, BREM contained a number of fascist and fascist sympathizers in key staff positions.

Kempei. Japanese Military Police. Created in 1881 to investigate disciplinary and criminal problems within the armed forces, but the sphere of its activities gradually extended to civilian circles. Particularly active and reputedly ruthless during the 1930s and early 1940s throughout the Japanese Empire and occupied areas. Dissolved in 1945.

Mladorossy. Young Russia movement founded on solidarist principles in Paris by Alexander Lvovich Kazem-Bek around 1930. Moribund after World War II.

NORM *(Natsionalnaya Organizatsiya Russkikh Mushketerov)*. National Organization of Russian Musketeers. A teenage order of storm troopers founded around 1924 by V. S. Barishnikov in Harbin. Cooperated with Russian fascist organizations during the late 1920s and through the 1930s.

NTS *(Natsionalno Trudovoi Soyuz)*. National Toilers' Alliance. A solidarist émigré organization founded by M. A. Georgievsky in 1932. Influential among Russian communities in Yugoslavia and Bulgaria, it had ambivalent relations with Germany during World War II.

RFO *(Rossiiskaya Fashistskaya Organizatsiya)*. Russian Fascist Organization. Founded by students at the Harbin Juridical Institute in 1925 and eventually dominated by Konstantin Rodzaevsky. Became the Russian Fascist Party (RFP) in 1931.

RFP *(Rossiiskaya Fashistskaya Partiya)*. Russian Fascist Party. Established in 1931 as an outgrowth of the Russian Fascist Organization (see above). Based in Harbin, it was briefly—and nominally—led by General Vladimir Kosmin, but Konstantin Rodzaevsky wielded the most influence, particularly when the party opted to collaborate with the Japanese in 1932. Merged

375

with Vonsiatsky's VFO (see below) in 1934 to form the All-Russian Fascist Party (VFP).

RFS *(Rossiisky Fashistsky Soyuz).* Russian Fascist Union. Name adopted by the All-Russian Fascist Party (VFP) in 1938 and retained until the Union's dissolution by the Japanese in 1943.

ROND *(Rossiiskoye Natsionalno-Sotsialisticheskoye Dvizheniye).* Russian National Socialist Movement. An organization of self-proclaimed Russian Nazis established in Berlin in 1933. Led briefly by A. P. Svetozarov and subsequently by "Prince" Bermondt-Avalov. Although slavishly loyal to Hitler, ROND was tolerated only intermittently by the Gestapo and apparently dissolved in the wake of the Nazi-Soviet Pact in 1939.

soratnik. A Russian expression for "comrade," although with somewhat different overtones than *tovarishch,* which has been used in the Soviet Union. Sometimes translated as "brother-in-arms." Employed by Russian fascists throughout the world to refer to each other, unless they happened to be members of rival parties.

Tokumu Kikan. "Special Services Organ." A field unit conducting, as its title implies, a variety of secret assignments ranging from intelligence to sabotage. Responsible to the Second Department (Intelligence) of the Imperial Japanese Army's General Staff. In August 1940, absorbed into Kwantung Army Intelligence.

VFO *(Vserossiiskaya Fashistskaya Organizatsiya).* All-Russian Fascist Organization. Created by Anastase Vonsiatsky in Thompson, Connecticut, in 1933, the VFO merged with Rodzaevsky's RFP to form the All-Russian Fascist Party (VFP) in 1934.

VFP *(Vserossiiskaya Fashistskaya Partiya).* All-Russian Fascist Party. Created by the merger of Vonsiatsky's VFO and Rodzaevsky's RFP in 1934. After the Vonsiatsky-Rodzaevsky schism in 1935, Rodzaevsky retained the name for his Harbin-based party until 1938, when it was rechristened Russian Fascist Union (RFS).

VNRP *(Vserossiiskaya Nationalno-Revoliutsionnaya Partiya).* All-Russian National Revolutionary Party. Name of Vonsiatsky's Connecticut-based party from 1935, the year of his expulsion from the VFP, until 1941, when he transferred leadership of the VNRP to Konstantin Steklov in Shanghai. Thereafter, the VNRP lapsed into oblivion.

vozhd. A Russian word that has been translated as "chief," "captain," or "leader" but carries overtones of the German expression *"Führer."* Rodzaevsky and Vonsiatsky both claimed to be *vozhd* of all Russian fascists. During the 1930s, Stalin was periodically called *vozhd* in some of the more fulsome domestic accolades.

Notes

In the interest of space, sources cited in the Notes are given in abbreviated form. For full information on each source, published and archival, see the Bibliography.

The following abbreviations are used throughout the Notes for archival sources:

BFOA   British Foreign Office Archives, Public Record Office, London.
DAI   Records of the Deutsches Ausland-Institut, Stuttgart. National Archives, Washington.
EOT   Records of the Reich Ministry for Occupied Eastern Territories. National Archives, Washington.
GFMA   German Foreign Ministry Archives, Bonn.
GSS   Records of the Reich Leader of the SS and Chief of the German Police. National Archives, Washington.
IMTFE   International Military Tribunal for the Far East, Tokyo. Center for Research Libraries, Chicago.
JAA   Japanese Army Archives, [formerly] Library of Congress, Washington.
JFMA   Japanese Foreign Ministry Archives, Tokyo.
PCA   Providence College Archives, Providence, Rhode Island.
USDJ   United States Department of Justice Archives, National Archives, Washington.
USDS   United States Department of State Archives, National Archives, Washington.
VP   Vonsiatsky Papers, St. Petersburg, Florida.

Foreword

Pages

xvi   Chile and fascism: "Save democracy and Chilean patriots from the fascists!" *Izvestiya*, December 5, 1973.

xvi   Thomas E. Dewey called a "fascist": Stone, *They Also Ran,* 433.
xvi   "external fascism": Manchester *Guardian Weekly,* March 7, 1976.
xvii   "fascism, pure and simple": Honolulu *Advertiser,* July 5, 1975.
xvii   "fascist pig" media: *Time,* June 17, 1974.
xvii   "Red fascism": Jacques de Launay, *Fascisme rouge* (Bruxelles: Editions Montana, 1954).
xvii   "objective fascists": *Time,* May 14, 1973.
xvii   "social fascists": Stalin, *Sochineniya,* VI, 282, cited in Laqueur, *Russia and Germany,* 136; Lyons, *Assignment in Utopia,* 634. For another interesting Soviet use of "social fascism," see Eugen Varga et al., *Sotsial-fashizm* (Moscow: Partizdat, 1932).
xvii   Chinese call Kremlin "social fascists": "Leninism or Social Imperialism," *People's Daily,* April 22, 1970. *Soviet World Outlook,* I (March 15, 1976), 8.
xvii   Stalin as "crypto-fascist": Gregor, *The Fascist Persuasion,* 185.
xvii–xviii My general discussion of the nature of fascism is drawn largely from the papers in S. J. Woolf, ed., *The Nature of Fascism* and from Otto-Ernst Schüddekopf, *Fascism.*
xvii   Stalinist Russia as fascist regime: Gregor, *The Fascist Persuasion,* 184–86. Bertoni, *Il trionfo del Fascismo nell' URSS,* as discussed by Oreste Mosca in *Antieuropa* (1939), 589–98.
xvii   Derzhavin on fascism: Louis Fischer, *The Road to Yalta* (New York: Harper & Row, 1972), 10.
xvii–xviii Ehrenburg on fascism: Arthur Richard, *Modern Quotations* (New York: Dover, 1947), 193.
xviii   Croce on fascism: George L. Mosse, "Fascism and the Intellectuals," in Woolf, *The Nature of Fascism,* 205.
xviii   "a synthesis of the lessons . . .": *Natsiya,* I (April 1932) as quoted by Oberländer, "The All-Russian Fascist Party," 158.
xix   Soviet reluctance to use term "German national socialists": Laqueur, *Russia and Germany,* 23.
xix   "sensitive, delicate subject": Nicholas V. Riasanovsky to author at the annual meeting of the American Association for the Advancement of Slavic Studies, Atlanta, October 9, 1975.
xxii   Notice in New York Russian daily: *Novoye Russkoye Slovo,* February 24–27, 1976.

1. The Russian Diaspora

1   Herzen quotation: Herzen, *Memoirs,* II, 686.
1–2   Russian refugee movements: Simpson, *Refugee Problem,* 62–83. Williams, *Culture in Exile,* 111. Tulsky, *Manchzhuriya,* 19. Volkmann, *Die russische Emigration,* 1, 4–5, 122. Balakshin, *Final v Kitae,* I, 9; II, 10.
2   Ungern-Sternberg: Pozner, *Bloody Baron,* 34–35.
2   Execution of imperial family: Walsh, *Fall of the Russian Empire,* 189.
3   Alexander trying to meet Wilson and Balfour: Alexander, *Always a Grand Duke,* 43–50.
3   George V and Queen Marie kindness to Romanovs: Marie, *Princess in Exile,* 9–18.
3   King Christian X and Empress Dowager Marie: Vorres, *Last Grand Duchess,* 169.
3–4   Romanov expertise on revolutions: Alexander, *Always a Grand Duke,* 108–9.

4   Gentleman and Paris landlord: *Ibid.,* 25–29.
4   Alexander's numismatic collection: *Ibid.,* 58–59.
4   "My former friends . . .": Lobanov-Rostovsky, *Grinding Mill,* 381.
4   Nabokov on two good friends: Nabokov, *Speak, Memory,* 277.
4   "Tragic" titled Russian at soirées: Alexander, *Always a Grand Duke,* 259.
5   "from peasant Socialist to White general": Nabokov, *Speak, Memory,* 262.
5   "I guess you Russians didn't do very much": Lobanov-Rostovsky, *Grinding Mill,* 381.
5   Allied victory parade: Alexander, *Always a Grand Duke,* 65–66.
5   Prince Yusupov: Marie, *Princess in Exile,* 102–5. Alexander, *Always a Grand Duke,* 112–13. *New York Times,* September 28, 1967; March 12, 1970.
6   Grand Duke Dmitry: *New York Times,* March 8, 1942.
6   Cinderella: Alexander, *Always a Grand Duke,* 241.
6   Alexander refusing Lowenstein offer: *Ibid.,* 187.
6   Alexander on lecture circuit: *Ibid.,* 269–86.
6   Marie's embroidery: Marie, *Princess in Exile,* 168 ff.
6   Dmitry selling champagne: *Ibid.,* 158. *New York Times,* March 8, 1942.
7   "Michael Romanoff": *New York Times,* September 2, 1971.
7   "The Angel": *1940 Britannica Book of the Year,* 726.
7   Cossacks in exile: Longworth, *Cossacks,* 315–17. Marie, *Princess in Exile,* 134.
7–8   Iliodor in exile: Massie, *Nicholas and Alexandra,* 526.
8   Colonel to general in Los Angeles: Day, *Russians in Hollywood,* 20–24.
8   Russian women in exile: Abrikossow, *Revelations,* 168, 208. Marie, *Princess in Exile,* 236. Wagatsuma, "Skin Color," 426–27. Kawabata, *Snow Country,* 91.
8–9   Dependence: Alexander, *Always a Grand Duke,* 3–4. Nabokov, *Speak, Memory,* 246, 276–77. Dorfman, "White Russians," 167.
9   Nansen passport holder like a "criminal on parole . . .": Nabokov, *Speak, Memory,* 276.
9   White Russian vulnerability in Far East: Dorfman, "White Russians," 167.
9   Empress Dowager Marie withdrawal: Alexander, *Always a Grand Duke,* 133–34, 209.
10   Paris cafe encounter: *Ibid.,* 70–72.
10–11 Émigré factions: Wraga, "Russian Emigration," 39–46.
11   Émigré hostility to Romanovs: Marie, *Princess in Exile,* 96, 138.
12   "Had Nicholasha advised the Czar . . .": Alexander, *Once a Grand Duke,* 145.
12–13 Cyril and Victoria: Cyril, *My Life,* 168–74, 213ff. Alexander, *Always a Grand Duke,* 145–46.
13   Victoria and NSDAP: Laqueur, *Russia and Germany,* 62, 110–11.
13   1922 "German Day": Maser, *Hitler,* 325–26.
13   Cyril supporters: Williams, *Culture in Exile,* 213–16.
13–14 Cyril at St. Briac: Alexander, *Always a Grand Duke,* 135–44.
14   Doubts about Cyril: Vorres, *Last Grand Duchess,* 171, 182, 239n.
14   Alexander on émigré divisiveness: *Always a Grand Duke,* 69–70.
15   "I don't hope to go back to Russia": Day, *Russians in Hollywood,* 16.

II. Genesis of the Émigré Right in Europe

16   Hitler quote: International Military Tribunal, *Trial of the Major War Criminals Before the International Military Tribunal,* xxxix (Nuremberg, 1949), 371.

16   Union of Russian People: Rogger, "Was There a Russian Fascism?" Rogger, "The Formation of the Russian Right."

17   Purishkevich called first Russian fascist: Laqueur, *Russia and Germany*, 81 ff. Lyubosh, *Russky Fashist, passim.* P. A. Stolypin, Russian premier (1906–11), has also been called the first Russian fascist. See F. T. Goriachkin, *Pervy Russky Fashist: Pyotr Arkadievich Stolypin* (Harbin: Merkury, 1928).

17   Purishkevich as a "tragic clown": Miliukov, *Political Memoirs*, 150.

18–20   Scheubner-Richter: Laqueur, *Russia and Germany*, 52–68, 105–6. Williams, *Culture in Exile*, 164–67, 174–81, 216–20. Volkmann, *Die russische Emigration*, 51–52. Hitler, *Mein Kampf*, xiii.

19–20   Bad Reichenall Congress: Laqueur, *Russia and Germany*, 64. Williams, *Culture in Exile*, 176–81.

20–23   Rosenberg: Laqueur, *Russia and Germany*, 68–79. Williams, *Culture in Exile*, 168–72.

20   Goebbels called Rosenberg "the Reich philosopher": Speer, 125.

22   Vinberg: Laqueur, *Russia and Germany*, 114–18.

22   Rosenberg on Russian émigrés: *Völkischer Beobachter*, April 7, 1923, as cited by Laqueur, *Russia and Germany*, 75.

22   Russians should seek their destiny in Asia: *Mythus des zwanzigsten Jahrhunderts* (Berlin, 1930), 601, as cited by Laqueur, *Russia and Germany*, 73, 335.

23   Schickedanz: Williams, *Culture in Exile*, 168–72. Laqueur, *Russia and Germany*, 60n, 64.

23   Rosenberg-Goebbels rivalry: Williams, *Culture in Exile*, 335–37. Goebbels, *Diaries*, 331, 516.

23   Ukrainians and Nazis: Laqueur, *Russia and Germany*, 156. Williams, *Culture in Exile*, 220.

23–24   Decline of Russian émigré population in Germany: Williams, *Culture in Exile*, 285.

24   Biskupsky "one of the most universally disliked men of the Russian emigration": *Ibid.*, 93.

24–25   Biskupsky character and activities: *Ibid.*, 95, 97–101, 165–66, 175–6, 212, 347–50. Laqueur, *Russia and Germany*, 67, 88, 108–9, 112. Volkman, *Die russiche Emigration*, 61–2, 67, 75, 79. Irene Bulazel, interview, January 4, 1974.

25   Biskupsky and Himmler: GSS, T-175, R-58 (October 18, 1935).

25   Russian Auxiliary: Alexandrov, *Journey*, 175–77, 184–85, 393–96.

25–26   ROND: "Georgievsky Report," in BFOA, FO 371, 29531/N802, 34–5. GSS, T-175, R-58 (October 18, 1935). *Sevodnya*, September 19, 1933, in VP, IV, 14.

26   Bermondt-Avalov: Ariadna Delianich, interview, August 28, 1974. Williams, *Culture in Exile*, 91–95, 334. Volkmann, *Die russische Emigration*, 62–74, 90.

26–27   Schwarz-Bostunich: Laqueur, *Russia and Germany*, 122–25.

27   Kaminsky: Dallin, "The Kaminsky Brigade," 249–80.

27–28   Vlasov: Fischer, *Soviet Opposition to Stalin, passim.* Thorwald, *The Illusion, passim.* Strik-Strikfeldt, *Against Stalin and Hitler, passim.*

28   Krasnov: Tschebotarioff, *Russia*, 298–308.

28   Younger generation of émigrés: Wraga, "Russian Emigration," 41–43.

28–29   Italian fascism and youth: Ledeen, *Universal Fascism*, xiii, xviii, 4, 37ff.

29   European intellectuals and fascism: Hamilton, *The Appeal of Fascism, passim.*

29   "Fascism is what China now most needs": Eastman, "Fascism in Kuomintang China," 4.

29   Ethiopian Pacific Movement: *Time,* August 23, 1943.
29   On solidarism: Gins, *Na Putiakh, passim.*
29–30   NTS: U.S., Department of State, "NTS: The Russian Solidarist Movement."
          [Note: sometimes NTS is said to stand for *Narodno-Trudovoi Soyuz* or Popular
          Toilers' Alliance.]
30   Young Russia movement: Williams, *Culture in Exile,* 332–33.
30   Strasser appeal to émigrés: Alexandrov, *Journey,* 174.

III. White Ghettos in China

31   Stalin quote: to Japanese Foreign Minister Matsuoka Yōsuke, April 13, 1941.
          Lensen, *Strange Neutrality,* 19.
31   Solzhenitsyn quote: *GULAG Archipelago,* 143.
31–32   For Siberia in the Russian Civil War, see Simpson, *Refugee Problem,* 78–80.
          Footman, *Civil War in Russia.* Fleming, *Fate of Admiral Kolchak.* Ossendowski,
          Beasts, Men, and Gods, 10–39.
32–33   Semenov: U.S. Senate, *The Deportation of Gregorii Semenov.*
33   Ungern-Sternberg: Pozner, *Bloody Baron,* 105–72. Alioshin, *Asian Odyssey,* 229–
          30.
33   Russians prefer China: Abrikossow, *Revelations,* 294.
33–34   Russian on Yap: Kodama Michiko, interview, September 13, 1977.
35–36   Émigré life in Shanghai: Balakshin, *Final v Kitae,* I, 10, 17, 108, 325–31.
          Lidin, "Russkaya emigratsiya v Shankhae." JAA, T955, F25001. Ilina,
          Vozvrashcheniye, II, 2.
36   Russian girls in Shanghai bars: Abend, *Treaty Ports,* 155.
36   Stanovoi brothers as con men: *China Weekly Review,* April 7, 1934, 233.
36–37   Tientsin and Tsingtao: Balakshin, *Final v Kitae,* I, 235–40. Abend, *My Life
          in China,* 107.
37   "Cradle of conflict": Owen Lattimore, *Manchuria: Cradle of Conflict* (New York:
          Macmillan, 1932).
38   Chang Tso-lin's French chateau: Suleski, "Manchuria under Chang Tso-
          lin," 8.
38   Chang's executions: McAleavy, *Dream of Tartary,* 158–9. Vespa, *Secret Agent
          of Japan,* 17.
38   Chang Tso-lin's Packard: Suleski, "Manchuria under Chang Tso-lin," 8–9.
39   Chang Tso-lin and Russian émigrés: Balakshin, *Final v Kitae,* I, 104, 265.
          China Weekly Review, September 12, 1936. *New York Times,* March 17, 1940.
39   Chang Tsung-ch'ang: Boorman, *Biographical Dictionary of Republican China,*
          I, 123–25.
39   Nechaev Detachment: Balakshin, *Final v Kitae,* I, 266–67.
40   Harbin development: *Dictionnaire Historique et Géographique de la Mandchourie,*
          211–15. *N.Y.K. Official Guide,* 11–16. *Directory and Chronicle for China* (1933),
          492. "White Russians in Manchukuo," 19–21. Arikawa, "Harbin," 53–55.
40–42   Harbin's seven towns: Arikawa, "Harbin," 55–56.
42   Traffic on bridge between Pristan and Novy Gorod: Swift, *Ninety Li a Day,*
          118.
42   Ikon in Harbin Central Railway Station: undated manuscript [April 1976?],
          Lydia Schmüser memoirs.
42   Sunbei: Pernikoff, *"Bushido,"* 120.
42–43   Harbin atmosphere: Olga Bodisco, interview, June 11, 1975. Ivan Toropov-
          sky, interview, June 27, 1975. Nicholas Slobodchikoff, interview, August

27, 1974. Peter Berton, conversation, October 13, 1975. Lydia Schmüser, letters and memoirs, March 10 to May 26, 1976.

43 Cheap pheasant and caviar: Olga Bodisco, interview, June 11, 1975. Lydia Schmüser letter, March 30, 1976.

43 Alcazar Restaurant: Lydia Schmüser, letter to author, May 4, 1976.

43 Putevaya, red light district: Pernikoff, *"Bushido,"* 22.

43–44 Harbin émigré groups: Balakshin, *Final v Kitae*, I, 110–11, 178–79, 184–87. JAA, T955, F25003, JFMA, A 6.5.0.1–2 (June 25, 1937). "Georgievsky Report," in BFOA, FO 371, 29531/N802, 37.

44 Kosmin and Brotherhood of Russian Truth: "Rodzaevsky Affidavit," in IMTFE, Prosecution Document no. 2364, 6.

44 Harbin's counterrevolutionary urgency: Balakshin, *Final v Kitae*, I, 263.

44 Russian refugees blamed Allies for plight: *Literary Digest*, July 28, 1923, 21.

44 Soviet pressure on Chinese to extradite "White Guards": Lensen, *Damned Inheritance*, 125, 128, 150.

44–45 Soviet infiltration of émigré groups: Balakshin, *Final v Kitae*, I, 102–3. Nicholas Petlin, interview, August 29, 1974.

45 "Radishes": Dorfman, "White Russians," 167.

45 Émigré mutual suspicion: Olga Bodisco, interview, June 11, 1975.

45 Harbin smuggling and contraband: Balakshin, *Final v Kitae*, I, 106–7. Olga Bodisco, interview, June 11, 1975.

46 Deaths exceed births: Simpson, *Refugee Problem*, 502, 506.

46 George Hanson's "arsenal": Snow, "Japan Builds," 81.

46 Automatic rifles on golf course: Carr, *Riding the Tiger*, 106–7.

46 Harbiner in Los Angeles: Day, *Russians in Hollywood*, 9.

46 *Hunghutze:* Petro-Pavlovsky, "Manchurian Racketeer." Swift, *Ninety Li a Day*, 208.

46 Kinney and bandits: Edward Tiffany, "Henry W. Kinney: Japan's Barometer in Manchuria." Unpublished M.A. thesis, University of Hawaii, 1974.

46 Chang Tso-lin execution of *hunghutze:* McAleavy, *Dream of Tartary*, 158–59.

47 Émigré poverty, unemployment in Harbin: Simpson, *Refugee Problem*, 502. Pernikoff, *"Bushido,"* 19.

47 Poverty and vulnerability as conditions that made fascism appealing to Harbin émigrés: Nicholas Petlin, interview, August 29, 1974.

iv. The Boy from Blagoveshchensk

48 "Song of Igor" quote: Alexander Porfirevich Borodin, *Le Prince Igor: Paroles russes du compositeur* (New York: M. P. Belaieff, 1960), 175.

48–49 Blagoveshchensk: Gaunt, *Broken Journey*, 209–23. Meakin, *Ribbon of Iron*, 228–36. *Guide to the Great Siberian Railway* (New York, 1900), 411.

49 Rodzaevsky childhood and family: Neonilla [Rodzaevsky] Yalisheva, interview, August 27, 1974. Nicholas Petlin, interview, August 29, 1974. Nicholas Petlin letters to author, October 28, November 8, 1974.

49 Rodzaevsky flight from Blagoveshchensk: his own explanation: Balakshin, *Final v Kitae*, II, 129. Soviet version: *Pravda*, August 28, 1946. Rodzaevsky as OGPU agent: Mutanchiang consular report of February 18, 1943, in JFMA, A 6.5.0.1–2. Pernikoff, *"Bushido,"* 65.

50 Fate of Rodzaevsky's parents: Nicholas Petlin, letters to author, October 28, November 8, 1974. Neonilla Yalisheva, interview, August 27, 1974.

50   Harbin Juridical Institute: Balakshin, *Final v Kitae,* I, 110. Nicholas Slobodchi-
        koff, interview, August 27, 1974.
50   Gins: Gins, *Na Putiakh,* 101 ff. Balakshin, *Final v Kitae,* I, 110. Nicholas Petlin,
        letter, January 10, 1975.
50–51   Nikiforov: Nicholas Petlin, interview, August 29, 1974 and letter, January
        10, 1975. Balakshin, *Final v Kitae,* I, 112. Oberländer, "All-Russian Fascist
        Party," 160.
51   Korablev, Pokrovsky, Rumiantsev and formation of RFO: Nicholas Petlin,
        letter, January 25, 1975. Balakshin, *Final v Kitae,* I, 112. *Natsiya,* February
        1938, 5–6.
51–52   Rodzaevsky physique and character: Nicholas Petlin, interviews on August
        29, 1974 and October 10, 1976, and letter of October 28, 1974. Neonilla
        Yalisheva, interview, August 27, 1974. Lahiri, "Russian Fascists in Harbin."
        Balakshin, *Final v Kitae,* I, 195.
52–53   Matkovsky: Nicholas Petlin, interview, August 29, 1974. Nicholas Slobodchi-
        koff, interview, August 27, 1974. Neonilla Yalisheva, interview, August
        27, 1974. Balakshin, *Final v Kitae,* I, 188–94.
53   *Nashe Trebovaniya: Natsiya,* February 1938, 6.
53   Musketeers: Nicholas Petlin, letter, February 20, 1976.
53   RFO activities: Harbin consular report (June 17, 1935), JFMA, A 6.7.0.1–
        2. *Natsiya,* May 1934, 30. Nicholas Petlin, interview, August 29, 1974,
        and letter, January 22, 1975. Oberländer, "All-Russian Fascist Party," 160–
        61.
53–54   Soviet pressure on Changs regarding "White Guards": Lensen, *Damned Inher-
        itance,* 125, 150.
54   Changs and RFO: Nicholas Petlin, interview, August 29, 1974.
54   Rodzaevsky expulsion from Juridical Institute: Nicholas Petlin, interview,
        August 29, 1974, and letter, January 10, 1975.
54   "I am head of the Russian fascists": anecdote related by Nicholas V. Riasa-
        novsky to author, October 9, 1975. Nicholas Petlin judged this anecdote
        "plausible" in a conversation with the author on October 10, 1976.
54   Rodzaevsky intimidated Institute into granting him a diploma. Pernikoff,
        "Bushido," 144.
55   RFP founding: *Natsiya,* April 1932. Balakshin, *Final v Kitae,* I, 112–13. Nicho-
        las Petlin, letter, January 10, 1975.
56–57   RFP program: Oberländer, "All-Russian Fascist Party," 161–62. Taradanov,
        Azbuka Fashizma, 76–89.
57   Rodzaevsky's views on fascism: Rodzaevsky lecture of September 25, 1932,
        reproduced in *Natsiya,* nos. 3–4 (1932). Taradanov, *Azbuka Fashizma,* 63–
        75.
57–58   Fascist roots in Russian history: Taradanov, *Azbuka Fashizma,* 53. Ivanov,
        "Russky Fashizm," *Natsiya,* January 1936, 4–6. Oberländer, "All-Russian
        Fascist Party," 169, 171–73. According to Nicholas Petlin (interview, Au-
        gust 29, 1974), Anatoly Dudukadov, a "brain of the RFP," excelled at
        adorning fascism with indigenous Russian roots.
57   Spiridovich on Zubatov: Oberländer, "All-Russian Fascist Party," 171.
58   Tsarina and swastika: Rollin, "La Svastika de l'Impératrice." While in exile
        in Holland, Kaiser Wilhelm II also exhibited an interest in the swastika
        and wrote about it in a book on Chinese symbols published in Leipzig
        in 1934. *New York Times,* January 28, 1934.

58   RFP anti-Semitism: Taradanov, *Azbuka Fashizma,* 33–34, 40.

58   "Jewish state capitalism": Rodzaevsky, *Kritika,* 64.

58   *Der Stürmer* cartoons: *Nash Put* issues of November 7, 1935, and March 11, 1937.

58   Stalin as "concubine of American capitalists and Jews": Tsitsihar consul Uchida Gorō report on RFP to Hirota Kōki, July 16, 1934, in JFMA, A.6.5.0.1–2.

v. The Japanese Connection

60   Kawai quotation: Kawai, Tatsuo, *The Goal of Japanese Expansion* (Tokyo: Hokuseido Press, 1938), 63–4.

60–62   Japanese in Manchuria: Background material is based upon Ogata, *Defiance in Manchuria;* Storry, *Double Patriots;* and Crowley, *Japan's Quest for Autonomy,* 82–121.

62   Doihara in Harbin: IMTFE, *Proceedings,* 15,715.

62   Henry P'u-Yi and Doihara: Brackman, *Last Emperor,* 177–81.

63   Émigrés welcomed Japanese in Harbin: Balakshin, *Final v Kitae,* I, 163. Pernikoff, *"Bushido,"* 17, 38–40. Vespa, *Secret Agent of Japan,* 27. Jones, *Manchuria since 1931,* 77.

63   Cyril applauded Japanese occupation: Balakshin, *Final v Kitae,* I, 163. Cyril also exchanged congratulatory telegrams with the RFS. *Natsiya,* no. 3–4 (1932), 1.

64   Japanese "tourists" in Russian church: Pernikoff, *"Bushido,"* 181.

63–64   Japanese treatment of émigrés: Jones, *Manchuria since 1931,* 76–79. "The White Russians in Manchukuo," 16–32. An Old Emigrant, "Truth about Russian Emigrants in Manchukuo," *Manshūkokushi,* II, 1245–48.

64   *Stukachi:* Pernikoff, *"Bushido,"* 66.

64   Greek spy at Hotel Moderne: Vespa, *Secret Agent of Japan,* 226.

64–65   Rivalry among Harbin police agencies: Lensen, *Damned Inheritance,* 320. Vespa, *Secret Agent of Japan,* 148.

65   *Tokumu Kikan:* Berton, et al., *Japanese Training,* 55. Vespa, *Secret Agent of Japan,* 45, 84.

65   *Kempei:* Pernikoff, *"Bushido,"* 55, 84, 191.

65   *Kokumin shimbun* exposure of police corruption: *China Critic,* October 18, 1934. *New York Times,* October 18, 1934.

65   Yagi: Vespa, *Secret Agent of Japan,* 255.

65n   Japanese take Russian names: *Ibid.,* 114.

66   Opium in Manchukuo, airplane leaflets: Stewart, "Drugging a Nation," 662.

66   "several hundred shops" sell opium: Snow, "Japan Builds a New Colony," 84.

66   Opium through holes and for tots: Vespa, *Secret Agent of Japan,* 103. Pernikoff, *"Bushido,"* 102–9.

66   Opium production and control: IMTFE, *Proceedings,* 15,856–58; 40,593–96. *Manchoukuo Year Book, 1934,* 715–16.

67   Prostitution monopoly: Vespa, *Secret Agent of Japan,* 97, 102. Pernikoff, *"Bushido,"* 101–2.

67   "They came down from the trees too soon": Nicholas Slobodchikoff, interview, August 27, 1974.

67   Japanese search for émigré figurehead: Balakshin, *Final v Kitae,* I, 114.

68   Semenov "behind the times": affidavit of *Tokumu Kikan* Colonel Ukai Yoshio [alias Kamazu], IMTFE, *Proceedings,* 23,484–88.

68   Gondatti refusal to collaborate and medal incident: Vespa, *Secret Agent of Japan,* 68.

68   Kislitsyn as a "cultured . . . honest man": Pernikoff, *"Bushido,"* 147. See also Balakshin, *Final v Kitae,* I, 184–85.

68   Kislitsyn as an "empty-headed, vainglorious parasite": Vespa, *Secret Agent of Japan,* 65.

68–69 "What we want is young men . . .": quoted ibid., 54–55.

69   Kosmin as *Tokumu Kikan* tool: "Rodzaevsky Affidavit," IMTFE, Prosecution Document No. 2364, 6 (hereafter "Rodzaevsky Affidavit").

69   Rodzaevsky and *Tokumu Kikan:* "Rodzaevsky Affidavit," 6–7.

69–70 Akikusa Shun: "Akikusa Affidavit," IMTFE, Prosecution Document No. 1983, 1–2 (hereafter "Akikusa Affidavit"). *Tokyo saiban,* I, 506. IMTFE, *Proceedings,* 7,707–8.

70   Akikusa respected in Russian community: Nicholas Petlin, interview, August 29, 1974. Neonilla Yalisheva, interview, August 27, 1974.

70   Nakamura: Vespa, *Secret Agent of Japan,* 34 f. Pernikoff, *"Bushido,"* 24–28, 61, 114. Nicholas Petlin, in a letter dated December 10, 1975, described Nakamura as having a "pleasant personality."

70–71 Nakamura summons White Russians to his shop: Pernikoff, *"Bushido,"* 24–28.

71   RFP leadership split: *Natsiya,* no. 2 (February 1936), 8. Nicholas Petlin, interview, August 29, 1974, and letter of January 22, 1975. Balakshin, *Final v Kitae,* I, 114, 126.

71   Pokrovsky interned by *Kempei:* Pernikoff, *"Bushido,"* 63.

71   Kolosova published poetry in the Harbin journal *Rubezh* ["Boundary"].

71   Kosmin and Komatsubara: "Rodzaevsky Affidavit," 12.

72   Kosmin ejection from RFP: Pernikoff, *"Bushido,"* 153–58. "Akikusa Affidavit," 12.

vi. The Manchurian Mafia

73   Vespa quotation: *Secret Agent of Japan,* 209.

73–74 RFP branch proliferation: Imamura to Hirota, November 2, 1933, in JFMA, A.6.5.0.1–2.

74   *Natsiya* actually published in Harbin: *Tokyo saiban,* I, 504.

74   "Professor" V. Nosach-Noskov: *Natsiya,* no. 5 (1934), 1–4.

74   Dozorov and Semena poems: *Natsiya,* no. 6 (June 1937), 64.

74   Rosenberg in *Natsiya:* See Rosenberg's article on B'nai B'rith in no. 3–4 (1932), 37–38.

74   French recruiting poster: *Natsiya,* March 1937.

74   Taradanov and Kibardin as close associates of Matkovsky: Petlin, letter, January 22, 1975.

74–75 *Azbuka Fashizma.* 2d ed. Shanghai: Izd. "Nash Put," 1935, 22–23, 107.

75   *What Is to Be Done?: Chto Delat?* I am grateful to Professor Erwin Oberländer for bringing this pamphlet to my attention and for permitting me to reproduce his copy of it.

75–76 RFP uniform and salute: Taradanov, *Azbuka Fashizma,* 107.

76   RFP songs: *Ibid.*, 109. Petlin, *S Pesnei k Pobed.*
76   Nicholas II and Preobrazhensky Regiment: Alexander, *Once a Grand Duke,* 166.
76   Verses of "Rise Up with Us, Brothers": *Azbuka Fashizma,* 109. Nicholas Petlin, letter, January 10, 1975.
77   RFP peer groups: Nicholas Petlin, letter, January 22, 1975. Oberländer, "All-Russian Fascist Party," 162.
77   "See how they turned little Italy into a powerful state": *Natsiya,* no. 3–4 (1932), 3.
77   Bolotov: Ishii (Shanghai consul-general) to Hirota, December 12, 1935, in JFMA, A.6.5.0.1–2. Nicholas Petlin, interview, August 29, 1974. Pernikoff, *"Bushido,"* 150–51 (calling Bolotov "Vorotoff").
77   Bolotov gambling casino above *Nash Put:* Nicholas Petlin, interview, August 29, 1974.
78   Bolotov was "kill-crazy" *(satsujinkyō):* Ishii to Hirota, December 12, 1935, in JFMA, A.6.5.0.1–2.
78   *Kempei* use of émigrés for illegal activities: Vespa, *Secret Agent of Japan,* 52, 60.
79   White Russians and Lytton Commission: *Ibid.,* 149 ff, 237.
79   Jews in Manchuria: Dicker, *Wanderers and Settlers,* 22–27. DAI report dated October 19, 1941, DAI 809, T-31, R-510, frame 5273047.
79   "Betar": Peter Berton, conversation, October 13, 1975.
79   *Kempei* and kidnapping of Chinese, Jews: Pernikoff, *"Bushido,"* 145 ff. Vespa, *Secret Agent of Japan,* 60–61, 240.
80   Kofman case: Balakshin, *Final v Kitae,* I, 211.
80   Rodzaevsky accused of being Kofman murderer: Vespa, *Secret Agent of Japan,* 200–204. According to Nicholas Slobodchikoff (interview, August 27, 1974), however, the Japanese did not force Rodzaevsky into violence.
81–89   Kaspé case: Balakshin, *Final v Kitae,* I, 211–23.
81   Window display in Kaspé's jewelry shop: Lydia Schmüser memoirs (part 2), 97. Peter Berton, conversation, October 13, 1975.
83   Martinov: Nicholas Petlin, interview, August 29, 1974. *China Weekly Review,* July 18, 1936, 246.
83   Kaspé kidnapping as *Kempei*-sponsored operation: Pernikoff, *"Bushido,"* 191, 201–2. Vespa, *Secret Agent of Japan,* 209. Balakshin disagrees (*Final v Kitae,* I, 217n).
83   Rodzaevsky withdrew from Kaspé kidnapping: Pernikoff, *"Bushido,"* 203–4.
84   Zaitsev "going hunting": Nicholas Petlin, interview, August 29, 1974.
84   Kaspé abduction: Balakshin, *Final v Kitae,* I, 213–14 (based largely upon Martinov's recollections).
84   Lydia Chernetskaya (Shapiro), daughter of a wealthy contractor, Abram Chernetsky. Peter Berton, conversation, October 13, 1975.
85   Martinov called upon Josef Kaspé: Balakshin, *Final v Kitae,* I, 215.
86   Nakamura called back Rodzaevsky: Pernikoff, *"Bushido,"* 206.
87–88   Oi Fukashi: *Ibid.,* 205. Vespa, *Secret Agent of Japan,* 213.
89   Kaufman speech: Vespa, *Secret Agent of Japan,* 219.
89   Rodzaevsky caused *Kempei* embarrassment over Kaspé case through *Nash Put:* Balakshin, *Final v Kitae,* I, 221.
89   RFP membership growth: *Contemporary Manchuria,* September 1937, 28.

VII. A Russian Cinderella

91   Alexander quote: *Always a Grand Duke,* 76.

92   Vonsiatsky family: *Fashist,* no. 43 (June 1938). VP, I, 1–4. "Vonsiatsky Affidavit" (December 2, 1941) in USDJ, file #202600–2871 (hereafter "Vonsiatsky Affidavit"). Alexis Sherbatoff, interview, June 18, 1975.

92   Subsequently notable prisoners: author's visit to Warsaw Citadel, April 29, 1977.

92–93   A. N. Vonsiatsky's assassination: *Varshavskoye Slovo,* August 19 [O.S.], 1910. VP, I, 3. *Fashist,* no. 17 (June 1935).

93   Fate of Vonsiatsky family members: Andre A. Vonsiatsky, interview, June 7, 1974. *Fashist,* no. 27 (July–August 1936), 2.

93–94   Vonsiatsky in Russian Civil War: "Vonsiatsky Affidavit," 1. Grozin, *Zashchitniya Rubashki,* 264, 266.

93   Vonsiatsky's war wounds: Andre A. Vonsiatsky, interview, June 7, 1974. Bannerman report (July 29, 1937), USDS file #800.00B-Vonsiatsky (hereafter "Vonsiatsky USDS file"). Hartford *Courant,* July 5, 1937.

94   Watermelon incident: Andre A. Vonsiatsky, interview, June 7, 1974.

94   March toward Ekaterinodar as fascist symbol and rallying cry: Oberländer, "All-Russian Fascist Party," 163.

94   Evacuation to Crimea: "Vonsiatsky Affidavit," 1.

94   Vonsiatsky and Lyuba Muromsky: *Ibid.,* 1–2. Lyuba Muromsky to U.S. attorney general (circa February 1922) in USDJ, file #202600–2871 (hereafter "Bigamy File"). *New York Times,* August 4, 1923.

94   Move to Constantinople: "Vonsiatsky Affidavit," 2. Providence *Sunday Journal,* January 6, 1935. Putnam *Patriot,* May 14, 1942.

95   Vonsiatsky to France and England: Andre A. Vonsiatsky, interview, June 7, 1974.

95   Yusupov life-style in London: Marie, *Princess in Exile,* 102–4. Alexander, *Always a Grand Duke,* 112–13.

95   Vonsiatsky as "guest of Prince Yusupov": Vonsiatsky interview with FBI special agent L. L. Meunier on May 9–10, 1942, presented as evidence at a federal grand jury hearing in Hartford, Connecticut, on May 15, 1942. USDJ, file #202600–2871, "Grand Jury Hearings," 146 (hereafter "Grand Jury Hearings").

95   Vonsiatsky at Folies Bergères: Andre A. Vonsiatsky, interview, June 7, 1974.

95   Ambition to marry money or become movie star: Fred Portunato, letter, July 19, 1974.

95   Cinderella in reverse: Alexander, *Always a Grand Duke,* 241.

96   Norman B. Ream and family: Robert C. Ream to Marion Ream Vonsiatsky, November 7, 1938, in "Vonsiatsky Papers," PCA. Frank Decker testimony, "Grand Jury Hearings," 268, 270. Thomas Watson, interview, December 27, 1973. *New York Times,* February 10, 1915. *New York Herald,* February 4, 1922. *National Cyclopedia of American Biography,* XVI (1937), 358.

96   Marion Ream birthplace, birthday, physique: Marion Ream Stephens, United States passport, issued September 2, 1919. "Vonsiatsky Papers," PCA.

97   Marion Ream character: Thomas Watson, interview, December 27, 1973. Helen Roshak, interview, December 27, 1973. Frank Decker testimony, "Grand Jury Hearings," 268–75. Marion de Floresz testimony, "Grand

Jury Hearings," 702. Hartford *Times,* June 23, 1942. *Windham County Observer,* November 13, 1963.

97   Marion Ream and Redmond Stephens: Redmond Stephens file, "Vonsiatsky Papers," PCA. VP, I, 25.

97–98   Redmond Stephens letter to Marion: Redmond Stephens file, "Vonsiatsky Papers," PCA.

98   Marion-Redmond divorce: Henry S. Robbins to Marion Stephens, April 6, 1918. *Ibid.*

98   Redmond Stephens bequest: Lester L. Falk to Marion Vonsiatsky, February 17, 1931. *Ibid.*

98   Marion in France: Red Cross file, "Vonsiatsky Papers," PCA.

98   Marion and Vonsiatsky met in dance hall: Thomas Watson, interview, December 27, 1973.

98   Marion's attraction to Vonsiatsky: Prudence Kwiecien, interview, June 7, 1975. According to John Bigelow (interview, June 8, 1975), Marion felt like an "indulgent mother" toward Vonsiatsky.

99   Vonsiatsky and Elliott Bacon: Meunier testimony, "Grand Jury Hearings," 146.

99   "Memoirs of a Monarchist": "Zapiski Monarkhista," *Posledniya Novosti,* June 24, 1921. Lev Mamedov testimony, "Grand Jury Hearings," 119. Louis Nemzer memorandum on Vonsiatsky (December 19, 1941) in USDJ, file #202600–2871.

100   Émigré press reaction to "Memoirs": *Rul,* July 6, 1921. *Volya Rossy,* July 5, 1921. *Golos Rossy,* June 29, 1921. *Novoye Russkoye Slovo,* July 19, 1921. *Posledniya Novosti,* July 3, July 8, 1921. *Novoye Vremya,* September 7, 1921.

100   French police on Vonsiatsky's *permit de séjour:* Lyuba Muromsky affidavit, "Bigamy File."

100   Vonsiatsky arrival in New York: Justice Department memo (July 15, 1941), in USDJ, file #202600–2871.

100   Quota Act and restriction of Russian immigrants: Simpson, *Refugee Problem,* 468–69, 609.

100   Ream connections in government circles: opening statement to the federal grand jury, Thomas J. Dodd, "Grand Jury Hearings," 5–6.

100   John R. Gladding as Hughes classmate: Paul F. Mackesey (Brown University Alumni Office), letter, January 15, 1974. Gladding as Hughes correspondent in June, 1921: Paul T. Heffron (Hughes Papers, Library of Congress), letter, February 25, 1974.

100   Gladding persuaded Hughes to get Vonsiatsky residence permit: Thomas Watson, interview, December 27, 1973.

100   Hughes responsible for Vonsiatsky getting residency permit: Vonsiatsky to Meunier (May 9–10, 1942) as recalled by Meunier, an FBI special agent, in testimony before federal grand jury on May 15, 1942. "Grand Jury Hearings," 146.

100–101 Gladding in later years regretted helping Vonsiatsky via Hughes: Thomas Watson, interview, December 27, 1973.

101   Vonsiatsky affection for Hughes: *Fashist,* no. 6 (January, 1934). According to Andre A. Vonsiatsky (interview on June 7, 1974), his father often spoke fondly of Hughes and kept a letter from the secretary of state among his prized possessions. On August 16, 1976, Andre Vonsiatsky wrote the author: "I still have not found the letter you asked for, but I do know it

did exist. I can remember my father telling me how Charles Evan [*sic*] Hughes helped Marion with his immigration. I will continue my search for the letter."

101   Vonsiatsky at Carolyn Hall, 1921: Philadelphia *Evening Bulletin,* January 31, 1922.

101   Marion's attitude toward Vonsiatsky: Prudence Kwiecien, interview, June 7, 1975. John Bigelow, interview, June 8, 1975.

101   Louis M. Ream's elopement with Eleanor Pendleton (1911): *American Pictorial,* February 8, 1922, in VP, I, 108.

102   Marion-Vonsiatsky wedding: *New York Times,* February 1, 1922. *New York Tribune,* February 1, 1922. *Philadelphia Inquirer,* February 1, 1922. Clippings of regional and international press in VP, I, 24–26; II, 71–72.

102   Vonsiatsky self-description to press: *New York Times,* February 1, 1922. VP, I, 25.

102   Honeymoon in Quebec: VP, I, 25.

103   Vonsiatsky as Eddystone apprentice: "Vonsiatsky Affidavit," 2. "Grand Jury Hearings," 6–7. *New York Times,* February 1, 1922. VP, I, 38.

104   Lyuba Muromsky bigamy complaint: "Bigamy File." *New York Times,* April 26, 1922. *Philadelphia Inquirer,* April 25, 1922.

104   Ream attempt to pay off Muromsky: Louis Nemzer memo (December 19, 1941), page 31, in USJD, file #202600–2871.

104   Ecclesiastical court declared Yalta marriage void: *New York Tribune,* December 7, 1922. "Vonsiatsky Affidavit," 2.

104   Marriages in White-occupied areas: Williams, *Culture in Exile,* 146.

105   Muromsky arrival in New York: *New York Times,* January 28, 1923.

105   Muromsky press interview: Chester, Pa. *Morning Republican,* July 25, 1923, in VP, II, 49.

105   New York Supreme Court decision: *New York Times,* August 4, 1923.

105   Marion and Anastase move to Thompson: "Vonsiatsky Affidavit," 2–3.

106   Quinnatisset Farm: deed in possession of Richard E. Snow. Examined, June 7, 1975.

106   "Nineteenth Hole" name: Frank Decker testimony, "Grand Jury Hearings," 270.

106   Vonsiatsky love of golf: Mooza Pookhir testimony, "Grand Jury Hearings," 393. Thomas Watson, interview, December 27, 1973. John Bigelow, interview, June 8, 1975.

106   1924 musical soirée: Putnam *Patriot,* February 1 and 8, 1924. John Bigelow, interview, June 8, 1975.

108   Vonsiatsky's musical comedies: Putnam *Patriot,* July 24, 1925. VP, III, 7, 8.

108   Costume balls, unpublished novel, lectures: VP, II, 106; III, 7–8. Andre A. Vonsiatsky, interview, June 7, 1974.

108   Vonsiatsky fancy tastes: Wesley Griswold, letter, January 14, 1974. E. T. Nolan testimony, "Grand Jury Hearings," 372.

108   Vonsiatsky's airplane: Putnam *Patriot,* July 12, September 2, 1927.

108   "Alex" and "Mama" nicknames: VP, XXIII, 27. Thomas Watson, interview, December 27, 1973.

108   Vonsiatsky love of cars: W. H. Towne testimony, "Grand Jury Hearings," 532. Thomas Watson, interview, December 27, 1973.

108   Vonsiatsky at Brown: Milton E. Noble (Brown University registrar), letter, March 11, 1974. Lev Mamedov testimony, "Grand Jury Hearings," 131.

109   Goalposts, Pierce-Arrow, traffic violations, and Prince Albert: Andre A. Von-siatsky, interview, June 7, 1974. Philadelphia *Evening Bulletin,* March 24, 1923.

109   Haircuts and "Jimmy, give me hat!": James W. B. Kelley, letter, August 18, 1976.

109   Ream family disapproval of Vonsiatsky: Frank Decker testimony, "Grand Jury Hearings," 264.

109   Vonsiatsky's allowance: "Vonsiatsky Affidavit," 4. Norman B. Watson testimony, "Grand Jury Hearings," 438. Marion de Floresz testimony, "Grand Jury Hearings," 698.

109–110 Robert C. Ream disapproval of Vonsiatsky: Richard Barton testimony, "Grand Jury Hearings," 488–89.

110   "like a Hottentot at a meeting of the D.A.R.": James W. B. Kelley, letter, August 18, 1976.

110   Vonsiatsky as dancing partner: Prudence Kwiecien, interview, June 7, 1975.

110   "lavender eyes": Prudence Kwiecien, quoting Leila Holt remark made circa 1922. Telephone interview, May 22, 1976.

110   Quinnatisset Farm guestbook quotations: "Vonsiatsky Papers," PCA.

111   Louis and Mary Ream tumult: Hartford *Times,* February 28, 1925. VP, II, 102. Prudence Kwiecien, interview, June 7, 1975. John Bigelow, interview, June 8, 1975. The Hartford *Times* placed the party in Pomfret, but John Bigelow recalled that it took place in Thompson. Mary Weaver's diary (consisting mostly of German poetry) is among the Vonsiatsky papers at PCA.

111   Vonsiatsky naturalization: Justice Department memo (July 15, 1941), in USDJ, file #202600–2871.

111   Lev and Natasha Mamedov: Helen Roshak, interview, December 27, 1973. Andre A. Vonsiatsky, interview, June 7, 1974.

111   Mamedov and Stalin: John Bigelow, interview, June 8, 1975.

112   The Russian Bear: Thomas Watson, interview, December 27, 1973. Mary S. Killiam testimony, "Grand Jury Hearings," 332–33. Boston *Herald,* April 7, 1933. A brochure on the Russian Bear was kindly supplied by Richard E. Snow (undated note, received on June 23, 1975).

112   Anastase and Marion relax at Russian Bear: Frank Decker testimony, "Grand Jury Hearings," 273.

113   Vonsiatsky entertained Prince Paul: Webster *Evening Times,* November 7, 1925 in VP, II, 102.

113   Vonsiatsky never called himself "count" in front of Romanovs: Nikita N. Romanoff, telephone interview, June 15, 1975.

113   Grand Duke Alexander: Alexander, *Always a Grand Duke* and *Once a Grand Duke.* Vorres, *Last Grand Duchess,* 172.

113–114 Grand Duke Alexander at Nineteenth Hole: Nikita N. Romanoff, telephone interview, June 15, 1975.

114   Prince Theodore: VP, XIII, 45. Wesley Griswold testimony, "Grand Jury Hearings," 135. Hartford *Times,* January 24, 1938. Providence *Evening Bulletin,* June 2, 1930.

114   Vonsiatsky/Prince Theodore auto tour: VP, III, 45–47.

114   Prince Nikita election as "Tsar": Alexander, *Always a Grand Duke,* 127.

114   Prince Nikita character and career: *New York Times,* June 15, 1931; September 24, 1974. Hartford *Courant,* September 23, 1934.

114–115   Nikita, Vonsiatsky, and the Nicholas II Military Academy: *Tsarsky Vestnik,* August 17, 1930; April 23, 1931. VP, III, 22, 26.
115   Nikita's 1931 visit to Nineteenth Hole: Putnam *Patriot,* September 10, 1931.
115   Nikita described as an "ardent fascist": Wesley Griswold, writing in the Hartford *Courant,* September 23, 1934.

VIII. New England's Russian Duce

116   Vonsiatsky quote: to a Hartford *Courant* reporter in 1927, reprinted in the Hartford *Courant* on September 23, 1934.
117   Biography of Vonsiatsky's father: Nikolai Nikolaevich Breshko-Breshkovsky, *Goluboi Mundir.* VP, III, 60.
117   "weary of picking apples": *Windham County Observer,* November 18, 1927.
117   General Kutepov: Lehovich, *White Against Red,* 197, 368, 423, 433–34.
117   Vonsiatsky support of Kutepov: Meunier testimony, "Grand Jury Hearings," 147, 162–63.
117   Kutepov "one of the founders of Russian fascism": *Fashist* (November 1935).
117–118   Brotherhood of Russian Truth: Meunier testimony, "Grand Jury Hearings," 147–48.
118   Vonsiatsky at 1928 Republican rally for Hoover: Putnam *Patriot,* September 20, 1928.
118n   "Between 1922 and 1933 . . ." and "Russian military souvenirs": "Vonsiatsky Affidavit," 3.
119   Vonsiatsky's U.S. Army officer commission: Chief of Staff Douglas MacArthur to Cordell Hull, March 26, 1935 in USDS, file #800.00B-Vonsiatsky. Vonsiatsky's Officer Reserve Corps identification card (no. 0–272813) is now in the possession of Andre A. Vonsiatsky.
119   Machine gun from Abercrombie & Fitch: "Vonsiatsky Affidavit," 4.
119   Machine gun installed on stairway landing: Wesley Griswold, letter, January 14, 1974.
119   Vonsiatsky training at Baltimore camp: Putnam *Patriot,* August 7, 1930. VP, III, 5.
119   Rifle purchases: "Vonsiatsky Affidavit," 3. Charles J. Scott (Francis Bannerman employee) testimony, "Grand Jury Hearings," 243–59.
119   Riot guns and tear gas billies: FBI Report of March 20, 1939, 8.
119   Stone annex construction: Richard E. Snow, conversation, June 7, 1975. Author's observations during visits to Quinnatisset Farm, December 27, 1973; June 7–8, 1975.
119–121   Military Room: Hartford *Courant,* September 23, 1934. R. C. Bannerman reports of November 10, 1934 and July 29, 1937 in USDS, file #800.00B.
121   Vonsiatsky resignation from Brotherhood: *Novaya Zarya,* July 12, 1932. Meunier testimony, "Grand Jury Hearings," 148–51.
121   Vonsiatsky low opinion of General Miller: Meunier testimony, "Grand Jury Hearings," 147.
121   Vonsiatsky quote on forming own party: *Ibid.,* 151.
122   Vonsiatsky articles on 1932 presidential election: *Novaya Zarya,* November 5, 1932. *Novoye Russkoye Slovo,* November 1, 1932.
122   Miliukov's "Is this stupidity or treason?": Treadgold, *Twentieth Century Russia,* 119.
122   Kunle background: Putnam *Patriot,* June 26, 1941.

123   Paula Kunle and Prince Demidov: Boris de Rosmaritza, letters of July 4
             and July 21, 1975.
123   Kunle nicknamed "Coontz": Anne Kenney, interview, December 26, 1973.
123   Formation of VFO: Meunier testimony, "Grand Jury Hearings," 151–52.
             "Vonsiatsky Affidavit," 5.
123   Mamedov title: Lev Mamedov testimony, "Grand Jury Hearings," 102–4,
             113.
124   Marion's honorary titles: Grozin, Zashchitniya Rubashki, 134.
124   Fashist finances: FBI Report of March 20, 1939.
124   Norman B. Watson duties: Norman B. Watson testimony, "Grand Jury Hear-
             ings," 416 ff, 462, 477.
124–125   Fashist style: observations of issues deposited at Slavonic Collection, New
             York Public Library.
125   "I'm so happy to become a Russian fascist": Fashist, no. 8 (March
             1934), 1.
125   Vonsiatsky on peasants: Oberländer, "All-Russian Fascist Party," 164. Vonsi-
             atsky, Osnovy, 10–19.
126   Vonsiatsky conception of fascism as anticommunism: Ibid., 164. Norwich
             Bulletin, October 16, 1941.
126   "To my mind . . . ": Vonsiatsky, quoted by Meunier, "Grand Jury Hearings,"
             162.
126   "The German, Italian, and Russian fascisms . . . ": Norwich Bulletin, October
             16, 1941.
126   Vonsiatsky on swastika: FBI Report, March 20, 1939.
126   "Why should I change it just because Hitler adopted it?": Vonsiatsky as
             quoted in Mooza Pookhir testimony, "Grand Jury Hearings," 396.
126   Vonsiatsky and reversed swastika: James W. B. Kelley, letter, August 18,
             1976. One of the pamphlets published by Vonsiatsky in 1934 (Mikhail
             Grott, "Tactics of Russian Fascists" [in Russian]) has a reverse swastika
             on the back. But Vonsiatsky seems to have used both forms at different
             times.
126   VFO salute and titles: Louis Nemzer memo (December 19, 1941) in USDJ,
             file #202600–2871.
126–127   Tune and lyrics of VFO anthem, "Raise the Banner!": Fashist, May 1935.
127   Recordings of "Raise the Banner!" are among the material disinterred from
             the hen coop at Nineteenth Hole. "Vonsiatsky Papers," PCA.
127   Vonsiatsky's imitation of Hitler's oratorical style: Richard McCauley testi-
             mony, "Grand Jury Hearings," 64. Report of August 11, 1942 from Von-
             siatsky's prison file (#3775-H).
127   Recordings of Vonsiatsky's speeches: "Vonsiatsky Papers," PCA.

IX. Toward a Fascist United Front

131   "to see what was going on" in Germany: Meunier testimony, "Grand Jury
             Hearings," 160.
131   Vonsiatsky at Adlon: Thomas J. Dodd, "Grand Jury Hearings," 13.
132   Berlin meeting: Fashist, no. 5 (December 1933).
132   Kazem-Bek attitude toward Vonsiatsky: Alexis Sherbatoff, interview, June
             18, 1975.
132   ROND article about Vonsiatsky: Probuzhdeniye Rossy, October 1, 1933.

133   Friends urge Vonsiatsky to see top Nazis: Meunier testimony, "Grand Jury Hearings," 160.

133   Berlin conference hailed in Europe: *Mladorosskaya Iskra,* October 1, 1933. *Rossiya,* October 4, 1933.

133   Harlem Russians demonstrate against Vonsiatsky: *Novy Mir,* November 11, 1933.

133–134   *Fashist* quotes: issue of April, 1934.

134   Koverda and Voikov: *Ibid.* Dennen, *White Guard Terrorists,* 13.

134   *Fashist* quotes: reprinted in *Daily Worker,* December 29, December 31, 1934; January 4, 1935.

134–135   *Daily Worker* attacks on Vonsiatsky: October 19, 1931; June 13, 1932.

135   Ivanoff-Krivkoff incident: USDS, file #3600.1121-Krivkoff, Ivanoff, later incorporated into USDS, file #800.00B-Vonsiatsky.

136   "The Center": FBI Report, March 20, 1939.

136   VFO membership criteria quote: Meunier testimony, "Grand Jury Hearings," 156.

136   M. M. Grott: FBI reports of March 20, 1939, and February 28, 1940. Grott pamphlets among "Vonsiatsky Papers," PCA.

137   Vonsiatsky differs with Grott on Jewish question: Meunier testimony, "Grand Jury Hearings," 160.

137   Bogoslovsky: *Fashist,* no. 48 (March 1939). For a portrait, see *Fashist,* no. 34 (July 1937), 4.

137   Mrs. Bogoslovsky made flags and arm bands: Michael Kapral testimony, "Grand Jury Hearings," 190.

137   Novozhilov: *Fashist,* no. 37 (November 1937), 20.

137   Natasha Novozhilov a favorite of Marion's: Helen Roshak, letter, August 8, 1975.

137   Doombadze: Meunier testimony, "Grand Jury Hearings," 155.

137   Semens: Alexander Tzuglevich testimony, *Ibid.,* 239.

137   San Francisco supporters: *Fashist,* no. 22 (November 1935). Dennen, *White Guard Terrorists,* 9.

138   Dakhov: *Fashist,* no. 22 (November 1935) and no. 36 (October 1937). Meunier testimony, "Grand Jury Hearings," 154–55.

138   *Rus: Nash Put,* November 21, 1934.

138    $5.65 from Edmonton: *Fashist,* no. 22 (November 1935), 21.

138   Vonsiatsky and Rodzaevsky "simultaneously" discovered fascism: Hartford *Courant,* September 23, 1934.

139   Early published indication of RFP interest in Vonsiatsky: *Nash Put,* October 18, 1933.

139   Rodzaesky letter to Vonsiatsky: Oberländer, "All-Russian Fascist Party," 162.

139   Vonsiatsky acceptance "in the name of 2,000 VFO members": *Ibid.,* 164.

140   Vanderbilt Hotel gathering: Boris de Rosmaritza, letter, July 4, 1975. Dennen, *White Guard Terrorists,* 17.

140   Pelley approached Vonsiatsky: Meunier testimony, "Grand Jury Hearings," 138.

140   SS *President Van Buren* passenger list: Honolulu *Star Bulletin,* March 9, 1934.

140   San Francisco statements and Japanese interest: *Morning Oregonian* (March 7, 1934) and letter from Nakamura Yutaka to Hirota Kōki, March 8, 1934, JFMA, A 6.5.0.1–2.

140   150,000 troops against USSR: *Osaka Mainichi,* March 23, 1934.

x. Harbin Summit

141   Vonsiatsky quote: *Fashist,* no. 11 (July 1934), 2.

141   Rodzaevsky and Matkovsky in Tokyo: Morishima Morito (Japanese consul general in Harbin) to Foreign Minister Hirota Kōki, April 2, 1934; Hirota to Morishima, April 9, 1934. JFMA, A.6.5.0.1–2.

141   Rodzaevsky-Vonsiatsky discussions in Tokyo: report of police officer Fujinuma Shōhei to Home Minister Yamamoto Tatsuo, April 10, 1934, in JFMA, A.6.5.0.1–2 (hereafter "Fujinuma Report").

142   *Tokumu Kikan* pressure on Rodzaevsky to cooperate with Semenov: Rodzaevsky Affidavit of April 11, 1946, IMTFE, Prosecution Document no. 2364, 10 (hereafter "Rodzaevsky Affidavit").

142   Protokoll Number 1: Oberländer, "All-Russian Fascist Party," 165.

143   Vonsiatsky references to meeting with Araki: Belgrade newspaper, *Politika,* July 17, 1934 in USDS, file #800.00B-Vonsiatsky A./9. Meunier testimony, "Grand Jury Hearings," 165.

143   Araki's rhetoric: Crowley, *Japan's Quest for Autonomy,* 203–4. Hata, *Reality and Illusion,* 6–7.

143   Araki headed Harbin *Tokumu Kikan: Tokyo saiban,* I, 504.

143   Araki rumored to have embraced Orthodoxy: Alexis Sherbatoff, telephone interview, June 18, 1975.

143   Araki and Troyanovsky: Lensen, *Damned Inheritance,* 374.

143   Araki regret about Siberian Intervention: remark made to General Ishiwata and published in *Kokumin shimbun* on August 14, 1941, as quoted in IMTFE, *Proceedings,* 7,303–4; 40,600.

144   Vonsiatsky-Araki meeting: as Vonsiatsky recounted to FBI special agent Meunier on night of May 9–10, 1942, Meunier testimony, "Grand Jury Hearings," 165. Vonsiatsky to State Department special agent R. C. Bannerman, November 7, 1934, as recounted in Bannerman's report of November 10, 1934 in USDS, file #800.00B.

144   Vonsiatsky's visa problem: Meunier testimony, "Grand Jury Hearings," 165.

145   Vonsiatsky departure from Yokohama: "Fujinuma Report."

145   Rodzaevsky-Araki meeting: *ibid.* In his affidavit of April 11, 1946 (Rodzaevsky Affidavit, 3), Rodzaevsky recollected his meeting with Araki as having taken place in March 1934. This could have been an error, or he could have been referring to an earlier meeting.

145   Rodzaevsky address at Yokohama Railroad Station: report of Yokoyama Tsuenari (governor of Kanagawa prefecture) to Home Minister Yamamoto Tatsuo, April 14, 1934. Copy filed in JFMA, A.6.5.0.1–2.

145   Rodzaevsky-Semenov talks in Dairen: Rodzaevsky to Vonsiatsky, April 20, 1934, in Kahn, *Sabotage!,* 76–77.

145–146 Vonsiatsky illness in Shanghai: *Nash Put,* April 27, 1934.

146   Vonsiatsky and Jewish physician: Andre A. Vonsiatsky, interview, June 7, 1974.

146   Vonsiatsky in Dairen: Edwin S. Cunningham (American consul general, Shanghai) to Secretary of State Cordel Hull, "Activities and Movements of Anastase Andre von Siatsky and Marion Ream von Siatsky," May 17, 1934, USDS, file #800.00B.

146–148 Rodzaevsky letter to Vonsiatsky: An English translation of the complete letter was published in Kahn, *Sabotage!* (77–78). In that book, a photograph of the first and last segments of the Russian original was placed opposite the English translation (76). Comparison of the Russian text in the photograph with the English translation reveals several omissions and discrepancies that cannot be ascribed solely to mistranslation. Moreover, those sections of the letter that are omitted in the photograph—points d through g and the next three and a half paragraphs—seem implausible from circumstantial evidence. *Sabotage!* does not identify the source of the letter, nor did the letter show up among Vonsiatsky's files in the National Archives, the Providence College Archives, the Federal Archives and Records Center, etc. In response to an inquiry about the provenance of the letter, Albert E. Kahn replied (letter, February 20, 1976) that he could not recall how he had acquired the document or where it now might be. On the basis of the photograph, I have corrected and made additions to Kahn's English translation, but cannot vouch for what has been omitted from the photograph.

148–149   Vonsiatsky speech at Dairen Russian Club: *The Manchurian Daily News,* April 23, 1924, an enclosure in Cunningham to Hull, May 17, 1934, USDS, file #800.00B.

148   Vonsiatsky's hands trembled: Alexis Sherbatoff, interview, June 18, 1975.

149   Possible Vonsiatsky-Semenov meeting in Dairen: "Fujinuma Report," JFMA, A.6.5.0.1–2.

150   Vonsiatsky-Kurbsky conversation: *Nash Put,* April 27, 1934. Translations appended to USDS, file #800.00B.

150–151   Vonsiatsky reception in Harbin: Cabot Coville (American consul, Harbin) to Hull, May 18, 1934, USDS, file #800.00B. *Nash Put,* April 26, 1934. Hartford *Courant,* September 23, 1934.

151–152   Vonsiatsky press conference and speech at Harbin Russian Club: Coville to Hull, May 18, 1934, based on "a reliable Russian émigré" present at the lecture. USDS, file #800.00B. *Nash Put,* April 27, 1934. *Natsiya,* no. 5 (May 1934).

153   Vonsiatsky's subsequent activities in Harbin: *Natsiya,* no. 5 (May 1934), 31. Coville to Hull, May 18, 1934, USDS, file #800.00B.

153–154   State Department following Vonsiatsky's activities: Hull to Cunningham, May 3, 1934; Cunningham to Hull, May 17, 1934; Grew to Hull, May 16, 1934; Coville to Hull, May 18, 1934; Cunningham to Hull, May 23, 1934. USDS, file #800.00B.

154–155   Vonsiatsky's second visit to Shanghai; Cunningham to Hull, May 17, 18, 1934, USDS, file #800.00B. Shanghai consul general to Hirota, May 26, 1934, in JFMA, A.6.5.0.1–2. Balakshin, *Final v Kitae,* I, 335.

155   Vonsiatsky invited audience to tea at Cathay Hotel: Vonsiatsky interview with David Karr, July 27, 1939. Karr testimony, "Grand Jury Hearings," 35.

155   Steklov: "Vonsiatsky Affidavit," 8. JAA, T-955, F-25009. Meunier testimony, "Grand Jury Hearings," 153–54.

156   Vonsiatsky in Italy: Alexis Sherbatoff, interview, June 18, 1975.

157   Prince Theodore acts as Vonsiatsky's chauffeur in Paris: *Ibid.*

157   Vonsiatsky spoke before two thousand in Berlin: *Fashist,* no. 14 (December 1934–January 1935), 10.

157   Vonsiatsky "made a fool of himself" and looked "tipsy": Wainwright Abbott to Hull, August 2, 1934, in USDS, file #800.00B.

157   New York Police Department file showed that Vonsiatsky met with top Nazis in 1934: Mitchell S. Solomon report of April 1, 1941, in USDJ, file #202600–2871.

157–158   Vonsiatsky met Rosenberg in 1934: David Karr testimony on May 14, 1942, "Grand Jury Hearings," 36, recalling an interview with Vonsiatsky on July 27, 1939, during which Vonsiatsky had said (in response to a question about whether he had met government leaders in Berlin): "Yes, I saw Rosenberg, but it was just for a chat at tea."

158   Vonsiatsky described as a "Russian Hitler": Henri Rollin in Le Temps, August 24, 1934.

xi. Schism

159   Mussolini quote: Arthur Richard, Modern Quotations (New York: Dover, 1947), 193.

159   New Higher Party School in Harbin: Oberländer, "All-Russian Fascist Party," 165. Nash Put, September 13, 1936.

159   Vonsiatsky remarks to Griswold: Hartford Courant, September 23, 1934.

160   Rodzaevsky considered Vonsiatsky an alfons (gigolo): Ilina, Vozvrashcheniye, II, 292.

160   Mamedov called Rodzaevsky "a crook": Mamedov testimony, "Grand Jury Hearings," 121.

160–161   Semenov as a divisive issue: Meunier testimony, "Grand Jury Hearings," 153. G. F. Hudson, "Japan and the White Russian Emigration in the Far East," memorandum to R. A. Butler, M. P. and E. O. Coote (Northern Department, British Foreign Office), BFOA, FO 371, 29531/N3890, July 17, 1941, 3 (hereafter "Hudson Memo").

160   Rodzaevsky advised by Akikusa to cooperate with Semenov: Rodzaevsky Affidavit of April 11, 1946, IMTFE, Prosecution Document no. 2364, 10 (hereafter "Rodzaevsky Affidavit"). IMTFE, Proceedings, 7, 695.

161   "If the Jews want to be our friends . . .": Vonsiatsky to Wesley Griswold. Hartford Courant, September 23, 1934.

161   "Well, our attitude toward the Jews depends on their attitude toward us . . .": Vonsiatsky to David Karr, July 27, 1939. Karr testimony, "Grand Jury Hearings," 38.

161   Oswald Mosley hired Jewish boxer: Schüddekopf, Fascism, 38.

161   Jewish firm in New York made Vonsiatsky's uniforms: Norman B. Watson testimony, "Grand Jury Hearings," 431.

161   Weinbaum at Nineteenth Hole: FBI report of March 20, 1939, 6. R. C. Bannerman report on November 10, 1934, 10 in USDS, file #800.00B. Both sources refer to the editor of Novoye Russkoye Slovo incorrectly (FBI says "Weinberg," State Department report says "Weinman"). The correct name was provided by Andrei Sedych (current editor-in-chief) in a letter dated July 2, 1976.

162   Vonsiatsky quotations: Hartford Courant, September 23, 1934.

163   National Revolution cannot be "waged according to the instructions . . .": Fashist, no. 21 (October 1935), 2, as quoted in Oberländer, "All-Russian Fascist Party," 167.

163   Rodzaevsky wooed monarchists: Oberländer, "All-Russian Fascist Party," 160, 172n.

163   "There will be no titles . . . in Fascist Russia": Hartford *Courant,* September 23, 1934.

163–164   "We have not asked them": *Ibid.*

164   *Nash Put* attack on Vonsiatsky: The entire text of the December 11 issue's attack was translated into English and sent by the American consul general in Harbin, Walter A. Adams, to Hull on December 12. USDS, file #800.00B.

165   Third Congress of Russian Fascists, Harbin (1935): *Natsiya,* no. 8 (August 1935), 47–55 for resolutions.

166   Vonsiatsky accused Rodzaevsky of being tool of Japan: Vonsiatsky, *Otvet Kritiku,* 9, 11, 16. *Fashist,* no. 30 (January 1937), 17; no. 36 (October 1937), 6.

166   Accusation that Bolotov murdered Kaspé, act ordered by Rodzaevsky: *Fashist,* no. 31 (Feburary 1937), 14–15.

166   First trial of Kaspé kidnappers: *China Weekly Review,* July 18, 1936.

166   Second trial: *Ibid.,* June 27, 1936.

166   *Nash Put* petition for clemency: *China Weekly Review,* July 18, 1936.

167   Hsinking Supreme Court decision: *Ibid.*

167   International uproar over kidnappers' release: *Pravda,* February 15, 1937. *New York Times,* February 16, 1937. Dicker, *Wanderers and Settlers,* 37.

167   Rodzaevsky seen as winner in schism with Vonsiatsky: Ivan S. Georgievsky, "Memorandum on the Russian Emigration" (August 17, 1941), in BFOA, FO 371, 29531/N802, 36.

167–168 Moscow *Fashist:* A copy of the first issue (January 1, 1935) is deposited at the Hoover Institution at Stanford.

168   "the crime of the century": Conquest, *The Great Terror,* 43.

168   Vonsiatsky hailed Kirov's assassin: *Fashist,* no. 14 (December 1934–January 1935).

169   *Pravda* on Vonsiatsky: An English translation of the article appeared in the December 26 issue of Moscow *Daily News.*

170   "What does one life in 20,000 matter?": Hartford *Courant,* September 23, 1934.

170   Vonsiatsky asked for police protection: Urquhart testimony, "Grand Jury Hearings," 365.

170   Vonsiatsky bought bulletproof vest: Hartford *Courant,* July 5, 1937.

170   German shepherds: Emil Lajeunesse testimony, "Grand Jury Hearings," 565. Richard E. Snow, interview, June 7, 1975.

170   Lady Astor: VP, I, 67.

170–171 False staircase and underground study: Andre A. Vonsiatsky, interview, June 7, 1974. Robert Rovatti, conversation in Putnam, December 27, 1973. Author examined the premises on June 8, 1975.

171   "Good Luck John": Norman B. Watson testimony, "Grand Jury Hearings," 467.

xii. Metastasis

172   Chapter quotation: Japanese consul in Manchouli to Minister of Foreign Affairs Arita Hachirō, November 6, 1936, in JFMA, A.6.5.0.1–2.

173   Population figures for Soviets and Whites in Manchukuo: Mantetsu, Sōsaishitsu jinjika [South Manchurian Railway Co., Director's Office, Per-

sonnel Section], "Zai-Man Rōjin ni kansuru chōsa" [Survey of Russians in Manchukuo], Dairen, 1939 (hereafter "SMR Report").

173–174 Akikusa approached Rodzaevsky, Matkovsky: Akikusa Shun affidavit, June 14, 1946, IMTFE, Prosecution Document no. 1983, 11–12 (hereafter "Akikusa Affidavit"). Konstantin Rodzaevsky affidavit, April 11, 1946, IMTFE, Prosecution Document no. 2364, 10 (hereafter "Rodzaevsky Affidavit").

174–175 Evening of BREM establishment: Balakshin, Final v Kitae, I, 180–81.

175 BREM structure: Ibid., 181. Nagaoka Hanroku (acting consul general in Harbin) to Hirota Kōki, January 17, 1935, in JFMA, A.6.5.0.1–2.

175 Ivan Mikhailov: Svit, Ukrainsko-yaponski vzaemini, 105. Peter Berton, conversation, October 13, 1975.

176 Decline of number of Soviet citizens in Manchukuo after 1935: "SMR Report."

176 Fascists expanded their power through BREM: Harbin consul general to Satō Naotake, May 20, 1937; Mutanchiang acting consul to Foreign Minister Tani Masayuki, February 18, 1943, in JFMA, A.6.5.0.1–2.

176 BREM departments staffed by fascists: Balakshin, Final v Kitae, I, 181–82.

177 White Russians trapped in Manchukuo: Ilina, Vozvrashcheniye, II, 58.

177 BREM and Hiroshimaya: China Weekly Review, September 5, 1936.

177 BREM and E. Y. Tchurin: Ibid., July 4, 1936; November 17, 28, 1936.

177 BREM finances: IMTFE, Proceedings, 7,709.

177 VFP finances: Mutanchiang acting consul to Tani Masayuki, February 18, 1943, in JFMA, A.6.5.0.1–2.

177 Rodzaevsky's clothing: Nicholas Petlin, letter, October 28, 1974.

177–178 Concordia Association: Peattie, Ishiwara Kanji, 168–74.

178 Concordia Association Russian section: Manshūkokushi, II, 1247. Balakshin, Final v Kitae, I, 184.

178 Rodzaevsky on "VFP-Kyōwakai brotherhood": Rodzaevsky speech at Hailar (September 14, 1936) as reported by Hailar consul Gotō Rokurō to Arita Hachirō, September 25, 1936, in JFMA, A.6.5.0.1–2. "Rodzaevsky Affidavit," 8.

178 Rodzaevsky's VFP membership claims: Oberländer, "All-Russian Fascist Party," 168.

178 Actual VFP membership about ten thousand: Nicholas Petlin, letter, November 8, 1974.

178 VFP membership growth among CER employees: Nicholas Petlin, letter, November 8, 1974.

178–179 Demographic shifts in Manchukuo: "SMR Report."

179 Rodzaevsky efforts to enlist cooperation of local schoolteachers and recruit youth, and resulting friction with Cossacks: Hailar consul general Gotō to Arita, October 6, 1936, in JFMA, A.6.5.0.1–2.

179 Cossacks in northern Manchuria: Kaigorodov, "Russkiye v Trekhreche," 140–49. Fukuda, Hoku-Man no Roshiyajin buraku.

179 Akikusa advised Rodzaevsky to compose his differences with Semenov: "Rodzaevsky Affidavit," 10.

179–180 Third Congress on Russian Fascists—open and secret policy toward Cossacks: Harbin consul general Satō Shōshirō to Hirota, July 17, 1935, in JFMA, A.6.5.0.1–2.

180 Fascist-Cossack alliance: Hailar acting consul Mimura Tetsuo to Hirota, February 7, 1938, ibid.

181   White Russian community in Shanghai: Japanese Imperial Army, General Staff, Intelligence (Shanghai Branch), "Zaiko hakkei Rōjin no genjō" [Present condition of White Russians in Shanghai], September 7, 1939, in JAA, T-955, R-113, frames 24997–25012.

181   VFP in Shanghai: Balakshin, *Final v Kitae*, I, 335, 338, 341, 380.

181–182 VFP in Tientsin: memorandum by L. P. Mouravieff and Chief of Police, British Municipal Council, Tientsin, November 22, 1937, in BFOA, FO 371, 22157/2900.

182   VFP in Karafuto: Karafuto governor Imamura Takeshi to Foreign Minister Hirota Kōki, Home Minister Yamamoto Tatsuo, and Colonization Minister Nagai Ryūtarō, November 2, 1933, in JFMA, A.6.5.0.1–2.

182   VFP branches in Japan: Satō to Hirota, July 17, 1935, *ibid.* Nicholas Petlin, interview, August 29, 1974.

182   Rodzaevsky inaugurated party operations in Europe in 1934: "Russische Emigranten und Faschisten, Nationalkomitee der Weissrussen," in GFMA, Gesandtschaft Bern, Aktenzeichen Russland 2 (1941), 138.

183   VFP representatives around the world: *Natsiya* (February 1938), 1.

183   "Palestine for the Palestinians!": *Nash Put,* January 14, 1937. The VFP "ambassador-at-large" for the Middle East was Leonid Alexeev.

184   VFP support of Italy: *Nash Put,* November 14, 1935; January 17, 1937.

184   Rodzaevsky reception for Italian ambassador: *Manchuria,* May 15, 1938.

184–185 SS report on VFP: GSS, T-175, R-58, frame 2573988.

185–186 Establishment of VFP branch in Berlin: *Natsiya* (February 1938), 1.

185   Erwin von Schultz in Harbin: Hsinking consul general Nakano Kō'ichi to Arita, June 18, 1936, in JFMA, A.6.5.0.1–2.

185   Germans in Asia: U.S. Department of State, Division of European Affairs, *National Socialism* (Washington, 1943), 421.

185   Germans in Manchukuo: "SMR Report."

185   Germans in Harbin: DAI, T-81, R-510, frame 5273100.

185   DAI and Russian fascists: *Izvestiya,* June 15, 1937.

185–186 Boris Tedli: "Russische Emigranten und Faschisten," GFMA, Gesandtschaft Bern, Aktenzeichen Russland 2 (1941), 112, 119. Williams, *Culture in Exile,* 340. *Nash Put,* May 24, 1936.

186   Rurik von Kotzebue: "Russischen Emigranten und Faschisten," op. cit., 65.

186   Tedli appointed "European leader" of VFP (1936): Williams, *Culture in Exile,* 342.

186   Tedli as "European and African" leader of RFS: "Russische Emigranten und Faschisten," *op. cit.,* 138.

XIII. National Revolution Far Eastern Style

188   White partisans in 1920s: Balakshin, *Final v Kitae,* I, 116–24.

189   Japanese spies in Siberia: Kondō Kan'ichi, *Shiberia supai nikki* ["Diary of a Siberian Spy"] (Tokyo: Chūō Shoin, 1974).

189   Major Kanda plans (1928): IMTFE, *Proceedings,* 620–37.

190   Japanese and Verzhbitsky: Balakshin, *Final v Kitae,* I, 120–21, 170.

190   Soviet agents in Beaumonde, Yara cafes: *Ibid.,* I, 106.

190   CER employees harassed by Japanese: *New York Times,* January 28, 1934.

190   *Dalbank* employee death: *Ibid.,* March 22, 1936.

190   Cossack pacification: *China Weekly Review,* September 12, 1936.

190n   Repatriated ex-CER employees arrested by NKVD as Japanese spies: Solzhenitsyn, *GULAG Archipelago*, 72.

191   Rodzaevsky prediction on National Revolution: *Natsiya*, no. 6 (June 1935), 1.

191   VFP Three-Year Plan: *Chto Delat?* esp. pp. 34–35.

191   VFP radio broadcasts to USSR from Tsitsihar: Tsitsihar consul Uchida Gorō to Hirota, June 17, 1935, in JFMA, A.6.5.0.1–2.

192   Tōyama sent Rodzaevsky a sword: Konstantin Rodzaevsky affidavit, April 11, 1946, IMTFE, Prosecution Document no. 2364, 9 (hereafter "Rodzaevsky Affidavit").

192   *Tokumu Kikan* recruitment of White Russians: Balakshin, *Final v Kitae*, I, 124, 170.

192   Yurenev protest and Horinouchi answer: Japan, Gaimushō, O-A Kyoku, *Nisso kōshō shi*, 252. *New York Times*, April 29, 1936.

193   Major Suzuki approached Rodzaevsky on VFP commando unit: "Rodzaevsky Affidavit," 10. IMTFE, *Proceedings*, 7,697.

193–194   VFP raid in Chita (November 7, 1936): Manchouli consul general Gotō Yasushi to Foreign Minister Arita Hachirō, November 20, 1936, in JFMA, A.6.5.0.1–2.

194   Abortive VFP attack on Soviet consulate in Harbin: Gotō to Arita, November 6, 9, 1936, *ibid.*

194   Soviet reaction: *Amurskaya Pravda*, November 22, 1936, as reported *ibid.*

194   Harbin war scare: *China Weekly Review*, November 7, 1936.

196   Kosmin detachments: "Rodzaevsky Affidavit," 12.

196   Creation of the Asano Brigade: *Ibid.*, 12. Akikusa Shun affidavit, June 14, 1946, IMTFE, Prosecution Document no. 1983, 10 (hereafter "Akikusa Affidavit"). Japan, Bōei-chō, Bōei Kenshujo, Senshishitsu, *Kantōgun*, II, 53.

197   Asano Brigade pay and uniforms: IMTFE, *Proceedings*, 7,707.

197   Gurgen Nagolen: Balakshin, *Final v Kitae*, I, 234. Petlin, interview, August 29, 1974.

197   Higuchi-Rodzaevsky conversation: "Rodzaevsky Affidavit," 2.

197   Hata-Rodzaevsky conversation: *Ibid.*

197   Envoys from Araki, Itagaki: *Ibid.*, 5. Araki's envoy was a White Russian identified (in Japanese phonetic symbols) only as "Porochyov," in JFMA, A.6.5.0.1–2.

198   Okhotin as Asano Brigade recruiter: Nicholas Petlin, interview, August 29, 1974.

198–199   Asano Brigade members at Nomonhan: "Rodzaevsky Affidavit," 12. IMTFE, *Proceedings*, 7,698. *New York Times*, March 17, 1940.

199   Rodzaevsky explanation for nonoccurrence of National Revolution by May 1, 1938: "To the Russian People," an undated pamphlet (in Russian) intercepted by British censorship, in BFOA, FO 371, 29531.

199–200   Lyushkov defection: Coox, *"L'Affaire* Lyushkov."

200   Matkovsky faction: Nicholas Petlin, letter, January 10, 1975.

200–201   Rodzaevsky-Matkovsky split at Fourth Congress: *Ibid.* Harbin consul general Tsurumi Ken to Arita Hachirō, February 2, 1939, in JFMA, A.6.5.0.1–2.

201–202   Rodzaevsky in Japan (April–May 1939): "Rodzaevsky Affidavit," 3. "Akikusa Affidavit," 2, 4. IMTFE, *Proceedings*, 7,694, 7,701–2. Police report to Home Minister Kido Kōichi, May 3, 1939, in JFMA, A.6.5.0.1–2.

203   Call for "Far Eastern National Front": *Nash Put,* August 10, 1939.
204   Nazi-Soviet pact and RFS membership: Shanghai consul to Matsuoka Yōsuke,
          May 21, 1941, in JFMA, A.6.5.0.1–2.
204   Tedli hailed Nazi-Soviet pact: "Russische Emigranten und Faschisten,"
          GFMA, Gesandtschaft Bern, Aktenzeichen Russland 2 (1941), 80.
204   Tedli deported from Germany: Williams, *Culture in Exile,* 360.
205   Kwantung Army caution after Nomonhan: Young, "Nomonhan Incident,"
          100.
206   Rodzaevsky visit to Tokyo (October 1939): "Rodzaevsky Affidavit," 4.
206   White Russian leaders forced to leave Harbin during boundary commission
          talks (1940): *New York Times,* January 30, 1940.
206   *Tokumu Kikan* banquet for BREM and General Imamura remarks: *Ibid.*
207   White Russian units organized by Semenov for Wang Ching-wei: *New York
          Times,* February 1, 1940; March 17, 1940.
207   30,000 White Russians under arms by 1941: *Ibid.,* March 17, 1940.
207–208   Boris Shepunov and incident at Mutanchiang: Nicholas Petlin, undated
          manuscript (circa 1975). Petlin, interview, August 29, 1974. Petlin, letter,
          May 14, 1976. Balakshin, *Final v Kitae,* I, 205–6. Leshko, *Russkiye v
          Manchzhugo,* 19. Balakshin places the incident in 1942, but Petlin recalls
          that it occurred in 1940.

xiv. Connecticut Capers

209   Advertising quote: from a brochure for the Russian Bear. This brochure
          was kindly brought to my attention by Richard E. Snow.
210   Vonsiatsky in khaki at black-tie dinner: Fred Portunato, letter, July 19, 1974.
210   Better that Alex be occupied than at loose ends: FBI report, February 28,
          1940.
210   Marion's hearing faltered: Frank Decker testimony, "Grand Jury Hearings,"
          263, 268, 273.
211   "Alex, whatever you are saying . . .": Marion de Floresz testimony, *ibid.,*
          695.
211   Marion and Alex mostly apart: Michael Kapral testimony, *ibid.,* 199. Mooza
          Pookhir testimony, *ibid.,* 394.
211   Steve Roshak sympathetic to both Alex and Marion: Helen Roshak, telephone
          interview, May 22, 1976.
212   Sadie Locke: Norman B. Watson testimony, "Grand Jury Hearings," 476.
          Prudence Kwiecien, telephone interview, May 22, 1976.
212   Watson salary and duties: Norman B. Watson testimony, "Grand Jury Hear-
          ings," 416 ff.
212   Michael Kapral: Kapral testimony, *ibid.,* 188.
212   Kunle popularity: Helen Roshak, interview, December 27, 1973.
212   Kunle "soft-spoken": Alexis Sherbatoff, interview, June 18, 1975.
212   "It's like being admitted to an audience with the Führer": Providence *Bulletin,*
          July 2, 1937.
213   "The Russian Fascist Party is the automobile . . .": Providence *Sunday Jour-
          nal,* January 6, 1935.
213   Number of Vonsiatsky followers: "twenty thousand": *Ibid.* "One million":
          Providence *Bulletin,* July 2, 1937. "Can one count . . .": Hartford *Courant,*
          September 23, 1934. "We agreed never to reveal . . .": to David Karr

of *The Hour,* July 27, 1939, as quoted in Karr testimony, "Grand Jury Hearings," 34.

213 Harry Raymond at Nineteenth Hole: R. C. Bannerman report (July 29, 1937), USDS, file #800.00B. VP, XI, 72.

213–214 Richard McCauley: McCauley testimony, "Grand Jury Hearings," 52–71. U.S. District court, District of Connecticut, Hartford. *USA* v. *Anastase A. Vonsiatsky, et al.* (No. 6763 Criminal), 2–3.

214 George Connell: Connell testimony, "Grand Jury Hearings," 72–100.

214 James Bakker: Bakker testimony, *Ibid.,* 614–32. James W. B. Kelley, letter, August 18, 1976.

214 Alex was an accomplished mimic: Andre A. Vonsiatsky, interview, June 7, 1934.

215 Vonsiatsky's traffic tickets: Philadelphia *Evening Bulletin,* March 24, 1923. Providence *Journal,* October 21, 1930. VP, I, 27, 35; III, 8.

215 Vonsiatsky-Nolan friendship: Elton Thomas Nolan testimony, "Grand Jury Hearings," 369, 375–76.

215 Vonsiatsky-Urquhart friendship: Ross Urquhart testimony, *ibid.,* 358, 362.

215–216 Vonsiatsky tear gas to Connecticut State Police: Vonsiatsky to Edward J. Hickey, March 19, 1941; Hickey to Vonsiatsky, March 21, 1941, USDJ file #202600–2871. Ross Urquhart testimony, "Grand Jury Hearings," 350–52.

216 Land grant offer: Vonsiatsky to Hickey, June 11, 1940, USDJ file #202600–2871.

216 Vonsiatsky had agents in forty-three countries: David Karr testimony, "Grand Jury Hearings," 39.

216 Three million copies of *Fashist:* Louis Nemzer memo, December 19, 1941, USDJ file #202600–2871.

217 Reverend Alexander Tzuglevich: Tzuglevich testimony, "Grand Jury Hearings," 224–29.

217–218 Bible School: Tzuglevich testimony, *ibid.,* 217–20. Meunier testimony, *ibid.,* 161–62. New York consul general Iguchi Sadao to Matsuoka Yōsuke, November 25, 1940, in JFMA, A.6.5.0.1–2.

218 Tzuglevich-Bogoslovsky feud: Michael Kapral testimony, "Grand Jury Hearings," 200.

218 Young Avantgarde Camp: *Fashist,* no. 45 (August–September, 1938), 20. Kapral testimony, "Grand Jury Hearings," 200.

218 Mamedov impersonating a woman: Nikita Nikitivich Romanoff, telephone interview, June 15, 1975.

218 "Japan is the only country . . .": Hartford *Courant,* September 23, 1934.

218 "They do not seek a single foot of Russian territory . . .": quoted in "The Near East and India" (July 26, 1934), an enclosure in Abbot to Hull, August 3, 1934, USDS, file #800.00B.

218 Vonsiatsky decried Kwantung Army: R. C. Bannerman report, July 29, 1937, in USDS, file #800.00B.

219 Vonsiatsky and Allen: U.S. Congress, House Committee on Un-American Activities, *Hearings,* VI (1939), 4153.

219 Vonsiatsky and Pease: Lavine, *Fifth Column,* 146

219 Vonsiatsky and Pelley: Thomas J. Dodd in "Grand Jury Hearings," 238–39. *Pelley's Weekly,* September 23, 1936. *Fashist,* no. 30 (January 1937), 24.

219 "Our status obliges us . . .": *Fashist,* no. 43 (June 1938).

219   "I would not like to see the United States become fascist": Vonsiatsky
       to David Karr, July 27, 1939. Karr testimony, "Grand Jury Hearings,"
       39.

219   Vonsiatsky saw best chance for propaganda on left so as to become known
       in USSR: R. C. Bannerman report, July 29, 1937, in USDS, file #800.00B.

220   "Stalin is the best fascist of them all": *Novoye Russkoye Slovo,* May 6, 1938.

220   "Trotsky is my automatic ally": Vonsiatsky to David Karr, July 27, 1939.
       Karr testimony, "Grand Jury Hearings," 35.

220   "100 percent sincere socialist": Bridgeport *Sunday Herald,* February 21, 1937.

220   Vonsiatsky wrote Trotsky: Andre A. Vonsiatsky, interview, June 7, 1974.

220   "He is very frank, but not always consistent": George Connell testimony,
       "Grand Jury Hearings," 80.

221   Vonsiatsky tossed money on store counter: Beatrice Peloquin, interview,
       December 26, 1973.

221   Vonsiatsky's monocle and swagger stick: Prudence Kwiecien, interview, June
       8, 1975.

221   Booming voice and temper: Richard E. Snow, interview, June 7, 1975.

221   "man of destiny," "world trio," etc.: Grozin, *Zashchitniya Rubashki,* 91.

222   Racetrack: Putnam *Patriot,* June 11, 1942.

222   Wax image as national shrine: Hartford *Times,* June 23, 1942.

222   Postage stamps: samples given to author by Andre A. Vonsiatsky, June 8,
       1974.

222   Tsarist currency: Putnam *Patriot,* June 11, 1942.

222   Kutepov Relief Fund: VP, VII, 33.

222   Bounty on Miller's abductor: Hartford *Courant,* September 25, 1937.

222   Shooting gallery: David Karr testimony, "Grand Jury Hearings," 29. Meunier
       testimony, *ibid.,* 143.

223   Murder sweepstakes: Karr testimony, *ibid.,* 41.

223–224 Vonsiatsky practiced speeches in bathtub: Andre A. Vonsiatsky, interview,
       June 7, 1974.

224   Seven hundred model battleships: Putnam *Patriot,* June 11, 1942.

224   Turtles: James W. B. Kelley, letter, August 18, 1976. Hartford *Times,* June
       23, 1942.

225   Olshevsky "secret agent of the GPU": *Fashist* (November 1935).

225   Carrier pigeons: Richard E. Snow, interview, June 7, 1975.

225   Girl friends: Michael Kapral testimony, "Grand Jury Hearings," 199.

225   "Alex was not very discriminating . . .": John Bigelow, interview, June 8,
       1975.

225   Vonsiatsky flings in New York: Thomas Watson, interview, December 27,
       1973. Richard E. Snow, interview, June 7, 1975.

225   Vonsiatsky stayed at Vanderbilt: Norman B. Watson testimony, "Grand Jury
       Hearings," 449.

225   Vonsiatsky and Howe-Marot girls: Prudence Kwiecien, interview, June 7,
       1975. Helen Roshak, interview, December 27, 1973. Millicent Beausoleil,
       December 27, 1973.

225   Marion caught Vonsiatsky in middle of wild party: Helen Roshak, interview,
       December 27, 1973.

226   "She finally realized she was stuck . . .": Frank Decker testimony, "Grand
       Jury Hearings," 273.

226   Vonsiatsky's objectives for Fourth of July weekend: R. C. Bannerman report,
       July 29, 1937, in USDS, file #800.00B.

226   Efforts to boost attendance: Francis Quinlan testimony, "Grand Jury Hearings," 196.

226–228   Fourth of July weekend: testimony of Francis Quinlan, Richard McCauley, James Bakker, Alexander Tzuglevich, *ibid.*, 203 f, 56 f, 618 f, 228 f. Hartford *Courant*, July 5, 1937. Putnam *Patriot*, July 8, 1937. Providence *Bulletin*, July 2, 1937.

226   GRIM GROUP . . .: Hartford *Courant*, July 5, 1937.

227   "The Communists . . .": Hartford *Courant*, July 5, 1937.

228   Unidentified airplanes: *Ibid.*

228   Prince Theodore delayed by ten thousand Lithuanians: Putnam *Patriot*, July 8, 1937.

228   Prince Theodore on fascism: Hartford *Courant*, July 7, 1937. Putnam *Patriot*, July 8, 1937. Karr testimony, "Grand Jury Hearings," 40.

228   "the present form of government in Russia . . .": Hartford *Courant*, July 7, 1937.

xv. Mounting Storm

230   Dickstein quote: *Congressional Record*, 75th Congress, First Session, July 27, 1937. 9971.

230   Twenty investigations of Vonsiatsky: Louis Nemzer memo, December 19, 1941, in USDJ, file #202600–2871.

232–233   Relevant passage of Roosevelt-Litvinov Agreement: U.S. Department of State, *Establishment of Diplomatic Relations with the Union of Soviet Socialist Republics* (Washington, 1933), 5.

233–234   R. C. Bannerman investigation and report of November 10, 1934: USDS, file #800.00B.

234   "clean bill of health": *Washington Star*, December 21, 1934.

234   Dennen attack on Kelley and Vonsiatsky: Dennen, *White Guard Terrorists in the U.S.A.*, 6 ff. Reprinted from the April and May 1935 issues of *Soviet Russia Today*.

234   "a murderer of the Russian workers": *Ibid.*, 7.

234   Vonsiatsky "was acclaimed and feted by Rosenberg": *Ibid.*, 22.

234   "There are at least a million . . .": *Ibid.*, 28.

234–235   Dennen booklet as model for Vonsiatsky's commissioned biography: Compare *White Guard Terrorists* and Grozin's *Zashchitniya Rubashki.*

235   State Department–War Department correspondence on Vonsiatsky's commission: Hull to Dern, March 13, 1935. MacArthur to Hull, March 26, 1935. USDS, file #800.00B. War Department file #G-2/10110–2712. MacArthur made no allusion in his March 26 letter to Hull as to why Vonsiatsky was not reappointed. However, an unsigned Justice Department memo dated July 15, 1941, states that Vonsiatsky's commission was not renewed "because of his connection along political lines" (file #202600–2871).

235   State Department–attorney general correspondence on Vonsiatsky: Hull to Cummings, May 18, 1935. Cummings to Hull, June 17, 1935. USDJ, file #202600–2871.

235   "flagrant violation of the pledge of noninterference given us on November 16": Hull, *Memoirs*, I, 305.

236   Angry Pittsburgh *Press* reader on Vonsiatsky's "private army": A. M. Cooper to Department of State, May 26, 1937, USDJ, file #202600–2871.

236   Answer to angry reader: McMahon to Cooper, June 11, 1937. *Ibid.*

236   ". . . a motley crew of fascists, subversive elements . . .": Morris Kominsky to Aimee [sic] Forand, July 3, 1937. *Ibid.*

237   ALAWAF, FSU, IWO as Communist-front organizations: See Appendix ("Communist Organizations") of Palmer, ed., *The Communist Problem in America.* The Appendix, based upon a list compiled in the late 1940s by Attorney General Tom C. Clark, distinguishes "Communist Organizations" from "Communist-front Organizations," placing the ALAWAF, FSU, and IWO in the former category. However, in 1944, the House Committee on Un-American Activities put the three in the "Communist-front" category (U.S. House of Representatives, Special Committee on Un-American Activities, 78th Congress, 2d Session, *Appendix,* Part IX, 412–29, 758–62, 849–914). Whittaker Chambers called the IWO "Communist-controlled" (*Witness,* 271). Louis Francis Budenz described it as "formed and controlled by Communists" (*Men Without Faces,* 191).

237   ALAWAF protests: Huntington to Citron, Maloney, Hull, July 19, 1937. USDS, file #202600–2871.

237   FSU protests: Randolph to Maloney, July 12, 15; Randolph to Cummings, July 29, 1937. *Ibid.*

237   IWO write-in campaign: Michael Ambrazevich to Hull, Roosevelt, July 17. Letters to Hull from Nicholas Chugay, John Juried, George Fishman, A. Bekeshka, A. Pronevich, S. Zukowsky.

237   Vonsiatsky "uses his home for the purpose of an arsenal . . ": Nicholas Kutzko to Franklin Delano Roosevelt, July 20, 1937. *Ibid.*

237   "The Russian National Revolutionary Fascist Party is a menace": William Weiner to Cordell Hull, July 23, 1937. *Ibid.*

237–238   Samuel Dickstein: *New York Times,* April 23, 1954. *Congressional Record,* January 5, 1937, 23.

238   Dickstein July 9, 1937, radio broadcast attack on Vonsiatsky: *Appendix to the Congressional Record,* vol. 81, part 10 (Washington, 1937), 1761.

238   "The Nazis, the Black Shirts, the Fascists . . .": *Congressional Record,* July 26, 1937, 7635.

238   "50,000 Fascists" within the state of Connecticut: *Ibid.,* July 27, 1937, 9971.

238–241   Second Bannerman visit to Nineteenth Hole: R. C. Bannerman report, July 29, 1937, USDS, file #800.00B.

240–241   Investigation of Vonsiatsky gun purchases: C. L. Willard to T. F. Fitch, July 29, 1937. Fitch to Bannerman, July 28, 1937. *Ibid.*

241   State Department–attorney general correspondence on Vonsiatsky: McMahon to Hull, July 30, 1937. Morse to attorney general, August 12, 1937. McMahon to Hull, August 17, 1937. USDJ, file #202600–2871.

241   Internal Revenue alerted about Vonsiatsky: McMahon to Commissioner of Internal Revenue, August 10, 1937. *Ibid.*

241   FBI alerted to Vonsiatsky: McMahon to Joseph B. Keenan (assistant to the attorney general), August 7, 1937. Keenan to J. Edgar Hoover, August 13, 1937.

241   FBI special agent Starr interview with Vonsiatsky: Louis Nemzer memo (December 19, 1941), USDJ, file #202600–2871.

242   Starr report submitted to attorney general: Justice Department memo ("Russian National Revolutionary Party"), July 15, 1941. USDJ. *Ibid.*

242   Vonsiatsky watched Hitler enter Vienna: Richard McCauley testimony, "Grand Jury Hearings," 68.

242   Vonsiatsky entertained by General Shkuro: Lionel S. Meunier testimony, *ibid.*, 162.

242   "he has an arsenal and a little army of his own": John C. Metcalfe testimony, House Committee on Un-American Activities, *Hearings*, III, 2381.

242   Vonsiatsky felt slighted about being ignored by Dies Committee: Bridgeport *Sunday Herald*, July 23, 1939.

242n   Second world tour uneventful (1936): Naval Intelligence reports of March 27, June 3, June 8, 1936. USDJ, file #202600–2871.

243   Vonsiatsky in Los Angeles and San Francisco: Naval Intelligence report, January 24, 1939. USDJ. *Ibid.* Los Angeles Times, January 17, 1939.

243–244   Vonsiatsky in Honolulu: Honolulu *Star Bulletin*, January 28, 1939. Honolulu *Advertiser*, January 29, 1939.

244   Vonsiatsky in Shanghai: *North China Herald*, March 1, 1939. Ilina, *Vozvrashcheniye*, 292. *Fashist*, no. 49 (April–May 1939), 2, 5. Vonsiatsky gave a talk at the Park Hotel on February 17, which he later reprinted in Thompson. Vonsiatsky, *Rech Soratnika A. A. Vonsiatskovo*. Miura to Arita, March 8, 1939, in JFMA A.6.5.0.1–2.

244   Steklov's newspaper considered anti-Japanese: Japanese Army General Staff, Intelligence (Shanghai Branch), "Zaiko hakkei Rōjin no genjō" ["Present condition of White Russians in Shanghai,"] September 7, 1939, in JAA, T-955, R-113, frame 24997.

244   Vonsiatsky's biography: Grozin, *Zashchitniya Rubashki*. Grozin's book carried a portrait of Marion (facing p. 128) painted by V. Podgursky.

245   Third Reich banned VNRP: Karr testimony, "Grand Jury Hearings," 37–38, 69. FBI report, March 20, 1939. Justice Department Memorandum dated July 15, 1941, USDJ, file #202600–7821.

245   Young Vonsiatsky follower intimidated by Gestapo: FBI special agent Meunier testimony, "Grand Jury Hearings," 168.

245   Vonsiatsky motives for courting Bund: Vonsiatsky to David Karr, July 27, 1939, as testified to by Karr, "Grand Jury Hearings," 44. Louis Nemzer memo (December 19, 1941) in USDJ, file #202600–2871.

245–246   Fritz Kuhn: *New York Times*, February 2, 1953. August Klapprott testimony, "Grand Jury Hearings," 804.

246   Kuhn claimed uniform modeled on that of American Legion: Lavine, *Fifth Column*, 157.

246   Kuhn invited Vonsiatsky to Hippodrome rally: Karr testimony, "Grand Jury Hearings," 170. Some sources (Karr, Vonsiatsky, FBI report of March 20, 1939) place the rally at Madison Square Garden. As reported by The *New York Times* (February 13, 1937), however, it took place at the Hippodrome.

246   Mamedov at rally: Although Vonsiatsky made no mention of Mamedov being at the Hippodrome rally, Mamedov himself later testified under oath that he was there. *USA* v. *Vonsiatsky* (Criminal 6763), 4.

247   Melnikov and the Russian National Union: Balakshin, *Final v Kitae*, I, 115.

247   Vonsiatsky behavior at rally: FBI report, March 20, 1939. Vonsiatsky to Karr, July 27, 1939, as testified by Karr, "Grand Jury Hearings," 170.

247   Camp Siegfried opening: *New York Times*, May 22, 1939.

248   Vonsiatsky at Camp Siegfried: Karr testimony, "Grand Jury Hearings," 50. Klapprott testimony, *ibid.*, 811.

248   Kunze visited Nineteenth Hole several (five) times in June, July 1939: Mame-

dov testimony (July 30, 1942), *USA* v. *Vonsiatsky* (Criminal 6763—typescript), 58. The typescript of Criminal 6763 (Federal Archives and Records Center) differs in some areas from the printed transcript of Criminal 6763 (in USDJ, file #202600–2871). All references are to the printed transcript unless otherwise noted.

248 Vonsiatsky called Kunze "Wilhelm Gerhardavich": *USA* v. *Vonsiatsky* (Criminal 6763), 146.

248–249 Kuhn, Kunze, Wheeler-Hill drop by Nineteenth Hole: Kuhn testimony (August 16, 1939), House Committee on Un-American Activities, *Hearings,* VI, 3708. Vonsiatsky to Karr, as testified by Karr, "Grand Jury Hearings," 171. Louis Nemzer memo (December 19, 1941), USDJ, file #202600–2871.

248 Louis Marshall Ream avoided crossing road to meet Vonsiatsky, Kuhn: Frank Decker testimony, "Grand Jury Hearings," 261.

249 Kuhn indictment for larceny: *New York Times,* May 24, 1939 (for Dewey role, *New York Times,* May 9, May 18, 1939).

249–250 Webster incident: *Ibid.,* July 17, 18, 1939. *Newsweek,* October 30, 1939. *The Hour,* no. 7 (July 30, 1939).

250 "Attempted putsch": Bridgeport *Sunday Herald,* July 23, 1939.

250 Vonsiatsky, Kuhn at Webster courthouse: *New York Times,* July 21, 1939.

250 Vonsiatsky brought libel suits against press: INS special agent Mitchell S. Solomon report on Vonsiatsky, April 1, 1941, USDJ, file #202600–2871.

251 Role of McCauley in supplying photos to *The Hour:* Richard McCauley testimony, *USA* v. *Vonsiatsky* (Criminal 6763—typescript), 56.

251 Karr-McCauley affidavit of August 2, 1939: "Grand Jury Hearings," 47–48.

251 "To the best of my knowledge . . .": Albert E. Kahn, letter, May 18, 1976.

251 ACANP telegram to Frances Perkins: Justice Department memo, July 15, 1941, in USDJ, file #202600–2871.

251 Dodd to Martin Dies on Vonsiatsky: *New York Times,* August 19, 1939. Similar appeals to Dies were made in *Novaya Zarya* (August 9, 1939) and the Bridgeport *Sunday Herald* (August 13, 1939).

252 Dickstein on Vonsiatsky: Dickstein to Hull, August 21, 1939. Hull to Dickstein, August 30, 1939. Hull to Murphy, August 30. USDJ, file #202600–2871.

252 FBI special agent lived two years in Putnam: Putnam *Patriot,* September 10, 1942.

252 Attorney general obtained Vonsiatsky's income tax returns: Frank Murphy to Henry Morgenthau, Jr., March 29, 1939.

252 Vonsiatsky's machine gun registered: FBI report, March 20, 1939.

252 "failed to disclose any information which would indicate that Vonsiatsky is receiving [foreign support]": FBI report, February 28, 1940.

253 ". . . any such drilling would be visible . . ." FBI report, February 28, 1940.

253 Holtzoff and INS reports: Justice Department memorandum, July 15, 1941, USDJ, file #202600–2871.

253 Rogge to Dickstein, September 13, 1939: USDJ, file #202600–2871.

254 Vonsiatsky hailed Nazi-Soviet Pact: *Fashist,* no. 54 (October–November 1939).

254 Tkoch told FBI that Vonsiatsky was working for Communists: Justice Department memorandum, July 15, 1941, USDJ, file #202600–2871.

254   "Drang nach Ossining": Lavine, *Fifth Column in America,* 161.
254   Mamedov quit VNRP: Lev Beck Mamedov testimony, *USA* v. *Vonsiatsky* (Criminal 6763—typescript), 60.
254   Kunle quit VNRP, went to California: Justice Department memorandum, July 15, 1941, USDJ, file #202600–2871.
254   Vonsiatsky told FBI agent about VNRP membership drop: *Ibid.*
255   Vonsiatsky gave machine gun to Nolan: Vonsiatsky to Hickey, June 7, 1940, USDJ, file #202600–2871.
255   Manifesto of July 4, 1940: "Vonsiatsky Affidavit," 6–7. Justice Department memorandum, July 15, 1941, USDJ, file #202600–2871.
255–256 Vonsiatsky foresaw U.S. involvement in European war after Lend-Lease Act passed (March 11, 1941): Vonsiatsky to Steklov, March 17, 1941, in *Fashist,* no. 63 (July–September 1941), 2. This letter was translated and included in Louis Nemzer's memorandum of December 19, 1941, USDJ, file #202600–2871.
256   Vonsiatsky ordered Steklov to take over VNRP: *Ibid.*
256   Varieties of public Vonsiatskiana: *Liberty,* September 30, 1939. Lavine, *Fifth Column in America,* 137–48 (Vonsiatsky ran arms to Franco, 146). *The Hour,* nos. 7, 8, (August 15, 1939), 12 (September 23, 1939), 18 (November 4, 1939), 27 (January 13, 1940), 29 (January 27, 1940), and 58 (August 17, 1940).
256   New York City Police Department file on Vonsiatsky: Mitchell S. Solomon report, April 1, 1941, USDJ, file #202600–2871.
256   Youngstown, Ohio informant: Louis Nemzer memorandum, December 19, 1941. *Ibid.*
256   Rochester, New York, informant: Mitchell S. Solomon report, April 1, 1941. *Ibid.*
257   Kahn made *The Hour* files available to investigators: *Ibid.*
257   "You see, in those bygone days . . .": Albert E. Kahn, letter, February 20, 1976.
257   Kenneth Watson as an informant: Louis Nemzer memorandum, December 19, 1941, USDJ, file #202600–2871.
257   Mordecai Ezekiel input: T. B. Shoemaker (deputy commissioner, Immigration and Naturalization Service) to Wendell Berge, January 31, 1941. *Ibid.*
257   Mitchell S. Solomon report on Vonsiatsky (April 1, 1941): USDJ, file #202600–2871.

xvi. Year of the Apocalypse

259   Rodzaevsky quote: Order no. 3, Rodzaevsky to Vladimir Shelikhov, June 27, 1941, intercepted by Imperial Censorship Bermuda, BFOA, FO 371, 29531/N6760.
259   Vonsiatsky quote: *Novaya Zarya* (San Francisco Russian daily), July 26, 1941. English translation of the article deposited in USDJ, file #202600–2871.
259   Émigré reactions to German invasion of USSR: Fischer, *Soviet Opposition to Stalin,* 19. Balakshin, *Final v Kitae,* I, 409.
259   "that blind naïveté which let one misconceive of Hitler as a potential liberator": Avinov, *Pilgrimage Through Hell,* 193.
259   Prince Trubetskoi petition: *Nordschleswigsche Tageszeitung,* July 3, 1941, enclosure in DAI, T-81, R-551, frame 5325649.

259–260   Tedli efforts to return to Germany: "Russische Emigranten und Fascisten," 111, 137 ff, in GFMA, Gesandtschaft Bern, Aktenzeichen Russland 2.

260   Rodzaevsky reaction to German attack: *Nash Put,* July 20, 1941, intercepted by Canadian Postal Censorship, translated, and eventually deposited in BFOA, FO 371, 29531/N6760.

260–261   Rodzaevsky's letters and cables to Europe: BFOA, FO 371, 29531/N6760.

260n   *Nash Put* offices moved from Harbin to Shanghai: *Tokyo saiban,* I, 504.

261   Wehrmacht plans for dividing USSR with Japan: Meskill, *Hitler and Japan,* 109–13.

261   "Third down and five yards to go!": Frank Decker testimony, "Grand Jury Hearings," 263.

261   "If Hitler comes out against Russia . . .": Vonsiatsky, *Osnovy Russkavo Fashizma,* 24.

262   Vonsiatsky telegram to Stalin: Naval Intelligence report, November 6, 1941, in USDJ, file #202600–2871.

263   Kunle death: Putnam *Patriot,* June 26, 1941.

263   Indignant at Kunle about to be cremated "like garbage": Andre A. Vonsiatsky, interview, June 7, 1974.

263   Vonsiatsky mausoleum: *Ibid.* Helen Roshak, telephone interview, May 22, 1976. Bridgeport *Sunday Herald,* July 6, 1941. James Bakker testimony, "Grand Jury Hearings," 625. Visits by author, 1973–75.

264   Kunze, Klapprott visit to Nineteenth Hole (February 1941): August Klapprott testimony, "Grand Jury Hearings," 768, 771, 814.

264   New Jersey indictment of Bundists: *New York Times,* February 1, 4, 1941.

264   Bundists at Kunle's funeral: Louis Nemzer memorandum, December 19, 1941, USDJ, file #202600–2871.

264   Kunze background and need for money: Kunze testimony, *USA* v. *Vonsiatsky* (Criminal 6763), 190–94, 575.

264–265   ". . . after the outbreak of the war": Vonsiatsky to Meunier, as testified by Meunier, "Grand Jury Hearings," 171–2.

265   Vonsiatsky paid Kunze $2,800: *Ibid.,* 172. Kunze testimony, *USA* v. *Vonsiatsky* (Criminal 6763), 144–45. Louis Nemzer memorandum, December 19, 1941, USDJ, file #202600–2871.

265   *Free American* eulogy of Kunle: Nemzer memorandum, December 19, 1941, USDJ, file #202600–2871.

265–266   Vonsiatsky and Kunze agree to meet in Chicago: Meunier testimony, "Grand Jury Hearings," 172.

266   Kunze letter to Vonsiatsky: *USA* v. *Vonsiatsky* (Criminal 6763), 144–45.

266   Nakamura Hitoshi: Meunier testimony, "Grand Jury Hearings," 165. Thomas J. Dodd, *Ibid.,* 239–40. Mamedov called Nakamura a "count" (*ibid.,* 125), yet it appears from Dodd's discussion of their correspondence and Vonsiatsky's own remarks that Nakamura Hitoshi was an executive in a shipping company. Examination of *Nippon shinshiroku* and *Teikoku shinshiroku* for 1939 and 1940 revealed three Nakamura Hitoshis living in Tokyo, but none were in the shipping business. Unfortunately for purposes of tracing, "Nakamura" is an extremely common name in Japan.

266   Vonsiatsky "especially friendly" with Nakamura Fusako: Vonsiatsky to Meunier, as testified by Meunier, "Grand Jury Hearings," 165.

267   Fusako at Nineteenth Hole (1936): Lev Beck Mamedov testimony, "Grand Jury Hearings," 125. Norman B. Watson testimony, *ibid.,* 422.

267   Vonsiatsky and Fusako spoke to each other in French: George Connell testimony, *ibid.*, 90.

267n   Nakamura Fusako's photograph is currently among Vonsiatsky's papers in St. Petersburg, Florida.

267   Marion's friends disturbed about Fusako's being at Nineteenth Hole (1940): Frank Decker testimony, "Grand Jury Hearings," 266. Michael Kapral noted (*ibid.*, 192–93) that Vonsiatsky also invited a Japanese girl student from the Howe-Marot School.

267   Vonsiatsky and Fusako to New Haven for Brown-Yale game: George Connell testimony, *ibid.*, 88. Philip King (headwaiter, Taft Hotel) testimony, *ibid.*, 186–87.

267   Takita Momoyo: *USA* v. *Vonsiatsky* (Criminal 6763), exhibit 27 (*Tatsuta maru* passenger list from San Francisco collector of customs), 58. Vonsiatsky to Meunier, as testified by Meunier, "Grand Jury Hearings," 167.

267   Possibility that Vonsiatsky was to meet another woman: *USA* v. *Vonsiatsky* (Criminal 6763), 20.

267   *Tatsuta maru* delayed: *Ibid.*, 58.

267   Vonsiatsky registered at Mark Hopkins under assumed name: Thomas J. Dodd, "Grand Jury Hearings," 16.

268   Vonsiatsky-Serebrennikov conversation: Serebrennikov testimony, *USA* v. *Vonsiatsky* (Criminal 6763), 58. For translation of *Novaya Zarya* article, see USDJ, file #202600–2871.

269–270   Alexius Pelypenko: *USA* v. *Vonsiatsky* (Criminal 6763), 656–57; (Criminal 6763—typescript), 72–77. T. Harry Walnut, *The Molzahn Case*, booklet in USDJ, #202600–2871.

269   Prince Stephan: Goebbels, *Diaries*, 356.

270n   Willumeit-Pelypenko meeting: Willumeit testimony, "Grand Jury Hearings," 836. Pelypenko testimony, *USA* v. *Vonsiatsky* (Criminal 6763), 7.

270–271   Bismarck Hotel meeting: Willumeit testimony, "Grand Jury Hearings," 834–45. Vonsiatsky to Meunier, as testified by Meunier, *ibid.*, 166. Kunze testimony, *USA* v. Vonsiatsky (Criminal 6763), 594–95. Willumeit testimony, *ibid.*, 623. Louis Nemzer memorandum, December 19, 1941, USDJ, file #202600–2871.

270   Vonsiatsky did not speak German: Pelypenko testimony, *USA* v. *Vonsiatsky* (Criminal 6763), 23.

271   Vonsiatsky's version of Pelypenko's two visits to Nineteenth Hole (including quotations): Meunier testimony, "Grand Jury Hearings," 166–67.

271–272   Pelypenko version of Bismarck Hotel meeting, two visits to Nineteenth Hole, and call on Japanese embassy: Pelypenko testimony, "Grand Jury Hearings," 510 ff. Pelypenko testimony, *USA* v. *Vonsiatsky* (Criminal 6763), 12, 19–21. M. E. Schaeffer report to J. Edgar Hoover, October 15, 1941, USDJ, #202600–2871. Louis Nemzer memorandum, December 19, 1941, *ibid.*

272n   Pelypenko on number present at Bismarck Hotel meeting: five (George Froboese present): Pelypenko to FBI, Louis Nemzer memorandum, USDJ, file #202600–2871; four: Pelypenko testimony, *USA* v. *Vonsiatsky* (Criminal 6763), 22.

272n   Colonel Kobayashi Gunji: Ōkurashō, *Shokuinroku* (1939), 125.

273   Pelypenko withholding information from FBI and concentrating on crypto-Nazi Ukrainians: INS special agent Mitchell S. Solomon to Sylvester Pindyck (INS commissioner), September 15, 1941, USDJ, file #202600–2871.

274   Andy Mamedov joined RAF: Richard McCauley testimony, "Grand Jury Hearings," 61.

274   Next issue of *Fashist* to be published in Moscow: Bridgeport *Sunday Herald*, August 17, 1941, cited in Nemzer memo, December 19, 1941, USDJ, file #202600–2871.

274   "improving the Quinnatisset Country Club": Putnam *Patriot*, May 14, 1942.

275   Kunze watched closely by other Bundists: Shaeffer report to J. Edgar Hoover, October 15, 1941. Paxman report to J. Edgar Hoover, September 23, 1941. USDJ, file #202600–2871.

275   Kunze reelected at Bund convention: *Ibid.*

275   Kunze promised to remain in U.S. if reelected: Willumeit testimony, "Grand Jury Hearings," 847.

275   Kunze's New Jersey fine paid by Bund membership: Klapprott testimony, "Grand Jury Hearings," 797.

275   Vonsiatsky neither criminal nor foreign agent: Justice Department memo, July 15, 1941, USDJ, file #202600–2871.

276   "someone prominent in the National Councils of the Bund": page 29 of Nemzer memo, December 19, 1941, *ibid.*

276   Special Defense Unit: Nemzer memo of November 25, 1941. *Ibid.*

276   Bisgyer letter to Vonsiatsky: referred to in Mitchell to Bisgyer, October 27, 1941. *Ibid.*

276   Vonsiatsky's and Marion's bank accounts blocked: "Vonsiatsky Affidavit," 9.

277   Andrew Mamedov death: Norwich *Bulletin*, October 16, 1941.

277   VNRP "more or less a one-man affair": Mitchell to Justice Department, October 27, 1941. USDJ, file #202600–2871.

277–278 Mitchell-Kane correspondence: *Ibid.*

277   "Race-hatred" law unconstitutional: *New York Times*, December 6, 1941.

277   Kunze flight to Mexico on November 6: Kunze testimony, *USA* v. *Vonsiatsky* (Criminal 6763), 606.

277   Kunze postcard to Vonsiatsky: Meunier testimony, "Grand Jury Hearings," 172.

278   Kunze letter to Vonsiatsky (December 8): *USA* v. *Vonsiatsky* (Criminal 6763), 146.

279   VNRP registration questionnaire: USDJ, file #202600–2871.

279   Akivisson on Vonsiatsky: DeWitt C. Poole "secret memorandum" to attorney general, December 9, 1941, USDJ, *ibid.*

279   Anti-Defamation League on Vonsiatsky: Arnold Forster to Bisgyer, December 3, 12, 1941; Miles M. Goldberg to Bisgyer, December 8, 1941. USDJ, *ibid.*

279   "cabinet full" of documents and Vonsiatsky's "confession to the commission of seven murders": Forster to Bisgyer, December 12, 1941. *Ibid.*

280   ". . . it may well be that this very resemblance to a comic opera character . . .": Louis Nemzer memorandum, December 19, 1941. *Ibid.*

xvii. Mime and Punishment

281   Dodd quote: "Grand Jury Hearings," 25.

281   Vonsiatsky rifles to Civil Defense Company: Hartford *Times*, May 9, 1942. *Windham County Observer*, May 13, 1942.

282   "a dangerous element in this country": *Congressional Record,* March 18, 1942, 2668.

282   Urquhart warned Vonsiatsky: Anne V. Kenney, interview, December 26, 1973.

282   FBI raid: Hartford *Times,* May 9, 1942. Hartford *Courant,* May 10, 1942. New York *Herald Tribune,* May 10, 1942. *New York Times,* May 10, 1942. Putnam *Patriot,* May 14, 1942.

282   Vonsiatsky thought that Marion was entertaining: *Windham County Observer,* May 13, 1942.

283   Vonsiatsky eager to help agents: *Ibid.*

283   Vonsiatsky talked all night with Meunier, Mahan: Meunier testimony, "Grand Jury Hearings," 145–75.

283   Other VNRP *soratniki* visited by FBI: *New York Times,* May 14, 1942. San Francisco *Examiner,* May 10, 1942.

283   Vonsiatsky knew only what he read in the press: Hartford *Times,* May 11, 1942.

283   Vonsiatsky avoided signing statement drawn up by Meunier: Meunier testimony, "Grand Jury Hearings," 175–76.

283   "an elaborate wardrobe of fascist uniforms": Hartford *Courant,* May 12, 1942.

283   Catalogue of effects taken away in truck: *New York Times,* May 14, 1942. Hartford *Times,* May 14, 1942.

283   Office left stripped: Putnam *Patriot,* May 14, 1942.

284   Justice Department linguists brought up from Washington: Hartford *Times,* May 14, 1942.

284–285 Dodd background: *Who's Who in U.S. Politics* (New York, 1952), 92. *New York Times,* June 28, 1966. Boyd, *Above the Law,* 8–9.

284–285 "Dodd learned, in a sort of trial by combat . . .": Boyd, *Above the Law,* 9.

285   Kahn helped Dodd on Vonsiatsky case: Albert E. Kahn, letter, February 20, 1976.

286   Federal grand jury members, court judge: Hartford *Times,* May 14, 1942.

286   "it is a matter that we believe very gravely concerns the safety of this government . . .": Robert P. Butler, "Grand Jury Hearings," 3.

286   "I have been acting almost eight years . . .": *Ibid.,* 3–4.

286–287 Dodd summary of Vonsiatsky background: *Ibid.,* 4–26. Dodd's mention of "registered mail to Alaska" is puzzling and not subsequently substantiated. The phrase is probably traceable to Pelypenko.

287   "Vonsiatsky, not so long ago . . .": Dodd, *ibid.,* 25.

290   Pelypenko dropped name of Prince Stephan: *Ibid.,* 517.

290   Vonsiatsky as "director of the German—of the Japanese—spy ring in this country": Pelypenko, *ibid.,* 525.

290   Vonsiatsky "in charge of German espionage in Canada": Pelypenko, *ibid.,* 572.

290   Vonsiatsky agents on Kodiak Island, at Sitka: Pelypenko, *ibid.,* 516.

290   "I spit upon American citizenship": Pelypenko quoting Vonsiatsky, *ibid.,* 518.

290   Outburst against "Polacks" and FBI supervisor: Pelypenko, *ibid.,* 526–27.

291   "Anything else? . . . We don't need you anymore": Dodd, *ibid.,* 581.

291   Dodd saw Rodzaevsky and Semenov as members of VNRP: Dodd, *ibid.,* 65.

291   Dodd linked "Hiroshita" to Hirohito: *Ibid.,* 105.

291   Dodd on Michael Karpovich: *Ibid.,* 310.

291   "I knew he was a great man for publicity . . .": Nolan, *ibid.,* 376.
291   "Well, he is a darn fool . . .": Urquhart, *ibid.,* 356.
292   "I didn't take these things seriously": Connell, *ibid.,* 78.
292   "The impression that I have makes it difficult for me to conceive of his movement as being serious . . .": Bakker, *ibid.,* 627–28.
292   Vonsiatsky as kind, fair, and a good American citizen: Watson, *ibid.,* 473–74. Sisson, 498.
292   "If Mr. Hitler wishes me to represent Germany in Russia, I am willing to go": Vonsiatsky quoted by de Floresz, *ibid.,* 700.
292   "everybody looked on him as more or less a joke": de Floresz, *ibid.,* 699.
293   "just a lot of soap bubbles": Pookhir, *ibid.,* 396.
293   "Is there anything the matter with your memory?": Dodd, *ibid.,* 76.
293   "it seems as though there might be some other information which your men should have obtained": Dodd, *ibid.,* 363.
293   "All these conversations you had with him over the years": Dodd, *ibid.,* 375–76.
293   "You are a United States citizen and a soldier . . .": Dodd, *ibid.,* 627.
293   "I would like to correct you, sir": Bakker, *ibid.,* 627.
293   "It might mean your head": Dodd, *ibid.,* 632.
294   "Don't you think . . .": Dodd, *ibid.,* 430.
294   "And you sit here and pretend . . .": Dodd, *ibid.,* 430.
294   "I don't know whether you are dumb . . .": Dodd, *ibid.,* 453.
294   "You get out of here . . .": Dodd, *ibid.,* 484.
295   Bill of Indictment (June 10, 1942): included in Criminal 6763 file at Federal Archives and Records Center, Waltham.
295   Keegan on Ream lawyers: to FBI agents Kane and Crocker. USDJ, file #202600–2871.
295   Martin W. Littleton, Sr. and Harry Thaw case: *New York Times,* June 26, July 11, July 24, 1906; February 23, 1947; December 20, 1934.
295–296 Martin W. Littleton, Jr.: Hartford *Times,* June 20, 1942. *New York Times,* August 31, 1966.
296   "he is considered somewhat deranged . . .": FBI report, March 20, 1939.
296   "ill-balanced, hysterical teuto-polak": Schüddekopf, *Fascism,* 126.
296–297 Littleton's attempt to have Vonsiatsky certified insane: Hartford *Times,* June 6, 1942. Hartford *Courant,* June 6, 7, 1942. *Windham County Observer,* June 10, 1942. Putnam *Patriot,* June 11, 1942. Kenneth Watson, "Tells of Efforts to Put Spy Suspect in Insane Asylum," New York *World-Telegram,* June 16, 1942.
297   Vonsiatsky's arrest in Providence: *New York Times,* June 7, 9, 1942. New York *Herald Tribune,* June 7, 1942. Hartford *Courant,* June 7, 1942.
297   Vonsiatsky was getting a haircut at time of arrest: Providence *Journal,* June 7, 1942. According to Helen Roshak, Vonsiatsky was with Natasha Novozhilov, daughter of Ivan Novozhilov, ex-VNRP representative in Boston (letter, August 8, 1975).
297   Vonsiatsky's behavior in Providence jail: report of U.S. Marshal Neal D. Murphy, Criminal 6763 file, Federal Archives and Records Center.
298   Arraignment scene: Hartford *Times,* June 11, 1942.
298   Littleton account of Vonsiatsky's madness: Hartford *Courant,* June 11, 1942. New York *World-Telegram,* June 15, 1942. New York *Journal-American,* June 15, 1942. New York *Daily Mirror,* June 15, 1942.

298   "We think he is guilty of what we charge him with . . .": Dodd, as quoted by Kenneth Watson in New York *World-Telegram,* June 15, 1942.

299   "Either Anastase Vonsiatsky is one of the most curious lunatics in the country, . . .": *Ibid.*

299   Dodd petition to cancel Vonsiatsky's citizenship: Hartford *Courant,* June 13, 1942. *New York Times,* June 14, 1942.

299   Vonsiatsky "drawn and haggard" when sentenced: Hartford *Times,* June 23, 1942. See also Hartford *Courant,* June 23, 1942. *New York Times,* June 23, 1942.

299–300   Dodd, Littleton, Smith statements: Hartford *Courant,* June 23, 1942.

300   Fine revoked: *New York Times,* June 25, 1942.

300–301   "Operation Pastorius": *New York Times,* June 28, 30, 1942.

301   Dodd saw possible Neubauer-Vonsiatsky link: Hartford *Times,* June 30, 1942.

301   Sentences of Bundists: Criminal 6763 file, Federal Archives and Records Center.

301   Kunze arrest in Mexico City: *New York Times,* July 4, 5, 1942. Kunze testimony, *USA* v. *Vonsiatsky* (Criminal 6763), 568.

301–302   George A. Kennedy testimony on Araki Sadao: *USA* v. *Vonsiatsky* (Criminal 6763), 115–6.

302   Dodd insinuation that Ebell had foreknowledge of Pearl Harbor attack: *Ibid.,* 598–99.

302   "a great injustice," "the uncorroborated version . . . ," "the prosecution stooped to deceit . . .": Walnut, "The Molzahn Case," i, in USDJ, file #202600–2871.

302   Vonsiatsky friends inducted into the army with unusual dispatch: Alexis Sherbatoff, interview, June 18, 1975.

302   Steps taken to strip Vonsiatsky of citizenship: New York *Herald Tribune,* December 17, 1942. *New York Times,* December 17, 1942. *The Hour,* no. 137 (June 27, 1942), also urged that Vonsiatsky be deported after serving a prison term.

302   Vonsiatsky's infected tooth: report of U.S. Marshal Bernard Fitch, July 14, 1942, in Criminal 6763 file, Federal Archives and Records Center.

302   "a penitentiary selected by the Attorney General": U.S. District Court, Connecticut Division, "Judgment and Commitment," June 23, 1942.

302   Vonsiatsky did not know his destination: *Windham County Observer,* July 22, 1942.

303–305   Reports of Vonsiatsky's behavior at Springfield: "Medical Record of A. A. Vonsiatsky," No. 3775-H, Medical Center for Federal Prisons, Bureau of Prisons, United States Department of Justice.

Note on locating and using the above records: After being told by John W. Ream (letter, November 27, 1973) that Vonsiatsky had been imprisoned in Leavenworth, inquiries were sent to the United States Penitentiary at Leavenworth, Kansas, and the United States Disciplinary Barracks at Fort Leavenworth, Kansas, with negative results. An inquiry to the National Personnel Records Center in St. Louis for Vonsiatsky's records also yielded no result (his files were apparently destroyed in a fire that damaged the Center on July 12, 1973). On January 17, 1974, however, Pasquale J. Ciccone, M.D., director of the Medical Center for Federal Prisoners in

Springfield, Missouri, wrote that Vonsiatsky had been confined at that institution. Further correspondence with the Medical Center and the Bureau of Prisons indicated that Vonsiatsky's records could not be released except by authorization of next of kin (letter of Assistant General Counsel Clair A. Cripe, March 14, 1974). On April 10, 1974, Andre A. Vonsiatsky gave such authorization. The Bureau of Prisons released the records to Mr. Vonsiatsky (letter of Norman A. Carlson, June 3, 1974), who generously passed them on to the author to be used without restrictions.

305   Marion's visits to Vonsiatsky in prison: Thomas Watson, interview, December 27, 1973.

306   Dickstein on Vonsiatsky: *Congressional Record,* July 1, 1942, 5905.

306   Hynd on Vonsiatsky: *Passport to Treason,* 187, 214, 217.

307   Derounian on Vonsiatsky: Carlson, *Under Cover,* 177–79.

307   Kahn on Vonsiatsky: *Sabotage!,* 70–79.

307   "actively conspiring with the German American Bund": *Ibid.,* 72.

307   "addressed large meetings of Bund Storm Troopers . . .": *Ibid.,* 73.

307   "conferred with Alfred Rosenberg, Dr. Goebbels, . . .": *Ibid.,* 75.

307   "His last visit to Tokyo was in 1941; . . .": *Ibid.,* 74.

307–308   "Shortly before Japan attacked the United States, . . .": *Ibid.,* 78.

308   "Scarcely a week passed . . .": *Ibid.,* 73–74.

308   "I was fighting Nazis, and I didn't bother too much about amenities": Albert E. Kahn, letter, February 20, 1976.

308   Vonsiatsky in Lanny Budd series: Sinclair, *Presidential Agent,* 515.

308–309   Walter Winchell on Vonsiatsky: *Liberty,* August 1, 1942.

309   Foley on Vonsiatsky: *Ibid.,* November 28, 1942.

309   Vonsiatsky and plan to divide up U.S. along Rocky Mountains: A clipping of Springfield's *Sunday News & Leader* article (March 23, 1943) is pasted in Vonsiatsky's scrapbook in St. Petersburg.

xviii. Last Tango in Harbin

310   "Even with the devil, always against Bolsheviks!": Rodzaevsky as quoted by Nicholas Petlin, letter, January 10, 1975.

311   Petlin left party in July 1941 over disagreement with Rodzaevsky about cooperation with Germany: Petlin, interview, October 10, 1976.

311n   Lydia Malkova: Nicholas Petlin, letter, October 28, 1974, and interview, October 10, 1976.

311   Germans wooed White Russians in Manchukuo: Umezu Yoshijirō (Japanese ambassador to Manchukuo and commander of the Kwantung Army) to Foreign Minister Tōgō Shigenori, April 28, 1942, in JFMA, A.6.5.0.1–2.

311   Erwin von Schultz and Tedli: "Russische Emigranten und Faschisten, Nationalkomitee der Weissrussen," 119 in GFMA, Gesandtschaft Bern, Aktenzeichen Russland 2.

311   Conference of pro-Nazi Russian émigrés in Berlin: EOT, T-454, R-17, frame 682.

312   "The Russians can never have their national state": Himmler to Schellenberg, GSS, T-175, R-68, frame 2584410.

312   Rosenberg's plans for Russia: Shirer, *Rise and Fall of the Third Reich,* 832–34.

312   Hitler's plans for Russia: *Ibid.,* 942. But it has also been noted that Hitler was "wholly unwilling to think in political terms of any post-Stalin organization of the USSR" (Fischer, *Soviet Opposition to Stalin,* 10).

312n   Wehrmacht plans to occupy Russia to Yenisei: Meskill, *Hitler and Japan,* 109–13.

312   Hitler joke about Stalin knowing how to handle Russians: Speer, *Inside the Third Reich,* 306.

312   Prohibition of Russian translations: Dallin, *German Rule in Russia,* 525n.

313   Japanese flags over the Urals: Matsuoka supposedly stated, "It is my hope to hoist Japanese flags on the Ural range," in a speech at an SMR construction site on December 21, 1936. Quoted by *China Weekly Review,* January 9, 1937.

314   Vlasevsky and Kislitsyn pledge total support for Japan: Balakshin, *Final v Kitae,* I, 233–34.

314–315   Otsu plan: IMTFE, *Proceedings,* 40,599–600.

315–316   Kwantung Army plans to utilize White Russians for combat: *Ibid.,* 7,662–70. Japan, Bōei-chō, Bōei Kenshujo, Senshishitsu, *Kantōgun,* II, 53 (hereafter, *Kantōgun*).

316   *Kantokuen* and White Russians: *Kantōgun,* II, 54. Lieutenant General Yanagita Genzō testimony, "Trial of White Guard Leaders and Japanese Spies," *Pravda,* August 28, 1946. Colonel Asada Saburō testimony, *Pravda,* August 29, 1946.

316   Rodzaevsky supervised drafting of anti-Soviet pamphlets: Konstantin Rodzaevsky affidavit, April 11, 1946, IMTFE, Prosecution Document no. 2364, 13 (hereafter, "Rodzaevsky Affidavit").

316   Colonel Niimura to Rodzaevsky on invasion of Siberia: *Ibid.,* 4.

316   Major General Doi to Rodzaevsky about BREM being future Russian government: *Ibid.,* 10.

316   Living conditions in Harbin, winter 1942–43: Lydia Schmüser, letter, May 4, 1976 and memoirs, part II, 140.

317   Rodzaevsky's family: Neonilla Yalisheva, interview, August 27, 1974. Vladimir Rodzaevsky, telephone interview, November 7, 1976.

317–318   Drunken *Kempei* thugs beating up *soratniki:* Nicholas Petlin, referring to the fate of Nikolai Gorlov in an interview, August 29, 1974.

318   Bolotov end: Pernikoff, *"Bushido,"* 151.

318   Gestapo arrest of Russian fascists: Mutanchiang consul to Tani Masayuki, February 18, 1943, in JFMA, A.6.5.0.1–2.

318   The Sorge ring: Johnson, *An Instance of Treason.* Deakin and Storry, *The Case of Richard Sorge.*

318   A Japanese diplomat in Manchukuo: Perhaps significantly, the extended consular report suggesting that Rodzaevsky was a Soviet spy emanated from Mutanchiang. Mutanchiang (in eastern Manchukuo between Harbin and Pogranichnaya) was the base of Boris Shepunov, a monarchist mafioso and bitter enemy of Rodzaevsky. Shepunov had been responsible for the execution of twenty-four RFS *soratniki* in 1940 (falsely accused of being Soviet agents), and it would not be surprising if he had continued to fill the ears of the local Japanese consul with similar accusations. For the consular report: Mutanchiang consul to Foreign Minister Tani Masayuki, February 18, 1943, in JFMA, A.6.5.0.1–2.

319   Rodzaevsky arrested by *Kempei:* Balakshin, *Final v Kitae,* II, 128.

319   Semenov open letter to Vlasov: Tsutsui (Japanese ambassador to Rumania) to Foreign Minister Shigemitsu Mamoru, May 24, 1943; Shigemitsu to Sakamoto (consul general in Harbin); May 26; Sakamoto to Shigemitsu, May 29; Shigemitsu to Tsutsui, June 1. JFMA, A.6.5.0.1–2.

320   End of Russian Fascist Union: Balakshin, *Final v Kitae*, I, 419; II, 219. Shanghai consulate police report no. 5060, August 18, 1943, in JFMA, A.6.5.0.1–2.

320   90 percent of White Russians pro-Soviet: Shanghai consul Yano to Shigemitsu, February 15, 1944, in JFMA, A.6.5.0.1–2.

320   Forces underlying pro-Soviet upsurge: *Ibid.* Stewart, "Manchuria Today," 79–80. Balakshin, *Final v Kitae*, II, 32–33.

320   Rush to acquire Soviet citizenship: Yamada Otozō (Japanese ambassador to Manchukuo and commander of the Kwantung Army) to Shigemitsu, December 4, 1944, in JFMA, A.6.5.0.1–2.

320   Émigré youths tried to enlist in Red Army: J. Gershevich, interview, June 17, 1972.

320   Merchants and bankers praise USSR: Yamada to Shigemitsu, December 4, 1944, in JFMA, A.6.5.0.1–2.

321   Radio *Otchizna:* Balakshin, *Final v Kitae*, II, 30–31.

321   *Kharbinskaya Pravda:* According to Balakshin, Matkovsky was involved with this underground paper. *Final v Kitae*, II, 31.

321   White Russian disaffection and desertions: Yamada to Shigemitsu, April 20, 1945, in JFMA, A.6.5.0.1–2.

321   Kislitsyn died of illness in 1944: Balakshin, *Final v Kitae*, I, 185.

321   Akikusa reassigned to Harbin: Akikusa Shun affidavit, June 14, 1946, IMTFE, Prosecution Document no. 1983, 3.

321–322   Émigré reactions to Germany's surrender: Balakshin, *Final v Kitae*, II, 27.

322   Story of fate of White Russians in Iran and impact on émigrés in Far East: Satō Naotake (Japanese ambassador to USSR) to Tōgō Shigenori, May 1, 1942, in JFMA, A.6.5.0.1–2.

322   Radio *Otchizna* announcement on White Russian male mobilization: Balakshin, *Final v Kitae*, II, 32.

322–323   Soviet preparations for invasion: Malinovsky, *Final*, 80–89.

323–324   Condition of Kwantung Army on eve of Soviet attack: *Kantōgun*, II, 383–91. Garthoff, "Soviet Intervention in Manchuria," 62–63.

324   Kwantung Army predictions about when USSR would enter war: *Kantōgun*, II, 350. Garthoff, "Soviet Intervention in Manchuria," 61.

324   "honor its commitments to the Allies under the Yalta Agreements": Malinovsky, *Final*, 47.

xix. Fatal Conversion

326   Rodzaevsky quote: Balakshin, *Final v Kitae*, II, 129.

326–327   Vlasevsky, Rodzaevsky, Matkovsky behavior on August 9: *Ibid.*, II, 101–2.

327   Collapse of Kwantung Army: *Kantōgun*, II, 411–48. Malinovsky, *Final*, 165–222.

328   Debate within BREM about evacuation offer: Balakshin, *Final v Kitae*, II, 102–4.

329   Rodzaevsky plans for flight: *Ibid.*, 105.

329–330   Harbin Railroad Station scene: *Ibid.*, 105–7.

330–332   Flight to Tientsin: *Ibid.*, 107–12.
333   Rodzaevsky's reception in Tientsin: *Ibid.*, 113–15.
333   Soviet occupation of Harbin: Malinovsky, *Final*, 273–82. *Kantōgun*, II, 466.
333   Japanese casualties, missing: *Kantōgun*, II, 464, 469, 487–90.
333–334   Soviet version of Semenov's capture: Malinovsky, *Final*, 300.
334   Émigré accounts of Semenov's arrest: Balakshin, *Final v Kitae*, II, 141–42.
334   Cossacks welcomed Red Army: Kaigorodov, "Russkiye v Trekhreche," 149.
334   Nagolen as Soviet intelligence officer: Nicholas Petlin, interview, August 29, 1974. Balakshin, *Final v Kitae*, I, 234.
334   Ex-fascists rush for Soviet passports: Balakshin, *Final v Kitae*, II, 114, 273–74.
335   Rodzaevsky's psychological transformation: *Ibid.*, II, 115–18.
335–340   "One Week Resurrecting the Soul": *Ibid.*, II, 119–35. Neonilla Yalisheva, Rodzaevsky's second wife, maintained in an interview on August 27, 1974 that the letter was spurious. Her view is shared by Rodzaevsky's son, Vladimir (letter, April 15, 1977). In *Final v Kitae*, Balakshin wrote (II, 122n) that there were three copies of the letter to Stalin: one was given to Patrikeev, the second was lost, and the third was donated by the late A. P. Vorobchuk-Zagorsk to the Museum of Russian Culture in San Francisco. The museum's director, Nicholas Slobodchikoff, was unable to locate the document; however, he recalled (letter, August 24, 1976) seeing a copy of it, adding that its authenticity was also testified to by the late Nicholas Kossoff (a former colonel in the Manchukuoan Army) and by Anatoly Skripkin, who was evacuated from Harbin with Rodzaevsky. On October 11, 1976, Slobodchikoff also suggested that a former *Nash Put* reporter named Iliodor Karnaukh would vouch for the letter. Both Skripkin and Karnaukh are alive but were not available for comment. Professor Erwin Oberländer quoted the letter ("All-Russian Fascist Party," 173) as if it were genuine. Nicholas Petlin, a former RFS *soratnik* who knew Rodzaevsky well and married Rodzaevsky's first wife, remarked in an interview on October 10, 1976 that the letter was "possible," given Rodzaevsky's state of mind in August 1945. The letter is sometimes referred to as "The Train Goes South," presumably because it germinated in Rodzaevsky's mind during his southward flight from Harbin to Tientsin.
340   Russian collaboration in World War II: Fischer, *Soviet Opposition to Stalin.* Thorwald, *The Illusion: Soviet Soldiers in Hitler's Armies.* Petrov, *My Retreat from Russia.*
341–342   Forced repatriation in Europe: Bethell, *The Last Secret*, 32–33, 117, 136–65.
342   NKVD lists of émigrés to be picked up: Balakshin, *Final v Kitae*, II, 30, 140, 143–44.
343   Soviet plenipotentiary in Shanghai announced forgiveness: Solzhenitsyn, *GULAG Archipelago*, 264.
343–344   Patrikeev: Balakshin, *Final v Kitae*, II, 144–46.
344–345   Patrikeev and Vlasevsky: *Ibid.*, II, 148–50.
345–351   Patrikeev's successful "hunt" for Rodzaevsky: *Ibid.*, II, 151–70. Balakshin based much of his narrative on interviews with Nikolai Martinov.
351–352   Description of Ulrikh: Institute for Study of the USSR, *Biographic Directory of the USSR* (New York, 1958), 687. Lyons, *Assignment in Utopia*, 568. Solzhenitsyn, *GULAG Archipelago*, 289–90.

351–354   Trial proceedings: *Pravda*, August 28, 29, 30, 1946. "Trial of the Japanese Agents," *USSR Information Bulletin*, vol. VI, no. 60 (September 11, 1946), 23. *New York Times*, August 29, 30, 31, 1946.

354   Rodzaevsky shot in Lubyanka cellar: Balakshin, *Final v Kitae*, II, 120. This assertion, made without supporting documentation, must be regarded as conjectural. Strictly speaking, the exact location of Rodzaevsky's execution is not known.

xx. Transmutation

355   Bulwer-Lytton: Evan Esar, ed., *Dictionary of Humorous Quotations* (New York: Horizon, 1953), 134.

355   Vonsiatsky remark on future plans: "I probably would not stay in Russia after a successful change in the form of government. I would probably come back to play golf on the links of Thompson!" Vonsiatsky to FBI special agent G. J. Starr, September 24, 1937, as quoted in Louis Nemzer memo (December 19, 1941), USDJ, file #202600–2871.

355   Conditional release for good behavior: New York *Herald Tribune*, February 28, 1946. New York *Journal-American*, February 28, 1946. According to Marion's former butler, Fred Portunato, Ream money shortened Vonsiatsky's term (letter, July 19, 1974); nevertheless, this would appear to be unlikely.

355–356   No signs of paranoia but some physical afflictions: ward surgeon's report, February 26, 1946. Prison file (#3775-H) of A. A. Vonsiatsky.

356   Soviet military victories caused Vonsiatsky to lose hope for a National Revolution: ward surgeon report, February 16, 1945. *Ibid.*

356   Vonsiatsky's arrival in Providence: Providence *Evening Bulletin*, February 28, 1946.

356   Vonsiatsky retained U.S. citizenship: Hartford *Courant*, April 4, 1946.

356–357   Social ostracism, loneliness on golf course: Prudence Kwiecien, interview, June 7, 1975.

357   Faithful friendship of Orlando: Andre A. Vonsiatsky, interview, June 7, 1974.

357   Vonsiatsky off to Hollywood after expiration of term: *Novaya Zarya*, August 27, 1947.

357   "I bore the cross for Russian émigrés": Vonsiatsky as quoted in *Novoye Russkoye Slovo*, September 6, 1947.

357   Stories of Vonsiatsky's amorous dalliances were recounted by most of the residents of Putnam and Thompson whom I interviewed between December 1973 and May 1976.

358   Vonsiatsky vacationed in St. Petersburg with Mamedovs: *Novaya Zarya*, January 24, 1948.

358   Natasha moved to St. Petersburg in part because she liked the name: St. Petersburg *Times*, June 8, 1953.

358   Description of Priscilla Royster: from a North Carolina driver's license (#961259), issued on June 2, 1949. Examined at Vonsiatsky home in St. Petersburg, June 7, 1974. Helen Roshak, interview, December 27, 1973.

358   "Sweetsky" and "Natsiya": letter from Anastase to Priscilla, July 16, 1950. VP.

358   Vonsiatsky moved permanently to St. Petersburg in 1950: Andre A. Vonsiatsky, interview, June 7, 1974. Putnam *Patriot*, February 10, 1965.

358   Question of Anastase-Marion divorce: John W. Ream, letter, November 27, 1973. Irving Myron, telephone interview, December 27, 1973. Helen Roshak, interview, December 27, 1973. Prudence Kwiecien, interview, June 7, 1975.

359   "Aunt Marion": Andre A. Vonsiatsky, interview, June 7, 1974.

359   Canasta match challenge: Providence *Evening Gazette,* November 10, 1949.

359   Entertaining royalty: St. Petersburg *Independent,* April 4, 1951.

359   "They pretend not to listen . . .": *Ibid.,* September 6, 1956.

359   Tsar Nicholas II Museum: St. Petersburg *Times,* June 8, 1953.

360   Vonsiatsky's letter on Gestapo, NKVD: St. Petersburg *Independent,* June 8, 1954.

360   Vonsiatsky considered FDR a Communist: *Rasplata,* v.

360n   Refusal to use Roosevelt dimes: Andre A. Vonsiatsky, interview, June 7, 1974.

360   Dodd lectured to right-wing groups: *New York Times,* June 28, 1966. In this connection, Drew Pearson described Dodd as a "bargain-basement McCarthy" (Boyd, *Above the Law,* 25). Albert E. Kahn, Dodd's onetime ally against Vonsiatsky, wrote on May 20, 1974, that Dodd became "one of the most reactionary members of the U.S. Senate."

360   Vonsiatsky on Dodd: *Rasplata,* vii, 49–52.

360   "We will not talk politics or religion in this house": Andre A. Vonsiatsky, interview, June 7, 1974.

361   Vonsiatsky at home: *Ibid.*

361   Marion's Tucson home: David H. Houghtaling to Marion Vonsiatsky, December 8, 1958, "Vonsiatsky Papers," PCA.

361   Marion crippled by arthritis: Anne V. Kenney, interview, December 26, 1973. According to Kenney, Marion used an electric lift instead of climbing stairs.

362   "My beloved, I press you to my heart": Anastase to Marion, March 22, 1960. Letter in possession of Helen Roshak.

362n   Marion's income, 1958–59: "Vonsiatsky Papers," PCA.

362   Marion's 1958 will: Probate Court Records, North Grosvenor Dale, Connecticut. Vol. 33, p. 432.

362n   Marion's estate (1963): *Ibid.,* Vol. 33, pp. 440–42.

362   Codicil to 1958 will: *Ibid.,* Vol. 33, p. 438; Vol. 36, p. 323.

362   Check for one half of Priscilla's unpaid Carte Blanche account: "Vonsiatsky Papers," PCA.

362   Vonsiatsky cried at Marion's funeral: Helen Roshak, interview, December 27, 1973.

362–363 Vonsiatsky at auction: undated and unidentified newspaper clipping sent by Fred Portunato, July 19, 1974. The clipping is probably from the Putnam *Patriot* or the *Windham County Observer.* Richard E. Snow, interview, June 7, 1975.

363   Kunle removed from mausoleum: Helen Roshak, letter, June 2, 1976. Prudence Kwiecien, letter, June 27, 1976. Thomas Watson, interview, December 27, 1973.

363   Vonsiatsky's death: Andre A. Vonsiatsky, interview, June 7–8, 1974. Florida State Board of Health, Bureau of Vital Statistics, "Certificate of Death: Anastase Andreyevich Vonsiatsky, file #65–009755."

364   Mamedov's death: Florida State Board of Health, Bureau of Vital Statistics, "Certificate of Death: Leo H. Mamedoff, file #66–010589."

364   Priscilla's death: *Ibid.*, "Certificate of Death: Edith Priscilla Vonsiatsky, file #66–016822."

364   Natasha's death: *Ibid.*, "Certificate of Death, Natalie Mamedoff, file #68–051661."

364   Vonsiatsky's diary: Vonsiatsky conversation with David Karr (August 2, 1939) as testified by Karr, "Grand Jury Hearings," 48, USDJ, file #202600–2871. Anastase A. Vonsiatsky, interview, June 7, 1974.

364   Okhotin's death: Neonilla Yalisheva, interview, August 27, 1974.

364   Matkovsky: According to Neonilla Yalisheva (*ibid.*) and Nicholas Slobodchikoff (interview August 27, 1974), Matkovsky died in the USSR.

364   Razhev and Kibardin: Nicholas Petlin, letter, January 22, 1975.

364   Rumiantsev and Taradanov: *Ibid.* Balakshin, *Final v Kitae*, II, 290.

364–365   Migunov and Kaufman: Nicholas Petlin, interview, August 29, 1974. Kaufman, *Lagerny Vrach,* passim.

365   Petlin experiences: Nicholas Petlin, interview, August 29, 1974; October 10, 1976.

365   Rodzaevsky's family: Neonilla Yalisheva, interview, August 27, 1974. Vladimir Rodzaevsky, telephone interview, November 7, 1976.

366   Cossack Restaurant: Neonilla Yalisheva, letter, undated, received on January 14, 1975.

366   Tzuglevich: Eugene J. Kerno, letter, June 2, 1976.

366   Prince Theodore: Nikita Nikitivich Romanoff, telephone interview, June 15, 1975.

366   Prince Nikita: *New York Times,* September 24, 1974. *Novoye Russkoye Slovo,* September 15, 1974.

366   Dodd and Hickey: Meridan *Record,* July 8, 1949.

366–367   Dodd's political nemesis: Boyd, *Above the Law,* 238, 258. *New York Times,* June 21, 1966; June 24, 1967.

367   Harbin: John Burns, "In Modern Harbin," Toronto *Globe and Mail,* December 14, 1973. *New York Times,* January 3, 1974. *Manshūkokushi,* II, 1,248.

368   Ammunition in ceiling, human mannequin in trunk: Richard E. Snow, interview, June 7, 1975.

368   Four crates from hen coop: currently deposited in the Providence College Archives, Providence, Rhode Island.

Postmortem

371   Vonsiatsky and Japanese submarine: Weyl, *Battle Against Disloyalty,* 174.

371   "global Ukrainian conspiracy": Farago, *Game of the Foxes,* 443–45.

371   "Nazi agent": Marcus, *Father Coughlin,* 209.

371   Rodzaevsky a patriot: Neonilla Yalisheva, interview, August 27, 1974.

371   Rodzaevsky "vain, gullible, and stupid—but not criminal": Nicholas Slobodchikoff, interview, August 27, 1974.

372   "Alex would have made a brilliantly successful condottiere": Alexis Sherbatoff, telephone interview, June 18, 1975.

Bibliography

I. State Archives

Germany. Foreign Ministry Archives. Political Archive, Bonn.
Germany. Records of the Deutsches Ausland-Institut, Stuttgart. Microfilm, U.S. National Archives.
Germany. Records of the Reich Leader of the SS and Chief of the German Police. Microfilm, U.S. National Archives.
Germany. Records of the Reich Ministry for Occupied Eastern Territories. Microfilm, U.S. National Archives.
Great Britain. Foreign Office Archives. Public Record Office, London.
International Military Tribunal for the Far East. Proceedings, Documents, and Exhibits. Center for Research Libraries, Chicago.
Japan. Army-Navy Archives. Microfilm, Library of Congress.
Japan. Foreign Ministry Archives. Gaimushō Gaikō Shiryōkan, Tokyo.
Japan. South Manchurian Railway Company Archives. Microfilm, Library of Congress.
United States. Department of Justice Archives. U.S. National Archives.
United States. Department of Justice. Bureau of Prisons. Prison File of Anastase A. Vonsiatsky.
United States. Department of State Archives. U.S. National Archives.
United States District Court. District of Connecticut, Hartford. *United States of America* v. *Anastase A. Vonsiatsky et al.* . . ." Federal Archives and Records Center, Waltham, Massachusetts.
United States. State of Connecticut. Windham County. Probate Court Records. North Grosvenor Dale, Connecticut.

II. Private Papers And Unpublished Manuscripts

Felix Patrikeev. "The Origins and Nature of Russian Émigré Society in Manchuria, up to the Far Eastern Crisis of 1931–1933." Undated manuscript received in August 1977 from the author.
Nicholas Petlin. Letters and manuscripts. Author's files.
Marion Ream. Papers and correspondence, 1914–1963. Providence College Archives, Providence, Rhode Island.
Lydia B. Schmüser. Memoirs, 1910–1947. Los Angeles.

423

Ronald Stanley Suleski. "Manchuria under Chang Tso-lin." Unpublished Ph.D. dissertation, University of Michigan, 1974.

Anastase A. Vonsiatsky. Papers, 1922–1963. Providence College Archives, Providence, Rhode Island.

Anastase A. Vonsiatsky. Papers and scrapbooks, 1910–1965. St. Petersburg, Florida.

iii. Published Material

Abend, Hallett. *My Life in China, 1926–1941.* New York: Harcourt, Brace & Co., 1943.

———. *Treaty Ports.* Garden City, N.Y.: Doubleday, 1944.

Abrikossow, Dmitrii I. *Revelations of a Russian Diplomat.* Edited by George Alexander Lensen. Seattle: University of Washington Press, 1964.

Agabekov, Georges. *OGPU: The Russian Secret Terror.* New York: Brentano's, 1931.

Agursky, Mikhail. "Russian Nationalism and the Jewish Question," in Moshe Davis, ed., *World Jewry and the State of Israel.* New York: Arno, 1977.

Alexander, Grand Duke of Russia. *Always a Grand Duke.* New York: Farrar & Rinehart, 1933.

———. *Once a Grand Duke.* New York: Farrar & Rinehart, 1932.

Alexandrov, Victor. *Journey Through Chaos.* New York: Crown, 1945.

Alioshin, Dmitri. *Asian Odyssey.* New York: Henry Holt, 1940.

An Old Emigrant. "The Truth abut the Russian Emigrants in Manchukuo." *Contemporary Manchuria,* III, 3 (1939), 62–82.

Arikawa, M. "Harbin: Cosmopolitan City of the Far East." *The Japan Magazine,* XXIV, 3 (1934), 53–56.

Asahi Shimbun Hotei Kishadan, ed. *Tokyo saiban* ["Tokyo Trial"]. 3 vols. Tokyo, 1962.

Avinov, Marie. *Marie Avinov: Pilgrimage Through Hell, An Autobiography.* Told by Paul Chavchavadze. Englewood Cliffs, N.J.: Prentice-Hall, 1968.

Balakshin, Pyotr P. *Final v Kitae: Vozniknoveniye, Razvitiye, i Ischeznoveniye Beloi Emigratsii na Dalnem Vostoke* ["Formation, Development, and Disintegration of the White Russian Emigration in the Far East"]. 2 vols. San Francisco: Kn-vo Sirius, 1958–59.

Berton, Peter, Paul Langer, and Rodger Swearingen. *Japanese Training and Research in the Russian Field.* Los Angeles: University of Southern California Press, 1956.

Bethell, Nicholas. *The Last Secret.* New York: Basic Books, 1974.

Boorman, Howard L., ed. *Biographical Dictionary of Republican China.* 4 vols. New York: Columbia University Press, 1967–71.

Boyd, James. *Above the Law.* New York: New American Library, 1968.

Brackman, Arnold C. *The Last Emperor.* New York: Charles Scribner's Sons, 1975.

Breshko-Breshkovsky, Nikolai Nikolaevich. *Goluboi Mundir* ["Blue Uniform"]. Riga: M. Didkovsky, 1930.

Budenz, Louis Francis. *Men Without Faces.* New York: Harper & Bros., 1950.

Bukhov, Arkhady. "Karerka" ["Little Careerist"]. *Krokodil,* no. 11 (April 1936).

Byas, Hugh. *Government by Assassination.* New York: Alfred A. Knopf, 1942.

Byrnes, Garrett D. "Leader of 20,000 Russian Fascists Awaits 'The Day.'" Providence *Sunday Journal,* January 6, 1935.

Carlson, John Roy [Arthur Derounian]. *Under Cover.* Philadelphia: Blakiston, 1943.

Carr, Harry. *Riding the Tiger: An American Newspaperman in the Orient.* New York: Houghton Mifflin, 1934.

Chambers, Whittaker. *Witness.* New York: Random House, 1952.

China Critic (Shanghai). 1932–41.

China Weekly Review (Shanghai). 1932–39.

Chto Delat? Nasha Fashistskaya Trekhletka protiv Kommunisticheskikh Piatiletok ["What Is to Be Done? Our Fascist Three-Year Plan versus the Communist Five-Year Plan"]. Harbin: "Nash Put," 1935.

Conquest, Robert. *The Great Terror.* New York: Macmillan, 1968.

Contemporary Manchuria (Dairen), 1932–40.

Coox, Alvin D. "*L'Affaire* Lyushkov: Anatomy of a Defector." *Soviet Studies,* XIX, 1 (January 1968), 405–20.

Crowley, James B. *Japan's Quest for Autonomy: National Security and Foreign Policy, 1930–1938.* Princeton: Princeton University Press, 1966.

Cyril Vladimirovich, Grand Duke of Russia. *My Life in Russia's Service—Then and Now.* London: Selwyn & Blount, 1939.

Dallin, Alexander. *German Rule in Russia, 1941–1945: A Study in Occupation Policies.* New York: St. Martin's Press, 1957.

————. "The Kaminsky Brigade: A Case-Study of Soviet Disaffection." In Alexander and Janet Rabinowitch, eds., *Revolution and Politics in Russia.* Bloomington: Indiana University Press, 1972, 243–80, 386–96.

Day, George Martin. *The Russians in Hollywood: A Study in Culture Conflict.* Los Angeles: University of Southern California Press, 1934.

Deakin, F. W., and G. R. Storry. *The Case of Richard Sorge.* New York: Harper & Row, 1966.

Dennen, Leon. *White Guard Terrorists in the U.S.A.* New York: Friends of the Soviet Union, 1935.

Dicker, Herman. *Wanderers and Settlers in the Far East: A Century of Jewish Life in China and Japan.* New York: Twayne, 1962.

Dictionnaire Historique et Géorgraphique de la Mandchourie. Lucien Gibert, ed. Hong Kong: Imprimerie de la Société des missions-étrangères, 1934.

Dorfman, Ben. "White Russians in the Far East." *Asia* (March 1935), 166–72.

Eastman, Lloyd. "Fascism in Kuomintang China: The Blue Shirts." *The China Quarterly,* no. 49 (January–March 1972), 1–31.

Farago, Ladislas. *The Game of the Foxes.* New York: David McKay, 1971.

Fashist (Putnam, Connecticut). 1933–41.

Fischer, George, ed. *Russian Émigré Politics.* New York: Free Russia Fund, 1951.

Fischer, George. *Soviet Opposition to Stalin: A Case Study in World War II.* Cambridge: Harvard University Press, 1952.

Fleming, Peter. *The Fate of Admiral Kolchak.* London: Hart Davis, 1963.

Foley, Tom. "Cracking Down on the Screwball." *Liberty,* November 28, 1942, 30–31, 57.

Footman, David. *Civil War in Russia.* London: Faber, 1961.

Foster, Ludmila A., comp. *Bibliography of Russian Émigré Literature: 1918–1968.* 2 vols. London: G. K. Hall, 1970.

Fukuda, Shinsei. *Hoku-Man no Roshiyajin buraku* ["Russian Settlements in Northern Manchuria"]. Tokyo: Tama Shobō, 1942.

Garthoff, Raymond L. "The Soviet Intervention in Manchuria, 1945–46," in Garthoff, ed., *Sino-Soviet Military Relations.* New York: Praeger, 1966.

Gaunt, Mary. *A Broken Journey.* London: Lippincott, 1919.

Gins [Guins], Georgy Konstantinovich. *Na Putiakh k Gosudarstvu Budushchevo: ot Liberalizma k Solidarizmu* ["On the Road to the State of the Future: From Liberalism to Solidarism"]. Harbin: N. E. Chinareva, 1930.

Goebbels, Paul Joseph. *The Goebbels Diaries, 1942–1943.* Edited and translated by Louis P. Lochner. New York: Doubleday, 1948.

Goriachkin, F. T. *Pervy Russky Fashist: Pyotr Arkadievich Stolypin* ["The First Russian Fascist: P. A. Stolypin"]. Harbin: Merkury, 1928.

Gregor, A. James. *The Fascist Persuasion in Radical Politics.* Princeton: Princeton University Press, 1974.

Grew, Joseph C. *Ten Years in Japan.* New York: Simon & Schuster, 1944.

Griswold, Wesley S. " 'Down with Communism!' Battle Cry of All-Russian Fascists. Their Militant World Leader Is A. A. Vonsiatsky of Thompson." Hartford *Courant,* September 23, 1934.

Grott, Mikhail Mikhailovich. *Borba za Rossiyu* ["Struggle for Russia"]. Putnam [Conn.]: VNRP, 1938.

———. *O Nashei Tainoi Rabote* ["About Our Secret Work"]. Putnam [Conn.]: VNRP, n.d.

———. *Sluzhu Rossy!* ["I Serve Russia!"]. Putnam [Conn.]: VNRP, n.d.

———. *Taktika Russkikh Fashistov* ["Tactics of Russian Fascists"]. Putnam [Conn.]: VNRP, n.d.

Grozin, N. N. *Zashchitniya Rubashki* ["Protective Shirts"]. Shanghai: Vseobshchy Russky Kalendar, 1939.

Guide to the Great Siberian Railway (1900). By A. I. Dmitriev-Mamonov and A. F. Zdziarski. Reprint of St. Petersburg edition. Newton Abbot, Devon (U.K.): David & Charles, 1971.

Hamilton, Alastair. *The Appeal of Fascism: A Study of Intellectuals and Fascism, 1919–1945.* New York: Macmillan, 1971.

Harper, Samuel N. *The Russia I Believe In: The Memoirs of Samuel N. Harper, 1902–1941.* Chicago: Univeristy of Chicago Press, 1945.

Hata, Ikuhiko. *Reality and Illusion: The Hidden Crisis between Japan and the U.S.S.R., 1932–1934.* New York: East Asian Institute, Columbia University, 1967.

Herzen, Alexander. *My Past and Thoughts: The Memoirs of Alexander Herzen.* 4 vols. Translated by Constance Garnett. New York: Alfred A. Knopf, 1968.

Hitler, Adolf. *Mein Kampf.* New York: Reynal & Hitchcock, 1941.

The Hour (New York). 1939–42.

Hull, Cordell. *The Memoirs of Cordell Hull.* 2 vols. New York: Macmillan, 1948.

Hynd, Alan. *Passport to Treason: The Inside Story of Spies in America.* New York: Robert M. McBride, 1943.

Ilina, Natalya Yosifovna. *Vozvrashcheniye* ["Return"]. 2 vols. Moscow: Sov. Pisatel, 1958, 1966.

Japan. Bōei-chō, Bōei Kenshujo, Senshishitsu [Defense Agency, Defense Research Institute, War History Room]. *Kantōgun* [Kwantung Army]. 2 vols. Tokyo, 1969–74.

Japan. Gaimushō, O-A Kyoku [Foreign Ministry, Europe-Asia Bureau]. *Nisso kōshō-shi* ["History of Soviet-Japanese Negotiations"]. Tokyo: Gannandō, 1969 (original printing, 1942).

Japan. Ōkurashō [Ministry of Finance]. *Shokuinroku* ["Register of Officials"]. Tokyo, 1934–41.

Johnson, Chalmers. *An Instance of Treason: Ozaki Hotsumi and the Sorge Spy Ring.* Stanford, Calif.: Stanford University Press, 1964.

Jones, F. C. *Manchuria since 1931.* London: Royal Institute of International Affairs, 1949.

Kahn, Albert E., and Michael Sayers. *The Great Conspiracy: The Secret War Against Soviet Russia.* Boston: Little, Brown, 1946.

———. *Sabotage! The Secret War Against America.* New York: Harper & Bros., 1942.

Kaigorodov, A. M. "Russkiye v Trekhreche: po Lichnym Vospominaniyam" ["Russians in San-Hsing: From Personal Recollections"]. *Sovetskaya Etnografiya* ["Soviet Ethnography"], no. 2 (March–April 1970), 140–49.

Kaliamin, M. V. *Natsionalnoye Khoziaistvo Budushchei Rossy* ["National Economy of Future Russia"]. Harbin: "Nash Put," 1936.

Kaufman, A. I. *Lagerny Vrach* ["Camp Doctor"]. Tel-Aviv: AM-OVED, 1973.

Kharbinskoye Vremya (Harbin). 1932–44.

Kislitsyn, Vladimir Alexandrovich. *V Ogne Grazhdanskoi Voiny: Memuary* ["In the Fire of the Civil War: Memoirs"]. Harbin: "Nash Put," 1936.

Kranzler, David. *Japanese, Nazis and Jews: The Jewish Refugee Community of Shanghai, 1938–1945.* New York: Yeshiva University Press, 1976.

Lahiri, Amar. "Russian Fascists in Harbin." *Pictorial Orient,* IX (February 1941), 40–42.

Laqueur, Walter. "Fascism—The Second Coming." *Commentary,* vol. 61, no. 2 (February 1976), 57–62.

———, ed. *International Fascism.* New York: Harper & Row, 1966.

———. *Russia and Germany: A Century of Conflict.* London: Weidenfeld and Nicolson, 1965.

Lattimore, Owen. *Manchuria, Cradle of Conflict.* New York: Macmillan, 1932.

Lavine, Harold. *Fifth Column in America.* New York: Doubleday, Doran, 1940.

Ledeen, Michael Arthur. *Universal Fascism: The Theory and Practice of the Fascist International, 1928–1936.* New York: Howard Fertig, 1972.

Lehovich, Dimitry V. *White Against Red.* New York: N. W. Norton & Co., 1974.

Lensen, George Alexander. *The Damned Inheritance: The Soviet Union and the Manchurian Crises, 1924–1935.* Tallahassee: The Diplomatic Press, 1974.

———. *The Strange Neutrality: Soviet-Japanese Relations during the Second World War, 1941–1945.* Tallahassee: The Diplomatic Press, 1972.

Leshko, O. *Russkiye v Manchzhugo* ["Russians in Manchukuo"]. Shanghai, 1937.

Lidin, N. "Russkaya Emigratsiya v Shankhae" ["The Russian Emigration in Shanghai"]. *Russkiya Zapiski* ["Russian Notes"], II (1937), 308–19.

Lobanov-Rostovsky, Prince A[ndrei]. *The Grinding Mill: Reminiscences of War and Revolution in Russia, 1913–1920.* New York: Macmillan, 1935.

Longworth, Philip. *The Cossacks.* London: Constable, 1969.

Lyons, Eugene. *Assignment in Utopia.* New York: Harcourt, Brace, 1937.

Lyubosh, S. B. *Russky Fashist* ["Russian Fascist"]. Leningrad, 1925.

McAleavy, Henry. *A Dream of Tartary: The Origins and Misfortunes of Henry P'u Yi.* London: Allen & Unwin, 1963.

Malinovsky, R. Ya. *Final.* Moscow: Nauka, 1966.

Malkin, Maurice L. *Return to My Father's House.* New Rochelle, N.Y.: Arlington House, 1972.

Manchoukuo Year Book, 1934. Tokyo: East Asiatic Economic Investigative Bureau, 1934.

Manchuria (Dairen). 1931–40.

Manshūkokushi Hensan Kankōkai [Society for the Publication of Manchukuo's History], ed. *Manshūkokushi* ["History of Manchukuo"]. 2 vols. Tokyo, 1971.

Marcus, Sheldon. *Father Coughlin.* Boston: Little, Brown, 1973.

Marie, Grand Duchess of Russia. *Education of a Princess: A Memoir.* New York: Blue Ribbon Books, 1930.

————. *A Princess in Exile.* New York: Viking, 1932.

Maser, Werner. *Hitler: Legend, Myth, & Reality.* New York: Harper & Row, 1974.

Massie, Robert K. *Nicholas and Alexandra.* New York: Atheneum, 1967.

Matankin, Alexander. *K Ustroistvu Budushchi Rossy* ["Toward Organizing the Future of Russia"]. Berlin: Budushchaya Rossiya, 1931.

Meakin, Annette M. B. *A Ribbon of Iron.* London: Archibald & Constable, 1901.

Meskill, Johanna Menzel. *Hitler and Japan: The Hollow Alliance.* New York: Atherton Press, 1966.

Miliukov, Paul. *Political Memoirs, 1905–1917.* Edited by Arthur P. Mendel. Ann Arbor: University of Michigan Press, 1967.

Mosca, Oreste. "Il trionfo del Fascismo in Russia e l'opera della medaglia d'oro Renzo Bertoni." *Antieuropa* (Roma, 1939), Anno 10, 589–98.

Nabokov, Vladimir. *Speak, Memory.* London: Weidenfeld and Nicolson, 1967.

Nash Put (Harbin) 1932–41. (Shanghai) 1941–43.

Natsiya (Shanghai and Harbin). 1932–43.

Novaya Zarya (San Francisco). 1936–50.

Novoye Russkoye Slovo (New York). 1933–74.

N.Y.K. Official Guide, 1937–38. Tokyo: Taikansha, 1938.

Oberländer, Erwin. "The All-Russian Fascist Party." *Journal of Contemporary History.* I, 1 (1966), 158–73.

Ogata, Sadako. *Defiance in Manchuria: The Making of Japanese Foreign Policy, 1931–1932.* Berkeley: University of California Press, 1964.

Ossendowski, Ferdinand. *Beasts, Men and Gods.* New York: E. P. Dutton, 1922.

Ōtani Keijirō, *Showa Kempeishi* ["History of Kempei in the Showa Period"]. Tokyo: Misuzu Shobō, 1966.

Palmer, Edward W., ed. *The Communist Problem in America.* New York: Thomas Y. Crowell, 1951.

Peattie, Mark R. *Ishiwara Kanji and Japan's Confrontation with the West.* Princeton: Princeton University Press, 1975.

Pernikoff, Alexandre. *"Bushido": The Anatomy of Terror.* New York: Liveright, 1943.

Petlin, N. N., ed. *S Pesnei k Pobed* ["With Songs toward Victory"]. Harbin: Russkoye Pechatnoye Delo, 1935.

Petro-Pavlovsky, W. "A Manchurian Racketeer." *Atlantic Monthly,* vol. 151 (January 1933), 43–51.

Petrov, Vladimir. *My Retreat from Russia.* New Haven: Yale University Press, 1950.

Pospielovsky, Dimitry V. "Russian National Thought and the Jewish Question." *Soviet Jewish Affairs,* vol. 6, no. 1 (1976), 3–17.

Pozner, Vladimir. *Bloody Baron: The Story of Ungern-Sternberg.* New York: Random House, 1938.

Presseisen, Ernst L. *Germany and Japan: A Study in Totalitarian Diplomacy, 1933–1941.* The Hague: Martinus Nijhoff, 1958.

Putnam *Patriot* (Putnam, Connecticut). 1924–65.

Quinlan, Francis L. "Grim Group of Russian Fascists at Conclave in Thompson, Ponder 'Independence' for Native Country." Hartford *Courant,* July 5, 1937.

Rodzaevsky, Konstantin V. *Kritika Sovetskovo Gosudarstva* ["Criticism of the Soviet State"]. 2 vols. Shanghai: Vserossiiskaya Fashistskaya Partiya, 1935–37.

Rogger, Hans. "The Formation of the Russian Right." *California Slavic Studies,* III (1964), 66–94.

———. "Was there a Russian Fascism? 'The Union of the Russian People.'" *Journal of Modern History,* XXXVI (1964), 398–415.

Rogger, Hans, and Eugen Weber, eds. *The European Right.* Berkeley: University of California Press, 1965.

Rollin, Henri. "La Svastika de l'Impératrice," in Rollin, ed., *L'Apocalypse de notre temps.* Paris: Gallimard, 1939.

Rossiya (New York). 1934–39.

Rubezh (Harbin). 1927–45.

Schüddekopf, Otto-Ernst. *Fascism.* New York: Praeger, 1973.

Semenov, Ataman [Grigory Mikhailovich]. *O Sebe* ["About Myself"]. Harbin: Zarya, 1938.

Shirer, William L. *The Rise and Fall of the Third Reich.* New York: Simon & Schuster, 1960.

Simpson, Sir John Hope. *The Refugee Problem.* London: Oxford University Press, 1939.

Sinclair, Upton. *Presidential Agent.* New York: Viking Press, 1944.

Snow, Edgar. "Japan Builds a New Colony." *Saturday Evening Post,* February 24, 1934, 12, 80–85.

Solzhenitsyn, Aleksandr. *The GULAG Archipelago.* New York: Harper & Row, 1974.

———. *The GULAG Archipelago, Two.* New York: Harper & Row, 1975.

Speer, Albert. *Inside the Third Reich.* New York: Macmillan, 1970.

Stewart, Reverend John. "Manchuria Today." *International Affairs,* XX, 1 (January 1944), 68–80.

Stewart, Marguerite McElveen. "Drugging a Nation." *Christian Century,* vol. 51 (May 16, 1934), 662–64.

Stone, Irving. *They Also Ran.* Rev. ed. New York: New American Library, 1968.

Storry, Richard. *The Double Patriots.* London: Chatto and Windus, 1957.

Strik-Strikfeldt, Wilfried. *Against Hitler and Stalin.* New York: John Day, 1973.

Svit, Ivan [John V. Sweet]. *Ukrainsko-yaponski vzaemini, 1903–1945* ["Ukrainian-Japanese relations, 1903–1945"]. New York: Ukrainian Historical Association, 1972.

Swift, David W., ed. *Ninety Li a Day.* Taipei: Orient Cultural Service, 1975.

Taradanov, G. V. *Azbuka Fashizma* ["ABC of Fascism"]. 2d ed. Shanghai: Izd. "Nash Put." 1935.

Thorwald, Jürgen. *The Illusion: Soviet Soldiers in Hitler's Armies.* Translated from the German by Richard and Clara Winston. New York: Harcourt Brace Jovanovich, 1975.

Tokyo saiban [Tokyo trial]. Ed., Asahi Shimbun Hōtei Kishadan. 3 vols. Tokyo: Tokyo Saiban Kankōkai, 1962.

Treadgold, Donald W. *Twentieth Century Russia.* 2d ed. Chicago: Rand McNally, 1964.

"Trial of the Japanese Agents." *USSR Information Bulletin,* VI, no. 60 (September 11, 1946), 23.

Tschebotarioff, Gregory P. *Russia, My Native Land.* New York: McGraw-Hill, 1964.

Tulsky, S. *Manchzhuriya.* Moscow: Voenizdat, 1932.

United States Congress. *Congressional Record, 1937–42.* Washington: Government Printing Office, 1937–42.

United States Congress, House, Special Committee on Un-American Activities. *Investigation of Un-American Propaganda Activities in the United States: Hearings.* Washington: Government Printing Office, 1938–39.

United States Congress. 74th Congress. First Session. *Investigation of Nazi and Other Propaganda.* House Report 153. Washington: Government Printing Office, 1934.

United States. Department of State, Division of European Affairs. *National Socialism.* Washington: Government Printing Office, 1943.

United States. Department of State. "NTS: The Russian Solidarist Movement." Washington: Department of State Intelligence Research Office, Series 3, No. 76, 1951.

United States Senate. *The Deportation of Gregorii Semenov.* [reprint] Hong Kong: Beamur International, 1972.

U.S.S.R., Tsentralny Komitet, KPSSSR [Central Committee, Communist Party of the USSR], Institut Marksizma-Leninisma [Institute of Marxism-Leninism]. *Istoriya Velikoi Otechestvennoi Voiny Sovetskovo Soiuza* ["History of the Great Patriotic War of the Soviet Union"]. Vol. 5. Moscow, 1963.

Vespa, Amleto. *Secret Agent of Japan.* Boston: Little, Brown, 1938.

Vinogradov, A. A. *SSSR Sevodnya i Zavtra* ["USSR Today and Tomorrow"]. Harbin: "Natsiya," 1940.

Volkmann, Hans-Erich. *Die russische Emigration in Deutschland, 1919–1929.* Würzburg: Holzner, 1966.

Vonsiatsky, A. "Zapiski Monarkhista" ["Memoirs of a Monarchist"]. *Posledniya Novosti,* June 24, 1921.

Vonsiatsky, Anastase Andreivich. *Osnovy Russkavo Fashizma* ["Bases of Russian Fascism"]. Shanghai: Dalne-Vostochnavo Tsentra VNRP, n.d. [circa 1939].

———. *Otvet Kritiku* ["Answer to a critic"]. Putnam, Conn.: VNRP, 1936.

———. *Rasplata* ["Retribution"]. São Paulo, 1960.

———. *Rech Soratnika A. A. Vonsiatskovo, Shankhai, 17 Feb 1939* ["Speech of Soratnik A. A. Vonsiatsky, Shanghai, February 17, 1939"]. Putnam, Conn.: VNRP, 1939.

Vorres, Ian. *The Last Grand Duchess.* New York: Charles Scribner's Sons, 1964.

Wagatsuma, Hiroshi. "The Social Perception of Skin Color in Japan." *Daedalus,* Spring 1967, 407–43.

Walsh, Edmund A. *The Fall of the Russian Empire.* New York: Blue Ribbon Books, 1927.

Weber, Eugen. *Varieties of Fascism.* Princeton: Van Nostrand, 1964.

Weyl, Nathaniel. *The Battle Against Disloyalty.* New York: Thomas Y. Crowell, 1951.

"The White Russians in Manchoukuo." *Contemporary Manchuria,* I, 3 (September 1937), 16–32.

Williams, Robert C. *Culture in Exile: Russian Émigrés in Germany, 1881–1941.* Ithaca: Cornell University Press, 1972.

Winchell, Walter. "Americans We Can Do Without." *Liberty,* August 1, 1942.

Windham County Observer. 1924–65.

Woolf, S. J., ed. *The Nature of Fascism.* New York: Vintage Books, 1969.

Wraga, Ryszard. "Russian Emigration after Thirty Years' Exile," in George Fischer, ed., *Russian Émigré Politics.* New York: Free Russia Fund, 1951, 35–50.

Wrangel, General Baron Peter N. *Always with Honor.* New York: Robert Speller & Sons, 1957.

Young, Katsu. "The Nomonhan Incident: Imperial Japan and the Soviet Union." *Monumenta Nipponica,* XXII (1967), 82–102.

Zarya (Harbin). 1931–41.

Index

433